Essentials of Conservation Biology

Essentials of
Conservation Biology

THIRD EDITION

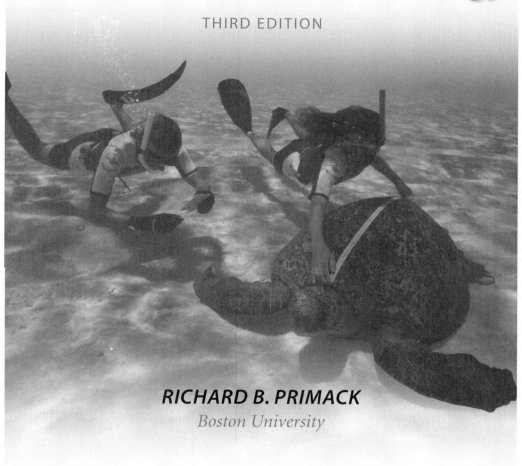

RICHARD B. PRIMACK
Boston University

Sinauer Associates, Inc. Publishers
Sunderland, Massachusetts U.S.A.

About the Cover

In a protected feeding and nesting area around Rocas Atoll, about 220 km from the coast of Brazil, Brazilian scientists measure the length of an endangered green turtle (*Chelonia mydas*). They will permanently tag the turtle as part of a comprehensive conservation effort by Projeto TAMAR (see Box 1 in Chapter 1). Photograph used by permission of BANCO DE IMAGENS/PROJETO TAMAR.

Essentials of Conservation Biology, Third Edition
Copyright ©2002 by Sinauer Associates, Inc.
ISBN 0-87893-719-6

Credits for Part Opener Photographs

Part I: Photograph courtesy of Projeto TAMAR Image Bank. Part II: Photograph by Scott Kraus, New England Aquarium. Part III: Photograph by Milla Jung. Part IV: Photograph by Bill Campbell. Part V: Photograph from the University of Wisconsin Arboretum and Archives. Part VI: Photograph by Robert Schoen/Northeast Sustainable Energy Association.

Library of Congress Cataloging-in-Publication Data

Primack, Richard B., 1950-
    Essentials of conservation biology / Richard B. Primack.-- 3rd ed.
        p.   cm.
    Includes bibliographical references (p.   ) and index.
    ISBN 0-87893-719-6 (hardcover)
    1. Conservation biology. I. Title.
QH75 .P752 2002
333.95'11--dc21   2002008076

Printed in U.S.A.

5   4   3   2

This book is dedicated to those who teach conservation biology, ecology, and environmental sciences, whose efforts will inspire future generations to find the right balance between protecting biological diversity and providing for human needs.

Brief Contents

Contents

II Valuing Biodiversity 85

V *Practical Applications 413*

VI   *Conservation and Human Societies 547*

Preface

The United Nations has declared the year 2001–2002 to be International Biodiversity Year, in recognition of the immense value of the living world. Conservation biology is the field that seeks to study and protect the living world and its biological diversity. The field emerged during the last 25 years as a major new discipline to address the alarming loss of biological diversity throughout the world. The threats to biological diversity are all too real, as most recently demonstrated by the extinction of Spix's macaw in Brazil and a subspecies of red colobus monkey in West Africa. At the same time, our need to gain greater knowledge of the diversity of life was highlighted by the discovery in 2002 of an entirely new order of insects in remote mountains of Namibia in southwestern Africa.

Evidence of the explosive increase of interest in conservation biology is shown by the rapidly increasing membership in the Society for Conservation Biology, the great intellectual excitement displayed in many journals and newsletters, and the large numbers of new edited books and advanced texts that appear almost weekly. In the United States, a major grant by one of the founders of the Intel Corporation has been used to establish a Center for Applied Biodiversity Science, and a Global Biodiversity Information Facility is being developed as an online resource to coordinate international conservation efforts.

Such interest extends to university students, who continue to enroll in introductory conservation biology courses. The publication of the first (1993) and second (1998) editions of *Essentials of Conservation Biology* provided a comprehensive textbook for this subject. (The *Primer of Conservation Biology*'s first (1995) and second (2000) editions filled the need for a "quick" guide for those who want a basic familiarity with conservation biology.) This third edition of *Essentials* attempts to provide a thorough introduction to the major concepts and problems of the field. Like its predecessors, it is designed for use in courses of conservation biology, and also as a supplemental text for general biology, ecology, wildlife biology, and environmental policy courses. The book is also intended to serve as a detailed guide for professionals who require a comprehensive background in the subject.

This third edition reflects the excitement and new developments in the field. It provides coverage of the latest information available on a number of topics, including the global hot spots of biodiversity that have been identified as targets for conservation efforts and a new system of classification for endangered species. The third edition also highlights new approaches culled from the literature on such topics as species reintroductions, population viability analysis, protected areas management, and integrated conservation and community development projects.

In keeping with the international approach of conservation biology, I feel it is important to make the field accessible to as wide an audience as possible. With the assistance of Marie Scavotto and the staff of Sinauer Associates, I have arranged an active translation program, beginning in 1995 with translations into German (as *Naturschutzbiologie*) and Chinese in 1997. However, it became clear to me that the best way to make the material accessible was to create regional or country-specific translations, identifying local scientists to become coauthors and to add case studies, examples, and illustrations from their own countries and regions that would be more relevant to the intended audience. To that end, in the past seven years, editions of *Essentials* have appeared in Hungarian (with Tibor Standovar) and Spanish (with Ricardo Rozzi, Peter Feinsinger, Rodolfo Dirzo, and Francisca Massardo); the *Primer* has appeared in Japanese (with Hiromi Kobori), in Indonesian (with Jatna Supriatna, Mochammad Indrawan, and Padmi Kramadibrata), in Vietnamese (with Pham Binh Quyen, Vo Quy, and Hoang Van Thang), in Korean (with Dowon Lee, Z. Kim, Y. Sohn, J. H. Shin, and J. C. Chae), in Brazilian Portuguese (with Efraim Rodrigues), in Czech (with Pavel Kindlmann and Jena Jersakova), and in Spanish (with Joandomenec Ros). Editions of *Essentials* and the *Primer* in French, Greek, Arabic, Italian, Thai, Russian, Romanian, and Mongolian, and for India, Africa, and Madagascar are currently in some stage of planning or production. The MacArthur Foundation and the Conservation, Food and Health Foundation have provided funds for several of these translations. It is my hope that these translations will help conservation biology develop as a discipline with a global scope. At the same time, examples from these translations find their way back into the English language editions, enriching the presentation.

I hope that readers of this book will want to find out more about the extinction crisis facing species and biological communities and how they can take action to halt it. I encourage readers to take the field's activist spirit to heart—use the Appendix to find organizations and sources of information on how to help. If readers gain a greater appreciation for the goals, methods, and importance of conservation biology, and if they are moved to make a difference in their everyday lives, this textbook will have served its purpose.

Acknowledgments

Individual chapters or groups of chapters in this edition were reviewed by Ruth Allard, Edith Allen, Jonathan Ballou, Laurie Bingaman Lackey, Katrina Brandon, Phil Cafaro, Linus Chen, Don Falk, Elizabeth Farnsworth, Peter Feinsinger, Richard Frankham, Kevin Gaston, David Hulse, Pamela Jagger, Devra Kleiman, Bill Laurance, David Lindenmayer, Kathy MacKinnon, John Marzluff, Jeffrey McNeely, Elliott Norse, Stuart Pimm, J. Michael Scott, R. David Simpson, Arthur Small, Brandie Smith, and Stanley Temple.

Numerous people offered specialized input that helped make the boxes and cases studies current and accurate. I would particularly like to recognize the contributions of Kamal Bawa, Peter Dunwiddie, Jim Estes, Jack Ewel, Jerry Franklin, Frances James, Daniel Janzen, Les Kaufman, Brian Miller, Peter Neuenschwander, Tom Power, George Schaller, Steve Shimek, Doug Smith, Lisa Sorenson, Bob Steneck, Lou Toth, and Kent Whealey.

Tamah Hunt was the principal research assistant and organizer for the project, with additional help from Jean Nguyen, Jamie Bechtel, Vivi Tran, Luba Zhaurova, and Daniel Primack. Kerry Falvey provided invaluable help in the production of the book, with numerous suggestions on how to make the book friendlier to student readers. Michele Ruschhaupt did a fine job laying out the book, and Andy Sinauer and the rest of the Sinauer staff helped to transform the manuscript into a finished book. Special thanks are due my wife Margaret and my children Daniel, William, and Jasper for encouraging me to fulfill an important personal goal by completing this book. I would like to recognize Boston University for providing me with the facilities and environment that made this project possible and the many Boston University students who have taken my conservation biology courses over the years. Their enthusiasm and suggestions have helped me to find new ways to present this material. And lastly, I would like to express my great appreciation to my coauthors in other countries who have worked with me to produce conservation biology textbooks in their own languages, which are critical for spreading the message of conservation biology to a wider audience.

RICHARD PRIMACK
BOSTON, MA
JUNE, 2002

PART I

Major Issues That Define the Discipline

Chapter

1

What Is Conservation Biology?

opular interest in protecting the world's biological diversity—including its amazing range of species, its complex biological communities, and the genetic variation within species—has intensified during the last few decades. It has become increasingly evident to both scientists and the general public that we are living in a period of unprecedented biodiversity loss. Around the globe, biological communities that took millions of years to develop, including tropical rain forests, coral reefs, temperate old growth forests, and prairies, are being devastated by human actions. Thousands, if not tens of thousands, of species and millions of unique populations are predicted to go extinct in the coming decades (Smith et al. 1993; Mace 1995; Lawton and May 1995; Levin 2001). Today's mass extinctions are unlike mass extinctions in the geological past, in which tens of thousands of species died out following massive catastrophes such as asteroid collisions with the Earth and dramatic temperature changes—today's extinctions have a human face. Never before in the history of life have so many species and biological communities been threatened with extinction in so short a period of time. Never before has such devastation been caused by beings who claim reason, a moral sense, and free will as their unique and defining characteristics. Worse still, the threats to biological diversity are accelerating due to the demands of a rapidly increasing human population and its rising material consumption.

Unless something is done to reverse the trend of human-caused extinctions, wonderful species that exemplify the natural world for us—such as giant pandas, butterflies, songbirds, and whales—soon will be lost forever from their wild habitats. Additionally, many thousands, possibly millions, of less conspicuous plant, fungi, and invertebrate species will join them in extinction unless their habitats and populations are protected. The loss of these seemingly inconspicuous species may prove to be devastating to the planet and its human inhabitants because of their role in maintaining biological communities.

In addition to the species extinctions, the natural hydrologic and chemical cycles that people depend on for clean water and clean air have been disrupted by deforestation and land clearing. The soil erosion and pollution that results from agriculture and sewage discharges cause massive damage to rivers, lakes, and oceans. The very climate of our planet Earth has been disrupted by a combination of atmospheric pollution and deforestation. Genetic diversity within species has decreased as populations are reduced in size, even among species with seemingly healthy populations. The main threat humans pose to the diversity of life is our destruction of natural habitat, which stems from the growth of the human population and our ever-increasing use of resources. Such habitat destruction includes the clear-cutting of old-growth forests in the temperate zone and in rain forests in the Tropics, overuse of grasslands for pasture, draining of wetlands, and pollution of freshwater and marine ecosystems. Even when parcels of natural habitat are preserved as national parks, nature reserves, and marine protected areas, extreme vigilance is required to prevent the extinction of their remaining species because their numbers have been so dramatically reduced in the past that they are now particularly vulnerable to extinction. Also, the environment in the habitat fragments is so altered from its original condition that a site may no longer be suitable for the continued existence of certain species.

There are many other threats facing modern ecosystems, including climate change and invasive species. Efforts to protect a species in one area may be severely crippled as a result of a rapid climate change to which the species cannot adapt (see Chapter 9). Also, biological communities have been particularly devastated by the introduction of exotic species, which are either deliberately brought in from another area and established by people, such as domesticated animals and ornamental plants, or are brought in accidentally, such as weed species and other pests. In many cases, these species have become invasive (see Chapter 10) and have displaced and eliminated native species, particularly on islands.

Another major threat to biological diversity is the use of modern technology to overharvest animals and plants for local and international markets. Entire forest, grassland, and ocean communities have been emptied of their animal life, and in many cases, their plant life as well.

Powerful technologies that have been developed by Western societies allow alteration of the environment on a regional and even a global scale. Some of these transformations are intentional, such as the creation of dams and the development of new agricultural land, but other changes, such as air pollution, overgrazing of grasslands, and damage to seabed habitats during fishing, are by-products of our activities. Unregulated dumping of chemicals and sewage into streams, rivers, and lakes has polluted major freshwater and coastal marine systems throughout the world and has driven significant numbers of species into extinction. Pollution has reached such high levels that even large marine environments, such as the Mediterranean Sea, the Gulf of Mexico, and the Persian Gulf, which were once assumed to be able to absorb pollution with no negative effects, are threatened with the loss of whole suites of formerly common species. Some inland water bodies, such as the Aral Sea, have been completely destroyed along with the many unique fish species that lived in them. Air pollution from factories and cars has turned rainwater into an acid solution that weakens and kills plant life and, in turn, the animals that depend on those plants. Scientists have warned that levels of air pollution have become severe enough to alter global climate patterns and strain the capacity of the atmosphere to filter out harmful ultraviolet radiation. The results of these events on biological communities are enormous and ominous; they are also the stimuli for the growth of conservation biology.

Scientists now realize that many of the threats to biological diversity are synergistic—that is, the negative effects of several independent factors—logging, fire, poverty, and overhunting, for instance—combine additively or even multiplicatively (Myers 1987). Also, the threats to biological diversity will almost certainly threaten human populations, because humans are dependent on the natural environment for raw materials, food, medicines, and even the water they drink.

The New Science of Conservation Biology

Some people feel discouraged by the avalanche of species extinctions and the wholesale habitat destruction occurring in the world today. But it is possible—and indeed necessary—to feel challenged to find ways to stop the destruction. Actions taken—or bypassed—during the next few decades will determine how many of the world's species and natural areas will survive. People may someday look back on the closing years of the twentieth century and the first decade of the twenty-first century as an extraordinarily exciting time, when a handful of determined people saved numerous species and some entire biological communities.

Conservation biology is a new, integrated science that has developed in response to the desire to face this challenge. It has three goals: first, to document the full range of biological diversity on Earth; second, to investigate human impact on species, communities, and ecosystems; and third, to develop practical approaches to prevent the extinction of species, to maintain genetic variation within species, and to protect and restore biological communities and their associated ecosystem functions (Wilson 1992; Meffe and Carroll 1997).

Conservation Biology Complements the Traditional Disciplines

Conservation biology arose because the traditional applied disciplines of resource management alone were not comprehensive enough to address the critical threats to biological diversity. Agriculture, forestry, wildlife management, and fisheries biology have been concerned primarily with developing methods to manage a small range of species for the marketplace and for recreation. These disciplines generally were not concerned with the protection of the full range of species and biological communities, or perhaps they regarded this as a secondary issue. Conservation biology complements the applied disciplines and provides a more general theoretical approach to the protection of biological diversity. It differs from these disciplines in its primary goal of long-term preservation of the entire biological community, with economic factors secondary.

The academic disciplines of population biology, taxonomy, ecology, and genetics constitute the core of conservation biology, and many conservation biologists have been drawn from these ranks. In addition, many leaders in conservation biology have come from zoos and botanical gardens, bringing with them experience in maintaining and propagating species in captivity. Because much of the biodiversity crisis arises from human pressures, conservation biology also incorporates ideas and expertise from a broad range of other fields (Figure 1.1) (Reaka-Kudla et al. 1996; Levin 2001). For example, environmental law and policy provide the basis for government protection of rare and endangered species and critical habitats. Environmental ethics provides a rationale for preserving species. Ecological economists provide analyses of the economic value of biological diversity to support arguments for preservation. Ecosystem ecologists and climatologists monitor the biological and physical characteristics of the environment and develop models to predict environmental responses to disturbance. Social sciences, such as anthropology, sociology, and geography, provide methods to involve local people in actions to protect their immediate environment. Because it draws on the ideas and skills of so many separate fields, conservation biology can be considered a truly multidisciplinary approach.

Another crucial difference between conservation biology and other academic disciplines is that conservation biology attempts to provide

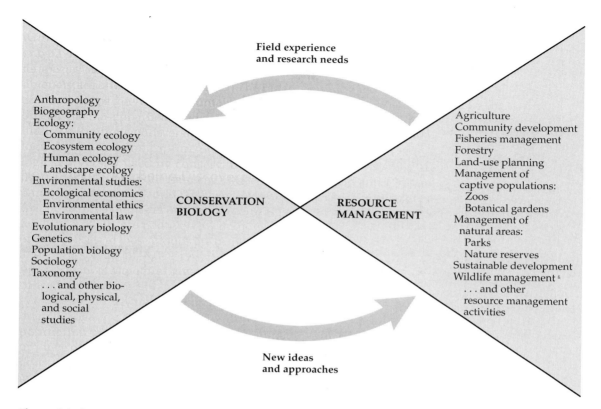

Field experience
and research needs

Anthropology
Biogeography
Ecology:
    Community ecology
    Ecosystem ecology
    Human ecology
    Landscape ecology
Environmental studies:
    Ecological economics
    Environmental ethics
    Environmental law
Evolutionary biology
Genetics
Population biology
Sociology
Taxonomy
    . . . and other bio-
    logical, physical,
    and social
    studies

**CONSERVATION
BIOLOGY**

**RESOURCE
MANAGEMENT**

Agriculture
Community development
Fisheries management
Forestry
Land-use planning
Management of
    captive populations:
    Zoos
    Botanical gardens
Management of
    natural areas:
    Parks
    Nature reserves
Sustainable development
Wildlife management
    . . . and other
    resource management
    activities

New ideas
and approaches

Figure 1.1 Conservation biology represents a synthesis of many basic sciences (left) that provide principles and new approaches for the applied fields of resource management (right). The experiences gained in the field in turn influence the direction of the basic sciences. (After Temple 1991.)

specific issues with solutions that can be applied in actual field situations (Box 1). These issues involve determination of the best strategies for protecting rare species, design of nature reserves, development of programs to maintain genetic variability in small populations, and reconciliation of conservation concerns with the needs of local people. The critical test for conservation biology is whether it can preserve and restore species and biological communities.

Conservation Biology Is a Crisis Discipline

Decisions on conservation questions are being made every day under severe time pressures. Conservation biologists and scientists in related fields are well-suited to provide the advice that governments, businesses, and the general public need in order to make crucial decisions, but because of time constraints, scientists are often compelled to make decisions on

BOX 1 *A Comprehensive Approach to Sea Turtle Conservation: Projeto TAMAR in Brazil*

Sea turtles are in trouble: In many countries of the world, populations have shrunk to less than 1% of their original sizes. Turtle populations have been devastated by a combination of factors, including destruction of their habitat due to coastal development, harvesting of adult turtles and turtle eggs for food, and high mortality due to entanglement in fishing gear. Like many tropical countries, Brazil has come to recognize the importance of protecting its sea turtles. Its conservation program provides a comprehensive approach to saving these fascinating and mysterious creatures.

Sea turtles spend their whole lives at sea, with only the females returning to land to lay eggs on remote, sandy beaches. Because so much of it is spent in the sea, little was known about the turtle life cycle until recently. This information was desperately needed, as the Brazilian government found out when it set out to design its conservation program: No one knew which sea turtles were found in Brazil, how many there were, where they lived, and how local people were affecting them. To overcome this lack of basic information, in 1980 the Brazilian government established the National Marine Turtle Conservation Program, called Projeto TAMAR, Portuguese for TArtarugas MARinhas ("marine turtles" in English) (Marcovaldi and Marcovaldi 1999). The project began with a two-year survey of Brazil's 6000-km long coastline, using boats, horses, and foot patrols combined with hundreds of interviews with villagers. The survey found three main zones of turtle nesting beaches along 1100 km of the coastline between Rio de Janeiro and Recife, with loggerhead turtles (*Careta careta*) the most abundant and four other species also present. The green turtle (*Chelonia mydas*) was the only species nesting on Brazil's offshore islands.

The interviews with villagers and observations of beaches revealed that adult turtles and turtle eggs were being intensively harvested, with 100% of the eggs often collected. Interviews also showed that despite this widespread harvesting, turtles were *not* the primary sources of income or protein for local fishermen.

Other results were also a cause for grave concern. Increased human activities on the nesting beaches were scaring females away before they laid their eggs. In many areas, the construction of resorts, houses, commercial developments, and beach roads directly damaged and reduced the available nesting area on beaches. The shadows cast by the buildings also changed the temperature of the sand, which is a critical determinant of sex in hatching turtles. In certain developed beaches, most of the emerging turtles were males. Additionally, the light from the buildings at night disoriented emerging hatchlings; instead of heading straight to the ocean, they often would wander in different directions and become exhausted. For many hatchlings, this delay proved fatal: Along the way, they were often killed by birds and other predators. For the young turtles that did make it to sea, many were caught in the nets of fishermen—both in Brazil's coastal waters and throughout the Atlantic Ocean—and suffocated to death.

Information from the TAMAR survey was critical to legislation passed in 1986 in Brazil that led to the complete protection of sea turtles and to the establishment of two new Biological Reserves and a Marine National Park to protect nesting beaches on the islands. Once the distribution of turtles and nesting areas were established, and the threats to turtles identified, TAMAR was able to move forward with its objectives on the ground, with funding provided by the Brazilian government, the leading Brazilian oil company, an international development bank, and other conservation organizations.

Projeto TAMAR chose an innovative and comprehensive approach to protecting the turtles. First, they established conservation sta-

BOX 1 *(continued)*

tions at each of the main nesting beaches. Within these areas, the Brazilian government allowed TAMAR to have complete responsibility and control of the beaches. Each station focuses on a conservation area where turtles nest and a more limited, intensive conservation area near the station. Each station has a manager, several university interns, and local employees. Over 85% of TAMAR's employees are former fishermen who bring their knowledge of turtles to bear on conservation. The local employees have become strong local advocates for the sea turtles, because their wages from Projeto TAMAR and the related tourist industry are linked to the continuing presence of these animals.

The stations' personnel regularly patrol the intensive conservation areas on foot and by vehicle, measuring turtles for size and permanently flipper-tagging all adults observed on the beach. All nests encountered are numbered. In places where predators are abundant, nests are covered with wire mesh fitted with small gaps to allow hatchlings to emerge. In places where disturbances by predators and people are too constant to allow natural hatching, the eggs are collected and brought to

Employees of Projeto TAMAR carving wooden turtles for sale to tourists at their education centers. The sale of such souvenirs provides additional revenue to the project. (Photograph courtesy of Projeto TAMAR Image Bank.)

nearby hatchery areas for reburial. Local employees are responsible for patrolling 5-km sections of the beach in the conservation areas, recording information about the turtles, and digging threatened nests for reburial in the hatchery areas. Baby turtles emerging from the hatcheries are allowed to enter the ocean just as if they were emerging from a natural nest.

Because of protection provided by the project, around 70% of turtle nests are allowed to hatch at their original locations. In addition to these efforts on the coastline, TAMAR has worked with the Brazilian government to protect and manage the nesting beaches on the offshore islands. TAMAR divers have also begun to tag and monitor turtles in coastal waters.

Projeto TAMAR currently operates 21 conservation stations along Brazil's coastline, and employs over 400 people, predominantly local villagers. TAMAR now protects over 4000 turtle nests each year, and has protected around 40,000 nests and approximately 2 million eggs in total over the years since its inception.

The project has also extended its mission to include protecting turtles caught in fishing nets while in their coastal feeding grounds. To this end, TAMAR provides information to local fishermen and villagers about the natural history, ecological importance, and legal protection of the turtles. Fishermen are given fishing gear that is designed to avoid capturing turtles. They are also taught techniques for reviving turtles caught in their nets so they will not suffocate. Due to their increasing appreciation of turtles and their awareness of the new laws, fishermen are cooperating with these policies. Another important component of this strategy involves providing fishermen an alternative livelihood—such as oyster and mussel culture—that they can turn to when fishing is poor so that they will not be tempted to return to catching turtles.

Projeto TAMAR plays a highly positive role in the villages where it operates. In many areas, TAMAR is the primary source of income

BOX 1 *(continued)*

for the local people, and it often provides childcare facilities and small medical and dental clinics. Villagers are employed in making crafts for sale to tourists, based on sea-turtle themes. To increase awareness of the program, TAMAR personnel give talks in village schools about marine conservation and organize hatchling-release ceremonies and local festivals.

Projeto TAMAR reaches a wide audience in Brazil through coverage in popular articles and on television programs. In addition, TAMAR operates special sea-turtle educational centers at three sites along the coast where thousands of tourists visit each year. The tourists get to see conservation in action, and they receive a large dose of conservation education and, in turn, support the project through their purchase of TAMAR T-shirts, towels, embroidery, and printed material. Additionally, through its establishment of an internship program, Projeto TAMAR has tried to involve the next generation of concerned conservationists in current projects, giving students a chance to experience success with a real-life conservation project. Hopefully, the awareness raised by Projeto Tamar will gradually extend to other conservation programs.

Projeto TAMAR has had much success. Although it has not prevented human-caused turtle deaths completely, it certainly has slowed population decline dramatically by protecting thousands of adult turtles, tens of thousands of nests, and millions of hatchlings. The project has also changed people's attitudes, both in coastal villages and in the wider Brazilian society. While keeping its focus on

Student interns and a child release turtle hatchlings. Interns gain valuable experience through their participation, in the process furthering project objectives. (Photograph courtesy of Projeto TAMAR Image Bank.)

turtle conservation, TAMAR has provided tangible social and economic benefits to rural people. Despite these many successes, there are still concerns that must be addressed: Turtles are still dying in fishing nets off Brazil's coast and elsewhere, and it is unknown if the protection given to the turtle nests will allow turtle populations to increase or even maintain their current levels. Major threats, such as those posed by fishing nets and coastal development, must still be dealt with if turtle populations are ever going to recover. However, by integrating conservation goals with local community development, Brazil's Projeto TAMAR has improved the future for sea turtles and for the local people involved with their conservation.

matters such as park design and species management without the thorough investigations that would normally be required. If they are unable or unwilling to offer such advice, decisions to act or not to act will be made with even less knowledge and concern for the needs of biological communities and endangered species. Consequently, conservation biologists must be willing to express an opinion and take a stand based on available evidence, accepted theory, comparable examples, and informed judgment.

Conservation Biology's Ethical Principles

Conservation biology rests on an underlying set of principles that are generally agreed on by members of the discipline (Soulé 1985). These principles cannot be proved or disproved, and accepting all of them is not a requirement for conservation biologists. For instance, religious fundamentalists who are active in the conservation movement but do not believe in the theory of evolution probably will not accept certain of these principles. Nonetheless, this set of ethical and ideological statements form the philosophical foundation of the discipline and suggest research approaches and practical applications. As long as one or two are accepted, there is enough rationale for conservation efforts.

- *The diversity of species and biological communities should be preserved.* The rich diversity of life should be protected, and in general, most people agree with this principle because they enjoy biological diversity. The hundreds of millions of visitors each year to zoos, national parks, botanical gardens, and aquariums testify to the general public's interest in observing different species and biological communities. Genetic variation within species also has popular appeal, as shown by dog shows, cat shows, agricultural expositions, flower exhibitions, and large numbers of specialty clubs (African violet societies, rose societies, etc.). At a local level, home gardeners pride themselves on how many types of plants they have in their gardens, while birdwatchers compete to see how many species they can see in one day or in their lifetimes. It has even been suggested that humans may have a genetic predisposition to like biological diversity, called **biophilia** (Wilson 1984; Kellert and Wilson 1993).

- *The untimely extinction of populations and species should be prevented.* The ordinary extinction of species and populations as a result of natural processes is an ethically neutral event. Through the millennia of geological time, the natural extinction of each species has tended to be balanced by the evolution of new species. The local loss of a population of a species likewise is usually offset by the establishment of a new population through dispersal. However, as a result of human activity the rate of extinction has increased by more than a hundredfold (see Chapter 7) (Lawton and May 1995; Lövei 2001). Virtually all of the hundreds of vertebrate species—and the presumed thousands of invertebrate species—that have gone extinct in the last century have been wiped out by humans.

- *Ecological complexity should be maintained.* Many of the most interesting properties of biological diversity are only expressed in natural environments. For example, complex coevolutionary and ecological relationships exist among tropical flowers, hummingbirds that visit the flowers to drink nectar, and mites that live in the flowers and use the hummingbirds' beaks as "buses" to go from flower to flower (Colwell 1986). These relationships would no longer exist if the animals and plants were housed separately and in isolation at zoos and botanical gardens. While the biological diversity of species may be partially preserved in zoos and gardens, the ecological complexity that exists in natural communities will be largely lost without the preservation of wild lands.

- *Evolution should continue.* Evolutionary adaptation is the process that eventually leads to new species and increased biological diversity. Therefore, allowing populations to continue to evolve in nature should be supported. Human processes that limit or even prevent populations from evolving, such as elimination of unique populations at the edge of a species range, should be avoided. Preserving species in captivity when they are no longer able to survive in the wild is important, but species are then cut off from their natural evolutionary process. In such cases, the species may no longer be able to survive in the wild if released.
- *Biological diversity has intrinsic value.* Species and the biological communities in which they live possess value of their own regardless of their economic, scientific, or aesthetic value to human society. This value is conferred not only by their evolutionary history and unique ecological role, but also by their very existence. This position is in sharp contrast to an economic viewpoint, which would assign a monetary value to each species or biological community on the basis of the goods and services that it provides or potentially could provide to humans. Such a purely economic viewpoint could lead to a decision to move forward with a development project and ignore the intrinsic value of biological diversity.

The Origins of Conservation Biology

The origins of conservation biology can be traced to religious and philosophical beliefs concerning the relationship between human societies and the natural world (Callicott 1994; Berkes 1999, 2001; McNeely 2001). In many of the world's religions, people are seen as both physically and spiritually connected to the plants and animals in the surrounding environment (Figure 1.2). In the Chinese Tao, Japanese Shinto, Hindu, and Buddhist philosophies, wilderness areas and natural settings are valued and protected for their capacity to provide intense spiritual experiences. These philosophies see a direct connection between the natural world and the spiritual world, a connection that breaks when the natural world is altered or destroyed by human activity. Strict adherents to the Jainist and Hindu religions in India believe that all killing of animal life is wrong. In Islamic teachings, people are given the sacred responsibility to be guardians of nature.

Biological diversity often has immediate significance to traditional societies whose people live close to the land and water. In Native Amer-

Figure 1.2 Tanah Lot is a Hindu temple on the island of Bali in Indonesia. Its coastal setting allows worshippers to experience the connection of the human spirit with the natural world. (Photograph by Gary J. James/Biological Photo Service.)

ican tribes of the Pacific Northwest, hunters underwent purification rituals in order to be considered worthy of hunting animals. The Iroquois, a Native American group, considered how their actions would affect the lives of their descendants after seven generations. Hunting and gathering societies, such as the Penan of Borneo, give thousands of names to individual trees, animals, and places in their surroundings to create a cultural landscape that is vital to the well-being of the tribe. This type of relationship to the natural world was described eloquently at the Fourth World Wilderness Congress in 1987 by the delegate from the Kuna people of Panama (Gregg 1991):

> For the Kuna culture, the land is our mother and all living things that we live on are her brothers in such a manner that we must take care of her and live in a harmonious manner on her, because the extinction of one thing is also the end of another.

In an ecological and cultural history of the Indian subcontinent, Gadgil and Guha (1992) argue that the belief systems, religions, and myths of hunter-gatherer societies and stable agricultural societies tend to emphasize conservation themes and the wise use of natural resources because these groups have learned over time to live within the constraints of a fixed resource base. In contrast, the belief systems of communities that raise livestock and rapidly expanding agricultural and industrial societies emphasize the rapid consumption and destruction of natural resources as a way to maximize growth and assert control over other groups. These groups move to new localities when the resources of any one place are exhausted. Modern industrial states represent the extreme of such societies. Their excessive and wasteful consumption involves the transportation of resources to urban centers in ever-widening circles of resource depletion.

European Origins

To the European mind, the prevalent view has been that God created nature for humans' use and benefit. In Genesis, the first book of the Bible, God instructs Adam and Eve to "be fruitful and multiply and fill the Earth and subdue it; have dominion over every living thing that moves upon the Earth." The biblical instruction supports a dominant tenet of Western philosophy: Nature should be converted into wealth as rapidly as possible and used for the benefit of humans. This point of view justifies nearly all land uses and implies that to leave land unused is to misuse God's gift—a foolish, if not downright sinful, mistake. In medieval Europe, wilderness was perceived to be useless land and was often believed to be inhabited by evil spirits or monsters, in contrast to the orderly qualities and appearance of agricultural landscapes (Nash 1990).

This anthropocentric (human-centered) view of nature led to the exploitation and degradation of vast resources in the regions colonized by European countries from the sixteenth century onward (Crosby 1986; Diamond 1999). In practice, the wealth and benefits that came from this policy accrued primarily to the citizens of the colonial powers, while the needs of non-European native peoples were largely disregarded. The long-term ramifications on the resources themselves were not considered either; the unexplored territories of the Americas, Asia, Africa, and Australia seemed so vast and rich that it was inconceivable to the colonial powers that their natural resources could ever be depleted.

An important element of the conservation movement did develop in Europe however, based on the experiences of scientific officers—often imbued with Romantic idealism—who were sent to assist in the development of colonies in the nineteenth century (Grove 1992). These scientists were trained to make detailed observations on the biology, natural history, geography, and anthropology of the colonial regions. Many of them expected to find the indigenous people living in wonderful harmony with nature. Instead, they found devastated forests, damaged watersheds, and poverty.

In European colonies throughout the world, perceptive scientific officers came to see that protection of forests was necessary to prevent soil erosion, provide water for irrigation and drinking, maintain wood supplies, and prevent famine. Some colonial administrators also argued that certain intact forests should remain uncut because of their necessary role in ensuring a steady supply of rainfall in adjacent agricultural areas—foreshadowing modern concern with global climate change. Such arguments led directly to conservation ordinances. On the Indian Ocean island of Mauritius, for example, the French colonial administration in 1769 stipulated that 25% of landholdings remain forested to prevent erosion, degraded areas be planted with trees, and forests growing within 200 meters of water be protected. On the Caribbean island of Tobago, British officers set aside 20% of the land as "reserved in wood for rain" (Grove 1992). Various colonial governments passed laws in the late eighteenth century regulating the pollutants being discharged by indigo and sugar mills, in order to prevent water pollution and the destruction of fish populations.

These experiences and experiments on small tropical islands had considerable influence on British scientists working in India, who issued a report in 1852 urging the establishment of forest reserves throughout the vast subcontinent in order to avert environmental calamities and economic losses. In particular, the report linked deforestation to decreased rainfall and water supplies, resulting in famine among the local people. The report was embraced by the leadership of the British East India Company, who could see that conservation made good economic sense. During the mid–nineteenth century, Indian state governments established an extensive system of forest reserves protected and managed by professional foresters. This system was widely adopted in other parts of the colonial world, such as Southeast Asia, Australia, and Africa, and it influenced forestry in North America as well. The irony is that, prior to colonization, indigenous peoples in these regions often had well-developed systems of natural resource management that were swept aside by the colonial governments (Poffenberger 1990; Gadgil and Guha 1992).

Many of the themes of contemporary conservation biology were established in European scientific writings of a century or more ago (Grove 1992). The possibility of species extinction was demonstrated by the loss of wild cattle (*Bos primigenius,* also known as the aurochs) from Europe in 1627 and the extinction of the dodo bird (*Raphus cucullatus*) in Mauritius in the 1680s (Figure 1.3) (Szafer 1968). To address the problem of the decline and possible extinction of wild cattle, Polish authorities in 1564 established a nature reserve that prohibited hunting. This nature reserve represented one of the earliest deliberate European efforts to conserve a species. While this action failed to preserve wild cattle (the progenitor of modern cattle), the nature reserve protected the sole remaining population of the wisent, also known as the European bison (*Bison bonasus*).

In Europe, expression of concern for the protection of wildlife began to spread widely in the late nineteenth century (Galbraith et al. 1998).

Figure 1.3 Humans witnessed the extinction of the dodo, a flightless bird found only on the remote island of Mauritius in the Indian Ocean. The dodo was extinct within 80 years of humans colonizing the island.

The combination of both an increasing area of land under cultivation and more widespread use of firearms for hunting led to a marked reduction in wild animals.

In Britain, many culturally and ecologically significant species became extinct in the wild around this time: great bustards (*Otis tarda*), ospreys (*Pandion haliaetus*), sea eagles (*Haliaeetus albicilla*), and the great auk (*Pinguinus impennis*). Other species showed rapid declines. These dramatic changes stimulated the formation of the British conservation movement, leading to the founding of the Commons, Open Spaces and Footpaths Preservation Society in 1865, the National Trust for Places of Historic Interest and Natural Beauty in 1895, and the Royal Society for the Protection of Birds in 1899. Altogether, these groups have preserved over 500,000 hectare* (ha) of open land. In the twentieth century, government action produced laws such as the National Parks and Access to the Countryside Act, passed in 1949 for the "protection and public enjoyment of the wider countryside" and the Wildlife and Countryside Act, passed in 1981, for the protection of endangered species, their habitat, and the marine environment. Because of the intensive human use of the British landscape, conservation efforts in Britain have traditionally emphasized the preservation and management of relatively small fragments of land. Rare and declining habitats, such as the chalk grasslands of eastern and southern England continue to be a major concern in conservation efforts.

Many other European countries also have strong traditions of nature conservation and land protection, most notably Denmark, Austria, Germany, and Switzerland.

American Origins

Many of the themes of the American conservation movement can be seen in the novels of James Fenimore Cooper, written in the early nineteenth century. In books such as *The Pioneers*, *The Prairie*, and *The Deerslayer*, Cooper described the moral, spiritual, and aesthetic value of wilderness and deplored its thoughtless destruction. His frontier hero Leatherstocking condemns the exploiters of the Earth with the words: "They scourge the very 'arth with their axes. Such hills and hunting grounds have I seen stripped of the gifts of the Lord, without remorse or shame!"

Among the first major intellectual figures in the United States arguing for the protection of natural areas were the nineteenth-century philosophers Ralph Waldo Emerson and Henry David Thoreau (Callicott 1990). Emerson, in his writings on transcendentalism, argued that nature could be viewed as a temple in which people can commune with the spiritual world (Emerson 1836). He was influenced in his writing by

*For an explanation of the term hectare and other measurements, see Table 1.1.

TABLE 1.1 Some useful units of measurement

LENGTH

1 meter (m)	1 m = 39.4 inches
1 kilometer (km)	1 km = 1000 m = 0.62 mile
1 centimeter (cm)	1 cm = 1/100 m = 0.39 inch
1 millimeter (mm)	1 mm = 1/1000 m = 0.039 inch

AREA

square meter (m^2)	Area encompassed by a square, each side of which is 1 meter
1 hectare (ha)	1 ha = 10,000 m^2 = 2.47 acres 100 ha = 1 square kilometer (km^2)

MASS

1 kilogram (kg)	1 kg = 2.2 pounds
1 gram (g)	1 g = 1/1000 kg = 0.035 ounce

TEMPERATURE

$0°C = \frac{5}{9}(°F - 32)$

degree Celsius (°C)	0°C = 32° Fahrenheit (the freezing point of water) 100°C = 212° Fahrenheit (the boiling point of water) 23°C = 72° Fahrenheit ("room temperature")

Eastern religions, which emphasize the importance of natural beauty as an aid to spiritual enlightenment.

Thoreau was both an advocate for nature and an opponent of materialistic society, believing that people needed far fewer possessions than they sought. To prove his point, he lived simply in a cabin near Walden Pond, writing his ideas and experiences in a book—*Walden*, published in 1854—that has had a significant impact on many generations of students and environmentalists. Thoreau believed that the experience of nature was a necessary counterweight to the overrefining tendencies of civilization. In his collection of essays *Excursions* (1863) he argued emphatically that

> [in] wildness is the preservation of the world. Every tree sends its fibers forth in search of the Wild. The cities import it at any price. Men plow and sail for it. From the forest and wilderness come the tonics and barks which brace mankind. Our ancestors were savages. The story of Romulus and Remus being suckled by a wolf is not a meaningless fable. The founders of every state which has risen to eminence have drawn their nourishment and vigor from a similar wild source.

This concern for the preservation of wilderness, a large area that remains essentially unoccupied, unmanaged, and unmodified by human

John Muir
(1838–1914)

beings, is a continuing and dominant theme in the American conservation movement up to the present time (Meine 2001). It contrasts sharply with the traditional European view that landscapes develop over thousands of years through the interaction of human activities with land; therefore, further management is appropriate to reach conservation objectives (Cooper 2000).

Eminent American wilderness advocate John Muir used the transcendental themes of Emerson and Thoreau in his campaigns to preserve natural areas. According to Muir's **preservationist ethic,** natural areas such as forest groves, mountaintops, and waterfalls had great value in fostering religious and spiritual experiences and for emotional refreshment (Muir 1901). Muir believed that the spiritual values of nature were generally superior to the tangible material gain obtained by its exploitation.

The preservationist ethic emphasizes the needs of the philosophers, poets, artists, and spiritual seekers—who require the beauty and stimulus of nature for their development—over the needs of the mass society, who require jobs and material goods from the natural environment. Some see this view as undemocratic and elitist, arguing that it disregards the very real material needs of food, clothing, shelter, and employment, which may require economic exploitation of the wilderness. Yet one does not have to be wealthy, highly educated, or a member of the elite in order to look to nature to create art, compose a song or poem, search for peace of mind, or simply appreciate natural beauty—all human beings share these impulses, and Muir's arguments for the spiritual and artistic value of nature did not limit its access or its benefits to a single strata of society. That wilderness can benefit all of society can be seen today in the special programs such as Outward Bound that use experiences with nature and wilderness to challenge and enrich the character development and self-confidence of troubled teenagers and young adults, many of whom might otherwise succumb to drugs, crime, despair, or apathy.

In addition to advocating the preservation of nature on the grounds of human spiritual needs, Muir was among the first American conservationists to explicitly state that nature has **intrinsic value**—value in and of itself, apart from its value to humanity. Muir argued on biblical grounds that, since God had created nature and individual species, to destroy them was undoing God's work. In Muir's view, people have an equal place with all other species in God's scheme of nature (Muir 1916, p. 139):

> Why should man value himself as more than a small part of the one great unit of creation? And what creature of all that the Lord has taken the pains to make is not essential to the completeness of that unit—the cosmos? The universe would be incomplete without the smallest transmicroscopic creature that dwells beyond our conceitful eyes and knowledge.

Muir also viewed biological communities as assemblages of species evolving together and dependent on one another.* This **ecological–evolutionary perspective** foreshadows the views of modern ecologists, as well as those of the premier American conservationist, Aldo Leopold.

An alternative view of nature, known as the **resource conservation ethic,** was developed by Gifford Pinchot, the dynamic first head of the U.S. Forest Service (Callicott 1990; Norton 1991). According to Pinchot, the world consists essentially of two components, human beings and natural resources, and the latter should be used for the benefit of the former (Pinchot 1947). The proper use of natural resources, according to the resource conservation ethic, is whatever will further "the greatest good of the greatest number [of people] for the longest time." Its first principle is that resources should be fairly distributed among present consumers, and between present and future consumers. In this definition, we see the origins of sustainable use doctrines and modern attempts by ecological economists to put a monetary value on natural resources. As defined by the World Commission on the Environment and Development (1987), "sustainable development is development that meets the needs of the present without compromising the ability of future generations to meet their own needs." From the perspective of conservation biology, **sustainable development** is development that best meets present and future human needs without damaging the environment and biological diversity (Lubchenco et al. 1991).

Gifford Pinchot
(1865–1946)

The second principle of the resource conservation ethic is that resources should be used with efficiency—that is, they should be put to the best possible use and not wasted. Efficiency implies that there can be an ordering of uses with some favored over others, or possibly a "multiple use" of resources. In this view, appreciation of natural beauty and other aesthetic and intellectual experiences can be considered competing uses of nature, which in some situations will take precedence over material uses.

Although the resource conservation ethic can be linked to resource economics to determine the "best" or most profitable use of the land, such methods use market forces to determine value and thus have a tendency to minimize or even disregard the costs of environmental degradation and to discount the future value of the resources. Consequently, Pinchot argued that government bodies are needed to regulate and control natural resources such as forests and rivers with a long-term perspective to prevent their destruction. The resource conservation ethic

---

*Biological communities have even been described as "superorganisms," in which each species plays a vital role. The best known extension of this argument is the Gaia hypothesis, which asserts that the biological, physical, and chemical components of the Earth interact to regulate the characteristics of the climate and atmosphere (Lovelock 1988; Volk 1997).

came to dominate American thinking in the twentieth century because of its democratic social philosophy. Government bodies that manage natural resources for multiple use, such as the Bureau of Land Management and the U.S. Forest Service, are the legacy of this conservationist approach, in contrast to the generally preservationist philosophy of the National Park Service.

The resource conservation ethic was the philosophy initially embraced by the influential Aldo Leopold in his early years as a government forester. Eventually, however, he came to believe that the resource conservation ethic was inadequate and untrue, because it viewed the land merely as a collection of individual goods that can be used in different ways. Leopold began to consider nature as a landscape organized as a system of interrelated processes (Leopold 1939a) and remarked that

> [ecology] is a new fusion point for all of the sciences. . . . The emergence of ecology has placed the economic biologist in a peculiar dilemma: with one hand he points out the accumulated findings of his search for utility, or lack of utility, in this or that species; with the other he lifts the veil from a biota so complex, so conditioned by interwoven cooperations and competitions, that no man can say where utility begins or ends.

Aldo Leopold
(1887–1948)

Leopold eventually came to the conclusion that the most important goal of conservation is to maintain the health of natural ecosystems and ecological processes. Maintaining these ecological processes will ultimately give greater long-term value to humans than managing natural areas for particular resources only. As a result, he and many others lobbied successfully for certain parts of national forests to be set aside as wilderness areas (Nash 1982; Rolston 2000; Shafer 2001). He also considered humans to be part of the ecological community rather than standing apart from nature and exploiting it, as the proponents of the resource conservation ethic argued. Despite Leopold's philosophical shift, he remained committed to the idea that humans should be involved in land management, seeking a middle ground between overexploitation and total control over nature on the one hand, and complete preservation of land with no human presence or activity on the other.

Leopold's new synthesis has been termed the **evolutionary–ecological land ethic**. In his writings and in practice at his family farm, Leopold advocated a land use policy in which human use of natural resources was compatible with, or even enhanced, biological diversity (Leopold 1939b, 1949). He believed that developing woodlots, fields, and ponds could in many cases create a more complex, biologically richer environment than a completely natural environment. Leopold's vision of an integration of nature and human activities is in line with modern research suggesting that humans have been an integral part of most ecosystems of the world for thousands of years, even in the tropical rain forests.

Integrating human activity into preservationist philosophy also makes practical sense because complete exclusion of human impact from natural reserves has always been very difficult and is now becoming impossible due to human population growth, air pollution, and global climate change. An approach that combines ideas of both Leopold and Pinchot has been developed, known as **ecosystem management,** which places the highest management priority on maintaining the health of wild species and ecosystems.

Development of these philosophies has taken place alongside the growth of many U.S. conservation organizations, such as the Wilderness Society, the Audubon Society, Ducks Unlimited, and the Sierra Club; the development of the national and state park systems; and the passing of numerous environmental laws. Elements of each of these differing philosophies are present in contemporary writings, conservation organizations, and government policy in both the United States and in other countries. Many government departments charged with land management typically follow the resource conservation ethic; established conservation organizations as well as newer "radical" and "activist" organizations often follow the preservation ethic; and many academic conservation biologists advocate either the evolutionary–ecological land ethic or the preservation ethic. Disagreements over policy and practice among conservation organizations and among individual conservationists continue to reflect these long-term philosophical differences. Serious differences of opinion even occur within organizations. This continuing debate over elements of conservation philosophy and ethics is necessary in deciding how to balance the long-term needs of protecting biological diversity with the more immediate needs of modern society for natural resources.

Within the American conservation movement, there has also been a series of writers who prophetically warn about the increasing destruction of biological diversity and the natural environment (Nash 1990, Meine 2001). Early authors include G. P. Marsh with his *Man and Nature: Or, Physical Geography as Modified by Human Action* (1864), and Fairfield Osborn, author of *Our Plundered Planet* (1948). In more recent years, four influential books documenting this destruction are *Silent Spring,* by Rachel Carson (1962); *The Population Bomb,* by Paul Ehrlich and Anne Ehrlich (1968); *The Closing Circle,* by Barry Commoner (1971); and *The Arrogance of Humanism,* by David Ehrenfeld (1978). Other books in this vein include *Earth in the Balance: Ecology and the Human Spirit,* by former U.S. Vice President Albert Gore (1992) and *The Diversity of Life,* by E. O. Wilson (1992). These authors have found a receptive general audience and have galvanized citizens by the millions to join efforts to protect birds and other wildlife; to protect mountains, seashores, wetlands, and other habitats; and to stop environmental pollution.

A New Science Is Born

By the early 1970s, scientists were aware of the impending biological diversity crisis, but there was no central forum or organization to address the issue. The growing number of people thinking about conservation issues and conducting research needed to be able to communicate with each other to develop new ideas and approaches (Takacs 1996). Ecologist Michael Soulé organized the First International Conference on Conservation Biology in 1978, which met at the San Diego Wild Animal Park, so that wildlife conservationists, zoo managers, and academics could discuss their common interests (Gibbons 1992). At that meeting, Soulé proposed a new interdisciplinary approach that could help save plants and animals from the threat of human-caused extinctions. Subsequently, Soulé, along with colleagues including Paul Ehrlich of Stanford University and Jared Diamond of the University of California at Los Angeles, began to develop conservation biology as a discipline that would combine the practical experience of wildlife, forestry, and fisheries management with the theories of population biology and biogeography. In 1985, this core of scientists founded the Society for Conservation Biology.

Conservation Biology: A Dynamic and Growing Field

The field of conservation biology has set itself some imposing—and absolutely critical—tasks: to describe the Earth's biological diversity, to restore what is degraded, and to protect what is remaining. Fortunately, the field is up to such tasks. The indicators listed below show just how dynamic the field is today.

- *Conservation biology has resulted in government action, both nationally and internationally.* The protection of biological diversity has emerged as a major goal of many national governments, as shown by the widespread government action being taken on behalf of conservation biology: laws such as the U.S. Endangered Species Act and comparable laws in other countries, new national parks and protected areas, international treaties, and increased regulations on trade and harvesting of endangered species.
- *Conservation biology programs and activities are being funded as never before.* Major funding agencies have made conservation biology a primary recipient for funding. For example, projects involving conservation and environmental protection worth over $2 billion are currently supported by the Global Environment Facility, a special program established by the United Nations and the World Bank. Major foundations, such as the MacArthur Foundation, the Ford Foundation, and the Pew Charitable Trusts, also make conservation activities a major priority.
- *Conservation biology's goals have been adopted by traditional conservation organizations.* Large, established conservation organizations such as

An Initiative of *DIVERSITAS*
2001-2002

Figure 1.4 The logo for International Biodiversity Observation Year 2001–2002.

The Nature Conservancy, the World Wildlife Fund, and the Audubon Society, which formerly had a restricted set of priorities, have embraced the broader goals of conservation biology (Sawhill 1996).

- *Conservation biology's goals are being celebrated in a yearlong initiative.* The year 2001–2002 has been designated the International Biodiversity Observation Year, or IBOY 2001–2002, by DIVERSITAS (Figure 1.4), an international scientific body linked to the United Nations (Norris 2000). IBOY is promoting biodiversity science to the public and to government officials through large international projects involving site monitoring and information integration. Two such projects are Species 2000 and the Global Biodiversity Information Facility, which will produce a comprehensive list of all the 1.8 million known species in the world and related databases of species distribution, conservation status, habitat, and documented museum specimens (Edwards et al. 2000).

- *Conservation biology's aims and goals are reaching a broader audience through increased media coverage.* Popular magazines such as *National Geographic, National Wildlife, Scientific American,* and *Environment,* newspapers such as *The New York Times,* and nature television programs increasingly present the latest findings of the field to an even wider audience (Morell 1999).

- *Conservation biology courses and curricula are expanding in academe.* More than 50 American universities and numerous universities in other countries have established graduate programs in conservation biology; large numbers of courses are being taught at all levels (Jacobson et al. 1995; Wilson and Perlman 1999). This development in academe is driven by the interests of students, the changing research activities of professors, and the willingness of foundations to support new programs (Collett and Karakashain 1996).

- *Conservation biology has a rapidly expanding professional society.* The Society for Conservation Biology (SCB) has become one of the fastest-growing and most exciting societies in biology. The SCB now has approximately 5100 professional members, approaching the size of the 6500-member Ecological Society of America, which was founded more than 70 years ago. The growing membership in the SCB reflects the perceived relevance of this new discipline.

Ultimately, however, conservation biology must be judged by its ability to preserve biological diversity. When conservation biologists can confidently point to successful examples of species and biological communities that have been protected and restored using their methods—and not simply the methods of its parent disciplines—only then will we be able to consider conservation biology a success.

Summary

1. Thousands of species are going extinct, genetic variation is being lost, millions of populations are disappearing, and entire biological communities are being destroyed as a result of human activities. Conservation biology is a new, synthetic discipline combining basic and applied research to describe biological diversity, document the threats it faces from human activities, and develop methods to protect and restore biological diversity.

2. Conservation biology rests on a number of underlying assumptions that are accepted by most conservation biologists: biological diversity, including the range of species, genetic variation, biological communities, and ecosystem interactions, should be preserved; the extinction of species by human activities should be prevented; the complex interaction of species in natural communities should be maintained; evolutionary change should continue; and biological diversity has value in and of itself.

3. Conservation biology draws on religious and philosophical traditions. European scientists in the eighteenth and nineteenth centuries reacted to the destruction of forests and water pollution in their colonies by proposing some of the first environmental legislation. The decline and extinction of species in Europe led to the establishment of the first nature reserves and an active popular interest in conservation. In the United States, Ralph Waldo Emerson, Henry David Thoreau, and John Muir argued for the preservation of wilderness and the intrinsic value of species; Gifford Pinchot proposed developing a balance among competing natural resource needs for present and future societies; and Aldo Leopold advocated striking a balance between managing land for ecological processes and satisfying human needs. These philosophies still guide land management, and elements of them can be found in the current doctrines of conservation organizations and government departments.

For Discussion

1. What do you think are the major conservation and environmental problems facing the world today? What are the major problems facing your local community? How do you think these problems can be solved?

2. Consider the public land management and private conservation organizations with which you are familiar. Would you consider their guiding philosophies to be closest to the resource conservation ethic, the preservation ethic, or the evolutionary-ecological land ethic? What factors allow them to be successful or limit their effectiveness? Go to the library or contact these organizations for their publications if you need more information.

3. How would you characterize your own conservation philosophy? How did you come to hold those beliefs? How do you, or could you, put these beliefs into practice?

Suggested Readings

Berkes, F. 2001. Religious traditions and biodiversity. In *Encyclopedia of Biodiversity*, S. A. Levin (ed.), Vol. 5, pp. 109–120. Academic Press, San Diego, CA. Evidence is provided that religious traditions can be used to argue for conservation.

Callicott, J. B. 1990. Whither conservation ethics? *Conservation Biology* 4: 15–20. A summary of some major themes in conservation biology.

Collett, J. and S. Karakashain (eds.). 1996. *Greening the College Curriculum: A Guide to Environmental Teaching in the Liberal Arts*. Island Press, Washington, D.C. Environmental themes are becoming part of many university programs.

Earle, S. 1996. *Sea Change: A Message of the Oceans*. Ballantine Books, New York. A personal exploration of the oceans and a plea for their protection.

Kellert, S. R. and E. O. Wilson (eds.). 1993. *The Biophilia Hypothesis*. Island Press, Washington, D.C. A discussion of the hypothesis that people have an inherent predisposition to value biological diversity.

Levin, S. A. (ed.). 2001. *Encyclopedia of Biodiversity*. Academic Press, San Diego, CA. An amazing guide to the whole field.

Morell, V. 1999. The variety of life. *National Geographic* 195 (February): 6–32. Special issue on biodiversity includes this and other beautifully illustrated articles about biological diversity, threats to its existence, and key conservation projects.

Nash, R. 1990. *American Environmentalism: Readings in Conservation Biology*, 3rd Edition. McGraw-Hill, New York. Many writers in the past were concerned with the loss of species and natural resources.

Norris, S. 2000. A year for biodiversity. *BioScience* 50: 103–107. The United Nations designated 2001–2002 as the International Biodiversity Observation Year, with a wide range of projects included.

Reaka-Kudla, M. L., D. W. Wilson, and E. O. Wilson (eds.). 1996. *Biodiversity II: Understanding and Protecting Our Natural Resources*. National Academy Press, Washington, D.C. Essays in conservation biology by leading scientists.

Rolston, H. III. 2000. The land ethic at the turn of the millennium. *Biodiversity and Conservation* 9: 1045–1058. Aldo Leopold's land ethic is now evolving into a more all-encompassing Earth ethic.

Sawhill, J. C. 1996. Conservation science comes of age. *Nature Conservancy* (January/February): 5–9. This special issue beautifully presents the advances in the field to the educated public.

Shafer, C. L. 2001. Conservation biology trailblazers: George Wright, Ben Thompson, and Joseph Dixon. *Conservation Biology* 15: 332–344. U.S. Park Service biologists in the past were aware of many of the modern principles of conservation biology.

Soulé, M. 1985. What is conservation biology? *BioScience* 35: 727–734. A classic statement.

Takacs, D. 1996. *The Idea of Biodiversity*. The Johns Hopkins University Press, Baltimore. Critical evaluation of the philosophical and political basis of conservation biology, including interviews with leading figures.

Wilson, E. O. 1992. *The Diversity of Life*. Belknap Press of Harvard University Press, Cambridge, MA. An outstanding description of biological diversity, written for the general public.

Wilson, E. O. and D. L. Perlman. 1999. *Conserving Earth's Biodiversity*. Island Press, Washington, D.C. CD-ROM with video clips, maps, models, and essays.

Chapter

What Is Biological Diversity?

The protection of biological diversity is central to conservation biology, but the phrase "biological diversity" (or simply "biodiversity") can have different meanings. The World Wildlife Fund (1989) defines it as "the millions of plants, animals, and microorganisms, the genes they contain, and the intricate ecosystems they help build into the living environment." By this definition, which we will use in this book, biological diversity must be considered on three levels:

1. *Species diversity.* All the species on Earth, including bacteria and protists as well as the species of the multicellular kingdoms (plants, fungi, and animals).
2. *Genetic diversity.* The genetic variation within species, both among geographically separate populations and among individuals within single populations.
3. *Community diversity.* The different biological communities and their associations with the physical environment ("the ecosystem") (Figure 2.1).

All three levels of biological diversity are necessary for the continued survival of life as we know it, and all are important to people (Purvis and Hector 2000). Species diversity represents the entire range of evolutionary and ecological

Genetic diversity in a rabbit population

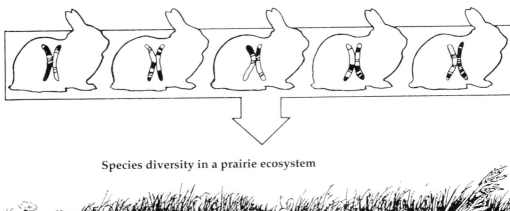

Species diversity in a prairie ecosystem

Community and ecosystem diversity across an entire region

Figure 2.1 Biological diversity includes genetic diversity (the genetic variation found within each species), species diversity (the range of species in a given ecosystem), and community/ecosystem diversity (the variety of habitat types and ecosystem processes extending over a given region). (From Temple 1991; drawing by T. Sayre.)

adaptations of species to particular environments. It provides people with resources and resource alternatives—for example, a tropical rain forest with many species produces a wide variety of plant and animal products that can be used as food, shelter, and medicine. Genetic diversity is necessary for any species to maintain reproductive vitality, resistance to disease, and the ability to adapt to changing conditions. In domestic plants and animals it is of particular value in the breeding programs necessary to sustain and improve modern agricultural species and resist diseases. Community-level diversity represents the collective response of species to different environmental conditions. Biological communities found in deserts, grasslands, wetlands, and forests support the continuity of proper ecosystem functioning, which provides crucial services to people, such as water for drinking and agriculture, flood control, protection from soil erosion, and filtering of air and water (Odum 1997). We will now examine each level of biodiversity in turn.

Species Diversity

Species diversity includes the entire range of species found on Earth. Recognizing and classifying species is one of the major goals of conservation biology. Yet how do biologists separate out individual species from the mass of creatures living on Earth, many of them small in size with few distinguishing features?

What Is a Species?

A species is generally defined in one of two ways. First, a species can be defined as a group of individuals that is morphologically,* physiologically, or biochemically distinct from other groups in some important characteristic (the **morphological definition of species**). Increasingly, differences in DNA sequences and other molecular markers distinguish species that look almost identical, such as bacteria. And second, a species can be defined as a group of individuals that can potentially breed among themselves in the wild and that do not breed with individuals of other groups (the **biological definition of species**). Because the methods and assumptions used are different, these two approaches to distinguishing species sometimes do not give the same results.

The morphological definition of species is the one most commonly used by **taxonomists,** biologists who specialize in the identification of unknown specimens and the classification of species (Box 2). Taxonomists collect specimens in the field and store them in one of the world's 6500 natural history museums (Figure 2.2). These permanent collections of approximately eight billion specimens form the basis of species descriptions and systems of classification. The biological definition of a species is the one most commonly used by **evolutionary biologists** because it emphasizes breeding and genetic relationships rather than phys-

---

*An individual's **morphology** is its form and structure—or, to put it more simply (if not totally accurately), its appearance.

(A)

(B)

Figure 2.2   (A) A botanist preparing a plant specimen while collecting in the Atlantic Coastal Forest of Brazil. The specimen will be flattened, dried, and mounted on paper. (Photograph by Donat Agosti.) (B) Natural history collections are stored in museums for use by scientists, such as these preserved birds in the Smithsonian Institution. (Photograph © Chip Clark/ National Museum of Natural History.)

ical features, which can be affected by the environment. In practice, however, the biological definition of species is difficult to use because it requires a knowledge of which individuals actually have the potential to breed with one another and their relationships to each other—information that is rarely available. As a result, practicing field biologists learn to designate one or more individuals that look different from other individuals and might represent a different species, sometimes referring to them as "**morpho-species**" or another such term until taxonomists can give them official scientific names (Oliver and Beattie 1996).

Problems in distinguishing and identifying species are more common than many people realize. For example, a single species may have several varieties that have observable morphological differences, yet the varieties are similar enough to be considered a single biological species. Different varieties of dogs, such as German shepherds, collies, and beagles, all belong to one species and readily interbreed despite the conspicuous morphological differences among them. Alternatively, closely related "sibling" species appear very similar in morphology and physiology, yet are biologically separate and do not interbreed. In practice, biologists often find it difficult to distinguish variation within a single

BOX 2 *Naming and Classifying Species*

Taxonomy is the science of classifying living things. The goal of modern taxonomy is to create a system of classification that reflects the evolution of groups of species from their ancestors (Hawksworth 2001). By identifying the relationships between species, taxonomists help conservation biologists identify species or groups that may be evolutionarily unique and/or particularly worthy of conservation efforts. Information about the taxonomy, ecology, morphology, distribution, and status of species is being organized into central databases, accessible via the Internet (Bisby 2000). In modern classification,

Similar species are grouped into a **genus** (plural, **genera**): the Blackburnian warbler (*Dendroica fusca*) and many similar warbler species belong to the genus *Dendroica*.

Similar genera are grouped into a **family:** all wood warbler genera belong to the family Parulidae.

(continued on next page)

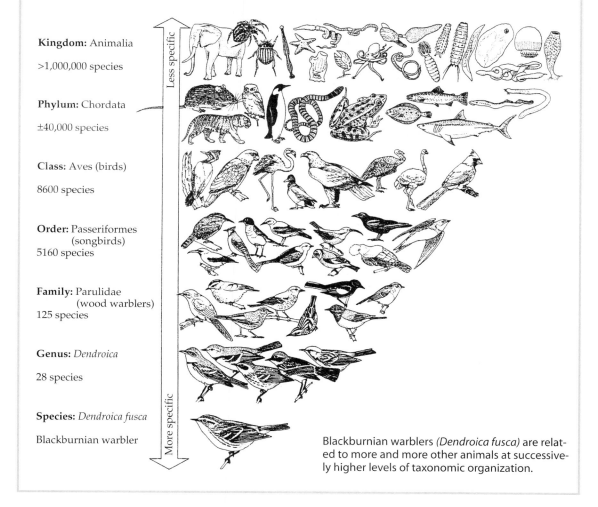

Kingdom: Animalia

>1,000,000 species

Phylum: Chordata

±40,000 species

Class: Aves (birds)

8600 species

Order: Passeriformes (songbirds)
5160 species

Family: Parulidae (wood warblers)
125 species

Genus: *Dendroica*

28 species

Species: *Dendroica fusca*

Blackburnian warbler

Less specific

More specific

Blackburnian warblers *(Dendroica fusca)* are related to more and more other animals at successively higher levels of taxonomic organization.

BOX 2 *(continued)*

Similar families are grouped into an **order:** all songbird families belong to the order Passeriformes.

Similar orders are grouped into a **class:** all bird orders belong to the class Aves.

Similar classes are grouped into a **phylum** (plural, **phyla**): all vertebrate classes belong to the phylum Chordata.

Similar phyla are grouped into a **kingdom*:** all animal classes belong to the kingdom Animalia.

Biologists throughout the world have agreed to use a standard set of names, called scientific, or Latin, names when discussing species. The use of scientific names avoids the confusion that can occur when using common names; the Latin names are standard across countries and languages. Scientific species names consist of two words. This naming system, known as **binomial nomenclature,** was developed in the eighteenth century by the Swedish biologist Carolus Linnaeus. In the scientific name for the Blackburnian warbler,

Dendroica fusca, Dendroica is the genus name and *fusca* is the species name. The genus name is somewhat similar to a person's family name in that many people can have the same family name (Sullivan), while the species name is similar to a person's given name (Jonathan).

Scientific names are written in a standard way to avoid confusion. The first letter of the genus name is always capitalized, whereas the species name is almost always lowercased. Scientific names are either italicized or underlined. Sometimes scientific names are followed by a person's name, as in *Homo sapiens* Linnaeus, indicating that Linnaeus was the person who first proposed the scientific name given to the human species. When many species in a single genus are being discussed, or if the identity of a species within a genus is uncertain, the abbreviations spp. or sp., respectively, are sometimes used (e.g., *Dendroica* spp.). If a species has no close relatives, it may be the only species in its genus. Similarly, a genus that is unrelated to any other genera may form its own family.

---

*Until recently, most modern biologists recognized five kingdoms in the living world: plants, animals, fungi, monerans (single-celled species without a nucleus and mitochondria, such as bacteria), and protists (more complex single-celled species with a nucleus and mitochondria). With the increasing sophistication of molecular techniques, biologists are now moving toward a

system of classification with three domains containing six kingdoms: Bacteria (common bacteria), Archaea (ancient bacteria that live in extreme environments, such as hypersaline environments, hot springs, and deep sea vents), and the Eucarya (all organisms with a membrane-bound nucleus, including animals, plants, fungi, and protists) (Coleman 2001).

species from variation between closely related species. For example, genetic analysis of New Zealand's unique reptile, the tuatara (*Sphenodon punctatus*), revealed that there are actually two distinct species of tuatara, both deserving scientific recognition and conservation protection (Daugherty et al. 1990). And scientists are still debating whether the African elephant is one widespread, variable species or is actually three separate species: a savannah species, a forest species, and a desert species.

To further complicate matters, individuals of related but distinct species may occasionally mate and produce **hybrids,** intermediate forms that blur the distinction between species. Sometimes hybrids are better suited to their environment than either parent species, and they can go on to form new species. Hybridization is particularly common among plant species in disturbed habitats. Hybridization in both plants and animals frequently occurs when a few individuals of a rare species are surrounded by large numbers of a closely related species. For example, the endangered Ethiopian wolf (*Canis simensis*) frequently mates with domestic dogs, and declining British populations of the European wildcat (*Felis silvestris*) are being swamped with genetic material due to matings with domestic cats. In the United States, protection of the endangered red wolf (*Canis rufus*) may be withdrawn because morphological and genetic evidence demonstrates that all of the remaining individuals are hybrids formed from extensive mating with common coyotes (*Canis latrans*) (Brownlow 1996).

Much more work is needed to catalog and classify the world's species. At best, taxonomists have described only one-third of the world's species, and perhaps only 1%. The inability to clearly distinguish one species from another, whether due to similarities of characteristics or to confusion over the correct scientific name, often slows down efforts at species protection. It is difficult to write precise, effective laws to protect a species if it is not certain what name should be used. At the same time, species are going extinct before they are even described. Tens of thousands of new species are being described each year, but even this rate is not fast enough. The key to solving this problem is to train more taxonomists, especially for work in the species-rich Tropics (Raven and Wilson 1992). We'll return to this topic later in the chapter.

The Origin of New Species

The biochemical similarity of all living species and the uniform use of DNA as the genetic code indicate that life on Earth probably originated only once, about 3.5 billion years ago. From one original species came the millions of species found on Earth today. The process of new species formation, known as **speciation,** continues today and will most likely continue into the future.

This process, whereby one original species evolves into one or more new and distinct species, was first described by Charles Darwin and Alfred Russel Wallace more than 100 years ago (Darwin 1859, Futuyma 1998). Their theory of the origin of new species is widely accepted today in the scientific community* and continues to be further refined and developed, along with the science of genetics. The wealth of new information that is continuously provided by the fossil record, along with the extensive modern research in molecular biology, has provided additional support for the ideas of Darwin and Wallace.

---

*That evolution occurs is regarded by virtually all biologists as fact. Several popular and scholarly books (e.g., Futuyma 1995, 1998; Mayr 1991) discuss religion-based arguments against evolution and why most scientists do not accept such arguments.

The theory of evolution is both simple and elegant. Imagine a population of a species—mountain rabbits living in Canada, for example. Individuals in the population tend to produce more offspring than can survive in that place. Most offspring will die before reaching maturity. In the population, one pair of rabbits will produce numerous litters of six or more offspring, yet on average, in a stable population, only two of those offspring will survive. Individuals in the population show variations in certain characteristics (such as fur thickness), and some of these characteristics are inherited; that is, they are passed from parents to offspring via genes. These genetic variations are caused both by mutations—spontaneous changes in the chromosomes—and by the rearrangement of chromosomes that occurs during sexual reproduction. Within the rabbit population, some individuals have thicker fur than others because of such genetic differences. These differences will enable some individuals to grow, survive, and reproduce better than others, a phenomenon sometimes referred to as "survival of the fittest." Our hypothetical thick-furred rabbits will be more likely to survive cold winters than rabbits with thinner fur. As a result of the improved survival ability associated with a certain genetic characteristic, the individuals possessing that characteristic will be more likely to produce offspring than the others; over time, the genetic composition of the population will change. After a series of cold winters, more thick-furred rabbits will have survived and produced thick-furred offspring, while more thin-furred rabbits will have died. Consequently, more rabbits in the population now have thicker fur than in previous generations. At the same time, another population of the same species living further south could be undergoing a gradual change toward thinner fur in response to warming conditions.

In the process of evolution, populations often genetically adapt to changes in their environment. These changes may be biological (new food sources, new competitors, new predators) as well as environmental (climate, water availability, soil characteristics). When a population has undergone so much genetic change that it is no longer able to interbreed with the original species from which it derives, the population can be considered a new species. This gradual transformation into another species is termed **phyletic evolution.**

In order for two or more new species to evolve from one original ancestor, there is usually a geographical barrier that prevents the movement of individuals between the various populations of a species (Bush 2001). For terrestrial species, these barriers may be rivers, mountain ranges, or oceans that the species cannot readily cross. Aquatic species adapt to particular lakes, rivers, or estuaries, which are separated from one another by land. Speciation is particularly rapid on islands. Island groups, such as the Galápagos and the Hawaiian Islands, are homes to many examples of insects and plants that were originally local populations of a single invading species. These local populations adapted genetically to the environments of particular unoccupied islands, mountains, and isolated valleys. Often in the absence of the competitors, predators, and parasites that affected them on the mainland, they diverged sufficiently from the original species to be considered separate species. This process of local adaptation and subsequent speciation is known as **adaptive radiation.** One of the best-known examples of adaptive radiation is that of the Hawaiian honeycreepers, a group of specialized bird species that apparently derives from a single pair of birds that arrived by chance in the Hawaiian Islands tens of thousands of years ago (Figure 2.3) (Scott et al. 1988).

The origination of new species is normally a slow process, taking place over hundreds, if not thousands, of generations. The evolution of new genera and families is an even slower process, lasting hundreds of thousands, or even millions, of years. However, there are mechanisms whereby new species can arise in just one generation without geographical separation. Unusual, unequal divisions of chromosome sets in plant re-

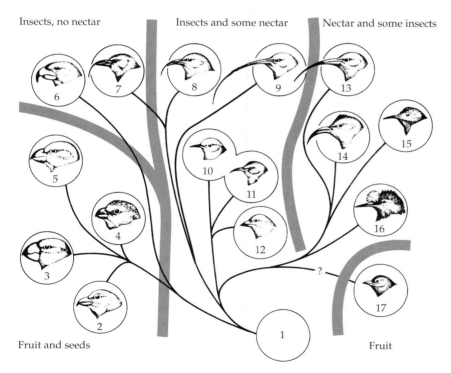

Figure 2.3 The Hawaiian honeycreeper family, a spectacular example of adaptive radiation, is thought to have arisen from one pair of birds that arrived on the islands (indicated by #1). The shape and size of bills are related to foods eaten: sharp for eating insects, thick for cracking seeds and eating fruit, long for feeding on nectar. Black lines indicate evolutionary relationships; gray bars indicate shifts in feeding habits. Numbered birds indicate different species. (After Cox 1993.)

production may result in offspring with extra sets of chromosomes; these offspring are known as **polyploids.** Polyploid individuals may be morphologically and physiologically different from their parents and, if they are well suited to the environment, may form a new species within the range of the parent species. Hybrids that result from mating between individuals of two different species can also form new species, especially when they have different characteristics from their parents and mate among themselves.

Even though new species are arising all the time, the present rate of species extinction is probably more than 100 times faster than the rate of speciation and may even be 1000 times faster. The situation is actually worse than this grim statistic suggests. First, the rate of speciation may actually be slowing down because so much of the Earth's surface has been taken over for human use and no longer supports evolving biological communities. As habitats decline, fewer populations of each species exist, and thus there are fewer opportunities for evolution (Myers and Knoll 2001). Many of the existing protected areas and national parks may be too small to allow the process of speciation to occur (Figure 2.4). Second, many of the species threatened with extinction in the wild are the sole remaining representatives of their genus or family; examples include the gorilla (*Gorilla gorilla*), rapidly declining throughout its range in Africa, and the giant panda (*Ailuropoda melanoleuca*) in China. The extinction of taxonomically unique species representing ancient lineages is not balanced by the appearance of new species.

Species Diversity and Its Measurement

Conservation biologists often want to identify locations of high species diversity. In the broadest sense, species diversity is simply the number of different species in a place. However, there are many other specialized, quantitative definitions of species diversity that ecologists have developed as a means of comparing the overall diversity of different communities at varying geographic scales (Hellmann and Fowler 1999; Leitner and Turner 2001). Often these approaches have as an underlying assumption that increasing levels of diversity lead to increasing levels of community stability and biomass production (Pimm 1991; Tilman 1999; McCann 2000). Research to test this assumption, though, has led to the conclusion that in the wild, no simple relationship between diversity, productivity, and stability exists. In controlled experiments in the greenhouse or gardens, or in simple grassland plant communities, increasing the number of species growing together generally leads to greater biomass production and resistance to drought. However, the significance of this result to the broader range of natural communities still needs to be convincingly demonstrated. Instead of linking directly to community stability and production, measures of biological diversity used or developed by field ecologists are often most useful for comparing particular groups

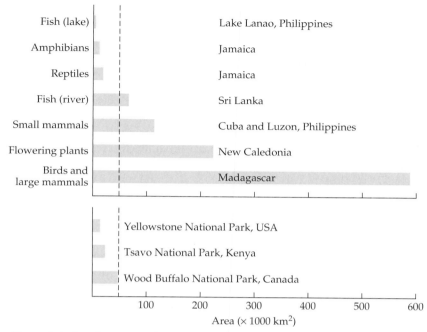

Figure 2.4 Certain groups of organisms apparently need a minimum area in order to undergo the process of speciation (upper graph). For example, for small mammals, the smallest islands (Cuba and Luzon) on which a single species is known to have given rise to two species are 100,000 km². The bottom graph shows the areas of some national parks. Even the largest national park shown (dotted line) is probably too small to allow for the evolution of new species of river fish, flowering plants, birds, or mammals, although it might be large enough for the continued evolution of lake fishes, amphibians, and reptiles. (After Soulé 1980.)

of species within or among communities. These researchers consider the diversity of plants, birds, or soil spiders separately.

At its simplest level, diversity has been defined as the number of species found in a community, a measure often called **species richness.** Quantitative indexes of biodiversity have been developed primarily to denote species diversity at three different geographical scales. The number of species in a certain community is described as **alpha diversity.** Alpha diversity comes closest to the popular concept of species richness and can be used to compare the number of species in particular places or ecosystem types, such as lakes or forests. For example, a 100-ha forest in Wisconsin has fewer tree species than a 100-ha patch of the Amazon rain forest; that is, the alpha diversity of the rain forest is greater. More highly quantitative indexes such as the Shannon diversity index take the relative abundance of different species into account and assign the highest diversity to communities with large numbers of species that are equally abundant and the lowest scores to communities in which there are either few species, or a large number of species, one or a few of which are much more abundant than the others. Because there is no universal agreement about which quantitative indexes are best to use or how to interpret them, they may be of less value to conservation biology than simply using the number of species.

Gamma diversity applies to larger geographical scales. It refers to the number of species in a large region or on a continent. Gamma diversity allows us to compare large areas that encompass diverse landscapes or a wide geographical area. For example, Kenya, with 1000 species of forest birds, has a higher gamma diversity than Britain, which has only 200 species.

Beta diversity links alpha and gamma diversity. It represents rate of change of species composition along an environmental or geographical gradient. For example, if each lake in a region contained different fish species, or if the bird species on one mountain were entirely different from the birds on neighboring mounts, then beta diversity would be high. However, if the species composition along the gradient does not change much ("the birds on this mountain are the same as the birds on the mountain we visited yesterday"), then beta diversity will be low. Beta diversity is sometimes calculated as the gamma diversity of a region divided by the average alpha diversity, though other measures also exist.

We can illustrate the three types of diversity with a theoretical example of three mountain ranges (Figure 2.5). Region 1 has the highest alpha diversity, with more species per mountain on average (6 species)

Figure 2.5 Biodiversity indexes for three regions, each with three mountains. Each letter represents a population of a species. Some species are found only on one mountain, while others are found on two or three mountains. Alpha, beta, and gamma diversity are shown for each region. If funds were available to protect only one mountain range, region 2 should be selected because it has the greatest gamma (total) diversity. However, if only one mountain can be protected, a mountain in region 1 should be selected because these have the highest alpha (local) diversity, with region 2 in second place because of the restricted distribution of its species, as shown by a high beta diversity.

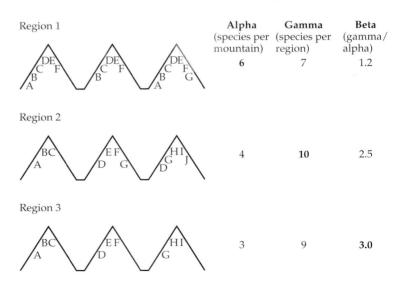

	Alpha (species per mountain)	Gamma (species per region)	Beta (gamma/ alpha)
Region 1	6	7	1.2
Region 2	4	10	2.5
Region 3	3	9	3.0

than the other two regions. Region 2 has the highest gamma diversity, with a total of 10 species. Dividing gamma by alpha, region 3 has a higher beta diversity (3.0) than region 2 (2.5) or region 1 (1.2), because all of its species are found on only one mountain each. In practice, indexes of diversity are often highly correlated. The plant communities of the eastern foothills of the Andes Mountains, for instance, show high levels of diversity at the alpha, beta, and gamma scales (Gentry 1986). These quantitative definitions of diversity are used primarily in the technical ecological literature and capture only part of the broad definition of biological diversity used by conservation biologists. However, they are useful for talking about patterns of species distribution and for comparing regions of the world. They are also valuable for highlighting areas that have large numbers of species requiring conservation protection.

Genetic Diversity

At each level of biological diversity—genetic, species, and community—conservation biologists study the mechanisms that alter or maintain diversity. Genetic diversity within a species is often affected by the reproductive behavior of individuals within populations (Tamarin 2001). A **population** is a group of individuals that mate with one another and produce offspring; a species may include one or more separate populations. A population may consist of only a few individuals or millions of individuals, provided that the individuals actually produce offspring. A single individual of a sexual species would not constitute a population. Neither does a group of individuals that cannot reproduce; for example, the last ten dusky seaside sparrows (*Ammodramus maritimus nigrescens*), native to the southeastern United States, did not constitute a true population because all of them were male.

What Is Genetic Diversity?

Individuals within a population usually are genetically different from one another. Genetic variation arises because individuals have slightly different forms of their **genes**, the units of the chromosomes that code for specific proteins. These different forms of a gene are known as **alleles**, and the differences originally arise through **mutations**—changes that occur in the deoxyribonucleic acid (DNA) that constitutes an individual's chromosomes. The various alleles of a gene may affect the development and physiology of an individual organism. Crop and animal breeders take advantage of this genetic variation to breed higher yielding, pest-resistant strains of domesticated species such as wheat, corn, cattle, and poultry.

Genetic variation increases when offspring receive unique combinations of genes and chromosomes from their parents via the **recombination** of genes that occurs during sexual reproduction. Genes are exchanged between chromosomes, and new combinations are created when chromosomes from two parents combine to form a genetically unique offspring. Although mutations provide the basic material for genetic variation, the random rearrangement of alleles in different combinations that characterizes sexually reproducing species dramatically increases the potential for genetic variation.

The total array of genes and alleles in a population is the **gene pool** of the population, while the particular combination of alleles that any individual possesses is its **genotype**. The **phenotype** of an individual represents the morphological, physiological, anatomical, and biochemical characteristics of the individual that result from the expression of its genotype in a particular environment (Figure 2.6). Some characteristics of humans, such as the amount of body fat and tooth decay, are strikingly influenced by the environment, while other characteristics, such as eye color, blood type, and forms of certain enzymes, are determined predominantly by an individual's genotype.

Sometimes individuals that differ genetically also differ in ways related to their survival or ability to reproduce, such as their ability to tolerate cold, as in our hypothetical example of rabbits, their resistance to disease, or the speed at which they can run away from danger. If individuals with certain alleles are better able to survive and produce offspring than individuals without these alleles, then **gene frequencies** in the population will change in subsequent generations. This phenomenon is called **natural selection**. In the example mentioned previously,

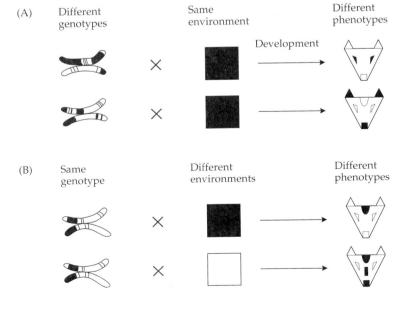

Figure 2.6 The physical, physiological, and biochemical characteristics of an individual—its *phenotype*—are determined by its genotype and by the environment (e.g., hot vs. cold climate; abundant vs. scarce food) in which the individual lives. (After Alcock 1993.)

(A) Different genotypes   Same environment   Different phenotypes

Development

(B) Same genotype   Different environments   Different phenotypes the rabbits in the cold climate are experiencing natural selection against thin, short fur.

The amount of genetic variability in a population is determined by both the number of genes that have more than one allele (**polymorphic genes**) and the number of alleles for each of these genes. The existence of a polymorphic gene also means that some individuals in the population will be **heterozygous** for the gene; that is, they will receive a different allele of the gene from each parent. All these levels of genetic variation contribute to a population's ability to adapt to a changing environment. Rare species often have less genetic variation than widespread species and, consequently, are more vulnerable to extinction when environmental conditions change.

In a wide variety of plant and animal populations, it has been demonstrated that individuals that are heterozygous have greater **fitness** than comparable individuals that are homozygous. This means that heterozygous individuals have greater growth, survival, and reproduction rates than homozygotes. The reasons for this appear to be that (1) having two different alleles gives the individual greater flexibility in dealing with life's challenges, and (2) nonfunctional or harmful alleles received from one parent are masked by the functioning alleles received from the other parent. This phenomenon of increased fitness in highly heterozygous individuals, also referred to as **hybrid vigor**, is widely known in domestic animals.

Populations of a species may differ genetically from one another in relative frequencies of alleles and even in types of allele forms for particular genes. These genetic differences may result from adaptation of each population to its local environment or simply from random chance. Unique populations of a species, particularly those found at the edges of a species range, are considered an important component of biological diversity and are worth protecting.

Although most mating occurs within populations, individuals occasionally move from one population to another, resulting in the transfer of new alleles and genetic combinations between populations. This genetic transfer is referred to as **gene flow**. Natural gene flow between populations is sometimes interrupted by human activities, causing a reduction in the genetic variation in each population. The importance of genetic variability to conservation biology is discussed at length in Chapters 11 and 12.

Genetic variation also occurs within domesticated plants and animals. In traditional societies, people preserved new plant forms that were well suited to their needs. Through generations of this process of **artificial selection,** varieties of species were developed that were productive and adapted to local conditions of soil, climate, and crop pests. This process has greatly accelerated in modern agriculture, with scientific breeding programs that manipulate genetic variation to meet present human needs.

(A)

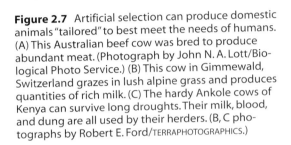

(B)

(C)

Figure 2.7 Artificial selection can produce domestic animals "tailored" to best meet the needs of humans. (A) This Australian beef cow was bred to produce abundant meat. (Photograph by John N. A. Lott/Biological Photo Service.) (B) This cow in Gimmewald, Switzerland grazes in lush alpine grass and produces quantities of rich milk. (C) The hardy Ankole cows of Kenya can survive long droughts. Their milk, blood, and dung are all used by their herders. (B, C photographs by Robert E. Ford/TERRAPHOTOGRAPHICS.)

Without genetic variation, improvements in agriculture would be more difficult. Advanced techniques of biotechnology enable even more precise use of genetic variation by allowing the transfer of genetic material between unrelated species. Thousands of varieties of crops, such as rice, potatoes, and corn, have been incorporated into the breeding programs of modern agriculture. Among animals, the huge numbers of breeds of domestic dogs, cats, chickens, cattle, sheep, and pigs are evidence of the ability of artificial selection to alter gene pools for the benefit of people (Figure 2.7). Genetic variation is also maintained in specialized collections of species used in scientific research, such as the *Drosophila* fruit fly stocks used in genetic studies; the tiny, fast-growing *Arabidopsis* mustard plants that are used in plant research; and the mice used in physiological and medical research.

Community Diversity

Communities are diverse, and this diversity is apparent even across a particular landscape. As we climb a mountain, for example, the structure of the vegetation and kinds of plants and animals present gradually change from those found in tall forest to those found in a low, moss-filled forest to alpine meadow to cold, rocky desert. As we move across the landscape, physical conditions (soil, temperature, precipitation, and so forth) change, and one by one the species present at the original location drop out and we encounter new species that were not found at the starting point. The landscape as a whole is dynamic and changes in response to the overall environment and the types of human activities that are associated with it.

What Are Communities and Ecosystems?

A **biological community** is defined as the species that occupy a particular locality and the interactions among those species. A biological community together with its associated physical environment is termed an **ecosystem.** Many characteristics of an ecosystem result from ongoing processes, including water cycles, nutrient cycles, and energy capture. Water evaporates from leaves, the ground, and other surfaces, to fall again elsewhere as rain or snow and replenish terrestrial and aquatic environments. Soil is built up from parent rock material and decaying organic matter. Photosynthetic plants absorb light energy, which is used in the plants' growth. This energy is captured by animals that eat the plants; the energy is then released as heat—both during the animals' life cycle and after the plants and animals die and decompose. Plants absorb carbon dioxide and release oxygen during photosynthesis, while animals and fungi absorb oxygen and release carbon dioxide during respiration. Mineral nutrients, such as nitrogen and phosphorus, cycle between the living and the nonliving compartments of the ecosystem. These processes occur at geographic scales ranging from square meters to hectares to square kilometers, all the way to regional scales involving tens of thousands of square kilometers (Poiani et al. 2000).

The physical environment, especially annual cycles of temperature and precipitation and the characteristics of the land surface, affects the structure and characteristics of a biological community and profoundly influences whether a site will be a forest, grassland, desert, or wetland. In aquatic ecosystems, physical characteristics such as water turbulence and clarity, and water chemistry, temperature, and depth affect the characteristics of the associated **biota** (a region's flora and fauna). The biological community can also alter the physical characteristics of an environment. For example, in a terrestrial ecosystem, wind speed, humidity, and temperature in a given location can be affected by the vegetation present there. Marine communities such as kelp forests and coral reefs can affect the physical environment as well (Box 3).

Within a biological community, species play different roles and differ in what they require to survive. For example, a given plant species might grow best in one type of soil under certain conditions of sunlight and moisture, be pollinated only by certain types of insects, and have its seeds

BOX 3 *Kelp Forests and Sea Otters: Shaping an Ocean Ecosystem*

Although the effects of human activities on the world's tropical and temperate forests have been given a lot of media attention in recent years, a third kind of forest has received very little notice—marine kelp forests. Although unsung in magazines and newspapers, these forests provide essential habitat for a diversity of species. Kelp forests are communities that develop mostly in the high-latitude coastal waters of the world's oceans around any of a number of species of marine brown algae, such as southern bull kelp (*Durvillaea antarctica*) and giant kelp (*Macrocystis pyrifera*). Enormous numbers of ocean fish, shellfish, and invertebrates depend on these forests for food and shelter (Estes 1996; Estes et al. 2001). Like terrestrial forests, kelp and seaweed communities inhibit erosion: The presence of kelp reduces the impact of waves and currents upon the shoreline, preventing destruction of coastal land. Despite their recognized value, kelp forests have disappeared over the last century at many localities in Alaska, British Columbia, and the Pacific Northwest of the United States.

The source of reduction is not as apparent as clear-cutting of terrestrial forests. Kelp is harvested in many countries by local people for subsistence, but this type of exploitation is fairly small-scale and does little harm to the kelp beds. Even large-scale harvesting of kelp for the food processing industry appears to have little long-term effect. The principal cause for kelp forest declines began over a century ago, with the harvesting of sea otters.

Sea otters (*Enhydra lutris*), once widespread throughout the Pacific, were all but exterminated by fur traders and later by fishermen who considered the otters competitors for valuable shellfish (sea otters also die when they get entangled in fishing nets). Sea otters eat large quantities of shellfish—as much as 25% of their body weight each day (Wolkomir 1995). In the absence of otters, populations of mussels, abalone, other shellfish, and sea urchins exploded, providing a greater harvest for the shellfish industry. However, sea

Forests of giant kelp provide the starting point and structure for a diverse biological community off the Pacific coast of North America. Sea otters are vital to the kelp community because they feed on invertebrates, such as sea urchins, that graze on the kelp. When the sea otters decline in number, sea urchin populations soar, resulting in grave damage to the kelp forests. (Illustration © Abigail Rorer. Reproduced with permission from *The Work of Nature* by Yvonne Baskin, Island Press, Washington, D.C.)

urchins feed voraciously on kelp; unchecked by predators, they created large "urchin barrens" where kelp forests formerly swayed.

Confined mostly to the far northern Pacific islands for decades, the sea otter is now protected in the United States and has begun to

BOX 3 *(continued)*

recolonize parts of its former range. The return of the sea otters has initiated a cascade of effects throughout the ecosystem with implications for the economy of the region's fisheries. Reductions in shellfish populations from sea otter predation have angered fishermen, but at the same time, the reduced herbivory by sea urchins has allowed kelp and other algae to grow back. Wherever otters have returned or have been reintroduced, significant changes have taken place in kelp communities: Usually within one or two years of the otters' return, formerly deforested areas are again dominated by kelp. Enhanced production of kelp has increased fish production and growth rates of suspension feeders, benefiting commercial and recreational fishing, though in many areas fish populations have been significantly re-

duced due to overharvesting (Paddack and Estes 2000). The disappearance of kelp beds in the last century and their subsequent recovery following the restoration of the sea otter demonstrates an important feature of ocean ecosystems: The loss of a single keystone species, no matter what its position on the food chain, can have a profound effect on every aspect of the system's ecological balance. The sea otter recovery is still fragile, however. Over the last decade, off the coast of western Alaska, killer whales have switched to feeding on sea otters, since their preferred prey of seals and sea lions has declined, perhaps in part due to overfishing (Estes et al. 2001). If the sea otters are eliminated again, it will have consequences for the whole kelp ecosystem.

dispersed by certain bird species. Similarly, animal species differ in their requirements, such as the types of food they eat and the types of resting places they prefer (Figure 2.8). Even though a forest may be full of vigorously growing green plants, an insect species that feeds only on one rare plant species may be unable to develop and reproduce because it cannot get the specific food that it requires. Any of these requirements may become a **limiting resource** when it restricts population size of the species. For example, a bat species with specialized roosting requirements—forming colonies only in small grottoes on the ceilings of limestone caves—will be restricted by the number of caves with the proper conditions for roosting sites.

In many communities, there may be occasional episodes when one or several resources become limited and vulnerable species are eliminated from the site. For example, although water is not normally a limiting resource to organisms living in a rain forest, episodes of drought lasting for weeks and even months occasionally do occur, even in the wettest forests. At these times, animal and plant species that need a constant supply of water may vanish. Or, bird species that are specialized to feed on flying insects may be unable to eat or to feed their young during days or weeks when unusually cold, wet, or windy weather prevents insects from flying; in this situation, the flying insects suddenly become the limiting resource for the bird population.

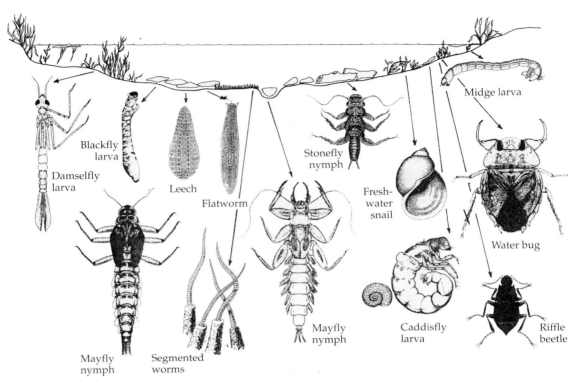

Blackfly larva

Damselfly larva

Leech

Flatworm

Stonefly nymph

Midge larva

Fresh-water snail

Water bug

Mayfly nymph

Segmented worms

Mayfly nymph

Caddisfly larva

Riffle beetle

Figure 2.8 In this illustration of a stream community in the Andean mountains, each animal species lives at different depths and in association with certain structural features. (From Roldán 1988.)

Ecological Succession

As a result of its particular requirements, behaviors, or preferences, a given species often ends up appearing at a particular time during the process of ecological succession. **Succession** is the gradual process of change in species composition, community structure, soil chemistry, and microclimatic characteristics that occur following natural and human-caused disturbance in a biological community. For example, sun-loving butterflies and annual plants most commonly are found early in succession, in the months or few years immediately following a hurricane or after a logging operation has destroyed an old-growth forest. At this time, with the tree canopy disrupted, the ground is receiving high levels of sunlight, with high temperatures and low humidity during the day. Over the course of decades, the forest canopy is gradually reestablished. Different species, including shade-tolerant, moisture-requiring wildflowers, butterflies whose caterpillars feed on these plants, and birds that nest in holes in dead trees, thrive in these mid- and late-successional stages. Similar cases of species firmly associated with either early, mid-, or late succession are found in other ecosystems, such as grasslands, lakeshores, and the intertidal zones of oceans. Human management patterns often upset the natural pattern of succession; for instance, grasslands overgrazed by cattle and forests from which all the large trees have been cut for timber no longer contain certain late-successional species.

Successional processes in modern landscapes might represent a combination of natural and human-caused disturbances. A grassland and forest community in the Rocky Mountains of Colorado, for instance, might be affected by natural fires, windstorms, and outbreaks of pest insects. Now succession in such a community is increasingly dominated by human-caused fires, cattle grazing, and road construction.

Species Interactions within Communities

The composition of communities is often affected by **competition** and **predation** (Gotelli 2001; Huxel and Polis 2001; Ricklefs 2001). Predators may dramatically reduce the densities of certain prey species and even eliminate some species from particular habitats. Indeed, predators may indirectly increase the number of prey species in a community by keeping the density of each species so low that severe competition for resources does not occur. A good example of this is the marine intertidal ecosystem in which a large sea star (starfish), *Pisaster*, feeds on 15 species of mollusks that cling to the rocks (Paine 1966). As long as the predatory sea star is present, competition among the mollusks for space on the rocks is reduced, since the mollusks are eaten too fast to achieve high population densities. Under these circumstances, all 15 species are able to occupy the intertidal rocks. If *Pisaster* is removed, however, the mollusks increase in abundance and start competing for space on the rocks. In the absence of predation, competition between species reduces the number of species; eventually only a few of the original 15 species remain, with some rocks taken over by just one species. In plant communities as well, species diversity is often higher when grazing by animals lessens competition than when grazers are absent (Harper 1977). Of course, overgrazing may completely destroy a community if all plants are eaten and the soil washes away. It is also possible that disease-causing organisms, and species we barely notice unless they attack us directly, profoundly influence community structure, reducing many species to low densities.

In many communities, predators keep the number of individuals of a particular prey species below the number that the resources of an ecosystem can support, a number termed the habitat's **carrying capacity.** If the predators are removed by hunting, fishing, or some other human activity, the prey population may increase to carrying capacity, or it may increase beyond carrying capacity to a point at which crucial resources are overtaxed and the population crashes. In addition, the population size of a species may often be controlled by other species that compete with it for the same resources; for example, the population size of terns that nest on a small island may decline or grow if a seagull species that uses the same nesting sites becomes abundant or is eliminated from the community.

Community composition is also affected when two species benefit each other in a **mutualistic relationship**. Mutualistic species reach higher densities when they occur together than when only one of the species is present. Common examples of mutualism are: fruit-eating birds and plants with fleshy fruit, flower-pollinating insects and flowering plants, the fungi and algae that together form lichens, and plants that provide both food and homes for the ants that protect them from pests (Figure 2.9) (Bawa 1990; Buchmann and Nabhan 1997). At the extreme of mutualism, two species that are always found together and apparently cannot survive without each other form a **symbiotic relationship**. For example, the death of certain types of coral-inhabiting algae in unusually

(A)   (B)

Figure 2.9 Mutualistic relationships. (A) This *Myrmecodia* in Borneo is an epiphyte—a plant growing on the surface of another plant. The plant produces a tuber at its base that is filled with hollow chambers, as seen in (B). The chambers are occupied by ant colonies, which use some chambers as nesting sites and some as "dumps" for wastes and dead ants. The plant absorbs the mineral nutrients it needs for growth from these "dumps," while the ants obtain a safe nest. In the epiphyte–tree relationship shown in (A), the epiphyte benefits while the tree it grows on neither benefits nor is harmed. (Photographs by R. Primack.)

high water temperatures in tropical areas, due to natural causes or human activities, may be followed by the weakening and subsequent death of their associated coral species.

Principles of Community Organization

Examining the feeding relationships among species provides an important way to understand how a community is organized. Further investigations demonstrate how these relationships can be disrupted by human activities.

TROPHIC LEVELS   Biological communities can be organized into **trophic levels** that represent ways in which energy is obtained from the environment (Figure 2.10).

- **Photosynthetic species** (also known as **primary producers**) obtain their energy directly from the sun. In terrestrial environments, higher plants, such as flowering plants, gymnosperms, and ferns, are responsible for most photosynthesis, while in aquatic environments, seaweeds, single-celled algae, and cyanobacteria (blue-green algae) are the most important. All of these species use solar energy to build the organic molecules they need to live and grow. Without the primary producers, species at the higher levels could not exist.
- **Herbivores** (also known as **primary consumers**) eat photosynthetic species. For example, in terrestrial environments, gazelles and grasshoppers eat grass, while in aquatic environments, crustaceans and fish eat algae. Because much plant material, such as cellulose and lignin, is indigestible to many animal species or is simply not eaten, only a small percentage of the energy captured by photosynthetic species is actually transferred to the herbivore level. The intensity of grazing by herbivores often determines the relative abundance of plant species and even the mass of plant material present.
- **Carnivores** (also known as **secondary consumers** or **predators**) kill and eat other animals. Primary carnivores (e.g., foxes) eat herbivores (e.g., rabbits), while secondary carnivores (e.g., bass) eat other carnivores (e.g., frogs). Since carnivores do not catch all of their potential prey, and since many body parts of the prey are indigestible, again only a small percentage of the energy of the herbivore trophic level is transferred to the carnivore level. Carnivores usually are predators, though some combine direct predation with scavenging behavior, and others, known as **omnivores,** include a substantial proportion of plant foods in their diets. In general, predators are larger and stronger than the species they prey on, but they usually occur in lower densities than their prey. In many biological communities, carnivores play a crucial role in keeping herbivore numbers in check and preventing overgrazing of plants.

Figure 2.10 A model of a field ecosystem showing its trophic levels and simplified energy pathways.

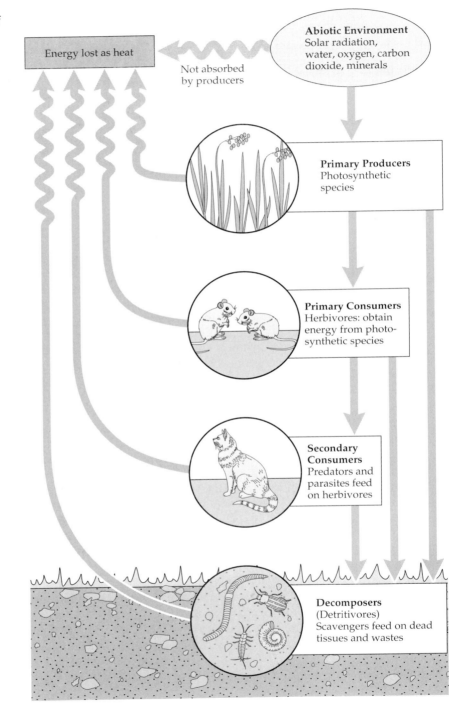

- **Parasites, pests,** and **disease-causing organisms** form an important subclass of predators. Parasites of animals, including mosquitoes, ticks, intestinal worms, protozoans, bacteria, and viruses, are small in size and do not kill their hosts immediately, if ever. Plants can also be attacked by parasites that include fungi, other plants (such as mistletoe and dodder), nematode worms, insects, bacteria, and viruses. Indeed, herbivores can be considered parasites of plants, since they eat parts of plants but often don't kill them outright. The effects of parasites range from imperceptibly weakening their hosts to totally debilitating or even killing their hosts over time. Parasites can strongly affect the density of host species. When host densities are low, parasites are less able to move from one host to another, and their effects on the host population are correspondingly weak. When host populations are at a high density, parasites spread readily from one host individual to the next, causing an intense local infestation of the parasite and a subsequent decline in host density. High densities of host populations sometimes occur in zoos and small nature reserves, making these places hazardous for many endangered species.
- **Decomposers** and **detritivores** are species, often much less conspicuous than herbivores and carnivores, that feed on dead plant and animal tissues and wastes ("detritus"), breaking down complex tissues and organic molecules. In the process, decomposers release minerals such as nitrates and phosphates back into the soil and water, where they can be taken up again by plants and algae. The most important decomposers are fungi and bacteria, but a wide range of other species plays a role in breaking down organic materials. For example, vultures and other scavengers tear apart and feed on dead animals, dung beetles feed on and bury animal dung, and worms break down fallen leaves and other organic matter. Crabs, worms, mollusks, fish, and numerous other organisms eat detritus in aquatic environments. If decomposers were not present, organic material would accumulate and plant growth would decline greatly.

FOOD CHAINS AND FOOD WEBS   As a consequence of less energy being transferred to each successive trophic level in biological communities, the greatest **biomass** (living weight) in a terrestrial ecosystem is usually that of the primary producers. In any community there tends to be more individual herbivores than primary carnivores, and more primary carnivores than secondary carnivores. For example, a forest community generally contains more insects and insect biomass than insectivorous birds, and more insectivorous birds than raptorial birds (birds such as hawks that feed on other birds). Most energy accumulated by each level is eventually broken down by decomposers.

Although species can be organized into these general trophic levels, their actual requirements or feeding habits within the trophic levels may

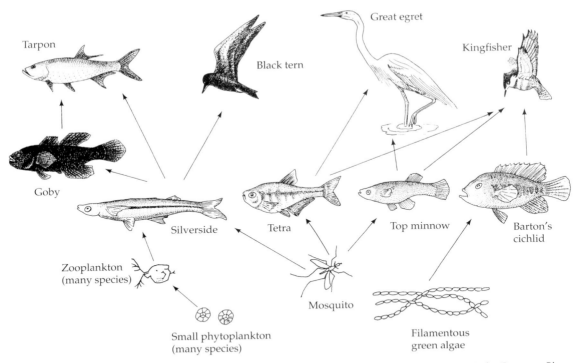

Figure 2.11 A diagram of an actual food web studied in Gatun Lake, Panama. Phytoplankton ("floating plants") such as green algae are the primary producers at the base of the web. Zooplankton are tiny, often microscopic, floating animals; they are primary consumers, not photosynthesizers, but they, along with insects and algae, are crucial food sources for fish in aquatic ecosystems. (Courtesy of G. H. Orians.)

be quite restricted. For example, a certain aphid species may feed only on one type of plant, and a certain lady beetle species may feed on only one type of aphid. These specific feeding relationships are termed **food chains.** The more common situation in many biological communities, however, is for one species to feed on several other species at the lower trophic level, to compete for food with several species at its own trophic level, and, in turn, to be preyed upon by several species at the next higher trophic level. Consequently, a more accurate description of the organization of biological communities is a **food web,** in which species are linked together through complex feeding relationships (Chapin et al. 2000; Hellmann 2001; Yodzis 2001)(Figure 2.11). Species at the same trophic level that use approximately the same environmental resources are considered to be a **guild** of competing species. For example, the many bird species that eat fruit in the temperate woodland make up a guild.

Keystone Species and Guilds

Within biological communities, certain species or groups of species with similar ecological features (guilds) may determine the ability of large numbers of other species to persist in the community. These **keystone species** affect the organization of the community to a far greater degree than one would predict, if considering only the number of individuals or the biomass of the keystone species (Figure 2.12) (Terborgh 1986; Power et al. 1996; Menge and Freidenburg 2001). Protecting keystone species and guilds is a priority for conservation efforts, because loss of a keystone species or guild will lead to loss of numerous other species as well.

Top predators may be keystone species, because predators often have marked influence on herbivore populations. The elimination of even a small number of individual predators, even though they constitute only a minute amount of the community biomass, may result in dramatic changes in the vegetation and a great loss in biological diversity (Pimm

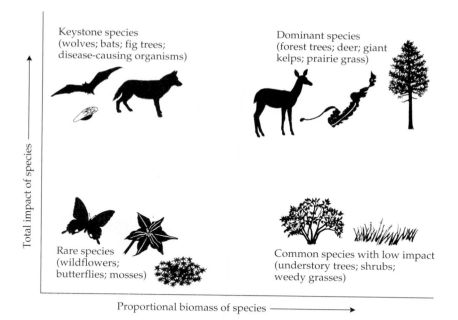

Figure 2.12 Keystone species, such as wolves, fig trees, bats, and disease-causing organisms, make up only a small proportion of the total biomass of a biological community, yet have a huge impact on the community's organization and survival. Many other species are not considered to be keystone species: rare species, such as some wildflowers, butterflies, and mosses, may have minimal impact on the biomass and on other species in the community; dominant species constitute a large proportion of the biomass and affect many other species in proportion to their biomass; some common species are plentiful in biomass, but have a relatively low impact on the community organization. (After Power et al. 1996.)

1991). For example, in some localities where gray wolves and other predators have been hunted to extinction by humans, deer populations have exploded. The deer severely overgraze the habitat, eliminating many herb and shrub species. The loss of these plants, in turn, is detrimental to the deer and to other herbivores, including insects. The reduced plant cover may lead to soil erosion, also contributing to the loss of species that inhabit the soil.

Bats called "flying foxes," of the family Pteropodidae, are another example of a keystone species (Figure 2.13). These bats are the primary pollinators and seed dispersers of many economically important tree species in the Old World tropics and Pacific Islands (Fujita and Tuttle 1991; Cox 2001). When bat colonies are overharvested by hunters, and the trees in which the bats roost are cut down, the bat populations decline. As a result, many of the tree species in the remaining forest fail to reproduce.

Species that extensively modify the physical environment through their activities, often termed "ecosystem engineers," are considered keystone species also (McLaren and Peterson 1994). For example, beavers build dams that flood temperate forests, creating new wetland habitat for many species. Earthworms may turn over many tons of soil per hectare each year, dramatically affecting soil fertility and thereby the plant and animal community. Leaf cutter ants in tropical and subtropical American forests dig extensive tunnels through the soil to build fungal gardens and, in the process, create new habitats for many subter-

Figure 2.13 Flying foxes—bats of the family Pteropodidae, such as this *Pteropus samoensis,* a fruit bat—are vital pollinators and seed dispersers in Old World tropical forest communities. (Photograph © Paul Cox.)

ranean species; their leaf-cutting activities also have a profound effect on the vegetation.

The importance of grazing animals in physically shaping communities is illustrated by the case of Caribbean coral reefs (Hughes 1994). On these reefs, many species of fish and sea urchins of the genus *Diadema* included algae in their diets, particularly those species of large, fleshy algae that were fairly uncommon prior to 1980. However, in the 1980s, overharvesting greatly depleted fish populations, and there was a massive die-off of *Diadema,* apparently caused by a viral epidemic. Without the fish and *Diadema* to control their numbers, the fleshy algae increased dramatically in abundance, covering and damaging the coral reefs. Pollution of coastal waters by human activities may have helped tip the ecological balance in favor of the algae by providing abundant nutrients for growth.

The importance of a keystone species or guild may hinge upon highly specialized relationships between the keystone species and other organisms. In many tropical forests, fig trees and fig vines (*Ficus* spp.) appear to be keystone species in the functioning of vertebrate communities. Fig flowers are pollinated by small, highly specialized fig wasps, which mature inside the developing fig fruit. Mature fig trees produce continuous fig crops, and generations of wasps are continually coming to maturity. As a consequence of this continuous fruit production, figs provide a reliable source of fruit to primates, birds, and other fruit-eating vertebrates throughout the year, even during dry seasons (Terborgh 1986). While fig fruits do not have the high energy content of many preferred lipid-rich fruits or the high protein content of an insect diet, during periods of drought the fig fruits serve as "famine food," which allows vertebrates to survive until their preferred foods are once more available. Even though fig trees and vines may be uncommon in the forest, and the fruit may constitute only a small percentage of the total vertebrate diet, their persistence is necessary to the continued functioning of many species in the vertebrate community. In this case, the fig trees are a keystone group because so many other species rely on them for food, and the health of the fig tree population rests on the health of their wasp pollinators. The mutualistic relationship between the trees and the wasps forms the foundation of the entire community's health.

Many keystone species play less obvious roles that are nevertheless essential to maintaining biological diversity (Wilson 1987). In addition to worms, other inconspicuous detritivores also play a significant role in the functioning of communities. For example, dung beetles exist at low density levels in tropical forests and constitute only a fraction of the biomass (Klein 1989). Yet these beetles are crucial to the community because they create balls of dung and carrion and bury them as a food source for their larvae (Figure 2.14). These buried materials break down rapidly, making nutrients available for plant growth. Seeds contained in

Figure 2.14 Dung beetles, also known as scarabs, are important keystone species in many communities. The beetles disperse and bury balls of dung and carrion, allowing the waste material to decompose quickly and making nutrients available for plant growth. Seeds are dispersed along with the dung, allowing new plants to flourish. (Illustration © Abigail Rorer. Reproduced with permission from *The Work of Nature* by Yvonne Baskin, Island Press, Washington, D.C.)

the dung of fruit-eating animals are also buried, which may facilitate seed germination and the establishment of new plants. In addition, by burying and feeding on dung, the beetles kill the parasites of vertebrates contained in the dung, thus helping keep the vertebrate populations healthy. Disease-causing organisms and parasites can also be examples of inconspicuous but nevertheless crucial species, because their presence reduces the density of their host species and keeps the biological community in balance.

As should be evident from our discussion thus far, the identification of keystone species has several important implications for conservation biology. First, the elimination of a keystone species or group from a community may precipitate the loss of other species (Sæther 1999). Losing keystones can create a series of linked extinction events, known as an **extinction cascade,** that results in a degraded ecosystem with much lower biological diversity at all trophic levels. This may already be happening in tropical forests where overharvesting has drastically reduced the populations of birds and mammals that act as predators, seed dispersers, and herbivores. While such a forest appears to be green and healthy at first glance, it is really an "empty forest" in which ecological processes have been irreversibly altered such that the nature of the forest will change over succeeding decades or centuries (Redford 1992).

Still in some cases, if the few keystone species in a community being affected by human activity can be identified, they can be carefully protected or even encouraged. For example, during selective logging operation, figs and other important fruit trees should be protected, while common trees that are not keystone species could be reduced in abundance with little permanent loss of biological diversity. Likewise, hunting in the logging area could be limited or stopped altogether.

Keystone Resources

Often nature reserves are compared and valued in terms of their size because, on average, larger reserves contain more species and habitats than smaller reserves. However, area alone does not ensure that a nature reserve contains the full range of crucial habitats and resources. Particular habitats may contain critical **keystone resources,** often physical or structural, that occupy only a small area yet are crucial to many species in the community. For example:

- *Salt licks and mineral pools* provide essential minerals for wildlife, particularly in inland areas with heavy rainfall. The distribution of salt licks can determine the abundance and distribution of vertebrates in an area.
- *Deep pools* in streams and springs may be the only refuge for fish and other aquatic species during the dry season, when water levels drop. For terrestrial animals, these water sources may provide the only available drinking water for a considerable distance.
- *Hollow tree trunks* are needed as breeding sites for many bird and mammal species. Suitable tree cavities are the limiting resource on the population size of many vertebrate species. The significance of nesting sites is demonstrated by the increase in breeding pairs that occurs when nesting boxes are provided and by the decline in population size of many species when dead and hollow trees are removed in managed forests (Newton 1994).

Keystone resources may occupy only a small proportion of a conservation area yet they are of crucial importance in maintaining many animal populations. The loss of a keystone resource could mean the rapid loss of animal species, particularly certain birds and mammals. When vertebrate species are lost, there could be an extinction cascade of plant species that depend on those animals for pollination and seed dispersal.

Ecosystem Dynamics

In the interaction of the biological community with the physical environment, key ecosystem processes include transfer of energy, production of biomass, cycling of carbon, nitrogen, and other nutrients, and the movement of water (Kratochwil 2000; Chu and Karr 2001; Diaz 2001). The concept of **ecosystem integrity** is important to conservation. Ecosystem integrity is the condition in which an ecosystem is free from human influences. An ecosystem that has lost some of its species and certain processes, such as the ability to retain water after storms and then release it slowly, has lost some of its integrity.

An ecosystem in which the processes are functioning normally, whether or not there are human influences, is referred to as a **healthy ecosystem.** In many cases, ecosystems that have lost some of their species will remain healthy because there is often some redundancy in the roles performed by ecologically similar species. Ecosystems that are able to remain in the same state are referred to as **stable ecosystems**. These systems remain stable either because of lack of disturbance or because they have special features that allow them to remain stable in the face of disturbance. Such stability despite disturbance could result from one or both of the following two features. **Resistance** is the ability to maintain the same state even with ongoing disturbance (e.g., despite an oil spill, a river ecosystem retains its major ecosystem processes), while **resilience** is the property of being able to return to the original state quickly after disturbance has occurred (e.g., following contamination by an oil spill and the deaths of many animals and plants, a river ecosystem returns to its original condition after two years).

Conclusion

The concepts of biological diversity described in this chapter can help identify species and places in need of protection. In addition, ecological principles are being used to formulate management strategies for biological communities. These topics will be further developed in later chapters. The next chapter will explore the distribution of biological diversity.

Summary

1. The Earth's biological diversity includes the entire range of living species, the genetic variation that occurs among individuals within a species, and, at a higher level, the biological communities in which species live, and their ecosystem-level interactions with the physical environment.

2. Species diversity, in its broadest sense, refers to the number of species found in a particular location. Species diversity is often measured with the goal of examining and comparing patterns of species distribution at local and regional levels. These measures are used chiefly for examining particular groups of species rather than the full range of species and interactions found in nature.

3. Genetic variation within species arises through the mutation of genes and the recombination of genes during sexual reproduction. Species with high levels of genetic variation may adapt most readily to a changing environment through the process of natural selection. In some cases, this process leads to the evolution of new species. In artificial selection, people alter gene pools to make domestic plants and animals more suitable for human use.

4. Within biological communities, species interact through processes such as competition, predation, and mutualism and occupy distinct trophic, or feeding, levels that represent the ways in which they obtain energy. Individual species often have specific feeding relationships with other species that can be represented as food chains and food webs.

5. Certain keystone species or groups may determine the ability of other species to persist in a community. These keystone species are sometimes top carnivores but also may be inconspicuous species. The loss of a keystone species from a community might result in a cascade of extinctions of other species.

6. Certain keystone resources, such as water holes, nesting sites, and salt licks, may occupy only a small fraction of a habitat, but can be crucial to the persistence of many species in an area.

For Discussion

1. How many species of birds, plants, insects, mammals, and mushrooms can you identify in your neighborhood? How could you learn to identify more? Do you believe that the present generation of people is more or less able to identify species than past generations?

2. Conservation efforts usually target genetic variation, species diversity, biological communities, and ecosystems for protection. Can you think of other components of natural systems that need to be protected? What do you think is the most important component of biological diversity?

3. Some examples of keystone species are top predators. Can examples of keystone species be found at all trophic levels and in each kingdom of the living world?

4. How could you manage a property, such as a degraded rangeland, a forest plantation, or a polluted lake, to restore all levels of biological diversity?

Suggested Readings

Bisby, F. A. 2000. The quiet revolution: Biodiversity informatics and the Internet. *Science* 289: 2309–2314. Databases are accumulating and organizing information on every known species and then making the information available on the Internet.

Brownlow, C. A. 1996. Molecular taxonomy and the conservation of the red wolf and other endangered carnivores. *Conservation Biology* 10: 390–396. Hybridization can blur species boundaries and create legal complications.

Buchmann, S. L. and G. P. Nabhan, 1996. *The Forgotten Pollinators.* Island Press, Washington, D.C. Wild species are vital pollinators of many crop species and endangered plants, as shown in this beautiful book.

Darwin, C. R. 1859. *On the Origin of Species.* John Murray, London. The classic work outlining a theory for the origin of new species, which became the paradigm for modern biological thought.

Fujita, M. S. and M. D. Tuttle. 1991. Flying foxes (*Chiroptera: Pteropodidae*): Threatened animals of key ecological and economic importance. *Conservation Biology* 5: 455–463. A case study of keystone species.

Futuyma, D. J. 1998. *Evolutionary Biology,* 3rd Edition. Sinauer Associates, Sunderland, MA. A sophisticated textbook that provides background material on the processes of evolution and speciation.

Gittleman, J. L., S. M. Funk, D. MacDonald, and R. K. Wayne. (eds.). 2000. *Carnivore Conservation.* Cambridge University Press, Cambridge. Carnivores are the subject of intense research as symbols of wildness and their role as keystone species.

Gotelli, N. J. 2001. *A Primer of Ecology,* 3rd Edition. Sinauer Associates, Sunderland, MA. Brief introduction, emphasizing theory and lucidly explained mathematics.

Kratochwil, A. (ed.). 2000. *Biodiversity in Ecosystems.* Kluwer Academic Publishers, Dordrecht, Netherlands. Focus on landscape conservation in southern and central Europe.

Myers, N. and A. Knoll. 2001. The biotic crisis and the future of evolution. *Proceedings of the National Academy of Sciences of the U.S.A.* 98: 5389–5392. Human alteration of the world is changing the process of evolution and may lead to unpredictable results.

Odum, E. P. 1997. *Ecology: A Bridge between Science and Society.* Sinauer Associates, Sunderland, MA. A classic brief text with updated examples.

Pimm, S. L. 1991. *The Balance of Nature.* University of Chicago Press, Chicago. An advanced text on the principles of community organization and their application.

Power, M., D. Tilman, J. A. Estes, B. A. Menge, et al. 1996. Challenges in the quest for keystones. *BioScience* 46: 609–620. An excellent review article, with strong coverage of theory and examples.

Purvis, A. and A. Hector. 2000. Getting the measure of biodiversity. *Nature* 405: 212–219. Biological diversity can be measured at different levels using different methods.

Ricklefs, R. E. 2001. *The Economy of Nature,* 5th Edition. W. H. Freeman and Co., New York. A well-written textbook on the basic principles of ecology.

Tamarin, R. H. 2001. *Principles of Genetics,* 7th Edition. Wm. C. Brown, Dubuque, IA. A good background text for learning the principles of population and molecular genetics.

Chapter

3

Where Is the World's Biological Diversity Found?

lthough planet Earth has an abundance of biological diversity, certain ecosystems have far more species than others. Certain groups of organisms are also especially rich in species, and scientists are discovering entire new biological communities in previously unexplored places. In this chapter we will examine the factors that determine the abundance and distribution of species throughout the world.

The most species-rich environments appear to be tropical rain forests, coral reefs, the deep sea, and large tropical lakes (WCMC 1992; Heywood 1995; Levin 2001). Tropical deciduous forests also have an abundance of species (Mares 1992), as do temperate shrublands with Mediterranean climates such as South Africa, southern California, southwestern Australia, Chile, and the countries of the Mediterranean Basin (Cowling et al. 1996). Much of the diversity of tropical rain forests is due to their great abundance of insects, but they also have many species of birds, mammals, and plants. In coral reefs and the deep sea, diversity is spread over a much broader range of phyla and classes. These marine systems contain representatives of 28 of the 33 animal phyla that exist today; 13 of these phyla exist only in the marine environment (Grassle 1991; Grassle 2001). In contrast, only one phylum is found exclusively in the terrestrial environment. Diversity in the ocean may be due to the great age, enormous area, degree of isolation of certain seas by intervening land masses, stability of the environment, and specialization on particular sediment types (Waller 1996; Lambshead and Schalk 2001). However, this traditional view of the "unchanging" sea is being reevaluated as a result of evidence that shows decreased deep-sea biodiversity during postglacial episodes (Rex 1997). Diversity in large tropical lakes is accounted for by the rapid evolutionary radiation of fishes and other species in a series of isolated, productive habitats (Kaufman 1992). High freshwater diversity is also found in complex river systems, with individual species having restricted distribution.

In temperate communities, great diversity is found among plant species in southwestern Australia, the Cape Region of South Africa, California, central Chile, and the Mediterranean Basin, all of which are characterized by a Mediterranean climate of moist winters and hot, dry summers. The Mediterranean Basin is the largest in area (2.3 million km²) and has the most plant species (25,000); the Cape Region of South Africa has an extraordinary concentration of unique plant species (8,550) in a relatively small area (70,000 km²). The shrub and herb communities in these areas are apparently rich in species due to their combination of considerable geological age, complexity of site conditions, and severe environmental

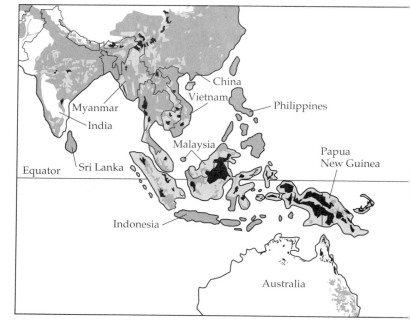

Figure 3.1 Tropical rain forests are found predominantly in wet, Equatorial regions of America, Africa, and Asia. Eight thousand years ago, tropical forests covered the entire shaded area, but human activities have resulted in the loss of a great deal of forest cover, shown in the darkest shade. In the lighter shaded area forests remain, but they are no longer true tropical forests; instead they are (1) secondary forests that have grown back following cutting (2) plantation forests such as rubber and teak, or (3) forests degraded by logging and fuelwood collection. Only in the regions shown in black are there still blocks of intact natural tropical forest large enough to support all of their biodiversity. (After Bryant et al. 1997.)

conditions. The frequency of fire in these areas also may favor rapid speciation (Richardson et al. 2001; Rundel 2001).

Two of the Most Diverse Ecosystems on Earth

Species richness is greatest in tropical ecosystems. Tropical rain forests on land and coral reefs in marine systems are among the most biologically diverse ecosystems on Earth and have become the focus of popular attention.

Tropical Rain Forests

Even though the world's tropical forests occupy only 7% of the land area, they contain over half the world's species (Caulfield 1985; Whitmore 1990). This estimate is based on limited sampling of insects and other arthropods, groups that are thought to contain the majority of the world's species (Figure 3.1). Estimates (we could call them educated guesses) of the number of undescribed insect species in tropical forests range from 5 million to 30 million (May 1992). If the 30 million figure is correct, it would mean that insects found in tropical forests may constitute over 90% of the world's species. Information on other groups, such as plants and birds, is much more accurate. For flowering plants, gymnosperms, and ferns, about 86,000 species occur in tropical America; 38,000 species

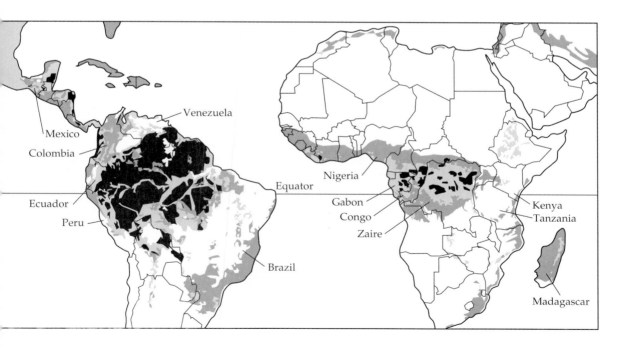

occur in tropical Africa and Madagascar; and 45,000 species occur in tropical Asia, including New Guinea and tropical Australia (Reid and Miller 1989). These numbers comprise about two-thirds of the estimated 250,000 plant species believed to exist worldwide. More than 100,000 of these plant species are found in tropical forests (Myers 1980).

About 30% of the world's bird species—1300 species in the American tropics, 400 species in tropical Africa, and 900 in tropical Asia—depend on tropical forests (Diamond 1985). This figure is probably an underestimate, since it does not include species that are only partially dependent on tropical forests (such as migrant birds), nor does it reflect the high concentrations of tropical forest birds living in restricted habitats, such as islands, that may be more vulnerable to habitat loss. In forested islands such as New Guinea, 78% of the nonmarine birds depend on the tropical forest for their survival.

Coral Reefs

Colonies of tiny coral animals build the large coral reef ecosystems—the marine equivalent of tropical rain forests in both species richness and complexity (Spalding et al. 2001)(Figure 3.2). Coral reefs include a wide range of diversity, with 32 of the world's 34 animal phyla present, in contrast to only 9 phyla represented as free-living species in tropical rain forests (Porter and Tougas 2001). One explanation for this richness is the high primary productivity of coral reefs, which produce 2500 grams of biomass per square meter per year in comparison with 125 $g/m^2/yr$ in the open ocean. The clarity of the water in the reef ecosystem allows sunlight to penetrate deeply so that high levels of photosynthesis occur in the algae living mutualistically inside the coral. Extensive niche special-

Figure 3.2 Coral reefs in tropical waters are built up from the skeletons of billions of tiny individual animals. The intricate coral landscapes create a habitat for many other marine species, such as these French grunts shoaling near the Elkhorn coral off Little Cayman, British West Indies. (Photograph © David Wrobel/ Biological Photo Service.)

ization among coral species and adaptations to varying levels of disturbance may also account for the high species richness found in coral reefs.

The world's largest coral reef is Australia's Great Barrier Reef, with an area of 349,000 km^2. The Great Barrier Reef contains over 350 species of coral, 1500 species of fish, 4000 species of mollusks, and 5 species of turtles, and provides breeding sites for some 252 species of birds (IUCN/UNEP 1988). Even though it occupies only 0.1% of its ocean surface area, the Great Barrier Reef contains about 8% of the world's fish species (Goldman and Talbot 1976). The Great Barrier Reef is part of the rich Indo–West Pacific region. The greater diversity of species in this region is illustrated by the fact that more than 2000 fish species are found in the Philippine Islands, compared with 448 species found in the mid-Pacific Hawaiian Islands, and 500 species around the Bahama Islands. In comparison to tropical coral reefs, the number of marine fishes in temperate areas is low: the mid-Atlantic seaboard of North America has only 250 fish species and the Mediterranean has fewer than 400 species. Most of the animals inhabiting coral reefs are small in size and poorly studied; tens of thousands of species or more still await discovery and description.

One notable difference between tropical forest species and coral reef species is that, unlike many tropical forest species that occupy large tropical forests in a specific part of the world, coral reef species are often widely dispersed, yet occupy a tiny percentage of the ocean's surface area. Only isolated islands, such as Hawaii, have numerous endemic species—species that are found in a particular location and nowhere else; fully 20% of Hawaiian coral species are endemic to the area (Hourigan and Reese 1987). Because coral reef species are more widely distributed, they may be less prone to extinction by the destruction of a single locality than are rain forest species. However, this assertion may be a taxonomic bias, because coral reef species are not as well known as terrestrial species. Recent research suggests that some widely distributed tropical marine species have genetically unique populations in certain geographical areas, which might eventually be considered to be a single species. As tropical reefs become damaged by human activity, the possibility that species of restricted range might be lost is cause for serious concern.

Patterns of Diversity

Patterns of diversity are known primarily through the efforts of taxonomists, who have methodically collected organisms from all areas of the world. These patterns, however, are known only in broad outline for many groups of organisms. For example, 80% of the beetle species collected in a study in Panama were new to science, even though Panama is one of the better-known areas of the Tropics (May 1992). This indicates the extent to which diversity patterns still need to be studied.

Almost all groups of organisms show an increase in species diversity toward the Tropics. For example, Thailand has 265 species of mam-

TABLE 3.1 Number of mammal species in selected tropical and temperate countries paired for comparable size

Tropical country	Area (1000 km^2)	Number of mammal species	Temperate country	Area (1000 km^2)	Number of mammal species
Brazil	8456	417	Canada	9220	193
DRC[a]	2268	450	Argentina	2737	320
Mexico	1909	491	Algeria	2382	92
Indonesia	1812	457	Iran	1636	140
Colombia	1039	359	South Africa	1221	255
Venezuela	882	323	Chile	748	91
Thailand	511	265	France	550	93
Philippines	298	158	United Kingdom	242	50
Rwanda	25	151	Belgium	30	58

Source: Data from WRI 2000.
[a]DRC = Democratic Republic of the Congo.

mals, while France has only 93, despite the fact that both countries have roughly the same land area (Table 3.1). The contrast is particularly striking for trees and other flowering plants: 10 ha of forest in Amazonian Peru or Brazil might have 300 or more tree species, whereas an equivalent forest area in temperate Europe or the United States would probably contain 30 species or less. In the case of tiger beetles (Cicindelidae), a widespread and well-known insect family, major tropical regions of the world have over 300 species, while temperate regions have less than 150 species (Pearson and Cassola 1992). Within a given continent, the number of species increases toward the Equator (Figure 3.3).

Particular groups of species are experimentally used as indicators of overall species diversity, so that locations of high species diversity can be rapidly identified (Beccaloni and Gaston 1995; Ricketts et al. 1999). At large spatial scales, there is a rough correspondence in the distribution of species richness between different groups of organisms. For example, in Africa, concentrations of birds, amphibians, and mammal species are each found in the same general areas: southern African shrubland, West African tropical forests and rivers, the Great Lakes region, and the Ethiopian highlands (Figure 3.4) (Bibby 1992). In North America, large-scale patterns of species richness are highly correlated for amphibians, birds, butterflies, mammals, reptiles, land snails, trees, all vascular plants, and tiger beetles; that is, a region with numerous species of one group will tend to have numerous species of the other groups. A combined index of butterflies, trees, and reptiles gives the best indication of overall species richness (Ricketts et al. 1999). On a local scale, this relationship may break down; for example, amphibians may be most diverse in wet, shady habitats, whereas reptiles may be most diverse in

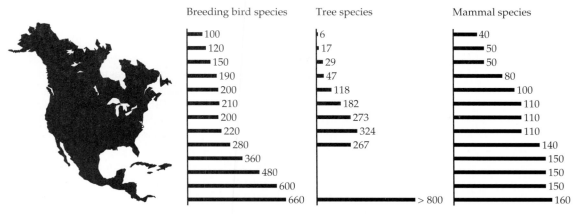

	Breeding bird species	Tree species	Mammal species
	100	6	40
	120	17	50
	150	29	50
	190	47	80
	200	118	100
	210	182	110
	200	273	110
	220	324	110
	280	267	140
	360		150
	480		150
	600		150
	660	> 800	160

Figure 3.3 In North America, as in all the continents, the numbers of bird, tree, and mammal species increase toward the Tropics. The numbers of species indicated in the bar graphs correspond to latitude in the map at left. Tree species diversity is not available for some lower latitudes. (From Briggs 1995.)

drier, open habitats. These patterns are also greatly weakened when the effects of latitude are removed. This is because greater concentrations of species tend to be found further south in North America. At a global scale, each group of living organisms may reach its greatest species rich-

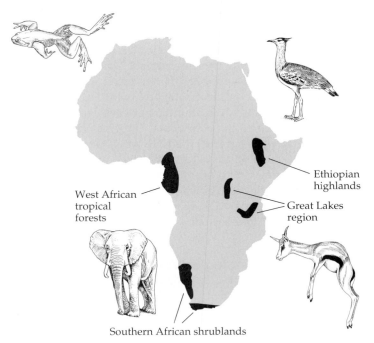

Figure 3.4 In Africa, concentrations of species of birds, amphibians, and mammals are found in the same general areas: the Ethiopian highlands, the African Great Lakes, West African tropical rain forests, and in the Mediterranean climate of southern Africa's shrublands. (Map after Bibby et al. 1992.)

Ethiopian highlands

West African tropical forests

Great Lakes region

Southern African shrublands

ness in a different part of the world due to historical circumstances or the suitability of the site to its needs.

Patterns of diversity in terrestrial species are paralleled by patterns in marine species, again with an increase in species diversity toward the Tropics. For example, the Great Barrier Reef off the eastern coast of Australia has 50 genera of reef-building coral at its northern end where it approaches the Tropics, but only 10 genera at its southern end, farthest away from the Tropics. In the case of sea squirts (tunicates), only 103 species are known to exist in the Arctic, but over 600 species have been identified in tropical waters. These increases in richness of coastal species toward the Tropics are paralleled by increases in planktonic species, such as foraminiferans, and increases in deep-sea species (Buzas and Culver 1991), though there are some groups of species that are most diverse in temperate waters.

Factors Affecting Species Richness

Local variation in climate, environment, topography, and geological age are factors that affect patterns of species richness (Huston 1994; Gaston 2000).

Variation in Climate and Environment

In terrestrial communities, species richness tends to increase with decreasing elevation, increasing solar radiation, and increasing precipitation. In some localities, species abundance is greatest at mid-elevations. The lower richness of plants and animals in Africa, in comparison with South America and Asia, may be due to a combination of lower past and present rainfall, the smaller total area of rain forest, and a longer period of human impact in Africa. Even within tropical Africa itself, areas of low rainfall in the Sahel have fewer species than forested areas with higher rainfall to the south. However, the extensive savannah areas of East and Central Africa have a richness and abundance of antelopes and other ungulate grazers not found on other continents. The greatest abundance of mammal species may occur at intermediate levels of precipitation rather than in the wettest or driest habitats (Western 1989; Mares 1992). Strong seasonal temperature fluctuations are another factor associated with large numbers of species in tropical communities (Scheiner and Rey-Benayas 1994). In the open ocean, species diversity reaches a peak at 2000 to 3000 m, with lower diversity closer to the surface and at greater depths.

Variation in Topography, Geological Age, and Habitat Size

Species richness can be greater where complex topography and great geological age provides more environmental variation which allows genetic isolation, local adaptation, and speciation to occur. For example, a species able to colonize a series of isolated mountain peaks in the Andes during

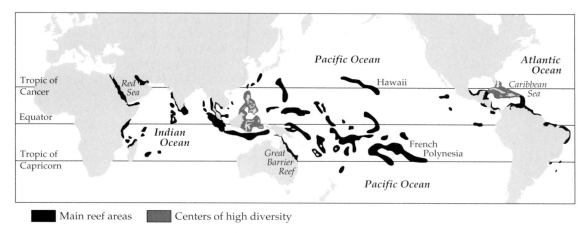

Figure 3.5 Global distribution of the coral reef biome. (After Wells and Hanna 1992.)

a period of favorable climate may eventually evolve into several different species, each adapted to its local mountain environment. A similar process could occur for fish and invertebrates occupying large drainage systems and lakes that become divided into several smaller systems. Examples include the Tennessee River system in the United States, the Mekong River in southeast Asia, and Lake Baikal in Siberia (Strayer 2001). Geologically complex areas can produce a variety of soil conditions with very sharp boundaries between them, leading to multiple communities and species adapted to one specific soil type or another.

Larger areas also can provide a greater range of habitats in which species can evolve and live. For example, coral species richness is several times greater in the Indian and West Pacific Oceans than in the western Atlantic Ocean, which is much smaller in area (Figure 3.5). More than 50 genera of coral exist in many of the Indo-Pacific areas, but only about 20 genera occur in the reefs of the Caribbean Sea and the adjacent Atlantic Ocean.

Why Are There So Many Species in the Tropics?

There is ample evidence demonstrating that tropical environments possess the greatest species diversity. Many theories have been advanced to explain this (Gaston 2000; Noble and Roxburgh 2001; Willig 2001). Following are some of the most reasonable theories:

1. Tropical regions receive more solar energy over the course of a year than temperate regions. As a result, many tropical communities have a higher rate of productivity than temperate communities, in terms of the number of kilograms of living material (biomass) produced

each year per hectare of habitat. This high productivity results in a greater resource base that can support a wider range of species.

2. The large geographical area of the Tropics, in comparison with the temperate zone, may account for the greater rates of speciation and lower rates of extinction than the temperate zones (Chown and Gaston 2000). This follows from the fact that the tropical areas north and south of the Equator are next to each other, while the temperate areas outside the Tropics are divided in two by the Tropics themselves.

3. Tropical communities are more stable than temperate communities, which have had to disperse in response to periods of glaciation. This greater stability has allowed the processes of evolution and speciation to occur uninterrupted in tropical communities in response to local conditions. In temperate areas, the scouring actions of glaciers and the frigid climate throughout the temperate region have destroyed many local species that might have evolved and have favored those species able to disperse long distances. Thus, a more stable period of evolution has allowed a greater degree of specialization and local adaptation to occur in tropical areas.

4. The warm temperatures and high humidity in many tropical areas provide favorable conditions for the growth and survival of many species. Entire communities of species can also develop in the tree canopies. In contrast, species living in temperate zones must have physiological mechanisms that allow them to tolerate cold and freezing conditions. These species may also have specialized behaviors, such as dormancy, hibernation, burrowing into the ground, or migration to help them survive the winter. The inability of many groups of plants and animals to live outside the Tropics suggests that these adaptations are not easily evolved.

5. Due to a predictable environment, species interactions in the Tropics are more intense, leading initially to greater competition among species and later to niche specialization. Also, tropical species may face greater pressure from parasites and disease because there is no winter to reduce pest populations. Ever-present populations of these parasites prevent any single species or group of species from dominating communities, creating an opportunity for numerous species to coexist at low individual densities. For example, tree seedlings are often killed by fungi and insects when they grow near other trees of the same species, often leading to wide spaces between adult trees of the same species (Harms et al. 2000). In many ways, the biology of the Tropics is the biology of rare species. In contrast, temperate-zone species may face reduced parasite pressure because the winter cold reduces parasite populations, allowing one or a few competitively superior species of plants and animals to dominate the community and exclude many other, less competitive species.

How Many Species Exist Worldwide?

Any strategy for conserving biological diversity must be based on a firm grasp of the numbers of species that exist in the world today and how those species are distributed (Figure 3.6A). At the present time, about 1.5 million species have been described in total. It is certain that *at least twice* this number of species remain undescribed, primarily in the Tropics, leading to an estimate of nearly 5 million species worldwide. We will return to this number later in the chapter when we examine the problems involved in estimating species.

New Species Are Being Discovered All the Time

Amazingly, around 20,000 new species are described each year. While certain groups of organisms such as birds, mammals, and temperate flowering plants are relatively well known, a small but steady number of new species in these groups are being discovered each year (Donoghue and Alverson 2000). Since 1991, six new species of primate have been found in Brazil, and three new species of lemur in Madagascar have been discovered. Five hundred to six hundred new species of amphibians are described each decade. More species of all groups will be found if scientists keep looking for them (Morell 1996).

In groups such as insects, spiders, mites, nematodes, and fungi, the number of described species is still increasing at the rate of 1–2% per year (May 1992). Huge numbers of species in these invertebrate groups, mostly in tropical areas but also in the temperate zone, have yet to be discovered and described (Figure 3.6B). Compounding the problem is the fact that, though most of the world's remaining undescribed species are probably insects and other invertebrates, only one-third of the world's 5000 taxonomists are now studying these groups.

Sometimes new species are discovered when further research, often involving the techniques of molecular systematics, reveals that what was originally thought to be a single species with a number of geographically distinct populations is really two or more species. Sometimes new species are discovered via "living fossils"—species known only from the fossil record and believed to be extinct until living examples are found in modern times. In 1938, ichthyologists throughout the world were stunned by the report of a strange fish caught in the Indian Ocean. This fish, subsequently named *Latimeria chalumnae,* belonged to a group of marine fish known as coelacanths that were common in ancient seas but were thought to have gone extinct 65 million years ago (Thomas 1991). Coelacanths are of particular interest to evolutionary biologists because they show certain features of muscles and bones in their fins that are comparable to the limbs of the first land animals. Biologists searched the Indian Ocean for 14 years before another coelacanth was found, off Grand Comoro Island between Madagascar and the African coast. Subsequent investigation has shown that there is a single population of about 200

Figure 3.6 (A) A total of 1,413,000 species have been identified and described by scientists; the majority of these are insects and plants. (Data from Wilson 1992.) (B) For major groups of organisms estimated to contain over 100,000 species, the numbers of described species are indicated by the shaded portions of the bars; the unshaded portions are estimates of the numbers of undescribed species. (Vertebrates are included for comparison.) The column on the right shows the accuracy of the estimates. The number of undescribed species is particularly speculative for the various groups of microorganisms. The number of identified species could eventually reach 5–10 million, or even 30–150 million. (After Hammond 1992.)

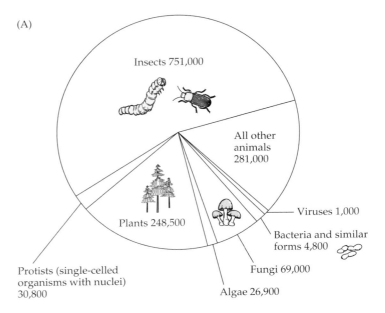

(A)

Insects 751,000

All other animals 281,000

Viruses 1,000

Bacteria and similar forms 4,800

Fungi 69,000

Algae 26,900

Plants 248,500

Protists (single-celled organisms with nuclei) 30,800

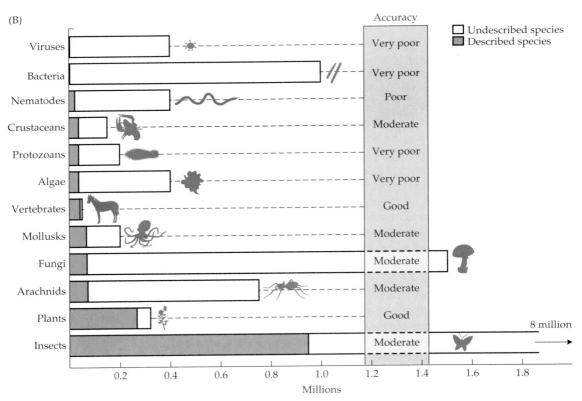

(B)

Accuracy

Undescribed species
Described species

Group	Accuracy
Viruses	Very poor
Bacteria	Very poor
Nematodes	Poor
Crustaceans	Moderate
Protozoans	Very poor
Algae	Very poor
Vertebrates	Good
Mollusks	Moderate
Fungi	Moderate
Arachnids	Moderate
Plants	Good
Insects	Moderate

8 million

Millions

individuals living in underwater caves approximately 200 m offshore of Grand Comoro Island (Fricke and Hissman 1990). In recent years, the Republic of Comores implemented a conservation plan to protect the coelacanths, including a ban on catching and selling the fish. In a remarkable footnote to this story, in 1998 a marine biologist working in Indonesia was astonished to see a coelacanth for sale in a local fish market. Although it is now known that a second population of coelacanths exists, it is not yet known whether the second population is the same species as that found in the Indian Ocean.

Recently Discovered Communities

In addition to new species, entire biological communities continue to be discovered, often in extremely remote and inaccessible localities. These communities often consist of inconspicuous species, such as bacteria, protists, and small invertebrates, that have escaped the attention of earlier taxonomists. Specialized exploration techniques have aided in these discoveries, particularly in the deep sea and in the forest canopy. Some recently discovered communities include:

- Diverse communities of animals, particularly insects, that are adapted to living in the canopies of tropical trees and rarely, if ever, descend to the ground (Wilson 1991; Moffat 1994; Lowman 1999). The use of technical climbing equipment, canopy towers and walkways, and tall cranes, is opening up this habitat to exploration (Figure 3.7).
- In 2002, scientists exploring in the remote Brandberg Mountains of Namibia in southwestern Africa discovered an entirely new insect order, distantly related to grasshoppers, stick insects, and praying mantids, subsequently named the Mantophatodea (Klass et al. 2002). The last time a new order of insects had been described was in 1915.
- Investigations of bacterial communities in remote locations using new sampling techniques have revealed a diversity of species previously unsuspected. The floor of the deep sea has unique communities of bacteria and animals that grow around geothermal vents (Box 4). Undescribed, active bacteria unrelated to any known species have even been found in marine sediments at depths of up to 6482 m, where they undoubtedly play a major chemical and energetic role in this vast ecosystem (Parkes et al. 1994; Li et al. 1999). Drilling projects have shown that diverse bacterial communities exist 2.8 km deep in the Earth's crust, at densities ranging from 100 to 100 million bacteria per gram of solid rock. Molecular genetic techniques have revealed these communities to be composed of numerous species, each with their own characteristic DNA (Fredrickson and Onstott 1996; Fisk et al. 1998). These bacterial communities are being actively investigated as a source of novel chemicals, for their potential usefulness in degrad-

(A)

(B)

Figure 3.7 (A) Biologists are gaining access to the diverse world of the rain forest canopy by using techniques borrowed from technical rock climbing. (Photograph courtesy of Nalini Nadkarni.) (B) Research is carried out in the tree canopy from a mobile platform attached to the arm of a tall crane. (Photograph by Marcos Guerra, courtesy of Joe Wright.)

ing toxic chemicals, and for insight into whether life could exist on other planets.

• Recent investigations of healthy tropical tree leaves have revealed an extraordinarily rich group of fungi that live inside the leaves. In a sample of 83 leaves, there appears to be over 340 distinct species of fungi (Arnold et al. 2000). Whether these fungi are parasites on the leaves or providing some benefit to the plants remains to be investigated.

Diversity Surveys: Collecting and Counting Species

Describing the diversity of major groups of organisms represents an enormous undertaking. Large institutions and teams of scientists often undertake biological surveys of entire countries or regions, which may involve decades—such work includes specimen collection in the field, identification of known species, descriptions of new species, and, finally, publication of the results so that others can use the information. Two such examples are the massive Flora of North America Project, based

BOX 4 *Conserving a World Unknown: Hydrothermal Vents and Oil Plumes*

Biologists are aware that many species exist that have not been adequately studied and described, a fact that frequently hampers conservation. In recent years, it has become apparent that there are entire communities that remain undiscovered in the more remote parts of the Earth. It is clear from the example of deep-sea hydrothermal vents that species, genera, and even families of organisms exist about which scientists know nothing. The biota of these vents were investigated in detail only in the last 15 years with the invention of technology that enables scientists to photograph and collect specimens from depths of over 2000 meters (Gage and Tyler 1991; Dover 2001). Such organisms pose a significant problem for conservationists: How does one go about conserving undiscovered or barely known species and communities?

Hydrothermal vents are temporary underwater openings in the Earth's crust. Extremely hot water (in excess of 150° C), sulfides, and dissolved minerals escape from these vents and support a profusion of species in the deepest parts of the ocean. Communities of large animals such as clams, crabs, fishes, and 2-m long tube worms (also known as pogonophorans) derive their energy from chemosynthetic bacteria, which are the primary producers of the vent ecosystem. The animals feed on the bacteria directly or the bacteria live symbiotically inside their bodies. The vents themselves are short-lived, spanning a few decades at most; however, the communities supported by these vents are thought to have evolved over the past 200 million years or more. Until deep-sea submersibles were developed in the 1970s, scientists were completely unaware of the communities that live around the vents. Since 1979, however, when the submersible *Alvin* was first used to examine the vents around the Galápagos Rift in the Pacific Ocean, 150 new species, 50 new genera, and 20 new families and subfamilies of animals—not including microorganisms—have been described (Lambshead and Schalk 2001). As investigation of deep-sea vents continues, more families will certainly be discovered, encompassing many new genera and species.

Like many terrestrial communities, hydrothermal communities vary according to differences in their local environment. Distribution of hydrothermal communities is dependent upon the character of the vents, including the temperature, chemical composition, and flow pattern of hydrothermal fluid issuing from the vents. Scientists studying hydrothermal species may work for decades, yet only acquire minimal knowledge of the dynamics of these communities because of the unique nature of the study sites: The vents are ephemeral, sometimes existing for only a few years, and inaccessible—they can be reached only with the use of expensive, specialized equipment. Work is just starting on the genetics of these species to determine their ability to disperse and colonize new vents.

Petroleum-seep communities, another little-known ecosystem like the assemblages at hydrothermal vents, exist at ocean depths far below the reach of sunlight. In this case, the initial source of energy comes from petrochemicals—oil—seeping from cracks in the ocean floor (Schneider 1995). Some of the same species that congregate around hydrothermal and petroleum-seep vents may also colonize the carcasses of large fish and marine mammals, such as whales, which sink to the bottom of the ocean floor; these unpredictable bonanzas of organic matter may provide crucial stepping stones for organisms to disperse among widely scattered hydrothermal vents and petroleum seeps.

Hampered by the inaccessibility of the sites and the cost of investigation, biologists nevertheless need to think ahead to conservation problems that might face these species in the future. Industrial pollutants, for example, have damaged ocean species in shallower waters and in theory could harm these communities as well. Deep-sea oil rigs might pump dry oil seeps and cause local extinctions. As whale and fish stocks decline, the corresponding de-

BOX 4 *(continued)*

crease in carcasses on the sea bottom may remove a critical resource necessary for the dispersal and maintenance of certain populations. How would conservationists respond to such a situation?

Though as yet these problems are strictly hypothetical, they illustrate a frustrating aspect of conservation biology: Too little is known about too many species and ecosystems to develop and implement specific measures that might prevent future extinctions. As time passes, new species, genera, and families continue to be added to the list of known organisms living on the Earth, but many others are probably lost before they are even discovered. How does conservation biology account for species and perhaps whole communities

that are still unknown but are nonetheless in need of conservation? Experience has shown that a specific conservation program created in ignorance of a species' behavior and biological needs can sometimes be worse than no program at all. Do we develop conservation programs despite our lack of information and hope for the best? Or do we continue our studies in the hope that the time lost will not prove fatal to the species? At this stage, there is only one definitive statement that can address these dilemmas: we know that restricting pollution has broadly positive effects on natural communities, so pollution abatement programs may offer the best conservation strategy in these situations, even when the biological communities are not thoroughly understood.

Part of a hydrothermal vent community. Large tube worms (*Riftia pachyptila*) dominate the ecosystem. Crabs and mussels also make their home here. The energy and nutrients that support this community are derived from the hydrogen sulfide and minerals emitted by volcanic vents. (Photograph by E. Kristoff/National Geographic Image Collection.)

at the Missouri Botanical Garden, and the Flora Malesiana in the Indo–Pacific region, organized by the Rijksherbarium in the Netherlands.

In conducting such surveys, scientists determine the identity and numbers of species present in an area by means of a thorough collection of specimens that has been compiled over an extended period of time. The collection is then carefully sorted and classified by specialists, often at museums. For example, a team from the Natural History Museum of London collected over one million beetles from a 500-ha lowland rain forest in the Dumoga–Bone National Park on Sulawesi, Indonesia, in 1985. This effort led to an initial list of 3488 species, large numbers of which were previously unknown to science. Subsequent museum work allowed the identification of 1000 more species, with as many as 2000 species remaining to be identified over the coming years and decades.

Estimating the Number of Species

Worldwide, the most diverse group of organisms appears to be the insects, with about 750,000 species described already—about half the world's total species (see Figure 3.6A). If we assume the number of insect species can be accurately estimated, then it may be possible to estimate the total number of species in the world. Entomologist Terry Erwin has attempted this by sampling entire insect communities in tropical America using insecticidal fogging of whole trees (Figure 3.8) (Erwin 1982). These studies have revealed an extremely rich and largely unde-

(A)

(B)

Figure 3.8 (A) A researcher uses insecticidal fog to sample the vast number of insect species in the canopy of a tropical forest. (Photograph © Mark Moffett/Minden Pictures.) (B) Back in the lab, a Costa Rican researcher begins the process of sorting, describing, and identifying specimens. (Photograph by Robert Colwell.)

scribed insect fauna in the tree canopies (Wilson 1991). Using the results of his tree-fogging work, Erwin (1982) attempted to estimate the number of insect species in the world. He reasons as follows: in Panama, 1200 species of beetles were collected from the canopy of a single tree species, *Luehea seemannii*. About 800 of these beetles were herbivorous. He estimated that 20% of these herbivorous beetles (160 species) are specialist feeders on this tree species. Since beetles represent 40% of all insect species, there may be a total of 400 species of specialized insects that feed in the canopy of each tree species. Erwin estimated that canopy species represent only about two-thirds of the insect species on the tree, suggesting that there are 600 insect species specializing on each plant species. Since there are about 50,000 species of tropical woody plants, there may be as many as 30 million species of insects alone.

Each step in this calculation is so speculative that many knowledgeable scientists do not accept it and keep to the earlier figure of about 5 million total species (Gaston 1991). For example, it may be the case that only 5% of insects are actually specialist feeders on only one plant species, leading to an estimate of only 7.5 million insect species. However, Erwin's work is very significant for a number of reasons: it calls attention to the large numbers of undescribed insect species, develops a new approach to estimating insect numbers, and emphasizes the relationships among plant and animal species.

Another approach to estimating biological diversity involves developing "rules" for determining how many species are involved in biological relationships (May 1992). For example, in Britain and Europe, where species are fairly well known, there are about six times more fungus species than plant species. If this general ratio is applicable throughout the world, there may be as many as 1.6 million fungus species, in addition to the estimated 250,000 plant species worldwide. Since only 69,000 fungus species have been described so far, it is possible that there are over 1.5 million fungus species waiting to be discovered, most of them in the Tropics (Hawksworth 1991). If it turns out that fungal diversity increases more rapidly toward the Equator, as some scientists have suggested (Frohlich and Hyde 1999), there may be as many as 9 million undescribed fungal species.

Yet another approach is to assume that each species of plant and insect, which together form the majority of currently known species, has at least one species of specialized bacteria, protist, nematode, and virus; hence the estimate of the number of total species worldwide should be multiplied by five—bringing it to 25 million, using traditional estimates, or to 150 million using Erwin's estimates. Perhaps biological communities have a number of common species that can be readily assessed and used to estimate the number of rare species that are harder to find. Developing such preliminary approaches is allowing estimates to be made of the number of species in communities while more rigorous sampling and identification is being performed.

UNDERREPRESENTED SPECIES   The difficulty of making estimates of species numbers is exacerbated by the fact that inconspicuous species have not received their proper share of taxonomic attention. Since inconspicuous species constitute the majority of species on Earth, the difficulty of finding and cataloging them delays a thorough understanding of the full extent of the planet's biological diversity.

Inconspicuous organisms, including small rodents, most insects, and microorganisms, are much less likely to be observed by chance outside their natural habitats, as the coelacanth was, or even *within* their native environments. For example, mites in the soil, soft-bodied insects such as bark-lice, and nematodes (roundworms) in both soil and water are small and hard to study. If properly studied, these groups could number in the hundreds of thousands of species: Since demonstrating the role of nematode species as root parasites of agricultural plants, scientists have dramatically increased their efforts to collect and describe these minute animals. Consequently, the catalog of this one group of organisms has grown from the 80 species known in 1860 to around 20,000 species known today. Most of the described nematode species are from northwestern European coastal regions; some experts estimate that there may be as many as 100 million species waiting to be described (Boucher and Lambshead 1995), though this number should be considered highly speculative. The number of trained specialists is the limiting factor in unlocking the diversity of this enormous group of species, as it is with so many other taxonomic groups.

Bacteria are also very poorly known (Dunlap 2001) and thus underrepresented in estimates of the total species on Earth. Only about 5000 species of bacteria are currently recognized by microbiologists, because they are difficult to grow and identify. However, work in Norway that analyzed bacterial DNA hints that there may be more than 4000 species in a single gram of soil and an equally large number of different species from marine sediments (Giovannoni et al. 1990; Ward et al. 1990). Such high diversity in small samples suggests that there could be thousands or even millions of undescribed bacteria species. Many of these unknown bacteria are probably very common and of major environmental importance. In the ancient kingdom of Archaea, which has been less studied in the past, even new bacteria *phyla* continue to be discovered.

Many inconspicuous species that live in remote habitats will not be found and cataloged unless biologists search for them. A lack of collecting, especially, has hampered our knowledge of the species richness of the marine environment (Grassle 2001)—a great frontier of biological diversity, with huge numbers of species and even entire communities still unknown—at least in part because it poses challenges for study. Marine invertebrate animals such as polychaete worms, for instance, are not well studied because they make the ocean bottom their home (Figure 3.9). Additionally, an entirely new animal phylum, the Loricifera, was described in 1983 based on specimens from the deep sea (Kris-

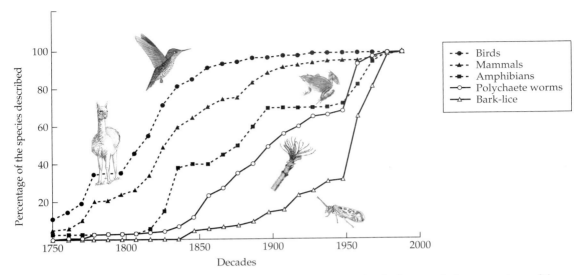

Figure 3.9 For five groups of Chilean animals, the cumulative percentage of the known species described from 1750 to 2000. Note that the majority of birds and mammals were largely described by 1900, and probably few new species remain to be discovered. In contrast, polychaete worms and bark-lice were largely neglected by early taxonomists and are only now being investigated and described. Amphibians are intermediate in their intensity of study. (After Simonetti and Rivera-Milla, in press.)

tensen 1983), and another new phylum, the Cycliophora, was first described in 1995 based on tiny, ciliate creatures found on the mouthparts of the Norway lobster (Figure 3.10) (Funch and Kristensen 1995). In 1999, the world's largest bacteria was discovered off the Namibian coast, with individual cells as large as the eyes of fruit flies (Schulz et al. 1999). Undoubtedly, more species, genera, families, orders, classes, and phyla (and perhaps even kingdoms!) are waiting to be discovered.

Considering that around 20,000 new animal species are described each year and perhaps 5 million more are waiting to be identified, the task of describing the world's species will not be completed for over 250 years if continued at the present rate! This underlines the absolutely critical need for more taxonomists.

The Need for More Taxonomists

A major problem the scientific community faces in describing and cataloging the biological diversity of the world is the lack of trained taxonomists able to take on the job. At the present time, there are only about 1500 taxonomists in the world who are competent to work with tropical

Figure 3.10 A new phylum, the Cyclio- phora, was first described in 1995. The phylum contains one vase-shaped species, *Symbion pandora* (around 40 of which are shown below), which attaches itself on the mouthparts of the Norway lobster, *Nephrops norvegicus* (inset). (Photographs courtesy of Reinhardt Kristensen, University of Copenhagen.)

species, and many of them are based in temperate countries. Unfortunately, this number is declining rather than increasing. When academic taxonomists retire, universities have a tendency to either close the position due to financial difficulties or replace the retiring biologist with a nontaxonomist. Many members of the younger generation of taxonomists are so preoccupied with the technology of molecular systematics and associated data analysis that they are neither interested nor capable of continuing the great tradition of discovering and cataloging the world's biological treasures. At least a fivefold increase in the number of field taxonomists focused primarily on describing and identifying tropical and marine species is needed to complete the task of describing the world's biological diversity (Gaston 1994). Much of this effort should be directed to lesser-known groups, such as fungi, bacteria, and invertebrates. And where possible, these taxonomists need to be based in tropical countries. Natural history societies and clubs that combine professional and amateur naturalists also can play a valuable role in assisting these efforts and in exposing the general public and student groups to the issues and excitement of biological diversity and encouraging people to become taxonomists.

Summary

1. In general, species richness is greatest in tropical rain forests, coral reefs, tropical lakes, the deep sea, and shrublands with a Mediterranean climate. In terrestrial habitats, species richness tends to be greatest at lower elevations and in areas with abundant rainfall. Areas that are geologically old and topographically complex also tend to have more species.

2. Tropical rain forests occupy only 7% of the Earth's land area, yet they are estimated to contain most of the Earth's species. The great majority of these species are insects not yet described by scientists. Coral reef communities are also rich in species, with many of the species widely distributed. The deep sea also appears to be rich in species, but is still not adequately explored.

3. About 1.5 million species have been described and at least twice that number remains to be described. Estimates of the total number of species range from 5–150 million. New biological communities are still being discovered, especially in the deep sea and the forest canopy. For example, spectacular communities that occupy deep-sea hydrothermal vents are major, recent discoveries.

4. While conspicuous groups, such as flowering plants, mammals, and birds, are reasonably well-known to science, other inconspicuous groups, particularly insects, bacteria, and fungi, have not been thoroughly studied. Recent attempts to collect all of the insects in the tropical forest canopy have yielded mostly undescribed species, suggesting that far more species exist than previously suspected.

5. There is a vital need for more taxonomists and field biologists to study, collect, classify, and help protect the world's biological diversity before it is lost.

For Discussion

1. What are the factors promoting species richness? Why is biological diversity diminished in particular environments? Why aren't species able to overcome these limitations and undergo the process of speciation?

2. Develop arguments for both low and high estimates of the total number of species in particular groups, such as bacteria, fungi, or nematodes. Read more about groups that you don't know well. Why is it important to identify and name all the species in a particular group?

3. If taxonomists are so important to documenting and protecting biological diversity, why are their numbers declining instead of increasing? How could societal and scientific priorities be readjusted to reverse this trend? Is the ability to identify and classify species a skill that every conservation biologist should possess?

4. Some scientists have argued that life may have existed on Mars, and recent drilling demonstrates that bacteria actually flourish in rocks deep under the Earth's surface. Speculate, as wildly as you can, about where to search for previously unsuspected species, communities, or novel life forms.

Suggested Readings

Boucher, G. and P. J. D. Lambshead. 1995. Ecological biodiversity of marine nematodes in samples from temperate, tropical, and deep-sea regions. *Conser-*

vation Biology 9: 1594–1605. Biologists grapple with deciding how many tiny worm species there are in the world.

Bryant, D., D. Nielson, and L. Tangley. 1997. *The Last Frontier Forests: Ecosystems and Economies on the Edge.* World Resources Institute, Washington, D.C. Authoritative report on the status and future of primary forests.

Cowling, R. M., P. W. Rundel, B. B. Lamont, M. K. Arroyo, and M. Arianoutsou. 1996. Plant diversity in Mediterranean climate regions. *Trends in Ecology and Evolution* 11: 362–366. A succinct review of patterns of species richness in these communities and threats to their continued existence.

Donoghue, M. J. and W. S. Alverson. 2000. A new age of discovery. *Annals of the Missouri Botanical Garden* 87: 110–126. In this article and others in the same special issue, scientists describe the numerous species still being discovered and described, even in the developed countries of the world.

Dunlap, P. V. 2001. Microbial diversity. In *Encyclopedia of Biodiversity,* S. A. Levin (ed.), Vol. 4, pp. 191–200. Academic Press, San Diego, CA. Even though bacteria are inconspicuous, they have tremendous biochemical diversity and an ancient lineage.

Fredrickson, J. K. and T. C. Onstott. 1996. Microbes deep inside the Earth. *Scientific American* 275 (4): 68–73. Exciting new finds of bacterial communities deep inside the Earth's rocky crust.

Gaston, K. J. 2000. Global patterns in biodiversity. *Nature* 405: 220–227. Advanced treatment of global patterns of species abundance.

Grassle, J. F. 2001. Marine ecosystems. In *Encyclopedia of Biodiversity,* S. A. Levin (ed.), Vol. 4, pp. 13–26. Academic Press, San Diego, CA. The marine environment has a greater diversity of animal phyla than the terrestrial environment.

Heywood, V. H. (ed.). 1995. *Global Biodiversity Assessment.* Cambridge University Press, Cambridge. This massive book comprehensively treats the subject, with chapters by leading scientists and a huge bibliography.

Hubbell, S. P. 2001. *Unified Theory of Biodiversity and Biogeography.* Princeton University Press, Princeton, NJ. Innovative new theory that seeks to combine biogeography and biodiversity theory to explain patterns of species richness.

Huston, M. A. 1994. *Biological Diversity: The Coexistence of Species on Changing Landscapes.* Cambridge University Press, Cambridge. Extensive review of the patterns and theories of biological diversity.

Lowman, M. D. 1999. *Life in the Treetops: Adventures of a Woman in Field Biology.* Yale University Press, New London, CT. Account of scientific research in the tropical forest canopy conducted while balancing work and family.

May, R. M. 1992. How many species inhabit the Earth? *Scientific American* 267 (4): 42–48. Excellent review of the arguments for different estimates of the number of species.

Spalding, M. D., C. Ravilious, and E. P. Green. 2001. *World Atlas of Coral Reefs.* The University of California Press, Berkeley, CA. Outstanding account of coral reefs in each area of the world.

Waller, G. (ed.). 1996. *Sealife: A Guide to the Marine Environment.* Smithsonian Institution Press, Washington, D.C. This is the book to start with if you want to learn about the marine environment in depth.

Whitmore, T. C. 1990. *An Introduction to Tropical Rain Forests.* Clarendon Press, Oxford. An authoritative short presentation by a leading scientist.

Wilson, E. O. 1991. Rain forest canopy: The high frontier. *National Geographic* 180 (December): 78–107. An authoritative and vivid account of diversity in the forest canopy.

Ecological Economics and Direct Economic Values

D ecisions on protecting species, communities, and genetic variation often come down to arguments over money: How much will it cost? And how much is it worth? The economic value of something is generally accepted as the amount of money people are willing to pay for it. But this is only one possible way of assigning value to things, including biological diversity. Ethical, aesthetic, scientific, and educational methods of valuation are available as well. However, government and corporate officials currently base major policy decisions on economic valuation. As a result, conservation biologists now use the methodology and vocabulary of economics in their arguments for the protection of diversity: It is easier to convince governments and corporations to protect biological diversity when there is an economic incentive to do so. When the loss of biological diversity is perceived to cost money, perhaps governments and corporations will act to prevent it.

Why Economic Valuation Is Needed

A major problem for conservation biology is that natural resources have often been undervalued. Thus, the costs of environmental damage have been ignored, the depletion of natural resource stocks disregarded, and the future value of resources discounted (Davidson 2000). Because the underlying cause of environmental damage is so often economic in nature, the solution must incorporate economic principles. **Ecological economics** is an emerging discipline, similar to environmental economics and resource economics, that integrates economic valuations of biological diversity with ecology, environmental science, sociology, and public policy (Barbier et al. 1994; Costanza et al. 1996; Masood and Garwin 1998; Dasgupta 2001). Governments need to allocate their resources in the most efficient manner possible, and a well-considered argument for the conservation of biological diversity that is grounded in economics will often effectively support arguments based on biological, ethical, and emotional grounds.

Before the trend of biodiversity loss can be reversed, its fundamental causes must be understood. What factors induce humans to act in a nonsustainable and therefore destructive manner? Usually, environmental degradation and species loss occur as a by-product of human economic activities. Forests are logged for revenue from timber sales. Species are hunted for personal consumption, sale, and sport. Marginal land is converted into cropland because people have nowhere else to farm. Species, either transported accidentally by commercial vessels or brought purposefully by people, invade islands and continents, often killing the local flora and fauna. An understanding of a few fundamental economic principles will clarify the reasons why people treat the environment in what appears to be a shortsighted, wasteful manner. One of the most universally accepted tenets of modern economic thought centers on the "voluntary transaction"—the idea that a monetary transaction takes place only when it is beneficial to both of the parties involved. For example, a baker who sells his loaves of bread for 50 dollars will find few customers. Likewise, a customer who is willing to pay only 5 cents for a loaf will soon go hungry. A transaction between seller and buyer will only occur when a mutually agreeable price is set that benefits both parties. Adam Smith, an eighteenth-century philosopher whose ideas are the foundation of much modern economic thought, wrote, "It is not upon the benevolence of the butcher, the baker, or the brewer that we eat our daily bread, but upon his own self-interest" (Smith 1909). All parties involved in an exchange expect to improve their own situation. The sum of each individual acting in his or her own self-interest results in a more prosperous society. Smith likened this effect to an "invisible hand" guiding the market—turning selfish, uncoordinated actions into increased prosperity and relative social harmony.

However, there is a notable exception to Smith's principle that directly applies to environmental issues (Fullerton and Stavins 1998). Smith assumed that the costs and benefits of free exchange are accepted and borne by the participants in the transaction. In some cases, however, associated costs or benefits sometimes befall individuals not directly involved in the exchange. These hidden costs or benefits are known as **external-ities.** Perhaps the most important and frequently overlooked externali-ty is the environmental damage that occurs as a consequence of human economic activity, such as the dumping of industrial sewage into a river as a by-product of manufacturing. The externalities of this activity are degraded drinking water, fewer fish safe to eat, and the loss of many species unable to survive in the polluted river. Where externalities exist, the market fails to benefit society as a whole. **Market failure** occurs when resources are misallocated, which allows a few individuals or businesses to benefit at the expense of the larger society. As a result, the society as a whole becomes *less* prosperous from certain economic activities, not more prosperous.

The fundamental challenge facing conservation biologists is to ensure that all the costs of economic behavior, as well as the benefits, are un-derstood and taken into account when decisions are made that will af-fect biological diversity. Companies, individuals, or other stakeholders involved in production that results in ecological damage generally do not bear the full cost of their activities. For example, the company that owns an electric power plant that burns coal and emits toxic fumes ben-efits from the sale of low-cost electricity, as does the consumer. Yet the hidden costs of this transaction—decreased air quality and visibility, in-creased respiratory disease for people and animals, damage to plant life, and a polluted environment—are distributed throughout society.

Another example is the almost unstoppable movement to convert un-developed land into agricultural land, residential neighborhoods, and industrial sites. Such activities create great wealth, often increasing the value of the land by 200 to 2500 times (Hulse and Ribe 2000). Yet the loss in species, ecosystem services, and quality of life for the surrounding human community is rarely considered in the rush to make a profit. Un-derstanding this imbalance is central to understanding market failure: The wide distribution of economic cost, combined with the concentrat-ed benefit to a small group, creates conflict between the economic realm and the ecological.

When people and organizations must pay for the consequences of their actions, they will be much more likely to stop damaging—or at least minimize their damage to—the environment (Repetto 1990, 1992; Arrow et al. 1995). Some suggestions designed to discourage behavior that dam-ages the environment include: charging taxes on air pollution caused by using fossil fuels, charging higher rates for water use and sewage dis-charge, preserving open land as compensation when another nearby site is developed, and paying for the damage caused when pesticides, her-bicides, and fertilizers are released into the environment. Many coun-tries of northern Europe have already put such ideas into action. In ad-dition, policy makers could create penalties for damaging biological

BOX 5 *Industry, Ecology, and Ecotourism in Yellowstone Park*

Yellowstone National Park is the oldest and most famous of the protected areas of the U.S. National Parks System. While federal policies affecting the natural landscape of the park often attract intense public scrutiny, policies that support the extraction of timber, oil, and other natural resources within the park and in nearby parts of Wyoming, Montana, and Idaho generally go unchallenged.

The industries that benefit from these policies argue that such activities are necessary for the economic health of the local communities surrounding the park, but recent studies indicate that this argument is increasingly less valid. The economic health of the communities surrounding Yellowstone has gradually become primarily dependent on the tourism industry and on the new residents and businesses that have moved to the area because of a perceived higher quality of life (Power 1991; Power and Barrett 2001). Though extractive industry was a significant force in the regional economy three decades ago, it may now be detrimental to the economic well-being of local residents because it harms what has become their major economic resource: the wildlife and natural landscape of Yellowstone Park.

One of the industries in Yellowstone that presently provides the largest boost to the economy of the region—ecotourism—is also the one that does the least damage to the ecosystem of the park. Ecotourism is not without drawbacks. The noise and pollution brought by the passage of millions of tourists annually, the disruption and alteration of animal behavior from constant exposure to the human presence, and the threat of human-caused soil erosion and fire are all side effects of the tourist trade. Accidental fires are perhaps the most visible and fearsome form of disturbance related to ecotourism; nevertheless, even the damage caused by these anthropogenic fires pales in comparison to the damage done by logging and mining activities. The reason that extractive industry is so much more damaging than ecotourism is simple: ecotourism, while it can pollute and alter habitats, does not actively destroy them.

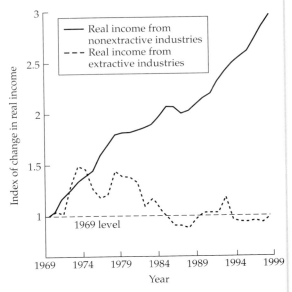

In the greater Yellowstone region, real income from extractive industries has fluctuated widely over the last 30 years but has not grown significantly, while real income from the rest of the economy—including recreation industries, tourism, service industries, and new residents, including retirees—has grown steadily, expanding by almost 200%. The region's economy has become increasingly independent of the extractive industries. The two income lines shown in the graph are standardized to equal a value of 1 in 1969, when extractive industries provided about 23% of the region's total income. By 1999 extractive industries provided only 9% of the region's total income. (From Power 1991 with new data from author.)

In contrast, logging and mining have many detrimental effects. Clear-cutting, a common logging practice in which forested slopes are simply cleared of trees, can induce massive sheet erosion, particularly if steps are not immediately taken to replace the vegetation removed during logging. The eroded silt builds up in streams, killing fish and other aquatic species, and the loss of nutrients retards regrowth of vegetation. Mining practices often introduce into the environment harmful chemical by-products, including cyanide. These

BOX 5 *(continued)*

Many people and businesses have been moving to the Yellowstone National Park area because of its natural beauty. People value a lifestyle filled with outdoor experiences, such as these visitors on the Yellowstone River boardwalk. (Photograph courtesy of the U.S. National Park Service.)

practices are ultimately not cost-effective for several reasons: (1) they lower the potential for future extraction by damaging the soil and water resources needed to regenerate timber; (2) they lower the region's potential for tourism, retirement communities, and new businesses by damaging the natural beauty of the area; and (3) they create hidden costs by lowering water quality for residents of the area, who must then pay more to have clean drinking water.

diversity and subsidies for preserving it, to make industries more mindful of how their actions impact the environment.

Assigning Economic Value to Biological Diversity

Most natural resources, such as clean air, clean water, soil quality, rare species, and even scenic beauty, are considered to be **common property resources**, collectively owned by society at large or owned by no one, with open access to everyone. These resources are rarely assigned a monetary value. People, industries, and governments use and damage these resources without paying more than a minimal cost, or sometimes paying nothing at all. This is a situation in which market failure occurs, described as **the tragedy of the commons**—in which the value of the common property resources is lost to all of society (Hardin 1968, 1985). In the more complete systems of "green" accounting (such as national resource accounting) that are being developed, the costs of depleting and damaging common property resources are included as part of the internal cost of doing business instead of being regarded as externalities. Using such accounting methods, the value of maintaining natural resources is often greater than the short-term benefit realized through resource extraction (Box 5).

In developing new accounting systems, conservation biologists and ecological economists also need to address discount rates, which are commonly used by economists to calculate what value natural resources will have at some point in the future. Economists use discount rates to assign a *lower current value* to resources or materials that will be used in the future (on the grounds that it is better for the society to have money now and invest it for greater wealth rather than leave natural resources unused). Economists often assign high discount rates (higher discount rates = lower current values) to natural resources (trees, wood, water, fish, wild game, etc.) in developing countries; that is, resources harvested at some point in the future will have a much lower value than equivalent resources harvested now. Such an approach leads to short-sighted decisions to use resources right away, and it minimizes the value of resources used in the future. This use of discounting propels development projects forward, when a more cautious approach would be to lower discount rates for natural resources in general, especially in developing countries, where local people rely on natural resources to survive.

Assigning monetary values to species, communities, and ecosystems has strengthened the conservation movement (Perrings 1995). In many cases, initial efforts have been simplistic, due to the difficulties of assigning economic values to variables such as the amelioration of global climate change and the future use of presently unused or even unknown species (Daly and Cobb 1989; Daily 1997). The hidden costs of environmental degradation that occur during income-producing activities, such as logging, agriculture, commercial fishing, and development of wetlands for commercial use, make it hard to determine the real value of natural resources (Repetto 1992). Economists continue to search for the most appropriate methods to determine the long-term costs associated with the disruption of a biological community by economic activity.

Evaluating Development Projects

In order to ensure that the costs of development are taken into account and carefully weighed, it is essential to review such projects and evaluate their potential effects *before* they proceed. Such reviews are the standard practice in most developed countries and are increasingly carried out in developing countries as well. International donor agencies may require such evaluations before projects are funded.

Cost–Benefit Analysis

Economists evaluate large development projects using **environmental impact assessments,** which consider the present and future effects of the projects on the environment. The environment is often broadly defined to include not only harvestable natural resources, but also air and water quality, the quality of life for local people, and the preservation of endangered species. In its most comprehensive form, **cost–benefit analysis** compares the values gained against the costs of the project or resource use (Hanley and Splash 1994; Perrings 1995). For example, during feasibility studies for a large logging operation that would remove a forest, an economist might assign monetary values to the cost of replacing naturally occurring resources—such as game meat, clean water and fish, a scenic walk through a grove of large trees, rare bird species, and wildflower populations—with resources obtained elsewhere. Alternatively, an economist might estimate what it would cost to restore the community or resource to its original condition. These different strategies are likely to have very different costs and produce very different results.

In one cost–benefit analysis, the competing uses of the terrestrial and marine environments in Bacuit Bay, Palawan, Philippines were modeled against three alternatives (Table 4.1). In the first option, logging, tourism, and fishing occur together. While logging provides more revenue than tourism and fishing when all three activities occur simultaneously, logging has strong negative impacts on the fishing industry and on tourism because it results in increased sedimentation that kills coral communities and the fish that depend on them. The second option protects forests through a ban on logging, and the fishing and tourist industries provide more revenue than when all three industries operate together (Hodgson and Dixon 1988). The third possible option involves the techniques of sustainable forestry. Logging is undertaken in a responsible and limited way to minimize environmental damage (such as by logging in small patches and avoiding steep slopes and streams, rivers, and the coast). If this third option were chosen, fishing, tourism, and logging might coexist without one industry compromising the economic benefits of the others. Although based on this analysis sustainable forestry appears to be the best long-term option, ultimately this was not considered realis-

TABLE 4.1 Cost–benefit analysis of three development options in Bacuit Bay, Palawan, Philippines

Development option	Amount of revenue[a] generated by:			Total revenue
	Tourism	Fisheries	Logging	
Option 1: Intensive logging until timber depleted[b]	$6	$9	$10	$25
Option 2: Logging banned; protected area established[c]	$25	$17	$0	$42
Option 3: Sustainable logging[d]	$24	$16	$4	$44

Source: After Hodgson and Dixon 1988.

[a] Revenues are in millions of dollars over a 10-year period.

[b] In this option, logging substantially decreases the revenues from tourism and fisheries. Timber is completely depleted after 5 years.

[c] In this option, tourism and fisheries are major sustainable industries.

[d] In this option, logging is allowed to proceed in an environmentally responsible manner. A buffer of trees is maintained near wetlands and streams, logging does not occur on steep slopes, construction of logging roads is minimized, and hunting is banned. There is minimal impact on fisheries and tourism, and the overall economic benefits are enhanced. (Real-life logging practices are rarely as benign as portrayed here.)

tic. In the end, Bacuit Bay was established as a marine sanctuary and has become a major tourist resort.

In theory, the outcome of such analysis is simple: If cost–benefit analysis shows that a project will be profitable, it should go forward, while unprofitable projects should be stopped. In practice, though, cost–benefit analyses are notoriously difficult to calculate because benefits and costs change over time and are hard to measure. For example, when a new paper mill is being constructed in a forested area, it is difficult to predict the future price of paper, the profitability of the industry, the future need for clean water, and the value of other plant and animal species in the forests being harvested. In the past, the natural resources used or damaged by large development projects were either ignored or were grossly undervalued. Now, there is an increasing tendency by governments, conservation groups, and economists to apply the **precautionary principle**; that is, it sometimes may be better to not approve a project that has some risk associated with it and err on the side of doing no harm to the environment than to harm it unintentionally or unexpectedly.

It would be highly beneficial to apply cost–benefit analysis to many of the basic industries and practices of modern society. Many economic activities appear to be profitable even when they are actually losing money, because governments subsidize industries involved in environment-damaging activities with tax breaks, direct payments or price supports, cheap fossil fuel, free water, and road networks—sometimes referred to as "perverse subsidies" (Myers and Kent 2001). These government subsidies promote specific industries, such as agriculture, fishing, and energy-production, and they may amount to $1.4 trillion dollars per year, or roughly 5% of the world economy (Myers 1998; Myers and Kent 2001). Without these subsidies, many environmentally damaging activities, such as farming on marginal lands, logging in remote areas, and inefficient and highly polluting energy use, would be reduced.

Natural Resource Loss and the Wealth of Societies

Attempts have been made to include the loss of natural resources in calculations of gross domestic product (GDP) and other indexes of national productivity (Daly and Cobb 1989; Repetto 1992). The problem with GDP is that it measures economic activity in a country without accounting for all the costs of nonsustainable activities (such as overfishing of coastal waters and poorly managed strip-mining), which cause the GDP to increase, even though these activities may be destructive to a country's long-term economic well-being. In actuality, the economic costs associated with environmental damage can be considerable and often offset the gains attained through agricultural and industrial development.

In Costa Rica, for example, the value of the forests destroyed during the 1980s greatly exceeded the income produced from forest products, so that the forestry sector actually represented a drain on the wealth of the country. Similarly, the costs associated with soil erosion in that country decreased the value of agriculture by 17%. In the United States, one controversial estimate shows that soil erosion costs the economy $44 billion every year in direct damage to agricultural lands and indirect damage to waterways and to human and animal health (Pimental et al. 1995). For the entire world, the cost of soil erosion is estimated to approach $400 billion per year. Even if these controversial estimates are eventually revised downward, the costs of soil erosion are enormous by any standard—and all such costs are underappreciated, and excluded from GDP calculations.

By excluding environmental costs and the loss of natural resources from economic analyses, many countries that appear to be achieving impressive economic gains actually may be on the verge of economic collapse. Unregulated national fisheries are a classic example of the need to monitor assets. Increased investment in fishing fleets may result in higher catches and impressive profits, but gradually leads to the overharvesting and destruction of one commercial species after another and, eventually, to the collapse of the entire industry. It would be easier to justify this activity if the profits were used to improve society through increased infrastructure, industrial development, job training, and education. However, a small number of people or companies often take most of the profits, while society as a whole often realizes only minor and temporary improvements.

The hidden costs associated with superficial economic gains are effectively demonstrated by the case of the *Exxon Valdez* oil spill in Alaska in 1989. The spill cost billions of dollars to clean up, damaged the environment, killed a large number of birds, fish, and marine mammals, and wasted 11 million gallons of oil. Yet the event was recorded as a *net economic gain* because expenditures associated with the cleanup increased the U.S. GDP and provided employment for cleanup crews hired throughout the United States. Without consideration of the hidden environmental costs and long-term damage to natural resources, a disaster like the *Valdez* spill can easily be misrepresented as economically beneficial.

Another attempt to account for natural resource depletion, pollution, and unequal income distribution in measures of national productivity is the development of the Index of Sustainable Economic Welfare (ISEW) (Daly and Cobb 1989). This index includes factors such as the loss of farmlands, the loss of wetlands, the impact of acid rain, the number of people living in poverty, and the effects of pollution on human health. Using the ISEW, the U.S. economy apparently did not improve during the period from 1956 to 1986 and actually declined from 1986 to 1994, even though the standard GDP index showed a dramatic gain. While a measure such as the ISEW is still in a preliminary stage, its early use suggests what conservation biologists have long feared: Many modern economies are achieving their growth only through the nonsustainable consumption of natural resources. As these resources run out, the economies on which they are based may be seriously disrupted.

An awareness of and involvement in assigning economic value to biological diversity is important for conservation biologists, although many would argue that any attempt to place a strictly monetary value on biological diversity is inappropriate and potentially corrupting, since many aspects of the natural world are unique and thus truly priceless (Ehrenfeld 1989; Bulte and van Kooten 2000). Supporters of this position point out that there is no way to assign monetary value to the wonder people experience when they see an animal in the wild or a beautiful natural landscape; nor can economic value realistically be assigned to the human lives that have been and will be saved through the medicinal compounds derived from wild species. In fact, economic models contribute much to the debate over the protection of biological diversity. It is to the advantage of conservationists to develop economic models—both to improve such models' accuracy and to appreciate their limitations, since these models often provide surprisingly strong support for the crucial role of biological diversity in local economies and for the need to protect natural communities. Economic models need to be presented to policy makers and incorporated into the regulations that will affect how development proceeds.

One Approach to Assigning Economic Value

A number of methods recently have been developed to assign economic values to genetic variability, species, communities, and ecosystems. In these methods, assignment of economic value can be done on three levels—the marketplace (or harvest) value of resources, the value provided by unharvested resources in their natural state, and the future value of resources. For example, we can assign economic value to the Southeast Asian wild guar (*Bos frontalis*), a wild relative of domestic cattle, based on: the meat currently harvested from its wild populations, the animal's value in the wild for nature tourism, and its future potential in domestic cattle breeding programs. As yet there is no universally accepted framework for assigning values to biological diversity, but a variety of new approaches have been proposed. Among the most useful is the framework used by McNeely et al. (1990) and Barbier et al. (1994), in which the use values of biodiversity are divided between **direct use values** (known to economists as **private goods**), which are assigned to products harvested by people (such as timber, seafood, and medicinal plants from the wild), and **indirect use values** (in economics, **public goods**), which are benefits provided by biological diversity and do not involve harvesting or destroying the resource (such as water quality, pollution control, ecosystem productivity, soil protection, recreation, education, scientific research, and regulation of climate). (Indirect use values are discussed in Chapter 5.) This framework also includes **option value**—the prospect for possible

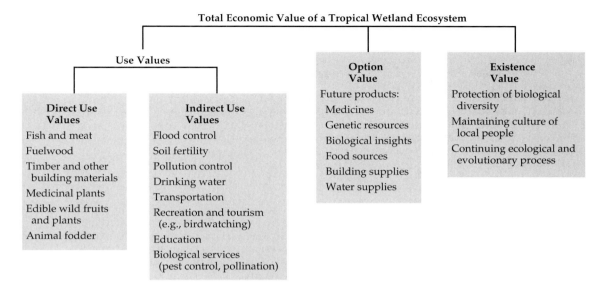

Figure 4.1 Evaluating the success of a development project must incorporate the full range of its environmental effects. This figure shows the total economic value of a tropical wetland ecosystem, including direct and indirect use value, option value, and existence value. The value of the wetland ecosystem is reduced when water is removed for irrigation of crops. When that lowered value is taken into account, the irrigation project may represent an economic loss. (Based on data in Barbier 1993.)

future benefits for human society (such as new medicines, possible future food sources, and future genetic resources). Option value is discussed further in Chapter 5. **Existence value** is another kind of value that can be assigned to biodiversity—for example, economists can attempt to measure how much people are willing to pay to protect a species from going extinct (Box 6). Figure 4.1 describes how these different values can be applied to a tropical forest ecosystem.

Direct Use Values

Direct use values (known in other frameworks as **commodity values**) can often be readily calculated by observing the activities of representative groups of people, by monitoring collection points for natural products, and by examining import and export statistics. Direct use values are further divided into **consumptive use value** for goods that are consumed locally, and **productive use value** for products that are sold in markets.

Consumptive Use Value

Goods such as fuelwood and game that are consumed locally and do not appear in the national and international marketplace are assigned con-

BOX 6 *How Much Is a Species Worth?*

I magine that a new species of lily has been discovered growing in a 25-ha meadow slated to be dug up for commercial development. Extensive searches of the area fail to find any other populations of the lily. Conservation organizations would like to save this species from extinction in the wild, but are not sure of its value. How much money is this species worth? How much money should be spent to save it? Some possible answers follow.

1. The species has no known value to people, and therefore no money should be spent to save it. Value: $0.

2. The species' value might be considered as equal to the value of the land, because saving the land is the key to saving the species. The willingness of conservation organizations to buy the land on which the species grows is an indication of the existence value of the species. Existence value: 25 ha at $4000 per ha = $100,000.

3. A local horticulturist is willing to pay for the exclusive right to collect 10% of the seeds of this species each year in order to propagate the species and sell the resulting plants for five years. He is willing to pay $5000 each year for this privilege. Productive use value: $5000 per year for 5 years = $25,000.

4. An average of two hundred botanists and nature lovers visit the site each year to see the plant, spending roughly $80 per person on local food, lodging, and supplies. Nature tourism value: 200 people at $80 = $16,000 per year.

5. The species' value might also be determined by calculating its future usefulness. Protecting this species preserves its option value. If we divide the estimated value of newly discovered plant products and genetic variation over the last 10 years by the estimated total number of plant species, we get an indication of the average value of each species. Option value: $100 billion of new plant products divided by 250,000 plant species = $400,000.

6. Suppose this particular species is found to produce a chemical that could have an enormous impact on human health and well-being. Perhaps the chemical prevents disease transmission in humans. Such a compound would be effective against a multitude of illnesses ranging from the minor (such as the common cold and chicken pox) to the devastating (such as malaria and AIDS). Or it might contain compounds that break down air- and waterborne toxins, rendering dangerous pollutants harmless. Such compounds would give this species incalculable value, as they could eliminate disease or reverse ecological damage caused by pollution. The lily might be the key to saving humanity from devastation. In such cases, the species would have a value equal to the total monetary value of all human economic activity. Estimated value: $100 trillion, or infinitely large.

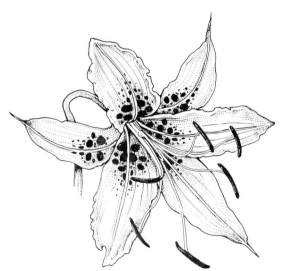

How do we determine what a newly discovered species might be worth?

sumptive use value. People living close to the land often derive a considerable proportion of the goods they require for their livelihood from the surrounding environment. These goods do not appear in the GDP of countries because they are neither bought nor sold. However, if rural people are unable to obtain these products, as might occur following environmental degradation, overexploitation of natural resources, or even creation of a protected reserve, their standard of living will decline, possibly to the point where they are forced to relocate.

Studies of traditional societies in the developing world show how extensively these people use their natural environment to supply themselves with fuelwood, vegetables, fruit, meat, medicine, rope and string, and building materials (Figure 4.2) (Myers 1983; Balick and Cox 1996; Cox 2001). One study of Amazonian Indians found that about half of the species of rain forest trees in the area were used for some specific product other than fuel (Prance et al. 1987; Dobson 1995). About 80% of the

(A)

(B)

Figure 4.2 (A) A wide variety of plants and other natural products are used in Chinese medicine. (Photograph © Catherine Pringle/Biological Photo Service.) (B) Wild animals, such as this wild bearded pig in Borneo, provide people with a crucial source of protein in many areas of the world. (Photograph by Richard Primack.)

world's population still relies principally on traditional medicines derived from plants and animals as their primary source of treatment (Tuxill 1999). More than 5000 species are used for medicinal purposes in China, while 2000 species are used in the Amazon basin (Schultes and Raffauf 1990; WRI/IUCN/UNEP 1992).

One of the most crucial requirements of rural people is protein, which they obtain by hunting wild animals for meat. In many areas of Africa, wild meat constitutes a significant portion of the protein in the average person's diet—about 40% in Botswana and about 75% in the Democratic Republic of the Congo (formerly Zaire) (Myers 1988). In Nigeria, over 100,000 tons of giant rats (*Cricetomys* sp.) are consumed each year, while in Botswana over three million kg of springhare (*Pedetes capensis*) are eaten per year. This wild meat includes not only birds, mammals, and fish, but adult insects, snails, caterpillars, and grubs. In certain areas of Africa, insects may constitute the majority of the dietary protein and supply critical vitamins. In areas along coasts, rivers, and lakes, wild fish represent an important source of protein. Throughout the world, 108 million tons of fish, crustaceans, and molluscs, mainly wild species, are harvested each year, with 91 million tons constituting marine catch and 17 million tons constituting freshwater catch (WRI 1998). Much of this catch is consumed locally.

Consumptive use value can be assigned to a product by considering how much people would have to pay if they had to buy an equivalent product when their local source was no longer available. One example of this approach was an attempt to estimate the number of wild pigs harvested by native hunters in Sarawak, East Malaysia. The study involved counting the number of shotgun shells used in rural areas and interviewing hunters to obtain two independent measures of animal harvest rates (Figure 4.2B). This pioneering study estimated that the consumptive value of the wild pig meat was a surprisingly large $40 million per year (Caldecott 1988). In many cases local people do not have the money to buy products in the market. In remote regions, markets may not exist at all. When the local resource is depleted, local people may be forced to change their livelihoods, migrate to other rural areas or cities, or may simply be faced with rural poverty.

Consumptive use value can also be assigned to fuelwood used for heating and cooking, which is gathered from forests and shrublands (Figure 4.3). In countries such as Nepal, Tanzania, and Malawi, most primary energy comes from fuelwood and animal dung. The value of these fuels can be determined by considering how much people would have to pay for kerosene or other fuels if they were unable to obtain fuel from their environment. In many areas of the world, rural people have consumed all local fuel sources but do not have the money to buy fuel from the market. This situation, the "poor man's energy crisis," forces the poor

Figure 4.3 One of the most important natural products required by local people is fuelwood, particularly in Africa and southern Asia. Here a woman in Nepal carries a load of kindling. (Photograph © Bill Kamin/Visuals Unlimited.)

to walk great distances to obtain fuel and leads to ever-widening circles of deforestation.

In the past, people developed ways of extracting resources from the natural environment that prevented overuse of renewable resources (Berkes 1999, 2001). Certain species of wild fruit trees were never allowed to be cut down; the breeding season of the year was taboo for hunting; families owned hunting territories that other families were not allowed to enter. These systems were organized at the village and tribal levels and were enforced through strong social pressures. For example, traditional Sherpa villages in Nepal had the custom of "shingo nava," in which men were elected to be forest guards. These men determined how much fuelwood people could collect and what trees could be cut and hence protected the common resources. People violating the village rules were made to pay fines, which were used to fund village activities.

Most of these traditional conservation systems have broken down as cash economies have developed. Local conservation strategies have also been eliminated by centralized or "top down" government decisions. People now frequently sell natural resources in town markets for money.

As social controls break down at the village level, the villagers, as well as outsiders, may begin to extract local resources in a destructive and nonsustainable manner. If the resources become depleted, many villagers may be forced to pay high prices in town markets for many of the products that they formerly obtained free from their natural environment. It is also true that access to town markets sometimes provides advantages to villagers that balance the loss of some local resources. For example, it sometimes allows local people to obtain higher prices for their products. With the cash, people may be able to establish their own businesses, educate their children, and have access to modern medical care.

Although dependency on local natural products is primarily associated with the developing world, there are rural areas of the United States, Canada, and other developed countries where hundreds of thousands of people are dependent on fuelwood for heating and on wild game and seafood for their protein needs. Many of these people would be unable to survive if they had to buy these necessities.

Productive Use Value

Products that are harvested from the wild and sold in both national and international commercial markets are assigned productive use value. Standard economic methods value these products at the price paid at the first point of sale minus the costs incurred up to that point, but they could also be valued at the final retail price of the products. The two methods give a wide range of values for the same product. For example, bark from the wild cascara (*Rhamnus purshiana*) gathered in the western United States is the major ingredient in certain brands of laxatives. The purchase price of the bark is about $1 million, but the final retail price of the medicine is $75 million (Prescott-Allen and Prescott-Allen 1986). Deciding the appropriate value for this product represents a basic problem for ecological economics.

The productive use value of natural resources is significant, even in industrial nations. Approximately 4.5% of the U.S. GDP depends in some way on wild species, about $350 billion for the year 2001. The percentage would be far higher for developing countries that have less industry and a higher percentage of the population living in rural areas.

The range of products obtained from the natural environment and sold in the marketplace is enormous: fuelwood, construction timber, fish and shellfish, medicinal plants, wild fruits and vegetables, wild meat and skins, fibers, rattan (a vine used to make furniture and other household articles), honey, beeswax, natural dyes, seaweed, animal fodder, natural perfumes, and plant gums and resins (Radmer 1996; Baskin 1997). There are large international industries associated with collecting tropical fish for the aquarium trade, tropical cacti, orchids, and other plants for the horticultural industry, and birds, mammals, amphibians, and reptiles for zoos and private collections.

In many cases, species have to be collected just once or a few times, because then they can be propagated in captivity. Only a few individuals are needed to establish entirely new populations, to be used for display purposes, to be used in the development of new medicines and industrial products, and to be used as biological control agents (Box 7). Wild relatives of domesticated crops can be collected and incorporated into modern breeding programs for genetic improvement. This occasional collection can be considered productive use value, or perhaps as option value, for their ability to maintain and improve economic activity. Species collected only in small numbers from the wild will be treated in the next chapter in the section on option value. Products gathered in large quantities from the wild are described below.

FOREST PRODUCTS   Wood is one of the most significant products obtained from natural environments, with an export value of around $135 billion per year (WRI 2000). The *total* value of wood products is far greater because most wood is used locally and is not exported. Wood products from the forests of tropical countries, including timber, plywood, and wood pulp, are being exported at a rapid rate to earn foreign currency, to provide capital for industrialization, to pay foreign debt, and to provide employment. In tropical countries such as Indonesia, Brazil, and Malaysia, timber products earn billions of dollars per year (Primack and Lovejoy 1995) (Figure 4.4A).

Nonwood products from forests, including game, fruits, gums and resins, rattan, and medicinal plants, also have a large productive use value (Figure 4.4B). These nontimber products are sometimes erroneously called "minor forest products"; in reality they are often very important economically and may even rival the value of timber. In a well-publicized study, researchers compared the productive use values of logged Amazonian tropical rain forests with those that are sustainably harvested for fruits and latex (Peters et al. 1989). For a species-rich rain forest in the Peruvian Amazon located 30 km from Iquitos, the net productive value of the forest was calculated at $490 per ha when used for timber production, compared to $6330 per ha when used for fruit and latex production. While it's true that the greatest profit in a *single year* can be made by harvesting and selling timber, no more timber can be harvested for decades. According to these calculations, the greatest long-term value comes from gathering fruit and latex, which can be brought to market and sold every year. The economic value of this land for cattle ranching is less than half the value obtained by collecting rain forest products. In this analysis, the net benefit of selective logging is also surprisingly low because of the damage it does to latex- and fruit-producing trees.

The method of valuation in the Peters et al. study assumes that there are stable and accessible markets for these nontimber forest products. Other subsequent analyses do not show such high values for these prod-

(A)

(B)

Figure 4.4 (A) The timber industry is a major source of revenue in many tropical countries. Here trees are harvested from rain forest in the Brazilian Amazon. (Photograph courtesy of William Laurance.) (B) Nontimber products are often important in local and national economies. Many rural people supplement their incomes by gathering natural forest products to sell in local markets. Here a Land Dayak family in Sarawak (Malaysia) sells wild honey and edible wild fruits. (Photograph by R. Primack.)

ucts (Gram et al. 2001). That's because the profitability of harvesting fruits and other forest products declines dramatically with increasing distances from large towns due to transportation costs, and the prices of these products may fall if more people bring the products to market due to an oversupply (Godoy et al. 1993; Godoy 2001). However, when the ecosystem value of the forest as a source of drinking water, flood control, and soil protection is combined with the value of nontimber products, maintaining and utilizing natural communities may still prove to be more productive than intensive logging, converting the forest into commercial plantations, or establishing cattle ranches (Panayotou and Ashton 1992; Daily 1997). Careful tree harvesting that minimizes damage to the surrounding biological community and the ecosystem services it provides, combined with gathering nontimber products, may be a profitable approach that justifies maintaining the land in forest.

THE NATURAL PHARMACY   Effective drugs are needed to keep people healthy, and they represent an enormous industry, with worldwide sales of around $300 billion per year (Grifo and Rosenthal 1997; Mateo et al. 2001). The natural world is an important source of medicines currently in use and possible future medicines. One species with great medicinal use is the rose periwinkle (*Catharanthus roseus*) from Madagascar

BOX 7 *Mighty Multitudes of Microbes: Not To Be Ignored!*

They're out there, and there are billions of them. They occupy cities, suburbs, countrysides, and forests; they're equally at home in spiffy high-rise hotels, filthy shanty towns, and barren deserts. They live in hospitals, restaurants, parks, theaters, and your digestive tract, as well as on mountaintops, in rain forests, and on seashores. They can be found swimming in the ocean's depths and warming themselves near volcanoes—they may even exist on Mars. The living world's quintessential jet-setters, we find them everywhere we look—or we would, if we could see at the microscopic level. Fortunately for the peace of mind of most people, we can't, so the billions of microbes that inhabit our world go unnoticed. Out of sight and out of mind, except when we're bothered by a cold or have gone too long without cleaning out the vegetable drawer in the refrigerator.

The word "microbe" is a catchall for thousands of species of bacteria, yeasts, protozoa, fungi, and the bacterialike species in the primitive kingdom Archaea.* A handful of soil can contain thousands, millions, even billions of each of these different types of microbes (Coleman 2001; Dunlap 2001), except for the Archaea, which at present are known only from extreme environments such as deep-sea thermal vents, coal deposits, highly salty environments, and hot springs (see Box 4). Few people realize how utterly essential these invisible critters are to our day-to-day existence. We tend to look on microbes as nuisances that pose a potential threat to our health—hence the proliferation of antibacterial soaps and antibiotic sprays on supermarket shelves.

In truth, most microbes either actively help us or at the very least do us little harm. Those microbes that do harm us—pathogens ranging from the annoying fungus that causes athlete's foot to the deadly viruses and protozoans that cause killer diseases such as AIDS and malaria—are fairly few in number when compared to the total range of microbes present in the world. On the other hand, we literally could not live without some of them. Microbes play a vital role in the production of foods such as bread, cheese, vinegar, yogurt, soy sauce, and tofu, and alcoholic beverages such as beer and wine. Bacteria in our gastrointestinal tract help break down the food we eat (Canby 1993). A few species of bacteria perform the vital biochemical function of transforming nitrogen gas from the atmosphere into a form that plants can take up from the soil as a nutrient. Such "fixed" nitrogen is essential for plant growth. Bacteria and fungi in the soil also aid in the decomposition of organic wastes, freeing up more nutrients such as phosphates, nitrates, carbon dioxide, and sulphates for plants to use as they grow. In short, without bacteria, there would be no plants—and thus no food or oxygen available for the animal kingdom, including humans.

In recent years, scientists have begun to appreciate that these organisms are important not only to sustain life as we know it, but also to assist in the conservation of threatened species. Some microbes have uses that may ultimately help reduce environmental pollution and habitat degradation. For instance, a major cause of the decline of many insect and bird species is the presence of harmful compounds in sprays used to control agricultural pests and pathogens. These chemicals harm important nonpest species either by killing them outright or by interfering with their ability to forage and reproduce; at the same time, many pests and pathogens have grown resistant to the compounds (NRC, 1996). As pesticides have become less effective, agronomists have begun turning to microbial solutions to solve pest problems. For example, the bacterial species *Bacillus thuringiensis* produces a toxin

---

*The term "microbe" also encompasses viruses, fragments of genetic material surrounded by a protective protein coat, which can invade the cells of other species and make copies of themselves. Viruses are not generally considered to be living, independent organisms.

BOX 7 *(continued)*

Bacteria can be genetically engineered to "eat" crude oil. In this laboratory simulation of an oil spill (left), adapted bacteria added to the spill (top, right) quickly reduce the area of the damaging pollutant (bottom right). (Photographs by Charles O'Rear.)

that kills some insect pests and *Agrobacterium radiobacter* inhibits the growth of a bacterial pathogen that attacks several important fruit and flower species. These bacteria can be sprayed on crops, or using the techniques of molecular biology, specific genes from bacteria can be incorporated into the cells of crop plants such as corn, potato, and tomato. The use of transgenic crops has improved crop yield, but some people believe that such dramatic alteration of species is morally wrong and potentially dangerous because of its unknown effects on other species.

Using microbes as biological controls is advantageous for two important reasons: First, they tend to be highly specific in what they will attack, so unlike chemicals, they are likely to harm only a narrow range of species. Though a microbe that causes disease in cabbage moth caterpillars could not be used, for instance, in an area also inhabited by an endangered butterfly, it could be used elsewhere without concern that it would harm beneficial insects such as bees or dragonflies. A second

advantage is that, like the pathogens they attack, microbes are capable of mutating into many different varieties. Unlike chemical pesticides, a microbe can be genetically altered to counteract the mutations of the pathogen; thus, although the pest species might become resistant to one strain of the bacterium used for biological control, additional strains can be developed to counteract the resistance. In addition to replacing harmful chemicals with microbes, bioengineering has allowed us to "train" microbes to perform tasks that are not feasible using technological means. For example, bacteria engineered to attack pollutants such as cyanide, crude oil, and creosote are used more and more often in cleaning up toxic waste sites (Canby 1993; Porazinska and Wall 2001). This use of microbes may become an important factor in reclaiming damaged habitat, possibly an essential component of future conservation efforts. It is ironic that the simplest, "lowest" life forms on Earth should be in a position to address problems created by the most complex and "highest" life form, humankind.

(Table 4.2). Two potent drugs derived from this plant are effective in treating Hodgkin's disease, leukemia, and other blood cancers. Treatment using these drugs has increased the survival rate of childhood leukemia from 10% to 90%. How many more such valuable plants will be discovered in the years ahead—and how many will go extinct before they are discovered?

Even in the case of medicines that are now produced synthetically by chemists, many were first discovered in a wild species used in traditional medicine (Cox 2001, Gerwick et al. 2001) (Figure 4.5). Extracts of willow tree bark (*Salix* sp.) were used by the ancient Greeks and by tribes of Native Americans to treat pain, leading to the discovery of acetylsalicylic acid—the painkilling ingredient in modern aspirin, one of our most important and widely used medicines. Similarly, the use of coca (*Erythoxylum coca*) by natives of the Andean highlands eventually led to the development of synthetic derivatives such as Novocaine and Xylocaine, commonly used as local anesthetics in dentistry and surgery. Many other important medicines were first identified in animals. Poisonous animals such as rattlesnakes, bees, and cone snails have been especially rich

TABLE 4.2 Twenty drugs first discovered in traditional medical practice

Drug	Medical use	Plant source	Common name
Ajmaline	Treats heart arrhythmia	*Rauwolfia* spp.	Rauwolfia
Aspirin	Analgesic, anti-inflammatory	*Spiraea ulmaria*	Meadow Sweet
Atropine	Dilates eyes during examination	*Atropa belladonna*	Belladonna
Caffeine	Stimulant	*Camellia sinensis*	Tea plant
Cocaine	Ophthalmic analgesic	*Erythroxylum coca*	Coca plant
Codeine	Analgesic, antitussive	*Papaver somniferum*	Opium poppy
Digitoxin	Cardiac stimulant	*Digitalis purpurea*	Foxglove
Ephedrine	Bronchodilator	*Ephedra sinica*	Ephedra plant
Ipecac	Emetic	*Cephaelis ipecachuanha*	Ipecac plant
Morphine	Analgesic	*Papaver somniferum*	Opium poppy
Pseudoephedrine	Decongestant	*Ephedra sinica*	Ephedra plant
Quinine	Antimalarial prophylactic	*Cinchona pubescens*	Chinchona
Reserpine	Treats hypertension	*Rauwolfia serpentina*	Rauwolfia
Sennoside A,B	Laxative	*Cassia angustifolia*	Senna
Scopolamine	Treats motion sickness	*Datura stramonium*	Thorn Apple
Strophanthin	Treats congestive heart failure	*Strophanthus gratus*	Rose Allamanda
THC	Antiemetic	*Cannabis sativa*	Marijuana
Toxiferine	Relaxes muscles during surgery	*Strychnos guianensis*	Strychnos plant
Tubocurarine	Muscle relaxant	*Chondrodendron tomentosum*	Curare
Vincristine	Treats pediatric leukemia	*Catharanthus roseus*	Rose periwinkle

Source: After Balick and Cox 1996.

Figure 4.5 Carrying on the traditions of his Mayan ancestors, Antonio Cue of Belize prepares useful medicines from plants that are growing in the local area. As is the case with many local people in the developing world who have knowledge of their flora and fauna, he is now working with scientists to determine if chemicals in these plants can be developed for use in modern medicine. (Photograph courtesy of M. J. Balick.)

sources of chemicals with valuable medical and biological applications (Carte 1996).

All of the 20 most frequently used pharmaceuticals in the United States are based on chemicals first identified in natural products. These drugs have a combined sales value of $6 billion per year. Twenty-five percent of the prescriptions filled in the United States contain active ingredients derived from plants, and many of the most important antibiotics, including penicillin and tetracycline, are derived from fungi and other microorganisms (Eisner 1991; Dobson 1995, 1998). Most recently, the fungus-derived drug cyclosporine has proved to be a crucial element in the success of heart and kidney transplants. As will be discussed in the next chapter, the natural world is being actively searched for the next generation of medicines and industrial products.

Even seemingly-unimportant species often possess tremendous value. Horseshoe crabs, for instance, were usually recognized only as clumsy creatures that seemed to move with difficulty in shallow water. At various times, humans have used them as cheap fish bait, poultry food, and agricultural fertilizer. In recent years, however, we have realized that horseshoe crab eggs and juveniles are greatly important as a food source to shorebirds and coastal fish. Without horseshoe crabs, these other species would decline. Additionally, horseshoe crab blood is now collected to make limulus amoebocyte lysate (LAL), which is used to detect bacterial contamination in medicines administered by injection. This chemical cannot be synthesized, and there is no other source besides horseshoe crabs. Without horseshoe crabs as a source of LAL, our ability to determine the purity of such medicines would be compromised. Due to the importance of horseshoe crabs in coastal ecology and their value as a source of LAL, there are currently harvesting restrictions for horseshoe crabs along the coastlines of the United States.

Summary

1. Conservation biologists and economists are developing a new method, called ecological economics, to assign monetary value to biological diversity and, in the process, are providing arguments for its protection. While some conservation biologists would argue that biological diversity is priceless and cannot and should not be assigned economic value, economic justification for biological diversity will play an increasingly important role in debates on the use of natural resources.

2. Many countries that appear to have annual increases in gross domestic product may have stagnant or even declining economies when the costs of development—depletion of natural resources and damage to the environment—are included in the calculations. More large development projects are being analyzed through environmental impact assessments and cost–benefit analyses before being approved. In addition, assigning economic value gives both the public and policy makers a frame of reference for understanding the magnitude of environmental degradation.

3. A number of methods have been developed to assign economic value to biological diversity. In one method, resources are divided between direct values, which are assigned to products harvested by people; indirect values, which are assigned to benefits provided by biological diversity that do not involve harvesting or destroying the resource; option value, which is assigned to the potential future value of biological diversity; and existence value, based on the willingness of society to pay for the protection of biological diversity.

4. Direct values can be further divided into consumptive use value and productive use value. Consumptive use value is assigned to products that are consumed locally, such as fuelwood, wild meat, fruits and vegetables, medicinal plants, and building materials. These goods can be valued by determining how much money people would have to pay for them if they were unavailable in the wild. When these wild products become unavailable, the living standard of the people who depend on them declines. Productive use value is assigned to products harvested in the wild and sold in markets, such as commercial timber, fish and shellfish, and wild meat.

For Discussion

1. Choose a recent large development project from your area, such as a dam, sewage treatment plant, or housing development, and learn all you can about it. Estimate the costs and benefits of this project in terms of biological diversity, economic prosperity, and human health. Who pays the costs and who receives the benefits? Consider other projects carried out in the past and determine their impact on the surrounding biological and human communities. (These are challenging questions that may be appropriate to tackle as a group activity.)

2. How do traditional (or rural) societies use and value biological diversity? What is the relative importance of biological diversity in both traditional and modern societies? How do these societies value biodiversity knowledge?

3. Suppose a medicinal plant used by traditional people in a remote area in Indonesia is investigated by a European pharmaceutical company and found to have huge potential as a new cancer medicine. Who will profit from the sale of this medicine under current practices? Can you suggest alternative methods to distribute the profits in a way that would be more equitable and that would increase the possibility of preserving Indonesia's biological diversity?

Suggested Readings

Balick, M. J. and P. A. Cox. 1996. *Plants, People and Culture: The Science of Ethnobotany.* Scientific American Library, New York. Fascinating story of traditional use of plants, filled with anecdotes and beautifully illustrated.

Barbier, E. B., J. C. Burgess, and C. Folke. 1994. *Paradise Lost? The Ecological Economics of Biodiversity.* Earthscan Publications, London. A clear introduction to this new field.

Baskin, Y. 1997. *The Work of Nature: How the Diversity of Life Sustains Us.* Island Press, Washington, D.C. Excellent semipopular account of the many benefits of preserving biological diversity.

Bulte, E. H. and G. C. van Kooten. 2000. Economic science, endangered species, and biodiversity loss. *Conservation Biology* 14: 113–119. Considers the limitations of economic arguments in preserving biological diversity; a good starting point for discussions.

Costanza, R., O. Segura, and J. Martinez-Alier. 1996. *Getting Down to Earth: Practical Applications of Ecological Economics.* Island Press, Washington, D.C. Leading authorities apply ecological economics to the issues of environmental health and sustainability.

Cox, P. A. 2001. Pharmacology, biodiversity and. In *Encyclopedia of Biodiversity,* S.A. Levin (ed.), Vol. 4, pp. 523–536. Academic Press, San Diego, CA. Good historical account of the contributions of the natural world to modern medicine.

Daily, G. C. (ed.). 1997. *Nature's Services: Societal Dependence on Ecosystem Services.* Island Press, Washington, D.C. Clear explanations of why maintaining species and ecosystems is critical to human societies.

Davidson, E. A. 2000. *You Can't Eat GNP: Economics as if Ecology Mattered.* Perseus Publishing, Cambridge, MA. Many current economic tools do not adequately value the service provided by the natural world.

Godoy, R. A. 2001. *Indians, Markets, and Rainforests: Theoretical, Comparative, and Quantitative Exploration in the NeoTropics.* Columbia University Press, New York. An examination of the value of forest products and factors contributing to deforestation in tropical Latin America; valuable for its descriptive method.

Grifo, F. and J. Rosenthal (eds.). 1997. *Biodiversity and Human Health.* Island Press, Washington, D. C. For a wide variety of reasons, maintaining human health and well-being depends on protecting biological diversity.

Myers, N. and J. Kent. 2001. *Perverse Subsidies: How Tax Dollars Can Undercut the Environment and the Economy.* Island Press, Washington, D.C. Governments are paying for destructive industries to continue.

Prescott-Allen, C. and R. Prescott-Allen. 1986. *The First Resource: Wild Species in the North American Economy.* Yale University Press, New Haven, CT. An innovative examination of the economic importance of wild species to a modern economy.

Tuxill, J. 1999. *Nature's Cornucopia: Our Stake in Plant Diversity.* World Watch Institute, Washington, D.C. Plants are crucial to both traditional and modern societies.

Chapter

Indirect Economic Values

As we discussed in Chapter 4, the components of biological diversity that provide economic benefits without being harvested and destroyed during use are said to have indirect use value. They are crucial to the continued availability of the natural products on which economies depend and societies function. Mountain forests, for example, prevent soil erosion and flooding that could damage human settlements and farmlands in nearby lowland areas; coastal estuaries provide rich harvests of fish and shellfish worth billions of dollars annually, and during severe storms, they provide protection for human coastal developments worth billions more.

Nonconsumptive Use Value

The great variety of environmental services that biological communities provide can be classified as having a particular type of indirect use value called **nonconsumptive use value** (because these services are not consumed). The nonconsumptive use value of ecosystem services is huge.

Economists are just beginning to calculate the nonconsumptive use value of ecosystem services at regional and global levels (Table 5.1) (Chichilnisky 1996; Daily and

TABLE 5.1 Estimated value of the world's ecosystems using ecological economics

Ecosystem[a]	Total area (millions of ha)	Annual local value (dollars/ ha/year)	Annual global value (trillions of dollars/year)
Coastal	3102	4052	12.6
Open ocean	33,200	252	8.4
Wetlands	330	14,785	4.9
Tropical forests	1900	2007	3.8
Lakes, rivers	200	8498	1.7
Other forests	2955	302	0.9
Grasslands	3898	232	0.9
Cropland	1400	92	0.1

Source: After Costanza et al. 1997
[a]Desert, tundra, urban, and ice/rock ecosystems not included.

Dasgupta 2001; Daily and Ellison 2002). These calculations are still at a preliminary stage, but they suggest that the nonconsumptive use value of ecosystem services is enormous, around $33 trillion per year, greatly exceeding the direct use value of biological diversity (Costanza et al. 1997). Because this amount is greater than the global gross national product of $18 trillion, the point can be made that human societies are totally dependent on natural ecosystems and they would not persist if these ecosystem services were permanently degraded or destroyed. The most important ecosystem services not accounted for in the current market system are waste treatment and nutrient retention, which are provided by wetlands and coastal areas and total $18 trillion per year. Many ecological economists are in sharp disagreement about how such calculations should be done, or if they even should be done at all (Masood and Garwin 1998). Using a different approach, Pimentel et al. (1997) came up with a much lower estimate for the global value of biodiversity, $3 trillion per year, indicating that much more work needs to be done on this topic. Biodiversity has been estimated to be worth $70 billion per year for Canada (Mosquin et al. 1995) and $319 billion per year for the United States (Pimentel et al. 1997).

The following is a discussion of some of the general benefits, derived from conserving biological diversity, that do not usually appear on the balance sheets of environmental impact assessments or in national GDPs.

Ecosystem Productivity

The photosynthetic capacity of plants and algae allows the energy of the sun to be captured in living tissue. The energy stored in plants is sometimes harvested by humans for use as food, fuelwood, and fodder. This plant material is also the starting point for innumerable food chains, from which many animal products are harvested by people. Human needs for natural resources dominate approximately 40% of the productivity of the terrestrial environment (Vitousek 1994; Vitousek et al. 1997). The destruction of the vegetation in an area through overgrazing by domestic animals, overharvesting of timber, or frequent fires will destroy the system's ability to make use of solar energy. Eventually it leads to the loss of production of plant biomass and the deterioration of the animal community (including humans) that lives at that site.

Likewise, coastal estuaries are areas of rapid plant and algal growth that provide the starting point for food chains leading to commercial stocks of fish and shellfish (see Table 5.1). The U.S. National Marine Fisheries Service has estimated that damage to coastal estuaries has cost the United States more than $200 million per year in lost productive value of commercial fish and shellfish and in lost nonconsumptive value of fish caught for sport (McNeely et al. 1990). Even when degraded or damaged ecosystems are rebuilt or restored at great expense, they often do not function as well as before and almost certainly do not contain their original species composition or species richness.

Scientists are actively investigating how the loss of species from biological communities affects ecosystem processes such as the total growth of plants, the ability of plants to absorb atmospheric carbon dioxide (CO_2), and the ability to adapt to global climate change (Baskin 1997; Chapin et al. 1998). This question was addressed experimentally at a grassland in Minnesota in which either 1, 2, 6, 8, 12, or 24 species were grown on 3 m × 3 m plots (Tilman 1999). The growth of plant material and the uptake of soil nutrients such as nitrogen was greater in plots with more species, clearly demonstrating the importance of species diversity to productivity (Figure 5.1). These results were further support-

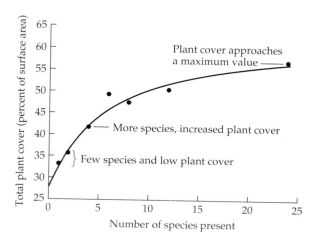

Figure 5.1 Varying numbers of prairie plant species were grown in experimental plots. The plots containing the most species had the greatest overall amount of growth, as measured by the total plant cover (the percentage of the total surface area occupied by plants) and total plant productivity (the total dry weight of plants on the plot). (After Tilman et al. 1996.)

ed by similar observations of nearby native grasslands. Plots with a greater diversity of species showed an increased ability to withstand drought and resist invasion by outside species. This research has been extensively replicated in European grasslands, pasture communities, and wetlands with similar results (Loreau and Hector 2001; Engelhardt and Ritchie 2001).

We know that species diversity is being reduced in major ecosystems as a result of human activities. At what point will the productivity of these ecosystems decline as well? We need to know the answer to this question before the world's forestry, ranching, agriculture, and fishing industries become critically damaged by the consequences of species decline. It is safe to assume that ecosystems with a lower diversity of species will be less able to adapt to the altered weather conditions associated with rising CO_2 levels and global climate change. For example, temperate forest ecosystems with few tree species to start with will likely show the effects of species loss quickly as their resident species are eliminated by exotic diseases and insects.

Protection of Water and Soil Resources

Biological communities are of vital importance in protecting watersheds, buffering ecosystems against extremes of flood and drought, and maintaining water quality (Likens 1991; Wilson and Carpenter 1999; Pimentel et al. 2000). Plant foliage and dead leaves intercept the rain and reduce its impact on the soil, and plant roots and soil organisms aerate the soil, increasing its capacity to absorb water. This increased water-holding capacity reduces the flooding that would otherwise occur after heavy rains and allows a slow release of water for days and weeks after the rains have ceased.

When vegetation is disturbed by logging, farming, and other human activities, the rates of soil erosion and even occurrences of landslides increase rapidly, decreasing the value of the land for human activities (Figure 5.2) (Pimentel et al. 1995). Damage to the soil limits the ability of plant life to recover from disturbance and can render the land useless for agriculture. In addition, silt (soil particles suspended in water from runoff) can kill freshwater animals, coral reef organisms, and the marine life in coastal estuaries. Erosion and flooding also make the water supplies for humans in the communities along the rivers undrinkable, leading to a increase in human health problems. Soil erosion increases sediment loads into the reservoirs behind dams, causing a loss of electrical output, and creates sandbars and islands, which reduces the navigability of rivers and ports.

Unprecedented catastrophic floods in Bangladesh, India, the Philippines, and Thailand have been associated with recent extensive logging in watershed areas. Flood damage to India's agricultural areas has led to massive government and private tree-planting programs in the

Figure 5.2 Logging and road construction on steep slopes leads to massive soil erosion and landslides, destroying a great deal of the economic value of the forest ecosystem. (Photograph by R. Primack.)

Himalayas. In the industrial nations of the world, wetlands protection has become a priority in order to prevent flooding of developed areas. In the region surrounding Boston, Massachusetts, the value of marshland has been estimated at $72,000 per hectare per year solely on the basis of its role in reducing flood damage (Hair 1988). The conversion of floodplain habitat to farmland along the Mississippi, Missouri, and Red Rivers, and elsewhere in the midwestern United States, is considered a major factor in the massive, damaging floods in past years.

In many areas of the developing world, people settle near natural water sources to obtain water for drinking, washing, and irrigation. As hydrologic cycles are disrupted by deforestation, soil erosion, and dam projects, and as water quality deteriorates due to pollution, people are increasingly unable to obtain their water needs from natural systems. The cost of boiling water, buying bottled water, or building new wells, rain catchment systems, water treatment plants, pipes, and water pumps gives some measure of the consumptive use value of water from surface sources. The government of New York City, for instance, paid $1.5 billion in the late 1980s to county and town governments in rural New York state to maintain forests on the watersheds surrounding its reservoirs and to improve agricultural practices. Water filtration plants doing the same job would have cost $8–9 billion (McKibben 1996).

Increases in waterborne disease and intestinal ailments, which currently affect half of the world's population, and the subsequent lost days of work that result from such illnesses, add to estimates of the economic value of water and the natural systems that provide it.

There is growing recognition of the fact that development of dams, reservoirs, and new croplands needs to include protection measures for natural communities located on the highlands above these projects in order to ensure a steady supply of high-quality water. For example, in Sulawesi, the Indonesian government borrowed $1.2 million from the World Bank to establish the Dumoga–Bone National Park to protect the watershed above a major agricultural project in the adjacent lowland (Wells and Brandon 1992). Combining development projects with watershed protection can make a critical difference in the conservation of biological communities, while also acknowledging the value provided by undeveloped land.

Climate Regulation

Plant communities are important in moderating local, regional, and probably even global climate conditions (Clark 1992; Couzin 1999). At the local level, trees provide shade and transpire water, which reduces the local temperature in hot weather. This cooling effect reduces the need for fans and air conditioners and increases people's comfort and work efficiency. Trees are also locally important because they act as windbreaks for agricultural fields and homes and reduce heat loss from buildings in cold weather.

At the regional level, transpiration from plants recycles rainwater back into the atmosphere so that it can return as rain. At the global level, loss of vegetation from large forested regions of the world such as the Amazon Basin and West Africa may result in a reduction of average annual rainfall (Fearnside 1990). In both terrestrial and aquatic environments, plant growth is tied into the carbon cycle. A reduction in plant life results in reduced uptake of carbon dioxide, contributing to the rising carbon dioxide levels that lead to global warming (Kremen et al. 1999). Plants are the "green lungs" of the planet, producing the oxygen on which all animals, including people, depend for respiration.

Waste Treatment and Nutrient Retention

Aquatic communities such as swamps, lakes, rivers, floodplains, tidal marshes, mangroves, estuaries, the coastal shelf, and the open ocean are capable of breaking down and immobilizing toxic pollutants, such as heavy metals and pesticides that have been released into the environment by human activities (Odum 1997). Fungi and bacteria are particularly important in this role. Waste treatment by these biological communities is estimated to be valued at around $2.4 trillion per year (Costanza et al. 1997). When these ecosystems are damaged and degraded, expensive pollution treatment facilities must be installed and operated to assume these functions.

Aquatic biological communities also play an important role in processing and storing the large amount of nutrients that enter the ecosystem as sewage or agricultural runoff, allowing these nutrients to be absorbed by photosynthetic organisms. These communities also provide a matrix for the bacteria that fix atmospheric nitrogen. These roles in nutrient processing and retention have an estimated value of $15.9 trillion per year, with coastal marine areas accounting for most of the total (Costanza et al. 1997).

An excellent example of the value of such an ecosystem is provided by the New York Bight, a 5200 km^2 (2000 square mile) bay at the mouth of the Hudson River. The New York Bight provides a free sewage disposal system into which the waste produced by 20 million people in the New York metropolitan area is dumped (Young et al. 1985). Until recently, the Bight was able to break down and absorb this onslaught of sewage because of the high degree of bacterial activity and tidal mixing in the area. However, the Bight is now showing signs of stress—fish die-offs and beach contamination—that suggest the system is overloaded. The system is being further strained by progressive filling in and development of real estate on the coastal estuaries and marshes, which are essential in the breakdown and assimilation process. As the New York Bight becomes overwhelmed and damaged by a combination of sewage overload and coastal development, an alternative waste disposal system of massive waste treatment facilities and giant landfills will have to be developed at a cost of tens of billions of dollars.

Species Relationships

Many of the species harvested by people for their productive use value depend on other wild species for their continued existence. For example, the wild game and fish harvested by people are dependent on wild insects and plants for their food. A decline in insect and plant populations will result in a decline in animal harvests. Thus, a decline in a wild species of little immediate value to humans may result in a corresponding decline in a harvested species that is economically important. Crop plants also benefit from birds and predatory insects, such as praying mantises, which feed on pest insect species that attack the crops (Pimentel et al. 1997). Insects act as pollinators for numerous crop species. About 150 species of crop plants in the United States require insect pollination of their flowers, often involving a mixture of wild insects and honeybees (Buchmann and Nabhan 1997). The value of these pollinators has been estimated to be around $20–40 billion per year. The value of wild insect pollinators will increase in the near future if they take over the pollination role of domestic honeybees, whose populations are declining due to disease and pests. Many useful wild plant species depend on fruit-eating animals, such as bats, birds, and primates to act as seed dispersers. Where these animals have been overharvested, fruits remain uneaten, seeds are not dispersed, and species head toward local extinction.

One of the most economically significant relationships in biological communities is that between many forest trees and crop plants and the soil organisms that provide them with essential nutrients. Fungi and bacteria break down dead plant and animal matter, which they use as their energy source. In the process, they release mineral nutrients, such as nitrogen, into the soil, where they can be used by plants for further growth. Mycorrhizal fungi greatly increase the ability of plant roots to absorb water and minerals, and certain mutualistic bacteria convert nitrogen into a form that can be taken up by plants. In return, the plants provide the mutualists with photosynthetic products that help them grow. The poor growth and dieback of many trees in certain areas of North America and Europe is attributable in part to the deleterious effects of acid rain and air pollution on soil fungi (Box 8).

Environmental Monitors

Species that are particularly sensitive to chemical toxins serve as "early warning indicators" for monitoring the health of the environment. Some species can even substitute for expensive detection equipment. Among the best-known indicator species are rock lichens, which absorb large amounts of chemicals in rainwater and airborne pollution (Hawksworth 1990). High levels of toxic materials kill lichens, so the distribution and abundance of lichens can identify areas of contamination around sources of air pollution, such as smelters. Conversely, certain conspicuous lichens grow only in old-growth forests and can be used to identify areas likely to contain rare and endangered species that are less conspicuous (Nilsson et al. 1995). Aquatic filter feeders, such as mollusks, are also effective in monitoring pollution because they process large volumes of water and concentrate toxic chemicals such as poisonous metals, PCBs, and pesticides in their tissues. The California Mussel Watch Program, started in 1977, has expanded to include 135 coastal and freshwater sites in which mussel (*Mytilus* sp.) and clam (*Corbicula fluminea*) tissues are sampled and analyzed for toxic compounds, highlighting areas of serious water pollution (Persson et al. 2000). Monitoring algal blooms in shallow marine waters can provide a warning of the contamination of shellfish by toxic species and potential health impacts on swimmers from encounters with poisonous species (Epstein 1998).

Recreation and Ecotourism

Ecosystems provide many recreational services for humans, such as the nonconsumptive enjoyment of nature through hiking, photography, and bird-watching (Duffus and Dearden 1990). The monetary value of

BOX 8   *The Decline of Fungi in the Forest: A Premonition of Disaster*

To many humans, fungi evoke images of rotting wood, spoiled food, mildewed rugs, and other damp, smelly, unpleasant things. Yet fungi may be vital to the continued existence of both temperate and tropical forests. Many fungi exist in symbiotic relationships with trees; these relationships are essential to the trees' health. Thus, the decline of many fungus species in recent decades is cause for great concern among biologists.

The best body of evidence for a decline among fungus species comes from Europe, where records of mushroom collecting date back to 1912. Scientists combined these records with long-term observations of different mushroom species and noticed a distinct decline in both the overall number of species and the population sizes of each species. One 20-year study in the Netherlands, for example, observed a significant drop in the average number of mushroom species found in 1000 m^2 plots: Roughly 65% of the species originally counted in the plots vanished during the study period (Cherfas 1991; Arnolds 1991). In addition, the population size of many species has declined, as has the size of individual mushrooms. Records for annual crops of edible chanterelle and bolete mushrooms in Germany and truffles in France indicate that the average size of both the crop and individual mushrooms has declined since 1950. The decline is not limited to edible mushrooms, however, ruling out overexploitation as a prime factor in this reduction. Similar declines among North American species are suspected, but because no data comparable to the European records exist, any estimates of declines and extinctions of North American fungi are pure guesswork.

Fungi extinctions have cataclysmic implications for forests worldwide. Many soil fungi live in a close symbiotic relationship with the roots of tree species. Experiments on tropical tree species have shown that some species cannot grow at all in the absence of fungi, and many others grow faster and are generally healthier with fungi than without (Medina and Huber 1992). In this association, fungi receive carbohydrates from the trees as food. In exchange, soil fungi improve the plant's resistance to insect attack, drought, and extremes of temperature, and they apparently increase the plant's ability to take up nutrients from the soil, which is vitally important in the nutrient-poor soils of the Tropics. Mass extinctions of fungi thus could conceivably precede large-scale losses of trees in both tropical and temperate forests.

(continued on next page)

Control   *G. rosea*   *G. margarita*   *A. spinosa*   *S. heterogama*

The presence of different mycorrhizal fungi greatly enhances the growth and health of tree seedlings. Seedlings of a savannah tree, *Clusia grandiflora*, from Venezuela were grown with various species of mycorrhizal fungi. The spindly, small seedlings on the left were grown as a control without fungi. Fungi in the species *Acaulospora spinsoa* and *Scutellospora heterogama* greatly enhanced seedling growth, whereas two species of fungi in the genus *Gigaspora* (*G. rosea* and *G. margarita*) had minimal effects. The inset shows the spores of a mycorrhizal fungus. (Photographs courtesy of Gisela Cuena.)

BOX 8 *(continued)*

These data present several questions for conservation biologists. First, how widespread is the problem? So far, the only long-term and relatively complete available data set is of European temperate forest fungi. Almost nothing is known of the condition of fungus species in the Americas or elsewhere. Second, what is causing the decline in fungus species? Investigations to date suggest the main cause is air pollution, including an increase in soil acidity and the deposition of excess nitrogen and sulfur on the soil (Lilleskov et al. 2001; Moore et al. 2001; Wallenda and Kottke 1998). The exact

problem is unclear: Does pollution damage the fungi directly, or does pollution-related damage to trees indirectly harm fungi by inhibiting symbiotic processes? Other factors negatively affecting native fungi include habitat destruction, changes in land use such as converting native forest to plantation forests, and intensification of agriculture such as converting meadows to cultivated fields. More specific information on fungal decline is needed before the third and most important question can be addressed: How can the trend be reversed?

these activities, sometimes called their amenity value, can be considerable (Figure 5.3). In the United States, there are 350 million visitors each year to U.S. national parks, wildlife refuges, and other protected public lands. These visitors engage in nonconsumptive activities such as sport fishing and camping, and in the process spend $4 billion on fees, travel, lodging, food, and equipment. The value of sport fishing alone in the United States has been estimated to be $6 billion per year, a surprisingly large figure.

In national and international sites known for their conservation value or exceptional scenic beauty, such as Yellowstone National Park, nonconsumptive recreational value often dwarfs the value generated or captured by all other economic enterprises, including extractive industries.

Figure 5.3 Wildlife is used in a variety of consumptive and nonconsumptive ways by both traditional and modern societies. The range of this use and the value of wildlife to people is increasing all the time. (After Duffus and Dearden 1990.)

Consumptive Uses
Commercial hunting • Sport hunting • Subsistence hunting • Commercial fishing • Sport fishing • Subsistence fishing • Fur trapping • Hunting for animal parts and pet trade • Indirect kills through other activities (pollution, by-catch, road kills) • Eradication programs for animals posing real or perceived threats

Low-Consumptive Uses
Zoos and animal parks • Aquariums • Scientific research

Nonconsumptive Uses
Birdwatching • Whale-watching • Photography trips • Nature walks • Commercial photography and cinematography • Wildlife viewing in parks, reserves and recreational areas

This value is even larger when the money spent off-site on food, lodging, equipment, and other goods and services purchased in the local area is included. For instance, mineral and timber harvesting, once regarded as key to the economic vitality of the area around Yellowstone National Park (Power 1991), are now less economically important than are the recreational activities and scenic beauty of the site, which attract the new businesses, temporary visitors, and retirees who now account for the majority of income and jobs in the area.

Even sport hunting and fishing, which in theory are consumptive uses, are in practice nonconsumptive, because the food value of the animals caught by fishermen and hunters is insignificant compared with the time and money spent on these activities. The increasingly common practice of sport fishermen releasing fish rather than keeping them emphasizes the recreational and nonconsumptive aspect of the activity. In many rural economies, such as those of East Africa, Alaska, and the southern United States, sport fishing and hunting generate hundreds of millions of dollars. The potential value of these recreational activities may be even greater than this number suggests, because many park visitors, fishermen, and hunters indicate that they would be willing to pay even higher usage fees to continue their activities.

Ecotourism is a special category of recreation involving people visiting places and spending money wholly or in part to experience unusual biological communities (such as rain forests, the African savannah, coral reefs, deserts, the Galápagos Islands, and the Everglades) and to view particular "flagship" species (such as elephants on safari trips) (Lindberg 1991; Ceballos-Lascuráin 1993). Tourism is among the world's largest industries (on the scale of the petroleum and motor vehicle industries). Ecotourism currently represents 10–50% of tourism, with an annual value of $600 billion–$3 trillion (Braithwaite 2001). Ecotourism is growing rapidly in many developing countries because people want to experience tropical biodiversity for themselves (Gössling 1999). One example of ecotourism's potential is Rwanda, which developed a gorilla tourism industry that until recent civil disturbances was the country's third largest foreign-currency earner. Ecotourism has traditionally been a key industry in East African countries such as Kenya and Tanzania, and is increasingly part of tourism in many American and Asian countries. In the early 1970s, an estimate was made that each lion at Amboseli Park in Kenya could be valued at $27,000 per year in tourist revenue, while the elephant herd was worth $610,000 per year (Western and Henry 1979). More recently, the viewing value of elephants in Kenya was estimated to be $25 million per year (Brown 1993).

The revenue provided by ecotourism has the potential to provide one of the most immediate justifications for protecting biological diversity, particularly when ecotourism activities are integrated into overall management plans (Wells and Brandon 1992, 1993; Southgate and Clark 1993). In Integrated Conservation Development Projects (ICDPs), local communities develop accommodations, expertise in nature guiding, local handicraft outlets, and other sources of income; the revenue income from ecotourism allows the local people to give up unsustainable or destructive hunting, fishing, or grazing practices (Figure 5.4). The local community benefits from learning new skills, employment opportunities, a greater appreciation for their environment, and the development of additional community infrastructure such as schools, roads, medical clinics, and stores.

To help protect biological diversity, ecotourism must provide a significant and secure income for its destination location. However, in a typical ecotourist package, only 20–40% of the retail price of the trip remains in the destination country, and only 0.01–1% is paid in entrance fees to native parks (Gössling 1999). For example, for a two-week trip costing $4000, somewhere between 40 cents and $40 would typically be paid in entrance fees. Even in well-known destinations, such as Komodo National Park in Indonesia, tourist revenues account for less than 10% of the park management budget (Walpole et al. 2001). Obviously, raising entrance fees and increasing tourist spending in the park and adjacent countryside is a priority for this industry.

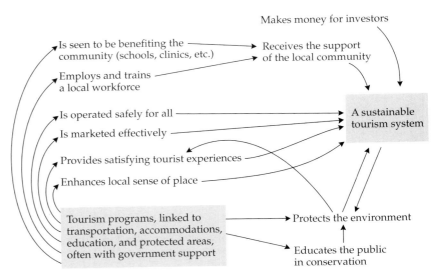

Figure 5.4 Ecotourism can provide an economic justification for protecting biological diversity and also can provide benefits to people living nearby. This diagram illustrates some of the main elements in a successful ecotourism program. (After Braithwaite 2001.)

Figure 5.5 In developing countries, facilities for ecotourists sometimes create a fantasyland that disguises and ignores the real problems those countries face. (From E. G. Magazin, Germany.)

A potential danger of this industry is that ecotourist facilities may provide a sanitized fantasy experience rather than helping visitors understand the serious social and environmental problems that endanger biological diversity (Figure 5.5). Another danger is that tourists themselves will unwittingly damage these sites—by trampling wildflowers, breaking coral, or disrupting nesting bird colonies, for instance—thereby contributing to the degradation and disturbance of sensitive areas. To take one example, hatching success was reduced by 47% when Adelie penguins (*Pygoscelis adeliae*) in the Antarctic were exposed to the typical activities of tourists (Giese 1996). At a wildlife refuge in Florida, the activity patterns of migrant ducks were disrupted at distances up to 80 m from areas frequented by tourists (Klein et al. 1995). Finally, the presence, affluence, and demands of tourists can transform the culture of traditional human societies in tourist areas. As local people increasingly enter a cash-based economy, their values, customs, and relationship to nature might be lost along the way.

Educational and Scientific Value

Many books, television programs, and movies produced for educational and entertainment purposes are based on nature themes (for example, Wilson and Perlman 1999; Morell 1999). Increasingly, natural history materials are being incorporated into school curricula. These educational materials are probably worth billions of dollars per year. These represent a nonconsumptive use value of biodiversity because nature is used as intellectual content in these materials. A considerable number of professional scientists, as well as highly motivated amateurs, are engaged in making ecological observations and preparing educational materials. In rural areas, these activities often take place in scientific field stations, which are sources of training and employment for local people. While these scientific activities provide economic benefits to the areas surrounding field stations, their real value lies in their ability to increase human knowledge, enhance education, and enrich the human experience.

Other Ways of Valuing Biodiversity

In addition to nonconsumptive use value, option value and existence value are two additional ways of valuing biological diversity. In this section we discuss these values in more detail.

Option Value

Recall from Chapter 4 that a species' potential to provide an economic benefit to human society at some point in the future is its option value. As the needs of society change, so must the methods of satisfying those needs, and such methods often lie in previously untapped animal or plant species. For example, the continued genetic improvement of cultivated plants is necessary not only for increased yield, but also to guard against pesticide-resistant insects and more virulent strains of fungi, viruses, and bacteria (Baskin 1997). Catastrophic crop failures often can be directly linked to low genetic variability: the 1846 potato blight in Ireland, the 1922 wheat failure in the Soviet Union, and the 1984 outbreak of citrus canker in Florida were all related to low genetic variability among crop plants (Plucknett et al. 1987). To overcome this problem, scientists are constantly substituting new, resistant varieties of agricultural species for susceptible varieties. The source of resistance often comes from genes obtained from wild relatives of crop plants, and from local varieties of the domestic species grown by traditional farmers.

The genetic improvement of crops is an ongoing process, and past improvements can give an indication of the potential for future improvements. Development of new crop varieties has a huge economic impact, and the option value of future improvements is similarly great. Genetic improvements in U.S. crops were responsible for increasing harvest values by an average of $1 billion per year from 1930 to 1980 (OTA 1987). Genetic improvements of rice and wheat varieties during the "Green Revolution" increased harvests in Asia by an estimated $3.5 billion per year (WCMC 1992). Genes for high sugar content and large fruit size from wild tomatoes from Peru have been transferred into domestic varieties of tomatoes, resulting in an enhanced value of $80 million to the industry (Iltis 1988). The discovery of a wild perennial relative of corn in the Mexican state of Jalisco has a huge option value: It is potentially worth billions of dollars to modern agriculture because it could lead to the development of a high-yielding perennial corn crop, thus eliminat-

BOX 9 *(continued)*

duced by 95%, an impressive achievement. The wasps bred quickly and dispersed well: Five months after one experimental release, *A. lopezi* had spread throughout most cassava fields up to a radius of 170 km. As long as mealybugs remained in an area, the wasps did too, keeping mealybug numbers and their damage down. Armed with evidence of this success, IITA, supported by international aid donors, embarked on a multiyear program of wasp releases and follow-up studies. Facilities were developed for raising up to 250,000 wasps per week. In collaboration with national partners, wasps were released in the most remote corners of Africa on about 150 occasions. Developing a technique for successfully releasing wasps from airplanes helped facilitate the release program. Today *A. lopezi* is found almost everywhere that cassava mealybugs are found in Africa. The tiny wasp has saved hundreds of millions of dollars in crop losses in some of the world's poorest countries (Zeddies et al. 2001). Farmers received free biological control of mealybugs, without the

dangers of pesticide poisoning and pollution to the surrounding environment.

The success of the campaign against the cassava mealybug convinced national governments and international aid donors of the usefulness of biological control efforts. Today IITA, with the same partners, has expanded its biological control programs to fight a number of important tropical pests, including cassava green mite, mango mealybug, corn borers, and water hyacinth. Such efforts continue worldwide.

The IITA search for a biological control agent for the cassava mealybug depended on the patient efforts of scientists and nonscientists from around the world. Bug hunting in South America, lab analysis and testing in England, field testing and release in Africa, and strong international funding were all necessary elements. Most important, biological control was possible because biological diversity had been preserved in Paraguay. This project has become one of the best documented biological control successes and serves as a beacon for new efforts to protect food crops and wild species.

to the new locality, where it can be released to act as a biological control agent. A classic example is the case of the prickly pear cactus (*Opuntia inermis*), a South American species introduced into Australia for use as a hedgerow plant. The cactus spread out of control and took over millions of hectares of rangeland. In the prickly pear's native habitat, the larvae of a particular moth species (*Cactoblastis cactorum*) feeds on the cactus. The moth was successfully introduced into Australia, where it has reduced the cactus to comparative rarity. Thus pristine habitats can be of great value as reservoirs of natural pest control agents.

As was discussed in Chapter 4, we are continually searching the biological communities of the world for new plants, animals, fungi, and microorganisms that can be used to fight human diseases or to provide some other economic value*, an activity referred to as "bioprospecting" (Cox and Balick 1994; Balick et al. 1996; Grifo and Rosenthal 1997;

---

*We discussed the productive use value of natural materials in Chapter 4; however, it is their future value as new products that also gives them value in the present time, so in this chapter we will discuss their option value.

Cox 2001). These searches are generally carried out by government research institutes and pharmaceutical companies. In 1987, the U.S. National Cancer Institute initiated a program costing $8 million to test extracts of thousands of wild species for their effectiveness in controlling cancer cells and the AIDS virus. To facilitate the search for new medicines and to profit financially from new products, the Costa Rican government established the National Biodiversity Institute (INBio) to collect biological products and supply samples to drug companies (Figure 5.6). The Merck Company has signed an agreement to pay INBio $1 million for the right to screen samples and will pay royalties to INBio on any commercial products that result from the research (Mateo et al. 2001). Expected royalties are difficult to calculate, but one estimate suggests a figure of $4.8 million per new drug developed (Reid et al. 1993). Another approach has been to target traditional medicinal plants and other natural products for screening, often in collaboration with local healers. The Glaxo Wellcome corporation, a Brazilian biotechnology company, and the Brazilian government recently signed a contract worth $3 million to sample, screen, and investigate approximately 30,000 plants, fungi, and bacteria from Brazil, with part of the royalties going to support scientific research and local community-based conservation and development projects (Neto and Dickson 1999).

Figure 5.6 Taxonomists and technicians at INBio sort and classify Costa Rica's rich array of species. In the offices shown here many species of plants and insects are cataloged. (Photograph by Steve Winter.)

Programs such as these provide financial incentives for countries to protect their natural resources and the knowledge of biodiversity possessed by indigenous inhabitants. One discovery in this search is a potent anticancer chemical in the Pacific yew (*Taxus brevifolia*), a tree native to North American old-growth forests. This chemical, called taxol, has greatly reduced the mortality rate from ovarian cancer. Another discovery is the ginkgo tree (*Ginkgo biloba*), a species that occurs in the wild in a few isolated localities in China. This species has long been used in traditional Chinese medicine. During the last 25 years, an industry valued at $500 million a year has developed around the cultivation of the ginkgo tree (Figure 5.7) and the manufacture of medicines made from its leaves, which are widely used in Europe, Asia, and increasingly in North America, to treat circulatory problems, including strokes, and to restore and maintain memory function (Del Tredici 1991).

The search for valuable natural products is wide-ranging: Entomologists search for insects that can be used as biological control agents, microbiologists search for bacteria that can assist in biochemical manufacturing processes, and wildlife biologists search for species that can

(A)

Figure 5.7 Ginkgo trees are preserved in the wild in the Tian Mu Shan forest reserve in China; no other wild populations exist. This species is the basis of a pharmaceutical business worth hundreds of millions of dollars each year. (B) Because of the valuable medicines made from their leaves, ginkgo trees are now cultivated as a crop. Each year the woody stems sprout new shoots and branches, which are harvested. (Photographs by Peter Del Tredici, Arnold Arboretum of Harvard University.)

(B)

potentially produce animal protein more efficiently and with less environmental damage than existing domestic species. The growing biotechnology industry is finding new ways to reduce pollution, to develop alternative industrial processes, and to fight diseases threatening human health. Innovative techniques in molecular biology are allowing unique, valuable genes found in one species to be transferred to another species. Both newly discovered and well-known species are often found to have exactly those properties needed to address some significant human problem. If biological diversity is reduced, the ability of scientists to locate and utilize a broad range of species will also be reduced.

A question currently being debated among conservation biologists, governments, environmental economists, and corporations is, "Who owns the commercial development rights to the world's biological diversity?" In the past, species were freely collected from wherever they occurred (often in the developing world) by corporations (almost always headquartered in the developed world). Whatever these corporations found useful in the species was then processed and sold at a profit, which was entirely kept by the corporation. An excellent example is provided by the immunosuppressant drug cyclosporin. Using the fungus *Tolypocladium inflatum,* the drug cyclosporin was developed into a family of drugs with sales of $1.2 billion per year by the Swiss Company Sandoz, which later merged to become Novartis (Svarstad et al. 2000). The fungus was in a sample of soil that was collected in Norway without permission by a Sandoz biologist on vacation. As of yet, Norway has not received any payment for the use of this fungus in drug production.

Countries in both the developing and developed world now frequently demand a share in the commercial activities derived from the biological diversity contained within their borders, and rightly so. Local people in developing countries, who have a knowledge of the use of species, protect them, and show them to scientists, should also share in the profits from any use of them. Writing treaties and developing procedures to guarantee participation in this process will be a major diplomatic challenge in the coming years.

How can the option value of species be determined? One way involves examining the impact on the world economy of wild species only recently utilized by humans. Consider a hypothetical example: Imagine that during the last 20 years, newly discovered uses of 100 previously unused plant species accounted for $100 billion of new economic activity in terms of increased agriculture, new industrial products, and improved medicines. Since there are presently 250,000 unused plant species, then a rough calculation might demonstrate that each presently unused plant species has the potential to provide an average of $400,000 worth of benefits to the world economy in the next 20 years. These types of calculations are now at a very preliminary stage, and they assume, for the sake of convenience, that the average value of a species can be determined.

While most species may have little or no direct economic value and little option value, a small proportion may have enormous potential value to supply medical treatments, to support a new industry, or to prevent the collapse of a major agricultural crop. If just one of these species goes extinct before it is discovered, it could be a tremendous loss to the global economy, even if the majority of the world's species were preserved. As Aldo Leopold commented:

> If the biota, in the course of aeons, has built something we like but do not understand, then who but a fool would discard seemingly useless parts? To keep every cog and wheel is the first precaution of intelligent tinkering.

The diversity of the world's species can be compared to a manual on how to keep the Earth running effectively. The loss of a species is like tearing a page out of the manual. If we ever need the information from that page in the manual to save ourselves and the Earth's other species, the information will be irretrievably lost.

Existence Value

Many people throughout the world care about wildlife and plants and are concerned for their protection. This concern may be associated with a desire to someday visit the habitat of a unique species and see it in the wild; alternatively, concerned individuals may not expect, need, or even desire to see these species personally or experience the wilderness in which they live. In either case, these individuals recognize an **existence value** in wild nature—the amount that people are willing to pay to prevent species from going extinct, habitats from being destroyed, and genetic variation from being lost. Particular species, the so-called "charismatic megafauna" such as pandas, whales, lions, elephants, bison, manatees, and many birds, elicit strong responses in people (Figure 5.8). Special groups have been formed to appreciate and protect butterflies and other insects, wildflowers, and fungi. People place value on wildlife and wild lands in a direct way by joining and contributing billions of dollars each year to conservation organizations that protect species. In the United States, $2.3 billion was contributed in 1990 to environmental wildlife organizations, with The Nature Conservancy, the World Wildlife Fund, Ducks Unlimited, and the Sierra Club topping the list (WCMC 1992). Citizens also show their concern by directing their governments to spend money on conservation programs and to purchase land for habitat and landscape protection. For example, the government of the United States has spent more than $20 million to protect a single rare species, the California condor (*Gymnogyps californianus*). The citizens of the United States have indicated in surveys that they are willing to spend around $19 per person per year (more than $5 billion per year in total) to protect a na-

Figure 5.8 For many people, the existence value of charismatic species, such as whales, is clear. Here people greet a minke whale that is being rescued after it became entangled in a trawler's gill net; the float behind the whale was attached to the net to keep the whale at the surface so it could breathe. Later, rescuers were able to release the whale from the netting. Most people find interacting with other species to be an educational and uplifting experience. Such meetings (which usually take place at greater distances, as in a more traditional "whale watch" setting, or on "photo safaris" in Africa) can enrich human lives. (Photograph by Scott Kraus, New England Aquarium.)

tional symbol, the bald eagle (*Haliaeetus leucocephalus*), a bird whose populations have suffered significant declines in the past but are now rebounding (Figure 5.9) (Perrings 1995).

Existence value can be attached to biological communities, such as temperate old growth forests, tropical rain forests, coral reefs, and prairie remnants, and to areas of scenic beauty. Growing numbers of people and organizations contribute large sums of money annually to ensure the continuing existence of these habitats. In Costa Rica, 91% of respondents said they would be willing to pay higher prices for water and electricity, if the money was used to protect environmental quality and biological diversity (Holl et al. 1995). In a survey relating to the spectacular, scenic Grand Canyon, which has been marred by sulfur dioxide air pollution from a nearby power plant, U.S. citizens indicated that they would be willing to pay $1.30–$2.50 per household per year to have improved pollution control equipment installed at the power plant—an amount

Figure 5.9 The bald eagle is a symbol of the United States. Many people have indicated a willingness to pay to protect its continued existence. (Photograph © John N. A. Lott/ Biological Photo Service.)

that translates into well over $100 million per year (Nash 1991b). Another survey, taken over a period of several years, showed approximately 80% of U.S. citizens approving of the statement, "environmental improvements must be made, regardless of the cost" (Ruckelshaus 1989). Current surveys continue to show that the public regards environmental protection as a high priority.

The money spent to protect biological diversity, particularly in the developed countries of the world, is on the order of hundreds of millions—if not billions—of dollars per year. This sum represents the existence value of species and communities. At present, many people do not extend existence value to include the full range of the world's species (Kellert 1996). Although a few insect species, such as the monarch butterfly (*Danaus plexippus*), receive protection and attention, the need to protect other invertebrates, much less single-celled bacteria and protists, is not even part of the public discussion. Conservation biologists need to continue to educate the public on the subject of biological diversity to raise awareness of the need to protect *all* species, not just mammals and birds. Similarly, people need to learn the value of protecting all biological communities, including ones that are not as well-known or popular, and populations that are genetically unique or have special value due to their proximity to urban centers.

Is Economic Valuation Enough?

Although the more complete systems of accounting being developed by ecological economics value common property resources and include them in the cost of doing business (instead of leaving them out, as in traditional accounting methods)(Levin 1996; Daily 1997), many environmentalists feel that ecological economics does not go far enough. For some, the use of green accounting methods still means acceptance of the present world economic system. These environmental thinkers advocate much stronger changes in our economic system, which is responsible for pollution, environmental degradation, and species extinctions at unprecedented rates.

They argue that the most damning aspect of this system is the unnecessary overconsumption of resources by a minority of the world's citizens at the same time that the majority of the world's people faces poverty. Given a world economic system in which millions of children die each year from disease, malnutrition, warfare, crime, and other factors strongly correlated with poverty, and in which thousands of unique species go extinct each year due to habitat destruction, major structural changes—not just minor adjustments—are needed.

As we will discuss in the next chapter, proponents of this view favor an alternative approach: dramatically lower the consumption of resources in the developed world, reduce the need to exploit natural resources, and greatly increase the value placed on the natural environment and biological diversity. Some suggestions for bringing this about include stabilization or reduction of the number of people in the world, much higher taxes on fossil fuels, penalties for inefficient energy use and pollution, support for public transportation and fuel-efficient vehicles, and mandatory recycling programs. Lands on which endangered species are present would have to be managed for biodiversity; private landowners would receive a government subsidy for maintaining the habitat. One of the greatest inefficiencies in the agricultural economies of Western countries is the production of meat and dairy products, so a switch to (or at least toward) vegetarianism would be more healthy for people and would reduce the impact on the environment. Restrictions could be placed on trade, so that only those products derived from sustainable activities could be bought or sold on national and international markets. Debts of developing countries could be reduced or dismissed and investment redirected to activities that provide the most benefits to the greatest number of impoverished people. Finally, financial penalties for damaging biological diversity and incentives for protecting biological diversity could be established and made so compelling that industries would be forced to protect the natural world. While the political will to carry out these policies may not be present today, perhaps at some point in the future they can be implemented and biological diversity can be truly protected.

Summary

1. Indirect use values can be assigned to aspects of biological diversity that provide economic benefit to people but are not harvested or damaged during use. One major group of indirect use values is nonconsumptive use values of ecosystems. These include ecosystem productivity (important as the starting point for all food chains); protection of water resources and soils; regulation of local, regional, and global climates; waste treatment and nutrient retention; the enhancement of commercial crops by wild species; and recreation.

2. Biological diversity features prominently in the growing recreation and ecotourism industry. The number of people involved in nature recreation and the amount of money spent on such activities are surprisingly large. In many countries, particularly in the developing world, ecotourism represents one of the major sources of foreign income. Even in industrialized countries, the economy in areas around national parks is increasingly dominated by the recreation industry. Educational materials and the mass media draw heavily on themes of biological diversity and create materials of considerable value.

3. Biological diversity also has an option value in terms of its potential to provide future benefits to human society, such as new medicines, biological control agents, and new crops. The biotechnology industry is developing innovative techniques to take advantage of new chemicals and physiological properties found in the living world.

4. People are often willing to pay money in the form of taxes and voluntary contributions to ensure the continued existence of unique species, biological communities, and landscapes; this amount represents the existence value of biological diversity.

For Discussion

1. Consider the natural resources people use where you live. Can you place an economic value on those resources? If you can't think of any products harvested directly, consider basic ecosystem services such as flood control, fresh water, and soil retention.

2. Ask people how much money they spend on nature-related activities. Also ask them how much they would be willing to spend each year to protect well-known species, such as bald eagles, grizzly bears, and songbirds; to save a rare, endangered freshwater mussel; and to protect water quality and forest health. Multiply the average values by the number of people in your city, your country, or the world to obtain estimates as to how much these components of biological diversity are worth. Is this an accurate method for gauging the economic value of biodiversity? How might you improve this simple methodology?

3. Imagine that the only known population of a dragonfly species will be destroyed unless money can be raised to purchase the pond where it lives and the surrounding land. How much is this species worth? Consider different methods for assigning a monetary value to this species and compare the different outcomes. Which method is best?

Suggested Readings

Buchmann, S. L. and G. P. Nabhan 1998. *The Forgotten Pollinators*. Island Press, Washington, D. C. Wild pollinators are crucial to agricultural production as described in this wonderful book.

Carte, B. K. 1996. Biomedical potential of marine natural products. *BioScience* 46: 271–286. Describes search for valuable new chemicals in marine organisms, from bacteria to mollusks.

Chapin III, F. S., O. E. Sala, I. C. Burke, J. P. Grime, et al. 1998. Ecosystem consequences of changing biodiversity. *BioScience* 48: 45-52. Investigations throughout the world provide evidence that reduced species diversity lowers ecosystem productivity.

Chester, C. C. 1996. Controversy over Yellowstone's biological resources. *Environment* 38(6): 10–15, 34–36. The national parks of the United States are potential sources of species with great economic value, but who owns the rights to use these species and what are the applicable laws?

Costanza, R., R. d'Arge, R. de Gros, S. Farber, et al. 1997. The value of the world's ecosystem services and natural capital. *Nature* 387: 253–260. High-profile article by top ecological economists estimates the total ecosystem services worldwide as worth around $32 trillion a year.

Daily, G. C. and K. E. Ellison. 2002. *New Economy of Nature: The Quest to Make Conservation Profitable*. Island Press, Washington, D.C. Ways of adjusting payments to protect biodiversity.

Heal, G. 2000. *Nature and the Marketplace: Capturing the Value of Ecosystem Services.* Island Press, Washington, D.C. Considers the idea that the people will pay more to preserve the value of ecosystems, rather that destroy them for short-term gain.

Levin, S. A. 1996. Economic growth and environmental quality. *Ecological Applications* 6: 12. Special issue of the journal devoted to discussion of environmental quality.

Mateo, N., W. Nader, and G. Tamayo. 2001. Bioprospecting. In *Encyclopedia of Biodiversity*, S. A. Levin (ed.), Vol. 1, pp. 471–488. Academic Press, San Diego, CA. The best examples of bioprospecting are described, along with a summary of how the approach works.

Moore, D., M. M. Nauta, S. E. Evans, and M. Rotheroe (eds.). 2001. *Fungal Conservation: Issues and Solutions.* Cambridge University Press, Cambridge. This edited volume helps to highlight what we need to learn to protect fungi and what we know about their role in ecosystem function.

Mosquin, T., P. G. Whiting, and D. E. McAllister. 1995. *Canada's Biodiversity: The Value of Life, Its Status, Economic Benefits, Conservation Costs and Unmet Needs.* Canadian Museum of Nature, Ottawa. Biodiversity provides $70 billion to Canada's economy, as described in this fascinating book.

Pimentel, D. C., L. Westra, and R. F. Noss (eds.). 2000. *Ecological Integrity: Integrating Environment, Conservation, and Health.* Island Press, Washington, D.C. Investigates the linkages between conservation and social justice.

Plotkin, M. J. 1993. *Tales of a Shaman's Apprentice.* Viking/Penguin, New York. Vivid account of ethnobotanical exploration and efforts to preserve medical knowledge.

Repetto, R. 1992. Accounting for environmental assets. *Scientific American* 266 (June): 94–100. Environmental degradation decreases national wealth.

Svarstad, H., H. C. Bugge, and S. S. Dhillion. 2000. From Norway to Novartis: cyclosporin from *Tolypocladium inflatum* in an open access bioprospecting regime. *Biodiversity and Conservation* 9: 1521–1541. Without any collecting permit or permission, a biologist collected the soil sample that led to a new group of drugs worth over $1 billion in annual sales.

Tilman, D. 1999. The ecological consequences of change in biodiversity: A search for general principles. *Ecology* 80: 1455–1474. Mixture of field data, experiments, and models used to demonstrate relationships among biodiversity, stability, productivity, and susceptibility to invasion, with implications for management.

Chapter

Ethical Values

A s was discussed in Chapters 4 and 5, the new discipline of ecological economics provides positive arguments in support of conservation that can be put to use in the policy arena. Although such economic arguments can be advanced to justify the protection of biological diversity, there are also strong ethical arguments for doing so (Vandeveer and Pierce 1994; Schmidtz and Willott 2001). While economic arguments often are assumed to be more objective or more convincing, ethical arguments have unique power: They have foundations in the value systems of most religions and philosophies and are readily understood by the general public (McPhee 1971; Bassett 2000). They may appeal to a general respect for life, a reverence for nature or specific aspects of it, a sense of the beauty, fragility, uniqueness, or antiquity of the living world, or a belief in divine creation. Indeed, to many, ethical arguments—because they are grounded in ethical values—provide the most convincing reasons for conservation.

Ethical Values of Biological Diversity

Many traditional cultures have successfully coexisted with rich local flora and fauna for hundreds of years because their societal ethics encourage personal responsibility and thoughtful use of resources. People in these societies feel duty-bound to respect wild animals and plants even as they harvest them or "borrow" their habitat for human purposes. Traditional beliefs often treat rivers, mountains, and other ecosystems as sacred places to be approached with reverence and an appreciation for what they are, rather than for what human beings can make of them (Callicott 1994).

Even in Western industrial societies, ethical arguments can and do convince people to conserve biodiversity. For example, in the United States the right of all species to continue to exist is strongly protected under the Endangered Species Act, and a judge ruling in a major court decision stated "that Congress intended endangered species to be afforded the highest of priorities" (Rolston 1988). As stated in the Endangered Species Act, the justification for this protection is the "aesthetic, ecological, educational, historical, recreational and scientific value" of species. As will be described in this chapter, the full range of ethical arguments includes many of these aspects of value. Significantly, economic value is not included in this legal rationale, and economic interests are explicitly stated to be of secondary importance when protecting species from extinction. According to the law, profits and economic values must be set aside when their pursuit threatens to extinguish a species. (The law does allow economic values to prevail in rare cases, but only if a so-called "God squad" of senior government officials rules that economic concerns are of overriding national interest.)

Ethical arguments are also important because although economic arguments by themselves provide a basis for valuing species, they can also provide grounds for extinguishing them or for saving one species and not another (Bulte and van Kooten 2001). According to conventional economics, a species with low population numbers, a limited geographical range, small physical size or unattractive appearance, no immediate use to people, and no relationship to any species of economic importance will be given a low value. Such qualities may characterize a substantial proportion of the world's species, particularly insects and other invertebrates, fungi, nonflowering plants, bacteria, and protists. Halting profitable developments or making costly attempts to preserve these species may not have any obvious economic justification. In fact, in some circumstances, economic justification could exist for destroying an endangered species, particularly an organism that causes disease or attacks crop plants.

Despite the economic justification, though, many people would make a case against it on ethical grounds, arguing that the conscious destruction of a natural species is morally wrong, even if it is economically profitable. Ethical arguments for preserving biological diversity resonate with people because they appeal to our nobler instincts, which do play a role in societal decision-making. Human societies have often made decisions based more on ethical values than on economic ones. Outlawing slavery, limiting child labor, and preventing cruelty to animals are three such examples.

If modern society adopted values that strongly support preserving natural environment and maintaining biological diversity, we could expect to see lower consumption of scarce resources, greater care in the use of those resources, and perhaps limits to further population growth. Unfortunately, however, modern Western societies generally take a different view. While demanding that human beings treat one another ethically, their primary attitude toward nature is: "anything goes"—people can use or destroy it as they see fit, as long as they do not harm human beings or take their property. In recent years, this attitude has been questioned. **Environmental ethics,** a vigorous new discipline within philosophy, has grown out of this questioning. It articulates a sense of the ethical value of the natural world (Rolston 1988; Armstrong and Botzler 1998; Primack and Cafaro 2001).

Ethical Arguments for Preserving Biological Diversity

Ethical arguments can be made for preserving all species, regardless of their economic value, and these arguments can form the basis for political action and changes in laws and corporate management. The following arguments, based on the intrinsic value of species and on our duty to other people, are important to conservation biology because they provide the rationale for protecting rare species and species of no obvious economic value:

EACH SPECIES HAS A RIGHT TO EXIST   All species represent unique biological solutions to the problem of survival. All are the living representatives of grand historical lineages, and all have their own beauty and fitness. For these reasons, the survival of each species must be guaranteed, regardless of its importance to humans. This statement is true whether the species is large or small, simple or complex, ancient or recently evolved; whether it is economically important or of little immediate economic value to humans; or whether it is loved or hated by humans (Box 10). Each species has value for its own sake—an **intrinsic value** unrelated to human needs or desires (Lee 1996). This argument suggests not only that we have no right to destroy any species, but also that we have a moral responsibility to actively protect species from going extinct as the result of our activities. This recognizes humans are part of the larger biotic community and assumes our respect for all other species and their right to exist.

Robert Elliot (1992) suggests that wild nature has the following properties that show its intrinsic value: "diversity, stability, complexity, beauty, harmony, creativity, organization, intricacy, elegance, and richness." These qualities of natural organisms are ones that we can appreciate—

BOX 10   *Sharks: A Feared Animal in Decline*

Of the many plants and animals threatened by human exploitation, one of the least loved is the shark. Public perception of these animals is based almost entirely upon news reports of attacks upon humans (which are actually quite rare; in the year 2000, only 79 shark attacks were confirmed worldwide, which resulted in 10 deaths) and gruesome media images that portray sharks as merciless, indiscriminate killers (e. g., the movie *Jaws*). For most people, a shark is little more than a terrifying triangular fin and a mouthful of very sharp teeth. For conservationists concerned with rapidly dwindling shark populations worldwide, the shark's bad reputation is a public relations nightmare.

When we contrast the 10 people killed worldwide per year by sharks with the estimated 100 million sharks killed per year by people, it is clear that people, by far, are the more dangerous species (Lemonick 1997). Sharks actually help people far more than they harm them. For example, shark's liver oil was an important source of vitamin A until it was synthesized in 1947; it is also used in cosmetics and is highly effective at shrinking human hemorrhoids, and is widely used in medicines for that purpose. The chemical squalamine found in the internal organs of dogfish has the ability to inhibit the growth of certain brain tumors in humans, and shark cartilage is being used as an alternative treatment for kidney cancer. The immune system of sharks is being intensively studied to learn the secret of why sharks have an unusually low incidence of cancer even when experimentally exposed to known carcinogens, information that may prove invaluable to humans in our battle against cancer. Their grace and power in the water, along with the medical benefits they provide or may provide in the future to people, would seem to warrant that sharks should be more appreciated by the public.

One quality that redeems these animals in the public eye is not one that encourages conservation: Sharks are a popular item on menus in Chinese restaurants. Shark fishing has become a booming business in the past decade. In Asia, shark-fin soup is a delicacy that has created high demand for several species of shark; dried shark fins may bring up to $300/kg (Fowler 2000). At these prices, a single fin of the giant basking shark (also known as the whale shark) could bring up to $10,000. The cruel and

Shark fishing in Florida. These sharks were caught by vacationers on a pleasure cruise, displayed for photographs, and then discarded. (Photograph © Paige Chichester.)

BOX 10 *(continued)*

wasteful practice called "finning," in which a captured shark is flung back into the water to die after its fins are amputated, has spurred some public sympathy for sharks and has led to a call for banning the practice. A more serious problem, however, is the tendency for sharks to become "by-catches" of commercial fishing using drift gill nets. More than half of the annual shark kills are related to accidental gill net catches; sharks caught in this manner are usually simply discarded.

High shark mortality has conservationists concerned for several reasons. Sharks mature very slowly, have long reproductive cycles, and produce only a few young at a time. Fish such as salmon (which have also been overharvested) can recover rapidly because of the large numbers of offspring they produce annually; sharks do not have this ability. A second problem is that harvesting of sharks by commercial and private fishing concerns is largely unregulated in many countries. Sharks are increasingly harvested for their meat, often used in fish-and-chips. Sharks are also targeted by sport fishermen because of their size and fierce reputation. A few countries, notably the United States, Australia, New Zealand, and Canada, have enacted legislation to stem shark losses, including a ban on finning, but other countries involved in commercial shark fishing either see no need for action or are delaying proposed regulations. The recent bans on catching large coastal sharks in United States waters is a step in the right direction, but allowing continued harvesting of smaller individuals and open-ocean sharks may prevent vulnerable species from recovering to their original numbers.

Finally, the decimation of shark populations is occurring at a time when very little is known about more than a handful of individual species. Though more than 350 species of sharks exist, management proposals often treat all sharks as a single entity because, lacking specific information, management by species is impossible. Species that have been studied, including the lemon shark (*Negaprion brevirostris*), have demonstrated a precipitous decrease in numbers of young observed in the past five years.

The decline of shark populations is a matter for concern in and of itself, but it is also an important factor in a larger problem. Sharks are among the most important predators in marine ecosystems; they feed upon a variety of organisms and are distributed throughout oceans, seas, and lakes worldwide. Terrestrial ecologists have already observed the benefits of predation for prey populations and the problems that occur when predators are removed from an ecosystem. The decline of sharks could have a significant, and possibly catastrophic, cascade effect upon marine ecosystems, allowing unwanted species to rapidly increase in numbers. Ironically, sharks have fulfilled their role for some 400 million years, making them one of the longest-lived groups of organisms on the planet; yet their future depends upon a change in human attitudes and perceptions. Conservationists have their work cut out for them. They must persuade world governments to look beyond the shark's terrifying aspect and act to preserve this diverse group of species that is vital to the health of the world's oceans.

and that call forth responses of personal restraint and active protection. In addition, naturalness itself might be seen as a valuable property, particularly in societies where wild nature is becoming more rare.

Opponents to this view counter that even though some people do value these qualities in nature, they are not morally required to do so (Ferry 1995). They argue that humans have a value beyond all other species' value, because only we are fully conscious, rational, and moral beings, and unless our actions affect other people, directly or indirectly, any treatment of the natural world is morally acceptable. It might seem strange to assign rights of existence and legal protection to non-human species, especially simple organisms, when they lack the self-awareness that we usually associate with the morality of rights and duties. How can a lowly moss or fungus have rights when it doesn't even have a nervous system? However, whether or not we allow them rights, species carry great value as the repositories of the accumulated experience and history of millions of previous life forms through their continuous, evolutionary adaptation to a changing environment (Rolston 2001). The premature extinction of a species due to human activities destroys this history and the natural process and could be regarded as a "superkilling" (Rolston 1989) because it kills future generations of the species and eliminates the processes of evolution and speciation.

Other writers, especially many animal rights activists, have difficulty assigning rights to species, even if they value the rights of individual animals (Regan 1992). Singer (1979), for one, argues that "species as such are not conscious entities and so do not have interests above and beyond the interest of individual animals that are members of a species." However, Rolston (1994) counters that on both biological and ethical grounds, species, rather than individual organisms, are the appropriate targets of conservation efforts. All individuals eventually die; it is the species that continues, evolves, and sometimes forms new species. In a sense, individuals are temporary representatives of species, thus species are more important than individuals.

This focus on the species challenges the modern Western ethical tradition of individualism. But the preservation of biodiversity seems to demand that the needs of endangered species take precedence over the needs of individuals. For example, the U.S. National Park Service killed hundreds of rabbits on Santa Barbara Island to protect a few plants of the endangered species Santa Barbara live-forever (*Dudleya traskiae*); in this case, one endangered species was judged to be more valuable than hundreds of individual animals of a common species (Figure 6.1).

ALL SPECIES ARE INTERDEPENDENT   Species interact in complex ways in natural communities. The loss of one species may have far-reaching consequences for other members of the community (Chapin et al. 2000; Tilman 2000): other species may become extinct in response, or the entire community may become destabilized as the result of cascades of species extinctions. For these reasons, if we value some parts of nature, we should protect all of nature. Even if we only value human beings, our instincts toward self-preservation should impel us to preserve biodiversity. When the natural world prospers, we prosper. We are obligated to conserve the system as a whole because that is the appropriate

Figure 6.1 Government agencies judged the continued existence of the endangered plant Santa Barbara live-forever (*Dudleya traskiae;* the tall plant at left) to be more valuable than the common rabbits on its island home. The rabbits, which fed on the plant's fleshy leaves (shown at the bottom right), were killed to stop their destruction of this fragile plant species. (Photograph by the U.S. National Park Service.)

survival unit (Rolston 2000; Aron and Patz 2001). When the natural world is harmed, we see countless examples of how people suffer in the form of widespread human health problems, such as asthma, food poisoning, waterborne diseases, and cancer, that can be caused or aggravated by environmental pollution.

In a colorful metaphor, Ehrlich and Ehrlich (1981) imagine that species are rivets holding together the "Earthship," which carries all species, including humans, in its travel through time. Species extinctions are like rivets popping out of the ship. While lost species may be more or less important, when enough species go extinct, the Earthship will crash, and all species on board will be harmed. This presents a new twist on the original Bible story, in which Noah built an ark at God's instruction to preserve each species. In this metaphor, the species (as rivets) prevent the Earthship/ark from crashing—instead of humans saving biodiversity, biodiversity saves the people.

PEOPLE HAVE A RESPONSIBILITY TO ACT AS STEWARDS OF THE EARTH   Many religious adherents find it wrong to allow the destruction of species, because they are God's creations. If God created the world, then presumably the species God created have value. Within the Jewish and Christian traditions, human responsibility for protecting animal species is explicitly described in the Bible as part of the covenant with God. The Book of Genesis describes the creation of the Earth's biological diversity as a divine act, after which "God saw that it was good" and "blessed them." In the story of Noah's Ark, God commanded Noah to save two of all species, not just the ones human beings found useful. God provided detailed instructions for building the ark, an early species rescue project, saying "Keep them alive with you." The prophet Muhammad, founder of Islam, continued this theme of human responsibility: "The world is green and beautiful and God has appointed you as His stewards over it. He sees how you acquit yourselves." Belief in the value of God's creation supports a stewardship argument for preserving biodiversity: Human beings have been given responsibility for God's creation and must preserve, not destroy, what they have been given.

Other religious traditions also support the preservation of nature (Callicott 1994; Bassett 2000; Science and Spirit 2001). For example, Hinduism locates divinity in certain animals, and recognizes a basic kinship between humans and other beings (including the transmigration of souls from one species to another). A primary ethical concept in Hinduism and other Indian religions, such as Jainism and Buddhism, is *ahimsa*—nonviolence or kindness to all life. To live by this ideal, many religious people become vegetarians and live as simply as possible. Of course, some religions articulate views that put human beings at the center of creation, supporting a domineering attitude toward nature. Since many people base their ethical values on a religious faith, the development of religious arguments in support of conservation might be effective in motivating people to conserve biodiversity (Nash 1991a; Oelschlaeger 1994). Five major religions, in fact, have stated that their faiths mandate the conservation of nature (Box 11).

PEOPLE HAVE A DUTY TO THEIR NEIGHBORS   Humans must be careful to minimize damage to their natural environment because such damage not only harms other species, it harms people as well. Much of the pollution and environmental degradation occurring today is unnecessary and could be minimized with better planning. Our duty to other humans requires us to live within sustainable limits (Norton 1991; Luper-Foy 1992). This goal can be achieved by people in the industrialized coun-

BOX 11 *Religion and Conservation*

n September 1986, an interfaith ceremony was held in the Basilica of St. Francis, in Assisi, Italy. It included "Declarations on Nature" by representatives of the five participating religions–Buddhism, Christianity, Hinduism, Islam, and Judaism. For the first time in history, leaders of these faiths declared that their religions mandate the conservation of nature. Excerpts from the five declarations follow.*

The Buddhist Declaration on Nature
Venerable Lungrig Namgyal Rinpoche, Abbot, Gyuto Tantric University

The simple underlying reason why beings other than humans need to be taken into account is that, like human beings, they too are sensitive to happiness and suffering . . . Many have held up usefulness to human beings as the sole criterion for the evaluation of an animal's life. Upon closer examination, one discovers that this mode of evaluation of another's life and right to existence has also been largely responsible for human indifference as well as cruelty to animals.

We regard our survival as an undeniable right. As co-inhabitants of this planet, other species too have this right for survival. And since human beings as well as other nonhuman sentient beings depend upon the environment as the ultimate source of life and wellbeing, let us share the conviction that the conservation of the environment, the restoration of the imbalance caused by our negligence in the past, be implemented with courage and determination.

The Christian Declaration on Nature
Father Lanfranco Serrini, Minister General, Order of Friars Minor (Franciscans)

To praise the Lord for his creation is to confess that God the Father made all things visible and invisible; it is to thank him for the many gifts he bestows on all his children. . . . By reason of its created origin, each creature according to its species and all together in the harmonious unity of the universe manifest God's infinite truth and beauty, love and goodness, wisdom and majesty, glory and power.

Man's dominion cannot be understood as license to abuse, spoil, squander or destroy what God has made to manifest his glory. That dominion cannot be anything other than a stewardship in symbiosis with all creatures . . . Every human act of irresponsibility towards creatures is an abomination. According to its gravity, it is an offence against that divine wisdom which sustains and gives purpose to the interdependent harmony of the universe.

The Hindu Declaration on Nature
Dr. Karan Singh, President, Hindu Virat Samaj

The Hindu viewpoint on nature is permeated by a reverence for life, and an awareness that the great forces of nature—the earth, the sky, the air, the water and fire—as well as various orders of life including plants and trees, forests and animals, are all bound to each other with the great rhythms of nature. The divine is not exterior to creation, but expresses itself through natural phenomena. The *Mahabharata* says that 'even if there is only one tree full of flowers and fruits in a village, that place becomes worthy of worship and respect.'

Let us declare our determination to halt the present slide towards destruction, to rediscover the ancient tradition of reverence for all life and, even at this late hour, to reverse the suicidal course upon which we have embarked. Let us recall the ancient Hindu dictum: 'The Earth is our mother, and we are all her children.'

*Text excerpts from World Wildlife Fund, 1999; used with permission. Art from Bassett, 2000; used with permission.

(continued on next page)

BOX 11 *(continued)*

The Muslim Declaration on Nature
Dr. Abdullah Omar Nasseef, Secretary General, Muslim World League

The essence of Islamic teaching is that the entire universe is God's creation. Allah makes the waters flow upon the earth, upholds the heavens, makes the rain fall and keeps the boundaries between day and night . . . It is God who created the plants and the animals in their pairs and gave them the means to multiply.

For the Muslim mankind's role on earth is that of a *khalifa*, viceregent or trustee of God. We are God's stewards and agents on Earth. We are not masters of this Earth; it does not belong to us to do what we wish. It belongs to God and He has entrusted us with its safekeeping . . . The *khalifa* is answerable for his/her actions, for the way in which he/she uses or abuses the trust of God.

The Jewish Declaration on Nature
Rabbi Arthur Hertzberg, Vice President, World Jewish Congress

The encounter of God and man in nature is conceived in Judaism as a seamless web with man as the leader and custodian of the natural world . . . Now, when the whole world is in peril, when the environment is in danger of being poisoned and various species, both plant and animal, are becoming extinct, it is our Jewish responsibility to put the defence of the whole of nature at the very centre of our concern.

We have a responsibility to life, to defend it everywhere, not only against our own sins but also against those of others. We are all passengers together in this same fragile and glorious world. Let us safeguard our rowboat—and let us row together.

tries taking strong actions to reduce their excessive and disproportionate consumption of natural resources. Why does an average person living in the United States or Canada need to use 9 times more energy per year than a person living in China, 17 times more than a person living in India and 76 times more than a person living in the Congo? Technology and social policy should be directed toward using natural resources in the most efficient manner possible to minimize human demands on the environment. For example, if paper products are used more efficiently and recycled, and logging is practiced more carefully, there will be far less soil erosion, flooding, and unnecessary destruction of forests.

PEOPLE HAVE A RESPONSIBILITY TO FUTURE GENERATIONS   If in our daily living we degrade the natural resources of the Earth and cause species to become extinct, future generations will pay the price in terms of a lower standard of living and quality of life. Rolston (1995) predicts, "[I]t is safe to say that in the decades ahead, the quality of life will decline in proportion to the loss of biotic diversity, though it is often thought that one must sacrifice biotic diversity to improve human life." To remind us to act more responsibly, we might imagine that we are borrowing the Earth from future generations who expect to get it back in good condition. As species are lost and wild lands developed, children are deprived of one of the most exciting experiences in growing up—the wonder of seeing "new" animals and plants in the wild.

RESPECT FOR HUMAN LIFE AND HUMAN DIVERSITY IS COMPATIBLE WITH A RESPECT FOR BIOLOGICAL DIVERSITY   Some people worry that recognizing an intrinsic value in nature requires taking resources and opportunities away from human beings. But a respect for biological diversity can be linked to greater opportunities for people (Kellert and Wilson 1993; Kelly 1994). Some of the most exciting developments in conservation biology involve supporting the economic development of disadvantaged rural people in ways that are linked to the protection of biological diversity. Helping poor people establish sustainable plots of cash crops and achieve a degree of economic independence sometimes reduces the need to overharvest wild species. Working with indigenous people to establish legal title to their land gives them the means to protect the biological communities in which they live. In developed countries, the environmental justice movement seeks to empower poor and politically weak people, who are often members of minority groups, to protect their own environment; in the process their well-being and the protection of biological diversity are enhanced (Westra and Wenz 1995).

Human maturity often leads to self-restraint and a respect for others. Environmentalists have argued that the further maturation of the human species will involve an "identification with all life forms" and "the acknowledgment of the intrinsic value of these forms" (Naess 1986). They envision an expanding circle of moral obligations, moving outward from oneself to include duties to relatives, the social group, all humanity, animals, all species, the ecosystem, and ultimately the whole Earth (Figure 6.2). Actions taken to protect species and biological communities should, whenever possible, benefit people as well. Conservation biologists need to be sensitive to the public perception that they care *more* about birds, turtles, or nature in general than they do about people. In some situations, protecting biological diversity may be incompatible with promoting human needs or human cultures. For example, if a tribe needed to hunt an endangered animal to maintain its way of life or simply to stay alive, an ethical dilemma would result (Davradou and Namkoong 2001). In such a situation, hopefully public discussions and government policy would be able to develop a compromise.

Some people argue that recognizing an intrinsic value in nature leads to absurdity. Because we must use nature, they say, we cannot recognize its intrinsic value that, by definition, would limit the ways in which we use it. Even people who are sympathetic to environmentalism and appreciate wild nature often resist granting it intrinsic value since this demands so much—If nature is wonderful and complex, as science and our own experiences tell us it is, how can we go on using it? But we must do

Figure 6.2 Environmental ethics holds that an individual has an expanding set of moral obligations, extending outward beyond the self to progressively more inclusive levels. (From Noss 1992.)

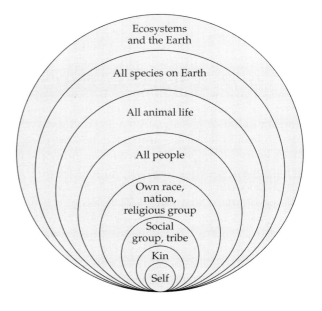

so to survive. In addition, the world is already filled with rules limiting our actions; adding another layer is tiresome. Finally, since so many modern lifestyles (especially in the developed world) depend to such a large extent on an ecologically destructive economic system, many despair of protecting the world and give up trying to live in an environmentally responsible manner.

These are legitimate concerns. Still, effective action to protect biological diversity is both possible and desirable. First, it is possible to use natural resources in a respectful and limited way: *It is necessary to use nature, but not all use of nature is necessary.* Second, while no one likes more rules, growing up and living moral lives involves recognizing our duty to others. Finally, it is possible to live in an environmentally responsible manner even in industrialized countries: It requires making a personal commitment to using less resources, having less of an impact on the environment, and helping to change society in a positive manner. If nature does in fact have intrinsic value, we should respect that value—whether doing so is convenient or not.

Enlightened Self-Interest: Biodiversity and Human Development

Economic arguments stress that preserving biological diversity *is in our material self-interest.* Ethical arguments based on the intrinsic value of wild nature and our duties to others stress that we should act altruisti-

cally toward nature *regardless of our material self-interest*. A second ethical framework appeals to our *enlightened self-interest*, arguing that preserving biodiversity and developing our knowledge of it will make us
better and happier people (Kellert 1996; Norton 2000; Van Wensveen
2000). The following points describe how protecting biological diversity is in our enlightened self-interest.

PROTECTING OUR LIFE-SUPPORT AND ECONOMY   It cannot be repeated
too often that biological diversity preserves our basic life-support systems of food production, water supply, oxygen replenishment, waste
disposal, soil conservation, and more. People will be healthier and happier in a clean, intact environment. We depend on this and should value
it. In addition to providing life-support, biodiversity allows us to create tremendous economic wealth, directly and indirectly, as detailed in
Chapters 4 and 5.

AESTHETIC AND RECREATIONAL ENJOYMENT   Nearly everyone enjoys
wildlife and landscapes aesthetically, and joy increases the quality of our
lives. The beauty of a field of wildflowers in Glacier National Park or a
migrating warbler on a spring morning in a city park enriches people's
lives. And for many people, experiencing nature means experiencing it
in an undisturbed setting: Simply reading about species or seeing them
in museums, gardens, and zoos does not suffice. Recreational activities
such as hiking, canoeing, and mountain climbing are physically, intel-
lectually, and emotionally satisfying. People spend tens of billions of dollars annually in these pursuits, proof enough of their value.

ARTISTIC AND LITERARY EXPRESSION   Throughout history, poets, writers, painters, and musicians of all cultures have drawn inspiration
from wild nature (Leopold 1949; Burks 1994; Howarth 2001). Nature
provides countless forms and symbols for painters and sculptors to
render and interpret (Figure 6.3). Poets have often found their greatest
inspiration in either wild nature or pastoral countrysides. Preserving
biological diversity preserves possibilities for all artists. It also allows
those of us who appreciate such creativity access to the sources and
experiences that inspire great artists. A loss in biological diversity
could very well limit the creative energies of people in the future and
thus restrict the development of human culture. For instance, if many
species of whales, butterflies, and orchids go extinct in the next few
decades, whole sets of imagery will be lost to the direct experience of
future generations of artists.

SCIENTIFIC KNOWLEDGE   Science and our growing knowledge of nature
are among humanity's greatest achievements. This knowledge is facilitated by the preservation of wild nature. Wild areas allow the study of

Figure 6.3 Rare wildflowers and butterflies are the inspiration for botanical sculptor Patrick O'Hara. In his studio in western Ireland, O'Hara molds, sculpts, and paints delicate porcelain scenes from nature that inspire an appreciation of conservation in a worldwide audience. (Photograph courtesy of Patrick O'Hara.)

natural ecological interactions. Wild species preserve the record of evolution. Young people are inspired to become scientists by personal contacts with wild nature, and those who do not become professional scientists can apply their basic knowledge of science to understanding their own local fields, forests, and streams (Orr 1994).

Three of the central mysteries in the world of science are how life originated, how the diversity of life found on Earth today came about, and how humans evolved. Thousands of biologists are working on these problems and are coming ever closer to the answers. New techniques of molecular biology allow greater insight into the relationships of living species as well as some extinct species, which are known to us only from fossils. However, when species become extinct, important clues are lost, and the mystery becomes harder to solve. For example, if *Homo sapiens'* closest living relatives—chimpanzees, bonobos, gorillas, and orangutans—disappear from the wild, we will lose important clues regarding human physical and social evolution (Whiten and Boesch 2001).

HISTORICAL UNDERSTANDING   Knowing nature, both scientifically and through personal experience, is a key to an understanding of human history (Thomashow 1996): In walking the landscapes our ancestors walked, we gain insight into how they experienced the world at a slower pace and without mechanized aids. We often forget just how recently humankind has moved to ultrafast transportation, fully illuminated cities that shut out the night, and other aspects of modern life. We need to preserve natural areas in order to develop our historical imaginations.

RELIGIOUS INSPIRATION   Many religions have traditions of "wandering in the wilderness" in order to commune with God or with spirits. Moses, Isaiah, Jesus, and St. Francis of Assisi, from the Western tradition, all sought out the solitude of wilderness. So have generations of Sioux, Ute, and Cheyenne vision seekers. Being in nature allows us to clear and focus our minds and, sometimes, experience the transcendent. When we are surrounded by the artifacts of civilization, our minds stay fully focused on human purposes and our everyday lives. Religion probably would not disappear from an environment totally tamed by humans, but it might become diluted for many.

Deep Ecology

Recognition of both the economic value and the intrinsic value of biological diversity leads to new limits on human action. This can make it seem like conservation is simply a never-ending list of "thou shalt nots," but many environmentalists believe that an understanding of our true self-interest would lead to a different conclusion:

> The crisis of life conditions on Earth could help us choose a new path with new criteria for progress, efficiency, and rational action.... The ideological change is mainly that of appreciating life quality rather than adhering to a high standard of living (Naess 1989).

In the past 200 years, the Industrial Revolution, with its accompanying technological advances and social changes, has generated tremendous material wealth and improved the lives of millions of people. But the law of diminishing returns seems to apply: For many in the developed world, heaping up further wealth at the expense of life quality makes little sense (Thoreau 1971; Shi 1985). Similarly, the continued loss of biodiversity and taming of the natural landscape will not improve people's lives. What is being lost is unique and increasingly more precious as monetary wealth increases and opportunities to experience nature diminish. Human happiness and human development require preserving our remaining biodiversity, not sacrificing it for increased individual or corporate wealth.

During the twentieth century, ecologists, nature writers, religious leaders, and philosophers have increasingly articulated an appreciation of nature and spoken of the need for changes in human lifestyles in order to protect it (Gore 1992; List 1993). Paul Sears, recognizing that a true belief in the value of nature would lead to questioning the destructive practices that are common in modern society and often taken for granted, called ecology a "subversive science." In the 1960s and 1970s, Paul Ehrlich and Barry Commoner demonstrated that professional biologists and academics could use their knowledge of environmental issues to create and lead political movements to protect species and ecosystems. Commoner even ran for President in 1980. Today religious leaders are revitalizing their followers with calls to combine social activism with environmental protection. Political movements such as these and the Green political parties in Europe and activist conservation organizations such as Greenpeace and EarthFirst! now appear throughout the world.

One well-developed environmental philosophy that supports this activism is known as **deep ecology** (Naess 1989; Sessions 1995). Deep ecology builds on the basic premise of biocentric equality, which expresses "the intuition... that all things in the biosphere have an equal right to live and blossom and to reach their own individual forms of unfolding" (Devall and Sessions 1985). Humans have a right to live and thrive, as do the other organisms with whom we share the planet. Deep ecologists oppose what they see as the dominant worldview, which places human concerns above all and views human happiness in materialistic terms (Table 6.1) (McLaughlin 1993).

Deep ecologists see acceptance of the intrinsic value of nature less as a limitation than as an opportunity to live better lives. Because present human activities are destroying the Earth's biological diversity, existing political, economic, technological, and ideological structures must change. These changes entail enhancing the life quality of all people—emphasizing improvements in environmental quality, aesthetics, culture, and spirituality rather than higher levels of material consumption. Improving adult literacy, organizing active nature hiking, bird-watching, and

TABLE 6.1 A comparison of beliefs of the dominant world view and those of deep ecology

Dominant worldview	Deep ecology
Humans dominant over nature	Humans live in harmony with nature
Natural environment and species are resources for humans	All nature has intrinsic worth, regardless of human needs
A growing human population with a rising standard of living	A stable human population living simply
Earth's resources are unlimited	Earth's resources are limited and must be used carefully
Ever-higher technology brings progress and solutions	Appropriate technology must be used with respect for the Earth
Emphasizes material progress	Emphasizes spiritual and ethical progress
Strong central government	Local control, organized according to ecosystems or bioregions

natural history clubs, encouraging people to have healthier lifestyles, and lobbying to reduce air pollution and sprawling development are some practical examples. The philosophy of deep ecology includes an obligation to work to implement needed programs through political activism and a commitment to personal lifestyle changes, in the process transforming the institutions in which we work, study, pray, and shop. Professional biologists, philosophers, and all concerned people (such as you?) are urged to escape from their narrow, everyday concerns and act and live "as if nature mattered" (Naess 1989).

Summary

1. Protecting biological diversity can be justified on ethical grounds as well as on economic grounds. The value systems of most religions, philosophies, and cultures provide justifications for preserving species. These justifications even support protecting those species with no obvious economic or aesthetic value to people.

2. The most central ethical arguments assert that humans have a duty to protect species based on their intrinsic value, unrelated to human needs. People do not have the right to destroy species and should take action to prevent their extinction.

3. Species, rather than individual organisms, are the appropriate target for conservation efforts; it is the species that evolves and undergoes speciation, whereas individuals are temporary representatives of the species.

4. Species interact in complex ways in biological communities. The loss of one species may have far-reaching negative consequences to that biological community and to human society.

5. People must learn to live within the ecological constraints of the planet. People must learn to minimize environmental damage and take responsibility for their actions, since they may harm humans as well as other species. People also have a responsibility to future generations to keep the Earth in good condition.

6. Protecting nature is in our enlightened self-interest. Biological diversity has provided generations of writers, artists, musicians, and religious thinkers with inspiration. A loss of species in the wild cuts people off from this wellspring of creative experience and impoverishes human culture. It also curtails recreational enjoyment, scientific knowledge, and self-understanding.

7. Deep ecology is a philosophy that advocates major changes in the way society functions in order to protect biological diversity and promote genuine human growth. Advocates of this philosophy are committed to personal lifestyle changes and political activism in the environmental movement.

For Discussion

1. Do living creatures, biological species, natural communities, and physical entities, such as rivers, lakes, and mountains, have rights? Can we treat them any way we please? Where should we draw the line of moral responsibility?

2. Do human beings have a duty toward individual animals, which lack self-awareness and toward plants, which lack a nervous system? Toward species of plants and animals? Natural communities? Mountains and streams? If so, what is the source of this duty? What is the sort of protection or respectful use appropriate for each of these groups?

3. What role does the consumption of resources, physical pleasure, the search for knowledge, artistic expression, recreation, and amusement play in your life? In a good human life in general? Does the preservation of biodiversity set limits on these human activities, or is it a prerequisite for our continued enjoyment of them?

4. What is your own environmental ethic? What is the source of your ethic? Reason? Emotion? Faith? Does it affect your life in any important way? Is it easy or hard to live up to?

5. If your house were on fire, you would try to rescue every family member inside. If even one person died, you would be devastated. Should we try to save every species threatened with extinction? Is the comparison valid?

Suggested Readings

Burks, D. C. (ed.). 1994. *Place of the Wild: A Wildlands Anthology.* Island Press/Shearwater Books, Washington, D.C. Leading advocates for wilderness protection reflect on the meaning and value of wilderness.

Callicott, J. B. 1994. *Earth's Insights: A Multicultural Survey of Ecological Ethics from the Mediterranean Basin to the Australian Outback.* University of California Press, Berkeley, CA. Comparison of the environmental ethics of religions throughout the world, including conceptions of nature and the value given to nonhuman beings.

Kellert, S. R. 1996. *The Value of Life: Biological Diversity and Human Society.* Island Press/Shearwater Books, Washington, D.C. Insightful examination of people's attitudes toward biological diversity, as affected by class, ethnicity, sex, and nationality; also, eloquent statement of the importance of biodiversity to human happiness.

List, P. C. (ed.). 2000. *Environmental Ethics and Forestry: A Reader.* Temple University Press, Philadelphia. Great selection of classic and contemporary articles on applying environmental ethics to forestry issues.

McPhee, J. 1971. *Encounters with the Archdruid.* Farrar, Straus, and Giroux, New York. Unique book describing an exchange of ideas between the leader of the Sierra Club and real-estate developers and mining engineers during wilderness backpacking trips.

Naess, A. 1989. *Ecology, Community, and Lifestyle: Outline of an Ecosophy.* Cambridge University Press, Cambridge. Good explanation of, and argument for, deep ecology by a leading proponent.

Norton, B. G. 2000. Biodiversity and environmental values: in search of a universal earth ethic. *Biodiversity and Conservation* 9: 1029–1044. Nature can be valued for its importance to people or its intrinsic value, and also for the creativity of its processes.

Rolston III, H. 1994. *Conserving Natural Value.* Columbia University Press, New York. A leading environmental philosopher lays out the ethical arguments for preserving biological diversity.

Schmidtz, D. and E. Willott (eds.). 2001. *Environmental Ethics: What Really Matters, What Really Works.* Oxford University Press, New York. Sixty-two selections, from classic articles to cutting-edge original research, that explore the principal issues in environmental ethics.

Shi, D. E. 1985. *The Simple Life: Plain Living and High Thinking.* Oxford University Press, New York. Traces the many ways Americans have pursued the ideal of simple yet rich living, from the Puritans and Quakers to Thoreau and modern back-to-the land philosophies.

Thomashow, M. 1996. *Ecological Identity: Becoming a Reflective Environmentalist.* MIT Press, Cambridge, MA. Through discussion and participatory learning, the author provides concerned teachers and students the tools needed to become reflective environmentalists.

Vandeveer, D. and C. Pierce. 1994. *The Environmental Ethics and Policy Book: Philosophy, Ecology, Economics.* Wadsworth Publishing Company, Belmont, CA. Excellent collection of essays by well-known authors.

Van Wensveen, L. 2000. *Dirty Virtues: The Emergence of Ecological Virtue Ethics.* Prometheus, New York. Provocative book that makes a strong connection between a healthy environment and human flourishing.

Whiten, A. and C. Boesch. 2001. The cultures of chimpanzees. *Scientific American* 284 (January): 61–67. Unique behavioral attributes of individual chimpanzee populations help us to understand human social evolution, but these attributes are diminished every time a local population is extirpated.

PART III

Threats to Biological Diversity

Extinction

W e live at a historic moment, a time in which the world's biological diversity is being rapidly destroyed. The present geological period has more species than any other, yet the current rate of extinction of species is greater now than at any time in the past. Ecosystems and communities are being degraded and destroyed, and species are being driven to extinction. The species that persist are losing genetic variation as the number of individuals in populations shrinks, unique populations and subspecies are destroyed, and remaining populations become increasingly isolated from one another.

The cause of this loss of biological diversity at all levels is the range of human activity that alters and destroys natural habitats to suit human needs. At present, approximately 40% of the net primary productivity of the terrestrial environment—roughly 25% of the total primary productivity of the world—is used or wasted in some way by people (Vitousek 1994). Genetic variation is being lost even in domesticated species, such as wheat, corn, rice, chickens, cattle, and pigs, as farmers abandon traditional agriculture. In the United States, about 97% of the vegetable varieties that were once cultivated are now extinct (Cherfas 1993). In tropical countries, farmers are abandoning their local varieties in favor of high-yielding varieties for commercial sale. This loss of variability among food plants and animals, and its implications for world agriculture, are discussed further in Chapters 14 and 20.

E. O. Wilson, one of the leading advocates of conservation biology, has argued that the most serious aspect of environmental damage is the extinction of species. Biological communities can be degraded, reduced in area, and their value to people lessened, but as long as all of the original species survive, communities retain the potential to recover. Similarly, genetic variation within a species is reduced when population size drops, but species can regain genetic variation through mutation, natural selection, and recombination. Unfortunately, once a species is eliminated, the unique genetic information contained in its DNA and the special combination of characters that it possesses are forever lost—its populations cannot be restored, the communities that it inhabited become impoverished, and its potential value to humans will never be realized.

The word "extinct" has many nuances and can vary somewhat depending on the context. A species is **extinct** when no member of the species remains alive anywhere in the world: "Bachman's warbler is extinct" (Figure 7.1). If individuals of a species remain alive only in captivity or in other human-controlled situations, the species is said to be **extinct in the wild.** "The Franklin tree is extinct in the wild but grows well under cultivation." In both of these situations the species are also considered to be **globally extinct.** A species is **locally extinct** or **extirpated** when it is no longer found in an area it once inhabited but is still found elsewhere in the wild: "The gray wolf once occurred throughout North America; it is now locally extinct in Massachusetts." Some conservation biologists speak of a species being **ecologically extinct** if it persists at such reduced numbers that its effects on the other species in its community are negligible: "Tigers are ecologically extinct because so few remain in the wild that their impact on prey populations is insignificant." In order to successfully maintain species, conservation biologists must identify the human activities that affect the stability of populations and drive species to extinction.

Past Mass Extinctions

The diversity of species found on the Earth has been increasing since life first originated. This increase has not been steady; rather, it has been characterized by periods of high rates of speciation followed by periods of minimal change and episodes of mass extinction (Wilson 1987; Raup 1992). This pattern is visible in the fossil record, which has been examined by scientists interested in determining the number of species and families in particular geological periods.

Figure 7.1 Bachman's warbler *(Vermivora bachmanii),* last seen in the 1960s, is an example of a Neotropical songbird that became extinct as a result of tropical deforestation in its wintering grounds. The Cuban forests in which this species overwintered were almost entirely cleared for sugarcane fields. The warbler is shown in this Audubon print with the flowering Franklin tree *(Franklinia altamaha).* The tree is now extinct in the wild, although it can still be found in arboretums and other cultivated gardens. (By John James Audubon; photograph from the Ewel Stewart Library, The Academy of Natural Sciences of Philadelphia.)

The evolutionary history of marine animals is better studied than terrestrial organisms because they often have hard body parts that are preserved in rocks formed from marine sediments. Marine animals first arose about 600 million years ago during the Paleozoic era. According to the fossil record, new families of marine animals appeared in rapid and steady succession during the next 150 million years. For the 200 million years that followed, the number of families was more or less constant at around 400. For the last 250 million years of the Mesozoic and Cenozoic eras, the diversity of families has steadily increased to its present number of over 700 families (Figure 7.2). The fossil record of marine animals demonstrates the slow pace of evolution, with new families appearing at a rate of roughly one per million years.

There have been five episodes of mass extinction in the fossil record, occurring at intervals ranging from 60–155 million years in length

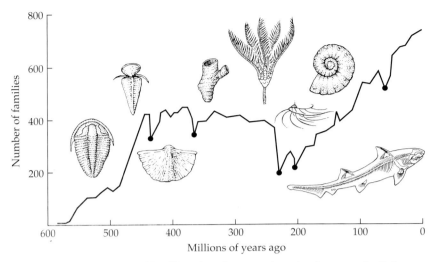

Figure 7.2 The number of families of marine organisms has been gradually increasing over geological time; this graph of their history clearly shows evidence of five episodes of mass extinction. (After Wilson 1989.)

(Figure 7.3). These episodes, which occurred during the Ordovician, Devonian, Permian, Triassic, and Cretaceous periods, could be called "natural" mass extinctions. The most famous is the extinction of the dinosaurs during the late Cretaceous, 65 million years ago, after which mammals achieved dominance in terrestrial communities. The most massive extinction took place at the end of the Permian, 250 million years ago, when 77–96% of all marine animal species are estimated to have gone extinct, as well as half of all extant families of animals. David Raup (1979) observed: "If these estimates are even reasonably accurate, global biology (for higher organisms at least) had an extremely close call." It is quite likely that some massive perturbation, such as widespread volcanic eruptions, a collision with an asteroid, or both, caused the dramatic change in the Earth's climate that resulted in the end of so many species. It took evolution about 50 million years to regain the number of families lost during the Permian extinction.

The Current, Human-Caused Mass Extinction

The global diversity of species reached an all-time high in the present geological period. The most advanced groups of organisms—insects, vertebrates, and flowering plants—reached their greatest diversity about 30,000 years ago. Since that time, however, species richness has decreased as one species has asserted its dominance. Humans have increasingly altered terrestrial and aquatic environments at the expense of other species in their need to consume natural resources. We are presently in the midst

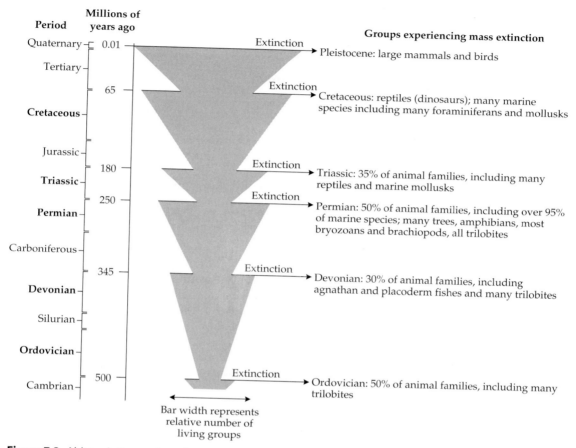

Figure 7.3 Although the total number of families and species of organisms has increased over the eons, during each of five episodes of natural mass extinction a large percentage of these groups disappeared. The most dramatic period of loss occurred about 250 million years ago, at the end of the Permian period. A sixth episode, beginning around 30,000 years ago up to the present time, incorporates the effects of hunting and habitat loss as human populations spread across the continents.

of a *sixth extinction episode*, this one caused by human activities rather than a natural disaster (Wilson 1989; Leakey and Lewin 1996; Lövei 2001).

The first noticeable effects of human activity on extinction rates can be seen in the elimination of large mammals from Australia and North and South America at the time humans first colonized these continents tens of thousands of years ago. Shortly after humans arrived, 74–86% of the megafauna—mammals weighing more than 44 kg (100 lbs)—became extinct. These extinctions probably were caused directly by hunting (Miller et al. 1999b; Martin 2001) and indirectly by burning and clearing forests and grasslands. On all continents, paleontologists and archaeologists have found an extensive record of prehistoric human alteration and destruction of habitat coinciding with high rates of species extinctions. For example, deliberate burning of savannahs, presumably to encourage plant growth for browsing wildlife and so to improve hunting, has been occurring for 50,000 years in Africa. A similar practice was observed in historic times among North American Plains Indians, who depended upon horses and buffalo for transportation and food. For thousands of years, the total area of natural grassland and forest in North America, Central America, Europe, and Asia has been steadily reduced to create pastures and farmlands to supply human needs.

Extinction rates are best known for birds and mammals because these species are conspicuous, that is, relatively large and well studied. Scientists have noted when these species are no longer found in the wild (Table 7.1). Extinction rates for the other 99.9% of the world's species are just rough guesses at present. However, extinction rates are uncertain even for birds and mammals because some species that were considered extinct have been rediscovered. For example, the Australian night parrot was last seen in 1912, and was presumed extinct before being rediscovered in 1979. It is also true that species presumed to be **extant** (still living) may actually be extinct. Some researchers have argued that the number of extinct species is probably higher than is generally known, because there are many remote areas scientists have not revisited to determine the status of rare species there (Whitten et al. 1987). In addition, in the last four centuries many species may have existed and gone extinct before we even discovered them.

How has human activity affected extinction rates in more recent times? One set of estimates based on the best available evidence is shown in Table 7.2. These estimates indicate, for example, that about 85 species of mammals and 113 species of birds have become extinct since the year 1600, representing 2.1% of known mammal species and 1.3% of known birds* (Reid and Miller 1989; Smith et al. 1993; Heywood 1995; Hilton-Taylor 2000). While these numbers may not seem alarming initially, the trend of these extinction rates is on the rise, with the majority of extinctions occurring in the last 150 years (Figure 7.4). The extinction rate for birds and mammals was about one species every decade during the period from 1600 to 1700, but it rose to one species every year during the period from 1850 to 1950. This increase in the rate of extinction indicates the seriousness of the threat to biological diversity.

Some evidence suggests a decline in the extinction rates for birds and mammals during the past few decades. This is mainly due to recent intensive efforts to save species from extinction. However, many species

---

*Only around 72 species of insects are known to have gone extinct, roughly 0.001% of the number of species in this taxon. However, this extremely low reported extinction rate is principally due to the poor state of our knowledge of this large group; many species may have gone extinct without scientists ever having been aware they existed.

TABLE 7.1 Some vertebrate species and subspecies that have gone extinct in North America since 1492 as a result of human activity

Common name	Scientific name	Region	Date of extinction
FISHES			
Yellowfin cutthroat trout	*Salmo clarki macdonaldi*	Colorado	1910
Silver trout	*Salvelinus agassizi*	New Hampshire	1930s
Blackfin cisco	*Coregonus nigripinnis*	Great Lakes	1960s
Tecopa pupfish[a]	*Cyprinodon nevadensis calidae*	California	1974
San Marcos gambusia	*Gambusia georgei*	Texas	1983
AMPHIBIANS			
Relict leopard frog	*Rana onca*	Utah, Arizona, Nevada	1960
Golden coqui	*Eleutherodactylus jasperi*	Puerto Rico	1980s
REPTILES			
Iguana	*Leiocephalus eremitus*	Navassa Island, West Indies	1800s
St. Croix racer	*Alsophis sancticrucis*	St. Croix, Virgin Islands	1900s
BIRDS			
Great auk	*Pinguinus impennis*	North Atlantic	1844
Labrador duck	*Camptorhynchus labradorium*	Northeastern North America	1878
Akialoa	*Hemignathus obscurus*	Hawaii	1895
Passenger pigeon	*Ectopistes migratorius*	Central and eastern North America	1914
Carolina parakeet	*Conuropis carolinensis*	Southeastern U.S.	1914
Heath hen	*Tympanuchus cupido cupido*	Eastern U.S.	1932
Dusky seaside sparrow	*Ammodramus maritimus nigrescens*	Southeastern U.S.	1987
MAMMALS			
Puerto Rican ground sloth	*Acratocnus odontrigonus*	Puerto Rico	1500
Puerto Rican paca	*Elasmodontomys obliquus*	Puerto Rico	1500
Atlantic gray whale	*Eschrichtius gibbosus gibbosus*	Atlantic Ocean	1750
Stellar's sea cow	*Hydrodamalis stellari*	Alaska	1778
Giant deer mouse	*Peromyscus nesodytus*	Channel Islands of California	1870
Sea mink	*Mustela macrodon*	New Brunswick; New England	1890
Florida red wolf	*Canis rufus floridianus*	Southeastern U.S.	1925
Texas gray wolf	*Canis lupus monstrabilis*	Texas, New Mexico	1942

Source: Data from Williams and Nowak, 1993.

[a]This fish became extinct even though it was protected by the U.S. Endangered Species Act.

not yet listed as extinct have been decimated by human activities and persist only in very low numbers. The fate of many such species is illustrated by the first reported extinction of a primate in the last 100 years, the Miss Waldron's colobus monkey (*Procolobus badius waldroni*) from Ghana and Côte d'Ivoire (Oates et al. 2000). Although for many species

TABLE 7.2 Recorded extinctions, 1600 to the present

Taxon	Recorded extinctions[a]				Approximate number of species	Percentage of taxon extinct
	Mainland[b]	Island[b]	Ocean	Total		
Mammals	30	51	4	85	4000	2.1
Birds	21	92	0	113	9000	1.3
Reptiles	1	20	0	21	6300	0.3
Amphibians[c]	2	0	0	2	4200	0.05
Fishes[d]	22	1	0	23	19,100	0.1
Invertebrates[d]	49	48	1	98	1,000,000+	0.01
Flowering plants[e]	245	139	0	384	250,000	0.2

Source: After Reid and Miller 1989; data from various sources.

[a]Numerous additional species have presumably gone extinct without ever being recorded by scientists.

[b]Mainland areas are those with landmasses of 1 million km² or greater (the size of Greenland or larger); smaller landmasses are considered islands.

[c]There has been an alarming decrease in amphibian populations in the last 20 years; some scientists believe that many amphibian species are on the verge of becoming extinct.

[d]The figures given are primarily representative of North America and Hawaii.

[e]The numbers for flowering plants include extinctions of subspecies and varieties as well as species.

it is true that a few individuals in scattered small populations might persist for years, decades, or centuries (for woody plants in particular, isolated individuals can persist for hundreds of years), their ultimate fate is extinction (Adams and Carwardine 1990; Tilman et al. 1994; Loehle and Li 1996). Remaining individuals of species that are doomed to extinction following habitat destruction have been called "the living dead"

Figure 7.4 Extinction rates during 50-year intervals for birds and mammals since 1600. Extinction rates have increased from 1800 to 1950, with some evidence of a decline during the last 50 years. (From Smith et al. 1993.)

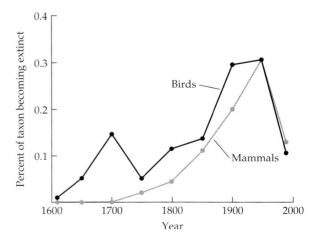

Figure 7.5 Only one individual remains alive in the wild of the hurricane palm, *Dictyosperma album* var. *conjugatum*, which is endemic to Round Island, Mauritius, in the Indian Ocean. This tree is doomed to extinction unless intensive management efforts are implemented at the site to establish new individuals. (Photograph courtesy of Michael Maunder.)

or "committed to extinction." (Figure 7.5). There are certainly many species in this category in the remaining fragments of forest in species-rich locations such as Madagascar and the Atlantic Forest of Brazil. Though technically the species is not extinct while these individuals live, the population is no longer reproductively viable, hence the species' future is limited to the lifespans of the remaining individuals (Gentry 1986; Janzen 1986, 2001). Evidence from forest fragments and parks indicates that, following the destruction of the surrounding habitat, species diversity of vertebrates may actually show a temporary increase as animals flee into the few remaining patches of forest (Bierregaard et al. 1992). However, the number of species falls over the next few weeks, months, and years as species begin to go extinct on a local scale and are not replaced by other species.

Extinction rates will remain high in the coming century because of the large number of threatened species. About 12% of the world's remaining bird species are threatened with extinction; the same percentage holds for mammal species. Table 7.3 shows certain animal groups for which the danger is even more severe, such as the family of lizards known as iguanas (Mace 1994). The threat to some freshwater fishes and mollusks may be equally severe (Williams and Nowak 1993). Plant species are also at risk, with gymnosperms (conifers, ginkgos, and cycads) and palms among the especially vulnerable groups.

The threat of extinction is greater for some groups of species than for others (see Chapter 8). Some groups are especially vulnerable for a combination of reasons, including high levels of human exploitation. For example, 10 of the world's 23 crocodile and alligator species face extinction not only because their habitat is disappearing, but also because they are overhunted for their meat and skins. Almost half of the world's primate species and one-third of the parrot species are threatened with extinction for similar reasons (Chapman and Peres 2001). Throughout

TABLE 7.3 Numbers of species threatened with extinction in major groups of animals and plants, and some key families and orders

Group	Approximate number of species	Number of species threatened with extinction	Percentage of species threatened with extinction
VERTEBRATE ANIMALS			
Fishes	24,000	752	3
Amphibians	3000	146	5
Reptiles	6000	296	5
Boidae (constrictor snakes)	17[a]	9	53
Varanidae (monitor lizards)	29[a]	11	38
Iguanidae (iguanas)	25[a]	17	68
Birds	9500	1183	12
Anseriformes (waterfowl)	109[a]	36	33
Psittaciformes (parrots)	302[a]	118	39
Mammals	4500	1130	25
Marsupialia (marsupials)	179[a]	86	48
Canidae (wolves)	34[a]	13	38
Cervidae (deer)	14[a]	11	79
PLANTS			
Gymnosperms	758	242	32
Angiosperms (flowering plants)	250,000	5390	2
Palmae (palms)	2820	925	33

Source: Data from Smith et al. 1993; Mace 1994; Hilton-Taylor 2000.
[a]Number of species for which information is available.

the world, large cat species (family Felidae) are hunted for sport, and for fur, and because they are perceived to be a threat to domestic animals and people. Slipper orchids, which have restrictive habitat requirements, are overharvested by plant collectors. In Europe, more non-marine molluscs have gone extinct than birds, mammals, reptiles, and amphibians together (Bouchet et al. 1999).

In most past geological periods, the extinction of existing species was balanced or exceeded by the evolution of new species. However, the present rate of human-caused extinction far surpasses the known rate of evolution. The known examples of recent rapid evolution—fruit flies adapting to localized environments or plants rapidly acquiring new characteristics when their chromosomes double during a peculiarity in meiosis—usually do not produce new families or orders. These unique evolutionary events require many generations on a timescale over hundreds of thousands, if not millions, of years. The famous naturalist William Beebe said, "[W]hen the last individual of any race of living things breathes no more, another heaven and another earth must pass before such a one can be again."

Background Extinction Rates

To better understand how calamitous present extinction rates are, it is useful to compare them to the natural extinction rates that would prevail regardless of human activity. What is the natural rate of extinction in the absence of human influence? Natural "background" extinction rates can be estimated by looking at the fossil record. In the fossil record, an individual species lasts about 1 to 10 million years before it goes extinct or evolves into a new species (Raup 1992). Since there are perhaps 10 million species on the Earth today, we can predict that 1–10 of the world's species would be lost per year as a result of a natural extinction rate of 0.0001–0.00001% per year. These estimates are derived from studies of wide-ranging marine animals, so they may be lower than natural extinction rates for species of narrow distribution, which are more vulnerable to habitat disturbance; however, they do appear to be applicable for terrestrial mammals (Raup 1992; Lawton and May 1995; Pimm et al. 1995). The current observed rate of extinction of birds and mammals of 1% per century (or 0.01% per year) is 100–1000 times greater than would be predicted based on background rates of extinction. Putting it another way, about 100 species of birds and mammals were observed to go extinct between 1850 and 1950, but the natural rate of extinction would have predicted that, at most, only 1 species would have gone extinct. Therefore, the other 99 extinctions can be attributed to the effects of human activity.

Some scientists have sharply questioned the accuracy of these estimates, saying that they are based on unfounded assumptions, such as the validity of comparing animals known from fossils with living animals and the validity of comparing marine mammals and terrestrial animals (Regan et al. 2001). However, even using a much more conservative approach with the available data, Regan and colleagues came up with a modern extinction rate that is still 36–78 times the background rate. Despite questions about the exact rates, no one disagrees that current extinction rates are far above background levels.

Extinction Rates on Islands

It should not come as a surprise that the highest species extinction rates during historic times have occurred on islands (see Table 7.2). These species often have a limited area, small population sizes, and a small number of populations. The high extinction rates on islands include the extinctions of birds, mammals, and reptiles during the last 350 years (WCMC 1992; Pimm et al. 1995). Further, numerous endemic plants of oceanic islands are extinct or in danger of extinction. (Endemic species, species found in one place and nowhere else, are particularly vulnerable to extinction. Endemic species are discussed in more detail in Chapter 8.)

Island species usually have evolved and undergone speciation with a limited number of competitors, predators, and diseases. When predatory species from the mainland are introduced onto islands, they frequently decimate the endemic island species, which have not evolved any defenses against them (Box 12; see also Chapter 8). Species extinction rates peak soon after humans occupy an island and then decline after the most vulnerable species are eliminated (Figure 7.6). Island plant species are also threatened, mainly through habitat destruction (Table 7.4). In Madagascar, 68% of the 9500 plant species are endemic, and 255 species are threatened with extinction (WRI 2000). In general, the longer an island has been occupied by people, the greater the percentage of extinct biota.

European colonization of islands has sometimes been more destructive than colonization by other peoples because European colonization includes greater amounts of clearing and the wholesale introduction of non-native species. For instance, between 1840 and 1880, more than 60 species of vertebrates, particularly grazing animals, such as sheep, were deliberately introduced into Australia, where they displaced native species and altered many communities. Over 1200 species of insects that have been brought into the United States. In the 1500s, the first European visitors to the Mascarene Islands (Mauritius, Reunion, and Rodrigues) released monkeys and pigs. These animals, and subsequent colonization by Dutch settlers, led to the extinction of the dodo bird, 19 other species of birds, and 8 species of reptiles. The impact of introduced predators on island species is highlighted by the example of the flightless Stephen Island wren, a bird that was endemic to a tiny island off New Zealand. Every Stephen Island wren on the island was killed by a

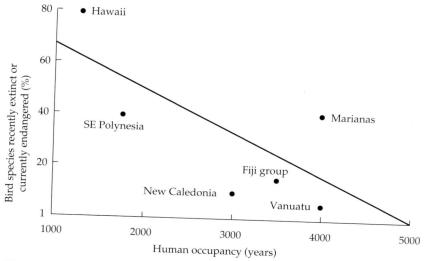

Figure 7.6 The proportion of recently extinct (that is, since the arrival of Europeans) or currently endangered bird species decreases as the length of time nonEuropean peoples have occupied an island group increases. This probably means that most sensitive species have already disappeared from those islands with long histories of human occupation. The seeming anomaly of the high recent extinctions in the Marianas group is due to the devastation caused by the recent introduction of the brown tree snake (see Chapter 10). (From Pimm et al. 1995.)

single cat belonging to the lighthouse keeper (Diamond 1984)—even one introduced predator can eliminate an entire species.

The vulnerability of island species is further illustrated when comparing the number of species that have gone extinct in mainland areas, on islands, and in the oceans from 1600 to the present (see Table 7.2).

TABLE 7.4 Number of plant species and their status for various islands and island groups

Island(s)	Native species	Endemic species	Percentage endemic	Number threatened	Percentage threatened
Fiji	1307	760	58	72	6
United Kingdom	1500	16	1	28	2
New Zealand	2160	1942	90	236	11
Jamaica	2746	923	33	371	14
Solomon Islands	2780	30	1	43	2
Sri Lanka	3000	890	30	436	15
Cuba	6004	3229	54	811	14
Philippines	8000	3500	44	371	5
Madagascar	9000	6500	72	189	2
Australia	15,000	14,074	94	1597	11

Source: Data from WRI 1998.

BOX 12 *Invasive Species and Extinctions in Island Ecosystems*

The problem of invasive, exotic species (as described in Chapter 10) is most pronounced in islands and archipelagos. The evolution of species in isolation from the mainland makes island species particularly vulnerable when competitors, predators, and diseases are introduced by human colonists or visitors. The fragility of species endemic to islands and archipelagos has been dramatically illustrated by the recent history of multiple extinctions and species decline in the Hawaiian and Galápagos archipelagos.

The two archipelagos have several features in common. Both are volcanic in origin, and both are a substantial distance from the nearest mainland coast. However, the entire Hawaiian chain, including the western seamounts, is some 63 million years older than the Galápagos (Loope et al. 1988) and has greater humidity and topographic diversity. Though the Hawaiian islands are five times as far from the mainland as the Galápagos, their age, climate, and topography combine to permit a higher level of biological diversity. Nevertheless, both archipelagos share a feature commonly found in island ecosystems: a high percentage of endemic species. Evolutionary radiation from relatively few colonizing species can produce an array of new species (see Chapter 2). An extreme instance of this type of rapid evolution occurred in Hawaii, where one or two colonizing species of fruit fly evolved into more than 800 different species (Howarth 1990). In addition to their unusual diversity, island ecosystems have particular value for evolutionary biologists as natural laboratories for the study of evolution. Charles Darwin's observations of finches in the Galápagos—observations from which he developed and supported his theory of the origin of new species—is a classic study of the rapid speciation common to islands.

But the same factors that make these island ecosystems so unique also leave them particularly vulnerable to invasions by exotic species. Introductions of exotic species to the Hawaiian and Galápagos islands have had dramatic and devastating effects on the endemic biota. In Hawaii, an initial wave of introductions, including Polynesian pigs, dogs, Polynesian rats, and a variety of plants, accompanied the colonization of the islands by the Polynesians approximately 1300 years ago. The initial human colonization of the Hawaiian archipelago is thought to have resulted in a wave of extinctions. At present, paleontologists have documented at least 62 species of birds that became extinct after the arrival of the Polynesians; plant and invertebrate taxa have yet to be examined (Olson 1989). Since the arrival of Europeans in 1778, many other alien species have had a powerful impact on native species. Black rats, domestic nonPolynesian pigs, feral dogs, cats, sheep, horses, cattle, goats, mongooses, and an estimated 2000 species of arthropods are some of the introduced species that have caused declines and extinctions among birds, insects, and plants in Hawaii in the past 200 years. In addition, numerous plant species brought to the islands have become naturalized, often outcompeting endemic taxa. The number of naturalized alien plant species in Hawaii is now greater than the number of native plant species. The impact of exotic species and habitat destruction has been so severe that Hawaii has the dubious distinction of having more recorded species extinctions than the entire rest of the United States.

The Galápagos archipelago has also experienced the effects of invasive, exotic species. Until recently, the overall inhospitality of these arid, rocky islands has limited the amount of human colonization, so the extent of destruction of endemic species is less than in Hawaii. Nonetheless, many species on these islands, particularly plants, are threatened by introduced species. Goats, cattle, and pigs are the primary culprits in the decline of many plant species; populations of goats on some islands are as high as 80,000, a number far in excess of what native plant species can withstand. Pigs consume the eggs of iguanas and turtles, including those of the endangered Pacific green turtle, which nests on the islands. Introduced

BOX 12 (continued)

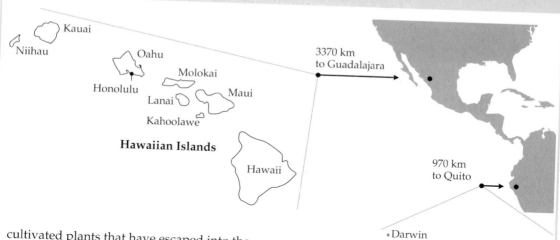

3370 km
to Guadalajara

970 km
to Quito

Hawaiian Islands

Kauai
Niihau
Oahu
Honolulu
Molokai
Lanai
Maui
Kahoolawe
Hawaii

Galápagos Islands

Darwin

Pinta
Isabela
Genovesa
San Salvador
Santa Cruz
San Cristóbal
Floreana
Española

cultivated plants that have escaped into the wild, including guava (*Psidium guajava*), quinine (*Cinchona succirubra*), and raspberries (*Rubus niveus*), crowd out many native species. The number of introduced plant species continues to increase and is strongly correlated with the rise in the human population (Mauchamp 1997). Even Darwin's famous finches are beginning to decline, with several species having already gone extinct. The government of Ecuador, which has jurisdiction over the Galápagos islands, recently declared the conservation of the Galápagos to be a national priority. This policy will have to be balanced against pressures to increase tourism and commercial fishing in the region.

As a first step toward protection, conservation biologists working in both archipelagos have been trying to eradicate some of the more prominent and destructive invasive species, particularly introduced mammals (Loope 1995). The hunting and removal of feral goats, pigs, and other ungulates is actively underway, while domestic stock is kept closely penned. Introduced herbs and trees are eliminated by herbicide sprays, felling, and burning. Over 75% of the management costs for Hawaii's protected areas are spent on the control of exotic species. These measures are sometimes effective against larger species. For example, when rat popula-

The oceanic archipelagos of Hawaii and the Galápagos have unique, rich, and severely threatened endemic biotas.

tions were controlled on Santa Cruz and Floreana in the Galápagos, nesting success of dark-rumped petrels increased from 0–7% to 67–72% (Powell and Gibbs 1995). Where pigs and other large animals have been eliminated from montane forests, the native species have recovered (Stone and Loope 1996). Control of invasive insects and other invertebrates and many herbaceous weeds is often far more difficult. Now that the problem of invasive species has been identified, the respective governments and conservation organizations are actively managing areas of the islands to protect, restore, and enlarge the original biological communities that remain.

Of the 726 species of animals and plants known to have gone extinct, 351 (about half of the total) were island species, even though islands represent only a small fraction of the Earth's surface (Smith et al. 1993).

Extinction Rates in Water

In contrast with the large amount of information we have on extinct terrestrial species, there are no documented cases of marine fish or coral species that have gone extinct during the last few thousand years. Only around 12 species—three marine mammals, five marine birds, and four mollusks—are known to have gone extinct in the world's vast oceans during historic times (Carlton et al. 1999). This number of extinctions is almost certainly an underestimate, since marine species are not nearly as well known as terrestrial species, but it may reflect a greater resiliency of marine species in response to disturbance. However, the significance of these losses may be greater than the numbers suggest. Many marine mammals are top predators, and their loss could have a major impact on marine communities. Some marine species are the sole species of their genus, family, or even order, so the extinction of even a few of them can possibly represent a serious loss to global biological diversity. The oceans were considered so enormous that it seemed unlikely that marine species could go extinct; and many people still share this viewpoint. However, as marine coastal waters become more polluted and species are harvested more intensely, even the vast oceans will not provide safety from extinction (Woodard 2000).

Also in contrast to terrestrial extinctions, the majority of freshwater fish extinctions have occurred in mainland areas rather than on islands because of the vastly greater number of species in mainland waters (Box 13). In North America, over one-third of freshwater fish species are in danger of extinction (Moyle and Leidy 1992). The fish of California are particularly vulnerable because of the state's scarcity of water and its intense development—7% of California's 115 types of native fish are already extinct and 56% are in danger of extinction (Moyle 1995). Large numbers of fish and aquatic invertebrates, such as mollusks, are in danger of extinction in the southeastern United States because of dams, pollution, irrigation projects, invasion of alien species, and general habitat damage (Figure 7.7).

Estimating Extinction Rates with the Island Biogeography Model

Studies of island communities have led to general rules on the distribution of biological diversity, synthesized as the **island biogeography model** by MacArthur and Wilson (1967). This model can be used to estimate future extinction rates, as we will see later in this section. The cen-

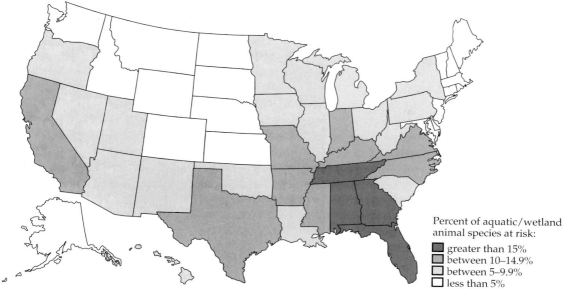

Percent of aquatic/wetland
animal species at risk:

■ greater than 15%
▨ between 10–14.9%
▢ between 5–9.9%
□ less than 5%

Figure 7.7 Dams, irrigation systems, polluted runoff from industry and agriculture, introduced species, and habitat destruction threaten as many as 23% of the aquatic species in the United States, including dozens of species of freshwater mussels, fish, and crayfish. The many endemic species of restricted range in the southeastern section of the country are most at risk. (After Stolzenburg 1996.)

tral observation that this model was built to explain is the **species–area relationship**: Islands with large areas have more species than islands with smaller areas (Figure 7.8). This rule makes intuitive sense because large islands will tend to have a greater variety of local environments and community types than small islands. Also, large islands allow greater geographic isolation, a larger number of populations per species, and larger sizes of individual populations, increasing the likelihood of speciation and decreasing the probability of local extinction of newly evolved as well as recently arrived species. The species–area relationship can be accurately summarized by the empirical formula:

$$S = CA^Z$$

where S is the number of species on an island, A is the area of the island, and C and Z are constants. The exponent Z determines the slope of the curve. The values for C and Z will depend on the types of islands being compared (tropical versus temperate, dry versus wet, etc.) and the types of species involved (birds versus reptiles, etc.). Z values are typically around 0.25, with a range from 0.15–0.35 (Connor and McCoy 1979, 2001).

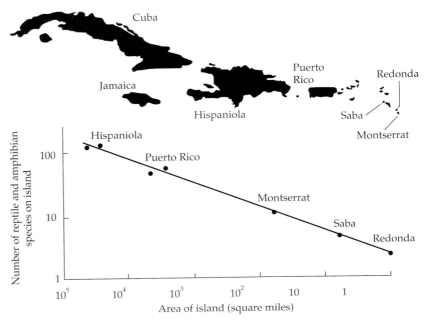

Figure 7.8 The number of species on an island can be predicted from the area of an island. In this figure, the number of species of reptiles and amphibians is shown for seven islands in the West Indies. The number of species on large islands such as Cuba and Hispaniola far exceeds that on the tiny islands of Saba and Redonda. (From Wilson 1989.)

Island species of restricted ranges, such as reptiles and amphibians, tend to have Z values near 0.35, while widespread mainland species tend to have Z values closer to 0.15. Values of C will be high in groups such as insects that are high in species numbers and low in groups such as birds that are low in species numbers.

The model has been empirically validated to the point of acceptance by most biologists (Quammen 1996): For numerous groups of plants and animals, it has been found to describe reasonably well the observed richness of species, explaining about half of the variation in numbers of species. Imagine the simplest situation, in which $C = 1$ and $Z = 0.25$, for raptorial birds on a hypothetical archipelago:

$$S = (1)A^{0.25}$$

The formula predicts that islands of 10, 100, 1000, and 10,000 km^2 in area would have 2, 3, 6, and 10 species, respectively. It is important to note that a tenfold increase in island area does not result in a tenfold increase in the number of species; with this equation, each tenfold in-

BOX 13 *Conserving Endemic Fish in Lake Victoria*

The extinction of individual species usually does not take place in isolation; too frequently, a species is lost in conjunction with many other component species of a damaged ecosystem. Ecological changes affecting single species can have a domino effect on other organisms, leading to catastrophic transformation of the entire ecosystem. This principle is illustrated by the recent, devastating changes in the ecology of Lake Victoria in East Africa. The lake, which is surrounded by Kenya, Tanzania, and Uganda, is one of the world's largest freshwater ecosystems. Until the early 1980s, it was also one of the most diverse in number of fish species. Prior to that time, Lake Victoria had over 400 endemic species of fishes in its waters and represented one of the most outstanding examples of rapid speciation (Kaufman and Cohen 1993; Goldschmidt 1996). At present, however, only one native species and two introduced species inhabit the lake in significant numbers; all of the remaining species are threatened, endangered, or extinct. Fortunately, populations of several species of Lake Victoria cichlids still exist in captivity, where they are being bred as part of a cooperative conservation program in hopes of eventual reintroduction. However, any reintroduction programs will not be successful unless the initial factors that drove the species to extinction are addressed.

The rapid losses of the endemic species have been correlated with an abrupt increase in the population of a single species of fish: the Nile perch, *Lates niloticus,* which was introduced into Lake Victoria in 1954 (with more serious attempts in the 1960s) to create a new food resource for the fishing industry. Based solely on this information, one might conclude that the Nile perch either consumed or outcompeted the native fishes, and was thus responsible for the recent losses. However, that is only partially correct. While the Nile perch has played a role in the decline of endemic fishes in the lake, subtle ecological forces have also contributed to the losses.

Lates niloticus, the Nile perch, was introduced into Lake Victoria as a food source in the 1950s and 1960s. It became a major factor in the eradication of the lake's rich cichlid fish fauna. (Photograph by John N. Rinne.)

The introduction of the Nile perch apparently did not have a significant impact on the Lake Victoria fish population until decades after its introduction. In 1978, Nile perch constituted less than 2% of the lake's annual fishing harvest. By 1986, however, this species was nearly 80% of the total catch (Kaufman 1992). The endemic species were virtually gone from the lake, and the Nile perch had undergone an

BOX 13 *(continued)*

abrupt population explosion. While the perch was a prime consumer of many of the smaller native fish species, the ascendancy of the Nile perch was more than simply a case of an introduced species running amok.

One clue that other factors were contributing to native fish losses was the change in the occurrence of algal blooms in the lake's shallower waters. Algal blooms had been observed at intervals throughout the lake's history, but the frequency of these events increased noticeably in the early 1980s, at the same time that the perch population explosion took place. Increases in algae are often associated with decreased oxygen levels in the lower depths of large bodies of water, which in turn makes the water less habitable for algae-eating fish. Prior to 1978, Lake Victoria had fairly high oxygen levels at all depths; because of these aerobic conditions, fish were able to survive even in the deepest waters of the lake, which in some places exceeds 60 m. Studies done from 1989 to 1992 revealed that Lake Victoria had severely depleted oxygen levels at depths below 25 m, and was in the process of becoming anoxic—completely lacking in oxygen—below a certain depth (Kaufman 1992). The anoxic conditions effectively reduced the available habitat within the lake; fish species that preferred the deeper regions of the lake may have died out as a result, either because they could not adapt to the different conditions of shallower water or because they were unable to escape shallow-water predators such as the Nile perch. The mystery does not end there, however; algal blooms had occurred before, without this devastating effect on the native fauna. Why did the mass extinctions occur this time?

The answer is probably a combination of factors. Initial high population levels of some native species in the 1960s and 1970s probably were related to high inputs of nutrients from agricultural runoff, sewage from towns and villages, and other anthropogenic sources. The majority of these endemic species were cichlids, which fed on the algae and other lake flora and fauna that increased because of the nutrient inputs. However, overfishing and predation by a rapidly expanding Nile perch population between 1978 and 1984 contributed to a rapid decline in native fish species diversity and abundance; as the cichlids decreased in numbers, the excess nutrients and reduced herbivory encouraged frequent algal blooms. Algal blooms from excess nutrients are in turn often followed by a depletion of oxygen as bacteria and fungi breakdown the dying alga; the whole process is known as **eutrophication.** The lack of oxygen in the lower depths of the lake drove the remaining native fish to shallower waters, where they were more vulnerable to fishing nets and ever-increasing numbers of Nile perch—and as the perch increased, the cycle continued in a downward spiral: fewer cichlids led to increased algal blooms, leading to decreased oxygen in deep water, which then further reduced the remaining cichlids. In the oxygen-poor water, a native shrimp species has now become common, and this is an important food for the perch now that cichlid numbers have declined (Stiassny 1996).

In 1990, the situation was compounded by the appearance and explosive spread of water hyacinth in Lake Victoria. Water hyacinth (*Eichornia crassipes*) is a floating water weed from South America, often introduced for its flowers, which are beautiful in small doses. Unfortunately this weed is extremely fecund under eutrophic conditions such as those that prevail in today's Lake Victoria. Now entire bays and inlets are sometimes covered by thick mats of hyacinth, choking breeding and nursery areas important to the cichlids. Property owners, fishermen, ferry boat operators, lakeside residents, and, of course, politicians are periodically up in arms about this singular and highly visible problem.

Restoration of the once-diverse Lake Victoria ecosystem is one of the most challenging problems facing conservation biologists today.

BOX 13   *(continued)*

Water hyacinth (*Eichornia crassipes*), an exotic weed, completely covers large areas of the surface of Lake Victoria in Africa. (Photograph by Les Kaufman.)

Transforming a eutrophic tropical lake of this size has never been attempted. If scientists are somehow successful in restoring oxygen levels, they must then deal with the different factors that contributed to the problem in the first place: excessive inputs of nutrients from human activity, overharvesting by fisheries, and the presence of the Nile perch. Recently, the World Bank and other donors joined forces to fund efforts by the three nations that border the lake to do just that. In this project, called the Lake Victoria Environmental Management Programme, funds are earmarked to deal with the different factors that contribute to the underlying problems.

There are many signs of hope. Overfishing and declines of Nile perch has been followed by local resurgence in a few of the indigenous cichlid species and even some native food fishes. There is evidence that the restrictions on the Nile perch fishery—which are in the best interests of that industry—will also help to restore native fishes. Finally, the three countries that border the lake have agreed that it is desirable to restore a multispecies fishery rather than try to rely on one species of exotic fish, Nile perch.

crease in island area increases the number of species by a factor of approximately 2. Actual data from three Caribbean islands can be used to illustrate the relationship: with increasing area, St. Nevis (93 km^2), Puerto Rico (8959 km^2), and Cuba (114,524 km^2) have 2, 10, and 57 species of anolis lizard, respectively; with a C of 0.5 and a Z of 0.35, the islands would be predicted to have 2, 12, and 30 species, respectively.

In their classic text, MacArthur and Wilson (1967) hypothesized that the number of species occurring on an island represents a dynamic equilibrium between the arrival of new species (and also the evolution of new species) and the extinction rate of existing species. Starting with an unoccupied island, the number of species will increase over time, since more species will be arriving (or evolving) than are going extinct, until

Figure 7.9 The island biogeography model describes the relationship between the rates of colonization and extinction on islands. The immigration rate (black curves) on unoccupied islands is initially high, as species with good dispersal abilities rapidly take advantage of the available open habitats. The immigration rate slows as the number of species increases and sites become occupied. The extinction rate (gray curves) increases with the number of species on the island; the more species on an island the greater the likelihood that a species will go extinct at any time interval. Colonization rates will be highest for islands near a mainland population source, since species can disperse over shorter distances more easily than longer ones. Extinction rates are highest on small islands, where both population sizes and habitat diversity are low. The number of species present on an island reaches an equilibrium when the colonization rate equals the extinction rate (circles). The equilibrium number of species is greatest on large islands near the mainland, and lowest on small islands far from the mainland. (After MacArthur and Wilson 1967.)

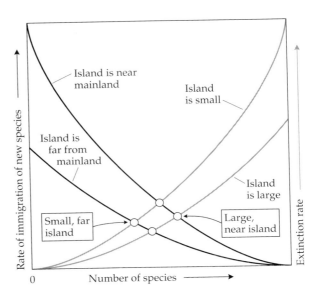

the rates of extinction and immigration are balanced (Figure 7.9). The arrival rate will be higher for large islands than small islands because large islands represent a larger target for dispersing animals to find and are more likely to have suitable open habitat available for colonization. The extinction rate will be lower on large islands than small islands because large islands have greater habitat diversity and a greater number of populations. The rate of immigration of new species will be higher for islands near to the mainland than for islands farther away, since mainland species are able to disperse to near islands more easily than to distant islands. The model predicts that for any group of organisms, such as birds or trees, the number of species found on large islands near a continent will be greater than that on small islands far from a continent.

Extinction Rates and Habitat Loss

Species–area relationships have been used to predict the number and percentage of species that would become extinct if habitats were destroyed (Simberloff 1992; Quammen 1996). The calculation assumes that, if an island has a certain number of species, reducing the area of natural habitat on the island would result in the island being able to support only a number of species corresponding to that on a smaller island (Figure 7.10). This model has great utility because it can be extended to national parks and nature reserves that are surrounded by damaged habitat. The re-

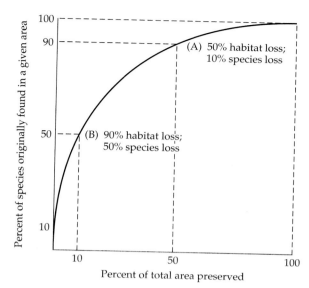

Figure 7.10 According to the island biogeography model, the number of species present in an area increases asymptotically to a maximum value. This means that if the area of habitat is reduced by 50%, the number of species lost may be 10% (A); if the habitat is reduced by 90%, the number of species lost may be 50% (B). The shape of the curve is different for each region of the world and for each group of species, but this model gives a general indication of the effect of habitat destruction on species extinctions and the persistence of species in the remaining habitat.

serves can be viewed as "habitat islands" in an inhospitable "sea" of unsuitable habitat. The model predicts that when 50% of an island (or habitat island) is destroyed, approximately 10% of the species occurring on the island will be eliminated. If these species are endemic to an area, they will become extinct. When 90% of the habitat is destroyed, 50% of the species will be lost; and when 99% of the habitat is gone, about 75% of the original species will be lost. The island of Singapore can be used as an example: Over the last 180 years, 95% of its original forest cover has been removed; the model estimates that around 30% of its forest species would be lost. In fact, between 1923 and 1998, 32% of Singapore's native birds were lost, with higher rates of loss for large ground birds and for insectivorous birds of the forest canopy (Castelleta et al. 2000).

Predictions of extinction rates based on habitat loss vary considerably, because each species–area relationship is unique. Because insects and plants in tropical forests account for the great majority of the world's species, estimates of present and future rates of species extinction in rain forests gives an approximation of global rates of extinction. At present rates of deforestation, 15% of the plant species in the Neotropics are predicted to eventually become extinct as a result of forest clearing between 1986 and 2000, and 12% of Amazon bird species are predicted to eventually go extinct (Simberloff 1986). If deforestation continues until all of the forests (except those in national parks and other protected areas) are cut down, about two-thirds of all plant and bird species will be driven to extinction.

Using the conservative estimate that 1% of the world's rain forests is being destroyed each year, Wilson (1989) estimated that 0.2–0.3% of all species—10,000–15,000 species using a total of 5 million species world-wide—will be lost per year, or 34 species per day. This estimate predicts that over the 10-year period from 1993 to 2003, approximately 125,000 species will become extinct. Other methods applied to the rates of extinction in tropical rain forests estimate a loss of between 2–11% of the world's species per decade (Reid 1992; Koopowitz et al. 1994). The variation in rates is due to the use of different estimates of the rate of deforestation, different values for the species–area curves, and different mathematical approaches. Extinction rates might in fact be higher because the highest rates of deforestation are occurring in countries with large concentrations of rare species, and large forest areas are increasingly being fragmented by roads and development projects (Balmford and Long 1994). We might lower extinction rates if these "hot spot" areas, particularly rich in endemic species, are targeted for conservation (Pimm and Raven 2000). Regardless of which estimate is the most accurate, all indicate that tens of thousands—if not hundreds of thousands—of species are headed for extinction within the next 50 years (Schmidt 1997). Such a rate of extinction is without precedent since the great mass extinction of the Cretaceous period 65 million years ago.

Assumptions and Generalizations in the Island Biogeography Model

Estimates of extinction rates based on the island biogeography model include a number of assumptions and generalizations that may limit the validity of this approach (Reid 1992; Simberloff 1992):

1. These estimates are based on typical values for the species–area curves. Groups of species with broad geographical ranges, such as marine animals and temperate tree species, will tend to have lower rates of extinction than species of narrow geographic distribution, such as island birds and freshwater fish.
2. The model assumes that all endemic species are eliminated from areas that have been largely cleared of forest. It is possible that many species can survive in isolated patches of forest and recolonize secondary forest that develops on abandoned land. A few primary forest species may also be capable of surviving in plantations and managed forests. Adaptation to managed forests is likely to be particularly significant in tropical forests that are being selectively logged on a large scale.
3. The species–area model assumes that areas of habitat are eliminated at random. In fact, areas of species richness are sometimes targeted for species conservation efforts and national park status. As a result, a greater percentage of species may be protected than is assumed in the species–area model.
4. The degree of habitat fragmentation may affect extinction rates. If remaining areas of land are divided into very small parcels or crossed

by roads, then wide-ranging species or species requiring large population sizes may be unable to maintain themselves. Also, hunting, clearing land for agriculture, and the introduction of exotic species may increase in fragmented forests, leading to further loss of species.

Other Methods for Calculating Extinction Rates

Another approach to estimating extinction rates uses information on projected declines in habitat, numbers of populations, and the geographical range of well-known individual species (Mace 1995). This approach uses empirical information to give a more accurate estimate of extinction rates for a smaller number of species. Applied to 725 threatened vertebrate species, this method predicts that some 15–20 species will go extinct over the next 100 years. Extinction rates are expected to be much higher in certain groups; within 100 years it is likely that half of the 29 threatened species in the deer family (Cervidae) will be extinct, as will 3 of the world's 10 threatened hornbill species (Bucerotidae).

The time required for a given species to go extinct following a reduction in area or fragmentation of its range is a vital question in conservation biology, and the island biogeography model makes no prediction as to how long it will take (Lawton and May 1995; Gibbs 2001). Small populations of some species may persist for decades or even centuries, even though their eventual fate is extinction. Another method, which compares predictions of species loss with historical examples, allows us to make estimates of when the extinctions will occur: Comparing predictions with historical examples from forests in Kenya, estimates have been made of the rates at which remaining forest fragments will lose their bird species. Of the species that will eventually be lost, the best estimates predict that half will be lost in 50 years from a 1000-ha fragment, while half will be lost in 100 years from a 10,000-ha fragment (Brooks et al. 1999). As a general rule, it seems that of the species that will eventually go extinct, half die off in the first 50 years (Pimm and Raven 2000). In situations in which there is widespread habitat destruction followed by recovery, such as in New England and Puerto Rico over the last several centuries, species may be able to survive in small numbers in isolated fragments and then reoccupy adjacent recovering habitat. Even though 98% of the forests of eastern North America were cut down, the clearing took place in a patchwork fashion over hundreds of years, so that forest always covered half of the area, providing refuges for mobile animal species such as birds.

Local Extinctions

In addition to the global extinctions that are a primary focus of conservation biology, many species are experiencing a series of local extinctions or extirpations across their range. Formerly widespread species are

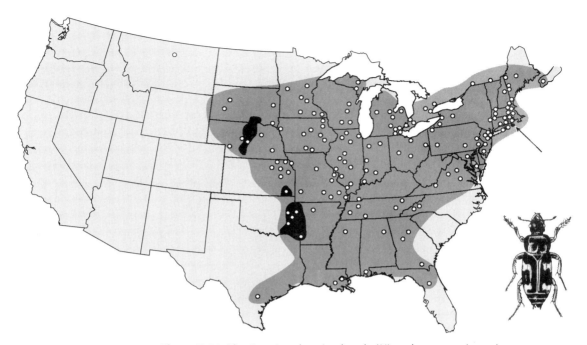

Figure 7.11 The American burying beetle (*Nicrophorus americanus*) was once widespread in the eastern and central United States (shaded area) but is now found only in four isolated populations (black areas; Block Island, in Long Island Sound, is highlighted with an arrow). Open dots represent past sites of collection, based on museum specimens. Note the isolated collections from central Montana, southern Texas, and southern Nova Scotia. Intensive efforts have been initiated to determine the cause of this decline and develop a recovery plan. (After Muths and Scott 2000.)

sometimes restricted to a few small pockets of their former habitat (Terborgh 1999). For example, the American burying beetle (*Nicrophorus americanus*), once found all across central and eastern North America, is now found only in four isolated populations (Figure 7.11) (Muths and Scott 2000). Biological communities are impoverished by such local extinctions. The Middlesex Fells, a local conservation area in metropolitan Boston, contained 338 native plant species in 1894; only 227 native species remained when the area was surveyed 98 years later (Drayton and Primack 1996). Fourteen of the plant species that were lost had been listed as "common" in 1894. A combination of forest succession, ground fires, trampling by hikers and mountain bikers, invasions by exotic species, and habitat fragmentation contributed to species losses in the Fells.

According to recent surveys by the U.S. Natural Heritage program, 4–8% of the plant species formerly found in Hawaii, New York, and Pennsylvania can no longer be found. In Britain, where species distributions are often known with great accuracy due to decades of collecting and research, an analysis of butterflies in one county showed that local extinctions over the last 25 years had eliminated 67% of the previously known localities of species, an astonishingly high rate of local loss (Thomas and Abery 1995).

IMPOVERISHED COMMUNITIES   The world's 5 million species are estimated to consist of 1 billion distinct populations, or around 200 populations per species (Hughes and Roughgarden 2000). While some species have just a few populations, other species might have thousands of populations. The loss of populations is roughly equal to the proportion of a habitat that is lost, so that the world's populations are being lost at a far higher rate than the loss of species (see Figure 7.10). When 90% of an extensive grassland ecosystem is destroyed, 90% of the populations of plant, animal, and fungus species there will also be lost. Tropical rain forests contain at least half of the world's species, and they are being lost at the rate of around 1% per year. This represents a loss of 5 million populations per year (1% of 500 million tropical forest populations), or around 30,000 populations per day.

These large numbers of local extinctions serve as important biological warning signs that something is wrong with the environment. Action is needed to prevent further local extinctions, as well as global extinctions. The loss of local populations not only represents a loss of biological diversity, but it diminishes the value of an area for nature enjoyment, scientific research, and the provision of crucial materials to local people in subsistence economies.

Summary

1. There are more species on Earth in the present geological period than have ever existed in the past. However, the current rate of species extinction is rapid and is comparable to the five past episodes of natural mass extinction found at intervals in the geological record.

2. The effect of human activity has been to drive many species to extinction. Since 1600, 2.1% of the world's mammalian species and 1.3% of its birds have gone extinct. The rate of extinction is accelerating, and many of the species still alive are teetering on the brink of extinction. The current observed rate of extinction for birds and mammals is estimated to be 100–1000 times greater than the rate that would be occurring naturally.

3. Island species have a higher rate of extinction than mainland species. Among aquatic species, freshwater species apparently have a higher extinction rate than marine species.

4. An island biogeography model has been developed to predict the equilibrium number of species that might be found on islands of different areas and distances from the mainland. This model has been used to estimate how many species would go extinct if human activity continues to destroy habitats at the present rate. The best evidence indicates that about 2–3% of the Earth's

species will be lost over the next 10 years, with a loss of about 10,000–15,000 species per year. Other empirical evidence on population declines and reductions in range support the prediction that the rate of extinction will remain high over the coming decades.

5. Individuals of long-lived species that remain alive in disturbed and fragmented habitats can be considered "the living dead." The individuals may persist for many years but will eventually die out due to a lack of reproduction.

6. Biological communities are becoming impoverished due to the local extinction of species. This, too, represents a loss of biodiversity.

For Discussion

1. Calculate the number of species expected on islands of various sizes, using several values of C (0.5, 1, 2, 4, etc.) and several values of Z (0.15, 0.25, 0.35, etc.). How many species will be lost on the largest island if native habitat is completely destroyed on 30%, 70%, 97%, and 98% of the island? What are the assumptions on which these calculations are based?

2. Why should conservation biologists, or anyone else, care if species go locally extinct if they are still found somewhere else?

3. If 50% of the species present today go extinct within the next 200 years, what is your estimate of how long it would take for the process of speciation to replace the lost number of species?

Suggested Readings

Adams, D. and M. Carwardine. 1990. *Last Chance to See.* Harmony Books, New York. A light but poignant account of the threat of imminent extinction facing many well-known species.

Goldschmidt, T. 1996. *Darwin's Dreampond: Drama in Lake Victoria.* MIT Press, Cambridge, MA. Personal account of working with an amazing group of fish—and then watching them go extinct.

Hilton-Taylor, C. (compiler). 2000. *2000 IUCN Red List of Threatened Species.* IUCN, Gland, Switzerland. Current information on the status of species; also available online.

Janzen, D. H. 1986. The eternal external threat. In *Conservation Biology: The Science of Scarcity and Diversity,* M. E. Soulé, (ed.), pp. 286–330. Sinauer Associates, Sunderland, MA. A superb essay on the causes of tropical extinctions, with vivid natural history examples.

Lawton, J. H. and R. M. May (eds.). 1995. *Extinction Rates.* Oxford University Press, Oxford. Superb short volume with leading authorities.

Leakey, R. and R. Lewin. 1996. *The Sixth Extinction: Patterns of Life and the Future of Humankind.* Doubleday, New York. Popular account of the mass extinctions by an anthropologist and a science writer.

Lövei, G. 2001. Extinctions, modern examples. In *Encyclopedia of Biodiversity,* S. A. Levin (ed.), Vol. 2, pp. 731–744. Academic Press, San Diego, CA. Examples of extinctions following first human contact and since 1600 A.D.

MacArthur, R. H. and E. O. Wilson. 1967. *The Theory of Island Biogeography.* Princeton University Press, Princeton, NJ. This classic text outlining the island biogeography model has been highly influential in shaping modern conservation biology.

Martin, P. S. 2001. Mammals (late Quaternary), extinctions of. In *Encyclopedia of Biodiversity,* S. A. Levin (ed.), Vol. 3, pp. 825–840. Academic Press, San Diego, CA. Large mammals went extinct on each continent and island following the arrival of humans.

Quammen, D. 1996. *The Song of the Dodo: Island Biogeography in an Age of Extinctions.* Scribner, New York. Popular account of early and modern explorations and of island biogeography theory.

Raup, D. M. 1992. *Extinction: Bad Genes or Bad Luck?* W. W. Norton & Company, New York. Clearly written overview of extinction, with an emphasis on geological processes.

Regan, H. M., R. Lupia, A. N. Drinan, and M. A. Burgman. 2001. The currency and tempo of extinction. *American Naturalist* 157: 1–10. An important paper examines the assumptions of past, present and future extinction rates.

Terborgh, J. 1999. *Requiem for Nature.* Island Press, Washington D.C. The multiple threats faced by biological diversity must be considered realistically and without illusions.

Wilson, E. O. 1989. Threats to biodiversity. *Scientific American* 261: 108–116. How extinction rates are increasing due to human activities.

Woodard, C. 2000. *Ocean's End: Travels through Endangered Seas.* Basic Books (Perseus Books Group), New York. A science journalist documents that even vast expanses of ocean are not protected from human impact.

Vulnerability to Extinction

Not all species have an equal chance of going extinct. Rare species are considered to be especially vulnerable to extinction, while common species are considered less so. But the term "rare" has a variety of meanings in the biological literature, each of which has a different implication for conservation biology (Goerck 1997; Stohlgren 2001).

Generally speaking, a species is considered rare if it (1) lives in a narrow geographic range, (2) occupies only one or a few specialized habitats, or (3) is found only in small populations. The first criterion, based on geographic area, is the most obvious: The Venus's-flytrap (*Dionaea muscipula*) is rare because it occurs only in the savannahs of the coastal plain of the Carolinas in eastern North America. Many geographically rare species occupy islands, and some may also occupy isolated habitats such as high mountain peaks in the middle of lowlands or lakes surrounded by a terrestrial landscape. Within their limited geographical range, however, a rare species may be locally abundant.

Related to the concept of rarity is the concept of endemism—that some species are found naturally in a single geographic area and no other place. This concept may seem

Figure 8.1 The Plymouth gentian (*Sabatia kennedyana*), a rare wildflower, is found only on the margins of coastal ponds in scattered locations in the eastern United States. At a few ponds, however, this species has large populations. (Photograph by Mark Primack.)

similar to one of the properties of rare species discussed above ("lives in a narrow geographic range"). But a species may be endemic to a large area and abundant throughout it. In contrast, a rare species such as the Venus's-flytrap is typically found only in a limited area (and could be considered a narrowly distributed endemic) (Figure 8.1). Or a rare species may be geographically rare in only part of its range. For example, the sweet bay magnolia (*Magnolia virginiana*) is reasonably common throughout the southeastern United States, but in the New England region it occurs in only one population of 100 individuals in one particular swamp in Magnolia, Massachusetts (Primack et al. 1986). Individual species may have always had a narrow geographic range, or they may have been more widespread at one time but became restricted due to human activities and habitat destruction.

A species may also be considered rare if it occupies only one or a few specialized habitats. Salt marsh cord grass (*Spartina patens*) is found only in salt marshes and not in other habitats; yet within this habitat, cord grass is quite common. This example contrasts with common species that are found in many different habitats, such as the dandelion (*Taraxacum officinale*), which occupies open meadows, roadsides, river edges, and mown lawns.

Finally, a species may be considered rare if it is found only in small populations. Mediterranean monk seals (*Monachus monachus*) are found over a wide area, but their populations are always small and isolated. A common species would have large populations at least occasionally.

These three criteria of rarity—narrow geographical range, specific habitat requirements, and small population size—can be applied to the entire range of species or to the distribution and abundance of species in a particular place (Rabinowitz et al. 1986). Such an approach can highlight priorities for conservation. Species with a narrow geographical range and specific habitat requirements that are always found in small populations require immediate habitat protection and, possibly, habitat management to maintain their few, fragile populations. This also applies, to a somewhat lesser degree, to species with larger populations. However, where species have a narrow geographical distribution but a broad habitat specificity, experiments in which individuals are transported to unoccupied but apparently suitable localities to create new populations may be a strategy worth considering (see Chapter 13), since these species may have been unable to disperse outside of their narrow geographical area. This suggestion is supported by a further study showing that plant species with poor dispersal abilities (no adaptation for long-distance dispersal) tend to have more aggregated populations in contrast to species with good dispersal ability (light, wind-dispersed seeds, or seeds dispersed by mammals and birds), which tend to have more widely dispersed populations (Quinn et al. 1994). Species with broad geographical ranges are less susceptible to extinction and less likely to need rescue efforts, since they tend to have more extant populations and more opportunities to colonize potentially suitable sites.

Endemic Species and Extinction

A species found naturally in a single geographic area and no other place is **endemic** to that location. Endemism is an extremely important factor in a species' risk of extinction. If the populations of an endemic species on Madagascar, or any isolated island, go extinct, the species will be globally extinct. In contrast, mainland species often have many populations distributed over a wide area, so the loss of one population is not catastrophic for the species. Even though 98% of the forests of eastern North America were logged or cleared for farming, for instance, no bird species went extinct because of habitat loss: Presumably the remaining forest fragments were sufficient to allow the species to survive until the forest grew back following the widespread abandonment of farming.

Expansion of an endemic species' geographical distribution that is caused deliberately or accidentally by humans is not considered part of the species' natural distribution. For example, the giant panda (*Ailuropoda melanoleuca*) is endemic to China, even though it now lives in zoos throughout the world. A species may be endemic to a wide geographical area (the black cherry tree [*Prunus serotina*] is endemic to the Western Hemisphere and is found across North, Central, and South America), or a species may be endemic to a small geographical area (the giant Komodo dragon [*Varanus komodoensis*] is endemic to several small islands in the Indonesian archipelago). Species that occupy a small area because they have only recently evolved from closely related species are designated **neoendemics;** examples include the hundreds of species of cichlid fish that occupy Lake Victoria. In contrast, **paleoendemics** are ancient species whose close relatives have all gone extinct; examples include the giant panda and the coelacanth. All such narrowly distributed endemic species are of concern for their potential to become extinct.

Isolated geographical units, such as remote islands, old lakes, and solitary mountain peaks, often have high percentages of endemic species. A high level of endemism is also evident in geologically old, continental areas with Mediterranean climates, such as southern Africa and California (Table 8.1). The biota of the entire continent of Australia has evolved in almost complete isolation, with 94% of its plant species endemic. Among the United States, it is not surprising that the geographically isolated Hawaiian islands have a large number of endemic species (Figure 8.2). Also, a landscape with rugged topography often leads to endemic species with restricted ranges. In contrast, equivalent areas that are not geographically isolated typically have much lower percentages of endemic species. For example, Panama is a small country but most (86%) of the species found there can also be found in neighboring countries. Germany and Belgium have few endemic species because virtually all of their species are found in neighboring countries. Similarly, the

TABLE 8.1 Total plant species and endemic plant species in selected regions

Region	Area (km^2)	Total number of species	Number of endemic species	% endemic species
Europe	10,000,000	10,500	±3500	33
Australia	7,628,300	15,000	14,074	94
Southern Africa	2,573,000	18,550	±14,800	80
Texas	751,000	4196	379	9
California	411,000	5046	1517	30
Germany	349,270	2600	6	<1
North and South Carolina	217,000	2995	23	1
Cape Region of South Africa	90,000	8578	5850	68
Panama	75,000	9000	1222	14
Belgium	30,230	1,400	1	<1

Source: After Gentry 1986; WRI 2000.

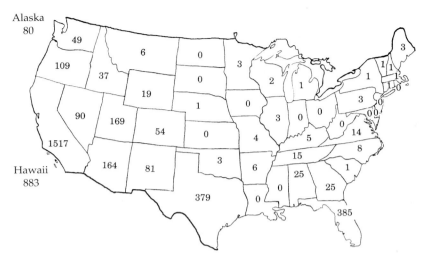

Figure 8.2 The number of plant species endemic to the different states varies greatly. For example, 379 plant species are found in Texas and nowhere else; New York, in contrast, has only one endemic plant species. California, with its large area and vast array of habitats, including deserts, mountains, seacoasts, old-growth forests, and myriad others, is home to more endemic species than any other state. There is a trend toward more endemic species in states further south. The island archipelago of Hawaii, far from the mainland, hosts many endemic species despite its small area. (From Gentry 1986.)

Carolinas in the southeastern United States share most of their species with adjoining areas. One of the most notable concentrations of endemic species is on the island of Madagascar, where the moist tropical forests are spectacularly rich in endemic species: 93% of 28 primate species, 99% of 144 species of frogs, and over 68% of the plant species on the island are found nowhere else but on Madagascar (WRI 2000). About 80% of Madagascar's land has been altered or destroyed by human activity, possibly putting almost half of the endemic species of birds and mammals in danger of extinction.

Species Most Vulnerable to Extinction

When environments are damaged by human activity, the ranges and population sizes of many species will be reduced, and some species will go extinct. Rare species must be carefully monitored and managed in conservation efforts (Box 14). Ecologists have observed that particular categories of species are most vulnerable to extinction, many of which

BOX 14 *Crisis after Crisis for the Black-Footed Ferret*

From time to time, the most dedicated and energetic efforts of conservationists are needed to prevent an endangered species from slipping away. In the case of the black-footed ferret (*Mustela nigrepes*), the species has repeatedly come to the brink of extinction. Several ferret population crises were brought about by well-intentioned but problem-plagued conservation efforts in the late 1970s and 1980s, and several near-calamitous crises resulted from the extreme sensitivity of this species to disease. Conflict between local, federal, and private agencies, all working to "save" the ferret, created a highly emotional atmosphere that made implementing a recovery plan difficult (Miller et al. 1996, 2000). Ultimately, the fact that the species still exists at all is amazing, despite the efforts of so many wildlife biologists working on the recovery plan.

Black-footed ferrets formerly existed on prairies throughout North America, from northern Mexico to southern Canada, feeding almost exclusively on prairie dogs (*Cynomys spp.*). Black-footed ferrets experienced a dramatic decline in their North American range during the first half of the twentieth century, due to agricultural development of their prairie habitat; a deliberate, government-endorsed program by ranchers to kill off the prairie dog, the ferret's main prey species; and a susceptibility to disease, particularly canine distemper. Even today the government efforts to eliminate prairie dogs conflict with programs protecting the ferret.

Biologists with the U.S. Fish and Wildlife Service attempted a captive breeding program in the mid-1970s using animals that had been captured from the only known wild population—a small colony in South Dakota (Clark 1989; Miller et al. 1996, 2000). The experiment was a failure, although it has provided valuable information about what went wrong. Four of the first six animals captured died almost immediately from vaccine-induced canine distemper, after their human handlers inoculated them. The vaccine had previously been demonstrated safe and effective in domestic ferrets, but the black-footed ferret proved high-

ly sensitive to the live-virus vaccine. More ferrets were taken from the wild and added to the captive population, but this group was apparently too closely related to form a viable gene pool and compatible breeding pairs. Tumors and diabetes, possibly related to inbreeding and old age, killed several of the captive ferrets. Only one of the captive females ever produced offspring, but none of her ten kits survived more than a few days. With the loss of both the captive population and the wild population in South Dakota by 1979, the species was thought to be completely extinct.

In the fall of 1981, however, a colony of 128 animals was located in Meeteetse, Wyoming. For four years, federal and state officials and conservation organizations argued over the best method of protecting the species, who would fund the program, who would be in control of the program, and even who would be allowed to participate! This delay proved costly to the ferrets. New census data in 1985 showed that the number of ferrets had dropped by 50% and the population was in immediate danger of extinction. A decision was made to capture some animals for breeding purposes. The first six black-footed ferrets captured in October 1985 died because two were infected in the wild with canine distemper. Tests of the wild ferrets showed that the disease was present in the colony.

At that point, biologists decided that drastic measures were required to save the ferret. All black-footed ferrets remaining in the wild were to be captured, vaccinated, quarantined, and sent to the Wyoming Game and Fish Department's captive breeding center in Sybille, Wyoming. The ferrets captured in late 1985 proved healthy, but a new obstacle to captive breeding was discovered. Only two males were initially present among the captive ferret population, both relatively young. Neither had ever mated before, and they showed no interest in the females during the first breeding season. In the summer of 1986, the Wyoming Game and Fish Department finally captured the last remaining wild ferrets, including an experienced adult male, and added them to the breeding colony.

BOX 14 *(continued)*

The lessons of past failures, supplemented by advice on breeding, diet, and housing provided by the Captive Breeding Specialist Group of the IUCN, finally paid off. Captive breeding led to a virtual population explosion among the ferrets: Between 1986 and 1991 the population jumped from 18 to 311 individuals. To prevent disease from wiping out the population, the ferrets were dispersed to several breeding centers around the country beginning in 1988 and were handled with extraordinarily strict hygienic precautions. Ferret numbers were sufficient in 1991 to permit the release of 49 animals into the wild in Wyoming, and an additional 159 were released in 1992 and 1993 in Montana, South Dakota, and Arizona. The ferrets were acclimated to the Wyoming site for ten days in cages before being allowed to enter their new habitat through a tunnel.

As of 2001, about 1200 ferrets have been released in the wild, but the success of the program remains in doubt. While some ferrets have been born in the wild, the populations are not growing at all sites. The reasons for these mixed results are not completely known, but are apparently due in part to attack by predators such as coyotes and owls. Releases of animals in South Dakota and Montana have had a higher rate of success by preconditioning the animals prior to release, which included acclimating the animals to the site in fenced enclosures with prairie dog burrows and killing coyotes in the area to reduce a potential predator. One serious problem is that prairie dogs, the ferret's main prey, are declining due to a combination of introduced disease (plague), hunting, and poisoning campaigns. Without good prairie dog populations to feed on, there is no hope of establishing viable ferret populations.

With reintroduction still an unproven technique, the captive breeding program has become even more important. Yet the number of new offspring in the program is apparently declining, possibly due to poor husbandry or failure to develop a genetically diverse breeding colony. The combination of declining species numbers and habitat destruction, combined with extreme susceptibility to disease and conflicting priorities among government departments and, private conservation groups, makes for a melancholy tale that may not have a happy ending for the black-footed ferret.

A young black-footed ferret born at the captive colony in Sybille, Wyoming. (Photograph by LuRay Parker, Wyoming Fish & Game Department.) Cages within enclosures allow ferrets to experience the range where they will eventually be released. The ferrets' caretaker is wearing a mask to reduce the chance of the ferrets' being exposed to human disease. (Photograph by LuRay Parker, Wyoming Fish & Game Department.)

are the defining characteristics of rare species (Terborgh 1974; Pimm et al. 1988; Gittleman 1994). These categories are as follows:

- *Species with a very narrow geographical range.* Some species occur at only one or a few sites in a restricted geographical range, and if that whole range is affected by human activity, the species may become extinct. Bird species on oceanic islands are good examples of species with restricted ranges that have become extinct or are in danger of extinction (Grant and Grant 1997); many fish species confined to a single lake or a single watershed have also disappeared (Figure 8.3).
- *Species with only one or a few populations.* Any one population of a species may become extinct as a result of chance factors, such as earthquakes, fire, an outbreak of disease, or human activity. Species with many populations are less vulnerable to extinction than are species with only one or a few populations. This category is linked to the previous category, because species with few populations will also tend to have a narrow geographic range.
- *Species in which population size is small,* sometimes called "the small population paradigm" (Caughley and Gunn 1996). Small populations are more likely to go locally extinct than large populations due to their greater vulnerability to demographic and environmental variation and loss of genetic variability (see Chapter 11); species that characteristically have small population sizes, such as large predators or extreme specialists, are more likely to become extinct than species that

Figure 8.3 Species of desert pupfish of the southwestern United States are highly endangered by the degradation and disappearance of their unique habitat—saline desert ponds. (Photograph by Ken Kelley, San Diego Zoo.)

typically have large populations. At the extreme are species whose numbers have declined to just a few individuals, or even only one.

Population size by itself seems to be one of the best predictors of the extinction rate of isolated populations (see Chapter 7) (Pimm et al. 1988). An excellent example is provided by the survival of bird species at the Bogor Botanical Garden in Java, a woodland and arboretum that has been isolated for 50 years (Diamond et al. 1987). At this site, only 25% of the birds that had small population sizes during the period from 1932 to 1952 survived into the 1980s, while all of the species that were initially common survived. The bird community of the Botanical Garden has also come to reflect the bird community of the surrounding disturbed countryside, indicating the significance of colonization in determining the species composition of isolated habitat fragments. These results were confirmed in studies of isolated forest fragments in Brazil: The persistence of individual forest species, after several decades of isolation, was related to the size of the forest fragment, the number of habitats found in the fragment, and the initial abundance of the species (Bierregaard et al. 1992). Larger fragments with more habitat diversity had more forest species than smaller, less diverse fragments, and species with high initial populations were far more likely to persist than species with low initial populations.

- *Species in which population size is declining,* sometimes called "the declining population paradigm." Population trends tend to continue, so a population showing signs of decline is likely to go extinct unless the cause of decline is identified and corrected (Schemske et al. 1994), as Charles Darwin pointed out more than 100 years ago in *On the Origin of Species* (1859):

> To admit that species generally become rare before they become extinct, to feel no surprise at the rarity of the species, and yet to marvel greatly when the species ceases to exist, is much the same as to admit that sickness in the individual is the forerunner of death—to feel no surprise at sickness, but when the sick man dies, to wonder and to suspect that he died of some deed of violence.

- *Species with low population density.* A species with low population density—few individuals per unit area—will tend to have only small populations remaining if its range is fragmented by human activities. Within each fragment the species may be unable to persist and will gradually die out across the landscape.
- *Species that need a large home range.* Species in which individual animals or social groups need to forage over a wide area are prone to die off when part of their range is damaged or fragmented by human activity.
- *Animal species with a large body size.* Large animals tend to have large individual ranges, require more food, and are more easily hunted by

humans. Top carnivores, especially, are often killed by humans because they compete with humans for wild game, sometimes damage livestock, and are hunted for sport. Within groups of species, often the largest species will be the most prone to extinction—that is, the largest carnivore, the largest lemur, the largest whale. In Sri Lanka, for example, the largest species of carnivores—leopards and eagles—and the largest species of herbivores—elephants and deer—are currently at the greatest risk of extinction (Erdelen 1988). Countering this effect, to some degree, is the tendency for these large species to live longer than smaller species. Also, in Neotropical forest mammals, large body size tends to be correlated with a wider geographic distribution and less vulnerability to habitat destruction in one place (Arita et al. 1990).

- *Species that are not effective dispersers.* Environmental changes prompt species to adapt, either behaviorally or physiologically, to the new conditions of their habitat. Species unable to adapt to changing environments must either migrate to more suitable habitat or face extinction. The rapid pace of human-induced changes often prevents adaptation, leaving migration as the only alternative. Species that are unable to cross roads, farmlands, and disturbed habitats are doomed to extinction as their original habitat becomes affected by pollution, exotic species, and global climate change. In particular, many animal species in isolated forest fragments are unwilling or unable to cross pastures and colonize unoccupied areas of forest. Dispersal is important in the aquatic environment as well, where dams, point sources of pollution, channelization, and sedimentation can limit movement. Limited ability to disperse, as well as more specialized habitat requirements, may explain why in the United States 68% of the freshwater fauna of mussels and snails are extinct or threatened with extinction in contrast to some 40% of freshwater fish species (which have the ability to swim actively) and around 20% of dragonfly species (which can fly between the aquatic sites needed by their larval stages) (Stein and Flack 1997).

  The importance of dispersal in preventing extinction is illustrated by two studies from Australia. The first, a detailed analysis of the vertebrates of Western Australia, revealed that modern extinctions were almost exclusively confined to nonflying mammals, with few extinctions recorded in birds and bats (Burbidge and McKenzie 1989). Among the birds, species that are unable to fly or are poor fliers showed the greatest tendency for extinction. In the second study, which examined 16 nonflying mammal species in Queensland rain forests, the most important characteristic determining the ability of species to survive in isolated forest fragments was their ability to use, feed on, and move through the intervening matrix of secondary vegetation (Laurance 1991). While large-bodied, long-lived, low-fecundity species initially appeared to be more vulnerable to extinction, this effect disappeared when the abundance of individual species in secondary vegetation was included in the analysis. This study highlights the importance of maintaining secondary vegetation to the survival of primary forest species.

- *Seasonal migrants.* Species that migrate seasonally depend on two or more distinct habitat types. If either one of these habitat types is damaged, the species may be unable to persist. The billion songbirds of 120 species that migrate each year between the northern United States and the American tropics depend on suitable habitat in both locations to survive and breed (see Figure 7.1). Also, if barriers to dispersal are created by roads, fences, or dams between the needed habitats, a species may be unable to complete its life cycle. Salmon species that are blocked by dams from swimming up rivers and spawning are a striking example of this problem. Many animal species migrate among habitats in search of food, often along elevational and moisture gradients. Herds of wild pigs, grazing ungulates, frugivorous vertebrates, and insectivorous birds are all examples of these. If these species are unable to migrate and thus are confined to one habitat type, they may not survive, or, if they do survive, they may be unable to accumulate the nutritional reserves needed to reproduce. Species that cross international barriers represent a special problem, in that conservation efforts have to be coordinated by more than one country. Imagine the difficulties of the tiny flock of Siberian cranes (*Grus leucogeranus*) that must migrate 4800 km each year from Russia to India and back, crossing six highly militarized, tense international borders.
- *Species with little genetic variability.* Genetic variability within a population can sometimes allow a species to adapt to a changing environment (see Chapters 2 and 11). Species with little or no genetic variability may have a greater tendency to become extinct when a new disease, a new predator, or some other change occurs in the environment. However, there are still limited examples from natural populations to support this hypothesis. Investigating the relationships among genetic variability, population persistence, and extinction is a crucial area for conservation biology in the future.
- *Species with specialized niche requirements.* Once a habitat is altered, the environment may no longer be suitable for specialized species. For example, wetland plants that require very specific and regular changes in water level may be rapidly eliminated when human activity affects the hydrology of an area. Soil arthropods and herbaceous plants may be eliminated when introduced livestock intensively graze native grasslands and, in the process, alter competitive relationships, change nutrient dynamics, and compact the soil. Species with highly specific dietary requirements are also at risk—for instance, there are species of mites that feed only on the feathers of a single bird species. If the bird species goes extinct, so do its associated feather mite species.

- Some species are confined to a single unusual habitat type that is scattered and rare across the landscape. Species are found, for example, in vernal pools in California, granite outcrops in the southeastern United States, and isolated high mountains in the northeastern United States, illustrating the importance of habitat preservation in the conservation of species with a narrow range.

- *Species that are characteristically found in stable, pristine environments.* Many species are found in environments where disturbance is minimal, such as in old stands of tropical rain forests and the interiors of rich temperate deciduous forests. When these forests are logged, grazed, burned, and otherwise altered, many native species are unable to tolerate the changed microclimatic conditions (more light, less moisture, greater temperature variation) and influx of exotic species. Also, species of stable environments tend to delay reproduction to an advanced age and produce only a few young. Following one or more episodes of habitat disturbance, such species are often unable to rebuild their populations fast enough to avoid extinction. When the environment is altered by air and water pollution, species unable to adapt to the destabilized physical and chemical environment will be eliminated from the community (Box 15). Coral reef species and freshwater invertebrates, such as crayfish, mussels, and snails, often cannot survive when their environments receive large inputs of sediment and sewage from human activities.

- *Species that form permanent or temporary aggregations.* Species that group together in specific places are highly vulnerable to local extinction (Reed 1999). For example, bats forage widely, but typically roost together in particular caves. Hunters entering these caves during the day can rapidly harvest every individual in the population. Herds of bison, flocks of passenger pigeons, and schools of spawning fish all represent aggregations that have been exploited and completely harvested by people. Temporary aggregations include schools of salmon and alewife moving up rivers to spawn; nets across rivers can catch virtually every fish and eliminate a species in a few days. Overly efficient harvesting of wild fruits from a cluster of neighboring trees for commercial markets can eliminate the seedlings that will grow into the next generation. Even though sea turtles may swim across vast stretches of ocean, egg collectors and hunters on a few narrow nesting beaches can threaten a species with extinction, as shown in Box 1. Many species of social animals may be unable to persist when their population size falls below a certain number; they may be unable to forage, mate, or defend themselves. Such species may be more vulnerable to habitat destruction than asocial species in which individuals are widely dispersed.

- *Species that have evolved in isolation and have not had prior contact with people.* As we discussed in relation to islands in Chapter 7, species that

BOX 15 *Why Are Frogs and Toads Croaking?*

At the First World Congress on Herpetology in 1989 in Canterbury, England, what had previously seemed like casual findings began to take on a disturbing significance: Scientists from around the world were seeing a decline in amphibian populations (Phillips 1990). A workshop to address this possibility, hastily put together in 1990, confirmed that evidence existed of widespread population crashes among numerous amphibian species. Species that had been common less than two decades ago were becoming rare, some to the point of near extinction. Although many scientists had only anecdotal evidence for the population crisis and explanations for the phenomenon were speculative, reports from the United States, Central America, the Amazon Basin, the Andes, Europe, and Australia repeated similar themes: Habitat destruction and pollution were contributing to the rapid declines of many species.

Amphibians may be particularly vulnerable to human disturbance because many species require two separate habitats, aquatic and terrestrial, to complete their life cycles. If either habitat is damaged, the species will not be able to reproduce. Amphibians, like many other taxa, are also sensitive to a number of global environmental problems, including climate changes, increased ultraviolet radiation, habitat fragmentation, chemical pollution, and acid rain (see Chapter 9). The latter two factors may be particularly dangerous to these animals: Chemical pollution can easily penetrate the thin epidermis characteristic of amphibians, while slight decreases in pH can destroy eggs and tadpoles.

Subsequent studies attempted to pinpoint a cause for the apparent global decline. The main explanation continues to be loss of habitat, particularly wetlands. For instance, the number of farm ponds, a favorite habitat for amphibians in Britain, has declined by 70% over the last 100 years. Research on the natterjack toad (*Bufo calamita*) in England, one of the most intensively studied amphibians, also supported the acidification hypothesis. Ponds that had formerly supported significant populations of the species had become gradually more acidic, a change that greatly increases the mortality of eggs and young toads (Beebee 1996). An increase in heavy metals and soot particles was associated with the acidification, indicating that the process was most likely related to industrial activities.

However, species in relatively undisturbed, protected areas elsewhere in the world have also exhibited declines. Introduced predatory fish, drought, epidemic disease, unusual climatic events, and increased ultraviolet radiation due to a decrease in the protective ozone layer were subsequently blamed for the decline of individual species (Blaustein and Wake 1995; Drost and Fellers 1996; Laurance et al. 1996; Davidson et al. 2001; Marsh 2001).

Despite an abundance of recent studies, scientists are still not sure whether amphibian species are declining on a global scale due to global causes or if they are declining on a local scale due to numerous separate causes (Alford et al. 2001). It is also true that what

Studies of the natterjack toad (*Bufo calamita*) and its habitat in England pointed to pollution and acidification of pondwater as a cause for the decline in numbers of this species. (Photograph by Richard Griffiths.)

BOX 15 *(continued)*

may appear to be a drastic decline in one population over the course of a few years may actually be a normal response to environmental variability. Because so little is known about amphibian population dynamics, it is difficult for short-term studies to distinguish between an ominous decline and a natural fluctuation in numbers. Furthermore, many species occur in remote areas, which are not easily studied. What is needed is a well-organized, long-term monitoring program to determine the status of amphibians (Young et al. 2001).

Much of the initial hubbub over amphibian declines occurred because amphibians are commonly perceived as being highly sensitive to environmental disturbance and could thus serve as an "indicator species" and give early warning of environmental damage. Few hard data exist to support this perception, however.

Although amphibian populations certainly have been affected in many areas by habitat degradation and destruction, it is unclear whether or not they have been affected disproportionately. Surveys suggest that around 5% of the world's amphibians are threatened with extinction; while this figure is cause for concern, it is comparable to the threat faced by reptiles (5%), and it is lower than the threats faced by birds (12%) and mammals (25%) (IUCN 1996). While this is certainly cause for grave concern, premature warnings about an amphibian crisis run the risk of drawing attention and resources away from other species that are at greater risk (Pechmann et al. 1994), such as primates and freshwater mussels. The drama over possible amphibian population declines highlights one of the dilemmas of conservation biology: balancing the need to act with the need to know more.

have experienced prior human disturbance and persisted have a greater chance of surviving than species encountering people, along with their associated animals and plants, for the first time (see Figure 7.6) (Balmford 1996). The rate of recent bird extinction is far lower on Pacific islands colonized in the past by Polynesians than on islands not colonized by Polynesians (Pimm et al. 1995). Similarly, Western Australia, which has only recently experienced intense human impact, has a modern extinction rate for plant species 10 times higher than the Mediterranean region, which has a long history of heavy human impact (Greuter 1995).

- *Species that are hunted or harvested by people.* Overharvesting can rapidly reduce the population size of a species (see Chapter 10). If hunting and harvesting are not regulated, either by law or by local customs, the species can be driven to extinction. Utility has often been the prelude to extinction.
- *Species that have closely related species that are recently extinct or are threatened with extinction.* Often groups of species are particularly vulnerable to extinction, such as primates, cranes, sea turtles, and cycads.

Characteristics of extinction-prone species are not independent; rather they group together into categories of characteristics. For example, species with a specialized diet tend also to have low population densities—both characteristics of extinction-prone species. The characteristics often vary among groups because of peculiarities of natural history: Butterflies differ from jellyfish and cacti in characters associated with vulnerability to extinction. By identifying characteristics of extinction-prone species, conservation biologists can anticipate the need for managing populations of vulnerable species. Those species most vulnerable to extinction may have the full range of characteristics, as David Ehrenfeld (1970) imagined:

> [A] large predator with a narrow habitat tolerance, long gestation period, and few young per litter [is] hunted for a natural product and/or for sport, but is not subject to efficient game management. It has a restricted distribution but travels across international boundaries. It is intolerant of man, reproduces in aggregates, and has nonadaptive behavioral idiosyncrasies.

There is another great need for identifying characteristics of threatened species: The greatest proportion of threatened species that have been identified so far are also in the most well-studied families, highlighting the point that only when we are knowledgeable about a species can we recognize the dangers it faces (Duncan and Lockwood 2001).

Conservation Categories

Identifying those species most vulnerable to extinction is essential to the work of conservation. To mark the status of rare and endangered species for conservation purposes, the International Union for the Conservation of Nature (IUCN) and the World Conservation Monitoring Centre (WCMC) have established 10 conservation categories (IUCN 1996; Colyvan et al. 1999); species in categories 3, 4, and 5 (critically endangered, endangered, and vulnerable) are considered to be threatened with extinction. These categories have proved to be useful at the national and international levels by directing attention toward species of special concern and identifying species threatened with extinction for protection through international agreements, such as the Convention on International Trade in Endangered Species (CITES), and through published Red Data Books and Red Lists of threatened species (Figure 8. 4).

1. *Extinct.* A species (or other taxa, such as subspecies or varieties) that is no longer known to exist.
2. *Extinct in the wild.* The species exists only in cultivation, in captivity, or as a naturalized population well outside its original range.
3. *Critically endangered.* Species that have an extremely high risk of going extinct in the wild in the immediate future.
4. *Endangered.* Species that have a high risk of extinction in the wild in the near future and may become critically endangered.
5. *Vulnerable.* Species that have a high risk of extinction in the wild in the medium-term future and may become endangered.

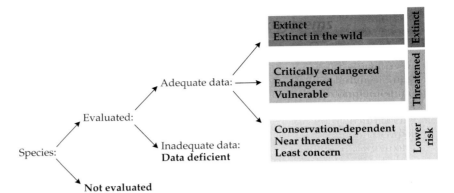

Figure 8.4 The IUCN categories of conservation status. This chart shows the distribution of the categories. Reading from left to right, they depend on 1) whether a species has been evaluated or not and 2) how much data is available for the species. If data are available, the species is then put into a category in either the lower risk, threatened, or extinct areas. (After Hilton-Taylor 2000.)

6. *Conservation-dependent*. The species is not currently threatened but is dependent on a conservation program, without which the species would be threatened with extinction.
7. *Near threatened*. The species is close to qualifying as vulnerable, but is not currently considered threatened.
8. *Least concern*. The species is not considered near threatened or threatened.
9. *Data deficient*. Inadequate information exists to determine the risk of extinction for the species.
10. *Not evaluated*. The species has not yet been assessed for its threat category.

These categories have proved problematic, though. Given the legal restrictions that accompany these assignments—and the resultant financial implications to landowners, corporations, and governments—the definitions of these categories needed clarification to prevent arguments over meaning. To correct this situation, the IUCN has issued refined, more quantitative definitions in a three-level system of classification based on the probability of extinction (IUCN 1996; Hilton-Taylor 2000; Gärdenfors 2001):

1. *Critically endangered species* have a 50% or greater probability of extinction within 10 years or 3 generations, whichever is longer.
2. *Endangered species* have a 20% or greater probability of extinction within 20 years or 5 generations.
3. *Vulnerable species* have a 10% or greater probability of extinction within 100 years.

Assignment of categories depends on having at least one of the following types of information:

1. Observable decline in numbers of individuals.
2. The geographical area occupied by the species, and the number of populations.
3. The total number of individuals alive, and the number of breeding individuals.
4. The expected decline in the numbers of individuals if current and projected trends in population decline or habitat destruction continue.
5. The probability of the species going extinct in a certain number of years or generations.

This new system eliminates the most serious problem of the old system—its subjective criteria. With greater numbers of people and organizations involved in assigning and evaluating threat categories, there was the potential for species to be arbitrarily assigned to particular categories. The new criteria for assigning categories are based on the developing methods of population viability analysis (see Chapter 12) and focus particularly on population trends and habitat condition. For example, a critically endangered species has at least one of the following characteristics: total population size less than 250 mature, breeding individuals and is expected to decline by 25% or more within 3 years or 1 generation; population size is less than 50 mature individuals; population has declined by 80% or more over the last 10 years or 3 generations, or is expected to decline that much; or the overall extinction probability is greater than 50% in 10 years or 3 generations. Species can also be assigned critical status as a result of restricted range of the species (less than 100 km^2 at a single location), observed or predicted habitat loss, ecological imbalance, or commercial exploitation (Figure 8.5). Using habitat loss in assigning categories is particularly useful for many species that are poorly known biologically, since species can be listed as threatened if their habitat is being destroyed. In practice, species are most commonly assigned to an IUCN category based on the area it occupies and the number of mature individuals it has; the probability of extinction is least commonly used (Gärdenfors et al. 2001).

The advantage of the revised system is that it provides a standard, quantitative method of classification by which decisions can be reviewed and evaluated by other scientists, according to accepted quantitative criteria and using whatever information is available. However, this method can devolve into arbitrary assignment if decisions have to be made with insufficient data. Gathering the data needed for proper assignment is expensive and time-consuming, particularly for developing countries and in rapidly changing situations. Regardless of this limitation, the new system of species classification is a distinct improvement and will assist attempts to protect species.

Figure 8.5 Yellow gentian (*Gentiana lutea*), a beautiful perennial herb of European mountain meadows, has roots that are collected for traditional medicine. Approximately 1500 tons of dried roots are used each year in a wide variety of preparations to stimulate digestion and to treat stomachache. Due to overharvesting and the resulting decline and destruction of many populations, the species is listed as endangered in Portugal, Albania, and certain regions of Germany and Switzerland, and as vulnerable in other countries, according to the IUCN's classification categories. Despite official regulation that restricts collection to designated areas, illegal harvesting continues. (Photograph by Bob Gibbons, Natural Image.)

TABLE 8.2 Percentage of species in some temperate countries that are threatened[a] with global extinction

Country	Mammals		Birds	
	Number of species	% threatened	Number of species	% threatened
Argentina	320	8.4	897	4.6
Canada	193	3.6	426	1.2
China	394	19.0	1100	8.2
Japan	132	22.0	>250	13.2
Russia	269	11.5	628	6.1
South Africa	247	13.4	596	2.7
United Kingdom	50	8.0	230	0.9
United States	428	8.2	650	7.7

Source: Data from WRI 1998.

[a]Threatened species include those in the IUCN categories "critically endangered," "endangered," and "vulnerable."

Using the new categories, the IUCN has evaluated and described the threats to about 7000 plant and 9500 animal species in its series of Red Data Books and Red Lists (IUCN 1990, 1996; Hilton-Taylor 2000). For animals, 3157 species are listed as threatened and 726 species are listed as critically endangered; for plants, 5531 species are listed as threatened and 992 species are listed as critically endangered. Included are numerous species of fish (700), amphibians (230), reptiles (450), mollusks (1800), insects (750), crustaceans (459), birds (2100), and mammals (2100). All bird species and most mammal species have been evaluated using the IUCN system because they are well known, but the levels of evaluation are lower for reptiles, amphibians, and fish (Vincent and Hall 1996). The evaluations of insects and other invertebrates, mosses, algae, fungi, and microorganisms are even less adequate.

The IUCN system has been applied to specific geographical areas and groups of species as a way of highlighting conservation priorities. As a group, mammals face a greater degree of threat than birds; comparing regions, in general, the species of Japan are more threatened than the species of South Africa, which are more threatened, in turn, than the species of the United Kingdom (Table 8.2). Applying IUCN categories to Malaysia, for instance, provides an example (Kiew 1991):

- A large number of Malaysian herb species are endemic to single localities, such as mountaintops, streams, waterfalls, or limestone outcrops. These species are threatened with extinction if their habitat is destroyed.

Reptiles		Amphibians		Plants	
Number of species	% threatened	Number of species	% threatened	Number of species	% threatened
220	2.3	145	3.4	9000	1.9
41	7.3	41	2.4	2920	22.2
340	4.4	263	0.4	30,000	1.1
66	12.1	52	19.2	4700	15.0
58	8.6	23	0.0	—	—
299	6.4	95	9.5	23,000	4.1
8	0.0	7	0.0	1550	1.8
280	10.0	233	10.3	16,302	11.3

- All five species of sea turtles in Malaysia are considered threatened due to a combination of habitat loss, egg collecting, hunting, pollution of marine waters, unregulated tourism, and entanglement in fishing nets.
- More than 80% of Malaysian Borneo's primate species are under some threat due to a combination of habitat destruction and hunting pressure.

To help focus attention on the threatened species most in need of immediate conservation efforts, the IUCN has begun to issue lists of the world's most threatened plants and animals. These lists include species of unique conservation value. Among the animals on the most-threatened list are the kagu (*Rhynochetos jubatus*), a rare flightless bird that is the symbol of New Caledonia; the kouprey (*Bos sauveli*), a primitive wild ox from Southeast Asia that has been hunted to near extinction; and the Orinoco River crocodile (*Crocodylus intermedius*), which has been decimated by illegal trade in hides. The plant list includes the giant *Rafflesia* of Sumatran rain forests, which produces a flower about 1 m across, and the African violet (*Saintpaulia ionantha*), the most common houseplant in the world, but only known in the wild from a few plants in fragments of mountain forest in central Tanzania.

In Switzerland, efforts are being made to identify those threatened (or Red List) species that are responding to conservation efforts (Gigon et al. 2000). The 317 species included in this "Blue List" have stable populations or are increasing in abundance. The method identifies species for which nature conservation and environmental protection techniques are known but have not been fully applied. The Blue List approach highlights successful conservation efforts and suggests further projects that might succeed (Figure 8.6).

Natural Heritage Data Centers

A program similar to the efforts of the IUCN and WCMC is the network of Natural Heritage Data Centers that covers all 50 of the United States, 3 provinces in Canada, and 14 Latin American countries (Jenkins 1996). This program, strongly supported by The Nature Conservancy, gathers, organizes, and manages information on the occurrence of more than 35,000 species and 7000 subspecies, as well as biological communities, referred to as elements of conservation interest. Elements are given status ranks based on a series of standard criteria: number of remaining populations or occurrences, number of individuals remaining (for species) or aerial extent (for communities), number of protected sites, degree of threat, and innate vulnerability of the species or community. On the basis of these criteria, elements are assigned an imperilment rank from 1 to 5, from critically imperiled to demonstrably secure, on a global, national, and regional basis. Species are also classified as "X" (extinct), "H" (known historically with searches ongoing), and "unknown" (uninvestigated elements).

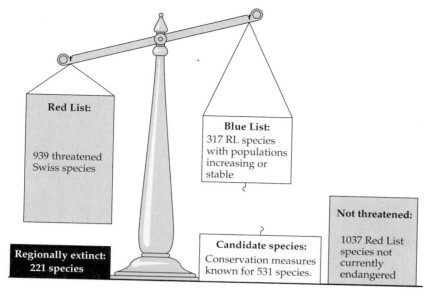

Figure 8.6 An innovative approach is being developed in three Swiss cantons to evaluate the current status of the species of plants and animals (filled boxes) that are currently on the Red List of threatened and extinct species. Of these, 317 species have been identified as stable or increasing in abundance, thanks to conservation and protection measures; these species form a "Blue List" of recovering species that have been removed from the Red List. Protection and conservation techniques are locally successful or known for 531 species: These species are future candidates for the Blue List. There are 1037 species on the Red List not currently listed as endangered, but in some cases abundances are declining, data are inadequate, or species are not responding to current conservation measures. The goal is to shift the balance as the Blue List lengthens. (After Gigon et al. 2002.)

    The Natural Heritage Data Centers and The Nature Conservancy approach has been applied in detail to the species of the United States. The results, given by Stein and Flack in *Species Report Card: The State of U.S. Plants and Animals* (1997) and supported by *Precious Heritage* by Stein et al. (2000), demonstrate that aquatic species groups, including freshwater mussels, crayfish, amphibians, and fish, are in greater danger of extinction than well-known groups of insects and vertebrates (Figure 8.7). Freshwater mussels are by far the most endangered species group, with 11.8% of these species presumed to be extinct already and almost 25% critically imperiled. Land plants are intermediate in degree of endangerment.

    This system has also been applied to the 4500 distinct ecological communities recognized in the United States. Only 25% of these can be considered as secure, with 26% listed as vulnerable, 31% as imperiled or severely imperiled, less than 1% as presumably eliminated, and 18% as not possible to evaluate (Stein et al. 2000). Concentration of endangered com-

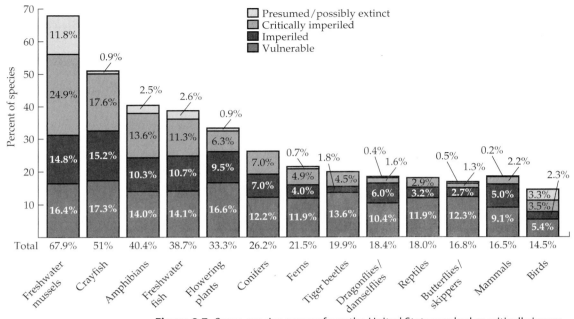

Figure 8.7 Some species groups from the United States ranked as critically imperiled, imperiled, or vulnerable (rankings 1–3, respectively, on a scale of 5) according to criteria endorsed by the Nature Conservancy. The graph also shows the percentage of species in each class that are presumed to be extinct. The groups are arranged with those at greatest risk on the left. (From Stein and Flack 1997.)

munities occur in Hawaii, the Willamette Valley of Oregon, and large areas of the Midwest and Southeast.

This system has proved extremely successful and useful in organizing between 300,000–400,000 records of species and ecosystems occurrence. Regional data centers are maintained by hundreds of workers and are consulted approximately 200,000 times a year for information to assist protection efforts on behalf of endangered species, environmental impact reports, scientific research, and land-use decisions. Organizing vast amounts of conservation information is an expensive, labor-intensive activity, but it is a crucial component of conservation efforts. It is imperative to know what species and biological communities are in danger and where they occur in order to protect them.

Summary

1. Rare species are more prone to extinction than common ones. A species can be considered rare if it has one of these three characteristics: it occupies a narrow geographical range, it occupies only one or a few specialized habi-

tats, or it is always found in small populations. Isolated habitats such as islands, lakes, and mountaintops often have many locally endemic species with narrow distributions.

2. Species most vulnerable to extinction have particular characteristics, including very narrow range, one or only a few populations, small population size, declining population size, and an economic value to humans, which leads to overexploitation. Additional characteristics include: low population density, a large home range, large body size, low rate of population increase, poor dispersal ability, migration among different habitats, little genetic variability, specialized niche requirements, a need for a stable environment, or typically found in large aggregations. An extinction-prone species may display several of these characteristics.

3. To highlight the status of species for conservation purposes, the IUCN has established 10 conservation categories, including three categories of threat: critically endangered, endangered, and vulnerable. This system of classification is now widely used to evaluate the status of species and establish conservation priorities. Designation of conservation categories depends on having quantitative information for species, such as number of individuals alive in the wild, number of extant populations, trends in population size, area occupied, and predicted future threats to the species.

For Discussion

1. Learn about a well-known endangered species, such as the bald eagle, the koala bear, the right whale, or the cheetah. Why are these particular species vulnerable to extinction? Use the IUCN criteria to determine the appropriate conservation category for one or more species.

2. Develop an imaginary animal, recently discovered, that is extraordinarily vulnerable to extinction. Give your species a whole range of characteristics that make it vulnerable; then, consider what could be done to protect it. Give your species a hypothetical set of population characteristics, natural history, and geographic range. Then apply the recently developed IUCN system to the species to determine its conservation category.

Suggested Readings

Balmford, A. 1996. Extinction filters and current resilience: The significance of past selection pressures for conservation biology. *Trends in Ecology and Evolution* 11: 193–196. Current extinction rates are highest for groups of species encountering people for the first time.

Cincotta R. P. and R. Engelman. 2000. *Nature's Place: Human Population and the Future of Biological Diversity.* Population Action International, Washington, D.C. Human populations are the major force causing the decline in biodiversity.

Gärdenfors, U., C. Hilton-Taylor, G. M. Mace, and J. P. Rodríguez. 2001. Classifying threatened species at national versus global levels. *Trends in Ecology and Evolution* 16(9): 511–516. IUCN Red Lists are being used at national levels to protect species.

Grant, P. R. and B. R. Grant. 1997. The rarest of Darwin's finches. *Conservation Biology* 11: 119–126. The mangrove finch has only a few small populations in a specialized habitat and now faces threats from human activity.

IUCN. 1996. *1996 IUCN Red List of Threatened Animals.* IUCN, Gland, Switzerland. Evaluation of 5205 animal species using new quantitative criteria, plus a wealth of other information.

IUCN. 2000. *Species: Newsletter of the Species Survival Commission.* IUCN, Gland, Switzerland. Concise descriptions of the activities of professional conservation biologists to protect species, organized by specialist groups.

Miller, B., R. P. Reading, and S. Forrest. 1996. *Prairie Night: Black-Footed Ferrets and the Recovery of Endangered Species.* Smithsonian Institution Press, Washington, D.C. An insider's look at an intensive recovery effort.

Rabinowitz, D., S. Cairnes, and T. Dillon. 1986. Seven forms of rarity and their frequency in the flora of the British Isles. In *Conservation Biology: The Science of Scarcity and Diversity,* M. E. Soulé (ed.), pp. 182–204. Sinauer Associates, Sunderland, MA. An influential paper describing patterns of rarity and their significance to conservation.

Reed, J. M. 1999. The role of behavior in recent avian extinctions and endangerments. *Conservation Biology* 13(2): 232–241. Certain bird behaviors make species vulnerable to extinction.

Stein, B. A. and S. R. Flack. 1997. *Species Report Card: The State of U.S. Plants and Animals.* The Nature Conservancy, Arlington, VA. The Nature Conservancy approach applied to the relatively well-known U.S. biota.

Stein, B. A., L. S. Kutner, and J. S. Adams (eds.). 2000. *Precious Heritage: The Status of Biodiversity in the United States.* Oxford University Press, New York. Analysis of the distribution of biodiversity in the United States and current threats.

Terborgh, J. 1974. Preservation of natural diversity: The problem of extinction-prone species. *BioScience* 24: 715–722. Why certain species are more vulnerable than others to extinction.

Vincent, A. C. J. and H. J. Hall. 1996. The threatened status of marine fishes. *Trends in Ecology and Evolution* 11: 360–361. Brief overview highlighting the lack of information on the status of most marine fishes.

Chapter

Habitat Destruction, Fragmentation, Degradation, and Global Climate Change

A s we've seen in Chapters 7 and 8, *Homo sapiens* poses perhaps the greatest threat of extinction to species and entire biological communities. Massive disturbances caused by people have altered, degraded, and destroyed the natural landscape on a vast scale, driving species and even communities to the point of extinction. The major threats to biological diversity that result from human activity are habitat destruction, habitat fragmentation, habitat degradation (including pollution), global climate change, the overexploitation of species for human use, the introduction of invasive species, and the increased spread of disease. In this chapter we will examine the threats we pose to the environment; in Chapter 10 we will discuss overexploitation, invasive species, and disease. Most threatened species face at least two or more of these threats, thus speeding their way to extinction and hindering efforts to protect them (Wilcove et al. 1998; Terborgh 1999; Stearns and Stearns 1999). Typically, these threats develop so rapidly and on such a large scale that species are not able to adapt genetically to the changes or disperse to a more hospitable location. Moreover, multiple threats may interact additively or even synergistically, such that their combined impact on a species is greater than their individual effects (Laurance and Cochrane 2001).

The Problem of Human Population Growth

These seven threats to biological diversity are all caused by an ever-increasing use of the world's natural resources by an expanding human population (Table 9.1). Only 15% of the land area in Europe remains unmodified by human activities. Up until the last few hundred years, the rate of human population growth had been relatively slow, with the birth rate only slightly exceeding the mortality rate. The greatest destruction of biological communities has occurred over the last 150 years, during which time the human population exploded from 1 billion in 1850 to 6 billion on October 12, 1998 (Figure 9.1). World population is 6.2 billion as of early 2002 and will reach an estimated 10 billion by the year 2050. Humans have increased in such numbers because birth rates have remained high while mortality rates have declined—a result of both modern medical achievements (specifically the control of disease) and the presence of more reliable food supplies. Population growth has slowed in the industrialized countries of the world, but it is still high in many areas of tropical Africa, Latin America, and Asia, where the greatest biological diversity is also found. If these countries implement effective programs of population control, human populations numbers could possibly peak at "only" eight billion in 2050 and then gradually decline.

People use natural resources, such as fuelwood, wild meat, and wild plants, and convert vast amounts of natural habitat for agricultural and residential purposes. Because some degree of resource use is inevitable, population growth is partially responsible for the loss of biological diversity (Krebs et al. 1999; Ayres 1999; Cincotta and Engelman 2000). All

---

TABLE 9.1 Three ways in which humans dominate the global ecosystem

1. LAND SURFACE
Human land use and need for resources have transformed as much as half of the Earth's ice-free land surface.

2. NITROGEN CYCLE
Each year human activities, such as cultivating nitrogen-fixing crops, using nitrogen fertilizers, and burning fossil fuels, release more nitrogen into terrestrial systems than is added by natural biological and physical processes.

3. ATMOSPHERIC CARBON CYCLE
By the middle of this century, human use of fossil fuels will have resulted in a doubling of the level of carbon dioxide in the Earth's atmosphere.

Source: Data from Vitousek 1994; Vitousek 1997.

else being equal, more people equals greater human impact and less bio-diversity. Nitrogen pollution is greatest in rivers with the highest human population densities, and the rates of deforestation are greatest in countries with the highest rates of human population growth. Therefore, some scientists have argued strongly that controlling the size of the human population is the key to protecting biological diversity (Hardin 1993; Myers 1998). However, population growth is not the only cause of species extinction and habitat destruction: overconsumption of resources is also responsible. Species extinctions and the destruction of ecosystems are not necessarily caused by individual citizens obtaining their basic needs. The rise of industrial capitalism and materialistic modern societies has greatly accelerated demands for natural resources, particularly in the developed countries. Inefficient and wasteful use and overconsumption of natural resources are major causes of the decline in biological diversity.

In many developing countries, local farm owners are often forced off their land by large landowners, business interests, and even the government, which is often backed up by the police and army. These local farmers often have no choice but to move to remote, undeveloped areas and attempt to eke out a living through shifting cultivation, destroying natural habitats, and hunting animals to extinction. Political instability, lawlessness, and war also force farmers off their land and into remote, undeveloped areas where they feel safer (Homer-Dixon et al. 1993).

Whether motivated by greed or indifference, once a community or nation begins exploiting resources for short-term gain, it is difficult to stop. Biological communities can often persist close to areas with high densities of people as long as human activities are regulated by local custom or government. The sacred groves that are preserved next to villages in Africa, India, and China are excellent examples of locally managed biological communities. Sometimes this regulation breaks down during war, political unrest, and social instability. When this happens, there may be a scramble to use up and sell resources that had been sustainably used for generations. The higher the density of people, the more closely their activities must be regulated, and the greater the destruction that can result from a breakdown in authority. The devastation that occurred in China's forests during the Cultural Revolution is a revealing example: Strict regulations against cutting trees were no longer enforced, so farmers cut down trees at a tremendous rate, stockpiling wood for fuel, construction, and furniture-making (Primack 1988).

People in industrialized countries (and the wealthy minority in the developing countries) consume a disproportionate share of the world's

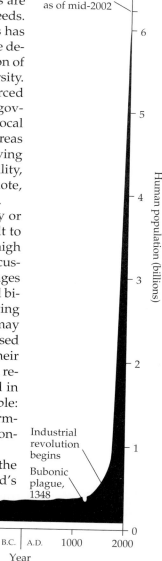

Figure 9.1 Human population has increased spectacularly since the seventeenth century. At current growth rates, the population will double in less than 40 years.

Figure 9.2 Citizens of the wealthy, developed countries of the world often criticize the poorer, developing nations for a lack of sound environmental policies but seem unwilling to acknowledge that their own excessive consumption of resources is a major part of the problem. (Cartoon by Scott Willis, © San Jose Mercury News.)

energy, minerals, wood products, and food (Myers 1997), and therefore have a disproportionate impact on the environment (Figure 9.2). Each year, the United States, with 5% of the world's population, uses roughly 30% of the world's natural resources. Each year the average U.S. citizen uses 17 times more energy and 79 times more paper products than the average citizen of India (WRI 2000).

The impact (I) of any human population on the environment is captured by the formula: $I = PAT$, where P is the number of people, A is the average income, and T is the level of technology (Rees 2001). It is important to recognize that this impact is often felt over a great distance; for example, a citizen of Germany, Canada, or Japan affects the environment in other countries through his/her use of foods and other materials produced elsewhere: The fish eaten quietly at home perhaps came from Alaskan waters where its capture contributed to the population decline of sea lions, seals, and sea otters; the chocolate cake and coffee consumed at the end of a meal in Italy or France accelerated the destruction of rain forest in Colombia. This linkage has been captured in the idea of the **ecological footprint**, defined as the influence a group of people has on both the surrounding environment and locations across the globe

TABLE 9.2 A comparison of ecological footprints for selected countries

Country	Population (millions)	Footprint (ha/person)[a]	Biocapacity (ha/person)[b]	Ecological deficit (if negative)[c]
India	950	1.1	0.7	−0.4
Indonesia	200	1.5	3.2	1.7
Brazil	161	2.5	11.5	9.0
China	1232	3.4	2.0	−1.4
Russia	148	5.3	4.0	−1.3
Japan	126	5.9	0.9	−5.0
Germany	82	6.2	2.4	−3.8
United Kingdom	58	6.2	1.8	−4.4
Canada	30	7.7	11.2	3.5
Australia	18	8.5	9.3	0.8
United States	269	12.2	5.5	−6.7
World[d]	5745	2.9	2.2	−0.7

Source: Redefining Progress, 2001.

[a]The ecological footprint is the number of hectares of land required to support the lifestyle of one person.

[b]Biocapacity is the number of hectares per person in a country.

[c]Countries with an ecological deficit (negative values) are using more natural resources than they have, resulting in environmental degradation within their own country and/or a need to obtain natural resources from other countries.

[d]The total ecological footprint of the world's human population.

(Rees 2001). A modern city in a developed country typically has an ecological footprint of between 290–1130 times its area (Table 9.2). For example, the city of Toronto, Canada, occupies an area of only 630 km², but each of its citizens requires the environmental services of 7.7 ha (0.077 km²) to provide food, water and waste disposal sites; with a population of 2.4 million people, Toronto has an ecological footprint of 185,000 km², an area equal to the state of New Jersey or the country of Syria. This excessive consumption of resources is not sustainable in the long term. If this pattern is adopted by the expanding middle class in the developing world, it will cause massive environmental disruption. The affluent citizens of developed countries must confront their excessive consumption of resources and reevaluate their lifestyles while at the same time offering aid to curb population growth and protect biological diversity in the developing world.

Habitat Destruction

The primary cause of the loss of organic diversity is not direct human exploitation or malevolence, but the habitat destruction that inevitably results from the expansion of human populations and human activities.

For the remainder of this century, land-use change will continue to be the main factor affecting biodiversity in terrestrial ecosystems, probably followed by climate change and the introduction of invasive species (Sala et al. 2000). The major threat to biological diversity is loss of habitat (Table 9.3), and the most important means of protecting biological diversity is habitat preservation. Habitat loss includes habitat destruction as well as habitat damage associated with pollution and habitat fragmentation. Habitat loss is known to be the primary threat to the majority of plants and animals currently facing extinction.

In many areas of the world, particularly on islands and in locations where human population density is high, most original habitat has been destroyed. Habitat disturbance has been particularly severe throughout Europe; south and east Asia, including the Philippines and Japan; southeastern and southwestern Australia; New Zealand; Madagascar; west Africa; the southeastern and northern coasts of South America; Central America; the Caribbean; and central and eastern North America. In many of these regions, more than 50% of the natural habitats have been disturbed or removed. In the United States, only 42% of the natural vegetation remains, and in many regions of the East and Midwest, less than 25% remains (Stein et al. 2000). Surveys in the United States have documented certain biological communities that have declined in area by 98% or more since European settlement (Noss et al. 1995): old growth stands

TABLE 9.3 Factors responsible for putting threatened species of the United States at risk of extinction

Threatened species group	Percentage of species affected by each factor[a]				
	Habitat degradation and loss	Pollution	Over-exploitation	Competition/predation from alien species	Disease
All species (1880 species)	85	24	17	49	3
All vertebrates (494 species)	92	46	27	47	8
Mammals (85 species)	89	19	47	27	8
Birds (98 species)	90	22	33	69	37
Amphibians (60 species)	87	47	17	27	0
Fishes (213 species)	97	90	15	17	0
All invertebrates (331 species)	87	45	23	27	0
Freshwater mussels (102 species)	97	90	15	17	0
Butterflies (33 species)	97	24	30	36	0
Plants (1055 species)	81	7	10	57	1

Source: Data from Wilcove et al. 1998.

[a]Species may be affected by more than one factor; therefore, rows do not sum to 100%. For example, 87% of threatened amphibian species are affected by habitat degradation and loss, and 47% of these same species are also affected by pollution.

in eastern deciduous forests; old-growth long-leaf pine (*Pinus palustris*) forests and savannahs in the southeastern coastal plain; ungrazed dry prairie in Florida; native grasslands in California; ungrazed sagebrush steppe in the Intermountain West; and streams in the Mississippi River floodplain. The principal habitat threats affecting endangered species, in order of decreasing importance, are agriculture (affecting 38% of endangered species), commercial developments (35%), water projects (30%), outdoor recreation (27%), livestock grazing (22%), pollution (20%), infrastructure and roads (17%), disruption of fire ecology (13%), and logging (12%) (Stein et al. 2000).

More than 50% of the wildlife habitat has been destroyed in many Old World tropical countries (WRI 2000). In tropical Asia, fully 65% of the primary forest habitat has been lost (Table 9.4). The two biologically rich countries of Malaysia and Indonesia still have about half of their primary forest habitats and are in the process of establishing extensive protected areas, though even in these countries, the forces of habitat destruction and degradation continue. Sub-Saharan Africa has similarly lost a total of about 65% of its forests, with losses being most severe in Rwanda (80%), Gambia (89%), and Ghana (82%). Two biologically rich

TABLE 9.4 Loss of forest habitat in some countries of the Old World tropics

Country	Current forest remaining (× 1000 ha)	Percentage of habitat lost	Percentage of current forest as frontier forest
AFRICA			
Democratic Republic of the Congo	135,071	40	16
Gambia	188	38	0
Ghana	1694	91	0
Kenya	3423	82	0
Madagascar	6940	87	0
Rwanda	291	84	0
Zimbabwe	15,397	33	0
ASIA			
Bangladesh	862	92	4
India	44,450	80	1
Indonesia	88,744	35	28
Malaysia	13,007	36	14
Myanmar (Burma)	20,661	59	0
Philippines	2402	94	0
Sri Lanka	1581	82	12
Thailand	16,237	78	5
Vietnam	4218	83	2

Source: Data from WRI 1998.

nations, Zimbabwe and the Democratic Republic of the Congo (former-ly Zaire), are relatively better off, retaining about half of their forests, al-though the recent civil war in the latter country has halted efforts to pro-tect and manage wildlife.

Present rates of deforestation vary considerably among countries, with particularly high annual rates of over 2% reported in such tropical coun-tries as Malaysia (2.4%), the Philippines (3.5%), Thailand (2.6%), Costa Rica (3.1%), El Salvador (3.3%), Haiti (3.5%), Honduras (2.3%), Nicaragua (2.5%), Panama (2.2%), and Paraguay (2.6%) (WRI 1998). As a result of habitat fragmentation, farming, logging, and other human activities, very little frontier forest—intact blocks of undisturbed forest large enough to support all aspects of biodiversity—remains in most Old World tropical countries. In the New World, the situation is somewhat better; 42% of Brazilian forest and 59% of Venezuelan forest are frontier forest. In the Mediterranean region, which has been densely populated by people for thousands of years, only 10% of the original forest cover remains. An im-portant point to remember here is that populations are lost in propor-tion to the amount of habitat that has been lost; even though the Mediter-ranean forest still exists in places, approximately 90% of the populations of birds, butterflies, wildflowers, frogs, and mosses that once existed are there no longer.

For many important wildlife species, the majority of habitat in their original range has been destroyed and very little of the remaining habi-tat is protected. For certain Asian primates, such as the Javan gibbon, more than 95% of the original habitat (and 95% of the populations!) has been destroyed, and some of these species are protected on less than 2% of their original ranges (WRI 2000). The orangutan, a great ape that lives in Sumatra and Borneo, has lost 63% of its range and is protected in only 2% of its range.

Threatened Rain Forests

The destruction of tropical rain forests has come to be synonymous with the loss of species. Tropical moist forests occupy 7% of the Earth's land surface but they are estimated to contain over 50% of its species (Myers 1986). Many of these species are important to local economies and have the potential for greater use by the entire world population. Rain forests also have regional importance in protecting watersheds and moderat-ing climate; they have local significance as the home to numerous in-digenous cultures; and they have global importance as sinks to absorb the excess carbon dioxide that is produced by the burning of fossil fuels.

These evergreen (or partly evergreen) forests occur in frost-free areas below about 1800 m in altitude and have at least 100 mm (4 inches) of rain per month in most years. They are characterized by a great richness of species and a complexity of species interaction and specialization un-paralleled in any other community. Tropical rain forests are easily degraded because the soils are often thin and nutrient-poor, and they erode readily in heavy rainfall. At present, there is considerable discussion in the scientific literature about the original extent and current area of tropical forests as well as rates of deforestation (WRI 2000). The original extent of tropical rain forests and related moist forests has been estimated at 16 million km^2, based on current patterns of rainfall and temperature (Myers 1984, 1986, 1991b; Sayer and Whitmore 1991). A combination of ground surveys, airplane photos, and remote-sensing data from satellites showed that in 1982 only 9.5 million km^2 remained, an area about equal in size to the continental United States. Another census in 1991 showed a loss of another 2.8 million km^2 during this 9-year period. Currently, approximately 150,000 km^2 of rain forest are being lost per year, an area larger than the state of Tennessee or the country of Guatemala; almost half of that amount is completely destroyed, with the remainder degraded to the point that the species composition and ecosystem processes of the community are greatly altered. This rate of deforestation represents approximately 1% of the original forest area lost per year. Other estimates are as high as 210,000 km^2 of forest being cleared and degraded each year (Laurance 1999). Despite the difficulty in obtaining accurate numbers, a general consensus exists that tropical deforestation rates are alarmingly high and are growing.

On a global scale, about 60% of rain forest destruction results from small-scale cultivation of crops by poor, landless farmers, most of whom moved to the agricultural frontier to practice temporary farming out of desperation or by way of government-sponsored resettlement programs (Myers 1991b). Some of this land is converted to permanent farm plantations and pastures, but much of the area is farmed using a method known as shifting cultivation. **Shifting cultivation** is a kind of subsistence farming, sometimes referred to as "slash-and-burn" agriculture, in which trees are cut down and then burned away and the cleared patches farmed for two or three seasons, after which soil fertility usually diminishes to the point where adequate crop production is no longer possible. The patches are abandoned and more natural vegetation must be cleared. Shifting cultivation is often practiced in such areas because the farmers are unwilling or unable to spend the time and money necessary to develop more permanent forms of agriculture on land that they do not own and may not occupy for very long. Included in this discussion is land degraded each year for fuelwood production, mostly to supply local villagers with wood for cooking fires. More than two billion people cook their food with firewood, so their impact is significant. About another 20% is destroyed through commercial logging in clear-cutting and selective logging operations. Around 10% more is cleared for cattle ranches (Figure 9.3). Clearing for cash-crop plantations (oil palm, cocoa, rubber, etc.) plus road building, mining, and other activities account for the remaining 5–10%. The relative importance of these enterprises

(A)

(B)

Figure 9.3 The displacement of rain forest for agricultural purposes can take many forms. (A) Shifting cultivation in West Africa: Gardens are hewn from the forest with slash-and-burn techniques. Indigenous peoples living at low densities have used such farming practices for centuries. However, when large numbers of people migrate into an area and practice shifting cultivation, rain forest destruction is vast. (Photograph © Charles Cecil/Visuals Unlimited.) (B) Rice paddies take over rain forest in southwestern India. (Photograph by R. Primack.)

varies by geographical region; logging is a significant activity in tropical Asia and America, cattle ranching is most prominent in tropical America, and farming is more important for the rapidly expanding population in tropical Africa (Bawa and Dayanandan 1997; Nepstad et al. 1999). In relative terms, the deforestation rate is greatest in Asia, at around 1.2% per year, while in absolute terms tropical America has the greatest deforestation rate: around 75,000 km^2 per year, due to its larger total area.

Extending the projection forward in time reveals that, at the current rate of loss, there will be virtually no tropical forest left after the year 2040, except in the relatively small protected areas and inaccessible areas of the Amazon basin, Congo River basin, and New Guinea. The situation is actually more grim than these projections indicate because the world's population is still increasing, and poverty is on the rise in many developing tropical countries, putting ever-greater demands on the dwindling supply of rain forest.

The destruction of tropical rain forests is caused frequently by demand in industrialized countries for cheap agricultural products, such as rubber, palm oil, cocoa, and beef, and for low-cost wood products (Myers 1997; Tucker 2000). During the 1980s, Costa Rica and other Latin American countries had some of the world's highest rates of deforestation as a result of the conversion of rain forests into cattle ranches (Dowling et al. 1992). Much of the beef produced on these ranches was sold to the United States and other developed countries to produce inexpensive hamburgers. Adverse publicity resulting from this "hamburger connection," followed by consumer boycotts, led major restaurant chains in the United States to stop buying tropical beef from these ranches. Even though deforestation continued in Latin America, the boycott was important in making people aware of the international connections promoting deforestation. A priority for conservation biology is to help provide the information, programs, and public awareness that will allow the greatest amount of rain forest to persist once the present cycle of destruction ends.

The story of Rondonia illustrates how rapid and serious rain forest destruction can be. This state in Amazonian Brazil was almost entirely covered by primary forest as late as 1975, with only 1200 km^2 cleared out of a total area of 243,000 km^2 (Myers 1986; Fearnside 1990, 1996). In the 1970s, the Brazilian government built a major highway system through Rondonia, including a network of lateral roads leading away from the highway into the forest. The government also provided lucrative tax subsidies to allow corporations to establish cattle ranches in the region and encouraged poor, landless people from coastal states to migrate to Rondonia with offers of free land. These incentives were necessary because the soils of the Amazon region are low in mineral nutrients, so new pastures and farmlands are usually unproductive and unprofitable. During this land rush, 10,000 km^2 of the forest was cleared by 1982, an additional 6000 km^2 was cleared by 1985, and a total of around 39,000 km2 by 1993, representing 16% of the total land area (Figure 9.4). By the late 1980s, the population of the state was growing at 16% per year, with deforestation increasing 37% per year. These rates of growth and deforestation are phenomenally high compared to most other parts of the world, whether industrial or developing. International protests against this environmental damage led the government to reduce its subsidies of the cattle industry. Reduced subsidies and a general economic recession

(A) N

Highway

City of
Rolim de Moura

(B)

Figure 9.4 (A) A satellite photo of a highway built through the Amazon rain forest in Rondonia; the area shown covers about 24,500 km². Note the lateral roads that provide access into the forest. (B) Tropical forests are cut down for a variety of reasons. In this case, indigenous people in the Amazon have cut down trees and burned them in preparation for planting their crops. Here a local chief stands in front of land that has been cleared. (Photograph by Milla Jung.)

somewhat decreased the rate of deforestation during the early 1990's, but the rate of deforestation has begun to increase again due to unusually dry weather in 1997 and 1998, which facilitated land clearing and burning (Nepstad 2001). Deforestation in the Amazon will also increase if the Brazilian government proceeds with its plan to build 7500 km of new paved road and associated transportation infrastructure, at a total cost of $45 billion (Laurance et al. 2001).

Other Threatened Habitats

The plight of the tropical rain forests is perhaps the most widely publicized case of habitat destruction, but other habitats are also in grave danger. Around 94% of temperate broadleaf forests have been disturbed by human activities, primarily farming and logging, with a comparable percentage for evergreen sclerophyllous forest consisting mainly of conifers (Hannah et al. 1995). Certain biological communities have lost more than 98% of their previous area due to human activities; among these are old-growth forests stands in eastern North America; native grasslands in California, and streams in the Mississippi river floodplains. We discuss a few of these threatened habitats below:

TROPICAL DECIDUOUS FORESTS   The land occupied by tropical deciduous forests is more suitable for agriculture and cattle ranching than the land occupied by tropical rain forests. The forests are also easier than rain forests to clear and burn. Moderate rainfall in the range of 250–2000 mm per year allows mineral nutrients to be retained in the soil where they can be taken up by plants. Consequently, human population density is five times greater in dry forest areas of Central America than in adjacent rain forests. Today, the Pacific Coast of Central America has less than 2% of its original extent remaining and less than 8% remains in Madagascar (Janzen 1988a; Laurance 1999).

GRASSLANDS   Temperate grasslands are another habitat type that has been almost completely destroyed by human activity. It is relatively easy to convert large areas of grassland to farmland and cattle ranches (Figure 9.5). Illinois and Indiana, for example, originally contained 15 million ha (37 million acres) of tallgrass prairie, but now only 1400 ha (3500 acres) of this habitat—one ten-thousandth of the original area—remain undisturbed; the rest has been converted to farmland (Chadwick 1993). This remaining area of prairie is fragmented and widely scattered across the landscape.

WETLANDS AND AQUATIC HABITATS   Wetlands are critical habitats for fish, aquatic invertebrates, and birds. They are also a resource for flood control, drinking water, and power production (Mitchell 1992; Moyle and Leidy 1992; Dugan 1993). Although many wetland species are widespread, some aquatic systems are known for their high levels of endemism (see Box 13 in Chapter 7).

Wetlands are often filled in or drained for development, or they are altered by channelization of watercourses, dams, and chemical pollution. All of these factors are affecting the Florida Everglades, one of the

(A)

(B)

(C)

◀ **Figure 9.5** Temperate grasslands are extremely valuable for protecting biological diversity and for agriculture. (A) A natural grassland with numerous native species on the National Bison Range, federally protected land in the state of Montana. (B) Cattle graze on natural grassland. (C) Overgrazed grassland takes on the appearance of a desert, and native species are eliminated. (Photographs courtesy of the U.S. Fish and Wildlife Service and the U.S. Forest Service.)

premier wildlife refuges in the United States, which is now on the verge of ecological collapse (Holloway 1994). Over the last 200 years, over half of the wetlands in the United States have been destroyed, resulting in 40–50% of the freshwater snail species in the southeastern United States becoming either extinct or endangered (Stein and Flack 1997). The state of California, with its wealth of endemic species, has lost around 91% of its wetlands, with comparable losses in the U.S. Midwest due to agricultural development. More than 97% of the vernal pools in California's San Diego County have been destroyed; these unusual wetlands fill up with water in the winter and dry out in the summer, and support a unique endemic biota. The majority of U.S. Pacific salmon stocks face moderate to high extinction risks as the rivers that they use to spawn are damaged and dammed (Naiman et al. 1995). In the United States, 98% of the country's 5.2 million km of streams have been degraded in some way to the point that they are no longer considered wild or scenic (Harrison and Stiassny 1999). Destruction of wetlands has been equally severe in other parts of the industrialized world, such as Europe and Japan. Only 2 of Japan's 30,000 rivers can be considered wild, without dams or some other major modification. In the last few decades, one of the major threats to wetlands in developing countries has been massive development projects organized by governments and often financed by international aid agencies involving drainage, irrigation, and dams.

MANGROVES   Mangrove forests are among the most important wetland communities in tropical areas. Composed of species that are among the few woody plants able to tolerate salt water, mangrove forests occupy coastal areas with saline or brackish water, typically where there are muddy bottoms. Such habitats are similar to salt marshes in the temperate zone. Mangroves are extremely important breeding grounds and feeding areas for shrimp and fish. In Australia, for example, two-thirds of the species caught by commercial fishermen depend to some degree on the mangrove ecosystem.

Despite their great economic value, mangroves are often cleared for rice cultivation and commercial shrimp and prawn hatcheries, particularly in Southeast Asia, where as much as 15% of the mangrove area has been removed for aquaculture. Mangroves have also been severely degraded by overcollecting wood for fuel, construction poles, and timber throughout the region. The loss of mangroves is extensive in some parts of South and Southeast Asia; the percentage of mangroves lost is particularly high for India (85%), Thailand (87%), Pakistan (78%), and Bangladesh (73%) (WRI 1994).

CORAL REEFS   Tropical coral reefs contain an estimated one-third of the ocean's fish species in only 0.2% of its surface area (see Chapter 3). Already 10% of all coral reefs have been destroyed and as many as 30% more could be destroyed in the next few decades (Birkeland 1997). Moreover, far larger areas of coral reef have been degraded by overfishing, overharvesting, pollution, and the introduction of invasive species. The most severe destruction is taking place in the Philippines, where a staggering 90% of the reefs are dead or dying. The main culprits are pollution, which either kills the coral directly or allows excessive growth of algae; sedimentation following deforestation; overharvesting of fish, clams, and other animals; and, finally, blasting with dynamite and releasing cyanide to collect the few remaining living creatures.

Extensive loss of coral reefs is expected within the next 40 years in tropical East Asia, the areas around Madagascar and East Africa, and throughout the Caribbean (Figure 9.6). In the Caribbean, a combination of overfishing, hurricane damage, pollution, and disease is responsible for a dramatic decline of a large proportion of the coral reefs

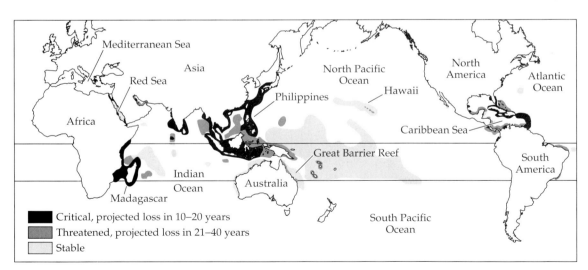

Figure 9.6 Extensive areas of coral will be damaged or destroyed by human activity over the next 40 years unless conservation measures can be implemented. (After Weber 1993.)

and their replacement by fleshy macroalgae (Hughes 1994). Elkhorn and staghorn corals, which were formerly common in the Caribbean and gave structure to the community, have already become rare in many locations.

Over the last 10 years, scientists have discovered extensive coral reefs living in cold water at depths of 300 m or more, many of which are in the temperate zone of the North Atlantic. These coral reefs are rich in species, with numerous species new to science. Yet at the same time that these communities are first being explored, they are being destroyed by trawlers, which drag nets across the seafloor to catch fish; at the same time, though, the trawlers are destroying the very coral reefs which protect and provide food for young fish.

Desertification

Many biological communities in seasonally dry climates are degraded by human activities into man-made deserts, a process known as **desertification** (Allan and Warren 1993; Reynolds 2001). These dryland communities include tropical grasslands, scrub, and deciduous forest, as well as temperate shrublands, such as those found in the Mediterranean region, southwestern Australia, South Africa, central Chile, and California. Dry areas cover around 47% of the world's land area, and they are home to around 1 billion people. Approximately 73% of these drylands are at least moderately desertified, with more than 25% of the productive capacity of their plant growth having been lost (Kaufman and Pyke 2001). While these areas initially may support agriculture, repeated cultivation, especially during dry and windy years, often leads to soil erosion and loss of water-holding capacity in the soil (Figure 9.7). Land may also be chronically overgrazed by domestic livestock and woody plants may be cut down for fuel (Fleischner 1994; Milton et al. 1994). Frequent fires during long dry periods often damage the remaining vegetation. The result is the progressive and largely irreversible degradation of the biological community and the loss of soil cover. Ultimately, formerly productive farmland and pastures take on the appearance of a desert. Desertification has been ongoing for thousands of years in the Mediterranean region and was known even to ancient Greek observers.

Worldwide, 9 million km^2 of arid lands have been converted to man-made deserts. These areas are not functional desert ecosystems but are wastelands, lacking the flora and fauna characteristic of natural deserts. The process of desertification is most severe in the Sahel region of Africa, just south of the Saharan Desert, where most of the native large mammal species are threatened with extinction. The human dimension of the problem is illustrated by the fact that the Sahel region is estimated to have 2.5 times more people (100 million currently) than the land can sustainably support. Further desertification appears to be almost inevitable, unless programs can be implemented involving sustainable and im-

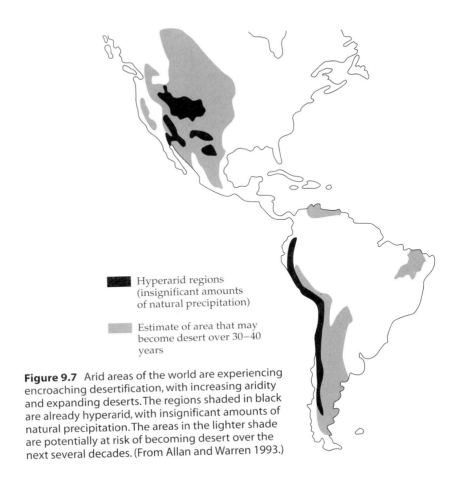

■ Hyperarid regions
(insignificant amounts
of natural precipitation)

■ Estimate of area that may
become desert over 30–40
years

Figure 9.7 Arid areas of the world are experiencing
encroaching desertification, with increasing aridity
and expanding deserts. The regions shaded in black
are already hyperarid, with insignificant amounts of
natural precipitation. The areas in the lighter shade
are potentially at risk of becoming desert over the
next several decades. (From Allan and Warren 1993.)

proved agricultural practices, the elimination of poverty, and population control (Hassan and Dregné 1997).

Habitat Fragmentation

In addition to outright destruction, habitats that formerly occupied wide
unbroken areas are now often divided into pieces by roads, fields, towns,
and a broad range of other human constructs. **Habitat fragmentation**
is the process whereby a large, continuous area of habitat is both reduced
in area and divided into two or more fragments (Figure 9.8) (Reed et al.
1996; Trombulak and Frissell 2000; Debinski and Holt 2000; Laurance
and Williamson 2001). When habitat is destroyed, a patchwork of habitat fragments may be left behind. These fragments are often isolated from
one another by a highly modified or degraded landscape and their edges

experience an altered set of conditions, referred to as the **edge effect**.
Fragments are often on the least desirable land, such as steep slopes,
poor soils, and inaccessible areas. Fragmentation almost always occurs
during a severe reduction in habitat area, but it can also occur when area
is reduced to only a minor degree if the original habitat is divided by
roads, railroads, canals, power lines, fences, oil pipelines, fire lanes, or
other barriers to the free movement of species (Figure 9.9). Forest habitats are sometimes deliberately fragmented by wildlife managers to create the open-edge habitats with new abundant plant growth that are
favored by deer and other wildlife. As discussed in Chapter 7, the island
model of biogeography is applicable to such situations: the habitat fragments resemble islands in an inhospitable, human-dominated sea.

Habitat fragments differ from the original habitat in two important
ways: (1) fragments have a greater amount of edge for the area of habitat (and thus a greater exposure to the edge effect), and (2) the center of
each habitat fragment is closer to an edge. A simple example will illustrate these characteristics and the problems they can cause.

Consider a square conservation reserve 1000 m (1 km) on each side
(Figure 9.10). The total area of the park is 1 km^2 (100 ha). The perimeter

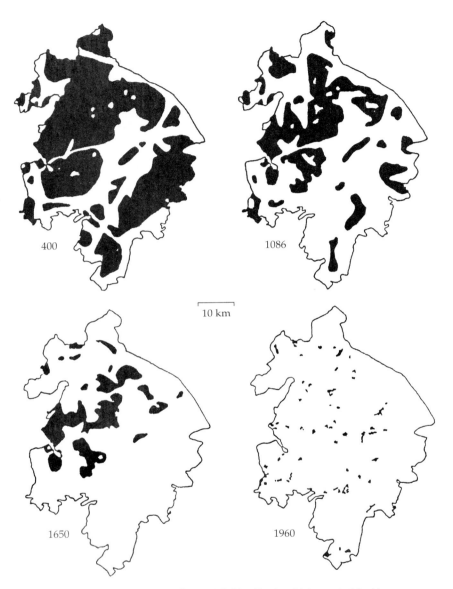

Figure 9.8 The forested areas of Warwickshire, England (shown in black), were fragmented and reduced in area—by paths, roads, agriculture, and human settle-ments—over the centuries from 400 A.D. (when Romans established villages and towns in the forested landscape and built roads between them) to 1960 A.D. (when only a few tiny forest fragments remained).

(or edge) of the park totals 4000 m. A point in the middle of the reserve is 500 m from the nearest perimeter. If the principle edge effect for birds in the reserve is predation from domestic cats and introduced rats, which forage 100 m into the forest from the perimeter of the reserve and pre-

(A)   Cape Cod National
      Seashore, Massachusetts

(B)   Yellowstone National
      Park, Wyoming/Montana

(C)   Great Smoky Mountains
      National Park,
      North Carolina/
      Tennessee

Figure 9.9 Even within national parks, fragmentation occurs when paved roads are built to allow access to visitors. Shown here are the park boundaries and paved roads (black lines) for three U.S. national parks (the parks are not shown to the same scale). (After Schonewald-Cox and Buechner 1992.)

(A)

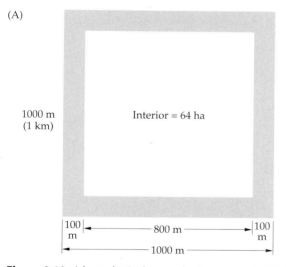

1000 m
(1 km)

Interior = 64 ha

100 m — 800 m — 100 m

1000 m

(B)

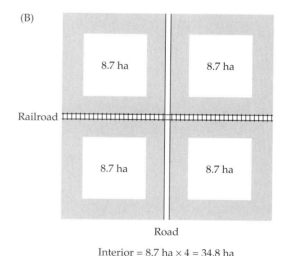

Railroad

8.7 ha   8.7 ha

8.7 ha   8.7 ha

Road

Interior = 8.7 ha × 4 = 34.8 ha

Figure 9.10 A hypothetical example shows how habitat area is severely reduced by fragmentation and edge effects. (A) A 1-km² protected area. Assuming edge effects (gray) penetrate 100 m into the reserve, approximately 64 ha are available as usable habitat for nesting birds. (B) The bisection of the reserve by a road and a railway, although taking up little in actual area, extends the edge effects so that almost half the breeding habitat is destroyed. Effects are proportionately greater when forest fragments are irregular in shape, as is usually the case.

vent forest birds from successfully raising their young, then only the reserve's interior—64 ha—is available to the birds for breeding. Edge habitat, unsuitable for breeding, occupies 36 ha.

Now imagine the park being divided into four equal quarters by a north–south road 10 m wide and by an east–west railroad track, also 10 m wide. The rights-of-way remove a total of 2 m × 1000 m × 10 m of area (2 ha) from the park. Since only 2% of the park is being removed by the road and railroad, government planners argue that the effects on the park are negligible. However, the reserve has now been divided into four fragments, each of which is 495 m × 495 m in area. The distance from the center of each fragment to the nearest point on the perimeter has been reduced to 247 m, which is less than half of the former distance. Since cats and rats can now forage into the forest from along the road and railroad as well as the perimeter, birds can successfully raise young only in the most interior areas of each of the four fragments. Each of these interior areas is now 8.7 ha, for a total of 34.8 ha. Even though the road and railroad removed only 2% of the reserve area, they reduced the habitat available to the birds by about half due to edge effects. The implications of this can be seen in the decreased ability of birds to live and breed in small forest fragments compared with larger blocks of forest (Figure 9.11).

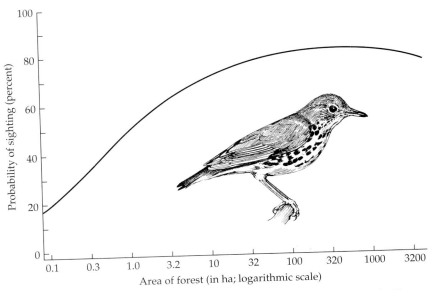

Figure 9.11 The probability of sighting a wood thrush in a mature forest in Maryland is only about 20% in a forest fragment of 0.1 ha; it increases to about 80% in a forest fragment over 100 ha in area. (From Robbins in Decker et al. 1991.)

In many areas of the world, human hunters are the most important predators. When habitat is fragmented by roads, hunters can use the road network to hunt more intensively in the habitat fragments and reach remote areas. There will be no refuge for the animals and their populations will decline.

The Effects of Fragmentation on Species Mobility

Habitat fragmentation results in a reduction of the area of the original habitat, a greater amount of edge habitat for a given area, a reduced distance to the nearest edge, and fragment isolation. Following fragmentation, the tendency for displaced animals to congregate in the remaining habitat fragments leads to a temporary increase in species numbers (Debinski and Holt 2000). However, over a period of years, species numbers in the fragments will show a gradual decline, a "relaxation" toward a lower value. The effects of habitat loss on biological diversity are clear: The habitat being destroyed may contain the only site for a particular species. However, as the above example demonstrates, habitat fragmentation also threatens the persistence of species in other subtle ways.

LIMITS TO DISPERSAL AND COLONIZATION   Fragmentation may limit a species' potential for dispersal and colonization (Trombulak and Frisell 2000) by creating barriers to normal dispersal and colonization processes. In an undisturbed environment, seeds, spores, and animals move passively and actively across the landscape. When they arrive in a suitable but unoccupied area, new populations begin to develop at that site. Over time, populations of a species may build up and go extinct on a local scale as the species disperses from one suitable site to another and the biological community undergoes succession. At a landscape level, a series of populations exhibiting this pattern of extinction and recolonization is sometimes referred to as a metapopulation (see Chapter 12).

When a habitat is fragmented, the potential for dispersal and colonization is often reduced. Many bird, mammal, and insect species of the forest interior will not cross even very short distances of open area (Figure 9.12) (Bierregaard et al. 1992; Laurance and Bierregaard 1997). If they do venture into the open, they may find predators such as hawks, owls, flycatchers, and cats waiting on the forest edge to catch and eat them. Agricultural fields 100 m wide may represent an impassable barrier to the dispersal of many invertebrate species. When mammal dispersal is reduced by habitat fragmentation, plants with fleshy fruits or sticky seeds that depend on animals for dispersal are also affected (Santos and Telleria 1994). As species go extinct within individual fragments through natural successional and metapopulation processes, new species will be unable to arrive due to barriers to colonization, and the number of species present in the habitat fragment will decline over time. Species that are able to live in and move across disturbed habitat will increase in abun-

Figure 9.12 A road and its parking loops (shown as heavy black lines) blocks the movement of a forest-dwelling beetle species, effectively creating two subpopulations. The circles represent points where beetles were trapped, with darker circles indicating beetle populations with greater density. The lines indicate the movement of "tagged" beetles. (After Mader 1984.)

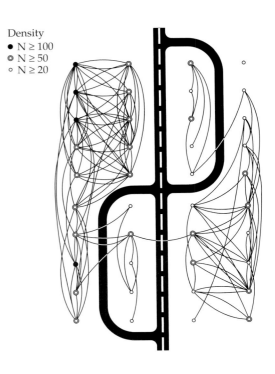

Density
● N ≥ 100
◉ N ≥ 50
○ N ≥ 20

dance in small, isolated fragments of undisturbed habitat. This is particularly true when the spaces between forest fragments are occupied by secondary forests and tree plantations, rather than pastures and cultivated fields (Gascon et al. 1999). Most of the world's national parks and nature reserves represent fragments of the original ecosystems which are now too small and isolated to maintain populations of many of the original species.

RESTRICTED ACCESS TO FOOD AND MATES Many animal species, either as individuals or social groups, need to move freely across the landscape to feed on widely scattered resources. A given resource may be needed only for a few weeks each year, or even only once in a few years, and when a habitat is fragmented, species confined to a single habitat fragment may be unable to migrate in search of that scarce resource over their normal home range. For example, orangutans, gibbons, and other primates typically remain in forests and forage widely for fruits. Finding scattered trees with abundant fruit crops may be crucial during episodes of fruit scarcity. Clearings and roads that break up the forest canopy may prevent these primates from reaching nearby fruiting trees, because the primates are unable or unwilling to descend to the ground and cross the intervening open landscape. Fences may prevent the natural migration of large grazing animals, such as wildebeest or bison, forcing them to overgraze unsuitable habitat, eventually leading to starvation and further degradation of the habitat.

Barriers to dispersal can also restrict the ability of widely scattered species to find mates, leading to a loss of reproductive potential for many animal species. Plants also may have reduced seed production if butterflies and bees are less able to migrate among habitat fragments to pollinate flowers.

DIVISION OF POPULATIONS   Habitat fragmentation may precipitate population decline and extinction by dividing an existing widespread population into two or more subpopulations in a restricted area (Rochelle et al. 1999). These smaller populations are then more vulnerable to inbreeding depression, genetic drift, and other problems associated with small population size (see Chapter 11). While a large area may support a single large population, it is possible that none of the smaller subpopulations will be sufficiently large to persist for a long period.

Edge Effects

Habitat fragmentation also changes the microenvironment at the fragment edge. Some of the more important edge effects include microclimatic changes in light, temperature, wind, humidity, and incidence of fire (Schelhas and Greenberg 1996; Laurance and Bierregaard 1997; Stevens and Husband 1998). Each of these edge effects can have a significant impact on the vitality and composition of the species in the fragment.

MICROCLIMATE CHANGES   Sunlight is absorbed and reflected by the layers of leaves in forest communities and other communities with dense plant cover. In forests, often less than 1% of the light energy may reach the forest floor. The forest canopy buffers the microclimate of the forest floor, keeping the forest floor relatively cool, moist, and shaded during the day, reducing air movement, and trapping heat during the night. When the forest is cleared, these effects are removed. As the forest floor is exposed to direct sunlight, the ground becomes much hotter during the day; without the canopy to reduce heat and moisture loss, the forest floor is also much colder at night and generally less humid. These effects will be strongest at the edge of the habitat fragment and decrease toward the interior of the fragment. In studies of Amazonian forest fragments, microclimate changes had strong effects up to 60 m into the forest interior, and increased tree mortality could be detected within 100–300 m of forest edges (Laurance and Bierregaard 1997; Laurance et al. 1998). Since species of plants and animals are often precisely adapted to temperature, humidity, and light levels, changes in these factors will eliminate many species from forest fragments. Shade-tolerant wildflower species of the temperate forest, late-successional tree species of the tropical forest, and humidity-sensitive animals, like amphibians, often are rapidly eliminated by habitat fragmentation because of altered environmental conditions, leading to a shift in the species composition of the community.

The habitat edge is usually the most altered region of the fragment (Figure 9.13). Edges may have very high daytime temperatures, when the angle of the sun is low, and very cold night temperatures due to the lack of buffering by other vegetation. However, a dense tangle of vines and fast-growing pioneer species grow up at the forest edge in response to these altered conditions and often create a barrier that reduces the effects of environmental disturbance on the interior of the fragment. In this sense, the forest edge plays an important role in preserving the composition of the forest fragment, but in the process the species composition of the forest edge is dramatically altered, and the area occupied by forest interior species is further reduced. Over time, the forest edge may be occupied by species of plants and animals different from those found in the forest interior. If a forest returns to the cleared area, either through natural growth of secondary forest or the establishment of a tree plantation, the forest fragments might be protected from change.

Wind changes can have a significant effect in fragmented forest habitats. In an intact forest, wind velocity is substantially reduced by the tree canopies; the wind moves strongly over the forest but is reduced to a gentle breeze within the forest. When a habitat is fragmented, the wind is able to enter and move through the forest. The impact of wind will be greatest at the forest edge, which is subject to the full force of it, but the effects on air movement may be felt over a considerable distance as well, particularly in flat terrain. The increased wind and air turbulence directly damages vegetation, particularly at the forest edge. Trees that have grown up in the forest interior with minimal wind stress will have leaves and branches stripped off by the wind or may be blown down (Laurance and Bierregaard 1997). Increased wind also leads to increased drying of the soil, lower air humidity, and higher water loss from leaf surfaces. This increased water stress may kill many interior plant species and reduce the production of seeds (Benitez-Malvido 1998). The overall result of wind effects may be to kill the trees along the forest edge, which will then be occupied by a new suite of species better adapted to the new conditions. Over time, with trees dying along the edge, the forest fragment will become smaller, and might eventually cease to exist (Gascon et al. 1999).

INCREASED INCIDENCE OF FIRE   Increased wind, lower humidity, and higher temperatures make fires more likely. Fires may spread into habitat fragments from nearby agricultural fields that are being burned regularly, as in sugarcane harvesting, or from the irregular activities of farmers practicing slash-and-burn agriculture. Forest fragments may be

(A)

Figure 9.13 (A) Forest clearing for pasture in Brazil results in sharp edges that change the rain forest microclimate. (Photograph by R. Bierregaard.) (B) Various effects of habitat fragmentation, as measured from the edge into the interior of an Amazon rain forest fragment. For example, disturbance-adapted butterflies migrate 250 m into the forest from an edge, and the relative humidity of the air is lowered within 100 m of the forest edge. (After Laurance and Bierregaard 1997.)

(B)

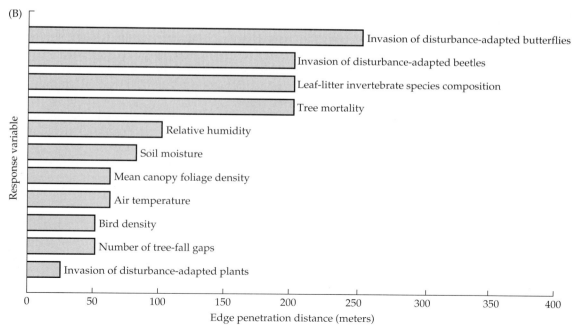

particularly susceptible to fire damage when wood has accumulated on the edge of the forest where trees have died or have been blown down by the wind. In Borneo and the Brazilian Amazon, millions of hectares of tropical moist forest burned during unusually dry periods in 1997 and 1998. A combination of factors contributed to these environmental disasters: forest fragmentation due to farming and selective logging, the accumulation of brush following selective logging, and human-caused fires (Cochrane et al. 1999; Goldammer 1999; Nepstad et al. 2001). Once a forest burns, sunlight can more readily dry out the ground, leading to a greater likelihood of further fires.

INTERSPECIES INTERACTION   Habitat fragmentation increases the vulnerability of the fragment to invasion by exotic and native pest species. The forest edge represents a high-energy, high-nutrient, disturbed environment in which many pest species of plants and animals can increase in number and then disperse into the interior of the fragment (Janzen 1983; Paton 1994). For example, the seeds of wind-dispersed plants may be blown great distances into the interior of the fragment and then colonize open, sunny areas where trees and shrubs have recently died, either from natural causes or because of the newly altered growing conditions. Butterflies that are adapted to disturbed habitats may be forced to migrate up to 250 m into the forest interior.

In the temperate regions of North America, omnivorous native animals such as raccoons, skunks, and blue jays may increase in population size along forest edges, where they can eat foods from both undisturbed and disturbed habitats (Yahner 1988). (Similar increases in nest predation occur on the edges of logged tropical forests [Cooper and Francis 1998].) These aggressive feeders seek out the nests of interior forest birds, often preventing successful reproduction for many bird species hundreds of meters from the nearest forest edge. Nest-parasitizing cowbirds, which live in fields and edge habitats, use habitat edges as an invasion point into forest interiors, where they lay their eggs in the nests of forest songbirds (Askins 1995). Similarly, predatory animals may decimate insect and amphibian populations that were inaccessible to them before fragmentation. Populations of deer and other herbivores can build up in edge areas, where plant growth is lush, eventually overgrazing the vegetation and selectively eliminating certain rare and endangered plant species for distances of several kilometers into the forest interior (Alverson et al. 1994).

POTENTIAL FOR DISEASE   Habitat fragmentation puts wild populations of animals in closer proximity to domestic animals. Diseases of domestic animals can then spread more readily to wild species, which often have no immunity to them. There is also the potential for diseases to spread from wild species to domestic plants, animals, and even people, once the level of contact increases. The effects of disease, and of exotic species in general, are more thoroughly examined in Chapter 10.

Two Studies of Habitat Fragmentation

An extensive literature on habitat fragmentation has developed over the last ten years. These studies show that habitat fragmentation changes the local environment, often resulting in the decline and loss of original species. The following are two such studies:

- The impact of habitat fragmentation was examined for eight bird species occupying chaparral and coastal sage scrub in southern California, an area undergoing rapid urban development (Crooks et al. 2001). In comparison with large fragments, small fragments (less than 10 ha in area) had higher rates of species extinction and lower rates of new species colonization. Bird species with high initial densities were less likely to go extinct in habitat fragments and were better able to persist in small fragments.
- Reindeer are one of the essential symbols of Scandinavian culture. The last remaining population of wild reindeer (*Rangifer tarandus tarandus*) lives in southern Norway (Nelleman et al 2001). Prior to 1900, the reindeer lived as a continuous herd, freely migrating throughout the mountain ranges of this region. Infrastructure developments and reindeers' tendency to keep 5 km away from human settlements and other structures, such as resort areas, roads, and power lines, have fragmented the population into 26 distinct herds (Figure 9.14). Only around 10% of the original range of reindeer is now found more than 5 km from such human structures. Because isolated herds are unable to migrate and consequently tend to overgraze the vegetation in their habitat fragment, herds must be actively managed by hunting to prevent local population increases. If additional roads, power lines, and resorts are built, the reindeer population will undergo further fragmentation and its long-term future will then be even more in doubt.

Habitat Degradation and Pollution

Even when a habitat is unaffected by overt destruction or fragmentation, the communities and species in that habitat can be profoundly affected by human activities (Smith 2001). Biological communities can be damaged and species driven to extinction by external factors that do not change the structure of dominant plants in the community, so that the damage is not immediately apparent. For example, in temperate deciduous forests, physical degradation of a habitat might be caused by frequent, uncontrolled ground fires; these fires might not kill the mature trees, but the rich perennial wildflower community and insect fauna

(A)

(B)

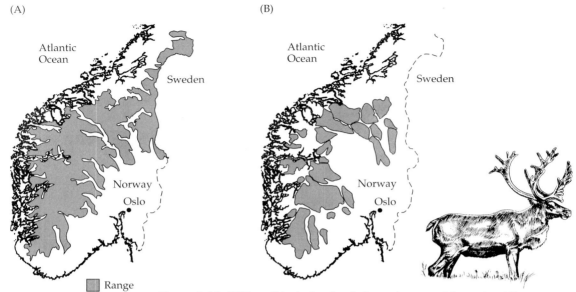

Figure 9.14 (A) The wild reindeer herds formerly roamed throughout the mountainous regions of southern Norway, with only one break in their range. (B) The range of reindeer has now been divided by roads, power lines, and other infrastructure, leading to 26 isolated subpopulations. (After Nelleman et al. 2001.)

on the forest floor would gradually become impoverished. Keeping too many cattle in grassland communities gradually changes the biological community, often eliminating many native species and favoring exotic species that can tolerate grazing and trampling. Frequent boating and diving among coral reefs degrade the community, as fragile species are crushed by divers' flippers, boat hulls, and anchors. Out of sight from the public, fishing trawlers drag across an estimated 15 million km² of ocean floor each year, an area 150 times greater than the area of forest cleared in the same time period. The trawling destroys delicate creatures such as anemones and sponges and reduces species diversity, biomass, and community structure (see Figure 9.16) (Watling and Norse 1998).

The most subtle and universal form of environmental degradation is pollution, commonly caused by pesticides, sewage, fertilizers from agricultural fields, industrial chemicals and wastes, emissions from factories and automobiles, and sediment deposits from eroded hillsides. These types of pollution are often not visually apparent even when they occur all around us, everyday, in nearly every part of the world. The general effects of pollution on water quality, air quality, and even the global climate are cause for great concern, not only because of the threats to biological diversity, but also their effects on human health (Edwards 1994). Although environmental pollution is sometimes highly visible and dra-

Figure 9.15 In the year 2000 an oil pipeline broke in Southern Brazil, spilling 4 million liters (1 million gallons) of oil into the Rio Iguaçu. Shown here are the polluted waters of the Iguaçu (left) merging with another river. (Photograph from *Jornal Gazeta do Povo*.)

matic, as in the case of the massive oil spill shown in Figure 9.15, it is the subtle, unseen forms of pollution that are probably the most threatening—primarily because they are so insidious.

Pesticide Pollution

The dangers of pesticides were brought to the world's attention in 1962 by Rachel Carson's influential book *Silent Spring*. Carson described a process known as **biomagnification**, through which dichlorodiphenyl-trichloroethane (DDT) and other organochlorine pesticides become concentrated as they ascend the food chain. These pesticides, used on crop plants to kill insects and sprayed on water bodies to kill mosquito larvae, were harming wildlife populations, especially birds that ate large amounts of insects, fish, or other animals exposed to DDT and its by-products. Birds with high levels of concentrated pesticides in their tissues, particularly raptors such as hawks and eagles, became weak and tended to lay eggs with abnormally thin shells that cracked during incubation. As a result of failure to raise young and the outright death of

BOX 16   *Pesticides and Raptors: Sentinel Species Warn of Danger*

Birds of prey such as the American bald eagle, the osprey, and the peregrine falcon are symbols evocative of power, grace, and nobility to people worldwide. When populations of these and other raptors began an abrupt decline shortly after World War II, concern for the birds prompted urgent research into the cause. In retrospect, these birds of prey were acting as sentinels, warning human society of a serious danger in the environment that was broadly affecting biological communities. The culprit was eventually identified as the chemical pesticide DDT (dichlorodiphenyltrichloroethane) and related organochlorine compounds such as DDE and dieldrin. DDT was first used as an insecticide during World War II to combat insectborne diseases among the troops. After the war ended, domestic use of the chemical exploded in an effort to control agricultural pests and mosquitoes; consequently, raptor populations plummeted.

Raptors are particularly vulnerable to these compounds because of their position at the top of the food chain. Toxic chemicals become concentrated at the top of the food chain through biomagnification: Pesticides are ingested and absorbed by insects and other invertebrates during pesticide application and remain in their tissues at fairly low concentrations. When fish, birds, or mammals eat a diet of these insects, the pesticides are further concentrated, eventually to highly toxic levels. For example, DDT concentrations might be only 0.000003 parts per million (ppm) in lake water and 0.04 ppm in zooplankton, but the concentrations rise to 0.5 ppm in minnows that eat zooplankton, 2.0 ppm in fish that eat the minnows, and 25 ppm in the fish-eating osprey. Birds such as the osprey (*Pandion haliaetus*) and the bald eagle (*Haliaetus leucocephalus*) are particularly susceptible because they rely heavily on fish, which concentrate the toxins draining into rivers and lakes from agricultural watersheds. Peregrine falcons (*Falco peregrinus*), which frequently feed on insectivorous birds and bats, are also vulnerable to the effects of biomagnification. DDT and its breakdown products cause eggshell thinning, inhibit proper development of the embryo, change adult bird behavior, and may even cause direct adult mortality. Dramatic evidence of the

A captive male peregrine falcon feeding young at the Cornell University "hawk barn" propagation facility. (Photograph courtesy of T. J. Cade, The Peregrine Fund.)

BOX 16 *(continued)*

damage done to raptors by DDT is the rapidity with which many U.S. populations recovered after DDT and other organochlorine pesticides were banned in 1972. The peregrine falcon has made an astonishingly strong recovery in many parts of the world (Cade et al. 1988; Enderson et al. 1995). Captive-bred peregrine falcons released within their former range have successfully established new breeding populations, often nesting on skyscrapers in urban areas. Ospreys and bald eagles have made a similar comeback. There are now over 5000 breeding pairs of eagles in the lower 48 states of the U.S., following a low of 417 pairs in 1963.

The unanticipated decline of raptor populations illustrates the dangers of indiscriminate introduction of chemicals into the environment. The unique sensitivity of raptors to pesticides warned of potential danger to humans as well. It should have been expected that a chemical toxic to insects might have a negative impact on other organisms. Chemicals known to be toxic to human and animal life are still being produced and finding their way into the environment. It has long been known that PCBs cause cancer, yet they continue to be used, for example, in the manufacture of electric transformers. As the use of new chemicals multiplies, so do the chances of unanticipated, harmful side effects. Observation of sentinel species—in this case, top predators that accumulate contaminants—may alert us to rising levels of harmful chemicals in the environment. But it may take the threat of another "silent spring" to motivate humankind to stop contaminating the environment with chemicals.

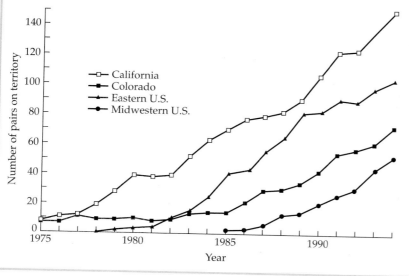

Following the banning of DDT in 1972, remnant peregrine populations in California and Colorado have gradually recovered with the help of population augmentation and nest protection. Populations in the East and Midwest were reestablished in their former range using captive-raised animals. (After Enderson et al. 1995.)

many adults, populations of these birds showed dramatic declines throughout the world (Box 16).

In lakes and estuaries, DDT and other pesticides became concentrated in predatory fish and in sea mammals such as dolphins. In agricultural areas, beneficial and endangered insect species were killed along with pest species. At the same time, mosquitoes and other targeted insects evolved resistance to the chemicals, so that ever-larger doses of DDT were required to suppress the insect populations. Recognition of this situation in the 1970s led many industrialized countries to ban the use of DDT and other chemically related pesticides. The ban eventually allowed the partial recovery of many bird populations, most notably peregrine falcons, ospreys, and bald eagles (Cade et al. 1988; Porteous 1992). Nevertheless, the continuing use of these classes of chemicals in other countries is still cause for concern, not only for endangered animal species, but also for the potential long-term effects on people, particularly the workers who handle these chemicals in the field and the consumers of the agricultural products treated with these chemicals. These chemicals are widely dispersed in the air and water and can harm plants, animals, and people living far from where the chemicals are actually applied. In addition, even in countries that outlawed these pesticides decades ago, chemicals persist in the environment, where they have a detrimental effect on the reproductive systems of aquatic vertebrates (McLachlan and Arnold 1996).

Water Pollution

Water pollution has negative consequences for people, animals, and all species that live in water: it destroys important food sources and contaminates drinking water with chemicals that can cause immediate and long-term harm to the health of people and other species coming into contact with the polluted water. In the broader picture, water pollution often severely damages aquatic communities (Figure 9.16). Rivers, lakes, and oceans are used as open sewers for industrial wastes and residential sewage. And higher densities of people almost always mean greater levels of water pollution. Pesticides, herbicides, oil products, heavy metals (such as mercury, lead, and zinc), detergents, and industrial wastes directly kill organisms living in aquatic environments. Pollution is a threat to 90% of the endangered fishes and freshwater mussels in the United States (Wilcove et al. 1998). An increasing source of pollution in coastal areas is the discharge of nutrients and chemicals from shrimp and salmon farms (Naylor et al. 1998).

Even if aquatic organisms are not killed outright, these chemicals can make the environment so inhospitable that species can no longer thrive. In contrast to a dump in the terrestrial environment, which has primarily local effects, toxic wastes in aquatic environments diffuse over a wide area. Toxic chemicals, even at very low levels in the water, can be lethal to aquatic organisms through the process of biomagnification. Many aquatic environments are naturally low in essential minerals, such as nitrates and phosphates, and aquatic species have adapted to the natural absence of minerals by developing the ability to process large volumes of water and concentrate these minerals. When these species process polluted water, they concentrate toxic chemicals along with the essential

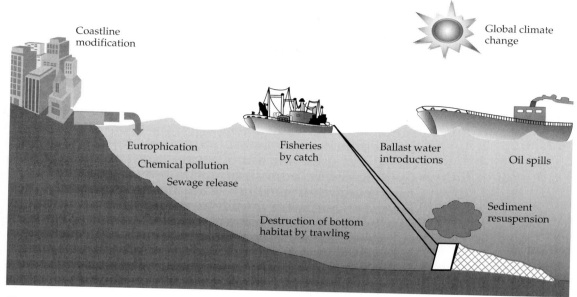

Figure 9.16 The aquatic environment faces multiple threats, as shown by this schematic view of damage to the ocean. Trawling is a fishing method in which a net is dragged along the ocean bottom by a boat, scooping up sea life but also damaging the structure of the community. (From Snelgrove 2001.)

minerals, which eventually poisons the plant or animal. Species that feed on these aquatic species ingest these concentrations of toxic chemicals.

Essential minerals that are beneficial to plant and animal life can become harmful pollutants at high levels. Human sewage, agricultural fertilizers, detergents, and industrial processes often release large amounts of nitrates and phosphates into aquatic systems, initiating the process of **eutrophication,** the result of human activity. Although small amounts of these nutrients can stimulate plant and animal growth, high concentrations of nutrients released through human activities often result in thick "blooms" of algae at the surface of ponds and lakes. These algal blooms may be so dense that they outcompete other plankton species and shade bottom-dwelling plant species. As the algal mat becomes thicker, its lower layers sink to the bottom and die. The bacteria and fungi that decompose the dying algae grow in response to this added sustenance and consequently absorb all of the oxygen in the water. Without oxygen, much of the remaining animal life dies off, sometimes visibly in the form of masses of dead fish floating on the water's surface. The result is a greatly impoverished and simplified community consisting of only those species tolerant of polluted water and low oxygen levels. This process of eutrophication can affect marine systems with large anthro-

Figure 9.17 In the 1970s, coral dominated Jamaica's reef ecosystems; 20 years later, algae have taken over these same areas. The shift is due to water pollution and the overharvesting of algae-eating fish. (After Hughes 1994.)

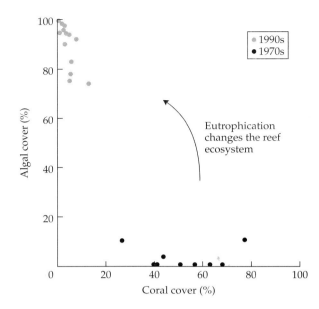

pogenic inputs of nutrients as well, particularly coastal areas and bodies of water in confined areas, such as the Gulf of Mexico, the Mediterranean, the North Sea and the Baltic Sea in Europe, and the enclosed seas of Japan (Malakoff 1998). In warm tropical waters, eutrophication favors algae, which grow over coral reefs and completely change the biological community (Figure 9.17).

Eroding sediments from logged or farmed hillsides can also harm aquatic ecosystems. The sediment covers submerged plant leaves and other green surfaces with a muddy film that reduces light availability and diminishes the rate of photosynthesis. Increasing water turbidity reduces the depth at which photosynthesis can occur and may prevent animal species from seeing, feeding, and living in the water. Sediment loads are particularly harmful to many coral species that require crystal-clear waters to survive. Corals have delicate filters that strain tiny food particles out of the clear water. When the water is filled with a high density of soil particles, the filters clog up and the animals cannot feed. Coral animals often have symbiotic algae that provide carbohydrates for the coral. When the water is filled with soil particles, there may be too little light for the algae to photosynthesize, and the corals will lose this source of energy.

Air Pollution

The effects of air pollution on forest communities have been intensively studied because of the great economic value of forests from wood production, protection of water supplies, and recreation (Hendrey 2001). In certain areas of the world, particularly northern Europe and eastern North America, air pollution damages and weakens many tree species—apparently both directly and indirectly—and makes them more susceptible to attacks by insects, fungi, and disease (Figure 9.18). When the trees die, many of the other species in a forest also become locally extinct. Even when communities are not destroyed by air pollution, species composition may be altered as more susceptible species are eliminated. Lichens—symbiotic organisms composed of fungi and algae that can survive in some of the harshest natural environments—are particularly susceptible to air pollution. Because each lichen species has distinct levels of tolerance to air pollution, the composition of the lichen community can be used as a biological indicator of the level of air pollution.

In the past, people assumed that the atmosphere was so vast that materials they released into the air would be widely dispersed and their effects would be minimal. But today several types of air pollution are so widespread that they damage whole ecosystems. These same pollutants also have severe impacts on human health, demonstrating again the com-

Figure 9.18 Forests in montane areas near concentrations of power plants and heavy industry are experiencing diebacks, thought to be caused in part by the effects of acid rain combined with nitrogen deposition, ozone damage, insect attack, and disease. These dead trees were photographed in Blue Ridge Parkway, North Carolina, in 1992. (Photograph © Cub Kahn/TERRAPHOTOGRAPHICS/Biological Photo Service.)

mon interests shared by people and nature. We discuss each of these air pollutants below.

ACID RAIN   Industries such as smelting operations and coal- and oil-fired power plants release huge quantities of nitrogen and sulfur oxides into the air, where they combine with moisture in the atmosphere to produce nitric and sulfuric acids. These acids become part of cloud systems and dramatically lower the pH (the standard measure of acidity) of rainwater, leading to the weakening and deaths of trees over wide areas. Acid rain, in turn, lowers the pH of soil moisture and water bodies, such as ponds and lakes, and also increases the concentration of toxic metals such as aluminum.

Acid rain is currently a severe problem in eastern North America, throughout Europe, but particularly in central Europe, and east Asia, particularly in China and Korea; within the next 50 years acid rain will also affect southeast Asia, western coastal India, and south central Africa (Kuylenstierna et al. 2001). In the United States alone, around 40 million metric tons of these compounds are released into the atmosphere each year (WRI 1998; Lynch et al. 2000). The heavy reliance of China on high-sulfur coal and the rapid increase in automobile ownership in Southeast Asia represent potential threats to biological diversity in this region, with the production of sulfur dioxide projected to double between 2000 and 2020 (WRI 1998).

Increased acidity alone damages many plant and animal species; as the acidity of water bodies increases, many fish either fail to spawn or die outright (Figure 9.19). Both increased acidity and water pollution are two contributing factors to the dramatic decline of many amphibian populations throughout the world. Most amphibian species depend on bodies of water for at least part of their life cycle, and a decline in water pH

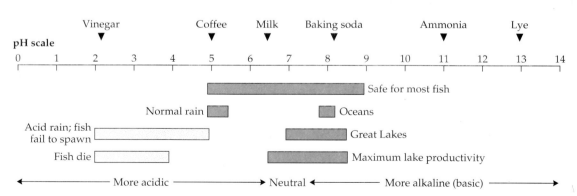

Figure 9.19 The pH scale, indicating ranges at which acidity becomes lethal to fish. Studies indicate that fish are indeed disappearing from heavily acidified lakes. (After Cox 1993, based on data from the U.S. Fish and Wildlife Service.)

causes a corresponding increase in the mortality of eggs and young animals (Blaustein and Wake 1995; Halliday 1998; Alford and Richards 1999). Acidity also inhibits the microbial process of decomposition, lowering the rate of mineral recycling and ecosystem productivity. Many ponds and lakes in industrialized countries have lost large portions of their animal communities as a result of acid rain. These damaged water bodies are often in supposedly pristine areas hundreds of kilometers from major sources of urban and industrial pollution: For example, acidification is evident in 39% of the lakes in Sweden and 34% of the lakes in Norway (Moiseenko 1994). While acidity of rain is decreasing in many areas due to better pollution control, it still remains a serious problem (Kerr 1998). In developing countries, such as China, the acidity of rain is increasing as the country powers its rapid industrial development through the use of fuels high in sulfur (Seip et al. 1999).

OZONE PRODUCTION AND NITROGEN DEPOSITION   Automobiles, power plants, and industrial activities release hydrocarbons and nitrogen oxides as waste products. In the presence of sunlight, these chemicals react with the atmosphere to produce ozone and other secondary chemicals, collectively called photochemical smog. Although ozone in the upper atmosphere is important in filtering out ultraviolet radiation, high concentrations of ozone at ground level damage plant tissues and make them brittle, harming biological communities and reducing agricultural productivity. Ozone and smog are detrimental to both people and animals when inhaled, so both people and biological communities benefit from air-pollution controls. When airborne nitrogen compounds are deposited by rain and dust, biological communities throughout the world are damaged and altered by potentially toxic levels of this nutrient. In particular, the combination of nitrogen deposition and acid rain is responsible for a decline in the density of soil fungi that form beneficial relationships with trees.

TOXIC METALS   Leaded gasoline (still used in many developing countries, and in the United Kingdom, despite its clear danger to human health), mining and smelting operations, and other industrial activities release large quantities of lead, zinc, and other toxic metals into the atmosphere. These compounds are directly poisonous to plant and animal life, and can cause permanent injury to children. The effects of these toxic metals are particularly evident in areas surrounding large smelting operations, where life has been destroyed for miles around.

Levels of air pollution are declining in certain areas of North America and Europe, but continue to rise in many other areas of the world. Increases in air pollution will be particularly severe in many Asian countries with dense (and growing) human populations and increasing industrialization. Hope for controlling air pollution in the future depends on building motor vehicles with dramatically lower emissions, increasing the development and use of mass transit systems, developing more efficient scrubbing processes for industrial smokestacks, and reducing overall energy use through conservation and efficiency measures. Many of these measures are already being actively implemented in European countries and Japan.

Global Climate Change

Carbon dioxide, methane, and other trace gases in the atmosphere are transparent to sunshine, allowing light energy to pass through the atmosphere and warm the surface of the Earth. These gases and water vapor (in the form of clouds) trap the energy radiating from the Earth as heat, slowing the rate at which heat leaves the Earth's surface and radiates back into space. These gases are called **greenhouse gases** because they function much like the glass in a greenhouse, which is transparent to sunlight but traps energy inside the greenhouse once it is transformed to heat (Figure 9.20). The similar warming effect of Earth by its atmospheric gases is called the **greenhouse effect.** We can imagine that these gases act as "blankets" on the Earth's surface: the denser the concentration of gases, the more heat trapped near the Earth, thus, the higher the planet's surface temperature.

The greenhouse effect allows life to flourish on Earth—without it the temperature on the Earth's surface would fall dramatically. Today, however, as a result of human activity, concentrations of greenhouse gases are increasing so much that scientists believe they are already affecting the Earth's climate (IPCC 2001). The term **global warming** is used to describe this increased temperature resulting from the greenhouse effect, and **global climate change** refers to the complete set of climate characteristics that are changing now and will continue to change in the future, including patterns of precipitation and wind.

During the past 100 years, global levels of carbon dioxide (CO_2), methane, and other trace gases have been steadily increasing, primarily as a result of burning fossil fuels—coal, oil, and natural gas (Gates 1993; IPCC 1996). Clearing forests to create farmland and burning firewood for heating and cooking also contribute to rising concentrations of CO_2. Carbon dioxide concentration in the atmosphere has increased from 290 parts per million (ppm) to 360 ppm over the last 100 years (Figure 9.21), and it is projected to double at some point in the latter half of this century. Even if the plans to reduce CO_2 production that were agreed

Figure 9.20 In the greenhouse effect, gases and water vapor form a blanket ▶ around the Earth that acts like the glass roof of a greenhouse, trapping heat near the Earth's surface. (From Gates 1993.)

(A)

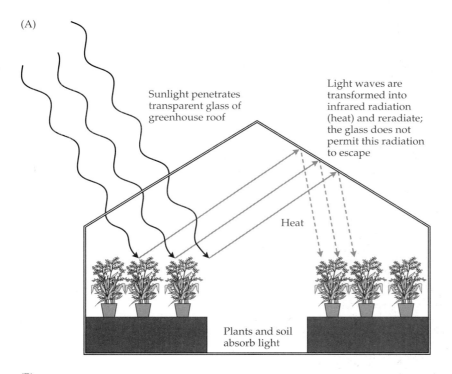

Sunlight penetrates transparent glass of greenhouse roof

Light waves are transformed into infrared radiation (heat) and reradiate; the glass does not permit this radiation to escape

Heat

Plants and soil absorb light

(B)

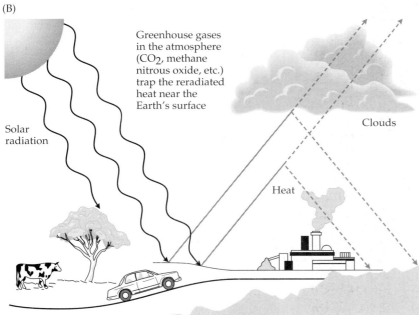

Greenhouse gases in the atmosphere (CO_2, methane nitrous oxide, etc.) trap the reradiated heat near the Earth's surface

Clouds

Solar radiation

Heat

Light waves are transformed into infrared radiation (heat) and reradiated

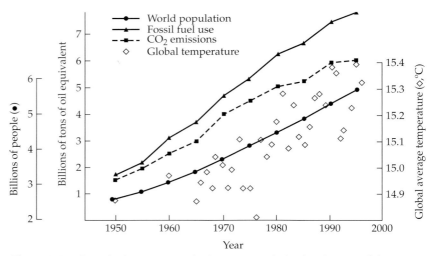

Figure 9.21 Over the last 50 years, the human population has increased dramatically. Increased fossil fuel use and forest destruction have led to greater release of carbon dioxide into the atmosphere. Most scientists believe the observed increase in global temperature is caused by increased atmospheric concentrations of carbon dioxide and other greenhouse gases. (After Houghton et al. 1996.)

upon by some countries at the 1997 Kyoto conference were implemented tomorrow, there would be little immediate reduction in present atmospheric CO_2 levels, because each CO_2 molecule resides in the atmosphere for an average of 100 years before being removed by plants and natural geochemical processes. Because of this time lag, levels of CO_2 in the atmosphere will continue to rise in the short term.

Another significant greenhouse gas is methane, which has increased from 0.9 to 1.7 ppm in the last 100 years as a result of rice cultivation, cattle production, microbial activity in dumps, the burning of tropical forests and grasslands, and release during fossil fuel production. Methane is far more efficient at absorbing heat than carbon dioxide, so that, even at low concentrations, methane is an important contributor to the greenhouse effect. Methane molecules persist in the atmosphere for even longer than does carbon dioxide. Reductions in methane levels will require changes in agricultural practices and improved pollution controls.

Most scientists believe that the increased levels of greenhouse gases have affected the world's climate and ecosystems already and that these effects will increase in the future (Table 9.5). An extensive review of the evidence supports the conclusion that global surface temperatures have increased by 0.6°C during the last century (Myneni et al. 1997; Schneider 1998; IPCC 2001). Some plant and animal species are changing their ranges and the timing of their reproductive behavior in response to these temperature changes. Evidence indicates that ocean water temperatures

TABLE 9.5 Some evidence for global warming

1. INCREASED INCIDENCE OF HEAT WAVES
Example: A July 1999 heat wave in the United States kills 250 people; Chicago registers a record temperature of 48°C (119°F).

2. INCREASED INCIDENCE OF DROUGHTS AND FIRES
Example: Severe summer droughts in 1998 are followed by massive wildfires in Indonesia, Central America, southern Europe, and the southern United States.

3. MELTING OF GLACIERS AND POLAR ICE
Example: In the Caucasus Mountains between the Black Sea and the Caspian Sea, half of all glacial ice has melted during the last 100 years.
Example: A 2992 km^2 section of previously stable Antarctic ice shelf collapses in 1999.

4. RISING SEA LEVELS
Example: Since 1938, one-third of the coastal marshes in a wildlife refuge in Chesapeake Bay has been submerged by rising seawater.

5. SPREAD OF DISEASE TO HIGHER ELEVATIONS
Example: In 1997, rising temperatures allowed malaria-carrying mosquitoes to extend their range into the Kenya highlands, killing hundreds of people.

6. EARLIER SPRING ARRIVAL
Example: One-third of English birds are now laying eggs earlier in the year then they did 30 years ago, and oak trees are now leafing out earlier than they did 40 years ago.

7. SHIFTS IN SPECIES RANGES
Example: Two-thirds of European butterfly species studied are now found farther northward by 35 to 250 km than recorded several decades ago.

8. POPULATION DECLINES
Example: Adelie penguin populations have declined by one-third over the past 25 years as their sea ice habitat melts away.

Source: After Union of Concerned Scientists 1999.

have also changed over the last 50 years: the Atlantic, Pacific, and Indian Oceans have increased in temperature by an average of 0.06°C (Levitus et al. 2000).

There is now a growing consensus among climatologists that the world climate will increase in temperature by an additional 1.4° to 5.8°C by 2100 as a result of increased levels of carbon dioxide and other gases. The increase could be even greater if carbon dioxide levels rise faster than predicted; it could be slightly less if all countries reduced their emissions of greenhouse gases in the very near future. The increase in temperature will be greatest at high latitudes and over large continents (Figure 9.22). Rainfall will increase globally, but will vary by region, with some regions showing decreases in rainfall. There will also probably be an increase in extreme weather events, such as hurricanes, flooding, and regional drought, associated with this warming (Karl et al. 1997). The

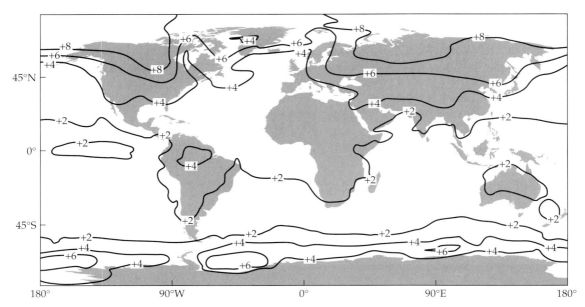

Figure 9.22 Complex computer models of global climate predict that temperatures will increase significantly (temperatures in 2071 to 2100 relative to the period from 1961 to 1990) when CO_2 levels double, which is projected to occur in the mid- to late part of this century. Predicted temperature increases, shown in °C, are greatest over continents and at high latitudes (i.e., closer to the poles). (After IPCC 2001.)

models of future weather patterns are rapidly improving to include: the role of the ocean in absorbing atmospheric carbon dioxide, how plant communities will respond to higher carbon dioxide levels and temperatures, the effects of increased levels of anthropogenic aerosols (airborne particles resulting from burning fossil fuels, wood, and other sources), and the role of cloud cover in reflecting sunlight. Even though details of global climate change are being debated by scientists, there is a broad consensus that the world's climate has started to change already and will continue to change substantially in coming decades.

Changes in Temperate and Tropical Climates

Global climate change is not a new phenomenon. During the past 2 million years, there have been at least 10 cycles of global warming and cooling. When the polar ice caps melted during warm periods, sea levels rose to well above their earlier levels, and species extended their ranges closer to the poles and migrated to higher elevations on mountains. During cold periods, the ice caps enlarged, sea levels dropped, and species shifted their ranges closer to the equator and to lower elevations. While many species undoubtedly went extinct during these repeated episodes of range changes, the species we have today are survivors of global climate change. If species could adjust to changes in global climate in the past, will species be able to adjust to the predicted changes in global climate caused by human alteration of the atmosphere?

It seems likely that many species will be unable to adjust quickly enough to survive this human-caused warming, which will occur far more rapidly than previous, natural climate shifts. It is likely that the consequences of a rise in temperature will be profound, probably profoundly negative.

As a result of global climate change, climatic regions in the northern and southern temperate zones will be shifted toward the poles. More than 10% of the plant species in many U.S. states will not be able to survive the new climatic conditions—if they are not able to migrate northward, they will die. This change has clearly begun already, with alpine plants found growing higher on mountains and migrating birds observed spending longer times at their summer breeding grounds (Walther 2002). In the coming century, global climate change is predicted to have a great impact on arctic boreal and alpine ecosystems as a result of warmer conditions and a longer growing season.

For the eastern deciduous forest of North America, plant species will have to migrate 100–530 km northward (or 1000–5300 m per year) to keep up with a predicted temperature increase of 1.4°–5.8°C over this century, (Davis and Zabinski 1992). Following the last glaciation and subsequent Pleistocene increase in temperature, tree species migrated back into North America at a rate of 10–40 km per century, or 100–400 m per year. Consequently, it seems likely that many species will be unable to disperse northward rapidly enough to track the changing climate (Hansen et al. 2001). Habitat fragmentation caused by human activities may further slow or prevent many species from migrating to new sites where suitable habitat exists (Figure 9.23). Many species of limited distribution and/or poor dispersal ability will undoubtedly go extinct, with widely distributed, easily dispersed species being favored in the new communities. Entire biological communities may become altered and degraded if the dominant species are not able to adapt to the changing conditions (Sala et al. 2000). Certain biological communities of the United States, such as the spruce–fir and the aspen–birch communities, may decline in area by more than 90% (Hansen et al. 2001).

The effects of global climate change on temperature and rainfall are expected to be less drastic in the Tropics than in the temperate zone (Bawa and Markham 1995; IPCC 2001). However, even small changes in the amount and timing of rainfall could have major effects on species composition, cycles of plant reproduction, and susceptibility to fire. The impact of such changes on populations of migratory birds could be quite dramatic. Some models suggest that hurricanes could become more severe and frequent in tropical areas, which would have major consequences for forest structure.

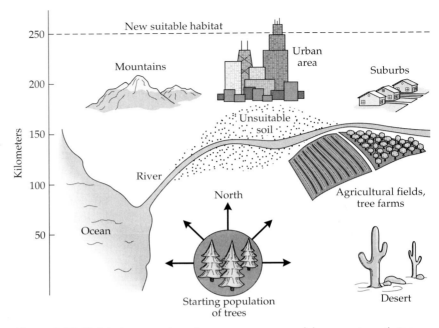

Figure 9.23 If global temperatures increase as some models suggest, north-temperate tree species will have to disperse hundreds of kilometers northward in order to find sites with a hospitable climate. Not only will these species encounter natural barriers such as mountains, oceans, rivers, and unsuitable terrain, but they face barriers created by people, such as agricultural fields, cities, suburbs, roads, and fences. (After Peters and Lovejoy 1992.)

Plants and Climate Change

Some plant species will adapt to utilize the increased carbon dioxide levels and higher temperatures to increase their growth rates, whereas other, less adaptable species will not and will decrease in abundance (Bazzaz and Fajer 1992; Harte and Shaw 1995). A substantial increase in plant growth has already been detected over large areas of northern high latitudes using satellite data (Myneni et al. 1997). Shifts in the populations of herbivorous insect species may be pronounced as their plant resources change. Unpredictable fluctuations in the populations of plant and insect species could lead to the extinction of many rare species and great population increases in some other species. In addition, many plant species will flower weeks earlier in the growing season. This could potentially disrupt the pollination systems of rare plant species that are visited by specialist pollinators, leading to reproductive failure.

Finally, the large areas where temperate agricultural crops, such as wheat and maize (corn), are now grown may have to be moved farther from the Equator and perhaps expanded as the climate changes. Many of the areas that will be potentially suitable for new agricultural land are currently protected conservation land such as national parks. This potentially creates a situation in which the protection of biological diversity directly competes with supplying the food needs of people.

Rising Sea Levels

Warming temperatures are already causing mountain glaciers to melt and the polar ice caps to shrink, and this process will continue and accelerate. As a result of this release of water over the next 100 years, sea levels are predicted to rise by 9–88 cm and flood low-lying, coastal communities. It is possible that rising sea levels could destroy or radically alter 25–80% of the coastal wetlands of the United States. The rise will occur so rapidly that many species will be unable to migrate quickly enough to adjust to changing water levels. The migration of wetland species, in particular species of coastal salt marshes, will be blocked where human settlements, roads, and flood control barriers have been built adjacent to wetlands. Squeezed between the rising sea and dense coastal developments, many species will no longer have a place to live. This will have major economic impacts as well because salt marsh habitat is among the world's most productive habitat for plant and animal life, and is a major breeding and nursery ground for commercial fish and shellfish.

In tropical areas, mangroves will be severely affected; seawater will be too deep in existing mangrove areas to allow the next generation of seedlings to become established. Much of the current land area of low-lying countries such as Bangladesh could be under water within 100 years. There is evidence that this process has already begun; sea levels have already risen by 10–20 cm over the last 100 years due to thermal expansion of the oceans and widespread melting of polar ice (IPCC 2001). Many low islands that were previously just above water are now just below the water level.

Rising sea levels are potentially detrimental to many coral reef species, which grow at a precise depth in the water with the right combination of light and water movement. Water levels rising at a rate of 88 cm per century translates into a rise in sea level of almost 1 mm per year—and 1 mm per year is about as fast as the fastest-growing corals can grow (Grigg and Epp 1989). Slow-growing coral reefs will be unable to keep pace with the rise in sea level and will gradually be submerged and die; only fast-growing species will be able to survive. Compounding this, the pace of coral growth might be slower than normal; increasing absorption of CO_2 by the ocean will make the water more acidic and inhibit the ability of coral animals to deposit the calcium used to build the reef structure.

Coral reefs are also threatened by rising seawater temperatures (Wilkinson et al. 1999). Abnormally high water temperatures in the Pacific Ocean and Indian Ocean in 1998 led to the death of the symbiotic algae that live inside coral and provide essential carbohydrates; subsequently, these "bleached" coral then suffered a massive dieback, with an estimated 70% coral mortality in Indian Ocean reefs (Sapp 1999). Even warmer conditions in the coming decades could be a disaster for many coral reefs.

The Overall Effect of Global Warming

Global climate change has the potential to radically restructure biological communities and change the ranges of many species. The pace of this change could overwhelm the natural dispersal abilities of species. There is mounting evidence that this process has already begun (see Table 9.5), with poleward movements in the distribution of bird and plant species, and reproduction occurring earlier in the spring (Parmesan et al. 1999; McCarty 2001; Schneider and Root 2001; Walther et al. 2002). Because the implications of global climate change are so far-reaching, biological communities, ecosystem functions, and climate need to be carefully monitored over the coming decades. Global climate change will also have an enormous impact on human populations in coastal areas, and in areas that usually experience large changes in temperature and rainfall. The poor people of the world will be least able to adjust to these changes and will suffer the consequences disproportionately.

It is likely that, as the climate changes, many existing protected areas will no longer preserve the rare and endangered species that currently live there (Kienast et al. 1998; McCarty 2001). We need to establish new conservation areas now to protect sites that will be suitable for these species in the future, such as sites with large elevational gradients. Potential future migration routes, such as north–south river valleys, need to be identified and established now. If species are in danger of going extinct in the wild because of global climate change, the last remaining individuals may have to be maintained in captivity. Another necessary strategy will be to transplant isolated populations of rare and endangered species to new localities at higher elevations and farther from the poles, where they can survive and thrive. Even if global climate change is not as severe as predicted, establishing new protected areas can only be good for the protection of biological diversity.

Although the prospect of global climate change is cause for great concern, it should not divert our attention from the massive habitat destruction that is the principal current cause of species extinction (Vitousek 1994; Kappelle et al. 1999): Preserving intact communities and restoring degraded ones are the most important and immediate priorities for conservation.

Summary

1. Massive disturbances to the environment caused by human activities are driving species, even communities, to the point of extinction. These impacts will increase in the future, mostly in the species-rich tropical countries, as the

human population reaches 8 billion or more around the year 2050. Slowing human population growth and reducing the overconsumption of resources are important elements of the solution to the biological diversity crisis.

2. The major threat to biological diversity is the loss of habitat, so to protect biological diversity we must preserve habitat. Many unique and threatened species have lost the greater areas of their habitat and are protected on only a tiny percentage of their original range. Species-rich tropical rain forests are currently being destroyed at a rapid rate. Extensive habitat destruction has occurred in tropical dry forests, wetlands in all regions of the world, coral reefs, and temperate grasslands.

3. Habitat fragmentation is the process whereby a large continuous area of habitat is both reduced and divided into two or more fragments. These fragments are often isolated from one another by modified or degraded habitat. Habitat fragmentation leads to the rapid loss of remaining species because it creates barriers to the normal processes of dispersal, colonization, and foraging. Particular fragments may lack the range of food types and other resources necessary to support permanent populations of certain species, or they may contain altered environmental conditions and increased levels of pests, which make them less suitable for the original species.

4. Environmental pollution eliminates many species from biological communities, even where the structure of the community is not obviously disturbed. Pesticides, sprayed to control insects, become concentrated in the bodies of birds, particularly raptors, leading to a decline in populations. Water pollution by petroleum products, sewage, and industrial wastes can kill species outright or gradually eliminate them. Excessive nutrient inputs can cause harmful algal blooms that damage aquatic communities. Acid rain, high ozone levels near the surface of the Earth, and airborne toxic metals are all damaging components of air pollution.

5. Global climate patterns may change within the coming century because of the large amounts of carbon dioxide and other greenhouse gases that are being produced by human activities such as the burning of fossil fuels. Predicted temperature increases could be so rapid during this coming century that many species will be unable to adjust their ranges and will go extinct. Low-lying coastal communities may be submerged by seawater if polar ice caps start to melt. Conservation biologists need to monitor these changes and take action when species cannot adapt to climate change.

For Discussion

1. Human population growth is sometimes blamed for the loss of biological diversity. Is this valid? What other factors are responsible, and how do we weigh their relative importance?

2. Excessive consumption of resources by people in developed countries is a major cause of the loss of biological diversity. An alternative is to "live simply, so that others may simply live," or to "live as if life mattered." Consider the absolute minimum of food, shelter, clothing, and energy that you and your family need to survive and compare it with what you now use. Would you be willing to change your lifestyle to preserve the environment and help others? How could an entire society change enough to benefit the environment?

3. What can an individual citizen do to improve the environment and conserve biodiversity? Consider the options, which range from doing no harm to becoming actively involved in large conservation organizations.

4. Consider the most damaged and the most pristine habitats near where you live. Why have some been preserved and others allowed to degrade?

5. Examine maps of parks and nature reserves. Have these areas been fragmented by roads, power lines, and other human constructs? How has fragmentation affected the average fragment size, the area of interior habitat, and the total length of edge? Analyze the effects of adding new roads or eliminating existing roads and developments from the parks and consider their biological, legal, political, and economic implications.

Suggested Reading

Askins, R. A. 2000. *Restoring North America's Birds: Lessons from Landscape Ecology.* Yale University Press, New Haven, CT. Various theories for bird decline are explored, with suggestions for restoration.

Ayres, E. 1999. *God's Last Offer: Negotiating for a Sustainable Future.* Four Walls Eight Windows, New York. The editor of *World Watch* magazine dramatically presents the overwhelming environmental crisis.

Carson, R. 1982. *Silent Spring.* Reprint, Penguin, Harmondsworth, England. This book describing the harmful effects of pesticides on birds heightened public awareness when it was first published.

Cincotta R. P. and R. Engelman. 2000. *Nature's Place: Human Population and the Future of Biological Diversity.* Population Action International, Washington, D.C. Human populations are the major force causing the decline in biodiversity.

Debinski, D. M. and R. D. Holt. 2000. A survey and overview of habitat fragmentation experiments. *Conservation Biology* 14: 342–355. Twenty fragmentation experiments reviewed, revealing a wide diversity of species responses and a need for long-term monitoring.

Edwards, M. 1994. Pollution in the former USSR: Lethal legacy. *National Geographic* 1994 (August): 70–98. Appalling, graphic examples of environmental neglect harming people and the environment.

Hansen, A. J., R. P. Neilson, V. H. Dale, C. H. Flather, et al. 2001. Global change in forests: Responses of species, communities, and biomes. *BioScience* 51(9): 765–779. Global climate will cause enormous changes in the distribution of species and communities.

Intergovernmental Panel on Climate Change (IPCC). 2001. *Climate Change 2001: Synthesis Report.* Cambridge University Press, Cambridge. A comprehensive presentation of the current state of our knowledge.

Laurance, W. F. and G. B. Williamson. 2001. Positive feedback among forest fragmentation, drought and climate change in the Amazon. *Conservation Biology* 15: 1529–1535. Article from a symposium on habitat fragmentation.

Laurance, W. F., M. A. Cochrane, S. Bergen, P. M. Fearnside, P. Delamônica, et al. 2001. The future of the Brazilian Amazon. *Science* 291: 438–439. Road construction in the Amazon will lead to the rapid loss of forest cover.

McCarty, J. P. 2001. Ecological consequences of recent climate change. *Conservation Biology* 15: 320–331. Global climate change is already affecting many species and communities and may soon cause extinctions.

Meyers, N. 1997. Consumption in relation to population, environment and development. *The Environmentalist* 17: 33–44. Overconsumption of resources in the developed world leads to poverty and environmental damage in the developing world.

Porter, J. and J. Tougas. 2001. Reef ecosystems: Threats to their biodiversity. In *Encyclopedia of Biodiversity,* S. A. Levin (ed.), Vol. 5, pp. 73–96. Academic Press, San Diego, CA. Reef ecosystems are the marine equivalent of tropical rain forests and their existence is similarly threatened.

Reed, R. A., J. Johnson-Barnard, and W. L. Baker. 1996. Fragmentation of a forested Rocky Mountain landscape, 1950–1993. *Biological Conservation* 75: 267–277. Case study presenting methods for analyzing quantitative trends in fragmentation.

Rees, W. 2001. Ecological footprint, concept of. In *Encyclopedia of Biodiversity*, S. A. Levin (ed.),. Vol. 2, pp. 229–244. Academic Press, San Diego, CA. People and cities can have impacts far beyond their immediate surroundings, as shown by this novel tool.

Schneider, S. 1998. *Laboratory Earth: The Planetary Gamble We Can't Afford to Lose.* Basic Books, New York. Leading authority clearly explains the complex ideas of global climate change and why it is vitally important to take action.

Smith, W. H. 2001. Pollution, overview. In *Encyclopedia of Biodiversity,* S. A. Levin (ed.), Vol. 4, pp. 731–744. Academic Press, San Diego, CA. Pollution can affect individuals, biological communities, and ecosystem processes.

Trombulak, S. C. and C. A. Frissell. 2000. Review of ecological effects of roads on terrestrial and aquatic communities. *Conservation Biology* 14(1): 18–30. Roads have a wide variety of negative impacts on biodiversity.

Tucker, R. P. 2000. *Insatiable Appetite: the United States and the Ecological Degradation of the Tropical World.* The University of California Press, Berkeley. Eating hamburgers and drinking coffee negatively affect tropical biodiversity.

Watling, L. and E. Norse. 1998. Disturbance of the seabed by mobile fishing gear: A comparison to forest clear-cutting. *Conservation Biology* 12: 1180–1197. Special section devoted to fishing impacts.

Walther, G. R., E. Post, P. Convey, A. Menzel, et al. 2002. Ecological responses to recent climate change. *Nature.* 416: 389–395. Review of the latest evidence for the impact of global climate change on biological systems.

Chapter 10

Overexploitation, Invasive Species, and Disease

E ven when biological communities appear intact, they may be experiencing significant losses as a result of human activities. In this chapter, we will discuss three threats to biological communities that are less obvious, but not less damaging than threats such as habitat destruction and loss. These three threats are: overexploitation of particular species, introduction of invasive species, and increased levels of disease transmission. These threats often follow habitat fragmentation and degradation, or are made worse by such factors. Global climate change will also make biological communities more vulnerable to these threats in the future.

Overexploitation

Overexploitation by humans has been estimated to currently threaten about a quarter of the endangered vertebrates in the United States and around half of the endangered mammals (Wilcove et al. 1998; Wilcove 1999). People have always hunted and harvested the food and other resources they need to survive, and as long as human populations were small and the methods of collection unsophisticated, people could sustainably harvest and hunt the plants and animals in their

(A)

(B)

Figure 10.1 (A) These fishermen are pulling a net to harvest fish on Mahe Island, Seychelles. Such traditional methods are often sustainable. (Photograph © G. J. James/Biological Photo Service.) (B) Modern methods of harvesting wildlife, however, have become so efficient that catches seriously deplete populations. In this case, large quantities of herring are being pumped into the hold of a fishing vessel in Sitka, Alaska. Note the additional vessels in the background. (Photograph © Gary C. Will/Visuals Unlimited.)

environment. However, as human populations have increased, our use of the environment has escalated and our methods of harvesting have become dramatically more efficient (Figure 10.1) (Redford 1992; Fitzgibbon et al. 1995; Cuarón 2001). In many areas, this has led to an almost complete depletion of large animals from many biological communities and the creation of strangely "empty" habitats.

Technological advances mean that, even in the developing world, guns are used instead of blowpipes, spears, or arrows for hunting in the tropical rain forests and savannahs. Whole villages are mobilized to systematically remove every usable animal and plant from a section of forest. Powerful motorized fishing boats and enormous "factory ships" harvest fish from the world's oceans and sell them on the global market. Small-scale local fishermen now have outboard motors on their canoes and boats, allowing them to harvest wider areas more rapidly. However, even in preindustrial societies, intense exploitation led to the decline and extinction of local species. For example, ceremonial cloaks worn by the Hawaiian kings were made from feathers of the mamo bird (*Drepanis* sp.); a single cloak used the feathers of 70,000 birds of this now-extinct species.

Traditional societies often imposed restrictions on themselves to prevent overexploitation of natural resources. For example, the rights to specific harvesting territories were rigidly controlled, hunting and harvesting in certain areas was banned. There were often prohibitions against harvesting female, juvenile, and undersized animals. Certain seasons of the year and times of the day were closed for harvesting. Certain efficient methods of harvesting were not allowed. (Interestingly enough, these restrictions, which allowed traditional societies to exploit communal resources on a long-term, sustainable basis, are almost identical to the rigid fishing restrictions currently imposed on and proposed for many fisheries in industrialized nations [Freese 1997; Colding and Folke 2001].) Among the most highly developed restrictions were those of the traditional or artisan societies of Micronesia and Polynesia (Johannes 1978). In these societies, the resources of the reef and lagoon were clearly defined and the possible consequences of overharvesting readily apparent. This is still true today in Tonga, where only the King is permitted to hunt flying foxes because their numbers have shrunk precipitously due to overharvesting.

Exploitation in the Modern World

Few self-imposed restrictions on using resources remain today. In much of the world, resources are exploited opportunistically (Mowat 1984; Chapman and Peres 2001). The lack of restraint applies to both ends of the economic scale—the poor and hungry as well as the rich and greedy. In previous chapters we have seen how corporations and the developed world take advantage of natural resources for a profit. If a market exists for a product, local people will search their environment to find and sell it. Sometimes traditional groups will sell the rights to a resource, such as a forest or mining area, for cash to buy desired goods. In rural areas, the traditional controls that regulate the extraction of natural products have generally weakened. Where there has been substantial human migration, civil unrest, or war, controls may no longer exist. In countries beset with civil conflict, such as Somalia, the former Yugoslavia, the

Democratic Republic of the Congo, and Rwanda, firearms have come into the hands of rural people. The breakdown of food distribution networks in countries such as these leaves the resources of the natural environment vulnerable to whoever can exploit them (Jones 1990). The most efficient hunter can kill the most animals, sell the most meat, and make the most money for himself and his family. Animals are sometimes even killed for target practice or simply to spite the government.

On local and regional scales, hunters in developing countries move into recently logged areas, national parks, and other areas near roads and legally and illegally shoot, trap, and collect wild mammals to sell as meat. Populations of large primates, such as gorillas and chimpanzees, ungulates, and other mammals, may be reduced by 80% or more by hunting, and certain species may be eliminated altogether (Wilkie and Carpenter 1999). The result is an empty forest: land with a mostly intact plant community that is lacking its animal community (Robinson et al. 1999). The decline in animal populations caused by the intensive hunting of animals has been termed the **bushmeat crisis** and is a major concern for wildlife officials in Africa. Solutions involve restricting the sale and transport of bushmeat, restricting the sale of firearms and ammunition, closing roads following logging, extending legal protection to key endangered species, establishing protected reserves where hunting is not allowed, and most importantly, providing alternative protein sources to reduce the demand for bushmeat (Bennett and Robinson 2000; Cuarón 2001).

Overexploitation of resources often occurs rapidly when a commercial market develops for a previously unexploited or locally used species. The legal and illegal trade in wildlife is responsible for the decline of many species (Fitzgerald 1989; Poten 1991). Worldwide trade in wildlife is valued at over $10 billion per year, not including edible fish (Hemley 1994). One of the most pervasive examples of this is the international trade in furs, in which hunted species, such as the chinchilla (*Chinchilla* spp.), vicuña (*Vicugna vicugna*), giant otter (*Pteronura brasiliensis*), and numerous cat species, have been reduced to low numbers. Overharvesting of butterflies by insect collectors, orchids, cacti, and other plants by horticulturists, marine mollusks by shell collectors, and tropical fish for aquarium hobbyists are further examples of whole biological communities being targeted to supply an enormous international demand (Table 10.1). It has been estimated that 500–600 million tropical fish are sold worldwide for the aquarium market, and many times that number are killed during collection or shipping (Simpson 2001). Parts of many rare animals such as bears and tigers are harvested and sold for their reported value as medicines and aphrodisiacs, particularly in East Asia. Major exporters are primarily in the developing world, often in the Tropics; most major importers are in the developed countries and East Asia, including Canada, China, the European Union, Hong Kong, Japan, Singapore, Taiwan, and the United States. The international trade in other

TABLE 10.1 Major targeted groups of the worldwide trade in wildlife

Group	Number traded each year[a]	Comments
Primates	26,000	Mostly used for biomedical research; also for pets, zoos, circuses, and private collections.
Birds	2–5 million	Zoos and pets. Mostly perching birds, but also legal and illegal trade in parrots.
Reptiles	2–3 million	Zoos and pets. Also 10–15 million raw skins. Reptiles are used in some 50 million manufactured products (mainly from the wild but increasingly from farms).
Ornamental fish	500–600 million	Most saltwater tropical fish come from the wild and may be caught using illegal methods that damage other wildlife and the surrounding coral reef.
Reef corals	1000–2000 tons	Reefs are being destructively mined to provide aquarium decor and coral jewelry.
Orchids	9–10 million	Approximately 10% of the international trade comes from the wild, sometimes deliberately mislabeled to avoid regulations.
Cacti	7–8 million	Approximately 15% of traded cacti come from the wild, with smuggling a major problem.

Source: Data from Hemley 1994, WRI 2000.
[a]With the exception of reef corals, refers to number of individuals.

animals is similarly large: 250,000 live snakes, 235,000 live parrots, and 26,000 primates are sold each year.

Besides a surprisingly large legal trade, billions of dollars are involved in the illegal trade of wildlife. A black market links poor local people, corrupt customs officials, rogue dealers, and wealthy buyers who don't question the sources that they buy from (Webster 1997). This trade has many of the same characteristics, the same practices, and sometimes the same players, as the illegal trade in drugs and weapons. Confronting those who perpetuate illegal activities has become a major and even dangerous job for international law enforcement agencies.

Commercial exploitation of natural resources often follows a common pattern of opportunism where there is increased dependency on technology, transportation, and new markets. The pattern usually occurs in the following sequence:

- The growth of towns, factories, logging camps, and mines creates a cash market for meat and other natural products.
- Traditional hunters and fishermen, who formerly harvested primarily for their own needs, begin to supply the cash market.
- The hunters and fishermen use the cash to buy guns and outboard motors for more efficient harvesting.
- Roads and motorboats allow middlemen to travel longer distances to bring the harvest to market and provide access to remote areas. Often, new marketable species are discovered and exploited as a result.

Figure 10.2 Seahorses are widely used as an ingredient in Chinese medicine and they have been overharvested for this purpose.

- Warehouses and refrigerators allow the catch to be accumulated at distant collection points prior to shipping.
- International buyers, eager sellers, and jet planes make a world market in wild species, further accelerating the overexploitation of natural resources.

Any number of examples could be given to illustrate this scenario: traditional hunters in remote areas of Borneo who supply the growing towns with wild boar meat, Malay fishermen using motorboats to collect edible jellyfish for sale in the high-priced Japanese market, and the depletion of wild game at increasing distances around mining towns in Africa. A striking example is the enormous increase in demand for seahorses (*Hippocampus* spp.; Figure 10.2) in China. The Chinese use dried seahorses in their traditional medicine, because it resembles a dragon and is believed to have a variety of healing powers. Around 20 tons of seahorses are consumed in China per year—roughly 6 million animals. Seahorse populations throughout the world are being decimated to supply this ever-increasing demand (Vincent 1994). Another example is the worldwide trade in frog legs; each year Indonesia exports the legs of around 94–235 million frogs to western European countries for luxury meals. There is no information on how this intensive harvesting affects frog populations, forest ecology and agriculture; and perhaps not surprisingly, the names of the frog species on the shipping labels are often wrong, which adds to the difficulty in quantifying the extent of the problem (Veith et al. 2000).

The pattern of overexploitation of plants and animals in many cases is distressingly similar. A resource is identified, a commercial market is developed for that resource, and the local human populace mobilizes to extract and sell the resource. As the supply diminishes, the price rises, creating a strong incentive to overexploit the resource. The resource is extracted so thoroughly that it becomes rare or even extinct, then the market identifies another species or another region to exploit. Commercial fishing and whaling demonstrates this pattern well, with the industry working one species after another to the point of diminishing returns (Box 17).

Maximum Sustainable Yield

Governments and industries often claim that they can avoid the overharvesting of wild species by applying modern scientific management. As part of this approach, an extensive body of literature has developed in wildlife and fisheries management and in forestry to describe the **maximum sustainable yield:** the greatest amount of a resource, such as Atlantic bluefin tuna (*Thunnus thynnus*), that can be harvested each year and replaced through population growth without detriment to the population. Calculations using the maximum population growth rate (r) and the carrying capacity (B) (the largest population or biomass that a given area can support) are used to estimate the maximum sustainable yield

BOX 17 *Endangered Whales: Making a Comeback?*

Whales are among the largest and possibly most intelligent animals on Earth, with complicated social organization and communication systems. The discovery of the whale's complex, unique songs captured the public imagination, resulting in strong public support for research on whales and for legal measures to protect them. But as public support has increased, has the situation for whales really improved?

Scientists have only recently begun to comprehend the complexity of whale behavior and ecology because studies of many whale species are difficult for several reasons. First, radio tracking devices commonly used for land animals are difficult to use in water, making it difficult to observe individuals and populations. Second, whales are often very far-ranging, traveling throughout the year from the tropical to polar seas. Finally, many whale species have become so rare that finding the animals in the open ocean is truly a needle-in-a-haystack search. Populations of numerous species, including the blue (*Balaenoptera musculus*), bowhead (*Balaena mysticetus*), humpback (*Megaptera novaenglie*), gray (*Eschrichtius robustus*), and right whales (*Eubalaena glacialis, E. japonica, and E. australis*), are estimated to have fewer than 35,000 individuals remaining (Darling 1988; Myers 1993).

Few ocean predators are capable of taking on the larger whales, so the greatest threat to all whale species for nearly four centuries has been humans. Until as recently as fifteen years ago, commercial whaling has been the single most significant factor leading to the decline of the larger whale species—a threat from which many have not yet recovered.

Commercial whaling began in the sixteenth century and reached its apex in the nineteenth and early twentieth centuries, when "baleen" (whalebone), spermaceti oil (oil from sperm whales), and oil made from whale blubber became important commercial products in the international marketplace. Several species hunted preferentially were pushed to the

Worldwide populations of whale species harvested by humans

Species	Numbers prior to whaling[a]	Present numbers	Main diet items
BALEEN WHALES			
Blue	200,000	9000	Plankton
Bowhead	56,000	8200	Plankton
Fin	475,000	123,000	Plankton, fish
Gray (Pacific stock)	23,000	21,000	Crustaceans
Humpback	150,000	25,000	Plankton, fish
Minke	140,000	850,000	Plankton, fish
Northern right	Unknown	1300	Plankton
Sei	100,000	55,000	Plankton, fish, squid
Southern right	100,000	1500	Plankton
TOOTHED WHALES			
Beluga	Unknown	50,000	Fish, crustaceans
Narwhal	Unknown	35,000	Fish, squid, crustaceans
Sperm	2,400,000	1,950,000	Fish, squid

Source: After Myers 1993; Sea World 2000.

[a]These numbers are highly speculative.

BOX 17   *(continued)*

brink of extinction. Right whales—so named because they were slow, easy to capture, and provided up to 150 barrels of blubber oil as well as abundant baleen, thus making them the "right" whale for whalers—were the first to bear the brunt of the industry. As the right whale declined in the eighteenth century, whalers turned to other species: the gray, humpback, and bowhead, and later the blue, were decimated in their turn.

Hunting of right whales was made illegal by international agreement in 1935, by which point they had been reduced to less than 5% of their original abundance. By 1946, faced with the imminent extinction of these and other important species, whaling nations created the International Whaling Commission (IWC) to regulate whale hunting. In 1974, the IWC instituted partial bans on whaling for parts of the world (and for certain species). These rules were violated so often that the IWC instituted a moratorium on all commercial killing of whales worldwide in 1986, against the protests of nations such as Japan, Norway, Russia, and Iceland. Some of these nations continued

hunting by employing a loophole in the IWC agreement allowing hunting of some abundant whale species, such as the southern minke whale, for scientific studies, but hunters regularly kill more whales than the agreement permits. Worse still, whalers frequently make illegal kills of protected species, often with the tacit approval of their governments (Taylor and Dunstone 1996; Twiss and Reeves 1999). Nevertheless, annual killings of whales have dropped dramatically since the 1986 ban.

Since the ban was instituted, different species have had variable recovery rates. Right whales, protected since 1936, have not recovered in either the North Atlantic or North Pacific. Humpback numbers, on the other hand, have more than doubled in some areas since the early 1960s, an increase of nearly 10% annually. Pacific gray whales appear to have recovered to their previous levels of about 23,000 animals after being hunted to less than 1000 whales. Despite continued hunting, minke whales appear to be quite abundant, with an estimated 850,000 individuals, even more than there were prior to hunting.

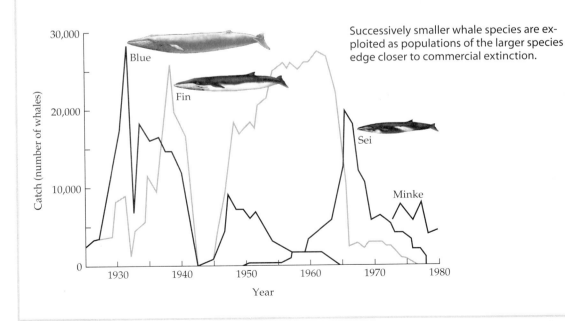

Successively smaller whale species are exploited as populations of the larger species edge closer to commercial extinction.

BOX 17 *(continued)*

Though the whaling ban has greatly reduced the most direct threat, other factors now contribute to whale mortality. At greatest risk is the North Atlantic right whale population, currently estimated at 1300 animals—far less than its original size. Right whales tend to ignore boats when feeding on the surface and are injured during collisions with large ships or when they become tangled in fishing gear. Recent efforts to limit injury and deaths related to human activities have included bans on gill nets in Florida calving grounds, as well as increased restrictions on fishing boats working in critical feeding areas off the coast of New England.

Many whales too small for large-scale commercial use, such as dolphins and porpoises, have shown substantial population declines as a result of deliberate as well as accidental capture. As fish become scarce due to overharvesting, some traditional societies are hunting dolphins in increasing numbers (Parfit 1995). Other rare marine animals, such as manatees, are also being targeted by fishermen. Nevertheless, accidental catches by commercial fishing boats still account for a high proportion of dolphin deaths. Dolphins in tropical waters of the eastern Pacific Ocean are particularly vulnerable to fishing-related fatalities because they often travel with schools of tuna; thousands of dolphins die in tuna nets each year. One approach to limit the by-catch killing of dolphins has been to establish international certification that tuna have been caught using "dolphin-friendly" methods and to label the tuna caught with such methods.

Small whales and dolphins living in estuarine and riverine habitats face additional threats because these areas are heavily used for shipping and boating, increasing the possibility of direct harm from collisions or entanglements, as well as indirect harm caused by chemical and noise pollution. Small whales appear to be highly sensitive to pollutants and carcinogens (particularly heavy metals and pesticides), which are present in greater concentrations in rivers and harbors than in the open sea. Tissue samples of St. Lawrence River belugas (*Huso huso*), for example, contain concentrations of carcinogenic PCBs 10–100 times higher than have been found in ocean-dwelling Arctic belugas (Beland 1996). Long-term exposure to high levels of pollutants exacts a heavy toll on the health of river-dwelling whales: Autopsies of over 70 beluga whales from the St. Lawrence indicate that the cancer rate among these whales was twice as high as in humans, with gastrointestinal cancers the most common form observed. Ailments found in these animals—illnesses not prevalent in Arctic Ocean belugas—include perforated stomach ulcers, thyroid and adrenal gland lesions, and a high incidence of infections.

In the coming years, whales and people will come into increasing conflict over marine resources. Fin, humpback, minke, and sperm whales eat the same fish and squid that commercial fishing fleets are harvesting intensively in the North Atlantic Ocean—in some cases, such as with cod and haddock stocks, to the point of collapse. In Japan, fisherman have organized killings of dolphins that they see as competitors for fish. As harvesting of marine resources becomes ever more efficient and as marine habitats are damaged and destroyed, it will grow increasingly difficult to find effective conservation strategies to protect whales and other marine species and to sustain ocean ecosystems.

(Y_{max}) (Bodmer et al. 1997; Beddington 2001; Essington 2001; Saltz 2001), which typically occurs when the population size is at around half the carrying capacity, or the biomass is half of its maximum value. The maximum sustainable yield can be estimated as:

$$Y_{max} = rB/4$$

For a growing population with *r* having a value of 2 (meaning the population is capable of doubling each year until it reaches carrying capacity), half of the biomass could theoretically be harvested each year. In highly controlled situations where the resource can be quantified, such as plantations of timber trees, it may be possible to approach maximum sustainable yield. However, in many real-world situations, harvesting a species at the theoretical maximum sustainable yield is not possible due to factors such as weather conditions, disease outbreaks, illegal harvesting, and damage to stock during harvesting. Attempts to harvest at high levels can lead to an abrupt species decline (Ludwig et al. 1993; Mace and Hudson 1999). Yield management of marine resources demonstrates some of the serious problems that can arise from careless applications of maximum sustainable yield figures.

PROBLEMS WITH YIELD MANAGEMENT: THE FISHING INDUSTRY   Worldwide, one-third of the world's major fish stocks have been classified as overfished. But fishing industry representatives use maximum sustainable yield calculations to support their position that harvesting levels of Atlantic bluefin tuna, for example, can be maintained at the present rate, even though the population of the species has declined by 90% in recent years (Safina 1993). In order to satisfy local business interests and protect jobs, governments often set harvesting levels too high, resulting in damage to the resource base. It is particularly difficult to coordinate international agreements and to monitor compliance with maximum sustainable yield limits when species migrate across national boundaries and through international waters. Illegal harvesting may result in additional resource removal not accounted for in official records, such has been occurring in the whaling industry and in fishing operations in Antarctic waters.

Further, a considerable proportion of the remaining stock may be damaged during harvesting operations. Another difficulty presents itself if harvest levels are kept fairly constant—often due to overly optimistic estimates of resource biomass—even though the resource base fluctuates; a normal harvest of a fish species during a year when fish stocks are low due to unusual weather conditions may severely reduce or destroy the species. In order to protect species from total destruction, governments are more frequently closing fishing grounds in the hopes that populations will recover (Safina 2001). For example, the Canadian fishing fleet continued to harvest large amounts of cod off Newfoundland during the 1980s, even as the population declined. As a result, cod stocks dropped to 1% of their original numbers, and the government was forced to close the fishery in 1992, eliminating 35,000 jobs (Barinaga 1995).

Many examples like these clearly demonstrate that management based on simplistic mathematical models of maximum sustainable yield are often inappropriate and invalid for the real world. Yield models should primarily be used to gain insight into fish stocks rather than to determine a single yield level that must be accepted. What *is* required is constant monitoring of stocks and the ability to adjust harvesting levels as appropriate. Once harvesting pressure is removed by government regulation, fishing stocks may take years to recover, because fish density may be too low for good reproduction, competing species may have established themselves, or most years may be unsuitable for reproduction. In some cases, fishing stocks have not recovered even many years after harvesting has been stopped completely.

For many marine species, direct exploitation is less important than the indirect effects of commercial fishing (Hofman 1995). Many marine vertebrates and invertebrates are caught incidentally as by-catch during fishing operations and are killed or injured in the process. Approximately 25% of the harvest in fishing operations is dumped back in the sea to die. The huge number of sea turtles and dolphins killed by commercial fishing boats as by-catch resulted in a massive public outcry and led to the development of improved nets to reduce these accidental catches. Even so, many marine animals die when they accidentally become entangled in discarded and lost fishing gear.

In the North Atlantic, one species after another has been overfished to the point of diminishing returns (Kendrick 1995). One of the most dramatic cases of overexploitation in recent years involves sharks (see Box 10 in Chapter 6). A similar situation has been documented among small cetacean species (dolphins and porpoises) in the southeastern Pacific. In the same way that the depletion of commercial fish in the North Atlantic has led to an increase in the harvesting of sharks, fishermen from coastal Peru are increasingly harvesting dolphins and porpoises for the local market now that southeastern Pacific fish stocks have been depleted. While these small cetaceans were previously caught incidentally by fishermen, the exploitation of porpoises and dolphins has become a common and deliberate practice (Parfit 1995).

What Can Be Done to Stop Overexploitation?

Perhaps as many overexploited species become rare it will no longer be commercially viable to harvest them, and their numbers will have a chance to recover. Unfortunately, populations of many species, such as the rhinoceros and certain wild cats, may already have been reduced so severely by the combination of hunting and habitat destruction that they will require vigilant conservation efforts to recover. In some cases, rarity even increases demand: As the rhinoceros becomes more rare, the price of its horn rises, making it an even more valuable commodity on the black market. In rural areas of the developing world, desperate people may search even more intensively for the last remaining marketable plants and animals to collect and sell in order to buy food for their families. Finding the methods to protect and manage the remaining individuals in such situations is a priority for conservation biologists. As described in Chapter 20, conservation projects linking the conservation of biodiversity and local economic development represent one possible approach. National parks, nature reserves, and other protected areas can be established to conserve overharvested species. When harvesting can be reduced or stopped by the enforcement of international regulations, such as the Convention on International Trade in Endangered Species (CITES), and comparable national regulations, species may be able to recover. Sea otters, elephants, and certain whale species provide hopeful examples of species that have recovered once overexploitation was stopped.

Invasive Species

Exotic species are species that occur outside their natural ranges because of human activity. The great majority of exotics do not become established in the places in which they are introduced because the new environment is not suitable to their needs. However, a certain percentage of species do establish themselves in their new homes, and many of these can be considered **invasive species**—that is, they increase in abundance at the expense of native species (Mack et al. 2000; Mooney and Hobbs 2000; Van Driesche and Van Driesche 2000). These invasive species may displace native species through competition for limiting resources. Introduced animal species may prey upon native species to the point of extinction, or they may alter the habitat so that many natives are no longer able to persist. Invasive exotic species represent threats to 49% of the endangered species in the United States, with particularly severe impacts on bird and plant species (Wilcove et al. 1998). The thousands of nonnative species in the United States are estimated to cause damages and losses amounting to $137 billion per year (Pimentel et al. 2000b). Many species introductions have occurred by the following means:

- *European colonization.* Settlers arriving at new colonies released hundreds of different species of European birds and mammals into places like New Zealand, Australia, and South Africa to make the countryside seem familiar and to provide game for hunting. Numerous species of fish (trout, bass, carp, etc.) have been widely released to provide food and recreation.
- *Horticulture and agriculture.* Large numbers of plant species have been introduced and grown as ornamentals, as agricultural species, or as pasture grasses. Many of these species escape from cultivation and become established in local communities.
- *Accidental transport.* Species are often transported unintentionally. For example, weed seeds are accidentally harvested with commercial seeds and sown in new localities; rats, snakes, and insects stow away aboard ships and airplanes; and disease, parasitic organisms, and insects trav-

el along with their host species, particular in the leaves and roots of plants. Ships frequently carry exotic species in their ballast: Soil ballast dumped in port areas brings in weed seeds and soil arthropods, and water ballast introduces vast numbers of bacteria, viruses, algae, invertebrates, and small fish. Large ships may hold up to 150,000 tons of ballast water, and with it the entire range of marine species (Ruiz et al. 1997, 2000). In one study, ballast water being released by ships into Coos Bay, Oregon, was found to contain 367 marine species originating in Japanese waters (Carlton and Geller 1993). Governments are now developing regulations to reduce the transport of species in ballast water, such as requiring ships to exchange their ballast water 320 km offshore in deep water before approaching a port.

- *Biological control.* When an exotic species becomes invasive, a common solution is to release an animal species from its original range that will consume the pest and control its numbers. While biological control is often dramatically successful, there are many cases in which a biological control agent has itself become invasive, attacking native species along with, or instead of, its intended target species. For example, a parasitic fly species (*Compsilura cocinnata*) introduced into North America to control invasive gypsy moths has been found to parasitize more than 200 native moth species, in many cases dramatically reducing population numbers.

Many areas of the world are strongly affected by exotic species. The United States currently has more than 20 species of exotic mammals, 97 species of exotic birds, 70 species of exotic fish, 88 species of exotic mollusks, 2000 species of exotic plants, and 2000 species of exotic insects (Figure 10.3). Exotic perennials completely dominate many North American wetlands: purple loosestrife (*Lythrum salicaria*) from Europe domi-

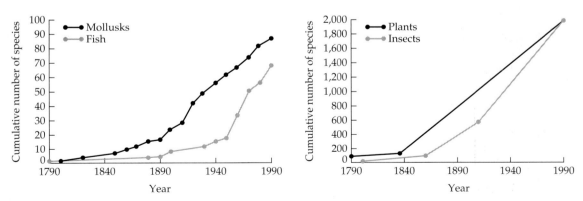

Figure 10.3 The number of exotic mollusk, fish, plant, and insect species in the United States has increased steadily over time. (After OTA 1993.)

nates marshes in eastern North America, while Japanese honeysuckle (*Lonicera japonica*) forms dense tangles in bottomlands of the southeastern United States. In southern Florida, introduced melaleuca trees (*Melaleuca quinquenervia*) already cover vast areas and are increasing their coverage by 16 ha per day, while Brazilian pepper (*Shinus terebinthifolius*) occupies over 100,000 ha (Simberloff et al. 1997). Introduced annual grasses now cover extensive areas of western North America rangelands and increase the probability of ground fires in the summer. When invasive species dominate a community, the diversity of native plant species and the insects that feed on them show a corresponding decline (Toft et al. 2001). Further, invasive species are many of the most serious agricultural weeds, costing farmers tens of billions of dollars a year in lost crop yield and extra weeding and pesticide expenses.

Insects introduced deliberately, such as European honeybees (*Apis mellifera*) and bumblebees (*Bombus* spp.), and accidentally, such as fire ants (*Solenopsis invicta*) and gypsy moths (*Lymantria dispar*), can build up huge populations. The effects of these invasive insects on the native insect fauna can be devastating (Porter and Savignano 1990). At some localities in the southern United States, the diversity of insect species declines by 40% following the invasion of exotic fire ants, with a similarly large decline for native birds (Figure 10.4). Introduced European worm species are currently outcompeting native species in soil communities across North America, with potentially enormous consequences to the rich underground biological communities and to the recycling of nutrients from the leaf litter to plants. In areas of human settlement, domestic cats may be one of the most serious predators of birds and small mam-

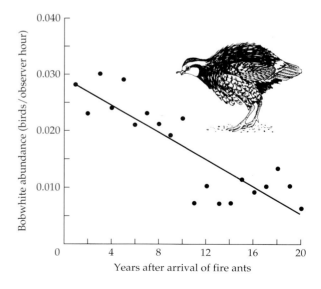

Figure 10.4 The abundance of northern bobwhites (*Colinas virginianus*) in Texas has been declining over a 20-year period following the arrival of the exotic red fire ant (*Solenopsis invicta*). The fire ants may directly attack and disturb bobwhites, particularly at the nestling stage, and may compete for food items, such as insects. (After Allen et al. 1995.)

mals: A placid house cat may be a fearsome hunter when let outdoors. Feral cats that must hunt for their own meals are especially damaging because of their ability to move far from human settlements.

Invasive Species on Islands

The isolation of island habitats encourages the development of a unique assemblage of endemic species (see Chapter 7), but it also leaves these species particularly vulnerable to depredations by invading species. Only a limited number of organisms are capable of crossing large expanses of water without human assistance. Thus, undisturbed island communities include few large mammalian predators and grazers, and organisms representing the highest trophic levels, such as mammalian carnivores, may be absent altogether. Because they evolved in the absence of selective pressures from mammalian predators and grazers, many endemic island species have evolutionarily lost defenses against these enemies, and they often lack a fear of them. Some birds have lost the power of flight and build their nests on the ground. Many island plants do not produce the bad-tasting, tough vegetative tissue that discourages herbivores, nor do they have the ability to resprout rapidly following damage.

Thriving endemic species often succumb rapidly when the selective pressures invasive species represent are introduced. Introduced animals have efficiently preyed upon endemic animal species and have grazed native plant species to extinction. Introduced plant species with tough, unpalatable foliage are better able to coexist with the introduced grazers than are the more palatable native plants, so the exotics begin to dominate the landscape as the native vegetation dwindles. Moreover, island species often have no natural immunities to mainland diseases. When exotic species arrive, they frequently carry pathogens or parasites that, though relatively harmless to the carrier, devastate the native populations.

The introduction of just one exotic species to an island may cause the local extinction of numerous native species. (Biogeographical models in which the arrival of one exotic species on an island results in the loss of one native species represent a great oversimplification.) Two examples illustrate the effects of introduced species on the biota of islands:

- *Plants of Santa Catalina Island.* Forty-eight native plant species have been eliminated from Santa Catalina Island off the coast of California, primarily due to grazing by introduced goats, pigs, and deer. One-third of the plant species currently found on the island are exotics. Removal of goats from part of the island has led to the reappearance of several native plant species.
- *Birds of the Pacific islands.* The brown tree snake (*Boiga irregularis*; Figure 10.5) has been introduced onto a number of Pacific islands where it is devastating endemic bird populations. The snake eats eggs, nestlings, and adult birds. On Guam alone, the brown tree snake has reduced ten endemic bird species to the point of extinction (Savidge

Figure 10.5 The brown tree snake (*Boiga irregularis*) has been introduced onto many Pacific islands, where it devastates populations of endemic birds. This adult snake has just swallowed a bird. (Photograph by Julie Savidge.)

1987). Visitors have remarked on the absence of birdsong: "between the silence and the cobwebs, the rain forests of Guam have taken on the aura of a tomb" (Jaffe 1994). Perhaps in an attempt to locate new prey, brown tree snakes have even attacked sleeping people. The government spends $4.6 million per year on attempts to control the brown tree snake population, so far without success.

Invasive Species in Aquatic Habitats

Freshwater communities are somewhat similar to oceanic islands in that they are isolated habitats surrounded by vast stretches of inhospitable and uninhabitable terrain. Exotic species can have severe effects on vulnerable lake communities and isolated stream systems (Mills et al. 1994). There has been a long history of introducing exotic commercial and sportfish species into lakes, such as the introduction of the Nile Perch into Lake Victoria in East Africa (see Box 13 in Chapter 7). Over 120 fish species have been introduced throughout the world into marine and estuarine systems and inland seas. Although some of the introductions have been deliberate attempts to increase fisheries, most of the introductions were the unintentional result of canal building and the transport of ballast water in ships (Baltz 1991). Often these exotic fish are larger and more aggressive than the native fish fauna, and they may eventually drive the local fish to extinction. The invasion of sea lampreys into the Great Lakes of North America severely damaged the commercial and sport fisheries, particularly lake trout; the United States and Canada currently spend $13 million each year to control this pest. In Madagascar, recent surveys of freshwater habitats were able to locate only five of the 28 known native freshwater fish of the island, with introduced fish dominating all of the freshwater habitats (Reinthal and Stiassny 1991; Benstead et al. 2000).

Besides fish, aggressive aquatic exotics can also include plants and invertebrate animals. The deliberate introduction of the freshwater opossum shrimp into the Flathead catchment of Montana was supposed to provide food for salmon (Figure 10.6); instead, the shrimp directly competed with the fish for stocks of zooplankton and led to a precipitous

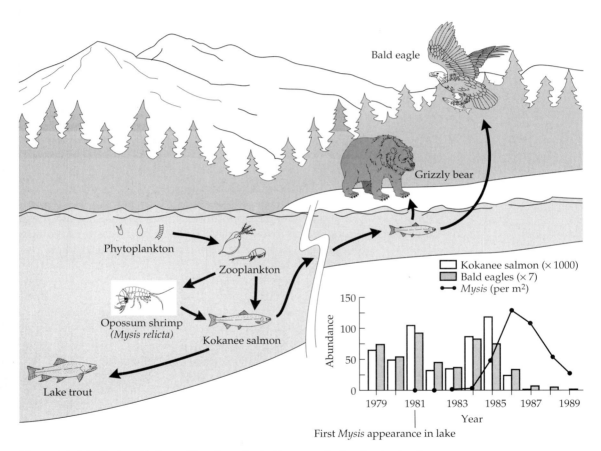

Figure 10.6 In Flathead Lake and its tributaries in Montana, the food web was disrupted by the deliberate introduction of opossum shrimp (*Mysis relicta*). The natural food chain consists of grizzly bears, bald eagles, and lake trout all eating kokanee salmon; kokanee eating zooplankton (cladocerans and copepods); and zooplankton eating phytoplankton (algae). Opossum shrimp, introduced as a food source for the kokanee salmon, ate so much zooplankton that there was far less food for the kokanee. Kokanee salmon numbers then declined radically, as did the eagle population that relied on the salmon. (After Spencer et al. 1991.)

Figure 10.7 (A) The zebra mussel (*Dreissena polymorpha*), a native of the Caspian Sea, was accidentally introduced into the Great Lakes and associated rivers in 1988. This shopping cart, which had been submerged in the Great Lakes, is thoroughly encrusted in zebra mussels. (Photograph courtesy of James F. Lubner, Ph.D., University of Wisconsin Sea Grant Institute.) (B) The North American comb jelly (*Mnemiopsis leidyi*) may look delicate and beautiful, but it is an aggressive feeder on fish larvae in the Black Sea. (Photograph © L. P. Madin.)

(A)

(B)

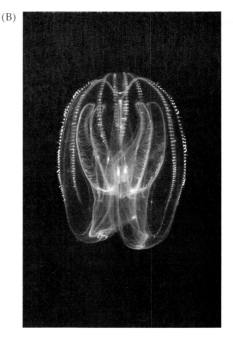

drop in salmon and bald eagle populations (Spencer et al. 1991). One of the most alarming recent invasions in North America was the arrival in 1988 of the zebra mussel (*Dreissena polymorpha*) in the Great Lakes. This small, striped native of the Caspian Sea apparently was a stowaway in the ballast tanks of a European tanker. Within two years zebra mussels had reached densities of 700,000 individuals per square meter in parts of Lake Erie, encrusting every hard surface and choking out native mussel species in the process (Figure 10.7A) (Stolzenburg 1992). One single individual of a native species was found with 10,000 tiny zebra mussels layered on it. This mussel has a prodigious capacity to reproduce: A single female can produce a million eggs per year, and the larval stage can disperse long distances in water currents. Zebra mussels are now spreading south throughout the entire Mississippi River drainage. As it spreads, this exotic species is causing enormous economic damage to fisheries, dams, power plants, water treatment facilities, and boats, as well as devastating the aquatic communities it encounters (Strayer et al. 1999). Merely keeping water intake pipes clear of zebra mussels will cost an estimated $3.1 billion over the next ten years (Vitousek et al. 1996).

Invasions can occur in marine ecosystems, as the case of the comb jelly (*Mnemiopsis leidyi*) demonstrates (Figure 10.7B). This species from North American coastal waters was first spotted in the Black Sea in Eastern Eu-

rope in 1982, where it had presumably been discharged from ship ballast (Travis 1993). The Black Sea has no predators or competitors of this
fish-eating comb jelly. Only 7 years later, in 1989, this species constituted 95% of the biomass of the Black Sea. The voracious appetite of this
jellyfish for fish larvae and for the zooplankton on which fish feed has
led to the collapse of a $250 million fishing industry and disruption of
the entire ecosystem. Another marine species being watched closely is
Cualerpa taxifolia, an invasive green algae. This species is spreading in
the northwestern Mediterranean, outcompeting native species of algae,
and has recently been discovered at two sites in California. In the United States, every estuary that has been carefully surveyed has been found
to contain between 70 and 235 exotic species; the actual numbers may
be much higher because many of the species were probably not recognized as exotic or were absent from the specific locations surveyed (Carlton 2001).

The Ability of Species to Become Invasive

Why are certain exotic species able to invade and dominate new habitats and displace native species so easily? One reason is the absence of
their natural predators and parasites in the new habitat to control their
population growth. For example, in Australia, introduced rabbits spread
uncontrollably, grazing native plants to the point of extinction, because
there were no effective checks on their numbers. Australian control efforts have focused in part on introducing diseases that help control rabbit populations elsewhere.

Exotic species may be better suited to take advantage of disturbed
conditions than native species. Human activity may create unusual environmental conditions, such as higher mineral nutrient levels, increased
incidence of fire, or enhanced light availability, to which exotic species
sometimes can adapt more readily than native species. The highest concentrations of invasive species are often found in the habitats that have
been most altered by human activity. For example, in western North
America, increased grazing by cattle and increased human-induced fire
provided the opportunity for the establishment of exotic annual grasses in areas formerly dominated by native perennial grasses. In Southeast
Asia, progressive degradation of forests results in a progressively smaller proportion of native species living in the habitat (Figure 10.8). When
habitats are further altered by global climate change, they will become
even more vulnerable to invasion.

"Invasive species" are generally defined as species that have prolif-
erated outside their native range, but some native species dramatically
flourish within their home ranges because they are suited to the ways in
which humans have altered the environment and are therefore almost
as much a source of concern as exotic invasive species (Soulé 1990). Within North America, fragmentation of forests, suburban development, and

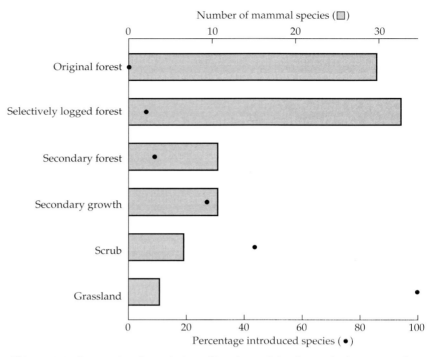

Figure 10.8 Progressive degradation of Southeast Asian forests by logging and farming not only decreases the number of species of nonflying native mammals, but increases the percentage of introduced species. Only introduced rats are present in the final grassland stage. (From Harrison 1968.)

easy access to garbage have allowed the numbers of coyotes, red foxes, and certain seagull species to increase. Native jellyfish have become far more abundant in the Gulf of Mexico because they use oil rigs and artificial reefs for spawning and feed on plankton blooms stimulated by nitrogen pollution. As these aggressive species increase, they do so at the expense of other local native species, such as the juvenile stages of commercially harvested fish. These unnaturally abundant native species represent a further challenge to the management of vulnerable species and protected areas.

Another special class of invasive species are those introduced species that have close relatives in the native biota. When invasive species hybridize with the native species and varieties, unique genotypes may be eliminated from local populations and taxonomic boundaries become obscured (Huxel 1999). This appears to be the fate of native trout species when confronted by commercial species. In the American Southwest, the Apache trout (*Oncorhynchus apache*) has had its range reduced by habitat destruction and competition with introduced species. The species has also hybridized extensively with rainbow trout (*O. mykiss*), an introduced sport fish (Dowling and Childs 1992). The entire population of the Leon Springs pupfish (*Cyprinodon bovinus*), a rare endemic of western Texas, shows evidence of hybridization with the introduced sheepshead minnow (*C. variegatus*); only one captive population of the Leon Springs pupfish was free of genetic contamination (Echelle and Echelle 1997).

Invasive species are considered to be the most serious threat facing the biota of the U.S. national park system. While the effects of habitat degradation, fragmentation, and pollution can potentially be corrected and reversed in a matter of years or decades as long as the original species are present, well-established exotic species may be impossible to remove from communities (Coblentz 1990). They may have built up such large numbers and become so widely dispersed and so thoroughly integrated into the community that eliminating them may be extraordinarily difficult and expensive. Also, the general public may resist efforts to control the numbers of introduced mammals that overgraze native plant communities. Animal rights groups, in particular, object to attempts to reduce large populations of deer, wild horses, mountain sheep, and wild boar. Yet sometimes these populations must be reduced if rare native species are to be saved.

The threats posed by invasive species are so severe that reducing the rate of their introduction needs to become a greater priority for conservation efforts (Carlton 2001; Bax 2001). Governments must pass and enforce laws and customs restrictions prohibiting the introduction of exotic species. Currently, vast sums are spent controlling widespread outbreaks of exotics, but inexpensive, prompt control and eradication efforts at the time of first sighting can stop a species from getting established in the first place (Simberloff 2001). Training citizens and protected-areas staff to monitor vulnerable habitats for the appearance of known invasive species and promptly implementing intensive control efforts can be an effective way to stop the establishment of a new species. A thoroughly researched program of biological control, using species from the exotic's original range, may be necessary in the overall strategy. In some cases, land-use practices may need to change in ways that favor the restoration of native species.

Disease

Another major threat to species and biological communities is the increased transmission of disease, a result of human activities (such as habitat destruction, which may increase disease-carrying vectors) and interaction with humans (such as populations of wild animals that acquire diseases from nearby populations of domestic animals and people; see Box 14 in Chapter 8). Infections by disease organisms are common in both wild and captive populations and can reduce the size and density of vulnerable populations. Disease organisms can also have a major impact on the structure of an entire biological community (Aguirre and Starkey 1994; McCallum and Dobson 1995; Daszak and Cunning-ham 1999; Deem et al. 2001). Infections may come from tiny microparasites, such as viruses, bacteria, fungi, and protozoa, or larger macroparasites, such as helminth worms and parasitic arthropods. While living inside the host, these parasites use and damage host tissue, weakening the host and lowering its chances of surviving and reproducing.

In some instances, human modifications to the environment have inadvertently increased the densities of disease-causing organisms (Cohn 1991; MacKenzie 2000). For example, biologists in Texas were puzzled by the increased winter deaths of sandhill cranes—the loss of 5000 birds over the winter of 1984 to 1985. Investigations revealed that the birds were eating unharvested, rotting peanuts on which a toxic fungus was growing. Thus, the increased cultivation of peanuts could be directly linked to increased crane mortality. To halt the spread of the fungus and save the cranes, farmers now plow under the unharvested peanuts left in their fields before the winter.

Within populations, individuals vary in their susceptibility to particular diseases. Conservation biologists may face this dilemma in practice: Either protect all individuals of a rare species from a potential disease in order to maintain population numbers and genetic variation or let natural selection take its course and allow the individuals that are genetically most susceptible to the disease die off. If the disease only kills a few individuals and the population is still large, the population may be more fit in the long term for having weathered the disease. However, if the disease kills large numbers of individuals and the population shrinks, then many potentially valuable alleles will be lost from the population and inbreeding depression may occur (see Chapter 11). It is often difficult to predict how virulent a disease will be in an isolated population of a rare species, especially if the environmental conditions and population have been altered by human activity.

The basic principles of epidemiology have three obvious practical implications for the captive breeding and management of rare species (Scott 1988):

1. A high rate of contact between host and parasite encourages the spread of disease.
2. Indirect effects of habitat destruction increase susceptibility to disease.
3. Species in conservation programs may contract diseases from related species and even from humans.

We'll examine each of these implications in turn, recognizing that increased levels of disease can be caused by multiple factors. First, a high rate of contact between the host (such as a mountain sheep) and the parasite (such as an intestinal worm) is one factor that encourages the spread of disease. In general, as host population density increases, the parasite load also increases, as expressed by the percentage of hosts infected and the number of parasites per host. In addition, a high density of the infective stages of a parasite in the environment of the host population can lead to increased incidence of disease. In natural situations, the level of infection is typically reduced when animals migrate away from their droppings, saliva, old skin, dead animals, and other infection sources. However, in unnaturally confined situations, such as habitat fragments, zoos, or even parks, the animals remain in contact with the potential sources of infection, and disease transmission increases (Loye and Carroll 1995). At higher densities, animals have abnormally frequent contact, and, once one animal becomes infected, the parasite can rapidly spread throughout the entire population.

Second, indirect effects of habitat destruction can increase an organism's susceptibility to disease. When a host population is crowded into a smaller area because of habitat destruction, there will often be a deterioration in habitat quality and food availability, leading to lowered nutritional status, weaker animals, and less resistance to infection. Young, very old, and pregnant individuals may be particularly susceptible to disease in such a situation. Crowding can lead to social stress within a species, which also lowers the animals' resistance to disease. For example, territorial animals such as mountain lions will fight, sometimes to the death, to prevent intrusion on their territories by other members of their species (Hornocker 1992). As the total area of habitat available to such animals decreases, fights and injuries become more frequent, lowering the animals' resistance to disease. Plant populations are similarly affected by fragmentation and degradation. Changes in plant microenvironments caused by fragmentation, stress caused by air pollution, and direct injury occurring during logging or other human activities directly lead to increased levels of disease in plant populations (Gilbert and Hubbell 1996). Aquatic species, including marine mammals, sea turtles, fish, coral animals, shellfish, and sea grasses also have exhibited increased levels of disease due to water pollution, injury, and unusual environmental perturbations (Kushmaro et al. 1996; Epstein 1998).

Third, in many conservation areas and zoos, species may come into contact with other species that they would rarely or never encounter in the wild, including humans, so that infections spread from one species to another (Figure 10.9). A species that is common and fairly resistant to a parasite can act as a reservoir for the disease, which can then infect a population of a highly susceptible species. For example, apparently healthy African elephants can transmit a fatal herpes virus to related Asian elephants when kept together in zoos (Richman et al. 1999). The Mauritius pink pigeon (*Columba mayeri*), endangered in the wild, is being bred in captivity at the Rio Grande Zoo. Because this species often aban-

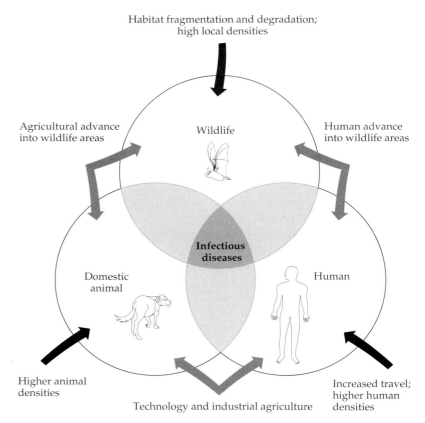

Habitat fragmentation and degradation;
high local densities

Wildlife

Agricultural advance
into wildlife areas

Human advance
into wildlife areas

**Infectious
diseases**

Domestic
animal

Human

Higher animal
densities

Increased travel;
higher human
densities

Technology and industrial agriculture

Figure 10.9 Infectious diseases—such as rabies, lyme disease, influenza, hantavirus, and canine distemper—spread among wildlife populations, domestic animals, and humans as a result of increasing population densities and the advance of agriculture and human settlements into wildlife areas. The figure illustrates the infection and transmission routes of the rabies virus—bats, dogs, and humans are all susceptible to the virus. The shaded areas of overlap indicate that diseases can be shared between the three groups. Black arrows indicate factors contributing to higher rates of infection; shaded arrows indicate factors contributing to the spread of disease among the three groups. (After Daszak et al. 2000.)

dons its eggs, domestic pigeons were used as foster mothers. Unfortunately, the pink pigeon chicks died after about one week due to infection by the herpes virus, which was carried by the otherwise healthy domestic pigeons.

Infected humans have been responsible for directly transmitting tuberculosis, measles, and influenza to orangutans, colobus monkeys, ferrets, and other animals (Thorne and Williams 1988). Certain emerging infectious disease vectors, such as human immunodeficiency virus (HIV) and Ebola virus, even appear to have even spread from wildlife populations to both humans and domestic animals. Once infected with exotic diseases, such captive animals cannot be returned to the wild without threatening the entire wild population. Captive Arabian oryx infected with the bluetongue virus of domestic livestock and orangutans with human tuberculosis could not be reintroduced into the wild as planned for fear of infecting free-ranging animals. Diseases can spread very rapidly between captive species kept in crowded conditions. An outbreak of herpes virus spread across the captive colony at the International Crane Federation, killing cranes belonging to several rare species. The outbreak was apparently related to a high density of birds in the colony (Docherty and Romaine 1983).

Disease also can spread from domestic animals into wild populations. A classic example from the late nineteenth century is that of rinderpest virus, which spread from domestic cattle to wild antelope, wildebeest, and other ungulates in eastern and southern Africa, killing off 75% of the animals. At Tanzania's Serengeti National Park, at least 25% of the lions were killed by canine distemper, a viral disease apparently contracted from one or more of the 30,000 domestic dogs living near the park (Morell 1994). For endangered species, such outbreaks can be the final blow: The last population of black-footed ferrets known to occur in the wild (see Box 14 in Chapter 8) was destroyed by the canine distemper virus.

Diseases transmitted to new parts of the world can decimate common species: North American chestnut trees (*Castanea dentata*), once common throughout the eastern United States, have been virtually obliterated by an ascomycete fungus carried by Chinese chestnut trees imported to New York City. Fungal diseases are also eliminating elm trees (*Ulmus americana*) and flowering dogwoods (*Cornus florida*) from these forests (Figure 10.10). Introduced diseases have particularly powerful adverse effects on endemic island species (see Box 12 in Chapter 7). An important factor in the decline and extinction of many endemic Hawaiian birds is the introduction of the mosquito *Culex quinquefasciatus* and the malaria protozoan *Plasmodium relictum capistranode*.

A number of actions can be taken to reduce the spread of disease:

1. Plants, animals, soils and other biological materials need to be inspected and, if needed, quarantined and appropriately treated before crossing borders.
2. Care must be taken to reduce the interaction of endangered species with humans, domesticated species, and closely related species. Such interactions can occur frequently in zoos, aquariums, and botanical gardens, or in small protected areas.
3. Endangered species need to be monitored to detect outbreaks of disease. If necessary, diseased individuals may have to be treated or removed from the population.
4. Appropriate living conditions and population densities will lower the susceptibility to disease vectors and reduce the rate of transmission.

Figure 10.10 Populations of flowering dogwood (*Cornus florida*) are declining in eastern North American forests because of anthracnose disease, which is caused by the introduced fungus *Discula destructiva*. (Photograph by Jonathan P. Evans.)

The Implications of Invasive Species and Diseases for Human Health

The presence of invasive species and disease-causing organisms also has serious, direct implications for humans. Not only do invading killer bees (*Apis mellifera scutellata*) and fire ants (*Solenopis invicta*) that are spreading in the New World displace the native insect species from their ecological niches, but they also can cause serious injuries to humans (Soulé 1990; Real 1996). The potential for the spread of serious pests and disease-causing organisms increases dramatically with the increasing movement of people, pets, wildlife, and materials from one part of the world to another. The phenomenon is already occurring: In North America, the increased abundance of the intestinal parasite *Giardia lamblia* in beavers and elk requires that water be purified before drinking, even in remote areas. The dramatic upsurge in Lyme disease and Rocky Mountain spotted fever, spread by infected ticks, and West Nile virus, spread by mosquitoes, has caused near-panic in some regions of the United States.

These examples are minor compared to the problems that will result from human-induced changes to the environment. Recent warm years have allowed many tropical disease-carrying insects to expand their ranges to higher elevations in tropical countries and further from the Equator. If world temperatures increase as predicted by global climate change models (see Chapter 9), the stage will be set for major range expansions of diseases now confined primarily to tropical climates (Epstein 1998). Warmer and more polluted aquatic environments and unusually heavy rains are already allowing waterborne diseases such as cholera to ravage previously unaffected human and animal populations, and this range expansion will probably continue (Epstein 1999).

There is a serious potential for the environment of the developed world to become a more dangerous place as stinging and disease-causing species arrive and thrive. In addition, if bird-watchers, hunters, swimmers, and hikers become frightened by and disenchanted with the outdoor experience, strong support for conservation efforts may be lost. Conservation biologists have an obligation to help prevent the spread of dangerous species that threaten both people and biological diversity. Conservation biologists also need to keep the public engaged in conservation-related activities, in part to counter media reports that exaggerate the dangers of the outdoors.

Conclusion

As we've seen in Chapters 7–10, a combination of factors acting simultaneously or sequentially can overwhelm a species. Consider, for example, the large freshwater mussel *Margaritifera auricularia.* This species was formerly known from Western Europe to Morocco, but now it only occurs in one population of 2000 individuals in an old canal of the Ebro River basin of northern Spain (Araujo and Ramons 2000). Its attractive shell and pearls have been used as ornaments by humans as far back as the Neolithic Age. Overcollecting, the main reason for the decline of the mussel, led to its disappearance from rivers in Central Europe in the fifteenth and sixteenth centuries; pollution, destruction of freshwater habitats, and overcollecting continue to reduce its range in recent times. The mussel is also affected by the loss of other species, since its larval stage needs to attach to the gill filaments of salmonid fish to complete its life cycle. The lack of small individuals in the Spanish population indicates that the species is unable to complete its life cycle under present conditions. To save this species, a comprehensive conservation plan must be implemented, including preventing overcollecting, controlling water quality, maintaining fish stocks, and protecting the habitat.

Threats to biological diversity come from a number of different sources, but their underlying cause is the same: the magnitude of destructive human activity. It is often easy to blame a group of poor, rural people or a certain industry for the destruction of biological diversity, but the real challenge is to understand the national and international linkages that promote the destruction and to find viable alternatives. These alternatives must include stabilizing the size of the human population, finding a livelihood for rural people in developing countries that does not damage the environment, providing incentives and penalties that will convince people and industries to value the environment, restricting international trade in products that are obtained by damaging the environment, and persuading people in developed countries to reduce their consumption of the world's resources and pay fair prices for products that are produced in a sustainable, nondestructive manner.

Summary

1. Overexploitation threatens about one-third of the endangered vertebrates in the world, as well as other groups of species. Poverty, more efficient methods of harvesting, and the globalization of the economy combine to exploit species to the point of extinction. Many traditional societies have customs to prevent overharvesting of resources, but these customs are breaking down.

2. Humans have deliberately and accidentally moved thousands of plant and animal species to new regions of the world. Some of these species have become invasive, increasing at the expense of native species. Island species are particularly vulnerable to invasive, exotic species. Aquatic communities throughout the world are often dramatically altered by the introduction of exotic fish and other exotic species.

3. Human activities may increase the incidence of disease in wild species. The levels of disease and parasites often increase when animals are crowded together and under stress in a nature reserve or a habitat fragment rather than being able to disperse over a wide area. Animals held in captivity in zoos are prone to higher levels of disease, which sometimes spreads between related species of animals. If diseased captive animals are returned to the wild, they may spread the disease to the wild population.

4. Species may be threatened by a combination of factors, all of which must be addressed in a comprehensive conservation plan.

For Discussion

1. Learn about one endangered species in detail. What is the full range of immediate threats to this species? How do these immediate threats connect to larger social, economic, political, and legal issues?

2. Control of invasive species may involve searching for parasites or predators of that species within its original range and releasing this parasite to control the invasive species at the new location. For example, attempts are currently underway to control exotic purple loosestrife in North America by releasing a European beetle species that eats the plant in its home area. What if this biological control agent begins to attack native species rather than its intended host? How might such a consequence be avoided? Consider the issues involved in a decision to institute a biological control program.

3. Why is it so difficult to regulate the fishing industry in many places and maintain a sustainable level of harvesting? Consider fishing, hunting, logging, and other harvesting activities in your region. Are these well managed? Try to calculate what the sustainable harvest levels of these resources would be and how such harvesting levels could best be monitored and enforced.

4. Develop a verbal or computer model of how disease spreads in a population. The rate of spread could be determined by the density of the host, the percentage of host individuals infected, the rate of transmission of the disease,

and the effects of the disease on the host's survival and rate of reproduction. How will an increase in the density of the host—caused by crowding in zoos or nature reserves, or an inability to migrate due to habitat fragmentation—affect the percentage of individuals that are infected and the overall population size?

Suggested Readings

Bax, N., J. T. Carlton, A. Mathews-Amos, R. L. Haedrich, et al. 2001. The control of biological invasions in the world's oceans. *Conservation Biology* 15: 1234–1246. The problem of marine invasive species may be enormous, and scientists are now deciding how to deal with it.

Chapman, C. A. and C. A. Peres. 2001. Primate conservation in the new millennium: The role of scientists. *Evolutionary Anthropology* 10: 16–33. Forest loss and hunting contribute to the decline and local extinction of primate populations.

Cuarón, A. 2001. A global perspective on habitat disturbance and tropical rain forest mammals. *Conservation Biology* 14: 1574–1579. A special issue focusing on mammals, with many excellent articles on hunting.

Daszak, P., A. A. Cunningham, and A. D. Hyatt. 2000. Emerging infectious diseases of wildlife—threats to biodiversity and human health. *Science* 287:443–449. Review of new diseases that spread among wildlife, humans, and domestic animals.

Epstein, P. R. 1998. *Marine Ecosystems: Emerging Diseases as Indicators of Change: Health of the Oceans from Labrador to Venezuela.* Harvard Medical School, Boston. Increased disease in marine ecosystems is associated with increased human impacts.

Ludwig D., R. Hilborn, and C. Walters. 1993. Uncertainty, resource exploitation, and conservation: Lessons from history. *Science* 260: 17, 36. Good, short explanation of why commercial exploitation so often destroys its resource base.

Mathiessen, P. 2000. *Tigers in the Snow.* North Point Press, New York. Account of heroic struggle to protect tigers from multiple threats, primarily in the Russian Far East.

Mooney, H. A. and R. J. Hobbs (eds.). 2000. *Invasive Species in a Changing World.* Island Press, Washington, D.C. Invasive species may be the greatest threat to threatened species.

Mowat, F. 1984. *Sea of Slaughter.* McClelland and Stewart, Toronto. Popular account of overexploitation by an outstanding Canadian author.

NOVA. 1997. *Kingdom of the Seahorse.* WGBH Science Unit, Boston, MA. A videocassette of the NOVA program on seahorse. Also see the program's companion website at NOVA online at: http://www.pbs.org/wgbh/nova/seahorse/

Pimental, D., L. Lach, R. Zuniga, and D. Morrison. 2000. Environmental and economic costs of nonindigenous species in the United States. *BioScience* 50(1): 53–65. Invasive species may cost the U.S. economy $137 billion per year.

Robinson, J. G., K. H. Redford, and E. L. Bennett. 1999. Wildlife harvest in logged tropical forests. *Science* 284: 595–596. Wildlife hunting by humans can greatly depress animal populations

Scott, M. E. 1988. The impact of infection and disease on animal populations: Implications for conservation biology. *Conservation Biology* 2: 40–56. An excellent review article.

Simpson, S. 2001. Fishy business. *Scientific American* 285(1): 82–89. Cyanide and other poisons are used in the Philippines and Indonesia to capture live fish for the aquarium trade, in the process damaging reefs; a new program is teaching less destructive methods.

Van Driesche, J. and R. Van Driesche. 2000. *Nature Out of Place: Biological Invasions in the Global Age*. Island Press, Washington, D.C. Visits around the world reveal that exotic species are taking over.

Vincent, A. 1994. The improbable seahorse. *National Geographic* 186(4): 126–140. The males get pregnant, but that does not save this unique and beautiful group of fish from overexploitation. Also see the well-done NOVA video.

Vitousek, P. M., C. M. D'Antonio, L. L. Loope, and R. Westerbrooks. 1996. Biological invasions as global environmental change. *American Scientist* 84: 468–478. Excellent review article describing impact of exotic species on ecosystems, human health, and the economy.

Webster, D. 1997. The looting and smuggling and fencing and hoarding of impossibly precious, feathered and scaly wild things. *The New York Times Magazine*, February 16, 1997, pp. 26–33, 48–49, 53, 61. Personal investigation of this $10 billion black market, focusing on Madagascar.

Wilcove, D. S. 1999. *The Condor's Shadow: The Loss and Recovery of Wildlife in America*. W. H. Freeman and Company, New York. Habitat destruction has threatened much of U.S. wildlife, but conservation efforts are now showing some progress.

PART *IV*

Conservation at the Population and Species Levels

11

Problems of Small Populations

N o population lasts forever. Changing climate, succession, disease, and a range of rare events ultimately lead every population to the same fate: extinction. The real questions to consider are whether a population goes extinct sooner rather than later, what factors cause the extinction, and whether other populations of the same species will continue elsewhere. Will a population of African lions last for more than 1000 years and go extinct only after a change in climate, or will the population go extinct after 10 years because of hunting by humans and introduced disease? Will individual lions from the original population start new populations in currently unoccupied habitat, or has all potential lion habitat disappeared because of new human settlements?

As we discussed in Chapter 7, the extinction of species as a result of human activities is now occurring more than 100 times faster than the natural rate of extinction—far more rapidly than new species can evolve. Because an endangered species may consist of just a few populations, or even a single population, *protecting populations is the key to preserving species;* it is often the few remaining populations of a rare species that are targeted for conservation efforts. In order to successfully maintain species under the restricted conditions imposed by human activities, conservation biologists must determine the stability of populations under different circumstances. Will a population of an endangered species persist or even increase in a nature reserve? Is the species in rapid decline and does it require special attention to prevent it from going extinct?

Many national parks and wildlife sanctuaries have been created to protect "charismatic" megafauna such as lions, tigers, rhinos, bison, and bears, which are important national symbols and attractions for the tourist industry. However, designating the habitats in which these species live as protected areas may not be enough to stop their decline and extinction, even when they are legally protected. Sanctuaries generally are created after most populations of the threatened species have been severely reduced by loss, degradation, and fragmentation of habitat, or by overharvesting. Under such circumstances, a species tends to dwindle rapidly toward extinction (Young et al. 2001). Also, individuals outside park boundaries remain unprotected and at risk. What, then, is the best strategy for protecting the few remaining populations of an endangered species? Are there special concerns for protecting small populations?

Essential Concepts for Small Populations

An adequate conservation plan for an endangered species requires the preservation of as many individuals as possible within the greatest possible area of high-quality, protected habitat (Caughley and Gunn 1996). To accomplish this, the planners, land managers, politicians, and wildlife biologists—who are trying to protect species from extinction with limited funds at their disposal—need specific guidelines (Lande 1995). Since these are generally unavailable, planners often must proceed without a firm understanding of the range and habitat requirements of a species. For example, how much long-leaf pine habitat does the red-cockaded woodpecker require? Is it necessary to protect 50, 500, 5000, 50,000, or more individuals to ensure the survival of the species? Furthermore, planners must reconcile conflicting demands on finite resources—somehow a compromise must be found that allows the economic development required by society while at the same time providing reasonable protection for biological diversity. This problem is vividly demonstrated by the current debate in the United States over the need to protect caribou and other wildlife in the vast Arctic National Wildlife Refuge and the equally compelling need to utilize the considerable natural resources of the area.

Minimum Viable Population (MVP)

In a groundbreaking paper, Shaffer (1981) defined the number of individuals necessary to ensure the long-term survival of a species as the **minimum viable population,** or **MVP**: "A minimum viable population for any given species in any given habitat is the smallest isolated population having a 99% chance of remaining extant for 1000 years despite the foreseeable effects of demographic, environmental, and genetic stochasticity, and natural catastrophes." In other words, MVP is the smallest population size that can be predicted to have a very high chance of persisting for the foreseeable future. Shaffer emphasized the tentative nature of this definition, saying that the survival probabilities could be set at 95%, 99%, or any other percentage, and that the time frame might similarly be adjusted, for example, to 100 or 500 years. The key point is that the MVP size allows a quantitative estimate to be made of how large a population must be to assure long-term survival.

Shaffer (1981) compares MVP protection efforts to flood control. It is not sufficient to use average annual rainfall as a guideline when planning flood control systems and regulating building on wetlands; instead, we recognize the need to plan for severe flooding, which may occur only once every 50 years. In protecting natural systems, we understand that certain catastrophic events, such as hurricanes, earthquakes, forest fires, volcanic eruptions, epidemics, and die-offs of food items, may occur at even greater intervals. To plan for the long-term protection of endangered species, we not only have to provide for their survival in average years, but also in exceptionally harsh years. An accurate estimate of the MVP size for a particular species often requires a detailed demographic study of the population and an analysis of its environment. This can be expensive and require months or even years of research (Soulé 1990; Thomas 1990). For vertebrates, some biologists have suggested that protecting at least 500–5000 individuals would adequately preserve genetic variability and would allow a minimum number of individuals to survive in catastrophic years and return to former levels (Lande 1988, 1995). For species with extremely variable population sizes, such as certain invertebrates and annual plants, it has been suggested that protecting a population of about 10,000 individuals would generally be an effective strategy.

Small population sizes are a reality for many species, particularly endangered species. For instance, a survey was done of two rare burrowing frog species in the genus *Geocrina*, which occur in swamps in southwestern Australia (Driscoll 1999). In one species, 4 of its 6 populations had less than 250 individuals, and in the other species 48 of 51 populations had less than 50 individuals. For Carter's mustard (*Warea carteri*), a rare annual plant of south-central Florida, 9 of 13 populations had a population size of less than 20 individuals (Evans et al. 2000).

Minimum Dynamic Area (MDA)

Once an MVP size has been established for a species, the **minimum dynamic area (MDA)**—the area of suitable habitat necessary for maintaining the minimum viable population—can be estimated by studying the home-range size of individuals and colonies of endangered species (Thiollay 1989). It has been estimated that reserves in Africa of

100–1000 km^2 are needed to maintain many small mammal populations (Schonewald-Cox 1983). To preserve populations of large carnivores, such as lions, reserves of 10,000 km^2 are needed.

One of the best-documented studies of MVP size tracked the persistence of 120 bighorn sheep (*Ovis canadensis*) populations (some of which have been followed for 70 years) in the deserts of the southwestern United States (Berger 1990, 1999). The striking observation is that 100% of the unmanaged populations with fewer than 50 individuals went extinct within 50 years, while virtually all of the populations with more than 100 individuals persisted within the same time period (Figure 11.1). No sin-

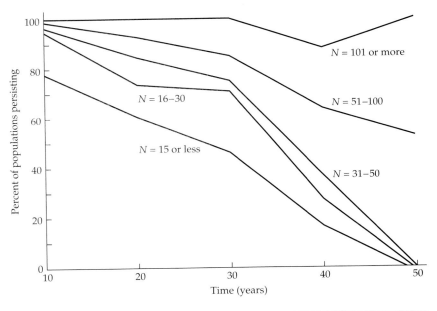

Figure 11.1 The relationship between initial population size (*N*) of bighorn sheep and the percentage of populations that persist over time. Almost all populations with more than 100 sheep persisted beyond 50 years, while populations with fewer than 50 individuals died out within 50 years. Not included are small populations that were actively managed and augmented by the release of additional animals. (After Berger 1990; photograph by Mark Primack.)

gle cause was evident for most of the populations that died out; rather, a wide variety of factors appears responsible for the extinctions. For bighorn sheep, the minimum population size is at least 100 individuals. Unmanaged populations below 50 could not maintain their numbers, even in the short term. Additional research on bighorn sheep populations suggests that populations have a greater chance of persisting when they occupy large habitats (which allow populations to increase in size) that are more than 23 km from domestic sheep, a source of disease (Singer et al. 2001). However, in other locations, habitat management by government agencies and the release of additional animals have allowed some other small populations to persist that might have gone extinct.

Field evidence from long-term studies of birds on the Channel Islands off the California coast supports the fact that large populations are needed to ensure population persistence; only bird populations with more than 100 breeding pairs had a greater than 90% chance of surviving for 80 years (Figure 11.2). In spite of most evidence to the contrary, however, small populations sometimes prevail: Many populations of birds apparently have survived for 80 years with 10 or fewer breeding pairs, and northern elephant seals have recovered to a population of 100,000 individuals after being reduced by hunting to only about 100 individuals in the late nineteenth century.

Exceptions notwithstanding, large populations are needed to protect most species, and species with small populations are in real danger of going extinct. Small populations are subject to rapid decline in numbers and local extinction for three main reasons:

1. Loss of genetic variability and related problems of inbreeding depression and genetic drift.
2. Demographic fluctuations due to random variations in birth and death rates.

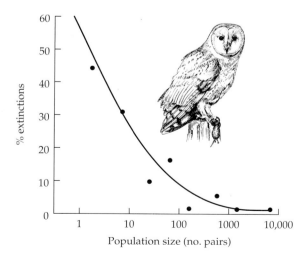

Figure 11.2 Extinction rates of bird species on the Channel Islands. Each dot represents the extinction percentage of all the species in that population size class; extinction rate decreases as the size of the population increases. Populations with less than 10 breeding pairs had an overall 39% probability of extinction over 80 years; populations of between 10–100 pairs averaged around 10% probability of extinction, and populations of over 100 pairs had a very low probability of extinction. (From Jones and Diamond 1976.)

3. Environmental fluctuations due to variation in predation, competition, disease, and food supply; and natural catastrophes that occur at irregular intervals, such as fires, floods, volcanic eruptions, storms, or droughts.

We'll now examine in detail each of these causes for decline in small populations.

Loss of Genetic Variability

As was described in Chapter 2, a population's ability to adapt to a changing environment depends on genetic variability, which occurs as a result of individuals having different alleles—different forms of the same gene. Within a population, the frequency of a given allele can range from common to very rare. New alleles arise in a population either by random mutations or through the migration of individuals from other populations.

In small populations, allele frequencies may change from one generation to the next simply because of chance—based on which individuals survive to sexual maturity, mate, and leave offspring. This random process of allele frequency change is known as **genetic drift**, and is a separate process from changes in allele frequency caused by natural selection (Hedrick 2000). When an allele occurs at a low frequency in a small population, it has a significant probability of being lost in each generation. For example, if a rare allele occurs in 5% of all the genes present (the "gene pool") in a population of 1000 individuals, then 100 copies of the allele are present (1000 individuals × 2 copies per individual × 0.05 allele frequency), and the allele will probably remain in the population for many generations. However, in a population of 10 individuals, only one copy of the allele is present (10 individuals × 2 copies per individual × 0.05 allele frequency) and it is possible that the rare allele will be lost from the population in the next generation.

Considering the general case of an isolated population in which there are two alleles of each gene in the gene pool, Wright (1931) proposed a formula to express the proportion of original heterozygosity remaining after each generation (H) for a population of breeding adults, which constitutes the **effective population size**, (N_e)—the size of the population as estimated by the number of its breeding individuals:*

$$H = 1 - 1/2\,N_e$$

---

*Factors affecting N_e, the effective population size, are discussed in detail beginning on page 310.

According to this equation, a population of 50 breeding individuals would retain 99% of its original heterozygosity after 1 generation:

$$H = 1 - 1/100 = 1.00 - 0.01 = 0.99$$

The proportion of heterozygosity remaining after t generations (H_t) is equal to

$$H_t = H^t$$

For our population of 50 animals, then, the remaining heterozygosity would be 98% after 2 generations (0.99×0.99), 97% after 3 generations, and 90% after 10 generations. A population of 10 individuals would retain 95% of its original heterozygosity after 1 generation, 90% after 2 generations, 86% after 3 generations, and 60% after 10 generations (Figure 11.3).

This formula demonstrates that significant losses of genetic variability can occur in isolated small populations, particularly those on islands and fragmented landscapes. However, the migration of individuals among populations and the regular mutation of genes tend to increase the amount of genetic variability within the population and balance the effects of genetic drift. The mutation rates found in nature—about 1 in 10,000 to 1 in 1,000,000 per gene per generation—may make up for the random loss of alleles in large populations, but they are insignificant in countering genetic drift in small populations of 100 individuals or less. Fortunately, however, even a low frequency of movement of individu-

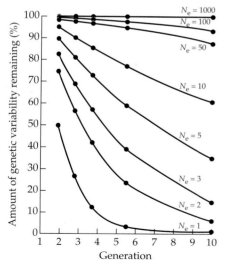

Figure 11.3 Genetic variability is lost randomly over time through genetic drift. This graph shows the average percentage of genetic variability remaining after 10 generations in theoretical populations of various effective population sizes (N_e). After 10 generations, there is a loss of genetic variability of approximately 40% with a population size of 10, 65% with a population size of 5, and 95% with a population size of 2. (From Meffe and Carroll 1997.)

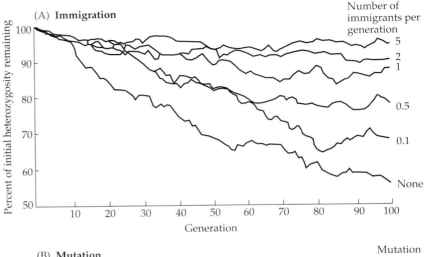

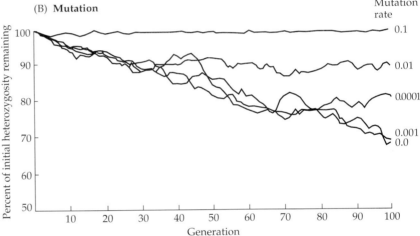

Figure 11.4 The effects of immigration and mutation on genetic variability in 25 simulated populations of size $N_e = 120$ individuals over 100 generations. (A) In an isolated population of 120 individuals, even low rates of immigration from a larger source population prevent the loss of heterozygosity from genetic drift. In the model, an immigration rate as low as 0.1 (1 immigrant per 10 generations) increases the level of heterozygosity, while genetic drift is negligible with an immigration rate of 1. (B) It is more difficult for mutation to counteract genetic drift. In the model, the mutation rate m must be 1% per gene per generation ($m = 0.01$) or greater to affect the level of heterozygosity. Since this mutation rate is far higher than what is observed in natural populations, mutation appears to play a minimal role in maintaining genetic variability in small populations. (From Lacy 1987.)

als between populations minimizes the loss of genetic variability associated with small population size (Figure 11.4) (Lacy 1987). If even one or two immigrants arrive each generation in an isolated population of about 100 individuals, the impact of genetic drift will be greatly reduced.

With 4–10 migrants arriving per generation from nearby populations, the effects of genetic drift are negligible (Mills and Allendorf 1996). Gene flow from neighboring populations appears to be the major factor preventing the loss of genetic variability in small populations of Galápagos finches (Grant and Grant 1992).

Field data also show that lower effective population size leads to a more rapid loss of alleles from the population. For example, the wind-pollinated dioecious conifer *Halocarpus bidwillii* of New Zealand naturally occurs in discrete populations in subalpine habitats. Protein electrophoresis was used to examine genetic variation in populations ranging from 10–400,000 individuals. There was a strong correlation between population size and genetic variation—large populations had the greatest levels of heterozygosity, percentage of polymorphic genes, and mean number of alleles per gene (Figure 11.5) (Billington 1991). Populations smaller than 8000 individuals appeared to suffer a loss of genetic variation, with the lowest variation in the smallest populations.

Unfortunately, rare and endangered species often have small, isolated populations, leading to a rapid loss of genetic variation. A review of studies of genetic variation in plants and animals found that small populations had less genetic variation than large populations in 22 out of 23 species (Frankham 1996). Genetic variation was also lower for endangered species and species with narrow ranges than for nonthreatened species and species with wide ranges. In some cases, entire species lacked genetic variation. An extensive review of genetic variation in plants showed that only 8 of 113 plant species had no genetic variation and these often had very limited ranges (Hamrick and Godt 1989). In the recently discovered Wollemi Pine in Australia, only 40 plants occur in two nearby populations. As might be predicted, an extensive investigation has failed to find any genetic variation in this species (Woodford 2000).

It seems safe to assume that to maintain genetic variability, conservation biologists should strive to preserve populations that are as large

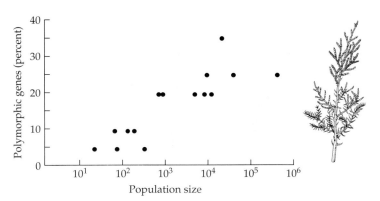

Figure 11.5 The level of genetic variability is directly correlated with population size in populations of *Halocarpus bidwillii*, a New Zealand coniferous shrub. This pattern holds true for the percentage of genes that are polymorphic as well as for the mean number of alleles per gene and the level of heterozygosity. Population size varies between 10 (10^1) and 1 million (10^6). (From Billlington 1991.)

as possible. But how big should a given population be? How many individuals are needed to maintain genetic variability? Franklin (1980) suggested that 50 reproductive individuals might be the minimum number necessary to avoid short-term inbreeding depression, the lower fitness that results from matings between closely related individuals. This figure is based on the practical experience of animal breeders, which indicates that animal stocks can be maintained with a loss of 2–3% of heterozygosity per generation. Wright's formula shows that a population of 50 individuals will lose only 1% of its heterozygosity per generation, which would be erring on the safe side. However, because this figure is based on work with domestic animals, its applicability to the wide range of wild species is uncertain.

Using data on mutation rates in *Drosophila* fruit flies, Franklin suggested that in populations of 500 reproductive individuals, the rate of new genetic variability arising through mutation might balance the variability being lost due to small population size. This range of values has been referred to as the **50/500 rule:** Isolated populations need to have at least 50 individuals and preferably 500 individuals to maintain genetic variability. This rule has been questioned by Lande (1995), who suggests that mutation rates may be lower than previously reported. If Lande is correct, then at least 5000 reproductive individuals must be protected to maintain the genetic variability and long-term survival of a population. While these formulae give us some practical guidelines, the ideal is still to protect as many individuals of rare and endangered species as possible to maximize their chance of survival.

Consequences of Reduced Genetic Variability

Small populations subjected to genetic drift have greater susceptibility to a number of deleterious genetic effects such as inbreeding depression, loss of evolutionary flexibility, and outbreeding depression. These factors may contribute to a decline in population size, leading to an even greater loss of genetic variability and a greater probability of extinction (Loeschcke et al. 1994; Avise and Hamrick 1996; Woodruff 2001).

INBREEDING DEPRESSION   A variety of mechanisms prevents inbreeding, mating among close relatives, in most natural populations. In large populations of most animal species, individuals do not normally mate with close relatives. They often disperse from their place of birth or are restrained from mating with relatives by behavioral inhibitions, unique individual odors, or other sensory cues. In many plants, a variety of morphological and physiological mechanisms encourage cross-pollination and prevent self-pollination. In some cases, particularly when population size is small and no other mates are available, these mechanisms fail to prevent inbreeding. Mating among parents and their offspring, siblings, and cousins, and self-fertilization in hermaphroditic species may result in **inbreeding depression,** a condition that is characterized by higher mortality of offspring, fewer offspring, or offspring that are weak, sterile, or have low mating success (Kirkpatrick and Jarne 2000; Ralls et al. 2001). These factors result in even fewer individuals in the next generation, leading to more pronounced inbreeding depression.

Evidence for the existence of inbreeding depression comes from studies of human populations (in which there are records of marriages between close relatives for many generations), captive animal populations, and cultivated plants (Darwin 1876; Nieminen et al 2001). In a wide range of captive mammal populations, matings among close relatives, such as parent–offspring mating and sibling mating, resulted on average in offspring with a 33% higher mortality rate than in noninbred animals (Figure 11.6) (Ralls et al. 1986, 1988). This lower fitness resulting from inbreeding is sometimes referred to as a "cost of inbreeding." Inbreeding depression can be a severe problem in small captive populations in zoos and domestic livestock breeding programs. But the effects of inbreeding in the wild, which are now being demonstrated, also appear to be significant. The scarlet gilia, *Ipomopsis aggregata,* provides an example. Plants that come from populations with fewer than 100 individuals produce smaller seeds with a lower rate of seed germination and exhibit greater susceptibility to environmental stress than do plants from larger popu-

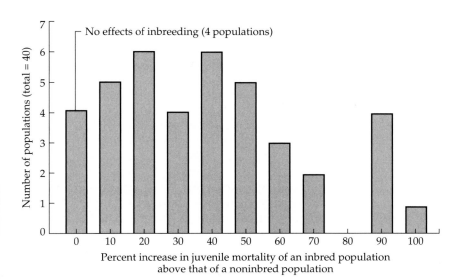

Figure 11.6 A high degree of inbreeding (such as matings between mother and son, father and daughter, brother and sister) results in a "cost of inbreeding." The data shown in the graph, based on a survey of 40 inbred mammal populations, express the cost as a percentage of increase in juvenile mortality above the juvenile mortality of outbreeding animals of the same species. (From Ralls et al. 1988.)

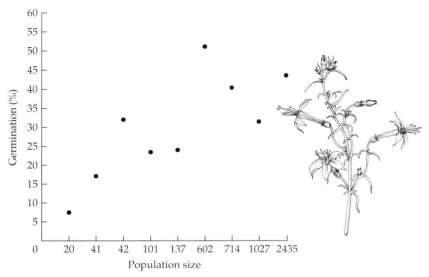

Figure 11.7 Seed germination in populations of the scarlet gilia (*Ipomopsis aggregata*) from montane Arizona is lower in small populations (fewer than 150 individuals) in comparison to larger populations. Seed germination is strongly reduced in the smallest populations. Populations are arranged from smallest to largest. (After Heschel and Paige 1995.)

lations (Figure 11.7) (Heschel and Paige 1995). Symptoms associated with inbreeding depression and loss of genetic variation are reduced when plants from small populations are cross-pollinated by hand with pollen from plants from large populations (Keller et al. 1994). In Illinois, isolated small populations of prairie chickens (*Tympanuchus cupido pinnatus*) were showing the effects of declining genetic variation and inbreeding depression, with lowered fertility and lowered rates of egg-hatching (Westemeier et al. 1998). When individuals from large, genetically diverse populations were released into the populations, egg viability was restored, demonstrating the importance of maintaining genetic variation.

In contrast with inbreeding, **outcrossing**—mating between individuals that are not closely related—not only increases the level of heterozygosity in a population but also results in many rare but harmful recessive alleles that arise by mutation to accumulate unexpressed in populations; as long as these alleles are rare, the function of the gene will be performed by the more common, dominant allele of the gene. When the population size of an outcrossing species declines, close relatives may be forced to inbreed because no other mates are available. This results in rare, harmful recessive alleles being expressed in the homozygous form that is the two alleles for a particular gene that are identical, resulting in offspring with lowered fitness. However, certain plant species, particularly weeds, are able to self-fertilize without any loss of fitness. Similarly, small inbred populations in the wild and in captivity have sometimes been able to persist for dozens of generations (Visscher et al. 2001). In these species, natural selection has presumably purged these harmful recessive genes from the population.

OUTBREEDING DEPRESSION   Individuals of different species rarely mate in the wild; there are strong ecological, behavioral, physiological, and morphological isolating mechanisms that ensure mating occurs only between individuals of the same species. However, when a species is rare or its habitat is damaged, **outbreeding**—mating between individuals of different species—may occur. Individuals unable to find mates within their own species may mate with an individual of a related species. The resulting offspring sometimes exhibit **outbreeding depression,** a condition that results in weakness, sterility, or lack of adaptability to the environment. Outbreeding depression may be caused by incompatibility of the chromosomes and enzyme systems that are inherited from the different parents (Thornhill 1993; Montalvo and Ellstrand 2001). To use an example from artificial selection, domestic horses and donkeys are commonly bred to produce mules. Although mules are not physically weak (on the contrary, they are quite strong, which is why humans find them useful), they are almost always sterile.

Outbreeding depression can also result from matings between different subspecies, or even matings between divergent genotypes or populations of the same species. Such mating might occur in a captive breeding program or when individuals from different populations are kept together in captivity. In such cases, the offspring of such different genotypes are unlikely to have the precise mixture of genes that allows individuals to survive and reproduce successfully in a particular set of local conditions. For example, when the ibex (*Capra ibex*) population of Slovakia went extinct, ibex from Austria, Turkey, and the Sinai were brought in to start a new population. These different subspecies mated and produced hybrids that bore their young in the harsh conditions of winter rather than in the spring, and consequently had a low survival rate. Outbreeding depression caused by the pairing of individuals from the extremes of the species' geographic range meant failure for the experiment. However, many other studies of animals have failed to demonstrate outbreeding depression or have even found the hybrids to be vigorous, suggesting that outbreeding depression is of less concern to conservation than inbreeding depression, the effects of which are well documented (Ralls et al. 2001).

Outbreeding depression may be especially significant in plants, where the arrival of pollen onto the receptive stigma of the flower is to some degree a matter of the chance movement of pollen by wind, insects, or another pollen vector. A rare plant species growing near a closely related common species may be overwhelmed by the pollen of the common species (Ellstrand 1992). The offspring of such hybridization events are often either sterile or poorly adapted to the environment of the parent species.

Even when hybrids produced by matings between a common and a rare species are not sterile, the genetic identity of the rare species becomes lost as its small gene pool is mixed into the much larger gene pool of the common species. The seriousness of this threat is illustrated by the fact that more than 90% of California's threatened and endangered plants occur in close proximity to other species in the same genus with which the rare plants could possibly hybridize. Such a loss of identity can also take place in gardens when individuals from different parts of a species' range are grown next to each other and are cross-pollinated, producing hybrid seed.

LOSS OF EVOLUTIONARY FLEXIBILITY Rare alleles and unusual combinations of alleles that confer no immediate advantages may be uniquely suited for a future set of environmental conditions. Loss of genetic variability in a small population may limit its ability to respond to new conditions and long-term changes in the environment, such as pollution, new diseases, and global climate change (Allendorf and Leary 1986; Falk and Holsinger 1991). A small population is less likely than a large population to possess the genetic variation necessary for adaptation to long-term environmental changes and so will be more likely to go extinct. For example, in many plant populations a small percentage of individuals have alleles that promote tolerance for high concentrations of toxic metals such as zinc and lead, even when these metals are not present (Antonovics 1976). If toxic metals become abundant in the environment due to pollution, individuals with these alleles will be better able to adapt to them grow, survive, and reproduce better than typical individuals; consequently, frequency of these alleles in the population increases dramatically. However, if the population has become small and the genotypes for metal tolerance have been lost, the population could go extinct.

Factors That Determine Effective Population Size

In this section we will discuss the factors that determine the effective population size, the size of the population as estimated by the number of its breeding individuals. The factors limiting the estimated number of breeding individuals in a population include unequal sex ratio, variation in reproductive output, and population fluctuations and bottlenecks.

The effective population size is lower than the total population size because many individuals do not reproduce, due to factors such as inability to find a mate, being too old or too young to mate, poor health, sterility, malnutrition, small body size, and social structures that restrict which individuals can mate. Many of the factors are initiated or aggravated by habitat degradation and fragmentation. Further, many plant, fungus, bacteria, and protist species have seeds, spores, or other structures in the soil that remain dormant unless stable conditions for germination appear. These individuals could be counted as members of the population, though they are obviously not part of the breeding population. Because of these factors, the effective population size (N_e) of breeding individuals is often substantially smaller than the actual population size (N). Because the rate of loss of genetic variability is based on the effective population size, the loss of genetic variability can be quite severe even in a large population (Kimura and Crow 1963; Lande and Barrowclough 1987; Nunney and Elam 1994). For example, consider a population of 1000 alligators with 990 immature animals and only 10 mature breeding animals, 5 males and 5 females; in this case, the effective population size is 10, not 1000. For a rare oak species, there might be 20 mature trees, 500 saplings and 2000 seedlings, resulting in a population size of 2520 but an effective population size of only 20. A smaller than expected effective population size can also exist when there is an unequal sex ratio, variation in reproductive output, or population fluctuations and bottlenecks, as described below. The overall impact of these factors can be substantial. A review of a wide range of wildlife studies revealed that the average effective population size was only 11% of total population size; that is, a population of 300 animals, seemingly large enough to maintain the population, might only have an effective population size of 33, indicating that it is in serious danger of extinction (Frankham 1996).

UNEQUAL SEX RATIO   A population may consist of unequal numbers of males and females due to chance, selective mortality, or the harvesting of only one sex by people. If, for example, a population of a monogamous (one male and one female forming a long-lasting pair bond) goose species consists of 20 males and 6 females, only 12 individuals, 6 males and 6 females, will be mating. In this case, the effective population size is 12, not 26. In other animal species, social systems may prevent many individuals from mating even though they are physiologically capable of doing so. Among elephant seals, for example, a single dominant male usually controls a large group of females and prevents other males from mating with them (Figure 11.8), whereas among African wild dogs, the dominant female in the pack often bears all of the pups.

The effect of unequal numbers of breeding males and females on N_e can be described by the formula

$$N_e = \frac{4N_m N_f}{N_m + N_f}$$

where N_m and N_f are the numbers of breeding males and breeding females, respectively, in the population. In general, as the sex ratio of breed-

Figure 11.8 A single male elephant seal (the larger animal with the extended snout, seen roaring in the center of the photograph) controls large numbers of females; thus the effective population size is reduced because only one male is providing genetic input. (Photograph by Frank S. Balthis.)

ing individuals becomes increasingly unequal, the ratio of the effective population size to the number of breeding individuals (N_e / N) also goes down (Figure 11.9). This occurs because only a few individuals of one sex are making a disproportionately large contribution to the genetic makeup of the next generation, rather than the equal contribution found in monogamous mating systems. For example, consider a population of seals that contains 6 breeding males and 150 breeding females, with each male mating with 25 females. The calculation demonstrates that the effective population size is actually comparable to a randomly mating population of 23 seals with similar numbers of males and females, not 156 seals, because of the relatively few males involved in mating:

$$N_e = \frac{(4)(6)(150)}{(6+150)} = \frac{3600}{156} = 23$$

VARIATION IN REPRODUCTIVE OUTPUT   In many species the number of offspring varies substantially among individuals. This phenomenon is particularly true in plants, where some individuals may produce a few seeds while others produce thousands. Unequal production of offspring leads to a substantial reduction in N_e because a few individuals in the present generation will be disproportionately represented in the gene

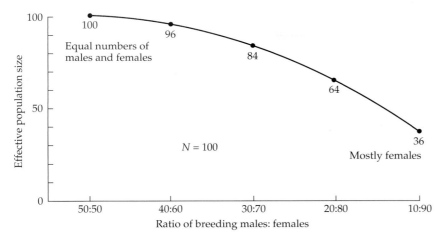

Figure 11.9 The effective population size (N_e) declines when the number of males and females in a breeding population of 100 individuals is increasingly unequal. N_e is 100 when 50 males and 50 females breed, but only 36 when 10 males and 90 females breed.

pool of the next generation. In general, the greater the variation in reproductive output, the more the effective population size is lowered. For a variety of species, Crow and Morton (1955) estimated that variation in offspring number reduces effective population size by a factor of 60–85%. In many annual plant populations that consist of large numbers of tiny plants producing one or a few seeds and a few gigantic individuals producing thousands of seeds, N_e could be reduced even more.

POPULATION FLUCTUATIONS AND BOTTLENECKS   In some species, population size varies dramatically from generation to generation. Particularly good examples of this are checkerspot butterflies in California (Murphy et al. 1990), annual plants, and amphibians. In extreme fluctuations, the effective population size is somewhere between the lowest and the highest number of individuals. The effective population size can be calculated over a period of *t* years using the number of individuals (*N*) breeding in any one year:

$$N_e = t/(1/N_1 + 1/N_2 + \ldots + 1/N_t)$$

Consider a butterfly population, monitored for five years, that has 10, 20, 100, 20, and 10 breeding individuals in the successive five years. In this case

$$N_e = 5/(1/10 + 1/20 + 1/100 + 1/20 + 1/10) = 5/(31/100) = 5(100/31) = 16.1$$

The effective population size over the course of 5 years is above the lowest population level of 10 but well below the maximum number of 100 and the arithmetic average population size of 32.

The effective population size tends to be determined by the years in which the population has the smallest numbers. A single year of drastically reduced population numbers will substantially lower the value of N. This principle applies to a phenomenon known as a **population bottleneck**, which occurs when a population is greatly reduced in size and rare alleles in the population are lost if no individuals possessing those alleles survive and reproduce (Barrett and Kohn 1991). With fewer alleles present and a decline in heterozygosity, the overall fitness of the individuals in the population may decline. A special category of bottleneck, known as the **founder effect**, occurs when a few individuals leave one population to establish another new population. The new population often has less genetic variability than the larger, original population (Figure 11.10). Bottlenecks can also occur when captive populations are established using relatively few individuals. For example, captive populations of rare desert pupfish were mostly established using fewer than 100 fish (Dunham and Minckley 1998).

The lions (*Panthera leo*) of Ngorongoro Crater in Tanzania provide a well-studied example of a population bottleneck (Packer 1992, 1997). The lion population in the crater consisted of 60–75 individuals until an outbreak of biting flies in 1962 reduced the population to 9 females and 1 male (Figure 11.11). Two years later, 7 additional males immigrated to the crater; there has been no further immigration since that time. The small number of founders, the isolation of the population, and the variation in reproductive success among individuals have apparently created a population bottleneck; even though the population increased to 75–125 animals in 1983, the population has since declined (Packer, per-

Figure 11.10   A new population started by only a few unrelated individuals is missing a substantial amount of the genetic variability of the source population. However, if the effective size of the founding population is more than 10 unrelated individuals, more than 90% of the genetic variability is preserved. If the population is started with a single breeding pair or just a pregnant female, giving an effective population size of two, the majority of the genetic variability is still preserved. This variability will be largely preserved if the population rapidly expands in size, but it will continue to be lost if population size remains very small. (From Foose 1983.)

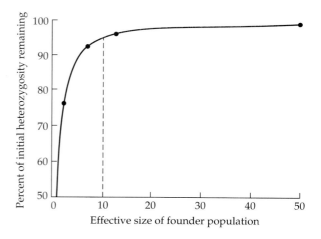

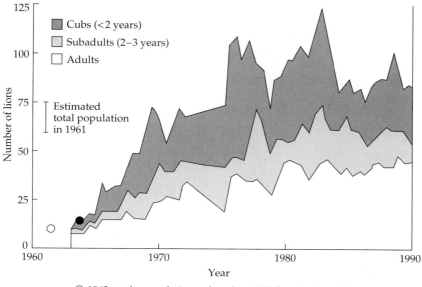

Figure 11.11 The Ngorongoro Crater lion population consisted of about 61 individuals in 1961 before crashing in 1962. Since that time the population had reached 125 individuals in 1983 before collapsing to 42 individuals in 2001. Small size, an isolated location, lack of immigration since 1964, and the impact of disease have apparently resulted in a loss of genetic variation caused by a population bottleneck. (From Packer et al. 1991.)

sonal communication). In comparison with the large Serengeti lion population nearby, the Crater lions show reduced genetic variability, high levels of sperm abnormalities (Figure 11.12), reduced reproductive rates, and increased cub mortality. Further genetic research on this population has been stopped because government officials have refused to grant permission for researchers to collect additional samples for analysis. The population is also vulnerable to outside influences: In February, 2001, the population dropped from 63 to 42 animals as a result of canine distemper virus spreading from domestic dogs kept by people living just outside the Crater area (Packer, personal communication).

Using protein electrophoresis, the rare aquatic annual plant *Howellia aquatilis* (Campanulaceae) was found to lack genetic variation, both among individuals within populations and among populations (Lesica et al. 1988). This lack of variation is thought to be due to fluctuations in population size and a tendency for flowers to self-fertilize. A similar lack of genetic variation is apparent in four populations of the rare Furbish's lousewort (*Pedicularis furbishiae*), an endemic plant of Maine (Menges

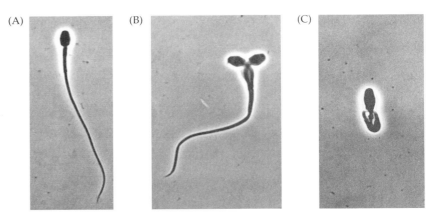

Figure 11.12 Males of the isolated and inbred population of lions at Ngorongoro Crater in Tanzania exhibit a high level of sperm abnormalities. (A) Normal lion sperm. (B) Bicephalic ("two-headed") sperm. (C) Nonfunctional sperm with a coiled flagellum. (Photographs by D. Wildt.)

1990). In this case, the lack of genetic variation is attributed to population bottlenecks resulting from a series of temporary populations established on riverbanks after colonization by a few seeds.

It should be noted that population bottlenecks do not always lead to greatly reduced heterozygosity. The effects of population bottlenecks will be most evident when the breeding population is reduced below 10 individuals for several generations. If the population expands rapidly in size after a temporary bottleneck, average heterozygosity in the population may be restored even though the number of alleles present is severely reduced (Nei et al. 1975; Allendorf and Leary 1986). An example of this phenomenon is the high level of heterozygosity found in the greater one-horned rhinoceros (*Rhinoceros unicornis*) in Nepal, even after the population passed through a bottleneck (Figure 11.13; see also Box 18). Population size declined from 800 individuals in Chitwan National Park to less than 100 individuals; fewer than 30 were breeding. With an effective population size of 30 individuals for one generation, the population would have lost only 1.7% of its heterozygosity after one generation. As a result of strict protection of the species by park guards, the population recovered to 400 individuals (Dinerstein and McCracken 1990). Similarly, the Mauritius kestrel (*Falco punctatus*) experienced a long population decline, with only one breeding pair remaining in 1974. An intensive conservation program, has allowed the population to recover to over 200 pairs today. Comparing the present birds with preserved museum specimens and kestrels living elsewhere, the Mauritius kestrel has only lost around 50% of its genetic variation after passing through this bottleneck (Groombridge et al. 2000).

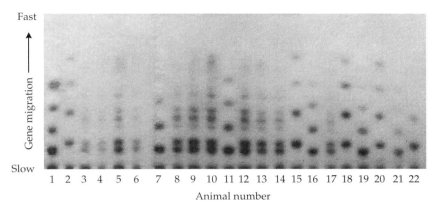

Fast

Gene migration →

Slow

1 2 3 4 5 6 7 8 9 10 11 12 13 14 15 16 17 18 19 20 21 22

Animal number

Figure 11.13 Starch gel electrophoresis reveals that the population of greater one-horned rhinoceroses (*Rhinoceros unicornis*) at Chitwan National Park in Nepal shows high levels of genetic variation. This technique is based on the fact that the proteins (in this case, an enzyme called LDH) produced by different alleles of a gene migrate at different rates across an electrically charged starch gel plate, appearing as bands at different distances from the starting point at the bottom of the gel. Each column represents one individual animal. Note that animals 10 and 11, for example, have bands at different positions, indicating that these two individuals are genetically different from each other for the enzyme LDH. (From Dinerstein and McCracken 1990.)

One way to estimate effective population size is by measuring the loss of heterozygosity over time in repeatedly censused populations (Fiumera et al. 2000). The rationale for this approach is that the rate of loss of heterozygosity over time due to genetic drift is directly correlated to N_e. This approach was used to examine eight large captive populations of *Drosophila melanogaster* flies using a technique for evaluating the number of variable alleles (Briscoe et al. 1992). All eight populations had been maintained separately with a population size of about 5000 individuals for between 8 and 365 generations. Despite the large population size, N_e varied between 185 and 253—only about 4% of the population size. The effective population size is severely reduced, presumably because of unequal breeding success; possibly a few males mated with the majority of reproductive females, and a small proportion of highly fertile females may have laid most of the eggs. These results and the others mentioned previously demonstrate that merely maintaining large population sizes is often insufficient to prevent the loss of genetic variation in both wild and captive populations. In the case of captive populations, genetic variation may be effectively maintained by controlling breeding, perhaps by subdividing the population, periodically removing dominant males to allow subdominant males the opportunity to mate, and allowing limited migration of individuals among subpopulations.

BOX 18 *Rhino Species in Asia and Africa: Genetic Diversity and Habitat Loss*

In recent decades, conservationists have focused extraordinary effort on restoring the numbers of rhinoceroses in parts of their original ranges. The task is monumental: the five species of rhinoceros that inhabit Asia and Africa, all critically endangered, represent ancient and unusual adaptations for survival. Habitat destruction and poaching represent serious threats to the three species of the Asian forests, while the illegal killing of rhinos for their horns is the main problem for the two African species.

Rhino losses are so severe that it is estimated that only 16,000 individuals of all five species survive today. These species only exist in a tiny fraction of their former range. The most numerous of the five is the white rhinoceros, *Ceratotherium simum*; this species numbers approximately 10,400 wild animals, although there are only 30 individuals of the distinctive northern subspecies. The rarest species—the elusive Javan rhinoceros, *Rhinoceros sondaicus*—is thought to number around 50 animals on the very western end of the island of Java, with another 7–10 in Vietnam. These two populations are genetically very distant (Fernando and Melnick, personal communication).

The overall decline of each species is alarming enough, but the problem is exacerbated by the fact that many of the remaining animals live in very small, isolated populations. The black rhino, *Diceros bicornis*, for example, numbers about 2700, but these individuals are in approximately 75 small, widely separated subgroups (Ashley et al. 1990). The existing populations of the Sumatran rhino (*Dicerorhinus sumatrensis*) each contain less than 100 individuals (Caughley and Gunn 1996), with the total species count under 300. Some biologists fear that these small populations may not be viable over the long term as a result of loss of genetic variability, inbreeding depression, and genetic diseases resulting from mating among closely related individuals.

The question of genetic viability in rhino populations is not as simple as it first appears.

Genetic diversity varies greatly among rhino species. Studies of the greater one-horned, or Indian, rhinoceros (*Rhinoceros unicornis*) in Nepal indicate that despite its small total population—an estimated 1500 animals—the genetic diversity in at least this population is extremely high (see Figure 11.13), contradicting the common assumption that small populations automatically have low heterozygosity. The combination of long generation times, high individual mobility, and the possibility that rhinos may have migrated into the park from a large area may have allowed the Indian rhino to maintain its genetic variability despite passing through a population bottleneck (Dinerstein and McCracken 1990; Melnick, personal communication). In contrast, six living subspecies of the black rhinoceros are believed to still exist, representing adaptations to local environmental conditions throughout the species' range. Certain of these subspecies appear to have very low genetic variability; in three cases—*D. bicornis brucii*, *D. bicornis longipes*, and *D. bicornis chobiensis*—only a few dozen animals remain to represent these variants (Ashley et al. 1990).

On the basis of genetic variability alone, one might assume that the Indian rhino has the advantage over the black rhino and is more likely to survive. However, the Indian rhino faces a different and possibly more deadly threat: habitat loss. Though no immediate threat of inbreeding exists for the Indian rhino, the critical pressure on this species' range since the nineteenth century has reduced its numbers dramatically, from possibly tens of thousands of animals to less than 1000 by the 1960s (Dinerstein and McCracken 1990). The geographic range of this animal, originally covering northern India, Pakistan, southern Nepal, Burma,

Each of the five rhinoceros species currently occupies only a tiny fraction of its former range, but their situations and their levels of endangerment vary greatly. (From Caughley and Gunn 1996.)

BOX 18 *(continued)*

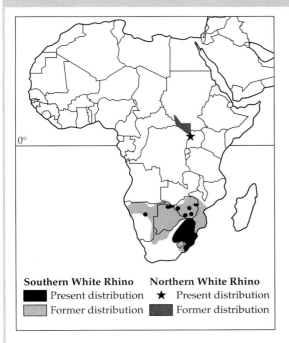

Southern White Rhino
■ Present distribution
▨ Former distribution

Northern White Rhino
★ Present distribution
▨ Former distribution

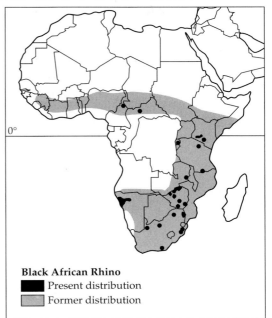

Black African Rhino
■ Present distribution
▨ Former distribution

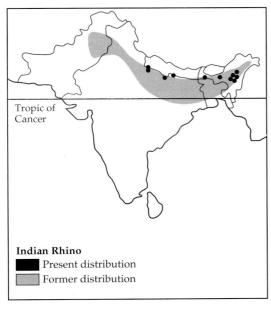

Indian Rhino
■ Present distribution
▨ Former distribution

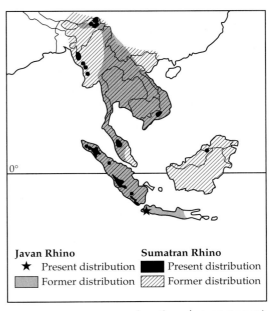

Javan Rhino
★ Present distribution
▨ Former distribution

Sumatran Rhino
■ Present distribution
▨ Former distribution

(continued on next page)

BOX 18 *(continued)*

and Bangladesh, has been almost completely taken over by human settlement. Indian rhino populations in parks and sanctuaries have increased dramatically and are genetically healthy; however, the species will always be limited to these small, heavily guarded remnant habitats, with no opportunity to return to its former range or numbers.

In contrast, much of the range of the black rhino in Africa is still open and is not likely to be subject to human encroachment at any time in the near future. A degree of heterozygosity could be maintained in the species by moving individuals between populations. If the black rhino population is managed for genetic diversity in this manner, it is conceivable that this species could be fully restored to its original numbers and much of its range. Yet the problem of microenvironmental adaptations remains: by placing black rhinos from a number of different locations together in a sanctuary to increase genetic diversity in the species, would the rhinos risk losing adaptive differences that might prove crucial to the survival of local subspecies? Analysis of mitochondrial DNA in populations of black rhinos (Ashley et al. 1990) indicates that in certain populations the relationship between most individuals is so close that the need to diversify the black rhino population outweighs any possible costs. Maintaining genetic diversity is contingent on controlling outside threats to the breeding population, including illegal poaching for their horns. Optimal park conditions must also be maintained to ensure that all adult individuals reproduce.

Genetic analysis has also been useful for making decisions on the conservation of the Sumatran rhinoceros, numbering less than 300 individuals and found in scattered populations. Analysis of mitochondrial DNA from blood and hair samples from eastern Sumatra, western Sumatra, peninsular Malaysia, and Borneo populations showed that the Borneo population represented a distinct lineage from the other three populations, which were genetically similar. The recommendation is that the Borneo rhinos be treated as a separate population for breeding and conservation purposes, whereas the other three populations could be managed as one conservation unit (Morales et al. 1997).

As this research makes evident, rhino conservation must be tailored to the specific circumstances of particular species and populations. The different species face a number of challenges with a variety of possible solutions. For species threatened with habitat loss, such as the Indian rhino, sanctuaries and habitat preservation may be the most important methods of preserving the species. Others, such as the black rhino, may require management to increase genetic diversity, including breeding programs in the wild and protection of the remnant populations. The rarest species, the Sumatran and Javan rhinos, may require a combination of approaches. They need habitat protection because both of these Asian species are under severe pressure from logging and conversion of forest to agricultural land, and they need breeding programs in the wild to increase and maintain genetic diversity. For each of these rhinos, there is no single, all-encompassing answer; the problems and circumstances of conserving the species must be evaluated individually.

Other Factors That Affect the Persistence of Small Populations

In this section we discuss some other factors that affect small populations. Small populations tend to go extinct because of the loss of genetic variation. In addition, they are vulnerable to extinction due to random variations in demography and the environment.

Demographic Variation

In an ideal, stable environment, a population would increase until it reached the carrying capacity (K) of the environment, at which point the average birth rate (b) per individual would equal the average death rate (d) and there would be no net change in population size. In any real population, individuals do not usually produce the average number of offspring: they might leave no offspring, somewhat fewer than the average, or more than the average. For example, in an ideal, stable giant panda population, each female would produce an average of two surviving offspring in her lifetime, but field studies show that rates of reproduction among individual females vary widely around that number. However, as long as population size is large, the average birth rate provides an accurate description of the population. Similarly, the average death rate in a population can be determined only by examining large numbers of individuals because some individuals die young and other individuals live a relatively long time. This variation in population size due to random variation in reproduction and mortality rates is known as **demographic variation** or **demographic stochasticity**.

Population size may fluctuate over time due to changes in the environment or other factors without ever approaching a stable value. In general, once population size drops below about 50 individuals, individual variation in birth and death rates begins to cause the population size to fluctuate randomly up or down (Menges 1992). If population size fluctuates downward in any one year due to a higher than average number of deaths or a lower than average number of births, the resulting smaller population will be even more susceptible to demographic fluctuations in subsequent years. Random fluctuations upward in population size are eventually bounded by the carrying capacity of the environment, and the population may fluctuate downward again. Consequently, once a population decreases because of habitat destruction and fragmentation, demographic variation becomes important and the population has a higher probability of declining more and even going extinct due to chance alone (in a year with low reproduction and high mortality) (Lacy and Lindenmayer 1995). Species with highly variable birth and death rates, such as annual plants and short-lived insects, may be particularly susceptible to population extinction due to demographic stochasticity. The chance of extinction is also greater in species that have low birth rates, such as elephants, because these species take longer to recover from chance reductions in population size.

As a simple example, imagine a population of three hermaphroditic individuals that each live for one year, need to find a mate, reproduce, and then die. Assume that each individual has a 33% probability of producing 0, 1, or 2 offspring, resulting in an average birth rate of 1 per individual; in this instance, there is theoretically a stable population. However, when these individuals reproduce, there is a 1-in-27 chance

$(0.33 \times 0.33 \times 0.33)$ that no offspring will be produced in the next generation and the population will go extinct. Consider also that there is a 1-in-9 chance that only 1 offspring will be produced in the next generation $(0.33 \times 0.33 \times 0.33 \times 3)$; because this individual will not be able to find a mate, the population will be doomed to extinction in the next generation. There is also a 22% chance that the population will decline to 2 individuals in the next generation. Thus, random variation in birth rates can lead to demographic stochasticity and extinction in small populations. Similarly, random fluctuations in the death rate can lead to fluctuations in population size. When populations are small, random high mortality in one year might eliminate the population altogether.

When populations drop below a critical number, deviations from an equal sex ratio may occur, leading to a declining birth rate and a further lowering of population size. For example, imagine a population of 4 birds that includes 2 mating pairs of males and females, in which each female produces an average of 2 surviving offspring in her lifetime. In the next generation, there is a 1-in-8 chance that only male or only female birds will be produced, in which case no eggs will be laid to produce the following generation. There is a 50% (8-in-16) chance that there will be either 3 males and 1 female or 3 females and 1 male in the next generation, in which case only 1 pair of birds will mate and the population will decline. For example, the last 5 surviving individuals of the extinct dusky seaside sparrow (*Ammodramus maritimus nigrescens*) were all males, so there was no opportunity to establish a captive breeding program. In Illinois, the last 3 individuals of the rare lakeside daisy (*Hymenoxys acaulis* var. *glabra*) remaining in the state are unable to produce viable seeds when cross-pollinated among themselves because they belong to the same self-infertile mating type (De Mauro 1993). Pollen has to be brought in from Ohio plants in order for the Illinois plants to produce seeds.

In many animal species, small populations may be unstable due to the inability of the social structure to function once the population falls below a certain size; this is known as the **Allee effect** (Keitt et al. 2001). Herds of grazing mammals and flocks of birds may be unable to find food and defend themselves against attack when numbers fall below a certain level. Animals that hunt in packs, such as wild dogs and lions, may need a certain number of individuals to hunt effectively. Many animal species that live in widely dispersed populations, such as bears, whales, spiders, and eagles, may be unable to find mates once the population density drops below a certain point. In this case, the average birth rate will decline, making the population density even lower and worsening the problem. In plant species, as population size decreases, the distance between plants increases; pollinating animals may not visit more than one of the isolated, scattered plants, resulting in the loss of seed production due to insufficient transfer of compatible pollen (Bawa 1990).

This combination of random fluctuations in demographic characteristics, unequal sex ratios, disruption of social behavior, and decreased population density contributes to instabilities in population size, which often leads to local extinction.

Environmental Variation and Catastrophes

Random variation in the biological and physical environment, known as **environmental stochasticity,** can also cause variation in the population size of a species. For example, the population of an endangered rabbit species might be affected by fluctuations in the population of a deer species that eats the same types of plants, fluctuations in the population of a fox species that feeds on the rabbits, and fluctuations in the populations of parasites and disease-causing organisms affecting the rabbits. Variation in the physical environment might also strongly influence the rabbit populations—rainfall during an average year might encourage plant growth and allow the population to increase, while dry years might limit plant growth and cause rabbits to starve. Environmental stochasticity affects all individuals in the population, unlike demographic stochasticity, which causes variation among individuals within in the population.

Natural catastrophes that occur at unpredictable intervals, such as droughts, storms, earthquakes, and fires, along with cyclical die-offs of the surrounding biological community, can cause dramatic fluctuations in population levels. Natural catastrophes can kill part of a population or even eliminate an entire population from an area. Numerous examples exist of die-offs in populations of large mammals; in many cases 70–90% of the population dies (Young 1994). Even though the probability of a natural catastrophe in any one year is low, over the course of decades and centuries, natural catastrophes have a high likelihood of occurring.

As an example of environmental variation, imagine a rabbit population of 100 individuals in which the average birth rate is 0.2 and an average of 20 rabbits are eaten each year by foxes. On average, the population will maintain its numbers at exactly 100 individuals, with 20 rabbits born each year and 20 rabbits eaten each year. However, if there are three successive years in which the foxes eat 40 rabbits per year, the population size will decline to 80 rabbits, 56 rabbits, and 27 rabbits in years 1, 2, and 3, respectively. If there are then three years of no fox predation, the rabbit population will increase to 32, 38, and 46 individuals in years 4, 5, and 6. Even though the same average rate of predation (20 rabbits per year) occurred over this six-year period, by introducing variation in year-to-year predation rates the rabbit population size declined by more than 50%. At a population size of 46 individuals, the rabbit population will go rapidly extinct when subjected to the average rate of 20 rabbits eaten by foxes per year.

Modeling efforts by Menges (1992) and others have shown that random environmental variation is generally more important than random demographic variation in increasing the probability of extinction in populations of small to moderate size. Environmental variation can substantially increase the risk of extinction even in populations showing positive population growth under the assumption of a stable environment (Mangel and Tier 1994). In general, introducing environmental variation into population models, in effect making them more realistic, results in populations with lower growth rates, lower population sizes, and higher probabilities of extinction. Menges (1992) introduced environmental variation into models of plant populations that had been developed by field ecologists working with palms. Considering only demographic variation, and before the inclusion of environmental variation, these plant models suggested that the MVP size, the number of individuals needed to give the population a 95% probability of persisting for 100 years, was about 140 mature individuals (Figure 11.14). When moderate environmental variation was included, however, the MVP size increased to 380 individuals, making protection of the species more difficult.

The interaction between population size and environmental variation was demonstrated using the biennial herb garlic mustard (*Alliaria peti-*

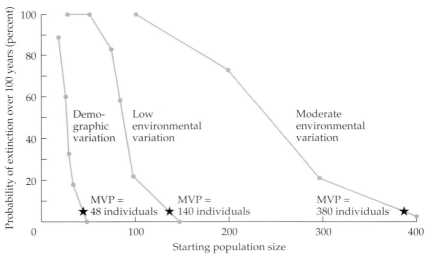

Figure 11.14 The effects of demographic variation, low environmental variation, and moderate environmental variation on the probability of extinction of a population of the Mexican palm, *Astrocaryum mexicanum.* (In this study, the MVP size, indicated by a star, was defined as the population size at which there is a less than 5% chance of the population going extinct within 100 years.) (From Menges 1992; data from Piñero et al. 1984.)

olata) as an experimental subject (Drayton and Primack 1999). Populations of various sizes were assigned at random to be either left alone as controls or experimentally eradicated by removing every flowering plant in each of the four years of the study. Overall the probability of an experimental population going extinct over the four-year period was 43% for small populations (≤ 10 individuals initially), 9% for medium size populations (>10 and ≤ 50), and 7% for large populations (>50 individuals). For control populations, the probability of going extinct for small, medium, and large populations is 11%, 0%, and 0%. Large numbers of dormant seeds in the soil apparently allowed most experimental populations to persist even when every flowering plant was removed in four successive years. However, small populations were far more susceptible to extinction than large populations.

Extinction Vortices

The smaller a population becomes, the more vulnerable it is to further demographic variation, environmental variation, and genetic factors that tend to lower reproduction, increase mortality rates, and so reduce population size even more and drive the population to extinction. This tendency of small populations to decline toward extinction has been likened to a vortex, a whirling mass of gas or liquid spiraling inward—the closer it gets to the center, the faster it moves. At the center of an **extinction vortex** is oblivion: the local extinction of the species. Once caught in such a vortex, it is difficult for a species to resist the pull toward extinction (Gilpin and Soulé 1986).

For example, a natural catastrophe, a new disease, or human disturbance could reduce a large population to a small size. This small population could then suffer from inbreeding depression with an associated lowered juvenile survival rate. This increased death rate could result in an even lower population size and more inbreeding. Similarly, demographic variation will often reduce population size, resulting in even greater demographic fluctuations and, once again, a greater probability of extinction.

These three forces—environmental variation, demographic variation, and loss of genetic variability—act together so that a decline in population size caused by one factor will increase the vulnerability of the population to the other two factors (Figure 11.15). For example, a decrease in orangutan population size caused by forest fragmentation may cause inbreeding depression, decreasing population size; decreased population size may then disrupt the social structure and the ability to find mates, leading to an even lower population size; the smaller population is then more vulnerable to further population reduction and eventual extinction caused by unusual environmental events. The widespread logging, drought, forest fires, and dense smoke cover in Borneo and Sumatra in

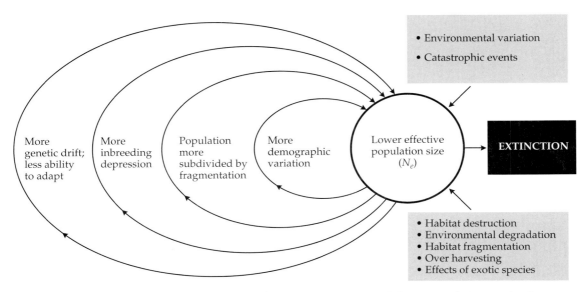

Figure 11.15 Extinction vortices progressively lower population size, leading to local extinctions of species. Once a population drops below a certain size, it enters a vortex, in which the factors that affect small populations tend to drive its size progressively lower. (After Gilpin and Soulé 1986 and Guerrant 1992.)

1997 are the types of environmental events that drive small populations to extinction. Many endangered species and their populations are being pulled into an extinction vortex because of human activities.

Once a population has declined to a small size, it will probably go extinct unless unusual and highly favorable conditions allow the population size to increase. Such populations require a careful program of population and habitat management, as described in later chapters, to reduce demographic and environmental variation and thus minimize the effects of small population size.

Summary

1. Biologists have observed that small populations have a greater tendency to go extinct than large populations. Small populations are subject to a more-rapid rate of extinction for three main reasons: loss of genetic variability and related problems of inbreeding depression and genetic drift, demographic fluctuations, and environmental variation or natural catastrophes. Experience with captive animals have led to some tentative rules: Isolated wild populations should have at least 50 to 500 breeding individuals to maintain genetic variability, though protecting 5000 individuals or more is preferable.

2. To protect small populations, we need to determine the effective population size, which is an estimate of the number of individuals that are actually producing offspring. The calculated effective population size is often much lower than simply the number of living individuals because (1) many individuals

are not reproducing; (2) there may be an unequal sex ratio; (3) there may be variation among individuals in number of offspring produced; and (4) populations may show large fluctuations in size over time.

3. Variations in reproductive and mortality rates can cause small populations to fluctuate randomly in size, leading to extinction. Environmental variation can also cause random fluctuations in population size, with infrequent natural catastrophes sometimes causing major reductions.

4. Once a population's size has been reduced by habitat destruction, fragmentation, and other human activities, it is even more vulnerable to random fluctuations in size and eventual extinction. The combined effects of demographic variation, environmental variation, and loss of genetic variability on small populations create an extinction vortex that tends to accelerate the drive to extinction.

For Discussion

1. Imagine a species that has four populations, consisting of 4, 10, 40, and 100 individuals. Using Wright's formula, calculate the loss in heterozygosity over 1, 2, 5, and 10 generations for each population. Calculate the effective population size for each population, assuming that there are equal numbers of males and females; then calculate it assuming different proportions of males and females. Allow the population size of each group to fluctuate at random around its average value. Calculate how this affects the loss of heterozygosity and the effective population size.

2. Construct a simple population model of a rabbit that has a stable population size (see page 323); then add environmental variation (such as severe winter storms or predation) and demographic variation (number of offspring produced per squirrel per year) and determine whether the population would be able to persist over time. Use the methods shown in the text, computer simulations (see Donovan and Welden [2002] and Shultz et al. [1999] for ideas), or random-number generators (flipping coins is the easiest).

3. Find out about species that are currently endangered in the wild. How are they or how might they be affected by the problems of small populations? Address genetic, physiological, behavioral, and ecological aspects, as appropriate.

Suggested Readings

Avise, J. C. and J. L. Hamrick (eds.). 1996. *Conservation Genetics: Case Histories from Nature.* Chapman and Hall, New York. Leading experts present current knowledge of genetics for many groups of organisms.

Caughley, G. and A. Gunn. 1996. *Conservation Biology in Theory and Practice.* Blackwell Science, Cambridge, MA. Strong presentation emphasizing quantitative analyses of vertebrate populations.

Donovan, T. M. and C. W. Welden. 2002. *Spreadsheet Exercises in Conservation Biology and Landscape Ecology.* Sinauer Associates, Sunderland, MA. A straightforward method for learning to build population models with some of the properties discussed in this chapter.

Falk, D. A. and K. E. Holsinger (eds.). 1991. *Genetics and Conservation of Rare Plants.* Oxford University Press, New York. Conservation efforts involving plants require some special considerations.

Frankham, R. 1996. Relationships of genetic variation to population size in wildlife. *Conservation Biology* 10: 1500–1508. Concise summary and literature review of 10 hypotheses.

Franklin, I. R. 1980. Evolutionary change in small populations. In *Conservation Biology: An Evolutionary-Ecological Perspective,* M. E. Soulé and B. A. Wilcox (eds.), pp. 135–149. Sinauer Associates, Sunderland, MA. Seminal paper outlining the problems of small populations.

Hedrick, P. W. 2000. *Genetics of Populations,* 2nd ed. Jones and Bartlett Publishers, Sudbury, MA. Excellent introduction to basic principles.

Lacy, R. C. 1987. Loss of genetic diversity from managed populations: Interacting effects of drift, mutation, immigration, selection, and population subdivision. *Conservation Biology* 1: 143–158. Clearly presented simulations of various realistic scenarios.

Menges, E. S. 1992. Stochastic modeling of extinction in plant populations. In *Conservation Biology: The Theory and Practice of Nature Conservation, Preservation and Management,* P. L. Fiedler and S. K. Jain (eds.), pp. 253–275. Chapman and Hall, New York. Clear presentation of extinction models.

Packer, C. 1992. Captives in the wild. *National Geographic* 181(April): 122–136. The story of Ngorongoro Crater lions, combining both natural history and genetics.

Ralls, K. S., R. Frankham, and J. Ballou. 2001. Inbreeding and outbreeding. In *Encyclopedia of Biodiversity,* S. A. Levin (ed.), Vol. 3, pp. 427–436. Academic Press, San Diego, CA.

Shultz, S. M., A. E. Dunham, K. V. Root, S. L. Soucy, S. D. Carroll, and L. R. Ginzburg. 1999. *Conservatioon Biology with RAMAS® EcoLab.* Sinauer Associates, Sunderland, MA. A set of computer exercises to accompany an undergraduate course in conservation biology, with an emphasis on population and management models.

Soulé, M. E. (ed.). 1987. *Viable Populations for Conservation.* Cambridge University Press, Cambridge. Leading authorities discuss the problems of small populations.

Young, A. G. and G. M. Clarke (eds.). 2001. *Genetics, Demography, and Viability of Fragmented Populations.* Cambridge University Press, New York. Case studies of animals and plants are used to illustrate the impact of fragmentation.

Chapter 12

Applied Population Biology

How can conservation biologists determine whether a specific plan to manage an endangered or rare species has a good chance of succeeding? Even without human disturbance, a population of any species can be stable, increasing, decreasing, or fluctuating in number. In general, widespread human disturbance destabilizes populations of native species, often sending them into sharp decline. But how can this disturbance be measured, and what actions should be taken to prevent or reverse it? This chapter discusses applied population biology, which seeks to answer these and other questions by examining the factors affecting the abundance and distribution of rare and endangered species.

In protecting and managing a rare or endangered species, it is vital to have a firm grasp of the ecology of the species, its distinctive characteristics (sometimes called its **natural history**), and the status of its populations and the dynamic processes that affect population size and distribution (its **population biology**). With more information concerning a rare species' natural history and population biology, land managers are able to more effectively maintain the species and identify factors that place it at risk of extinction. As will be discussed later in the chapter, this information can be used to make mathematical predictions of the ability of species to persist in a protected area and the impact of alternative management options.

To implement effective population-level conservation efforts, conservation biologists should try to answer as many questions as possible from the following categories (Gilpin and Soulé 1986). For most species, we're able to answer only a few of these questions without further investigation, yet management decisions may have to be made before this information is available or while it is being gathered:

- *Environment.* What are the habitat types where the species is found, and how much area is there of each? How variable is the environment in time and space? How frequently is the environment affected by catastrophic disturbance? How have human activities affected the environment?
- *Distribution.* Where is the species found in its habitat? Are individuals clustered together, distributed at random, or spaced out regularly? Do individuals of this species move and migrate among habitats or to different geographical areas over the course of a day or over a year? How efficient is the species at colonizing new habitats? How have human activities affected the distribution of the species?
- *Biotic interactions.* What types of food and other resources does the species need and how does it obtain them? What other species compete with it for these resources? What predators or parasites affect its population size? How have human activities altered the relationships among species in the community?
- *Morphology.* What does the species look like? What are the shape, size, color, surface texture, and function of its parts? How does the morphology of the species change over its geographical range? Do all of the individuals in the population look the same? How does the shape of its body parts relate to their function and help the species to survive in its environment? How large are new offspring, and are they different in appearance from adults?
- *Physiology.* How much food, water, minerals, and other necessities does an individual need to survive, grow, and reproduce? How efficient is an individual at using its resources? How vulnerable is the species to extremes of climate, such as heat, cold, wind, and rain? When does the species reproduce, and what are its special requirements during reproduction?
- *Demography.* What is the current population size, and what was it in the past? Are the numbers of individuals stable, increasing, or decreasing? Does the population have a mixture of adults and juveniles, indicating that recruitment of new individuals is occurring?
- *Behavior.* How do the actions of an individual allow it to survive in its environment? How do individuals in a population mate and produce

offspring? In what ways do individuals of a species interact, cooperatively or competitively?

- *Genetics.* How much variation occurs in morphological and physiological characteristics? How much of this variation is genetically controlled? What percentage of the genes are variable? How many alleles does the population have for each variable gene?

Methods for Studying Populations

Methods for the study of populations have developed largely from the study of land plants and animals. Research on small organisms such as protists, bacteria, and fungi have not been investigated in comparable detail. Species that inhabit soil, freshwater, and marine habitats are particularly poorly investigated for population characteristics. In this section we will examine how conservation biologists undertake their studies of populations, recognizing that methods need to be modified for each species.

Gathering Ecological Information

The basic information needed for an effort to conserve a species or determine its status can be obtained from three major sources: published literature, unpublished literature, and fieldwork.

PUBLISHED LITERATURE   Other people may have studied the same rare species (or a related species) or have investigated a habitat type. Library indices such as *BioSys, Biological Abstracts,* and *The Zoological Record* are often accessible by computer and provide easy access to a variety of books, articles, and reports. This literature may contain records of previous population sizes and distributions that can be compared with the current status of the species (Greenberg and Droege 1999). Sometimes sections of the library will have related material shelved together, so finding one book often leads to others. The World Wide Web on the Internet provides ever-increasing access to databases, electronic bulletin boards, journals, specialized discussion groups, and subscription databases such as the *ISI Web of Science.* Information on the Internet needs to be examined carefully to be sure of its accuracy, source, and data, because there is often no control over what is posted. Asking biologists and naturalists for ideas on references is another way to locate published materials. Checking indices of newspapers, magazines, and popular journals is also an effective strategy because results of important scientific research often appear first in the popular news media and are sometimes more clearly summarized there than in the professional journals.

Once one key reference is obtained, the bibliography often can be used to discover useful earlier references. The *Science Citation Index* (available online via the subscription database the *ISI Web of Science*), available in many libraries, is a valuable tool for tracing the literature forward in time; for example, many recent scientific papers on the Hawaiian monk seal can be located by looking at the current *Science Citation Index* for the name W. K. Kenyon, who wrote several important papers about the Hawaiian monk seal between 1959 and 1981. Any recent paper citing Kenyon will appear following a search of his name.

UNPUBLISHED LITERATURE   A considerable amount of information on conservation biology is contained in unpublished reports by individual scientists, enthusiastic citizens, government agencies, and conservation organizations such as national and regional forest and park departments, government fisheries and wildlife agencies, The Nature Conservancy, the IUCN, and the World Wildlife Fund. This so-called "gray literature" is sometimes cited in published literature or mentioned by leading authorities in conversations, lectures, or articles. For example, the unpublished series of Tropical Forest Action Plans contains some of the most comprehensive sources of information on conservation in tropical countries. Often a report known through word of mouth can be obtained through direct contact with the author. In addition, conservation organizations sometimes are able to supply additional reports not found in the published literature. (A list of environmental organizations and other information sources is found in the Appendix.)

FIELDWORK   The natural history of species usually must be learned through careful observations in the field. Fieldwork is necessary because only a tiny percentage of the world's species have been studied, and the ecology of a species often changes from one place to another. Only in the field can the conservation status of a species be determined, as well as its relationships to the biological and physical environment. Fieldwork for species such as the polar bear, the humpback whale, tropical trees, or bog orchids can be time-consuming, expensive, and physically arduous, but it is crucial for developing conservation plans for endangered species and can be exhilarating and deeply satisfying as well. There is a long tradition, particularly in Britain, of dedicated amateurs conducting excellent studies of species in their immediate surroundings with minimal equipment or financial support. While much natural history information can be obtained through careful observation, many of the technical methods for investigating populations are very specialized and are best learned by studying under the supervision of an expert or reading manuals (Rabinowitz 1993; Heyer et al. 1994; Wilson and Cole 1998).

The need for fieldwork is highlighted by a report on the conservation of the red panda, *Ailurus fulgens* (Figure 12.1). Despite the attractive appearance of this species, its unique taxonomic status within the mammals, and the threat of extinction over much of its Himalayan range, there was virtually no information about its field biology prior to 1990, when a study was conducted at Lantang National Park in Nepal (Yon-

Figure 12.1 The red panda (*Ailurus fulgens*), also known as the lesser panda. Although not as widely recognized among the general public as the giant panda (to which it is distantly related), the shy and attractive red panda is equally in danger of extinction. (Photograph by Jessie Cohen, National Zoological Park, Smithsonian Institution.)

zon and Hunter 1991). This study showed that the red panda is a specialist on fir-jhapra bamboo forests between 2800 and 3900 m, a habitat rare within the park. The population is probably less than 40 in the park and divided into at least 4 subpopulations. Red pandas produce only one cub per year, and these cubs suffer from a high mortality rate, mostly caused by accidental trampling by cattle. The red panda has a low-quality diet consisting mainly of bamboo leaves, seasonally supplemented with fruits and mushrooms. Fieldwork demonstrated that the precarious existence of the red panda in the Himalayas is due to its specialized habitat requirements, low density, population fragmentation, low-quality diet, low birth rate, and vulnerability to disturbance by cattle.

Monitoring Populations

To learn the status of a species of special concern, scientists must census its population in the field and monitor it over time (Figure 12.2). Census methods range from making a complete count of every individual to estimating population size using sampling methods. By repeatedly censusing a population on a regular basis, changes in the population can

(A)

(B)

(C)

be determined (Schemske et al. 1994; Primack 1998; Shultz et al. 1999). Long-term census records can help to distinguish long-term population trends of increase or decrease (possibly caused by human disturbance) from short-term fluctuations caused by variations in weather or unpredictable natural events. Consensus records can also determine if a species is showing a positive response to conservation management.

Monitoring effectively shows the response of a population to a change in its environment; for example, in a study discussed later in this chapter, a decline in an orchid species was shown to be connected with heavy

◀ **Figure 12.2** Monitoring populations requires specialized techniques suited to each species. (A) An ornithologist checks the health and weight of a piping plover on Cape Cod. Note the identification band on the bird's leg. (Photograph by Laurie McIvor.) (B) Botanists monitor tagged lady's slipper orchid plants (*Cypripedium acaule*) for their changes in leaf size and number of flowers over a ten-year period. As shown here, individual leaves are monitored for their rates of carbon dioxide uptake, a measure of photosynthetic rate and an index of plant health. Note the numbered aluminum tag, anchored to the ground by a wire. (Photograph by Richard Primack.) (C) Censusing fish populations on a tropical reef ecosystem. (Photograph © Simon Jennings.)

cattle grazing in its habitat. Observing a long-term decline in the species they study often motivates biologists to take vigorous action to conserve it (Box 19). Monitoring can also follow characteristics of the community and ecosystem, such as the density and biomass of plants and the pattern of water release into nearby streams (Feinsinger 2001).

Monitoring has a long history in temperate countries, particularly Britain (Goldsmith 1991), and it plays an increasingly important role in conservation biology. In North America, the Breeding Bird Survey has been censusing bird abundance at approximately 1000 transects over the past 30 years, and this information is now being used to determine the stability of migrant songbird populations over time (James et al. 1996). Some of the most elaborate projects involve establishing permanent research plots in tropical forests, such as the 50-ha site at Barro Colorado Island in Panama, to monitor changes in species and communities (Condit et al. 1992). The Barro Colorado studies have shown that many tropical tree and bird species are more dynamic in numbers than had previously been suspected, suggesting that estimates of their MVP sizes may need to be revised upward.

Monitoring studies are increasing dramatically as government agencies and conservation agencies have become more concerned with protecting rare and endangered species (Elzinga et al. 2001). Some of these studies are mandated by law as part of management efforts. The most common types of monitoring conducted are inventories and population demographic studies, with survey studies somewhat less frequently used.

INVENTORIES An **inventory** is a count of the number of individuals present in a population. It is an inexpensive and straightforward method. By repeating an inventory over successive time intervals, biologists can determine whether a population is stable, increasing, or decreasing in number. In addition to counting the number of plants that presently exist, an inventory of the only population of sweet bay magnolia (*Magnolia virginiana*) in Massachusetts (Primack et al. 1986) sought to answer such questions as: Is the population stable in numbers during the period for which inventory records exist? Has the population increased during the

BOX 19 *Three Primatologists Who Became Activists*

Human beings' closest living relatives are the great apes: chimpanzees, gorillas, and orangutans. Yet despite a fascination spanning centuries, most of what we know about them has been learned in the past 40 years. Much of our knowledge rests largely on the pioneering work of three primatologists: Jane Goodall, Dian Fossey, and Birute Galdikas, sometimes called the "trimates." Their contributions are all the more valuable because they came at a time when prominent female scientists were a rare breed. These women pioneered the long-term study of their respective subjects, and all three eventually came to devote much of their time to conservation efforts rather than to the sole pursuit of scientific knowledge.

The first of the trimates, Jane Goodall, began her study of chimpanzees in 1960 in Gombe, Tanzania. Her fieldwork quickly paid off. Within three months, she had witnessed activities no researcher had ever seen, including chimpanzees eating meat that they had killed and extracting termites from nests using plucked blades of grass. The latter finding caused a sensation: it was the first example of an animal other than a human using tools (Morell 1993). Goodall's method of naming (rather than numbering) individual animals and focusing on each individual's unique characteristics in order to explain group dynamics was criticized by some primatologists, but in time it became the standard. By patiently following chimpanzee groups across generations, she gained new insights into their social structure. In her sec-

ond decade of research, Goodall and her associates made more startling discoveries, including cannibalism within groups and elaborate, premeditated "warfare" between groups. Now entering its fifth decade, the work at Gombe is among the longest continuous field study of animal behavior ever undertaken.

The second trimate, Dian Fossey, began studying mountain gorillas in 1966 in Zaire, but within a year civil war forced her from her original study site. Persevering, she moved across the border into the Parc Nacional des Volcans in Rwanda, her research site and home for the next 18 years. According to her 1986 obituary in the journal *American Anthropologist*, Fossey's scientific writings "provided anthropologists and zoologists with the first precise information on the behavioral development and social organization of gorillas in the wild" (Hausfater and Kennedy 1986). She was the first researcher to note females transferring between groups and to document

"Trimates" Dian Fossey (left), Jane Goodall (center), and Birute Galdikas began by studying animal behavior but eventually devoted themselves to conservation activism. (Photograph courtesy of The Leakey Foundation.)

BOX 19 *(continued)*

males killing infant gorillas to bring females into estrus: two important keys to gorilla social dynamics. Like Goodall at Gombe, Fossey developed her study site, Karisoke, into a major center for field research.

Birute Galdikas, the youngest of the trimates, embarked on her pioneering work among orangutans in Borneo in 1971. Unlike chimps and gorillas, orangutans are largely solitary, making it difficult to study their social interactions or to habituate them to the presence of human observers. They are also the only arboreal great ape, and they often live in swamp forests, making finding and tracking them extremely difficult. Nevertheless, over years of patient study, Galdikas uncovered basic information on the orangutan diet, mapped home ranges, and cataloged their various vocalizations. She greatly added to the little that was known about the social life of this ape, documenting the sometimes lengthy courtships between males and females, maternal care-giving, and roving juvenile bands (Morell 1993). Like her fellow trimates, Galdikas' work led to the creation of a study center that has supported the work of new generations of scientists.

The scientific success of the trimates rested in part on the new study methods they developed, which allowed these researchers to study the effects of individual differences on group social dynamics. These new methods included long-term, multiyear observations of the same individuals, the habituation of primate groups to the presence of humans, much closer observation than had been attempted before, and an appreciation for the individuality of the animals being studied. Such methods, which led the researchers to develop empathy with the apes, ran counter to prevailing attitudes, which valued objectivity and emotional detachment as essential to "good science." For the work of the trimates, however, involvement with the study animals seemed less a barrier and more an aid to gaining scientific knowledge.

Empathy led the three researchers to fight for the conservation of the great ape species, all of which are endangered by poaching, habitat destruction, and human population growth. While her writings and well-publicized career helped increase popular knowledge about nature and support for its preservation, for many years Jane Goodall was content to concentrate on research and leave direct conservation work to others. Eventually her attitude changed as a result of the direct threats to chimpanzees in and around her study site. She remarked that "Gombe was still the best place in the world for me. But I came to realize the chimps needed me elsewhere. . . I knew I had to use the knowledge the chimps gave me in the fight to save them" (Miller 1995). Today Goodall devotes much of her time to conservation education and political advocacy, speaking out against habitat destruction, the illegal trade in chimpanzees, the hunting of chimpanzees for bushmeat, and the poor treatment of chimps in medical research.

Birute Galdikas also became actively involved in conservation issues. Throughout Borneo and Sumatra, forests are being cut down, leaving orangutans without any home. Disoriented and isolated animals are often illegally captured as pets or left to die in forest fragments. From her first years in Borneo, she helped rehabilitate ex-captive orangutans for release back into the wild, a process that can take years. The Orangutan Foundation International, which she directs, has established rehabilitation centers currently housing 500 orangutans and has already returned 800 orangutans back to the wild. (This approach has proved controversial, as it is uncertain if these reintroduced animals are still surviving in the wild.) Over time, more of her conservation work focused on habitat preservation, the key to preserving orangutans in the wild, and she was instrumental in halting logging within her study site, an area now designated as the Tanjung Puting National Park. Galdikas has worked to educate local residents,

BOX 19 *(continued)*

especially schoolchildren, about orangutans and the need to protect them, by building on local traditions of respect for these "people of the forest" (the Indonesian meaning of the word "orangutan") (Galdikas 1995).

Dian Fossey did not have the luxury of gradually developing into a conservationist. Like many other field scientists, she saw her study subjects being wiped out right before her eyes. The mountain gorillas were being slaughtered to collect trophy heads and hands for sale to tourists and to capture infants for European zoos. Gorillas were also being killed accidentally by snares set by local villagers to catch antelope, and farmers and cattle were steadily reducing and degrading the habitat both inside and outside the park. With only about 600 mountain gorillas remaining in two isolated populations, this gorilla subspecies is the most endangered of the great apes. Fossey publicized the fate of her gorillas in public lectures around the world and petitioned the Rwandan government and international bodies for their protection. But in the face of lax enforcement of park rules, she also practiced what she termed "active conservation"—destroying poachers' snares, shooting cattle pastured within the park, and leading armed an-

tipoaching patrols (Fossey 1990). Her murder in 1985 was probably motivated by her antipoaching activities. By the time of her death, Fossey had largely given up data collection and was focusing full time on "active conservation." Both her methods and her dismissal of science were criticized by some, but others saw her efforts as essential, even heroic, steps in salvaging a population at the brink of extinction. Under such conditions, her supporters argued, detailed scientific study is beside the point. The well-known zoologist George Schaller believes Fossey had her priorities in order: "When you have any kind of rare species, the first priority is to work for its protection. Science is necessarily secondary" (Morell 1986).

The contributions of these three scientists are, appropriately, threefold. First, they have created an astonishing body of knowledge on species that are our closest relatives. Second, they have made the international community aware of the dangerous plight of these species and have taken prominent, active, and self-sacrificing stands on behalf of the apes. Finally, they provide role models for young women, scientists, and students worldwide, inspiring them to enrich the scientific world with their own contributions.

last 20 years, when the overstory pine trees were cut to increase light levels? Are the plants fruiting, and are any seedlings present? Inventories of a community can be conducted to determine what species are currently present in a locality; a comparison of current occurrences with past inventories can highlight species that have been lost. Inventories conducted over a wide area can help to determine the range of a species and its areas of local abundance. Inventories taken over time can highlight changes in the range of species.

The most extensive inventories have been carried out in the British Isles by a large number of local amateur naturalists supervised by professional societies. The most detailed mapping efforts have involved recording the presence or absence of plants, lichens, and birds in a mosaic of 10-km squares covering the British Isles. The Biological Records Centre (BRC) at Monks Wood Experimental Station maintains and analyzes the 4.5 million distribution records, which contain information on 16,000 species. One part of these efforts involved the Botanical Society in the British Isles Monitoring Scheme, in which the British Isles were intensively surveyed from 1987 to 1988 by 1600 volunteers, who collected one million records of all plant species occurrences on a 10-km square grid (Rich and Woodruff 1996). When the 1987/1988 data were compared with a detailed survey from 1930 to 1960, it was found that numerous species of grasslands, heathlands, and aquatic and swamp habitats had declined in frequency, while introduced weed species had increased (Figure 12.3).

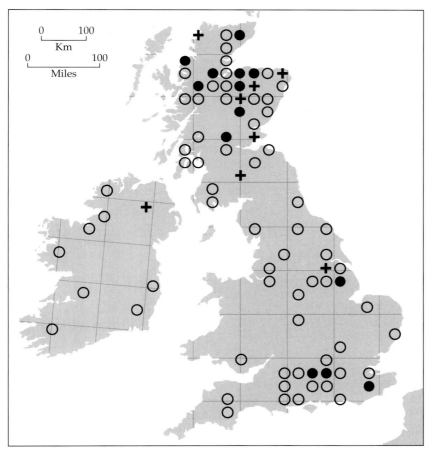

Figure 12.3 The British Isles Monitoring Scheme for *Gnaphalium sylvaticum*, the woodland cudweed. Large numbers of populations present from 1930 to 1960 were no longer present in the period from 1987 to 1988 (open circles), particularly in Ireland and England. Many populations in Scotland persisted during this interval (black dots), and there were few new populations (crosses). (From Rich and Woodruff 1996.)

SURVEYS   A **survey** of a population involves using a repeatable sampling method to estimate the number of individuals or the density of a species in part of a community. An area can be divided into sampling segments and the number of individuals in certain segments counted. These counts can then be used to estimate the actual population size. For example, the number of trees of the rare Florida torreya (*Torreya taxifolia*) was estimated in five separate ravine populations along the Apalachicola River of northern Florida and southern Georgia (Schwartz et al. 2000). A total of 365 trees were counted in the 1825 ha surveyed, leading to estimated tree density of 0.2 trees per ha. Because the total area of ravines is 20,370 ha, the maximum number of trees in the whole region is estimated to be 4063 trees (20,370 ha × 0.2 trees/ha). This estimate is a maximum because the density of trees is much lower away from the five known populations. A variety of survey methods has been used in Africa to document a sudden, widespread decline in wildlife populations, particularly large primates, as a result of hunting (Chapman and Peres 2001). A specialized type of survey involves the capture, marking, releasing, and recapture of animals to estimate population size and individual movement (see Mousson et al. 1999 for an example). Similar methods can be used for different species in a variety of ecosystems; for instance, the number of crown-of-thorns starfish can be counted in a series of 10 m × 10 m quadrats (plots) to estimate the total starfish population on a coral reef. A survey might also count the number of bats caught in mist nets per hour or the density of a particular crustacean species per liter of seawater.

Survey methods are used when a population is very large or its range extensive. Although survey methods are time-consuming, they are a methodical and repeatable way to examine a population and determine whether it is changing in size. Such methods are particularly valuable when the species being studied has stages in its life cycle that are inconspicuous, tiny, or hidden, such as the seedling stages of many plants or the larval stages of aquatic invertebrates. In the case of a Venus's-fly-trap population, scientists could census a series of small, 50 cm × 50 cm quadrats to determine the density of tiny seedlings on the ground. Soil samples could be taken at fixed survey points and examined in the laboratory to determine the density of seeds expressed as the number of seeds per cubic cm of soil. Disadvantages of survey methods are that they may be expensive (chartering a vessel to sample marine species), technically difficult (identifying poorly known immature stages in the life cycle), and inaccurate (sampling may miss or include infrequent aggregations of species). All of these disadvantages are present when conducting a survey in the deep-sea environment (Grassle 1991).

DEMOGRAPHIC STUDIES   **Demographic studies** follow known individuals in a population to determine their rates of growth, reproduction, and survival. Individuals of all ages and sizes must be included in such a study. Either the whole population or a subsample can be followed. In a complete population study, all individuals are counted, aged if possible, measured for size, sexed, and tagged or marked for future identification; their position on the site is mapped, and tissue samples sometimes are collected for genetic analysis. The techniques used to conduct a population study vary depending on the characteristics of the species and the purpose of the study. Each discipline has its own technique for following individuals over time; ornithologists band birds' legs, mammalogists often attach tags to an animal's ear, and botanists nail aluminum tags to trees (see Goldsmith 1991; Wilson and Cole 1998). Information from demographic studies can be used in life history formulae to calculate the rate of population change and to identify critical stages in the life cycle (Caswell 2001).

Demographic studies provide the most information of any monitoring method and, when analyzed thoroughly, suggest ways in which a site can be managed to ensure population persistence. The disadvantages of demographic studies are that they are often time-consuming, expensive, require repeated visits, and a knowledge of the species' life history. Demographic data gathered over time can be used to predict whether the population will be present at different future dates and what the population size will be. If the population is predicted to go extinct, estimates can be made of the extent to which the survival and reproductive rates need to be increased through site management to maintain or enlarge the population. Populations showing a pattern of decline and populations predicted to decline in the future are cause for special concern and action to prevent their extinction.

Demographic studies can provide information on the age structure of a population. A stable population typically has an age distribution with a characteristic ratio of juveniles, young adults, and older adults. The absence or low representation of any age class, particularly of juveniles, may indicate that the population is in danger of declining. Conversely, a large number of juveniles and young adults may indicate that the population is stable or even expanding. However, it is difficult to determine the age of individuals for species such as plants, fungi, and colonial invertebrates. A small individual may be either young or slow-growing and old; a large individual may be either old or unusually fast-growing and young. For these species, the distribution of size classes is often taken as an approximate indicator of population stability, but this needs to be confirmed by following individuals over time to determine rates of growth and mortality. It is significant that for many long-lived species, such as trees, the establishment of new individuals in the population is an episodic event, with many years of low reproduction and an occasional year with abundant reproduction. Careful analysis of long-term data on changes in the population over time is needed in order to distinguish short-term fluctuations from long-term trends.

In general, populations are stable when the growth rate is zero, that is, when the average birth rate equals the average death rate. While a population with an average growth rate of zero is expected to be stable over time and a growth rate above zero should lead to an expanding population, random variation in population growth rates in different years can lead to population decline and extinction even with a positive average growth rate (see Chapter 11).

Demographic studies can also indicate the spatial characteristics of a species, which might be very important to maintaining the vitality of separate populations. The number of populations of the species, movement among populations, and the stability of these populations in space and time are all important considerations. This is particularly true for species that occur in an aggregate of temporary or fluctuating populations linked by migration, known as a metapopulation (discussed in detail later in this chapter). Demographic studies can identify the core sites that support large, fairly permanent populations and supply colonists to temporary satellite areas.

Reproductive characteristics of populations—such as sex ratio, mating structure, percentage of breeding adults, and monogamous or polygamous mating systems—will also affect the success of conservation strategies and should be thoroughly analyzed. For example, a strategy to increase genetic diversity in a highly inbred population such as the lions of Ngorongoro Crater (see Chapter 11) might include introducing individuals from outside this population to mate with the inbred animals. But if the "migrant" individuals do not fit into the social dynamics of the group, they may not breed and may even be driven out or killed by the native population.

Finally, demographic studies can supply clues to the maximum carrying capacity of the environment. These studies are important in determining how large a population the environment can support before it deteriorates and the population declines. Nature reserves may have abnormally large populations of certain species due to the recent loss of adjoining habitat or the inability of individuals to disperse from the nature reserve. Due to limited available space, many nature reserves are expected to support large populations over long periods of time. Data that help define the maximum carrying capacity of the reserves are crucial to preventing population and environmental stress, particularly in circumstances where natural population control mechanisms such as predators have been eliminated by humans.

MONITORING: SOME CASE STUDIES   A few case studies provide an overview of how the various monitoring techniques have been used in the field.

- *Butterflies.* Long-term trends in the abundance of butterfly species in the Netherlands were analyzed using an inventory of 230,000 butterfly records from 1901 to 1986 (van Swaay 1990). Of 63 species analyzed, 29 species (46%) have declined in abundance or gone extinct. Most of the species that have declined in this century occupied nutrient-poor grasslands that now have largely been converted to agriculture. Because these declining species overwinter as larvae and produce only one generation a year, they are vulnerable to land-use changes.

- In Britain, butterfly inventories have been carried out on a grid of 2 km × 2 km squares covering Hertfordshire County (Thomas and Abery 1995). This amazingly detailed study documents a surprisingly high rate of local extinction—67% of the 2-km squares occupied by particular species before 1970 had no current population of that species.
- *Hawaiian monk seals.* Population inventories of the Hawaiian monk seal (*Monachus schauinslandi*) on the beach at several islands in the Kure Atoll have documented a decline from almost 100 adults in the 1950s to less than 14 in the late 1960s (Figure 12.4) (Gerrodette and Gilmartin 1990). The number of pups similarly declined during this period. On the basis of these trends, the Hawaiian monk seal was declared an en-

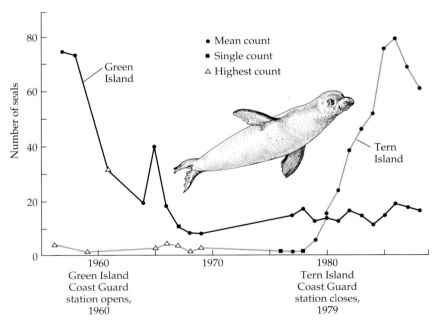

Figure 12.4 Inventories of Hawaiian monk seal populations on Green Island, Kure Atoll (black trace) and on Tern Island, French Frigate shoals (shaded trace) revealed that this species was in danger of extinction. Population counts were plotted from either a single count, the mean of several counts, or the maximum of several counts. Seal populations declined when a Coast Guard station was opened on Green Island in 1960; seal populations increased on Tern Island following the closing of a Coast Guard station in 1979. (After Gerrodette and Gilmartin 1990.)

dangered species in 1976 under the U.S. Endangered Species Act, and conservation efforts were implemented that reversed the trend for some populations. The Tern Island population showed a substantial recovery following the closing of a Coast Guard station in 1979, but started to decline again in the 1990s for unknown reasons. The Green Island population grew after its Coast Guard station was closed in 1994.

* *The early spider orchid.* This orchid (*Ophrys sphegodes*) has shown a substantial decline in range during the past 50 years in Britain. A nine-year demographic study showed that the plants were unusually short-lived for perennial orchids, with only half of the individuals surviving beyond two years (Hutchings 1987). This short half-life makes the species unusually vulnerable to unfavorable habitat changes. In one population in which the species was declining in numbers, demographic analysis highlighted soil damage by cattle grazing as the primary cause of decline. A change in land management to sheep grazing (sheep grazing causes less soil damage than cattle grazing) and restricting the sheep to graze only when the orchids are not flowering and fruiting has enabled the population to make a substantial recovery.

Population Viability Analysis

Predictions of whether a species has the ability to persist in an environment can be made using **population viability analysis** (**PVA**), an extension of demographic analysis (Akçakaya et al. 1997, 1999; Ferson and Burgman 2000; Harwood 2000; Bradbury et al. 2001). PVA can be thought of as risk assessment, using mathematical and statistical methods to predict the probability that a population or a species will go extinct at some point in the future. By looking at the range of a species' requirements and the resources available in its environment, vulnerable stages in the natural history of the species can be identified. PVA can be useful in considering the effects of habitat loss, habitat fragmentation, and habitat deterioration on a rare species. An important part of PVA is estimating how management efforts such as reducing (or increasing) hunting or increasing (or decreasing) the area of protected habitat will affect the probability of extinction. PVA can model the effects of augmenting a population through the release of additional individuals caught in the wild elsewhere or raised in captivity. PVA may be particularly useful when investigating species characterized by populations that fluctuate widely in size.

PVA begins by constructing a mathematical model of the population or species of concern using data on average mortality rates, average recruitment rates, and the current age (or size) distribution of the population (Possingham et al. 2001). The model can be readily constructed using a spreadsheet package, and it can be analyzed using the methods of matrix algebra. Because this initial model results in only one outcome—a population that is growing, declining, or stable—it is called a deterministic model. Environmental variability, as well as genetic and demographic variability, can then be added into the model by allowing model elements (such as the mortality rate) to vary at random between their observed range of annual values. Catastrophic events can be programmed to occur at random (Figure 12.5). Hundreds or thousands of simulations of individual populations can be run using this random variation to determine the probability of population extinction within a certain period of time or the mean time to extinction. Management regimes that affect population parameters can then be developed and analyzed (for example, a regime that increases adult survival by 10% and juvenile recruitment by 20%). Simulations of the impact of this management regime could be compared with the original population model to determine how it affects the probability that the population will persist in the future (Plissner and Haig 2000; Pfab and Witkowski 2000).

Existing computer-simulation packages such as VORTEX, ALEX, and RAMAS® can be used to run the models (Lindenmayer et al. 1995). Models can be tailored to include landscape information and a variety of independent environmental factors. The choice of models will depend on the goals of the analysis and the management options under consid-

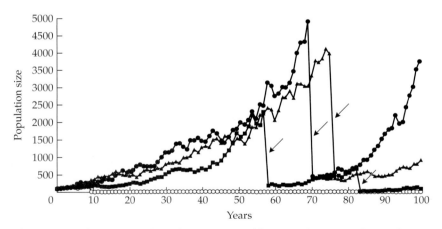

Figure 12.5 This PVA simulates the trajectory of four populations. Each population has an average growth rate of 5% per year, with fluctuations around this value due to demographic and environmental variation. In any one year, there is also a 2% chance of a catastrophe (indicated by arrows), in which 90% of the population dies. For example, one population (squares) experienced catastrophes in years 55 and 82. After a catastrophe strikes, population size is often so small that environmental and demographic variations cause the population to go extinct. All four populations have experienced at least one catastrophe. One population (open circles) went extinct after 10 years and a second population (squares) is on the verge of extinction after 100 years. (After Possingham et al. 2001.)

eration. A particularly useful feature of PVA is that the parameters of the model can be investigated using sensitivity analysis; a method that determines which parameter or combination of parameters most influences extinction probabilities. For example, sensitivity analysis might reveal that slight changes in adult mortality rates greatly affect the probability of extinction, whereas relatively large changes in juvenile mortality rates have minimal impact on the probability of extinction. Obviously, parameters that greatly influence the extinction rate should become the focus of conservation efforts, whereas parameters that have minimal effect on the extinction rate can be given less attention.

Such statistical models must be used with caution and a large dose of common sense (Harcourt 1995; Mann and Plummer 1999; Menges 2000). The results of some models can often change dramatically with different model assumptions and slight changes in parameters. Another problem is that models are still not sophisticated enough to include all possible parameters and cannot incorporate unanticipated future events. PVA does have value in demonstrating the possible impact of alternative management strategies. For this reason, attempts to utilize PVA as part of practical conservation efforts have already begun, as the following examples demonstrate. It will be valuable to revisit these studies in the future to determine if their predictions were accurate.

- *The Hawaiian stilt. Himantopus mexicanus knudseni* is an endangered, endemic bird of the Hawaiian islands (see photo in Box 26 in Chapter 18). Hunting and coastal development 70 years ago reduced the number of birds to 200, but protection has allowed recovery to the present population size of around 1200 individuals (Reed et al. 1998). The goal of government protection efforts is to allow the population to increase to 2000 birds. A PVA was made of the species' ability to have a 95% chance of persisting for the next 100 years. Models treated the stilts as one continuous population or six subpopulations inhabiting individual islands. Given the stilts' current positive growth under present conditions, the models predicted that stilt numbers will increase until they occupy all available habitat, but they will show a rapid decline if nesting failure and mortality of first-year birds exceed 70%, or if the mortality rate of adults increases above 30% per year. To keep mortality rates below these values will require the control of hunting and exotic predators and the maintenance of natural fluctuations in water levels. And most importantly, additional wetland needs to be protected in order for the goal of protecting 2000 stilts to be achieved.
- *African elephants.* Conservation efforts on behalf of the African elephant (*Loxodonta africana*) have taken on international importance because of the species' precipitous decline in numbers and its symbolic importance throughout the world as a representative of wildlife (see Box 29 in Chapter 21). A PVA of elephant populations in semiarid land at Tsavo National Park in Kenya indicated that a minimum

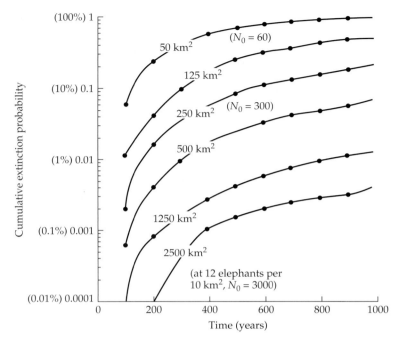

Figure 12.6 Cumulative probability of extinction (log scale) over time for elephant populations in different-sized protected areas. With a density of 12 elephants per 10 km^2, a 2500-km^2 protected area has an initial population (N_0) of 3000 elephants; the probability of extinction in 100 years is close to 0, and in 1000 years it is just 0.4%. A population in a protected area of 250 km^2 with an initial population of 300 elephants has a 20% probability of extinction in 1000 years. (After Armbruster and Lande 1993.)

reserve size of 2500 km^2 is needed to attain a greater than 99% probability of population persistence for 1000 years (Figure 12.6) (Armbruster and Lande 1993). At densities of about 12 animals per 10 km^2, this translates into an initial population size of about 3000 animals. At this reserve size, the model predicts that the population could tolerate a modest degree of harvesting without substantially increasing its probability of extinction.

- *Leadbeater's possum.* The most complete PVA ever undertaken is probably that of the Leadbeater's possum (*Gymnobelideus leadbeateri*), an endangered, arboreal marsupial inhabiting a rare type of eucalyptus forest in southeastern Australia (Lindenmayer 2000). Populations of this species are predicted to decline by more than 90% over the coming 20–30 years, due to habitat destruction caused by logging. Population models have been developed for the spatial distribution of habitat patches and dispersal corridors, den requirements, and forest dynamics. These models are based on extensive field research, and they have been used to estimate the impact of different logging management plans on the persistence of populations and the extinction of the species. The analyses all point to the need to manage the species at a landscape scale and over the entire present range of the species.

These examples illustrate the application of PVA to management situations. To be convincing, PVA must begin with a clear understanding of the ecology of the species, the threats it faces, and its demographic characteristics. In addition, the limitations of the model should be well understood (Morris and Doak 2002).

Metapopulations

Over time, populations of a species may become extinct on a local scale, while new populations may form nearby on other suitable sites. Many species of ephemeral habitats, such as streamside herbs, are characterized by a **metapopulation** (a "population of populations") that is made up of a shifting mosaic of populations linked by some degree of migration (Hanski et al. 1996; McCullough 1996; Hanski and Simberloff 1997). In some species, every population in the metapopulation is short-lived, and the distribution of the species changes dramatically with each generation. In other species, the metapopulation may be characterized by one or more **source populations** (core populations) with fairly stable numbers, and several **sink populations** (satellite populations) that fluctuate with arrivals of immigrants. Populations in the satellite areas may become extinct in unfavorable years, but the areas are recolonized, or rescued, by migrants from the more permanent core population when conditions become more favorable (Figure 12.7). Metapopulations might also involve relatively permanent populations that individuals occasionally move between. Metapopulation structures have a further complexity in migratory species in which there are separate summer breeding grounds and overwintering areas, which may or may not be shared

Figure 12.7 Possible metapopulation patterns, with the size of a population indicated by the size of the circle. The arrows indicate the direction and intensity of migration between populations. (After White 1996.)

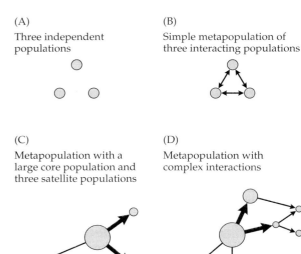

(A) Three independent populations

(B) Simple metapopulation of three interacting populations

(C) Metapopulation with a large core population and three satellite populations

(D) Metapopulation with complex interactions

among populations (Esler 2000). Metapopulations also lend themselves to modeling efforts, and various programs have been developed for simulating them (Hokit et al. 2001; Donovan and Welden 2002). In one approach, metapopulation dynamics can be simulated by using PVA combined with spatial information on multiple populations.

The target of a population study is typically one or several populations, but a metapopulation may need to be studied to acquire a more accurate portrayal of the species. Metapopulation studies recognize that local populations are dynamic; that is, the location of populations changes over time, and individuals can move between populations and colonize new sites. Sites within the range of the species may be occupied only because they are repeatedly colonized after local extinction occurs; a reduction in migration rates between sites, perhaps caused by intervening roads and farms, would gradually result in the permanent extinction of local populations across the range of the metapopulation. Metapopulation models recognize that infrequent colonization events and migration occur, which allows biologists to consider the impact of founder effects, genetic drift, and gene flow on the species. Even infrequent movement of individuals between populations can restore much of the lost genetic variation, in effect genetically "rescuing" a small population otherwise headed toward extinction (Ingvarsson 2001). The following two examples demonstrate how evaluating species on the metapopulation level has proved to be more useful in understanding and managing many species than evaluating them on the single-population level.

- *California mountain sheep.* Mountain sheep in the desert of southeastern California exhibit the shifting mosaic of populations best described as a metapopulation. These sheep have been observed migrating between mountain ranges and occupying previously unpopulated sites, and mountains that previously had sheep populations are now unoccupied (Figure 12.8). Maintaining migration routes between known population areas and potentially suitable sites is important in managing this species.
- *Furbish's lousewort.* The endemic Furbish's lousewort (*Pedicularis furbishiae*) occurs along a 200-km stretch of the St. John's River in northern Maine and New Brunswick, Canada, that is subject to periodic flooding (Menges 1990). Flooding often destroys some existing populations of this herb species but also creates exposed riverbank conditions suitable for establishing new populations. These populations eventually decline as the growth of shrubs and trees shade out the lousewort plants. Studies of any single population would give an incomplete picture of the species, because the current populations are short-lived. Dispersal of seeds from existing populations to newly exposed soil suitable for colonization is a feature of the species. The metapopulation is really the appropriate unit of study for this species, and the watershed is the appropriate unit of management.

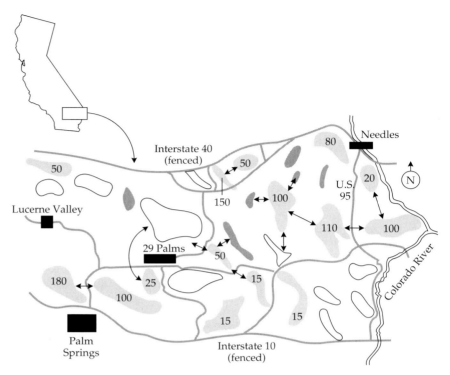

Figure 12.8 In 1990, mountain sheep in the southeastern California desert occupied the mountain ranges shown in light gray and had populations of the sizes indicated; open mountain ranges (the areas encircled by black lines) were unpopulated in 1990 but have had resident populations in the past. The mountains shown in dark gray have never had resident populations. Arrows indicate observed migrations of sheep. (After Bleich et al. 1990.)

In metapopulations, destruction of the habitat of one central, core population might result in the extinction of numerous smaller populations that depend on the core population for periodic colonization. Also, human disturbances that inhibit migration, such as fences, roads, and dams, might reduce the rate of migration among habitat patches and so reduce the probability of recolonization after local extinction. Habitat fragmentation resulting from these and other human activities sometimes has the effect of changing a large, continuous population into a metapopulation in which small, temporary populations occupy habitat fragments. When population size within each fragment is small and the rate of migration among fragments is low, populations within each fragment will gradually go extinct and recolonization will not occur (Lacy and Lindenmayer 1995; Lindenmayer and Lacy 1995).

Metapopulation models highlight the dynamic nature of population processes and show how eliminating a few core populations or reducing the potential for migration could lead to the local extinction of a species over a much wider area. This actually occurred with the California checkerspot butterfly (*Euphydryas* sp.): A large core population went extinct after an unmanaged grassland habitat underwent succession, followed soon after by the extinction of the satellite populations. Maintaining the butterfly would have required managing the site using periodic controlled fires or cattle grazing to keep the area in grassland. Effective management of a species often requires an understanding of these metapopulation dynamics and a restoration of lost habitat and dispersal routes (Hanski et al. 1996).

Long-Term Monitoring of Species and Ecosystems

Monitoring of populations needs to be combined with monitoring of other parameters of the environment. The long-term monitoring of ecosystem processes (such as temperature, rainfall, humidity, soil acidity, water quality, discharge rates of streams, and soil erosion) and community characteristics (species present, percentage of vegetative cover, amount of biomass present at each trophic level, etc.) allows scientists to determine the health of the ecosystem and the status of species of special concern. Such monitoring is needed to distinguish normal year-to-year fluctuations from long-term trends (Magnuson 1990; Primack 1992; Feinsinger 2001).

For example, many amphibian, insect, and annual plant populations are highly variable from year to year, so many years of data are required to determine whether a particular species is actually declining in abundance over time or merely experiencing a number of low population years that are in accord with its regular pattern of variation. In one instance, a salamander species' low population numbers (based on several years of low breeding numbers) initially made it appear to be very rare. But in a subsequent favorable year for breeding, its population numbers turned out to be surprisingly large (Pechmann et al. 1991). In another instance, 40 years of observation of populations of two flamingo species (*Phoenicopterus ruber*, the greater flamingo, and *Phoeniconaias minor*, the lesser flamingo) in southern Africa revealed that large numbers of chicks fledged only in years with high rainfall (Figure 12.9). However, the number of chicks fledging in the current populations is much lower than in the past, indicating that the species may be heading toward local extinction (Simmons 1996).

The fact that environmental effects may lag for many years behind their initial causes creates a challenge to understanding change in ecosystems. For example, acid rain, nitrogen deposition, and other components of air pollution may weaken and kill trees over a period of decades, increasing the amount of soil erosion into adjacent streams and ultimately making the aquatic environment unsuitable for the larvae of certain

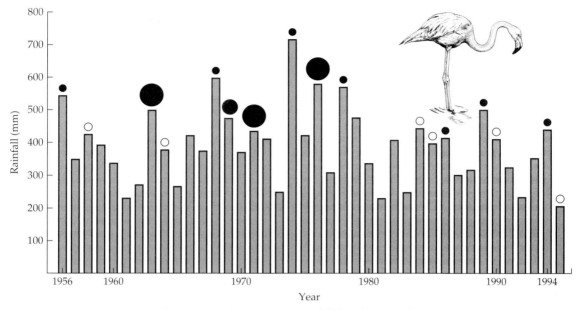

Figure 12.9 The bars show rainfall data from Etosha National Park for the years 1956 to 1995. The flamingo breeding events that occurred in those years are indicated by circles. Open circles indicate failed breeding events: Eggs were laid but no chicks hatched. The small, medium, and large black circles indicate, respectively, fewer than 100 chicks hatched, hundreds of chicks hatched, and thousands of chicks hatched. The last large hatching occurred in 1976. (From Simmons 1996.)

rare insect species. In this case, the cause (air pollution) may have occurred decades before the effect (insect decline) is detectable.

Acid rain, global climate change, vegetation succession, nitrogen deposition, and invasion of exotic species are all examples of processes often hidden from our short-term perspective that cause long-term changes in biological communities. Some long-term records are available from weather stations, annual census counts of birds, forestry plots, water authorities, and old photographs of vegetation, but the number of long-term monitoring efforts for biological communities is inadequate for most conservation purposes. To remedy this situation, many scientific research stations have begun to implement programs for monitoring ecological change over the course of decades and centuries. One program is the system of 172 Long-Term Ecological Research (LTER) sites established by the U.S. National Science Foundation (Figure 12.10) (Glazer 2001). Other programs involve the United Nations Man and the Biosphere system of Biosphere Reserves and the increasing number of community-level permanent research plots being established in tropical forests (see Chapter 20) (Dallmeier 1992; Glazer 2001).

Years		Research scales	Physical events	Biological phenomena
10^5	100 Millennia			Evolution of species
10^4	10 Millennia	Paleoecology and limnology	Continental glaciation	Bog succession Forest community migration
10^3	Millennium		Climate change	Species invasion Forest succession
10^2	Century		Forest fires CO_2-induced climate warming	Cultural eutrophication
10^1	Decade			Population cycles
10^0	Year		Sun spot cycle El Niño events Prairie fires Lake turnover Ocean upwelling	Prairie succession Annual plants Seasonal migration Plankton succession
10^{-1}	Month			
10^{-2}	Day	Most ecology	Storms Daily light cycle Tides	Algal blooms Daily movements
10^{-3}	Hour			

LTER is bracketed across the rows from Century (10^2) through Month (10^{-1}).

Figure 12.10 The Long-Term Ecological Research (LTER) program focuses on time scales ranging from years to centuries in order to understand changes in the structure, function, and processes of biological communities that are not apparent from short-term observations. (From Magnuson 1990.)

A major purpose of these programs is to gather essential data on ecosystem functions and biological communities that can be used to monitor changes in natural communities. Monitoring in these studies allows managers to determine if the goals of their projects are being achieved or if adjustments have to made in the management plans. Increasingly, monitoring of biological diversity is being combined with the monitoring of social and economic characteristics of the same area—for example, annual income, adequacy of diet, education level, and amount and value of plant and animal materials people obtain from nearby ecosystems—in recognition of the linkages between people and conservation (Kremen et al. 1994; Bawa and Menon 1997). For example, the World Wildlife Fund's Biodiversity Conservation Network Program brings together biologists, social scientists, government officials, and local leaders to develop comprehensive monitoring programs for conservation projects. People who live in the local area are incorporated into the monitoring program because they know the area well and have the greatest interest in ensuring that the area is well-managed (Danielsen et al. 2000). Long-term monitoring provides an early-warning system for disruption or decline of ecosystem functions and the social systems of humans that depend on them. Magnuson (1990) expressed the need for long-term monitoring as follows:

> In the absence of the temporal context provided by long-term research, serious misjudgments can occur not only in our attempts to understand and predict change in the world around us, but also in our attempts to manage our environment. Although serious accidents in an instant of mismanagement can be envisioned that might cause the end of Spaceship Earth (sensu Fuller 1970), destruction is even more likely to occur at a ponderous pace in the secrecy of the invisible present.

Summary

1. Protecting and managing a rare or endangered species requires a firm grasp of its ecology and its distinctive characteristics, sometimes called its natural history. This essential knowledge covers the species' environment, distribution, biotic interactions, morphology, physiology, demography, behavior, and genetics. This information can be obtained from the published and unpublished literature, or from fieldwork. Long-term monitoring of a species in the field can reveal temporal changes in population size and help to distinguish short-term fluctuations from long-term decline.

2. Population viability analysis (PVA) uses demographic, genetic, environmental, and natural-catastrophe data to estimate the probability of a population persisting in an environment. PVA can also be used to simulate the effects of various management actions.

3. Many species that reside in ephemeral habitats are characterized by metapopulations made up of a shifting mosaic of temporary populations that are linked by some degree of migration. In other species, the metapopulation may be characterized by one or more core populations with relatively stable numbers linked by dispersal to satellite areas with unstable, temporary populations.

4. Long-term monitoring efforts are now being developed throughout the world to follow changes in populations and communities over the course of decades and centuries. These programs will provide an early warning system for threats to species, communities, and ecosystem functions.

For Discussion

1. Read the paper on the Hawaiian stilt by Reed et al. (1998), the paper on the South African plant by Pfab and Witkowski (2000), or another PVA study. What are the strengths and weaknesses of PVA?

2. Construct models of various metapopulations using Figure 12.7 as a starting point. The simplest model would be an infinitely large core population that continuously sends out colonists to a satellite population, which is regularly destroyed by a catastrophic event such as a hurricane. Then include random variation in the frequency of hurricanes (destroying the population on average once every 4 years) and rate of colonization (sending out colonists on average once every 4 years). How realistic are your models?

3. Construct your own PVA of an endangered toad species. This species formerly occupied many large islands, but now occupies only one small, isolated island in the middle of the Atlantic Ocean. There are presently 10 toads on the island, and the island can support a maximum of 20 toads. In the spring, males and females form mating pairs, and each pair can produce 0, 1, 2, 3, 4,

or 5 offspring, all of which survive and reach maturity the following year (for example, flip 5 coins for each mated pair; the number of heads is the number of offspring). Individuals not mated because of uneven sex ratios do not breed. After breeding, the toads die. The sex of the offspring is assigned at random (for example, flip a coin for each animal with heads for males and tails for females, or use a random-number generator or simulation software such as VORTEX or RAMAS®).

4. Run 10 population simulations for 10 generations each and chart population size over time. What percentage of populations go extinct? Try making the conditions more severe by lowering the island's carrying capacity to 15 (or even 10), or by imposing a 50% mortality on offspring every third year due to an introduced rat. Examine the impact of supplying extra food to the toads, which would allow more offspring to be produced per breeding pair. Make different variants of this basic model, corresponding to different ecological, genetic, and life history constraints. Use a computer program if possible.

Suggested Readings

Caswell, H. 2001. *Matrix Population Models,* 2nd ed. Sinauer Associates. Sunderland, MA. Matrix models are the place to begin for predicting population trends.

Chapman, C. A. and C. A. Peres. 2001. Primate conservation in the new millennium: The role of scientists. *Evolutionary Anthropology* 10: 16–33. Forest loss and hunting contribute to the decline and local extinction of primate populations.

Donovan, T. M. and C. W. Welden. 2002. *Spreadsheet Exercises in Conservation Biology and Landscape Ecology*. Sinauer Associates, Sunderland, MA. Use of spreadsheets to model populations and metapopulations.

Elzinga, C. L., D. W. Salzer, J. W. Willoughby, and J. P. Gibbs. 2001. *Monitoring Plant and Animal Populations*. Blackwell Scientific, Oxford. Practical approaches for land managers.

Feinsinger, P. 2001. *Designing Field Studies for Biodiversity Conservation*. Island Press, Washington, D.C. A guide to establishing a field research program for the conservation of species and communities.

Ferson, S. and M. Burgman (eds.). 2000. *Quantitative Methods for Conservation Biology*. Springer-Verlag, New York. Reviews methods for PVA, metapopulation models, and other quantitative approaches.

Fossey, D. 1990. *Gorillas in the Mist*. Houghton Mifflin Company, Boston. Read the book, then watch the movie. Was she courageous or crazy?

Galdikas, B. 1995. *Reflections of Eden: My Years with the Orangutans of Borneo*. Little, Brown and Company, Boston. A personal approach to conservation by an unusual person.

Hanski, I., A. Moilanen, and M. Gyllenberg. 1996. Minimum viable metapopulation size. *American Naturalist* 147: 527–541. The applicability of metapopulation theory to conservation strategies.

Lindenmayer, D. B. 2000. Factors at multiple scales affecting distribution patterns and their implications for animal conservation—Leadbeater's Possum as a case study. *Biodiversity and Conservation* 9: 15–35. Probably the most completely modeled species; this article reviews the variety of techniques that have been used to model it.

Morris, W. F. and D. F. Doak. 2002. *Quantitative Conservation Biology: Theory and Practice of Population Viability Analysis*. Sinauer Associates, Sunderland, MA. Comprehensive treatment of population analysis and modeling.

Pfab, M. F. and E. T. F. Witkowski. 2000. A simple PVA of the Critically Endangered *Euphorbia clivicola* R. A. Dyer under four management scenarios. *Biological Conservation* 96: 263–270. This article presents an application of PVA that is easy to understand.

Possingham, H., D. B. Lindenmayer, and M. A. McCarthy. 2001. Population viability analysis. In *Encyclopedia of Biodiversity,* S. A. Levin (ed.), Vol. 4, pp. 831–844. Academic Press, San Diego, CA. Clear summary of a complex topic.

Reed, J. M., C. S. Elphick, and L. W. Oring. 1998. Life-history and viability analysis of the endangered Hawaiian stilt. *Biological Conservation* 84: 35–45. Strategies of land management and land acquisition are analyzed for their impact on population size.

Rich, T. C. G. and E. R. Woodruff. 1996. Changes in the vascular plant floras of England and Scotland between 1930–1960 and 1987–1988; the BSBI monitoring scheme. *Biological Conservation* 75: 217–229. Monitoring with an astonishing degree of precision.

Schemske, D. W., B. C. Husband, M. H. Ruckelshaus, C. Goodwillie, I. M. Parker, and J. M. Bishop. 1994. Evaluating approaches to the conservation of rare and endangered plants. *Ecology* 75: 584–606. Monitoring populations is crucial to the evaluation of conservation efforts.

Shultz, S. M., A. E. Dunham, K. V. Root, S. L. Soucy, S. D. Carroll, and L. R. Ginzburg. 1999. *Conservation Biology with RAMAS® EcoLab.* Sinauer Associates, Sunderland, MA. A set of computer exercises to accompany an undergraduate course in conservation biology, with an emphasis on population and management models.

Wilson, D. E. and R. F. Cole. 1998. *Measuring and Monitoring Biological Diversity: Standard Methods for Mammals.* Smithsonian Institution Press, Washington, D.C. Part of a series, this volume explains standard methods for gathering, analyzing, and presenting field data.

Chapter

13

Establishing New Populations

In Chapters 11 and 12 we discussed the problems conservation biologists face in preserving populations of endangered species. This chapter discusses some exciting conservation methods that try to address those problems. These include establishing new wild and semi-wild populations of rare and endangered species and increasing the size of existing populations. These important new approaches allow species that had been living only in captivity or in small, isolated populations to regain their ecological and evolutionary roles within the biological community.

Many species benefit from the complementary approaches of establishing new populations in the wild and developing captive breeding programs. Widely dispersed populations in the wild may be less likely to be destroyed by catastrophes (such as earthquakes, hurricanes, disease, epidemics, or war) than captive populations confined to a single facility or isolated wild populations occupying only a small area. Furthermore, increasing the number and size of populations for a species will generally reduce its probability of extinction.

Establishment programs are unlikely to be effective, however, unless the factors leading to the decline of the original wild populations are clearly understood and eliminated, or at least controlled (Bowles and Whelan 1994; Tutin et al. 2001). For example, the Guam rail has been eliminated from its home on the island of Guam because of predation by the introduced brown tree snake (see Figure 10.5). In order for an establishment program to be successful, the snake would have to be removed from the island, or the rail nests would have to be protected from the snake in some way. Since this is not possible at the present time, the birds are being introduced onto the nearby island of Rota where there are no snakes. Therefore, a crucial initial step in establishing new populations is to locate suitable unoccupied sites for the species or to create new sites.

Three Approaches to Establishing New Populations

Three basic approaches have been used to establish new populations of animals and plants. A **reintroduction program*** involves releasing captive-bred or wild-collected individuals into an ecologically suitable site within their historical range where the species no longer occurs. The principal objective of a reintroduction program is to create a new population in its original environment. For example, a program initiated in 1995 to reintroduce gray wolves into Yellowstone National Park aims to restore the equilibrium of predators and herbivores that existed prior to human intervention in the region (Box 20). Frequently, individuals are released near the site where they or their ancestors were collected to ensure genetic adaptation to their environment. Wild-collected individuals are also sometimes caught and later released elsewhere within the range of the species when a new protected area has been established, when an existing population is under a new threat and will no longer be able to survive in its present location, or when natural or artificial barriers to the normal dispersal tendencies of the species exist.

There are two other distinct types of release programs. An **augmentation program** involves releasing individuals into an existing population to increase its size and gene pool. These released individuals may be raised in captivity or may be wild individuals collected elsewhere. One special example of augmentation is "headstarting," an approach in which animals are raised in captivity during their vulnerable young stage and then are released into the wild. The release of sea turtle hatchlings

---

*Unfortunately, some confusion exists about the terms denoting the reintroduction of populations. These programs sometimes are called "reestablishments" or "restorations." Another term, "translocation," usually refers to moving individuals from a location where they are about to be destroyed to another site that often provides a greater degree of protection.

BOX 20 *Wolves Return to a Cold Welcome*

To the general public, "conservation" usually means saving endangered animal species on the verge of extinction—such as the California condor, with only around 120 remaining individuals, or the giant panda, whose numbers are estimated at less than 1100. Although it is critical to try to prevent species extinctions, the ultimate goal of conservation is to restore damaged ecosystems to their previous balanced, functional state. Sometimes that involves reintroducing species into ecosystems to restore them—species whose own numbers are not precarious and might not otherwise need reintroduction to protect them. An example of such a situation is the reintroduction of gray wolves into Yellowstone Park.

Until recently, Yellowstone National Park was an ecosystem out of balance, largely due to the systematic extermination of the Yellowstone gray wolf (*Canis lupus*) populations in the late 1800s and early 1900s. Wolves were believed to pose a threat to the herds of elk and other game animals inhabiting the park. The result of their extinction was a burgeoning population of elk and other herbivores, which damaged vegetation and starved during times of scarcity.

When the U.S. Fish and Wildlife Service proposed in 1987 that the gray wolf be reintroduced into Yellowstone National Park and surrounding government lands, known as the Greater Yellowstone Area (GYA), opposition erupted immediately. Ranchers in Montana, Wyoming, and Idaho argued that wolves would destroy livestock and possibly endanger humans as well (Fischer 1995). Hunters objected that wolves would reduce the supply of game animals, and logging and mining companies were concerned that the presence of a protected species would limit their ability to utilize resources on federal lands. Underpinning all these objections was the argument that the wolf, with an estimated population of 50,000 in Canada alone, is in no immediate danger of extinction. Furthermore, wolves had been steadily recolonizing the northern states, including Wisconsin and Michigan. To accommodate these concerns, it was agreed that any wolf population at Yellowstone would be designated "experimental, nonessential" and not be given special legal protection.

From a biological perspective, however, the wolf is necessary to restore ecological balance in the Yellowstone area. Wolves are needed to maintain the health of the elk herds by removing older, sick, and weak animals and to keep population levels below the environmental carrying capacity. Without these predators, herbivore herds become so dense that hundreds can starve in a winter. Releasing wolves into the GYA and carefully documenting their effect on elk behavior and numbers is necessary for the ecological health of the region.

In 1995 and 1996, two complete wolf packs, as well as a few individuals, were transferred from Canada to the area. The wolves were held in a large pens for ten weeks (to break their homing tendency) and then released. The wolves adapted well to the park, hunting prey and producing pups. As of the end of 2001, a total of 220 free-ranging wolves have formed 21 packs, and most reside almost exclusively within the GYA (Smith et al. 2001). Because of the good health of the animals, there are large numbers of pups (71 surviving pups in 2000 alone) and an expanding wolf population.

The wolves' activities are reshaping the ecological structure of the park. Elk are congregating in larger herds, and wolves are interacting with grizzly bears. The availability of carrion from wolf kills is affecting the dynamics of scavengers, from grizzlies to carrion beetles. Perhaps most importantly, wolves are having an impact on coyotes, which had an unusually high density without wolves. Wolves are killing coyotes and their pups, forcing them to change their denning behavior and driving them out of some areas. As one of the major attractions of Yellowstone National Park, wolves are having a positive economic impact as the featured subject of books and souvenirs sold to park visitors. The ecology and impact of wolves on the ecosystem has

BOX 20 *(continued)*

proved to be a subject worthy of intensive study, with the participation of numerous scientists and student volunteers.

Fears that wolves would kill large numbers of livestock remain largely unfounded. In 2000, the wolves killed a total of 7 cattle, 39 sheep, and 8 dogs—a small number given that there are 400,000 cattle alone living in the area. The number is also small in comparison with the millions of dollars invested in the project, its great ecological value to the Yellowstone area, and the tens of thousands of people who have visited the park or been exposed to the story of the Yellowstone wolves. These people may become supporters of the Yellowstone program or conservation programs like it as a result. In addition, an organization called Defenders of Wildlife has assumed responsibility for compensating ranchers for verified wolf kills, but reactions by ranchers remain mixed. Wolves

that attack livestock on private land have been captured by park officials and released onto government lands far away. Three wolves suspected of killing livestock in 2000 have also been killed by park officials. As the wolf population grows, however, so will the potential for depredations beyond park boundaries and for further conflict with ranchers.

The controversy surrounding the reestablishment of the wolf in Yellowstone reflects a dilemma central to conservation biology: how to balance environmental needs with human demands. When the *survival* of a species is at risk, the urgency of their argument works in conservationists' favor. In the case of the wolf, however, the problem does not appear to be clear cut because the species is not at risk, and for much of the general public, ecological equilibrium does not yet rank so high in their minds.

A gray wolf stalks an elk herd in Yellowstone National Park. As a result of the wolves' reintroduction to the park, elk have changed their behavior, becoming more vigilant while grazing. A keystone predator, the activity of the gray wolf has already altered the behavior and population numbers of many other species, including grizzly bears, coyotes, and carrion beetles. (Photograph by Bill Campbell.)

produced from eggs collected from the wild and raised in nearby hatcheries is an example of an augmentation program. An **introduction program** involves moving captive-bred or wild-collected animals and plants to areas suitable for the species outside their historical range. This approach may be appropriate when the environment within the known range of a species has deteriorated to the point where the species can no longer survive there, or when reintroduction is impossible because the factor causing the original decline is still present.

The introduction of a species to new sites needs to be carefully thought out in order to ensure that the species does not damage its new ecosystem or harm populations of any local endangered species. Care must be taken that released individuals have not acquired any diseases while in captivity that could spread to and decimate wild populations. For example, captive orangutans released into the forest in Borneo may have contaminated wild animals with hepatitis and tuberculosis acquired from people while in captivity. Also, a species may adapt genetically to the new environment where it is being released so that the original gene pool is not actually being preserved.

New populations can be established using different approaches and experimental treatments, which seek to help individuals make a successful transition to their new home—for example, giving supplemental food and water to the animals for a while as they learn about their new home; planting individual plants into a habitat from which competing plants have been removed. By carefully monitoring such experiments, existing management techniques can be evaluated and new techniques developed. These management techniques can then be applied to better manage existing natural populations of the species.

Considerations for Successful Programs

Establishing new populations is often expensive and difficult because it requires a serious, long-term commitment. The programs to capture, raise, monitor, and release California condors, peregrine falcons, and black-footed ferrets, for example, have cost millions of dollars and have required years of work. When the animals involved are long-lived, the program may have to continue for many years before its outcome is known.

Reintroduction programs can also become highly emotional public issues, as demonstrated by the California condor, the black-footed ferret, the grizzly bear, and the gray wolf programs in the United States, and comparable European programs. Programs are often criticized on many different fronts. They may be attacked as a waste of money ("Millions of dollars for a few ugly birds!"), unnecessary ("Why do we need wolves here when there are so many elsewhere?"), intrusive ("We just want to go about our lives without the government telling us what to do!"), poorly run ("Look at all the ferrets that died of disease in captivity!"), or unethical ("Why can't the last animals just be allowed to live out their lives in peace without being captured and put into zoos?").

The answer to all of these criticisms is straightforward: Although reintroduction is not appropriate for every endangered species, a well-run, well-designed captive breeding and reintroduction program may be the best hope for preserving a species that is about to become extinct in the wild or is in severe decline. It is crucial to explain the need and the goals of the program to local people and to convince them to support the program or, at least, not to oppose it (Reading and Kellert 1993; Milton et al. 1999). Providing incentives to the local community as a part of the program often is more successful than imposing rigid restrictions and laws.

There is an important genetic component in selecting animals for reintroduction programs. Captive populations may have lost much of their genetic variability. Genetic adaptations to the benign captive environment may occur in populations that have been raised for several generations in captive conditions (such as has occurred in the Pacific salmon [Waples and Teel 1990]) and may lower a species' ability to survive in the wild following release. Individuals have to be carefully selected to ensure against inbreeding depression and to produce the most genetically diverse release population. Also, to increase the chances that the individuals can survive, they must be selected from an environment and climate which are as similar as possible to the release site.

For some species, animals may require special care and assistance immediately to insure survival (Kleiman 1989). This approach is known as **soft release.** Animals may have to be fed and sheltered at the release point until they are able to subsist on their own, or they may need to be caged temporarily at the release point and introduced gradually, until they become familiar with the area. Social groups abruptly released from captivity without assistance such as food supplementation (**hard release**) may disperse explosively from the protected area, resulting in a failed establishment effort. Intervention may be necessary if animals appear unable to survive, particularly during episodes of drought or low food abundance. Even when animals appear to have enough food to survive, supplemental feeding may lead to increased reproduction and allow the population to increase. Outbreaks of diseases and pests may have to be monitored and dealt with. The impact of human activities in the area, such as farming and hunting, needs to be observed and possibly controlled. In every case a decision has to be made whether it is better to give occasional temporary help to the species or to force the individuals to survive on their own.

Successful reintroduction programs often have considerable educational value. In Brazil, conservation and reintroduction efforts to protect golden lion tamarins have become a rallying point for the protection of the last remaining fragments of the Atlantic coastal forest. In the Middle East and North Africa, captive-bred Arabian oryx have been successfully reintroduced into many desert areas that they formerly occupied. In Oman, in particular, the reintroduction of the oryx created an important national symbol and a significant source of employment for the local Bedouins who ran the program (Figure 13.1) (Stanley-Price 1989). However, despite almost two decades of successful management,

Figure 13.1 The Arabian oryx (*Oryx leucoryx*), almost extinct in the wild, is being reintroduced to many places in its former range. In Oman, an initial successful reintroduction was discontinued due to poaching of animals for private collectors. (Photograph by Ron Garrison, San Diego Zoo.)

the program in Oman was discontinued and all the animals brought back into captivity due to continuing thefts of animals to supply private collectors.

Establishment programs for common game species have always been widespread and have contributed a great deal of knowledge for the development of new programs for threatened and endangered species. A detailed study examined 198 bird and mammal establishment programs conducted between 1973 and 1986 which used both wild-caught and captive-reared animals. A number of significant generalizations were supported (Griffith et al. 1989):

1. Success was greater for releases in excellent quality habitat (84%) than in poor quality habitat (38%).
2. Success was greater in the core of the historic range (78%) than at the periphery of and outside the historic range (48%).
3. Success was greater with wild-caught (75%) than with captive-reared animals (38%).
4. Success was greater for herbivores (77%) than for carnivores (48%).

For these bird and mammal species, the probability of establishing a new population increased with the number of animals being released, up to about 100. Releasing more than 100 animals did not further enhance the probability of success. Certain of these results have been confirmed by a subsequent update and reanalysis (Wolf et al. 1996, 1998; Fischer and Lindenmayer 2000).

A second survey of reintroduction projects (Beck et al. 1994) used a more restricted definition of reintroduction: the release of captive-born animals within the historical range of the species. A program was judged a success if there was a self-maintaining population of 500 individuals. Using this restricted definition, only 16 out of 145 reintroduction projects were judged successful—a dramatically lower rate of success than the earlier survey, in which the majority of reintroductions were successful. An analysis consisting solely of ungulate reintroductions concluded that factors increasing the rate of success included: releasing at least 20 individuals, releasing a higher proportion of mature individuals, and having balanced sex ratios (Komers and Curman 2000). In many projects, success involves releasing large numbers of animals over many years. A survey of more than 400 releases of short-lived fish species into wild habitats of the western United States showed a success rate of around 26%, though incomplete information on many species made compiling and evaluating the results extremely difficult (Hendrickson and Brooks 1991). Reintroductions and translocations of endangered amphibians and reptiles appear to have an extremely low rate of success, perhaps due to highly specialized habitat requirements (Platenberg and Griffiths 1999).

Clearly, monitoring ongoing programs is crucial in determining whether efforts to establish new populations are achieving their stated goals. Key elements of monitoring involve determining if released individuals survive and establish a breeding population and then following that population over time to see if it increases in numbers of individuals and geographical range. Monitoring of important ecosystem elements is also needed to determine the broader impact of a reintroduction; for example, when a predator is introduced, it will be crucial to determine its impact on prey species and competing species, and its indirect impact on vegetation (Berger et al. 2001). Monitoring may need to be carried out over many years, even decades, because many reintroductions that initially appear successful eventually fail. For example, a reintroduction of topminnows into a stream in the western United States resulted in a large, viable population; however, a flood eliminated the population 10 years later (Minckley 1995). The costs of reintroduction need to be tracked and published to determine if reintroduction represents a cost-effective strategy. Also, the results of monitoring need to be published in scientific journals so that successful methods can be incorporated into new reintroduction efforts (Fischer and Lindenmeyer 2000).

Social Behavior of Released Animals

To be successful, both introduction and reintroduction programs must often address the behaviors of animals that are being released (Clemmons and Buchholz 1997). When social animals, particularly mammals and some bird species, grow up in the wild they learn from other members of their population—particularly their parents—about their environment and how to interact with other members of their species. They learn (often from their family group) how to search their environment for food and how to capture, gather, and consume it. For carnivores such as lions and wild dogs, hunting techniques are complex, subtle, and require considerable teamwork. To obtain the variety of food items necessary to stay alive and reproduce, frugivores such as hornbills and gibbons must learn seasonal migration patterns that cover a wide area.

When mammals and birds are raised in captivity, their environment is limited to a cage or pen, so exploration is unnecessary. Searching for food and learning about new food sources is not needed, since the same food items come day after day, on schedule. Social behavior may become highly distorted when animals are raised alone or in unnatural social groupings (i. e., in single-gender or single-age groups). In such cases, animals may lack the skills to survive in their natural environment and the social skills necessary to cooperatively find food, sense danger, find mating partners, and raise young.

To overcome these behavioral problems, captive-raised mammals and birds may require extensive training before and after release into the environment (Biggins et al. 1999). They must learn how to find food and shelter, avoid predators, and interact in social groups. Training techniques have been developed for several mammals and a few birds. Captive chimps, for instance, have been taught how to use twigs to feed on termites and how to build nests in captivity. Red wolves are taught how to kill live prey. Captive animals are taught to fear potential predators by pairing a frightening stimulus to a dummy predator when the dummy predator is shown.

Social interaction is one of the most difficult behaviors to teach captive-bred mammals and birds, because for most species the subtleties of social behavior are poorly understood. Nevertheless, some successful attempts have been made to socialize captive-bred mammals (Valutis and Marzluff 1999). In one technique, humans mimic the appearance and behavior of the wild species. This method is particularly important when dealing with very young animals. For example, captive-bred condor hatchlings were originally unable to learn normal social bonds with other condors because they had imprinted on their human keepers. Newly hatched condors are now fed with condor puppets and kept from the sight of visitors so they learn to identify with their own species rather than a foster species or humans (Figure 13.2). However, even with such training, when captive-raised condors are released into the wild in

Figure 13.2 California condor chicks raised in captivity are fed by researchers using puppets that look like adult birds. Conservation biologists hope that minimizing human contact with the birds will improve their chances of survival when they are returned to the wild. (Photograph by Mike Wallace, The Angeles Zoo.)

protected areas, they often congregate around buildings, causing damage and frightening people. In the future, captive-rearing of condors may have to take place in an enclosed outdoor area without any buildings to break this association.

When captive-bred animals are released into the wild as part of an augmentation program, developing social relationships with wild animals may be crucial to their success. They sometimes join existing social groups or mate with wild animals and so gain some knowledge of their environment. Failure to associate with wild birds during migration appears to be one of the reasons for the high mortality rate of captive-raised bald ibis (*Geronticus eremita*) (Akçakaya 1990). Killdeer chicks (*Charadrius vociferus*) raised in captivity by humans, cross-fostered by a related plover species in the wild, and then released into a natural population, however, did not behave appreciably differently from chicks reared by wild killdeer parents (Powell and Cuthbert 1993).

Animal Reintroduction Case Studies

The following case studies illustrate the various approaches to animal species reintroductions:

- *Red wolves.* Red wolves (*Canis rufus*) have been reestablished in the Alligator River National Wildlife Refuge in northeastern North Carolina through the release of 42 captive-born animals starting in 1987. Currently 80 animals occupy around 400,000 ha (one million acres) of government and private land. Animals in the program have produced pups, established packs, and survive by hunting deer, raccoons, rabbits, and rodents (Kelly and Phillips 2000). Even though the Red Wolf Recovery Program appears to be successful, many landowners remain unwilling to accept the presence of wolves on their land. A further difficulty is hybrid offspring, which are produced by mating between red wolves and coyotes, obscuring species boundaries.

- *Kemp's Ridley sea turtles.* Attempts have been made to stop the rapid decline of Kemp's Ridley sea turtles (*Lepidochelys kempii*) by collecting wild eggs from a Mexican beach, raising the hatchlings for one year in captivity, and releasing them in the wild on North Padre Island, Texas (Frazier 2000). Despite having released 22,000 "head-started" hatchlings between 1978 and 1988, only 32 turtles have returned to breed on the beaches, with at least 6 having come from the headstarting program. Due to the low rate of success and high cost of the program, large-scale releases of turtles were discontinued.

- *The kakapo.* The kakapo (*Strigops habraptilus*) is not only the largest parrot species in the world, it is also flightless, nocturnal, and solitary. The New Zealand kakapo was believed extinct because of introduced mammalian predators, but two small populations were discovered in the late 1970s. These populations were declining in numbers, requiring urgent action to save the species. Sixty-five kakapos were collected in the wild and released on three offshore islands that lacked most of their predators (Lloyd and Powlesland 1994). Breeding success on the island improved following supplemental feeding with apples, sweet potatoes, and native seeds. Unfortunately, chick survival is still low, but it is being improved by artificial incubation of eggs, raising chicks in captivity, and releasing young birds back into the wild.

- *Big Bend gambusia.* The Big Bend gambusia (*Gambusia gaigei*) was originally known from a single spring in Texas, which dried up in 1954 and eliminated the one known population. The fish was then discovered one year later in an artificial pond. A combination of captive breeding and releases into new artificial ponds helped the species survive a series of droughts and invasions by exotic fish. In 1983 the species was reestablished in its original spring, and the natural flow of the spring is now mandated under the management plan for this protected species (Minckley 1995).

Establishing New Plant Populations

Methods used to establish new populations of rare and endangered plant species are fundamentally different from those used to establish terrestrial vertebrate animal species and are still in the early stages of development (Falk et al. 1996; Primack and Drayton 1997). Animals can disperse to new locations and actively seek out the most suitable microsite conditions. In the case of plants, seeds are dispersed to new sites by agents such as wind, animals, water, or the actions of conservation biologists (Primack and Miao 1992); alternatively, either wild-collected or greenhouse-grown adults can be planted at the site to bypass the vulnerable seedling stage. Once a seed lands on the ground or an adult is planted at a site, it is unable to move, even if a suitable microsite exists just a few meters away. The immediate microsite is crucial for plant survival—if the environmental conditions are in any way too sunny, too shady, too wet, or too dry, either the seed will not germinate or the resulting plant will not reproduce or will die.

Disturbance in the form of fire or tree falls may also be necessary for seedling establishment in many species; therefore, a site may be suitable for seedling establishment only once every several years. Careful site selection is thus critical in plant reintroductions. Plants and seeds need to be obtained from a site as similar as possible to the new site to ensure that they are genetically suited to the conditions of the new site (Jones and Hayes 1999; Montalvo and Ellstrand 2001). However, just as with animal reintroductions, identifying the factors that caused the original decline in the plant species is critical for success. For example, in California many rare native plants are being outcompeted by introduced annual grasses. Developing management techniques to control or eliminate these grasses is an essential part of the reintroduction process (Guerrant and Pavlik 1998).

Plant populations typically fail to establish from introduced seeds at most sites that appear to be suitable for them. In one study, large numbers of seeds of six species of annual plants were planted at 48 apparently suitable sites (Primack 1996). Of these 48 attempts, new populations persisted for 2 years at only 5 sites, and for 6 years at only 1 site. At this single, apparently successful site, the population had increased to more than 10,000 individuals and had spread 30 m around the margins of a marshy pond (Figure 13.3). Subsequent attempts to establish new populations of 35 species of perennial herbs by sowing seeds at 173 apparently suitable sites had an even lower rate of success: No seedlings at all were seen at 167 of the 173 sites, and no individuals at all were seen for 32 of the 35 species.

To increase their chances of success, botanists often germinate seeds in controlled environments and grow the young plants in protected conditions (Figure 13.4). Only after the plants are past the fragile seedling stage are they transplanted into the wild. Planting has to be executed using the techniques appropriate to the species (planting depth, watering, time of day, time of year, site preparation, etc.) to ensure survival.

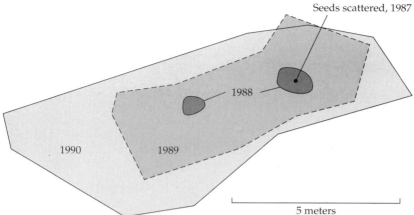

Figure 13.3 Sometimes a new plant population can be established by the introduction of seeds. In September 1987, 100 seeds of *Impatiens capensis*, an annual species of jewelweed, were introduced into an unoccupied site in Hammond Woods, near Boston, Massachusetts. The seeds were scattered within 1 m of a stake (black dot). In 1988, two groups of plants separated by several meters had established themselves (darkest gray areas). The populations continued to expand in 1989 (as shown by the limits in dashed lines) and 1990 (solid lines). By 1994, population size had reached to more than 10,000 individuals and had spread 30 m. (After Primack and Miao 1992.)

Transplanted seedlings and adults often flower and fruit one or more years earlier than plants growing from seed sown directly into the wild, which increases the potential for seed dispersal and the formation of a second generation of plants.

Figure 13.4 Seedlings of rare plant species being grown on a greenhouse bench: they were subsequently planted in the wild. Plant reintroductions from seed usually fail; they are often more successful when plants are grown from seeds or cuttings in a separate location and then transplanted into their new home site as seedlings or mature plants. (Photograph by R. Primack.)

Figure 13.5 A variety of methods
are being investigated to create
new populations of rare wildflower
species on U.S. Forest Service land
in South Carolina. Seeds are being
planted in a pine forest from which
the oak understory has been removed. Wire cages will be placed
over some plantings to determine
if excluding rabbits, deer, and other
animals will help in plant establishment. (Photograph by R. Primack.)

While transplanting seedlings and adults has a better chance of ensuring that the species survives at a new location, it does not perfectly
mimic a natural process, and the new population often fails to produce
seed and form the next generation. Plant ecologists are currently trying
to work out new techniques to overcome these difficulties, such as fencing to exclude animals, removal of some of the existing vegetation to reduce competition, controlled burning, planting other species to provide
shade and leaf litter in arid regions, and adding mineral nutrients to the
soil (Figure 13.5). Keys to success seem to be using as many sites as possible, using as many seeds or adult transplants as possible, and reintroducing species over several successive years at the same site (Primack
and Drayton 1997). Reintroductions require careful monitoring of the
numbers of seedlings and adults to determine if the project is a success.
A successful project would have a self-maintaining—or even growing—
population with subsequent generations of plants replacing the reintroduced individuals. As research on this rapidly developing topic is published and synthesized, the chances for successful plant reintroductions
will hopefully improve.

PLANT REINTRODUCTION CASE STUDIES   The following case studies illustrate the various approaches to plant species reintroductions:

- *The large-flowered fiddleneck* (*Amsickia grandiflora*) is an annual plant
  from northern California that has a narrow range. The species is in
  decline because livestock grazing and fire suppression—both human

activities—have favored exotic grasses over native plants. Experimental reintroductions of the fiddleneck were combined with different management treatments, including grass-specific herbicides and burning (Guerrant and Pavlik 1998). Management techniques that proved successful on the experimental populations were then applied to a declining natural population, resulting in a major increase in plant numbers (Figure 13.6).

- *The endemic Clanwilliam cedar* (*Widdringtonia cedarbergensis*) of South Africa has been declining in numbers due to its vulnerability to intense wild fires (Mustart et al. 1995). Along with moving toward a controlled fire regime of frequent, low-intensity fires, which the cedars often survive, an active program of population augmentation using seeds and seedlings is being carried out. In general, the survival of planted seedlings has been higher than sown seeds, and seedlings planted in the shade have done best.
- *Knowlton's cactus* (*Pediocactus knowltonii*) is a tiny, perennial cactus known only from one narrow hilltop location in northwestern New

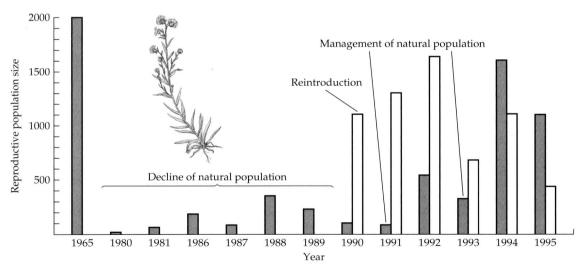

Figure 13.6 A natural population (dark gray bars) of *Amsickia grandiflora*, an endangered annual plant of northern California, was in severe decline during the 1980s as a result of competition with exotic annual grasses. A reintroduction was carried out at a second site, starting in 1990 (white bars), and was combined with various management treatments to eliminate exotics. Successful treatments were then applied to the natural population in 1991 and 1993, with major increases in plant numbers seen in 1992 and 1994. (After Guerrant and Pavlik 1998.)

Figure 13.7 Knowlton's cactus (*Pediocactus knowltonii*) growing in New Mexico. The coin shown for scale is 1.9 cm (0.75 in) in diameter. (Photograph courtesy of The Nature Conservancy.)

Mexico (Figure 13.7). Despite the fact that the site is now owned by The Nature Conservancy, this threatened species remains vulnerable to human disturbance from oil and gas exploration, livestock grazing, and removal of plants by collectors. To reduce the possibility of extinction, two nearby, comparable sites were selected for introductions in 1985. At one site, 150 individuals grown from cuttings were planted and watered. After 17 years, 40% of the plants are still alive, with about half of them flowering and fruiting, but still no second generation has grown up. With a different approach, only 8 plants had been produced from 408 seeds sown at the same site (Cully 1996).

Government Regulation of New Populations

The establishment of new populations raises some novel issues at the interaction of scientific research, conservation efforts, government regulation, and ethics. These issues need to be addressed because reintroduction, introduction, and augmentation programs will increase in the coming years as the biological diversity crisis eliminates more species and populations from the wild. Many of the reintroduction programs for endangered species will be mandated by official recovery plans set up by national governments (Tear et al. 1993). There are a number of problems surrounding national regulations of reintroduction programs.

First, programs and research increasingly are being hampered by endangered species legislation that restricts the possession and use of endangered species (Reinartz 1995; Falk et al. 1996). If government officials rigidly apply these laws to scientific research programs, which certainly was not the original intent of the legislation, the programs will be blocked, and any possible creative insights and new approaches that could have come out of them will be lost (Ralls and Brownell 1989). Projects to establish experimental populations have sometimes been delayed for more than five years while waiting for government approval. New scientific information is central to reintroduction programs and other conservation efforts. Government officials who block reasonable scientific projects may be doing a disservice to the organisms they are trying to protect. The potential harm to endangered species caused by carefully planned scientific research is relatively insignificant when compared with the actual massive loss of biological diversity being caused by habitat destruction and fragmentation, pollution, and overexploitation.

Experimental populations of rare and endangered species—those that are successfully created by reintroduction and introduction programs—are given various degrees of legal protection (Falk and Olwell 1992). The U.S. Endangered Species Act recognizes two categories of experimental populations: "Experimental, essential" populations are regarded as critical to the survival of endangered species and are as rigidly protected as naturally occurring populations. "Experimental, nonessential" populations are not considered essential to the survival of a species and are not protected under the Act. Designating populations as nonessential, as was done for the gray wolf release in the Greater Yellowstone area, means that local landowners are not limited by the provisions of the Act and may be less inclined to oppose the creation of an experimental population. The disadvantage of this designation is that landowners can shoot at or kill animals they perceive as a threat without any legal consequences.

Sometimes reintroduction programs are misused. In many cases, proposals are made by developers to create new habitat or new populations to compensate for the habitat damage or the eradication of populations of endangered species that occurred during a development project. This is generally referred to as **mitigation.** Mitigation is often directed at legally protected species and habitats. Proposals to establish new populations of endangered species merely for the convenience and profit of developers should be regarded with considerable skepticism. Claims that the loss of biodiversity can be mitigated are usually exaggerated. Given the poor success of most attempts to create new populations of rare species, protection of existing populations of rare species should be given the highest priority. While the replacement and restoration of damaged habitat such as wetlands may be beneficial, artificially created wetlands are generally neither as biologically rich nor as functionally useful as natural wetlands (in terms of water storage capacity and ability to break down sewage and other human pollutants, etc.). Legislators, environmental engineers, and scientists alike must understand that the establishment of new populations through reintroduction programs in no way reduces the need to protect the original populations of the endangered species. These original populations are more likely to have the most complete gene pool of the species and the most intact interactions with other members of the biological community.

Finally, conservation biologists must be able to explain the benefits and weaknesses of reintroduction programs in a way that government officials and the general public can understand, and they must address the legitimate concerns of those groups (Farnsworth and Rosovsky 1993). One way this can be facilitated is by biologists incorporating citizen groups, in particular school groups, into reintroduction efforts. When people have the experience of working on reintroduction projects, they become more knowledgeable about the issues and often become advocates for conservation.

Summary

1. One approach to protect endangered species involves establishing new wild populations of those species. New populations of rare and endangered species can be established in the wild using either captive-raised or wild-caught animals. Reintroduction involves releasing individuals within the historical range of the species; introduction involves release of individuals at a site outside of the historical range of the species; augmentation involves releasing individuals into an existing population to increase population size and genetic variability.

2. Mammals and birds raised in captivity may lack the skills needed to survive in the wild. Some species require social and behavioral training before release, and some degree of maintenance after release ("soft release"). Establishment of a new population of a rare bird or mammal species has a low chance of success, but is enhanced when the release occurs in excellent habitat within the historical range of the species and when using large numbers (up to 100) of wild-caught animals. Reintroductions of amphibians and reptiles also have a low rate of success.

3. Reintroductions of plant species require a different approach because of their specialized environmental requirements and inability to move. Current research focuses on improving site selection and habitat management.

4. Newly created populations of endangered species are sometimes given legal status as either "experimental, essential" or "experimental, nonessential" populations. Conservation biologists involved in establishing new populations of endangered species must be careful that their efforts do not weaken the legal protection currently given to natural populations of those species. Similarly, they must educate the public about the potential benefits and uncertainties of reintroduction efforts, which should never become an excuse for allowing a species to decline to the point of extinction in the wild.

For Discussion

1. How do you judge whether a reintroduction project is successful? Develop simple and then increasingly detailed criteria to evaluate a project's success. Use demographic, environmental, and genetic factors in your evaluation.

2. Design reintroduction projects involving a rodent species, an annual plant species, and a marine mollusk. What similarities and what differences would you expect in working with these three species?

3. Does our increasing ability to create new populations of rare and endangered species mean that we do not have to be concerned with protecting the known sites where these species occur? What are the costs and benefits of reintroduction programs?

4. Many endangered plant species are currently being propagated by commercial growers and botanical gardens and then sold (as both plants and seeds) to government agencies, conservation organizations, garden clubs, and the general public, who then in effect create new populations of these legally protected species (Reinartz 1995). There is little or no regulation of these sales or the subsequent plantings. What do you see as the advantages and disadvantages of this widespread activity? Should the propagation and planting of legally protected species be more closely regulated by the government?

5. What are the advantages and disadvantages of incorporating children into a local reintroduction project for wildflowers or butterflies? What concerns would their parents have?

Suggested Readings

Beck, B. B., L. G. Rapport, M. Stanley-Price, and A. Wilson. 1994. Reintroduction of captive-born animals. In *Creative Conservation: Interactive Management of Wild and Captive Animals*, P. J. Olney, G. M. Mace, and A. T. Feistner (eds.), pp. 265–286. Chapman and Hall, London. Critical analysis of animal reintroduction programs.

Berger, J., P. B. Stacey, L. Bellis, and M. P. Johnson. 2001. A mammalian predator-prey imbalance: Grizzly bear and wolf extinction affect avian neotropical migrants. *Ecological Applications* 11: 947–960. Without top predators, increased herbivore impact leads to the loss of bird diversity.

Bowles, M. L. and C. J. Whelan (eds.). 1994. *Restoration of Endangered Species: Conceptual Issues, Planning, and Implementation*. Cambridge University Press, Cambridge. Good mixture of case studies, reviews, and analysis.

Clemmons, J. R. and R. Buchholz (eds.). 1997. *Behavioral Approaches to Conservation in the Wild*. Cambridge University Press, New York. Conservation projects need to pay careful attention to animal behavior and to adjust management practices accordingly.

Falk, D. A., C. I. Millar, and M. Olwell (eds.). 1996. *Restoring Diversity: Strategies for Reintroduction of Endangered Plants*. Island Press, Washington, D.C. Policy, biology, legal issues, and case studies.

Farnsworth, E. J. and J. Rosovsky. 1996. The ethics of ecological field experimentation. *Conservation Biology* 7: 463–472. Ecologists need to be able to justify their research to the government and the public, and follow relevant regulations and laws.

Fischer, J. and D. B. Lindenmayer. 2000. An assessment of published results of animal relocations. *Biological Conservation* 96: 1–11. A review of 180 relocation studies highlights factors leading to success: using wild-caught animals, releasing more than 100 animals, and removing the original cause of population decline.

Frazier, J. 2000. Kemp's Ridley sea turtle (*Lepidochelys kempii*). In *Endangered Animals,* R. P. Reading and B. Miller (eds.), pp. 164–170. Greenwood Press, Westport, CT. This excellent books provides a factual description of the history of turtle programs.

Guerrant, E. O. and B. M. Pavlik. 1998. Reintroduction of rare plants: Genetics, demography and the role of ex-situ conservation methods. In *Conservation Biology: For the Coming Decade,* P. L. Fiedler and P. M. Kareiva (eds.), pp. 80–108. Chapman and Hall, New York. Theory and ideas, with examples from California.

Milton, S. J., W. J. Bond, M. A. DuPleissis, D. Gibbs, et al. 1999. A protocol for plant conservation by translocation in threatened lowland Fynbos. *Conservation Biology* 13: 735–743.

Minckley, W. L. 1995. Translocation as a tool for conserving imperiled fishes: Experiences in western United States. *Biological Conservation* 72: 297–309. Review of freshwater fish releases; also see other articles on fish conservation in this issue.

Primack, R. and B. Drayton. 1997. The experimental ecology of reintroduction. *Plant Talk* 11: 25–28. Investigation of the best methods for plant reintroduction in a wonderful magazine that is now the bulletin of the National Tropical Botanical Garden.

Reinartz, J. A. 1995. Planting state-listed endangered and threatened plants. *Conservation Biology* 9: 771–781. Legal and moral issues involved in selling and planting endangered species.

Snyder, N. and H. Snyder. 2000. *The California Condor: A Saga of Natural History and Conservation.* Academic Press, San Diego, CA. People struggling to save the condor have to contend with difficult political, legal, and financial issues.

Tutin, C. E. G., M. Ancrenaz, J. Paredes, M. Vacher-Vallas, et al. 2001. Conservation biology framework for the release of wild-born orphaned chimpanzees into the Conkouati Reserve, Congo. *Conservation Biology* 15(5): 1247–1257. A model framework for a proposed release.

Chapter *14*

Ex Situ Conservation Strategies

The best strategy for the long-term protection of biological diversity is the preservation of natural communities and populations in the wild, known as **in situ**, or on-site, **preservation.** Only in natural communities are species able to continue their process of evolutionary adaptation to a changing environment. Further, only populations in the wild are typically large enough to prevent the loss of genetic variability through genetic drift. However, in the face of increasing human activities, in situ preservation is not currently a viable option for many rare species, and species may decline and go extinct in the wild for any of the reasons already discussed: loss of genetic variation and inbreeding depression, demographic and environmental variability, insufficient habitat, deteriorating habitat quality, habitat fragmentation, competition from invasive species, disease, and excessive hunting and collecting.

If a remnant population is too small to maintain the species, is still declining despite conservation efforts, or if the remaining individuals are found outside of protected areas, then in situ preservation may not be effective. It is likely that the only way species in such circumstances can be prevented from going extinct is to maintain individuals temporarily in artificial conditions under human supervision (Kleiman et al. 1996). This strategy is known as **ex situ,** or off-site, **preservation**. Already a number of species that are extinct in the wild survive in captive colonies, such as the Père David's deer (*Elaphurus davidianus*) and Przewalski's horse (*Equus caballus przewalski*) (Figure 14.1). The beautiful Franklin tree (see Figure 7.1) grows only in cultivation and is no longer found in the wild. The long-term goal of many ex situ conservation programs is the eventual establishment of new populations in the wild, once sufficient numbers of individuals and a suitable habitat are available. As described in Chapter 8, a small group of wild-collected black-footed ferrets gave rise to a substantial captive colony, 1200 of which were returned to the wild to establish new populations.

Figure 14.1 (A) Père David's deer (*Elaphurus davidinus*) has been extinct in the wild since about 1200 B.C. The species remained only in managed hunting reserves kept by Chinese royalty and is now kept in captive herds. (B) Przewalski's horse (*Equus caballus przewalski*) does well in captivity, but is now probably extinct in the wild. This species was once abundant in Central Asia and is the last living species of wild horse. Animals are now being reintroduced into grassland habitats. (Photographs by Jessie Cohen, National Zoological Park, Smithsonian Institution.)

(A)

(B)

Ex situ facilities for animal preservation include zoos, game farms, aquariums, and private breeders, while plants are maintained in botanical gardens, arboretums, and seed banks. An intermediate strategy that combines elements of both ex situ and in situ preservation is the monitoring and management of populations of rare and endangered species in small, protected areas; such populations are still somewhat wild, but human intervention may be necessary occasionally to prevent population decline.

Ex situ and in situ conservation are complementary strategies (Robinson 1992). Individuals from ex situ populations can be periodically released into the wild to augment in situ conservation efforts (Figure 14.2). Research on captive populations can provide insight into the basic biology of the species and suggest new conservation strategies for in situ populations. Long-term, viable ex situ populations can also reduce the need to collect individuals from the wild for display and research. Captive-bred individuals on display can help to educate the public about the need to preserve the species and so protect other members of the species in the wild. The number of people visiting zoos is enormous; in the Unit-

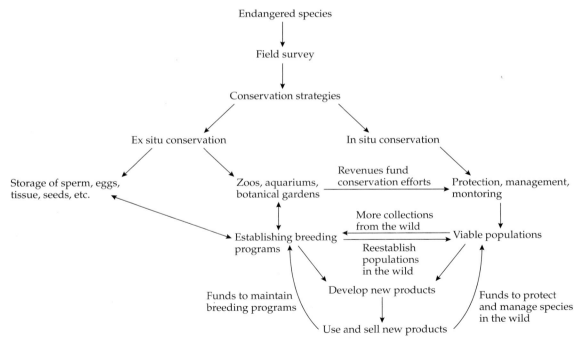

Figure 14.2 This model of biodiversity conservation shows the ways in which in situ (on site) and ex situ (off site) conservation efforts benefit each other and provide alternative conservation strategies. (After Maxted 2001.)

Figure 14.3 Modern zoos offer educational opportunities to the public in addition to serving as sanctuaries for animals. These visitors to the National Zoo meet camels during an animal feeding demonstration. (Photograph © Richard T. Nowitz/Photo Researchers, Inc.)

ed States alone, over 120 million people visit zoos every year (Figure 14.3). Zoos, aquariums, and botanical gardens, and the people that visit them, often contribute money to in situ conservation programs. In addition, ex situ programs can be used to develop new products that potentially can generate funds from profits or licensing fees to protect species in the wild. In situ preservation of species, in turn, is vital to the survival of species that are difficult to maintain in captivity, as well as to the continued ability of zoos, aquariums, and botanical gardens to display species.

Limitations of Ex Situ Conservation

Ex situ conservation has several important limitations. First, ex situ conservation is not cheap: The cost of maintaining African elephants and black rhinos in zoos is 50 times greater than protecting the same number of individuals in East African national parks (Leader-Williams 1990). The cost of maintaining zoos is enormous in comparison to many other conservation activities; for example, U.S. zoos cost around $1 billion per year to run. Also, ex situ programs protect only one species at a time. In contrast, when a species is preserved in the wild, an entire community of species consisting of thousands or tens of thousands of species is preserved, along with a range of ecosystem services. Nevertheless, ex situ conservation strategies are an important part of an integrated conservation strategy to protect endangered species and educate the public.

In addition to their expense and to the fact that only one species at a time is conserved, ex situ conservation efforts have additional basic limitations compared with in situ preservation (Snyder et al. 1996):

- *Population size.* To prevent genetic drift, ex situ populations of at least several hundred individuals need to be maintained. No one zoo can maintain such large numbers of any of the larger animals, and only a few vertebrate species are maintained in captivity at such numbers globally. In botanical gardens, only one or a few individuals of most species typically are maintained, especially in the case of trees.
- *Adaptation.* Ex situ populations may undergo genetic adaptation to their artificial environment. For example, animal species kept in captivity for several generations may exhibit changes in mouthparts and digestive enzymes due to the diet of zoo food; when the animals from this altered population are returned to the wild, they may have difficulty eating their natural diet.
- *Learning skills.* Individuals in ex situ populations may be ignorant of their natural environment and unable to survive in the wild. For example, captive-bred animals may no longer recognize wild foods as edible or their predators as dangerous, or be able to locate water sources if they are released back into the wild. This problem is most likely to occur among social mammals and birds in which juveniles learn survival skills and locations of critical resources from adult members of the population. Migratory animals will not know where or when to migrate.
- *Genetic variability.* Ex situ populations may represent only a limited portion of the gene pool of the species. For example, a captive population started using individuals collected from a warm lowland site may be unable to adapt physiologically to colder highland sites formerly occupied by the species.
- *Continuity.* Ex situ conservation efforts require a continuous supply of funds and a steady institutional policy. While this is also true to some extent for in situ conservation efforts, interruption of care in a zoo, aquarium, or greenhouse lasting only days or weeks can result in considerable losses of both individuals and species. Frozen and chilled collections of sperm, eggs, tissues, and seeds are particularly vulnerable to the loss of electric power. The break up of the former Soviet Union, the deterioration of the Russian economy, and civil wars in its outlying states illustrate how rapidly conditions can shift in a country. Zoos are not going to be able to maintain their animal collections under such circumstances.

- *Concentration.* Because ex situ conservation efforts are sometimes concentrated in one relatively small place, there is a danger of an entire population of an endangered species being destroyed by a catastrophe such as fire, hurricane, or epidemic.
- *Surplus animals.* Some species breed too easily in captivity. What should be done with surplus animals in captivity that no other zoo wants and that have no chance of surviving in the wild? This ethical issue must be addressed: the welfare of any animal taken into human custody is the responsibility of its captors, so it is often unacceptable to kill or sell an individual animal, particularly when each animal in a highly threatened species might represent a key component of the species' future survival.

In spite of these limitations, ex situ conservation strategies may prove to be the best—perhaps the only—alternative when in situ preservation of a species is difficult or impossible. As Michael Soulé says, "There are no hopeless cases, only people without hope and expensive cases" (Soulé 1987).

Ex Situ Conservation Facilities

The most common types of ex situ conservation facilities currently in use are zoos, aquariums, botanical gardens, and seed banks. In this section, we'll examine each of these facilities to determine their role in conservation programs.

Zoos

A current goal of most major zoos is to establish viable, long-term captive breeding populations of rare and endangered animals (Lyles 2001). Zoos have traditionally focused on maintaining large vertebrates—especially mammals—since these species are of greatest interest to the general public, whose entrance fees fund zoo budgets. These animals were typically displayed in cages, without any relationship to a natural environment. The emphasis on "charismatic" megafauna such as pandas, giraffes, and elephants tends to ignore the enormous threats to the huge numbers of insects and other invertebrates that comprise most of the world's animal species. However, charismatic species do influence public opinion favorably toward conservation. The world's 2000 zoos and aquaria are increasingly incorporating ecological themes and information about the threats to endangered species in their public displays and their research programs as part of the World Zoo Conservation Strategy, which seeks to link zoo programs with conservation efforts in the wild (Robinson 1992; Tarpy 1993; Olney and Ellis 1995).

The educational impact of zoos is potentially enormous, considering that they receive approximately 600 million visitors per year. Educational programs at zoos, articles written about zoo programs, and zoo field projects all direct public attention to animals and habitats of conservation significance. If, for example, the general public becomes interested in protecting giant pandas after seeing them in zoos and reading about them, then money may be donated, pressure may be exerted on governments, and eventually appropriate habitat in China may be set aside as protected areas (Box 21). At the same time, thousands of other plant and animal species occupying these environments will be protected.

Zoos, along with affiliated universities, government wildlife departments, and conservation organizations, presently maintain over 280,000 individuals of terrestrial vertebrates, representing 7000 species and subspecies of mammals, birds, reptiles, and amphibians (Table 14.1). While this number of captive animals may seem impressive, it is trivial in comparison to the numbers of domestic cats, dogs, and fish kept by people as pets. In the United States alone, about 50 million cats are kept as pets, over 100 times more than the world's total of zoo animals. Zoos could establish breeding colonies of even more species if they directed more of their efforts to smaller-bodied species such as insects, amphibians,

TABLE 14.1 Number of terrestrial vertebrates currently maintained in zoos according to the International Species Inventory System (ISIS)

Location	Mammals	Birds	Reptiles	Amphibians
Europe	44,195	55,620	9715	3314
North America	43,355	52,729	26,523	6606
Asia	7470	13,293	1755	34
Australia	4978	7789	2531	701
South America	539	574	575	7
Totals				
All species	102,180	132,982	41,476	10,676
Number of taxa[a]	1836	3452	1809	393
% wildborn	8	16	19	19
Rare species[b]	45,968	55,940	21,098	2272
Number of taxa	717	1089	1355	32
% wildborn[c]	7	19	19	3

Source: Data from ISIS (2002, unpublished) and Laurie Bingaman Lackey (2002, personal communication).

[a]The number of taxa is not exactly equivalent to species because many species have more than one subspecies listed.

[b]Rare species are those covered by the Convention of International Trade in Endangered Species.

[c]The percentage of individuals born in the wild is only approximate (particularly for reptiles and amphibians), since the origin of the animals is often not given.

BOX 21 *Love Alone Cannot Save the Giant Panda*

The giant panda (*Ailuropoda melanoleuca*) is one of the most familiar endangered species in the world. It is so well known and so beloved by millions of people that its image is the symbol for the World Wide Fund for Nature (also known as the World Wildlife Fund), a prominent international conservation organization. Despite its popular appeal, the panda's future is in jeopardy. As with many endangered species, disappearing habitat and illegal hunting are the most significant threats to its survival (Schaller 1993; Entwistle and Dunstone 2000; Zhi et al. 2000). Moreover, human pressure appears to exacerbate some of the unusual traits of the panda's physical and behavioral makeup that make this species particularly vulnerable to extinction.

One of the strangest features of panda biology is the species' diet of bamboo. Pandas share their ancestry with animals in the order of carnivores even though they don't eat meat, and they lack many of the anatomical adaptations such as an elongated digestive tract that enable other herbivores to use plant foods efficiently. Most herbivores also have symbiotic bacteria in their digestive systems that help break down cellulose, further improving digestive efficiency; pandas lack these organisms. Consequently, pandas must eat almost continually to obtain sufficient nutrients to survive.

To further complicate matters, pandas periodically must change their behavior in response to cyclical bamboo die-offs. Bamboo species reproduce in long-term cycles of anywhere from 15 to over 100 years; typically, nearly all individuals in a given species within a certain area will produce flowers and seeds in a single season, then die. Ten years are generally required before new plants are large enough for pandas to eat. Though pandas may usually prefer one particular species of bamboo above all others, during die-off events they will eat other bamboo species. In the past, on those uncommon occasions when two or three bamboo species flowered simul-taneously and bamboos died over a wide area, pandas would migrate long distances to find sufficient bamboo, especially in lowland areas. Now when agricultural areas prevent them from migrating to lowland areas, pandas have no recourse during bamboo die-offs. In the 1970s, when three species of bamboo flowered simultaneously, at least 138 pandas starved, and the population declined by more than 14%.

Following this catastrophe, in 1983 the Chinese government instituted a policy of searching for starving pandas during bamboo die-

Among the most beloved of all endangered species, the panda has become a symbol of conservation efforts. (Photograph by Jessie Cohen, National Zoological Park, Smithsonian Institution.)

BOX 21 *(continued)*

offs. The policy was not without its drawbacks. "Rescued" animals, many of which were captured unnecessarily, frequently ended up in zoos around the world, which competed for exhibition animals and offered large sums of money for them. This depleted the wild population further, and many of the giant pandas that ended up in zoos were not given the opportunity or the environment necessary for captive breeding.

Attempts to establish a self-sustaining captive breeding population were mostly unsuccessful until the last few years. Giant pandas are extremely selective in choosing mates, and pandas paired by zoos and other breeding facilities often prove incompatible, or the zoos do not provide the pandas with enough time or enough choices. Artificial insemination has been used to circumvent the pandas' choosiness, but even its success has been limited. Females go into heat only once every year, and are fertile for only two or three days. Cubs are born singly or in pairs and are

remarkably small and helpless, weighing just 110 grams (four ounces). A panda female usually raises only one cub at a time, even if she gives birth to two live cubs. Moreover, the 3–5 month pregnancy is followed by 5 months of nursing, and, since the female does not generally go into heat again immediately after she stops nursing, she misses a year's breeding season. Thus the rate of population growth is very slow even under the best conditions. Young pandas are dependent on their mothers for up to 22 months after birth, so injury, sickness, or death of the mother may mean the loss of the cub as well. Would-be panda breeders worldwide are still attempting to find out why captive pandas frequently do not mate or, in the case of many males, do not even come into heat.

Despite these problems, however, giant panda breeding has recently proved more successful, due in part to a better understanding of nutrition and housing needs. Between 1963, when China first began to breed captive pandas, and 1989, only 90 cubs were born, of which only 37 survived for more than 6 months. However, 22 cubs born between 1998 and 2000 in China have survived, a hopeful sign that some of these problems can be overcome; the captive population is still not expanding sufficiently, though. The captive-bred population is still not large

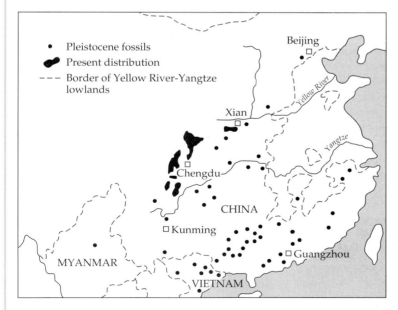

Pandas were once widely found in southern and eastern China, and even into Myanmar (Burma) and Vietnam. They are now restricted to a few areas along the eastern edge of the Tibetan Plateau. (After Schaller 1993.)

BOX 21 *(continued)*

enough to consider releasing individuals back into the wild. However, the captive breeding program is valuable in raising public interest and funds needed for in situ conservation. Currently, the three U.S. zoos with pairs of giant pandas on loan from China each contribute about $1 million per year for giant panda conservation programs in China. These contributions are required as part of the panda exchange program.

Fragmentation of habitat is another problem for the long-term survival of the species. The remaining wild pandas number around 1000 individuals and are scattered in about 25 small populations over an area of 13,000 km^2. As a result, the small populations, many with less than 30 individuals, may eventually suffer from inbreeding depression. Poaching pandas for their skins was formerly a serious problem that is now less common due to stiff penalties imposed by the Chinese government, but pandas still die in snares set for antelope, deer, and other game.

The Chinese government has put significant financial resources into setting aside more habitat for the remaining wild pandas. Currently, there are 33 reserves covering half of the pandas' current habitat. However, it will not be easy for the reserves to withstand the pressure of China's immense human population. The pandas need forest, bamboo, and protection from hunters—difficult resources to provide. Time will tell whether they will get what they need.

and reptiles, which are less expensive to maintain in large numbers than large-bodied mammals such as giant pandas, elephants, and rhinos (Balmford et al. 1996). Obviously a better balance must be reached between displaying large animals to draw many visitors and displaying smaller, lesser known animals that appeal less to the public but represent a greater proportion of the world's biodiversity.

Zoos, working with affiliated universities, government wildlife departments, and conservation organizations, are the logical choice for the development of captive populations of rare and endangered species because they have the needed knowledge and experience in animal care, veterinary medicine, animal behavior, reproductive biology, and genetics. Zoos and affiliated conservation organizations have embarked on a major effort to build facilities and develop the technology necessary to establish breeding colonies of these animals, and to develop the new methods and programs needed to reintroduce species in the wild (Conway et al. 2001). Some of these facilities are highly specialized, such as that run by the International Crane Foundation in Wisconsin, which is attempting to establish captive breeding colonies of all crane species. This effort has paid off. Currently, less than 20% of the terrestrial vertebrates kept in zoos have been collected in the wild, and this number is declining as zoos gain more experience (see Table 14.1). For endangered mammals, only around 7% of captive individuals were captured in the wild.

For common animals such as the raccoon and the white-tailed deer, there is no need to establish breeding colonies since individuals of these species can be readily obtained from the wild. The real need is for zoos to establish populations of rare species that can no longer be readily captured in the wild, such as the orangutan, Chinese alligator, and snow leopard.

CAPTIVE BREEDING METHODS AND TARGETS   The success of captive breeding programs has been enhanced by efforts to collect and disseminate knowledge about rare and endangered species. The Species Survival Commission's Conservation Breeding Specialist Group, a division of the IUCN, and affiliated organizations, such as the American Zoo and Aquarium Association and the European Association of Zoos and Aquaria, provide zoos with the necessary information for proper care and handling of these species, as well as updates on the status and behavior of animals in the wild (Wiese and Hutchins 1994). This includes data on nutritional requirements, anesthetic techniques to immobilize animals and reduce stress during transport and medical procedures, optimal housing conditions, vaccinations and antibiotics to prevent the spread of disease, and breeding records. This effort is being aided by a central database called ARKS, the Animal Record Keeping System, maintained by the International Species Inventory System (ISIS), which keeps track of all relevant information on 296,000 living specimens (and over 2 million ancestors of these animals) of 8000 species of animals at 576 member institutions in 54 countries. Such a database is an important tool in monitoring health trends in zoo populations.

Some rare species do not adapt or reproduce well in captivity. In most cases, better care of the animal's particular nutrition and housing needs has overcome these problems. In addition, new techniques are being developed to enhance the low reproductive rates of such species (Kleiman et al. 1996). Some of these come directly from human and veterinary medicine, while others are novel methods for particular species developed at special research facilities, such as the San Diego Zoo's Center for Reproduction of Endangered Species, and the Audubon Institute Species Survival Center in New Orleans. For example, if animal mothers are unable to raise their own young, foster parents from another species can sometimes raise their offspring. This **cross-fostering** can increase the reproductive success of certain species. Many bird species, such as the bald eagle, normally lay only one clutch of eggs per year, but if biologists remove this first clutch of eggs, the mother bird will lay and raise a second clutch. If the first clutch of eggs is given to another bird of a related species, two clutches of eggs will be produced per year for each rare female. This technique, known informally as "double-clutching," potentially doubles the number of offspring one female can produce.

Another aid to reproduction, similar to cross-fostering, is **artificial incubation.** If a mother does not adequately care for her offspring, or if the offspring are readily attacked by predators, parasites, or disease, humans may care for them during their vulnerable early stages. This approach has been tried extensively with egg-laying species such as sea turtles, birds, fishes, and amphibians: Eggs are collected and placed in ideal hatching conditions; the hatchlings are protected and fed during their vulnerable early stages; and the young are then released into the wild or raised in captivity. This approach is sometimes called "headstarting" (see Chapter 13).

Individuals of some animal species lose interest in mating while in captivity, and a zoo may have only one or a few individuals of a rare species such as the giant panda. In these circumstances, **artificial insemination** can be used when an isolated female animal comes into breeding condition, either on her own or after being chemically induced. Sperm is collected from suitable males, stored until needed at low temperatures, and then used for artificial insemination with a receptive female. While artificial insemination is performed routinely with many domesticated animal species, the exact techniques of sperm collection, sperm storage, recognition of female receptivity, and sperm delivery have to be worked out separately for each species in a conservation breeding program.

Embryo transfer has been accomplished successfully in a few rare animals such as the bongo, gaur, and Przewalski's horse. Superovulation, or production of multiple eggs, is induced using fertility drugs, and the extra eggs are surgically collected, fertilized with sperm, and surgically implanted into surrogate mothers, sometimes using related common species. The surrogate mother carries the offspring to term and then gives birth (Figure 14.4). In the future this technology may be used to increase the reproductive output of rare species.

Cutting-edge medical and veterinary technologies have the potential to develop innovative approaches for some species that are difficult to breed in captivity (Lanza et al. 2000). These include cloning individuals from single cells (when only one or a few individuals remain), cross-species hybridization (when the remaining members of a species cannot breed among themselves), induced hibernation and induced dormancy as a way of maintaining dormant populations, biochemical and surgical sexing of animals that have no external sex differences, and biochemical tracking of hormonal levels in urine and feces to determine the timing of sexual receptivity in females. One of the most unusual and controversial techniques involves freezing purified DNA, eggs, sperm, embryos, and other tissue of species on the verge of extinction in the hope that these can be used to reestablish the species at some time in the future, or at least contribute to breeding programs and scientific research (Ryder et al. 2000). This technique has sparked controversy because it gives the impression of being a "high-tech" solution to the problem of species extinction. However, many of these techniques are enormously

Figure 14.4 This bongo calf (*Tragelaphus euryceros*), an endangered species, was produced by embryo transfer using an eland (*Taurotagus oryxi*) as a surrogate mother at the Cincinnati Zoo Center for Reproduction of Endangered Wildlife. (Photograph © The Cincinnati Zoo.)

expensive and may not actually be able to produce healthy animals for certain species. In any case, "frozen zoos" are no substitute for in situ and ex situ conservation programs that preserve ecological relationships and behaviors that are necessary for survival in the wild.

As we discussed in Chapter 11, genetic inbreeding is an important problem in small populations (such as those found in zoos). Traditionally, captive populations in zoos were usually extensively inbred (Figure 14.5), but zoo managers are more careful now to avoid potential genetic problems when assigning mates. Modern zoos now use global computerized databases provided by ISIS and special studbooks to carefully track the genetic lineages of endangered captive animals to prevent pairing of related animals and avoid inbreeding depression as part of a species survival plan. Hundreds of studbooks currently exist, detailing European, North American, Japanese, Australian, and international cap-

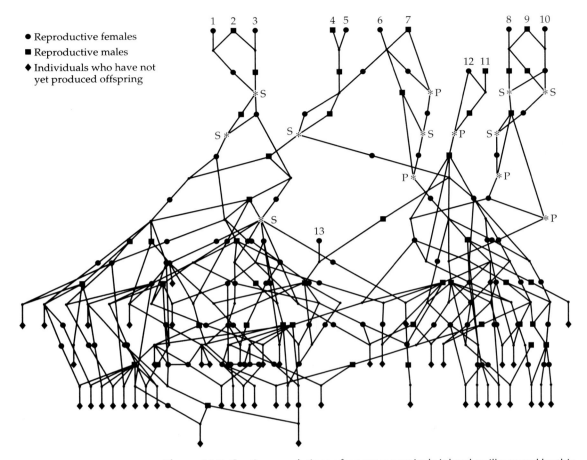

- ● Reproductive females
- ■ Reproductive males
- ◆ Individuals who have not yet produced offspring

Figure 14.5 Captive populations often are extensively inbred, as illustrated by this pedigree of a captive group of Przewalski's horses. The 13 "founder" individuals are indicated with numbers. Matings among close relatives become common; some sibling matings (S) and parent–offspring matings (P) are highlighted with asterisks. (After Thomas 1995.)

tive animals. The international studbook of giraffes, for example, lists 7000 living and deceased animals, along with all available information on parentage and genetic relationships. This system of pedigree construction can also be used to construct a breeding program to prevent the gradual loss of genetic diversity over time in small populations (see Chapter 11).

Ex situ conservation efforts have been increasingly directed at saving endangered species of invertebrates as well. One of the most striking examples is the partulid snails of the Pacific island of Moorea (Tudge 1992). All seven species of this snail family became extinct in the wild after a predatory snail was introduced to control an agricultural pest. Currently six of the seven partulid species survive only in a captive breeding program, with attempts being made to reintroduce the species into predator-free enclosures on Moorea. Many zoos are displaying colonies of butterflies, which are popular with the public.

Other important targets for captive breeding programs are breeds of domestic animals on which human societies depend for animal protein, dairy products, leather, wool, agricultural labor, transportation, and recreation. Even though enormous populations of domestic animals exist (over 1 billion cattle and 1 billion sheep, for example), diverse and distinctive breeds of domestic animals that have adapted to local conditions are rapidly dying out as traditional agricultural practices are abandoned and intensive, high-yield agriculture is emphasized. For example, out of 3831 breeds of ass, water buffalo, cattle, goat, horse, pig, and sheep that existed during the last 100 years, 16% have already become extinct and an additional 15% are rare and in danger of extinction (Hall and Ruane 1993). Preservation of the genetic variation from these local breeds for characteristics such as disease resistance, drought tolerance, general health, and meat production is crucial to animal breeding programs (Figure 14.6). Governments and conservation organizations are maintaining

Figure 14.6 Soay sheep are a relict breed (a breed of an otherwise extinct group) of sheep living in the St. Kilda Islands, off the coast of Scotland. Soays retain characteristics of the first sheep brought to Britain more than 5000 years ago, and some of these characteristics may be valuable for low-maintenance animal husbandry in the future: small size (25–36 kg); robust health; and the ability to shed their fleece. (Photograph by Stephen J. G. Hall.)

secure populations of some of these local breeds and developing frozen collections of sperm and embryos for later use. However, much more needs to be done to protect this global resource needed for healthy and productive domestic animals.

ETHICAL ISSUES   Ex-situ techniques provide technological solutions to problems caused by human activities. Often the cheapest solution and the one most likely to succeed is protection of the species and its habitat in the wild so that it can recover naturally. When this solution is not possible, ex situ methods are available to support those species that will become extinct without human intervention. When scientists consider ex situ methods, they need to answer a series of ethical questions (Norton et al. 1995):

1. How necessary and how effective are these methods for a particular species? Is it better for the last few individuals of a species to live out their days in the wild or to breed a captive population that may be unable to readapt to wild conditions?
2. Does a population of a rare species that has been raised in captivity and does not know how to survive in its natural environment really represent a victory for the species?
3. Are species held in captivity primarily for their own benefit, the economic benefit of zoos, or the pleasure of zoo visitors?

Even when the answers to these questions indicate a need for ex situ management, it is not always feasible to create ex situ populations of rare animal species. A species may have been so severely reduced in numbers that there is low breeding success and high infant mortality due to inbreeding depression. Certain animals, particularly marine mammals, are so large or require such specialized environments that the facilities for maintaining and handling them are prohibitively expensive. Many invertebrates have complex life cycles in which their diet changes as they grow and in which their environmental needs vary in subtle ways. Many of these species are impossible to raise given our present knowledge. Finally, certain species are simply difficult to breed, despite the best efforts of scientists. Two prime examples of this are the giant panda (see Box 21) and the Sumatran rhino; neither species reproduces well in captivity, though the rate of breeding has shown improvement over time. As a result of these considerations, zoos are increasingly embarking on projects to protect endangered species in the wild. In many cases, these projects are linked to exhibits or special projects within the zoo.

Aquariums

Public aquariums have traditionally been oriented toward the display of unusual and attractive fish, sometimes supplemented with exhibits and performances of seals, dolphins, and other marine mammals. However, as concern for the environment has increased, aquariums have made conservation a major educational theme. The need is great, since thousands of fish species are threatened with extinction. In North America alone, 24 species are known to have gone extinct since the arrival of European settlers, and 63 species are now classified as endangered (Williams and Nowak 1993). The rich fauna of the southern U.S. Gulf coastal plain, and the unique desert pupfish of the southwestern United States are in particular danger. Large-scale extinctions of fishes are occurring worldwide in places such as the African Great Lakes, the Andean lakes, Madagascar and the Philippines. Freshwater mollusks in the United States and throughout the world are also a priority for protection because of their restricted distributions and vulnerability to changes caused by water pollution, dams, and invasive species.

In response to this threat to aquatic species, ichthyologists, marine mammalogists, and coral reef experts who work for public aquariums are increasingly linking up with colleagues in marine research institutes, government fisheries departments, and conservation organizations to develop programs for the conservation of rich natural communities and species of special concern. Currently approximately 600,000 individual fish are maintained in aquariums, with most of these obtained from the wild. Major efforts are being made to develop breeding techniques so that rare species can be maintained in aquariums without further collection in the wild, and sometimes can be released back into the wild (Philippart 1995). These breeding programs utilize indoor aquarium facilities, seminatural water bodies, and fish hatcheries and farms.

Many of the techniques for fish breeding were originally developed by fisheries biologists for large-scale stocking operations involving trout, bass, salmon, and other commercial species. Other techniques were discovered in the aquarium pet trade, when dealers attempted to propagate tropical fish for sale. These techniques are now being applied to endangered freshwater fauna such as the pupfish and other desert fishes, stream fishes of the Tennessee River Basin, and cichlids of the African Great Lakes. Programs for breeding endangered marine fishes and coral species are still in an early stage, but this is a promising area of active research at the present time.

Aquariums have a particularly important role to play in the conservation of endangered cetaceans. Aquarium personnel often respond to public requests for assistance in handling whales stranded on beaches or disoriented in shallow waters. The lessons learned from working with common species may be used by the aquarium community to develop programs to aid endangered species. Extensive experience with captive populations of the bottle-nosed dolphin, the most popular aquarium species, is being applied to other species (Figure 14.7) (Ames 1991): Researchers are able to maintain colonies, breed them naturally or perform artificial insemination, hand-raise calves, and release captive-born animals into the natural environment. Techniques learned with dolphins

Figure 14.7 Breeding bottle-nosed dolphins (*Tursiops truncatus*) in captivity has provided aquarium personnel with valuable experience that can be applied to endangered cetacean species. Shown here are a mother and calf. (Photograph courtesy of Sea World.)

may eventually be applied to other endangered cetaceans such as the Chinese Yangtze River baiji, the Gulf of California vaquita, the Mediterranean striped dolphin, and local populations of harbor porpoise.

A practical problem in establishing populations of captive marine mammals is the requirement of large volumes of water. One possible solution is to use small, protected bodies of water to create habitats that are somewhat between wild and artificial conditions. This approach is being used to protect the baiji (*Lipotes vexillifer*), a rare dolphin that lives in the Yangtze River. This species has undergone a precipitous decline— only about 200 individuals now remain in the wild. The most obvious causes of the decline are the dams and floodgates that reduce fish populations and interfere with migration patterns and the injuries to dolphins that are caused by collisions with commercial fishing boats and their propellers. Water pollution may also disrupt the baiji's reproductive physiology, and the noise of motorboats and other industrial activity may interfere with the echolocation used by the baiji to find food and mates and avoid danger. The construction of the Three Gorges Dam on the Yangtze (see Box 30 in Chapter 21) may pose further threats. To protect the baiji, Chinese scientists have established experimental breeding reserves in oxbow lakes. While this species is normally found in moving river water rather than lakes, the lakes offer the baiji some protection from the most damaging aspects of human activity.

The ex situ preservation of aquatic biodiversity takes on additional significance due to the dramatic increase in aquaculture throughout the world. This aquaculture includes the extensive salmon, carp, and catfish farms of the temperate zones, the shrimp farms of the Tropics, and the 12 million tons of aquatic products grown in China and Japan. As fish, frogs, mollusks, and crustaceans increasingly become domesticated and are raised to meet human needs, it becomes necessary to preserve the genetic stocks needed to continue improvements in these species—and to protect them against disease and unforeseeable threats. Ironically, fishes and invertebrates that have escaped from aquaculture present major threats to the diversity of indigenous species because these exotic species can become invasive, spread disease, and hybridize with local species. A challenge for the future will involve balancing the need to increase human food production from aquaculture with the need to protect aquatic biodiversity from increasing human threats.

Botanical Gardens and Arboretums

Gardening is enjoyed by millions of people worldwide and has a history that dates back thousands of years. Kitchen gardens have long provided a source of vegetables and herbs for households. In ancient times, doctors and healers kept gardens of medicinal plants to treat their patients. In more recent centuries, royal families established large private gardens for their personal enjoyment, and governments established botanical gardens for the urban public. An **arboretum** is a specialized botanical garden focusing on trees and other woody plants. While the major purpose of many of these large gardens was the display of beautiful plants, they also illustrate the diversity of the living world and assist in the dissemination and propagation of plants that can be used in horticulture, agriculture, forestry, landscaping, and industry. In recognition of the vital role plants play in the economic activity of society, many European countries set up botanical gardens throughout their colonial empires. The world's 1600 botanical gardens now contain major collections of living plants and represent a crucial resource for plant conservation; they currently contain around 4 million living plants, representing 80,000 species—approximately 30% of the world's flora (Given 1995; Heywood 1995). When we add in the species grown in greenhouses, subsistence gardens, and hobby gardens, the numbers are increased. The world's largest botanical garden, the Royal Botanic Gardens, Kew, in England, has an estimated 25,000 species of plants under cultivation, about 10% of the world's total; 2700 of these are listed as threatened under the IUCN categories (Figure 14.8). In addition to living plants, botanical gardens and research institutes have developed collections of seeds, sometimes called **seed banks**, from both wild and cultivated plants that provide a crucial backup to their living collections. One of the most exciting new botanical gardens is the Eden Project in

Figure 14.8 The Royal Botanic Gardens, Kew, is well known for its training courses and research in plant conservation and horticulture. Here a training session is being conducted around a collection of desert plants inside the Princess of Wales Conservatory. (Photograph courtesy of the Royal Botanic Gardens, Kew.)

southwest England, which focuses on displaying and explaining over 5000 species of economically important plants in a series of giant greenhouse domes.

Botanical gardens increasingly focus their efforts on cultivating rare and endangered plant species, and many specialize in particular types of plants. The Arnold Arboretum of Harvard University grows hundreds of different temperate tree species. The New England Wildflower Society has a collection of hundreds of perennial temperate herbs at its Garden in the Woods location. In California, a specialized pine arboretum grows 72 of the world's 110 species of pines, and South Africa's leading botanical garden has 25% of South Africa's plant species growing in cultivation (Raven 1981).

In many ways, plants are easier to maintain in controlled conditions than animals. Adequate population samples can often be established from seeds, shoot and root cuttings, and other plant parts, and by using tissue-culture techniques. Most plants have similar basic needs for light, water, and minerals, which can be readily supplied in greenhouses and gardens. Adjusting light, temperature, humidity levels, soil type, and soil moisture to suit species is the main concern, but this is often easily determined through knowledge of the plant's natural growing conditions. Since plants do not move, they often can be grown in high densities. If space is a limiting factor, plants can be pruned to a small size. Plants can often be maintained outdoors in gardens, where they need minimal care and weeding to survive. Some perennial plants, particularly shrubs and trees, are long-lived, so that individuals can be kept alive for decades or centuries once they grow beyond the seedling stage. Species that are primarily inbreeders (self-fertilizing), such as wheat, need fewer individuals to maintain genetic variability than primarily outcrossing species such as maize or corn. Many plant species readily produce seeds on their own, which can be collected and germinated to produce more plants. Wind, insects, and other animals cross-pollinate many plants in botanical gardens, while other species naturally self-pollinate. Simple hand pollination is used to produce seed in some plant species. Many plants, particularly those found in the temperate zone, in dry climates, and those found growing in disturbed conditions, have seeds that can lie dormant for years—even decades—in cool, dry conditions.

Botanical gardens are in a unique position to contribute to conservation efforts because living collections in botanical gardens and their associated herbaria of dried plant collections represent the best sources of information we have on plant distribution and habitat requirements. The staff of botanical gardens are often recognized authorities on plant identification, distribution, and conservation status. Expeditions sent out by botanical gardens discover new species and determine the distribution and status of known species, while more than 250 botanical gardens maintain nature reserves that serve as important conservation areas in their own right. In addition, botanical gardens are able to educate an estimated 150 million visitors per year about conservation issues (IUCN/WWF 1989).

The conservation of endangered species is becoming one of the major goals of botanical gardens as well as zoos (Frankel et al. 1995). In the United States, conservation efforts by a network of 34 botanical gardens are being coordinated by the Center for Plant Conservation based at the Missouri Botanical Garden (Falk 1991). These botanical gardens maintain joint collections of 580 rare plant species. While most plant species occur in the Tropics, the United States has 3000 species that are threatened in some way, and perhaps 700 of these species are in danger of going extinct within 5–10 years. More than 450 of the threatened species are now being grown in cultivation in these botanical gardens. Their ultimate goal is the reintroduction of these species into the wild.

The Botanical Gardens Conservation Secretariat (BGCS) of IUCN attempts to coordinate conservation efforts by the world's botanical gardens. Priorities of this program involve creating a worldwide database to coordinate collecting activity and identify important species that are underrepresented or absent from living collections. Most botanical gardens are located in the temperate zone, even though most of the world's plant species are found in the Tropics. A number of major gardens do exist in places such as Singapore, Sri Lanka, Java, and Colombia, but establishing new botanical gardens in the tropics should be a priority for the international community, along with training local plant taxonomists, geneticists, and horticulturalists to fill staff positions.

SEED BANKS   Botanical gardens and research institutes have developed seed banks—collections of seeds from the wild and from cultivated plants. Seed banks have generally focused on the approximately 100 plant species that make up over 90% of human food consumption, but they are devoting more and more attention to a wider range of species that may be threatened with extinction or loss of genetic variability.

As mentioned above, seeds of most plant species can be stored in cold, dry conditions in seed banks for long periods of time and then later germinated to produce new plants (Figure 14.9) (Linington and Pritchard 2001). At low temperatures, a seed's metabolism slows down and the food reserves of the embryo are maintained. This property makes seeds extremely well-suited to ex situ conservation efforts since seeds of large numbers of rare species can be stored in a small space with minimal supervision and at a low cost. The U.S. Department of Agriculture (USDA) National Seed Storage Laboratory (NSSL) at Fort Collins, Colorado, stores some seeds in conditions as low as –196°C. The NSSL is part of the U.S. National Genetic Resource Program, which stores 450,000 seed samples from 8000 species. The Institute of Crop Germplasm in Beijing, China has over 300,000 seed collections. More than 50 other major seed banks exist in the world, many of them in developing countries, maintaining around 6 million seed samples (Maunder 2001). The focus of most of these facilities is on preserving the genetic variation needed for breeding purposes in crop species.

At present, somewhere between 10,000—20,000 wild plant species are represented in seed banks, less than 10% of the world's species. To deal with this collection gap, many botanical gardens have established seed banks to preserve genetic variation in wild species, particularly those in danger of extinction. These seed banks allow a greater range of genetic variation to be preserved than exists in their living collections. The most ambitious project is the Millennium Seed Bank Project of the Royal Botanic Gardens, Kew, which has a goal of conserving the seeds of 10% of the world's species by the year 2010. The particular focus of the collection will be on species from dry climates of the world and the flora of the United Kingdom. As of the year 2000, over 12,000 seed samples of 5000 species were in storage. Another project is a collaboration among the botanical gardens of Spain to provide a comprehensive seed bank for that country's plants. Seed banks are also expanding their collections

(A)

(B)

(C)

(D)

Figure 14.9 (A) The National Seed Storage Facility in Fort Collins, Colorado. (B) Seeds of many plant varieties are sorted, cataloged, and stored. Detailed labels describe the plant's characteristics and the place and date of collection. (C) At the National Seed Storage Facility, some seeds are stored in hermetically sealed packets at –20°C. (D) Seeds are also stored in liquid nitrogen at –196°C. (Photographs courtesy of the U.S. Department of Agriculture.)

to include the pollen of seed plants and the spores of ferns, mosses, fungi, and microorganisms.

While seed banks have great potential for conserving species, they are limited by certain problems (Hamilton 1994). If power supplies fail or equipment breaks down, an entire frozen collection may be damaged. Even seeds in storage gradually lose their ability to germinate, after energetic reserves are exhausted and harmful mutations are accumulated. Old seed supplies simply may not germinate. To overcome the gradual deterioration of quality, samples must be regenerated periodically by germinating seeds, growing new plants to maturity, controlling pollination, and storing new samples. The testing and rejuvenation of seed samples can be a formidable task for seed banks with large collections. Renewing seed vigor in species that have large individual plants and delayed maturity, such as trees, may be extremely expensive and time-consuming.

Approximately 10% of the world's plant species have recalcitrant seeds that either lack dormancy or do not tolerate low-temperature storage conditions and consequently cannot be stored in seed banks. Seeds of these species must germinate right away or die. Species with recalcitrant seeds are much more common in tropical forests than in the temperate zone, and the seeds of many economically important tropical fruit trees, timber trees, and plantation crops such as cocoa and rubber cannot be stored. Intensive investigations are underway to find ways of storing recalcitrant seeds; one possibility may be storing just the embryo from inside the seed, or the young seedling. (Figure 14.10). One of the few ways to preserve genetic variation in these species is to establish special

Figure 14.10 Cereal seedlings are checked for quality prior to their long-term cold storage. (Photograph courtesy of the U.S. Department of Agriculture.)

botanical gardens, known as **clonal repositories,** or clonal orchards, which require considerable area and expense. In the past, root crops such as cassava (manioc), yams, and sweet potatoes have not been well represented in seed banks because they often do not form seeds. Genetic variation in these species is being preserved by vegetative propagation in special gardens such as the International Potato Centre in Peru and the International Center for Tropical Agriculture in Colombia. This undertaking is crucial, as these root crops are very important in the diet of people in developing tropical countries. An alternative method of conserving this genetic variability involves the in situ preservation of traditional agricultural practices (see Chapter 20).

AGRICULTURAL SEED BANKS   Seed banks have been embraced by agricultural research institutes and the agricultural industry as an effective resource for preserving and using the genetic variability that exists in agricultural crops. Often resistance to particular diseases and pests is found in only one variety of a crop, known as a **landrace,** that is grown in only one small area of the world. Genetic variability is crucial to the agricultural industry's interest in maintaining and increasing the high productivity of modern crops and their ability to respond to changing environmental conditions such as acid rain, global climate change, and soil erosion. Researchers are in a race against time to preserve genetic variability because traditional farmers throughout the world are abandoning their diverse local crop varieties in favor of standard, high-yielding varieties (Altieri and Anderson 1992) (Box 22). This worldwide phenomenon is illustrated by Sri Lankan farmers, who grew 2000 varieties of rice until the late 1950s, when they switched over to five high-yielding varieties (Rhoades 1991). Agricultural researchers have been combing the world for landraces of major food crops that can be stored and later hybridized with modern varieties in crop improvement programs. Many of the major food crops such as wheat, maize (corn), oats, potatoes, soybeans, and other legumes are well represented in seed banks, and other important crops such as rice, millet, and sorghum are being intensively collected (Plucknett et al. 1987).

To better understand the value of agricultural seed banks, consider the following classic example. Rice crops in Africa were being devastated by a virus called grassy stunt virus strain 1. To find a solution to this problem, agricultural researchers grew wild and cultivated rice plants from thousands of seed samples obtained from collections around the world (Lin and Yuan 1980). One seed sample of wild rice from Gonda, Uttar Pradesh, India, was found to contain a gene for disease resistance. These wild plants were immediately incorporated into a major breeding program to transfer the gene for virus resistance into high-yielding varieties of rice. If the sample of wild rice had not been collected or had died out before being discovered, the future of rice cultivation in Africa would have been uncertain.

BOX 22 *Seed Savers and Crop Varieties*

Preserving genetic diversity is a major concern for conservation biologists, with good reason: Even among populations that seem healthy, low genetic diversity can leave a population vulnerable to disease, which can wreak potentially disastrous consequences for a threatened species. Many common crop plants, including the fruits and vegetables that most people eat regularly, are potentially threatened by low genetic diversity. The reason for this is simple: Commercial farming tends to emphasize a few varieties that have high yield and appeal to consumer preferences for flavor, shape, size, and color. As such, many unique varieties of common crops have been ignored and are now relatively uncommon, even rare. Some varieties might have died out altogether, if not for the activities of ordinary gardeners and plant breeders belonging to a small Iowa-based organization, founded in 1975, called Seed Savers Exchange (SSE).

SSE concentrates on preserving many little-known "heirloom" varieties of crop plants that were brought to North America by immigrants. SSE accomplishes this task in an ingenious yet simple way: it makes these varieties available to individual gardeners and plant breeders—hobbyists who garden for their own pleasure or benefit, as well as various university agricultural programs and historic preservation societies—through newsletters and catalogs. In the 20 years of its existence, SSE has organized a group of some 1000 individual gardeners and plant breeders responsible for preserving over 12,000 different varieties of crop plants, which are offered in the SSE catalog to other interested gardeners. More than 65% of these varieties are offered by only one grower, which shows just how unusual many of these varieties have become (Cherfas 1996).

Many of these plants have long and fascinating histories, particularly the heirloom plants that can be traced back for centuries—even millennia—in their native habitat. Some are still linked to ongoing cultural traditions: Peruvian farmers in isolated Andean villages, for example, grow varieties of potatoes that may have been handed down from generation to generation since pre-Columbian times, yet remain completely unknown in nearby regions. Other plants may be interesting to look at, have medicinal properties, or be unusually colorful or flavorful. These reasons alone are sufficient rationale for most gardeners to obtain these varieties. For many gardeners, the opportunity to grow rare, unusual, and interesting plants is one of the great pleasures of gardening, and SSE is an excellent source of such plants.

SSE works on a unique system: Members pay a nominal fee in exchange for a catalog that describes the varieties available and provides the names of growers who will supply seeds. SSE founders Kent and Diane Whealy run a farm in Iowa (appropriately called Heritage Farm) at which all of the different varieties available are grown. They have enlisted amateur and professional growers to act as curators for specific crops. These growers may produce hundreds of varieties of crops—melons, tomatoes, beans, or peppers, for example—for their own use, but they are specifically responsible for maintaining a smaller number of individual varieties and supplying seeds to others. To assure that no crop is left out because of habitat or climate limitations, growers are located in different parts of the United States and in different climatic zones.

SSE makes a phenomenal number of interesting and unique plants available to ordinary gardeners. One curator in Iowa offers almost 200 different types of squash and 53 varieties of watermelon. And for those growers seeking a particular variety—perhaps one they remember from childhood, but for which they have no name—the "Plant Finder Service," appearing annually in the *Seed Savers Harvest Edition,* publishes growers' descriptions of the plants they want and appeals to the general membership for help finding them. In the near future, even more information will be made available through a television program planned for PBS called *Seed Time,* which will focus on heirloom plants.

BOX 22 *(continued)*

The SSE produces the Garden Seed Inventory, an inventory of 245 seed catalogs and 6483 vegetable varieties. The headquarters of SSE is the Heritage Farm in Iowa, where many unusual and hard-to-find vegetable varieties are grown. The screen boxes enclose particular varieties and prevent cross-pollination between varieties.

The loss of the heirloom varieties that SSE hopes to protect could have serious consequences for the long-term sustainability of agriculture worldwide. As more and more acreage is devoted to a few common varieties of crops, the genetic diversity of crop species declines, and, as has been observed many times in populations of threatened animal and plant species suffering from poor genetic diversity, devastating bouts of disease or attacks by pests become an even more serious risk. The Irish potato famine of 1845 to 1846, in which more than a million people starved to death, was the result of a blight on the all-important potato crop, most of which was composed of a single variety. Had potato farmers used even 1% of the more than 2000 potato varieties available, it is possible that a few varieties would have proven resistant to the disease, which might have alleviated (if not averted) some of the human suffering.

Despite the fact that all societies are dependent on agriculture, few of the wealthy industrial nations put significant resources into in-

BOX 22   *(continued)*

vestigating the traits of the less-common strains of ordinary crop plants. The U.S.D.A., for example, operates its National Seed Storage Laboratory (NSSL) on an annual budget of around $30 million—meager by government standards, so little that it is not included as a separate line item when the budget is reviewed by Congress. NSSL is so underfunded and ignored that it is likely to fail in its most important mission: preserving and cataloging the thousands of known varieties of crop plants and their wild relatives. The likelihood of failure increases as time passes for one simple reason: As seeds grow older, they lose their viability and die. Many of the seeds in the collection are 20–40 years old, which means that as many as half of them might already have lost their viability, thus the unique genetic makeup of those seeds is irretrievably lost. The only way to avoid seed deterioration is to periodically germinate and multiply the varieties, but low funding ensures that the enormous task of maintaining all varieties is physically impossible because of the small NSSL staff. This could have serious consequences: for example, researchers seeking strains of wheat resistant to the Russian aphid, an introduced pest, had to sort through 10,000 varieties of wheat and related cereals stored in the

NSSL to find 30 resistant varieties, a task that took five years (and had a success rate of less than 0.3%). Had they waited a few years longer to begin the search, it is entirely possible that their rate of success would have been even lower as the older seeds lost their viability. Who can say what important traits may already have been lost?

Private organizations such as the SSE—which recently went international in an attempt to preserve heirloom plants all over the world, especially in Eastern Europe—have filled in the gap to an extent. Turning the garden hobbyist's enthusiasm into a tool for conservation, this organization has managed to spread the word to an attentive worldwide audience of gardeners, breeders, and agricultural research and teaching institutions. Nevertheless, loss of crop varieties is a serious threat to world food supplies and should be recognized and addressed by world food organizations such as the United Nations Food and Agriculture Organization, as well as by governments' agricultural departments and ministries. For all their valiant efforts, organizations such as Seed Savers Exchange/Seed Savers International have merely plugged the hole in the dike; unless the rest of the global village comes to their rescue, they will be unable to stop impending disaster.

Despite their obvious successes in collecting and storing material, agricultural seed banks have several important limitations. Collections are often poorly documented regarding the locality of collection and growing conditions. Many of the seeds are of unknown quality and may not germinate. Crops of regional significance as well as medicinal plants, fiber plants, and other useful plants are not as well represented, even though these are economically significant to tropical countries.

Wild relatives of crop species are one of the most important sources of genetic variation for use in breeding programs. For example, more than 20 wild species of potatoes have been used in the development of modern potato varieties. However, only about 2% of the collections in agricultural seed banks come from wild relatives of crop plants (Hoyt 1988). Only the wild relatives of wheat and potatoes are well represented in seed banks. The majority of wild relatives for major crops such as rice and cassava still remain to be adequately collected.

Seed banks are coordinated by the Consultative Group on International Agricultural Research (CGIAR) and the International Board for Plant Genetic Resources (IBPGR) (Fuccilo et al. 1998; Linington and Pritchard 2001). One of the largest seed banks in the world, with around 80,000 separate collections of rice seeds, is maintained by the International Rice Research Institute (IRRI), an organization instrumental in the development of high-yielding, Green Revolution crop varieties. Other specialized seed collections are held by the International Maize and Wheat Improvement Center (Centro Internacional de Mejoramiento de Maiz y Trigo, or CIMMYT) in Mexico, which holds 12,000 samples of maize and 100,000 samples of wheat, and by the Plant Genetic Resources Unit at the National Germplasm Repository in Geneva, New York.

A major controversy in the development of agricultural seed banks is who owns and controls the genetic resources of crops (Brush and Stabinsky 1996). The genes of local landraces of crop plants and wild relatives of crop species represent the building blocks needed to develop elite, high-yielding varieties suitable for modern agriculture. Approximately 96% of the raw genetic variation necessary for modern agriculture comes from developing countries such as India, Ethiopia, Peru, Mexico, Indonesia, and China, yet the corporate breeding programs for elite strains frequently are located in the industrialized countries of North America and Europe (Figure 14.11). In the past, genetic material was perceived as free for the taking: The staffs of international seed banks freely collected seeds and plant tissue from developing countries and gave them to research stations and seed companies. Seed companies then developed new strains through sophisticated breeding programs and field trials and sold their seeds at high prices to maximize profits that often totaled hundreds of millions of dollars a year, but the countries from which the original seeds were collected saw no profit from this activity.

Developing countries now argue that this practice is inequitable and possibly a holdover of a "colonial mentality" in which "dependent nations are robbed of diversity" (Goldstein in Shulman 1986). These countries question why they should share their genetic resources freely if they will have to pay for new seed varieties based on those genetic resources. In fact, all countries of the world benefit from the free exchange of genetic resources. The modern varieties developed by international breeding centers and now grown throughout the world have the best qualities of the landraces that were originally found in many different countries. Many countries contribute genetic resources to international breeding efforts, but they also receive benefits in terms of higher agricultural productivity. Indeed, two-thirds of the agriculture of developing countries is grown in crops that were first domesticated in other regions of the world.

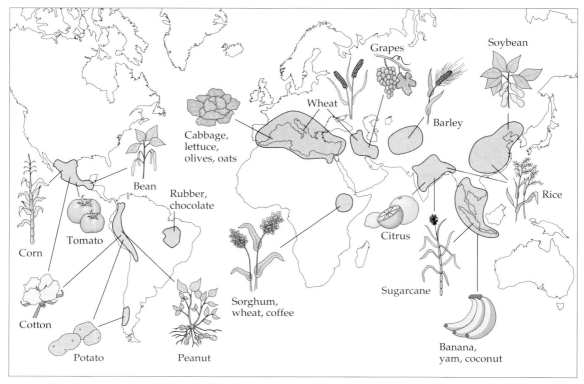

Figure 14.11 Crop species show high genetic diversity in certain areas of the world. These areas are often where the species was first domesticated or where the species is still grown in traditional agricultural settings. (Courtesy of Garrison Wilkes.)

In 1993, a group of countries drew up the Convention on Biological Diversity in an effort to provide a fair way of dealing with the situation. The Convention, signed by 170 countries, sets forth a general framework for sharing the financial benefits of genetic resources more fairly and gives incentives for countries that preserve biological diversity. Among the important policy recommendations of the Convention are the following:

- Countries have the right to control access to their biological diversity and should be paid for its use.
- Countries have a responsibility to inventory their biological diversity and protect it.
- Collectors must have permission to collect samples from the host country, the local community, and the land owners.
- As much as possible, research, breeding, processing, and production of new varieties should take place in the countries where the biological resources occur.

- The financial benefits, new products, and new varieties should be shared fairly with countries that contributed genetic resources used in the final product.

Many countries, international agencies, conservation organizations, and corporations are presently developing the financial and legal mechanisms to carry out the provisions of the Convention. Disagreements among these groups have been difficult to resolve, which has impeded implementation of the Convention. However, a few contracts have been negotiated, such as the one between the Costa Rican government and the Merck Company for the development of products based on species collected in the wild (see Chapter 4), and these will be followed carefully to determine if they are mutually satisfactory and to see if they can serve as models for future contracts.

SEED SAMPLING STRATEGIES   Botanical gardens and institutes are increasingly developing seed banks in addition to their collections of living plants. Strategies for collecting seeds from endangered and rare wild plants for storage in seed banks are influenced by the distribution of genetic variability because species that are genetically variable may require more extensive sampling to acquire most of their alleles than species that are more genetically uniform. Genetic variability includes the percentage of genes that are variable as well as the number of alleles per polymorphic gene (see Chapter 2). The most extensive information on genetic variation in plants comes from accumulated studies of allozyme variation in more than 400 species (Hamrick et al. 1991). These studies show that the most important factor in determining the total amount of genetic variation in a plant species is the geographical range of the species; widespread species have more than twice as much genetic variation as species of restricted range. Also, plant species have, on average, 78% of their genetic variability within populations and 22% of their variability among populations, though many species differ from these average values depending on their reproductive system and morphology. These data suggest strategies for protecting the gene pool of rare and endangered species by both in situ protection of carefully selected populations and a well-planned collection program for ex situ preservation.
   Using information on patterns of genetic variation, the Center for Plant Conservation (1991) has developed a list of five seed-sampling guidelines for conserving the genetic variability of endangered plant species. These guidelines could be modified for other groups of species such as animals, fungi, and microorganisms:

1. The highest priority for collecting should be species that (a) are in danger of extinction—that is, species showing a rapid decline in number of individuals or number of populations; (b) are evolutionarily or taxonomically unique; (c) can be reintroduced into the wild; (d) have

the potential to be preserved in ex situ situations; (e) have potential economic value for agriculture, medicine, forestry, or industry.

2. Samples should be collected from up to five populations per species to ensure a sampling of the genetic variability contained among populations. Where possible, populations should be selected to cover the geographical and environmental range of the species. For the 70% of endangered species that have five or fewer populations, all populations should be sampled.

3. Samples should be collected from 10–50 individuals per population. Sampling fewer than 10 individuals may miss alleles that are common in the population; sampling more than 50 may not result in enough new alleles to justify the effort. In general, sample sizes should be at the high end of the range when the population appears to be phenotypically variable, the site is heterogeneous, and the plants are outcrossing.

4. The number of seeds (or cuttings, bulbs, etc.) collected per plant is determined by the viability of the species' seeds. If seed viability is high, then only a few seeds need to be collected per individual; if seed viability is low, then many seeds per individual have to be collected.

5. If individual plants of a species have a low reproductive output, collecting many seeds in one year may have a negative effect on the sampled populations. This is particularly true for annuals and other short-lived plants. In these cases, a better strategy would be to spread the collecting over several years.

The CPC (1991) concludes:

Conservation collections are only as good as the diversity that they contain. Thus the forethought and methods that go into sampling procedures play a critical role in determining the ultimate quality of the collection, as well as its usability for purposes such as reintroduction and restoration. In the long run, the real significance of collections in biological conservation is their role in reinforcing the management and maintenance of natural populations. Collectors should view themselves not as 'preserving' static entities, but as providing a stepping-stone on the pathway to survival and evolution.

CONSERVING THE GENETIC RESOURCES OF TREES   Forestry is a huge, global industry that depends on the genetic variation found in trees for its long-term success (Ledig 1988; Rogers and Ledig 1996). Protecting the genetic variation found in forest trees requires a variety of in situ and ex situ methods. As with crop plants, trees are genetically variable, with each population often adapted to local conditions of climate, soil, and pests (Figure 14.12). Seeds collected from one geographic area and planted elsewhere under different environmental conditions may not develop into vigorously growing trees. The success of a forestry program depends

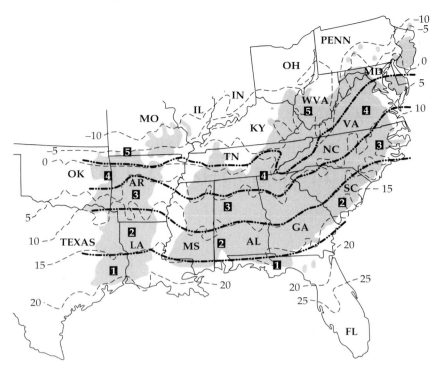

Figure 14.12 Five seed zones based on climate have been established for the shortleaf pine (*Pinus echinata*); seed zone boundaries are shown with heavy dashed lines. New tree plantations should be established using seeds from the same seed zone in order to have the best growth. The lighter dashed lines are minimum-temperature isotherms, which define areas with the same minimum temperatures (given in °F); for example, in typical winters the temperature in southern Florida does not drop below 25°F. (From Rogers and Ledig 1996.)

on establishing tree plantations from a good sample of seeds obtained from a suitable geographic location. For example, a plantation in a wet mountainous area requires seeds obtained from trees adapted to those conditions rather than to a dry, lowland site. The results of seed selection may not be known till years or decades later when a poor initial seed sample results in slow-growing, misshapen, disease-ridden trees with poor wood quality. Relying on wild-collected seeds for establishing plantations has its drawbacks because selective logging often removes the superior trees and leaves the inferior ones behind.

To conserve genetic variation in tree species, foresters have used cuttings and families of closely related seeds to establish plantations of superior genetic varieties, called **clone banks,** for long-term maintenance and research of commercially important tree species (Ledig 1988). For loblolly pine (*Pinus taeda*) alone, 8000 clones are being grown in clone banks in the southeastern United States. Selected trees are used to establish seed orchards for producing commercial seed. Storage of seeds is difficult for many important genera of trees such as oaks (*Quercus*) and poplars (*Populus*). Even pine seeds cannot be stored indefinitely and must eventually be grown as trees.

Preserving areas where commercial tree species occur naturally is an important way to protect genetic variability. International cooperation is needed in forestry research and conservation because commercial species are often grown far from their countries of origin. For example, loblolly pine (*Pinus taeda*) and Monterey pine (*Pinus radiata*) from North America are planted on 5.8 million ha of land outside that continent. In New Zealand 1.3 million ha are planted in Monterey pine, making it a key element in the national economy. In Hungary, 19% of the forested area is planted in North American shipmast locust (*Robinia pseudoacacia* var. *rectissima*), because the species produces durable wood and grows on degraded, low-nutrient sites. These forest plantations far from home still depend on natural populations of the species to supply the genetic variability required for continued improvements and survival in a hostile environment.

Conclusion

As more of the environment is dominated by human activities, ex situ preservation is playing an ever-greater role in protecting genetic variation and species. Species maintained in captivity and in cultivation are used with greater frequency in reintroduction projects and in restoring damaged ecosystems. Although ex situ programs are expensive, they do generate income—through the display of species in zoos, genetic improvements in domesticated species, and new products developed by the biotech and medical industries. Some of this income needs to be used to support the protection of biodiversity in the wild by funding the creation and management of protected areas, which is the topic of Part Five.

Summary

1. Some species that are in danger of going extinct in the wild can be maintained in artificial conditions under human supervision; this is known as ex situ, or off-site, preservation. These captive colonies can be used later to reestablish species in the wild.

2. Zoos are developing self-maintaining populations of many rare vertebrates, often using modern techniques of veterinary medicine to increase their reproductive rates. Currently zoos maintain approximately 280,000 individuals of 7000 species and subspecies, most of which were born in captivity. Collections are also being maintained of endangered breeds of domestic animals.

3. Marine mammalogists, ichthyologists, and coral reef experts who work for public aquariums are using breeding techniques and conservation pro-

grams for the protection of endangered fishes, marine mammals, and aquatic invertebrates.

4. The world's 1500 botanical gardens and arboretums now make it one of their main priorities to collect and grow rare and endangered species. The seeds of most species of plants can be stored for long periods of time under cold conditions in seed banks. Seed banks often specialize in the collection of major crop species, commercial timber species, and their close relatives in order to preserve material for genetic improvement programs.

For Discussion

1. What are the similarities and differences among the ex situ conservation methods used for plants, terrestrial animals, and aquatic species?

2. Would biological diversity be adequately protected if every species were raised in captivity? Is this possible? Practical? How would freezing a tissue sample of every species help to protect biological diversity? Again, is this possible and is it practical?

3. Are the arguments for preserving the genetic variability in domesticated species of animals and plants (and their close relatives) the same arguments we would put forward for saving endangered wild species?

4. How much of an ex situ conservation facility's resources should be devoted for conservation efforts in order for the institution to announce that it is involved in conservation? What sorts of conservation activities are appropriate for each institution? Visit such an institution and evaluate it for its conservation activities and efforts; use or modify some of the methods of Balmford et al. 1996.

Suggested Readings

Balmford, A., G. M. Mace, and N. Leader-Williams. 1996. Designing the Ark: Setting priorities for captive breeding. *Conservation Biology* 10: 719–727. Zoos should focus more on smaller-bodied species that breed well in captivity and are cheaper to maintain.

Brush, S. B. and D. Stabinsky (eds.). 1996. *Valuing Local Knowledge: Indigenous People and Intellectual Property Rights*. Island Press, Washington, D.C. Case studies of how local people can gain economic benefits from the species they know and protect.

Conway, W. G., M. Hutchins, M. Souza, Y. Kapentanakos, and E. Paul. 2001. *The AZA Field Conservation Resource Guide*. Zoo Atlanta, Atlanta, Georgia. Information on hundreds of projects supported or directed by zoo and aquarium personnel.

Frankel, O., A. Brown, and J. Burdon. 1995. *The Conservation of Plants*. Cambridge University Press, Cambridge. A comprehensive advanced treatment.

Fuccilo, D., L. Sears, and P. Stapleton. 1998. *Biodiversity in Trust: Conservation and Use of Plant Genetic Resources in CGIAR Centres*. Cambridge University Press, New York. A major international effort is being made to coordinate the conservation of plant genetic resources.

Given, D. R. 1995. *Principles and Practice of Plant Conservation*. Timber Press, Portland, OR. Good summary of plant conservation approaches.

Hancocks, D. 2001. *A Different Nature: The Paradoxical World of Zoos and their Uncertain Future*. University of California Press. Berkeley, CA. Criticism of traditional zoos, and a vision of zoos that are better for animals, people, and conservation.

Kleiman, D. G., M. E. Allen, K. V. Thompson, and S. Lumpkin. 1996. *Wild Mammals in Captivity: Principles and Techniques.* University of Chicago Press, Chicago. Leading experts give current information on a range of issues facing zoos.

Lanza, R. P., B. L. Dresser, and P. Damiani. 2000. Cloning Noah's Ark. *Scientific American* 283 (5): 84–89. Biotechnology might be an effective way to propagate certain rare species, but is it really the answer to the problem?

Linington, S. and H. Pritchard. 2001. Gene banks. In *Encyclopedia of Biodiversity*, S. A. Levin (ed.), Vol. 3, pp. 165–182. Academic Press, San Diego, CA. Overview of methods and principles of seed banks and collections of microorganisms.

Lyles, A. M. 2001. Zoos and zoological parks. In *Encyclopedia of Biodiversity*, S. A. Levin (ed.), Vol. 5, pp. 901–912. Academic Press, San Diego, CA. Explores the rise of the new zoo, which focuses on conservation.

Maunder, M. 2001. Plant conservation, overview. In *Encyclopedia of Biodiversity*, S. A. Levin (ed.), Vol. 4, pp. 645–658. Academic Press, San Diego, CA. Describes the importance of botanical gardens in plant conservation.

Norton, B. G., M. Hutchins, E. F. Stevens, and T. L. Maple. 1995. *Ethics on the Ark: Zoos, Animal Welfare, and Wildlife Conservation.* Smithsonian Institution Press, Washington, D.C. Vigorous examination of the ethical issues confronting modern zoos.

Philippart, J. C. 1995. Is captive breeding an effective solution for the preservation of endemic species? *Biological Conservation* 72: 281–295. Focus on rare and endangered fish species.

Rhoades, R. E. 1991. World's food supply at risk. *National Geographic* 179 (April): 74–105. A beautifully illustrated popular account of the decline of traditional agricultural varieties and the need for seed banks.

Ryder, O. A., A. McLaren, S. Brenner, Y. P. Zhang, and K. Benirschke. 2000. DNA banks for endangered animal species. *Science* 288: 275. Frozen tissue samples are presented as an alternative conservation strategy.

Snyder, N. F., S. R. Derrickson, S. R. Beissinger, J. W. Wiley, et al. 1996. Limitations of captive breeding in endangered species recovery. *Conservation Biology* 10: 338–348. Captive breeding programs should be initiated only if a species cannot survive in the wild without them.

Tarpy, C. 1993. Zoos: Taking down the bars. *National Geographic* 184 (July): 2–37. A great article on the new role of zoos in animal species conservation.

PART V

Practical Applications

Chapter

15

Establishing Protected Areas

rotecting habitats that contain healthy, intact biological communities is the most effective way to conserve
biological diversity. One could argue that it is ultimately the only way, because we have the resources and
knowledge to maintain only a small minority of the world's
species in captivity. In this chapter we will discuss the critical
first step in protecting biological communities—establishing
legally designated protected areas governed by laws and rules
that allow widely varying degrees of commercial resource
use, traditional use by local people, and recreational use
(Bruner et al. 2001). We'll begin our discussion by examining
existing protected areas and then will explore the steps involved in creating new ones.

The momentum to establish protected areas has been
increasing throughout the twentieth century and reached its
peak in the 1970s (Figure 15.1). The drop-off during the
1980s reflects the lack of political will on the part of citizens
and governments to designate more protected areas and the
perception that enough land has already been protected.
Protected areas will never cover a large percentage of the
Earth's surface—perhaps they will cover 10–15%, or slightly

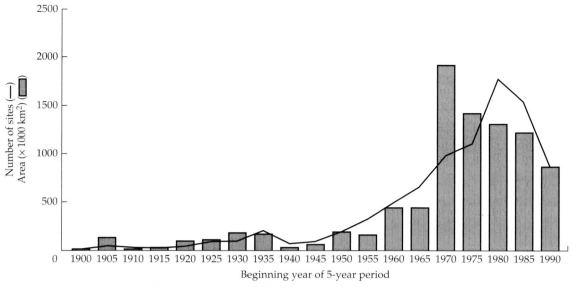

Figure 15.1 The solid line graphs the number of new protected areas worldwide since 1900 ; the bars indicate the area encompassed in new protected areas (in km^2) at 5-year intervals. (After McNeeley et al. 1994.)

more—because of the perceived needs of human society for natural resources. This limited area of protected habitat emphasizes the biological significance of the 10–20% of the land that is managed for resource production, described in greater detail in Chapter 18.

Existing Protected Areas

At least 160 countries—and perhaps more—currently have protected areas. Among the countries without protected areas as of the year 2000 are Syria, Yemen, Equatorial Guinea, and Guinea-Bissau. While it could be argued that all countries should have at least one national park, large countries with rich biotas and a variety of ecosystem types would obviously benefit from having many protected areas. As of 1998, around 10,706 IUCN protected areas (categories I–III; see the description on page 435 of this chapter) had been designated worldwide, covering some 6 million km^2, with an additional 47,097 partially protected areas (IUCN categories IV–VI) covering 7 million km^2* (Davey 1998). Although this total of 13 million km^2 may seem impressive, it represents only about 9% of the Earth's total

---

*Uncertainty about the number and size of protected areas stems from the different standards used throughout the world and the degree of protection actually given to a designated area.

land surface. Also, the world's largest park is in Greenland and covers 970,000 km^2, accounting for about 7% of the global area protected. Only 4% of the Earth's surface is *strictly protected* in scientific reserves and national parks. The measurements of protected areas in individual countries and on continents are only approximate because sometimes the laws protecting national parks and wildlife sanctuaries are not actually enforced, and sometimes sections of managed areas, which are not technically protected, are carefully protected in practice. Examples of the latter are the sections within U.S. national forests designated as wilderness areas. The coverage of protected areas varies dramatically among countries: There are high proportions of land protection in Germany (25%), Austria (25%), and the United Kingdom (19%), and surprisingly low proportions in Russia (1.2%), Greece (0.8%), and Turkey (0.3%).

Marine conservation has lagged behind terrestrial conservation efforts; even establishing priorities has proved difficult (Agardy 1997, 1999). Currently only 1% of the marine environment is included in protected areas, yet 20% of it needs to be protected in order to manage declining commercial fishing stocks (Costanza et al. 1998). Over 1300 marine and coastal protected areas have been established worldwide, protecting about 800,000 km^2 (Agardy 1997). Accounting for half of the total are the three largest marine protected areas: the Great Barrier Reef Marine Park in Australia, the Galápagos Marine Park, and the Netherlands' North Sea Reserve. About one-fourth of the 300 internationally recognized biosphere reserves includes coastal or estuarine habitats (Ray and Gregg 1991). Unfortunately, many of these reserves only exist on the map and receive little protection from overharvesting and pollution.

In the United States, only 12 marine sanctuaries have been designated, covering 46,548 km^2, in contrast to the 906 national forests, national parks, and wildlife refuges that total 1,657,084 km^2 (Lindholm and Barr 2001). Efforts to protect marine biological diversity have been hindered by the difficulty of identifying distinct biological communities and by the widespread migration and dispersal of marine species. In addition, opposition from fishing interests, the widespread impact of marine pollution, the difficulties of concluding international agreements, and the problems of policing large areas have also slowed efforts to establish effective marine reserves. Regulating the harvesting of fish that migrate in international waters has proven to be very difficult, and water pollution can damage extensive coastal areas and enclosed seas. These problems need to be seriously addressed (Norse 1993): The conservation community has identified marine conservation as a high priority, and urgent efforts are currently underway to protect marine biological diversity by establishing marine parks that seek to protect the nursery grounds of commercial species and maintain high-quality areas for recreational activities such as diving, swimming, and fishing. One approach to establishing marine protected areas involves protecting examples of each type of marine community. Determining biogeographical provinces for the marine environment is much more difficult than for the terrestrial environment because boundaries between realms are less sharp, dispersal of larval and adult stages is more widespread, and the marine environment is less well known (Grassle 1991). Marine biogeographical provinces are being identified using a combination of the distribution of related marine animals (coastal, shelf, ocean) as well as physical properties that affect ecology and distribution (currents, temperature). Urgent efforts are being made throughout the world to protect marine biological diversity in each one of these biogeographical provinces by establishing marine parks comparable to terrestrial parks (Kenchington and Agardy 1990). One such example is the Hol Chan Marine Reserve in Belize, which is proving invaluable to the rapidly growing ecotourism industry. The El Nido Marine Reserve along the coast of Palawan Island in the Philippines provides protection for the sea cow (also called the dugong), the hawksbill sea turtle, and the Ridley sea turtle.

Creating New Protected Areas

Protected areas can be established in a variety of ways, but the common mechanisms are: (1) by government action (usually at a national level, but often on regional or local levels as well); (2) through purchases of land by private individuals and conservation organizations such as the Audubon Society and The Nature Conservancy (Box 23); (3) via the established customs of indigenous people; and (4) through the development of biological field stations (which combine biodiversity protection and research with conservation education) by many universities and other research organizations.

While legislation and land purchases alone do not ensure habitat preservation, they lay the groundwork for it. Partnerships among governments of developing countries in the Tropics, international conservation organizations, multinational banks, and the governments of developed countries bring together funding, training, and scientific and management expertise to help establish new protected areas. Local people are often partners in these efforts (see Chapter 20). Traditional societies also have established protected areas to maintain their way of life or just to preserve their land. Many of these protected areas have been in existence for long periods and are linked to the religious beliefs of the people. National governments in many countries, including the United States, Canada, Colombia, Brazil, Australia, and Malaysia, have recognized the rights of traditional societies to own and manage the land on which they live, hunt, and farm, although in some cases recognition of land rights only results following conflict in the courts, in the press, and on the land.

BOX 23 *Ecologists and Real Estate Experts Mingle at The Nature Conservancy*

For nearly a century, nonprofit organizations such as the Sierra Club and the Audubon Society have sought to encourage the conservation of wild species and habitats. The number of these organizations has increased in recent decades at the local, national, and international levels. Of the many organizations that now fight to protect biological diversity, The Nature Conservancy (TNC) is set apart by a unique approach that applies the methods of private business to accomplish the conservation of rare species and habitats. Simply put, TNC either buys threatened habitat outright or shows landowners how managing their land for conservation can be as profitable as developing it.

Founded in 1951, TNC now has approximately one million members. TNC is not as widely known as some conservation organizations, nor is it as vocal. TNC advocates a nonconfrontational, businesslike approach that contrasts with the methods of some high-profile, activist conservation groups such as Greenpeace and EarthFirst! (Grove 1988). Still, its methods have been quietly successful: In the United States alone, TNC has set aside more than 5 million ha, much of which has eventually become state or national parks or wildlife refuges. Outside the United States, 33 million ha have been protected with their help.

TNC maintains a fund of over $160 million, created from private and corporate donations, with which they can make direct land purchases when necessary. Through these methods, the organization has created the largest system of private natural areas and wildlife sanctuaries in the world (The Nature Conservancy 1996). One such outstanding property is the 14 ha of land surrounding the shoals at Pendleton Island on Virginia's Clinch River (Stolzenburg 1992). These 300 meters of shoals have 45 species of freshwater mussels and may be among the richest localities for mussels in the world. The decision of TNC in 1984 to buy this small piece of land and get involved in cleaning up the Clinch River represented an important step in recognizing the importance of aquatic invertebrates to overall biological diversity.

TNC's approach is creative; like other land-trust organizations, if TNC cannot purchase land outright for the protection of habitat, it offers alternatives to landowners that make conservation financially attractive. Such alternatives include tax benefits in exchange for accepting legal restrictions, or conservation easements to prevent development. In other cases,

Paul Todd of The Nature Conservancy (left) discusses the management of the Silver Creek Preserve in Idaho with neighboring rancher Bud Purdee. (Photograph © Martha Hodgkins-Green.)

BOX 23 *(continued)*

the landowner can donate the land to TNC and retain lifetime occupancy, which in essence permits the owner to have a rent- and mortgage-free home and to receive a sizable tax deduction as well. TNC also seeks methods that allow the preserves it owns to support themselves financially. The cost of maintaining one South Dakota prairie preserve is partially defrayed by maintaining a resident bison herd. Grazing by bison enhances biological diversity in these grasslands, provided the herd does not become too large; when the herd grows to a size at which overgrazing becomes a possibility, the excess animals are sold. The sale of bison brings roughly $25,000 annually to the preserve.

In addition, TNC supports and encourages efforts to identify populations of rare and endangered species and to manage biological diversity in the United States (The Nature Conservancy 1996). Often TNC sells at cost or donates land it has purchased to state governments or federal agencies that will protect the land. Some parcels of land are so valuable that they have been designated as national wildlife refuges by the government. TNC also promotes state-level conservation through Natural Heritage Programs in all 50 states, which

originated as joint ventures between TNC and state governments (Jenkins 1996). TNC provides training for Heritage staff to inventory plant and animal populations in each state. The data are collected and recorded in a computerized database located in each state and at NatureServe, a TNC-affiliated data center; with this database, TNC biologists can keep track of the status of species and populations throughout the nation. When Natural Heritage Program biologists identify populations of species that are rare, unique, declining, or threatened, state agencies and TNC will have the information to make wise decisions.

TNC is distinguished from other conservation organizations by its businesslike approach. It generally refuses to bring lawsuits against projects encroaching on the habitat of endangered species, preferring to provide financial incentives to promote conservation. But the Conservancy's businesslike approach is successful largely because developers, who too often have no great love for environmentalists, respect and understand TNC's methods. The fundamental principle of TNC is, in essence, "Land conservation through private action." So far, the idea has proved to be sound.

Creating new protected areas requires the following steps, which we'll examine in detail in the following sections:

1. Identifying those species and biological communities that are the highest priorities for conservation.
2. Determining those areas of the world that should be protected to meet conservation priorities.
3. Linking new conservation areas to existing conservation networks using techniques such as gap analysis.

Identifying Priorities for Protecting Biodiversity

In a crowded world with limited natural resources and limited government funding, it is crucial to establish priorities for conserving biological diversity. While some conservationists would argue that no biological community and the species that make it up should ever be lost, the reality is that numerous species are in danger of going extinct, and there are not enough resources available to save them all. The real challenge lies in finding ways to minimize the loss of biological diversity in an environment of limited financial and human resources. Conservation planners must address three interrelated questions (Johnson 1995): What needs to be protected? Where should it be protected? and How should it be protected? Three criteria can be used to answer these questions and set conservation priorities:

1. *Distinctiveness.* A biological community is given higher priority for conservation if it is composed primarily of rare endemic species than if it is composed primarily of common, widespread species. A species is often given more conservation value if it is taxonomically unique— that is, the only species in its genus or family—than if it is a member of a genus with many species (Faith 1994; Vane-Wright et al. 1994). Similarly, a unique population of a species having unusual genetic characteristics that distinguish it from other populations of the species might be a greater priority for conservation than a more typical population.

2. *Endangerment.* Species in danger of extinction are of greater concern than species that are not; thus, the whooping crane, with only about 155 individuals, requires more protection than the sandhill crane, with approximately 500,000 individuals. Biological communities threatened with imminent destruction are also given priority (such as the forests of West Africa, the wetland ecosystems of the southeastern United States; and biological communities within the United States with numerous restricted-range species of butterflies and birds in southern Florida, southern Texas, and coastal California [Abbitt et al. 2000]).

3. *Utility.* Species that have present or potential value to people are given more conservation priority than species of no obvious use to people. For example, wild relatives of wheat, which are potentially useful in developing new, improved cultivated varieties, are given greater priority than species of grass that are not known to be related to any economically important plant. Biological communities of major economic value, such as coastal wetlands, are usually given greater priority for protection than less valuable communities such as dry scrubland.

By applying these criteria, the Komodo dragon of Indonesia (Figure 15.2) is an example of a species that fits all three categories: it is the world's largest lizard (distinctive); it occurs on only a few small islands of a rapidly developing nation (endangered); and it has major potential as a tourist attraction in addition to being of great scientific interest (utility). Appropriately, these Indonesian islands are now protected within

Figure 15.2 The carnivorous Komodo dragon (*Varanus komodoensis*) of Indonesia is the largest living monitor lizard. Many tourists want to see these animals in the wild. Protecting this endangered species was an important reason for establishing the Komodo National Park. (Photograph by Jessie Cohen, National Zoological Park, Smithsonian Institution.)

the Komodo National Park. The Western Ghats, a series of hills paralleling the southwestern coast of India, contain tropical forests that are similarly a high priority for conservation: These forests contain many endemic species, including the ancestors of several cultivated species (distinctive); many of the products from theses forests are necessary to the well-being of local villagers (utility); the forests perform vital watershed services that prevent flooding and provide hydroelectric power for the region (utility); and despite their importance, these forests are threatened by logging; by fires set by villagers to create forage for their animals; by the collection of fuelwood and other forest products; and by continuing fragmentation by human activities (endangered).

Prioritization Systems

Using the three criteria, several prioritization systems have been developed at both national and international levels to target both species and communities. These approaches are generally complementary; they differ more in their emphases than in fundamental principles.

SPECIES APPROACHES   One approach to establishing conservation priorities involves protecting particular species and in doing so protecting an entire biological community. Protected areas are often established to protect individual species of special concern, such as rare species, endangered species, keystone species, and culturally significant species; species that provide the impetus to protect an area and biological community are known as **focal species** (Linnell et al. 2000). One type of focal species is an **indicator species,** a species that is associated with an endangered biological community or set of unique ecosystem processes, such as the endangered northern spotted owl in the U.S. Northwest (Figure 15.3) or the red-cockaded woodpecker in the U.S. Southeast. The goal is that managing a site for indicator species will protect the range of species and ecosystem processes with the same distribution (Schwartz 1999; Lawton and Gaston 2001); for example, by protecting the red-cockaded woodpecker, the last remaining stands of old-growth, longleaf pine forest in the southeastern U.S. will also be protected. Of course, research must be conducted to establish that the designated indicator species is

Figure 15.3 The northern spotted owl (*Strix occidentalis caurina*) is an indicator species for old-growth forests in the Pacific northwest, a habitat coveted for its rich timber sources. Protecting the owl protects many other species in the same habitat. (Photograph by Jon Mark Stewart/Biological Photo Service.)

consistently associated with the full range of species and ecosystem processes, and in many cases, it might be more effective to designate a group of indicator species to ensure the protection of a biological community (Lawton and Gaston 2001).

Another type of focal species is **flagship species,** often known as the "charismatic megafauna." Many national parks have been created to protect flagship species, which capture public attention, have symbolic value, and are crucial to ecotourism. In the process of protecting flagship and indicator species, whole communities that may consist of thousands of other species and their associated ecosystem processes are also protected. Flagship and indicator species, whose protection automatically extends protection to other species and the community, are therefore, known as "umbrella" species. For example, Project Tiger in India was begun in 1973 after a census revealed that the Indian tiger was in imminent danger of extinction. The establishment of 18 Project Tiger reserves, combined with strict protection measures, has halted the rapid decline in the number of tigers and in so doing has also protected many important and endangered biological communities (Ward 1992).

The species approach follows from developing survival plans for individual species, which also identifies areas of high conservation priority. In the Americas, the Natural Heritage Programs and Conservation Data Centers are collecting data on rare and endangered species from all 50 U.S. states, 9 Canadian provinces, and 14 Latin American countries (Jenkins 1996; Stein et al. 2000). This information is being used to target new localities for conservation where there are concentrations of endangered species or where the last populations of a declining species exist. Another important program is the IUCN Species Survival Commission Action Plans. Approximately 7000 scientists are organized in over 100 specialist groups to provide evaluations and recommendations for mammals, birds, invertebrates, reptiles, fishes, and plants.

APPROACHES USING BIOLOGICAL DIVERSITY INDICATORS   Certain organisms are used as **biological diversity indicators** when specific data about whole communities are unavailable (Brooks et al. 2001). Diversity in plants and birds, for example, are sometimes (but not always) good indicators of the diversity of a community (Ricketts et al. 1999). Several analyses have put this principle into practice. For example, Terborgh and Winter (1983) identified areas of Colombia and Ecuador that had the greatest concentrations of bird species and proposed that these areas be made into protected areas. In another case, analysis of existing databases revealed that the protection of sites with endangered plants in the United States also would protect many endangered animal species—on a relatively small amount of the total U.S. land area (Dobson et al. 1997).

This approach is now being expanded in a systematic way. The IUCN Plant Conservation Office in England is identifying and documenting about 250 global centers of plant diversity with large concentrations of species (WWF/IUCN 1997; WWF 2000). The International Council for Bird Protection (ICBP) is identifying Endemic Bird Areas (EBAs): localities with large concentrations of birds that have restricted ranges (Stattersfield et al. 1998). To date, 218 localities containing 2451 restricted-range bird species have been identified (Figure 15.4). Many of these localities are islands and isolated mountain ranges that also have many endemic species of lizards, butterflies, and plants, and thus represent priorities for conservation. Further analysis has highlighted EBAs that contain no protected areas and thus require urgent conservation measures.

Another innovative project uses the detailed bird census records from Britain to identify potential sites for new nature reserves (Williams et al. 1996). Using 170,098 documented breeding records of 218 species located within 2827 census grid cells (each 10 km × 10 km) that cover all of Britain, three possible reserve systems were analyzed for their ability to protect breeding sites for British birds; each network included only 5% of the grid cells—approximately 5% of Britain's land area. These three systems were created to: (1) protect "hot spots" of richness that contain the most species, (2) protect hot spots of rare species (narrowly distrib-

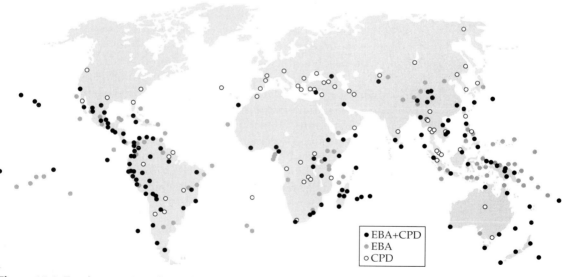

Figure 15.4 Two large projects have identified global centers of diversity. BirdLife International has identified Endemic Bird Areas (EBAs) that include concentrations of restricted-range species; and the Centers of Plant Diversity Project (CPD) has identified high concentrations of restricted-range plant species. There is considerable overlap between the areas of species concentration, with many of the sites found in tropical areas. Many EBAs are also found on islands, and CPDs are sometimes found in more temperate and Mediterranean climates. (From Stattersfield et al. 1998.)

uted endemics), and (3) protect sets of **complementary areas,** areas in which each new cell added to the set includes one or more additional species. The results of the analysis show that while selecting species hot spots results in the greatest number of bird species per grid cell, it misses 11% of Britain's rare bird species. In contrast, selecting for complementary areas protects all of the bird species and is probably the most effective conservation strategy. In addition to using birds, this approach could also be used to select new protected areas using mammals, plants, unique biological communities, or any other biodiversity component. The advantage of this approach is that each additional protected area adds to the total range of biological diversity protected (Balmford and Gaston 1999; Cabeza and Moilanen 2001). Despite their sophistication, such approaches are often regarded as impractical by land managers, who are preoccupied with nuts-and-bolts issues such as fund raising, public relations, and the development of management plans.

COMMUNITY AND ECOSYSTEM APPROACHES   A number of conservationists have argued that communities and ecosystems rather than species should be targeted for conservation (Grumbine 1994a; Harrop 1999). They claim that spending $1 million on habitat protection and the management of a self-maintaining ecosystem, for example, might preserve more species in the long run than spending the same amount of money on an intensive effort to save just one conspicuous species. Ecosystems benefit people by providing flood control, hydroelectric power, grazing for domestic animals, wood production, hunting and fishing, and recreation. Ecosystem conservation not only protects species as well as ecosystem services, it often is easy to demonstrate ecosystems' economic value to policy makers and the public.

Using this approach, new protected areas should try to ensure that representative sites of as many types of biological communities as possible are protected. A **representative site** includes the species and environmental conditions characteristic of the biological community. While no site is perfectly representative, biologists working in the field can identify suitable sites for protection.

National Priorities for Establishing Protected Areas

National governments are the most important force in establishing and managing protected areas today. The international conservation community can help to establish guidelines and find opportunities to protect biological diversity, but in the end national (and local) governments must determine their own priorities. Many countries are in the process of doing so or have recently prepared National Environmental Action Plans, National Biodiversity Action Plans, or Tropical Forest Action Plans.

The amount of money available to acquire and manage new national parks and protected areas is increasing substantially as a result of the creation of the Global Environment Facility (GEF) in 1991. The GEF provides around $500 million of new funding each year for environmental projects; approximately one-third of these funds are allocated for biodiversity projects. Large international conservation organizations are contributing additional funds and expertise. Conservation biologists can play a valuable role in the creation of new parks at the national level by using their field experience to identify and recommend new areas suitable for preservation.

Park management, a subject covered in detail in Chapters 17 and 18, is of central importance in ensuring that a protected area actually fulfills its goals and is not just a "paper park" that is soon destroyed and degraded. Furthermore, biological communities inside a protected area are not immune to outside forces such as hunting, pollution, poverty, and war, all of which may threaten their existence. In many cases, this means that if issues outside park boundaries are not addressed, biological diversity will continue to decline within protected areas.

Determining Which Areas Should Be Protected

The second major task in establishing protected areas is determining *which* areas to protect. It's obvious enough, but given the range of biological communities on Earth and the extent of human-caused habitat destruction, the task is daunting. Biological communities vary from the few that are virtually unaffected by human influence (such as communities found on the ocean floor or in the most remote parts of the Amazon rain forest) to those that are heavily modified by human activity (such as agricultural land, forest plantations, cities, and reservoirs). Even in the most heavily modified human environments, though, remnants of the original biota may still exist and thrive, and habitats with intermediate levels of disturbance present some of the most interesting challenges and opportunities for conservation biology because they often cover large geographical areas. For instance, considerable biological diversity may remain in selectively logged forests, heavily fished oceans and seas, and grasslands grazed by domestic livestock (Western 1989; Chapman et al. 2000).

Determining which areas of the world urgently need additional protection is critical. Resources, research, and publicity must be directed to those areas that require additional protection (Nias 2001). An analysis of 14 major terrestrial **biomes**—ecosystem types linked by the structure and characteristics of their vegetation, each of which supports unique biological communities—shows that the number of protected areas and the percentage of area they contain vary considerably (Table 15.1). Based on the information in Table 15.1, probably the greatest priority for conservation is increasing the area of protection for temperate grasslands and lake systems, because these communities are limited in area and only a small percentage of their area is protected (IUCN 1994; Ricketts et al. 1999).

TABLE 15.1 The relative numbers of protected sites and total area protected in 14 major biomes

Biome type	Total area (km^2)	Number of protected sites	Area protected (km^2)	% of area protected
Tundra (Arctic and alpine grasslands)	22,017,390	78	1,645,043	7.5
Warm deserts/semi-deserts	24,279,842	300	984,007	4.1
Mountain systems (e. g., Andes, Himalayas)	10,633,145	1277	852,494	8.0
Tropical dry forests/woodlands	17,312,538	799	817,551	4.7
Tropical rain forests and moist forests	10,513,210	506	538,334	5.1
Boreal forests and woodlands	15,682,817	429	487,227	3.1
Subtropical/temperate rain forests/woodlands	3,930,979	899	366,297	9.3
Cold deserts	9,250,252	136	364,720	3.9
Temperate broadleaf (deciduous) forests	11,216,660	1507	358,240	3.2
Island systems (e. g., Hawaii, Galápagos, etc.)	3,252,270	530	322,769	9.9
Tropical grasslands/savannahs	4,264,833	59	235,128	5.5
Temperate evergreen coniferous forests	3,757,144	776	177,584	4.7
Temperate grasslands	8,976,591	194	99,982	0.8
Lake systems (e. g., U.S. Great Lakes, African Great Lakes)	517,694	17	6635	1.3

Source: Data from IUCN 1994.

A variety of approaches are being developed to classify countries on the basis of their conservation needs (Dingwall et al. 1994). In a system developed by Dinerstein and Wikramanayake (1993), tropical Asian countries are classified into four categories on the basis of the percentage of their currently protected rain forest and the percentage of unprotected forest predicted still to be intact in 10 years (Figure 15.5). Category I countries (Brunei, Indonesia, Bhutan, and Malaysia) have large amounts of protected forest and will have remaining unprotected forests in the near future. The funding priority for these countries should be for park infrastructure, so that "paper parks" become real parks on the ground. Category II countries (Thailand, Sri Lanka, India, Nepal, Pakistan, and Taiwan) have many parks, but the remaining unprotected forest is disappearing rapidly. New parks need to be created before all of the unprotected forests and their associated species are eliminated. Category III countries (such as Papua New Guinea, Solomon Islands, and Laos) have a lot of forest but few protected areas, usually because of other national priorities and minimal financing from conservation organizations and developed countries. Funding the establishment of new parks would be a good investment. Category IV countries (Vietnam, the Philip-

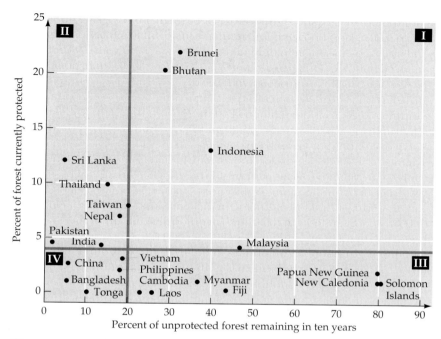

Figure 15.5 Distribution of Indo-Pacific countries based on (1) the percentage of their forests that are currently protected and (2) the percentage of unprotected forest predicted to remain intact in 10 years. The figure highlights countries in Category III with at least 20% forest cover but less than 4% of that protected; these are high-priority countries for establishing reserves. (After Dinerstein and Wikramanayake 1993.)

pines, China, Bangladesh, and Tonga) have little protected forest and little forest left to protect; the remaining unprotected areas are being degraded rapidly by human activities. Saving the remaining forest patches in these countries is an urgent conservation priority.

Centers of Biodiversity

Using another approach, The World Conservation Monitoring Centre, BirdLife International, Conservation International, the World Wildlife Fund and others have attempted to identify key areas of the world that have great biological diversity and high levels of endemism and are under immediate threat of species extinctions and habitat destruction: so-called "hot spots" for preservation (Figure 15.6). Using these criteria, Mittermeier et al. (1999) identified 25 global hot spots that together encompass the entire ranges of 44% of the world's plant species, 28% of the bird species, 30% of the mammal species, 38% of the reptile species, and 54% of the amphibian species, on only 1.4% of the Earth's total land sur-

(A)

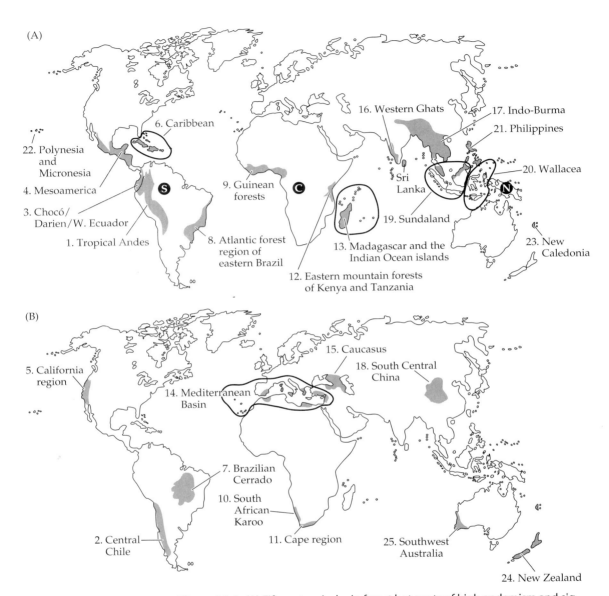

Figure 15.6 (A) Fifteen tropical rain forest hot spots of high endemism and significant threat of imminent extinctions. Numbered regions correspond to Table 15.4. The circled areas enclose four island hot spots: Caribbean, Madagascar, and Indian Ocean islands, plus Sundaland and Wallacea regions. The Polynesia/Micronesia region covers a large number of Pacific Ocean islands, including the Hawaiian Islands, Fiji, Samoa, French Polynesia, and the Marianas. Circled letters indicate the only three remaining tropical forest wilderness areas of any extent: S = South America, C = Congo Basin, N = New Guinea. (B) Ten hot spots in other ecosystems. The circled area encloses the Mediterranean Basin. (After Mittermeier et al. 1999.)

TABLE 15.2 A comparison of twenty-five global hot spots

	Original extent (× 1000 km²)	Percentage remaining	Percentage protected	Number of		
				Plants	Birds	Mammals
1. Tropical Andes	1258	25.0	6.3	45,000	1666	414
2. Central Chile	300	30.0	3.1	3429	198	56
3. Chocó/Darien/ Western Ecuador	261	24.2	6.3	9,000	830	235
4. Mesoamerica	1155	20.0	12.0	24,000	1193	521
5. California region	324	24.7	9.7	4426	341	145
6. Caribbean	264	11.3	15.6	12,000	668	164
7. Brazilian Cerrado	1783	20.0	1.2	10,000	837	161
8. Atlantic forest of Brazil	1227	7.5	2.7	20,000	620	261
9. Guinean forests of West Africa	1265	10.0	1.6	9000	514	551
10. South African Karoo	112	27.0	2.1	4849	269	78
11. Cape region of South Africa	74	24.3	19.0	8200	288	127
12. Eastern mountain forests of Kenya and Tanzania	30	6.7	16.9	4000	585	183
13. Madagascar and Indian Ocean islands	594	9.9	1.9	12,000	359	112
14. Mediterranean Basin	2362	4.7	1.8	25,000	345	184
15. Caucasus region east of the Black Sea	500	10.0	2.8	6,300	389	152
16. Western Ghats and Sri Lanka	182	6.8	10.4	4780	528	140
17. Indo-Burma	2060	4.9	7.8	13,500	1170	329
18. Mountains of south central China	800	8.0	2.1	12,000	686	300
19. Sundaland Island region	1600	7.8	5.6	25,000	815	328
20. Wallacea Island region	347	15.0	5.9	10,000	697	201
21. Philippines	301	8.0	1.3	7620	556	201
22. Polynesia/Micronesia	46	21.8	10.7	6557	254	16
23. New Caledonia	19	28.0	2.8	3332	116	9
24. New Zealand	271	22.0	19.2	2300	149	3
25. Southwest Australia	310	10.8	10.8	5469	181	54

Source: From Mittermeier et al. 1999.

face (Table 15.2). Because these hot spots also include more widespread species, they actually include about two-thirds of all nonfish vertebrates on the planet. Many of these hot spots are tropical rain forest areas, such as the Atlantic Coast of Brazil, the Chocó/Darien/Western Ecuador region, Mesoamerica, the Guinean forests of West Africa, the Western Ghats of India, and the Indo-Burma region. Island areas are also among these hot spots, including the Caribbean region, Madagascar, Sri Lanka, the Sundaland and Wallacea regions of Malaysia and Indonesia, the Philippines, New Caledonia, New Zealand, and the Polynesia region. Hot spots are also located in warm, seasonally dry areas in the temperate zone, such as the Mediterranean Basin, the California region, central Chile, the Cape region of South Africa, the Caucasus region, and southwest Australia. Remaining areas are the dry forests and savannahs of the Brazilian Cerrado, the eastern mountains of Kenya and Tanzania, the tropical Andes, and the mountains of south central China. These habitats originally covered 17 million km^2 but are now intact on only 2 million km^2, and protected on only 888,789 km^2, only 0.60% of the Earth's total surface. One of the Earth's major centers of biodiversity is the tropical Andes, in which 45,000 plant species, 1666 bird species, 414 mammal species, 479 reptile species, and 830 amphibian species persist in tropical forests and high-altitude grasslands on less than 1/4 of 1% of the Earth's total land surface. The hot-spot approach can also be applied to individual countries. In the United States, hot spots for rare and endangered species occur in the Hawaiian Islands, the southern Appalachians, the Florida Panhandle, the Death Valley region, the San Francisco Bay Area, and coastal and interior Southern California (Flather et al. 1998; Dobson et al. 1997; Figure 15.7).

Another valuable approach has been to identify 17 "megadiversity" countries (out of a global total of more than 230) that together contain 60–70% of the world's biological diversity: Mexico, Colombia, Brazil, Peru, Ecuador, Venezuela, the United States, the Democratic Republic of the Congo, South Africa, Madagascar, Indonesia, Malaysia, the Philip-

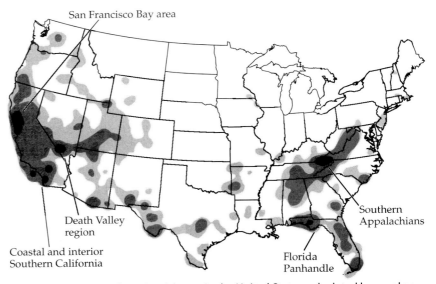

Figure 15.7 Peaks of species richness in the United States, calculated by employing an index that gives extra weighting to rare species. The Hawaiian Islands, not shown here, have the greatest concentration of rare species. Darker shading indicates greater concentrations of rare species. (After Stein et al. 2000.)

TABLE 15.3 "Top ten" rankings for countries with the largest number of species from well-known groups

Rank	Higher plants[a]	Mammals	Birds	Reptiles	Amphibians	Freshwater fish	Butterflies
1	Brazil 53,000	Brazil 524	Colombia 1815	Australia 755	Colombia 583	Brazil >3000	Peru 3532
2	Colombia 47,000	Indonesia 515	Peru 1703	Mexico 717	Brazil 517	Colombia >1500	Brazil 3132
3	Indonesia 37,000	China 499	Brazil 1622	Colombia 520	Ecuador 402	Indonesia 1400	Colombia 3100
4	China 28,000	Colombia 456	Ecuador 1559	Indonesia 511	Mexico 284	Venezuela 1250	Bolivia 3000
5	Mexico 24,000	Mexico 450	Indonesia 1531	Brazil 468	China 274	China 1010	Venezuela 2316
6	South Africa 23,000	USA 428	Venezuela 1360	India 408	Indonesia 270	DRC 962	Mexico 2237
7	Ecuador 19,000	DRC 415	India 1258	China 387	Peru 241	Peru 855	Ecuador 2200
8	Peru 19,000	India 350	Bolivia 1257	Ecuador 374	India 206	Tanzania 800	Indonesia 1900
9	PNG 18,000	Peru 344	China 1244	PNG 305	Venezuela 204	USA 790	DRC 1650
10	Venezuela 18,000	Uganda 315	DRC 1094	Madagascar 300	PNG 200	India 750	Cameroon 1550

Source: From Mittermeier et al. 1997.
Note: PNG = Papua New Guinea; DRC = Democratic Republic of the Congo; USA = United States of America.
[a]Flowering plants, gymnosperms, and ferns.

pines, India, China, Papua New Guinea, and Australia. At least some of these countries are possible targets for increased conservation attention and international funding (Table 15.3; Mittermeier et al. 1997). Clearly a current priority is to establish comparable hot spot analyses for freshwater and marine ecosystems.

Wilderness Areas

Wilderness areas are another high priority for establishing new protected areas. Large blocks of land that have been minimally affected by human activity, that have a low human population density, and are not likely to be developed in the near future are perhaps the only places on Earth where large mammals can survive in the wild. These wilderness areas potentially could serve as "controls," showing what natural communities are like with minimal human influence. For example, large protected areas of wilderness in the Chang Tang Reserve of the Tibetan

Plateau will be needed to preserve the remaining declining populations of the wild yak (*Bos grunniens*) from hunting, habitat encroachment, and hybridization with domesticated yaks (Schaller and Wulin 1996). In the United States, proponents of the Wildlands Project, a private conservation policy group, are advocating the management of whole ecosystems to preserve viable populations of large carnivores such as grizzly bears, wolves, and large cats (Noss and Cooperrider 1994). Three large tropical wilderness areas occupying 6.3% of the Earth's land surface also have been identified and established as conservation priorities (see Figure 15.6A) (Conservation International 1990; Bryant et al. 1997). It is important to emphasize that even these so-called "wilderness" areas have had a long history of human occupation and the structure of the forest and the densities of plants and animals have been affected by human activity. Following are three large tropical forest wilderness areas that are in danger of degradation:

- *South America.* One arc of wilderness containing rain forest, savannah, and mountains—but few people—runs through the southern Guianas, southern Venezuela, northern Brazil, Colombia, Ecuador, Peru, and Bolivia. The principal threat to this wilderness is the development of a modern road network, which will facilitate logging, migration, and agriculture (see Chapter 21). This combination will in turn lead to widespread forest fires.
- *Africa.* A large area of equatorial Africa centered on the Congo River basin has a low population density and undisturbed habitat, including large portions of Gabon, the Republic of the Congo, and the Democratic Republic of the Congo. Warfare and lack of government control prevents effective conservation activities in parts of the region.
- *New Guinea.* The island of New Guinea has the largest tracts of undisturbed forest in the Asian Pacific region despite the impacts of logging, mining, and transmigration programs. The eastern half of the island is the independent nation of Papua New Guinea, with 4.8 million people on 450,000 km^2 of land. The western half of the island, West Papua, is a province of Indonesia and has a population of only 2.2 million people on 345,670 km^2. Large tracts of forest also occur on the island of Borneo, but logging, plantation agriculture, an expanding human population, and the development of a transportation network are rapidly reducing the area of undisturbed forest there.

A problem for conservation protection is that these wilderness areas act as a magnet for landless people living elsewhere. These areas currently have over 75 million people (1.3% of the world's total in 6.3% of the land area), but the population is rising at 3.1% per year, more than twice the global rate, due in large part to immigration (Cincotta et al. 2000).

Once priorities are established, resources and personnel can be effectively directed to the most critical conservation areas. Prioritization should reduce the tendency of funding agencies, tropical scientists, and development officers to cluster together in a few politically stable, accessible countries with high-profile projects. The decision of the MacArthur Foundation, one of the largest private sources of funds for conservation activities, to concentrate on different areas of the world for several years at a time—a "moving spotlight" approach—is a valuable counter to the tendency to concentrate all resources on a few well-known places such as Costa Rica, Kenya, and Brazil.

How Much Protection Is Needed?

When a conservation area is established, a compromise must be struck between protecting biological diversity and ecosystem function and satisfying the immediate and long-term needs for resources of the local human community and its national government. At the outset, decisions must be made during the planning process regarding what human activities and how much human disturbance will be allowed. In general, when greater amounts of human disturbance are permitted, a narrower scope of biodiversity is preserved.

The IUCN System of Classification

The IUCN has developed a system of classifying protected areas that ranges from minimal to intensive use of the habitat by humans (Davey 1998, WRI 2000), with the following six categories:

I. *Strict nature reserves* and wilderness areas.* These areas protect natural organisms and natural processes in an undisturbed state, in order to have representative examples of biological diversity for scientific study, education, environmental monitoring, and maintenance of genetic variation. Included are two subcategories: (Ia) primarily includes nature reserves established for scientific research and monitoring; (Ib) primarily includes wilderness areas maintained for recreation, for subsistence economic activities, and to protect natural processes. This category currently includes 5201 sites covering 1,922,831 km^2.

II. *National parks.* These are large areas of outstanding scenic and natural beauty of national or international importance that are maintained for scientific, educational, and recreational use; they usually are not used for commercial extraction of resources. This category currently includes 3383 sites covering 4,001,463 km^2.

III. *National monuments and landmarks.* These are smaller areas designed to preserve unique natural areas of special national interest. This category currently includes 2122 sites covering 193,022 km^2.

---

*Protected areas that are managed primarily for biological diversity are often called nature reserves or nature sanctuaries.

IV. *Managed wildlife sanctuaries and nature reserves.* These are similar to strict nature reserves, but some human manipulation may be necessary to maintain the characteristics of the community. Some controlled harvesting may be permitted. This category currently includes 11,169 sites covering 2,460,110 km^2.

V. *Protected landscapes and seascapes.* These are areas that embody the harmonious interaction of people and the environment through the traditional, nondestructive use of natural resources while providing opportunities for tourism and recreation. Such areas may include grazing land, orchards, or villages. This category currently includes 5578 sites covering 1,057,450 km^2.

VI. *Managed-resource protected areas.* These areas allow for the sustained production of natural resources, including water, wildlife, grazing for livestock, timber, tourism, and fishing, in a manner that ensures the preservation of some aspects of biological diversity. These areas are often large and may include both modern and traditional uses of natural resources. This category currently includes 30,350 sites covering 3,601,447 km^2.

Of these categories, the first five can be defined as true protected areas, because their habitat is managed primarily for biological diversity. (However, a stricter definition would include only the first three categories.) Areas in the sixth category, managed-resource protected areas, are not administered primarily for biological diversity, though this may be a secondary goal. Managed-resource protected areas can be particularly significant because they are often much larger in area than protected areas, because they still may contain many or even most of their original species, and because protected areas are often embedded in a matrix of managed areas.

Establishing Protected Areas with Limited Data

In general, new protected areas should encompass biological communities that are rich in endemic species of restricted range, that contain community types underrepresented in other protected areas, that support threatened species, and that contain resources of potential use to people, such as species of potential agricultural or medicinal use or ecosystem services that are easily understood by the public. However, such data typically do not exist. One approach to supplementing the lack of data is to convene groups of biologists to pool their collective knowledge, identifying localities that should be protected (Hawksworth et al. 1997). Teams of biologists can be dispatched to poorly known areas to make an inventory of species. Where decisions on park boundaries have to be made quickly, biologists are being trained to make **rapid biodiversity assessments,** also known as **RAPs,** that involve mapping vegetation, making lists of species, checking for species of special concern,

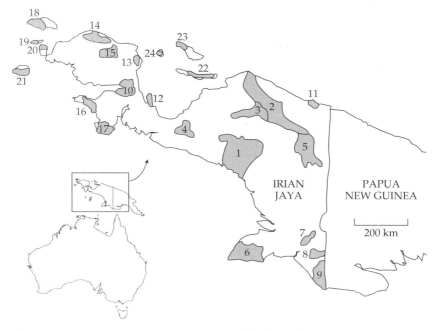

Figure 15.8 Reserves in West Papua approved by the Indonesian government as of 1983. In addition to the 24 large reserves indicated, an additional 11 smaller reserves were established. Reserves were positioned to include major habitat types, centers of endemism, and islands. (From Diamond 1986.)

estimating the total number of species, and looking out for new species and features of special interest (Oliver and Beattie 1993).

Another way of circumventing the lack of data is to base decisions on general principles of ecology and conservation biology, as described more completely in Chapter 16. For example, Jared Diamond (1986) was asked by the Indonesian government to help design a national park system covering Irian Jaya, the western half of New Guinea (Figure 15.8). On the surface this seemed like an impossible task, since much of the region had never been surveyed biologically. However, Diamond was able to propose a series of reserves based on sound conservation principles. The principles include protecting elevational gradients that encompass diverse habitats, the need for large parks to protect low-density species, the need to protect representative habitats in different climatic zones, and the need to protect individual biogeographical areas that have many endemic species.

Size and Effectiveness

A recent study shows that protected areas truly are effective in keeping land intact (Bruner et al. 2001). Land clearing in tropical forests in 86 national parks is far lower than in 88 control areas surrounding those parks (Figure 15. 9). But if protected areas cover only a small percentage of the total area of the world, how effectively can they preserve the world's species and biological communities? Concentrations of species occur at particular places in the landscape: along elevational gradients, at places where different geological formations are juxtaposed, in areas that are geologically old, and in places with an abundance of critical natural resources (e. g., streams and water holes in otherwise dry habitats; caves and hollow tree trunks that can be used by birds, bats, and other animals for nesting; salt licks that provide essential mineral nutrients) (Carroll 1992). New protected areas should also be sited along environmental gradients, so that a variety of biological communities are included. Such gradients could allow species dispersal as the global climate changes (Smith et al. 2001).

Often a landscape contains large expanses of a fairly uniform habitat type and only a few small areas of rare habitat types. Protecting biological diversity in such a case probably depends not so much on preserving large areas of the common habitat type as on including representatives of all the habitats in a system of protected areas (Shafer 1999). Conservation management plans for Sarawak, on the northwest coast of Borneo, have emphasized the need to distribute new national

Figure 15.9 Land clearing of tropical forests in 85 national parks is far lower than in 88 control areas surrounding those parks. More than 80% of the parks have almost-intact vegetation (<10% cleared), whereas less than 20% of nearby control areas have almost-intact vegetation. National parks also have much lower-than-average levels of hunting, logging, and grazing than surrounding areas. (After Bruner et al. 2001.)

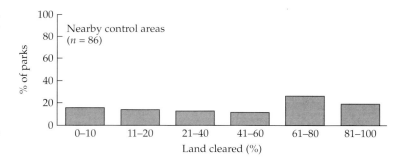

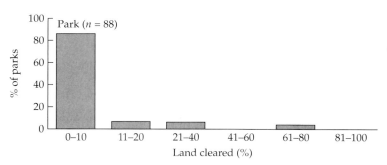

parks in order to cover all major vegetation types and biological communities (Kavanaugh et al. 1989). The following examples illustrate the potential effectiveness of protected areas of limited extent:

- Parks and wildlife sanctuaries cover only about 8% of Thailand but include 88% of its resident forest bird species (Rand 1985, reported in Reid and Miller 1989).
- The Indonesian government has designated 10% of Indonesia's land as protected area, with a goal of protecting populations of all native bird and primate species within its system of national parks and reserves.
- The 30 major protected areas in tropical Africa collectively include 67 of the 70 species of kingfishers, bee-eaters, rollers, hoopoes, and hornbills, with 90% of the species found in more than one park and 55% of the species found in more than five parks (IUCN/UNEP 1986). A similarly high percentage of other vertebrate groups are protected.
- A dramatic illustration of the importance of small protected areas is given by Santa Rosa Park in northwestern Costa Rica. This park covers only 0.2% of the area of Costa Rica, yet it contains breeding populations of 55% of the country's 135 species of sphingid moth. Santa Rosa Park is included within the 82,500-ha Guanacaste National Park, which has populations of at least 90% of the sphingid moth species in the country (D. Janzen, personal communication).

While these examples clearly show that well-selected protected areas can include many if not most of the species in a country, the long-term future of many species in these reserves, and even of the biological communities themselves, remains in doubt. Populations of many species may be so reduced in size that their eventual fate is extinction. Similarly, catastrophic events like fires, outbreaks of disease, and episodes of poaching can rapidly eliminate particular species from isolated reserves. Consequently, although the number of species existing in a park is an important indicator of the park's potential in protecting biodiversity, the real value of the park lies in its ability to support viable long-term populations of species and maintain healthy biological communities.

Linking New Protected Areas to Reserve Networks

The third major step in establishing protected areas is to link new protected areas to systems of existing protected areas, since biological diversity is protected most efficiently by ensuring that all major ecosystem types are included in such a system. These ecosystem types should include those that are unaffected by human activity as well as those disturbed by human activity that are similar in certain aspects of structure and function to their undisturbed condition (such as some managed rangelands and forests).

Gap Analysis

One way to determine the effectiveness of ecosystem and community conservation programs is to compare biodiversity priorities with existing and proposed protected areas (Olson and Dinerstein 1998; World Wildlife Fund 2000). This comparison can identify gaps in biodiversity preservation that need to be filled in with new protected areas. In the past, this was done informally by establishing national parks in different regions with distinctive biological communities (Shafer 1999). At the present time, a more systematic conservation planning process, known as **gap analysis,** is sometimes used (Margules and Pressey 2000). Gap analysis consists of the following steps:

1. Data are compiled on the species, ecosystems, and physical features of the region, which are sometimes referred to as **conservation units**. Information on human densities and economic factors can also be included.
2. Conservation goals are identified, such as the amount of area to be protected for each ecosystem or the number of individuals of rare species to be protected.
3. Existing conservation areas are reviewed to determine what is protected already and what is not (known as "identifying gaps in coverage").
4. Additional areas are identified to help meet the conservation goals ("filling the gaps").
5. These additional areas are acquired for conservation and a management plan is developed and implemented.
6. The new conservation areas are monitored to determine if they are meeting their stated goals. If not, the management plan can be changed or possibly additional areas can be acquired to meet the goals.

On an international scale, gap analysis is helping to identify for protection representative examples of all of the world's biological communities. Biogeographers have divided the world into seven terrestrial biogeographical realms (excluding the Antarctic). Each of these regions has numerous endemic species and genera, and each has been isolated from other regions for a considerable time by barriers of oceans, mountains, and deserts. These regions are the Nearctic (North America), Neotropical (Central and South America), Palearctic (Europe, most of Asia, North Africa), Indomalayan (India, Southeast Asia), Afrotropical (Africa south of the Sahara, Madagascar), Australian, and Oceanian (New Guinea and islands to the east). The percentage of total area occupied by protected areas is greatest for the Nearctic (12.4%) and the Indomalayan (8.1%) regions and lowest for the Palearctic (3.5%) and Australian (5.0%) regions. The seven regions are subdivided into 193 provinces. Although all biogeographical regions have some protected areas, 10 of the 193 provinces have no protected areas and 38 have less than 1% of their area protected (McNeely et al. 1994). These provinces should be targeted for new parks.

At the national level, maps of vegetation types and biological communities can be compared with maps showing lands under government protection (Wright et al. 2001). In the western United States, a comprehensive system of ecosystem mapping has been developed by the gap analysis programs of individual states. In the 148 million ha covered by this analysis, 73 distinct vegetation types are recognized. Maps of these vegetation types can be compared to maps of the 8% of government land legally maintained in a natural state (such as national parks, wilderness areas, and wildlife refuges). Of the 73 vegetation types, 25 (34%) had at least 10% of their total area in protected areas. Among the best protected are high-elevation vegetation types, such as alpine/subalpine meadows (44% protected) and subalpine spruce (26% protected), which are well represented in mountainous national parks. Of the 48 vegetation types not currently having at least 10% of their area protected, 43 of them have more than 20% of their area on government land that is managed for resource extraction, which is not surprising, since 62% of the western United States is publicly owned land. The management of some of these lands for conservation could extend government protection to 68 of the 73 vegetation types. For the remaining vegetation types—shadscale-grass-shrub, Sitka spruce, Oregon white oak conifer, westside Douglas fir, Chihuahuan grassland, and semidesert tobosa grassland—negotiations with private landowners would be required to establish protection. The most critical vegetation type is semidesert tobosa grassland, which occupies only 64,900 ha, of which less than 1% is on government land. It is important to remember that no one federal agency has a complete representation of U.S. ecosystem types on its land; certain government agencies, such as the Department of Defense and the Bureau of Land Management, which have priorities other than conservation, may be important in efforts to preserve biological diversity. Cooperation among federal agencies, state and local governments, and private landowners is key to protecting biological communities.

Another example of gap analysis at a more local level (Szaro and Johnston 1996) compared California vegetation maps with protected areas. The result showed that more than 95% of the alpine and subalpine habitats were in reserves, even though these habitats had relatively few rare plant populations. In contrast, less than 10% of the biologically rich mixed chaparral, grasslands, and coastal scrub were protected (Figure 15.10). Preservation efforts had been successful at maintaining certain types of habitat but others had been virtually ignored.

Amazonian Brazil has already lost about 10% of its original forest and continues to lose more each year (Fearnside and Ferraz 1995). Establishing new protected areas is an urgent priority because only 2.7% of the Amazon (13 million ha) is currently in reserves, and future plans call for increasing this to only 3.3%. A gap analysis of the Amazon reveals that 10 of the 38 distinct vegetation types of the region are not repre-

Figure 15.10 In California, most rare plants occur in low-elevation communities (such as mixed chaparral, grasslands, and coastal scrub), which are highly developed and are protected in less than 10% of their area. In contrast, high-elevation communities (subalpine and alpine communities and pine forests) are protected in more than 80% of their area, but few rare plants occur there. (After Szaro and Johnston 1996.)

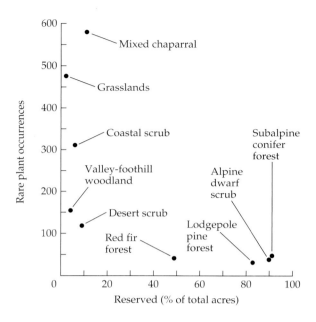

sented within protected areas. A series of reserves that is large enough to protect examples of each vegetation type and have viable populations of virtually all species has been proposed.

Geographic Information Systems (GIS) represent the latest development in gap analysis technology, using computers to integrate the wealth of data on the natural environment with information on species distributions (Sample 1994; Kremen et al. 1999; Heywood et al. 1998). GIS analyses make it possible to highlight critical areas that need to be included within national parks and areas that should be avoided by development projects. The basic GIS approach involves storing, displaying, and manipulating many types of mapped data such as vegetation types, climate, soils, topography, geology, hydrology, species distributions, human settlements, and resource use (Figure 15.11). This approach can point out correlations among the abiotic and biotic elements of the landscape, help plan parks that include a diversity of biological communities, and even suggest sites to search for rare and protected species. Aerial photographs and satellite imagery are additional sources of data for GIS analysis. In particular, a series of images taken over time can reveal patterns of habitat fragmentation and destruction that need prompt attention. These images can dramatically illustrate when current government policies are not working and need to be changed.

An ambitious attempt to apply GIS is the Eastside Ecosystem Management Project, which is charged with analyzing the ecosystem, bio-

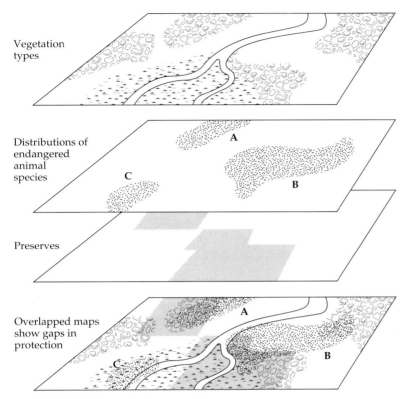

Vegetation types

Distributions of endangered animal species

A

C

B

Preserves

Overlapped maps show gaps in protection

A

C

B

Figure 15.11 Geographic Information Systems (GIS) provide a method for integrating a wide variety of data for analysis and display on maps. In this example, vegetation types, distributions of endangered animal species, and preserved areas are overlapped to highlight areas that need additional protection. The distribution of Species A is predominantly in a preserve, Species B is only protected to a limited extent, and Species C is found entirely outside of the preserves. (After Scott et al. 1991.)

diversity, and socioeconomic factors of the Columbia River Basin east of the Cascade Mountains (McLean 1995). One hundred specialists drawn from the U.S. Bureau of Land Management, the Forest Service, and other agencies are digitizing 10,000 maps that cover 600,000 km^2 and include 100 layers of information. The goal is to produce a management plan that addresses the overall needs of the region: preserving endangered species such as the northern spotted owl, preserving salmon and trout fisheries, maintaining the timber industry, and allowing for local economic development.

Summary

1. Protecting habitat is the most effective method for preserving biological diversity. Land can be protected by governments, private organizations such as The Nature Conservancy, groups of local people, or private individuals. Protected areas include nature reserves, national parks, wildlife sanctuaries, national monuments, protected landscapes and seascapes, and managed-resource protected areas.

2. About 9% of the Earth's surface is included in about 58,000 protected areas. Strictly protected areas occupy only 4% of the Earth's surface due to the per-

ceived needs of human society for natural resources. Therefore, the protection of biological diversity must be a priority on land and in water that is managed for resource production, including production forests, grazing lands, and fishing grounds.

3. Government agencies and conservation organizations have set priorities for establishing new protected areas based on the relative distinctiveness, endangerment, and utility of the species and biological communities that occur in an area. Many protected areas are established to safeguard indicator species of special concern, often preserving an entire community with its associated ecosystem processes.

4. International conservation organizations are identifying "hot spots" of large concentrations of animal and plant species. If these areas can be protected, then most of the world's biological diversity will be protected. Another conservation priority is protecting wilderness areas so that ecological processes and evolution can continue with minimal human impact.

5. Gap analysis is an approach that identifies additional protected areas that need to be added to an existing network of protected areas. New computer mapping technologies, known as Geographical Information Systems, can facilitate this process.

For Discussion

1. Obtain a map of a town, state, or nation that shows protected areas (such as nature reserves and parks) and multiple-use managed areas. Who is responsible for each parcel of land, and what is their purpose in managing it?

   a. Consider aquatic habitats in this region (ponds, marshes, streams, rivers, lakes, estuaries, coastal zones, etc.). Who is responsible for managing these environments, and how do they balance the need for protecting biological diversity with the needs of society for natural resources?

   b. If you could add protected areas to this region, where would you place them and why? Show their exact location, size, and shape, and justify your choices.

2. Imagine that the only population of a rare and declining flamingo species lives along the shore of an isolated lake. This lake has numerous unique species of fish, crayfish, and insects. The lake and its shores are owned by a logging company that is planning to build a paper mill on the shore where the flamingos nest. This mill will seriously pollute the lake and destroy the food eaten by the flamingos. You have $1 million to spend on conservation in this area. The company is willing to sell the lake and its shores for $1 million. An effective flamingo management program involving captive breeding, release of new individuals into the population, habitat improvement, and natural history studies would cost $750,000. Is it better to buy the land and not devote resources to managing and researching the flamingo? Or would it be better to manage the flamingo and allow the lake to be destroyed? Can you suggest other alternatives or possibilities?

Suggested Readings

Agardy, T. S. 1997. *Marine Protected Areas and Ocean Conservation*. R. G. Landes Company, Austin, Texas. A wide range of planning, design, and policy issues are discussed by a leading authority.

Bruner, A. G., R. E. Gullison, R. E. Rice, and G. A. B. da Fonseca. 2001. Effectiveness of parks in protecting tropical biodiversity. *Science* 291: 125–128. Parks are generally effective in reducing land clearing, logging, hunting and grazing; the most effective parks are better managed and are able to compensate local people.

Davey, A. G. 1998. *National System Planning for Protected Areas.* IUCN, Gland, Switzerland. Reliable, comprehensive data sets.

Heywood, I., S. Cornelius, and S. Carver. 1998. *An Introduction to Geographical Information Systems.* Prentice Hall, New Jersey. Good beginning textbook.

Lawton, J. H. and K. Gaston. 2001. Indicator species. In *Encyclopedia of Biodiversity*, S. A. Levin (ed.), Vol. 3, pp. 437–450. Academic Press, San Diego, CA. Indicator species can be used to highlight patterns of diversity, detect global climate change, and locate new protected areas.

Lindholm, J. and B. Barr. 2001. Comparison of marine and terrestrial protected areas under federal jurisdiction in the United States. *Conservation Biology* 15: 1441–1444. Marine areas are not as well-protected as terrestrial areas.

Margules, C. R. and R. L. Pressey. 2000. Systematic conservation planning. *Nature* 405: 243–253. Review of principles for developing a comprehensive set of conservation areas.

Mittermeier, R. A., N. Myers, P. R. Gil, and C. G. Mittermeier. 1999. *Hotspots: Earth's Richest and Most Endangered Terrestrial Ecoregions.* Cemex/Conservation International and the University of Chicago Press, Chicago. Lavish, large-format book with pictures and information on each region.

Nature Conservancy, The. 1996. *Designing a Geography of Hope: Guidelines for an Ecoregion-Based Conservation in The Nature Conservancy.* The Nature Conservancy, Arlington, VA. Clearly stated conservation philosophy for guiding land-acquisition policy.

Rabinowitz, A. 2000. *Jaguar. One Man's Struggle to Establish the World's First Jaguar Preserve.* Island Press, Covelo, CA. Sometimes one motivated individual makes a huge difference.

Scott, J. M., F. W. Davis, R. G. McGhie, R. G. Wright, et al. 2001. Nature reserves: do they capture the full range of America's biological diversity? *Ecological Applications* 11: 999–1007. Many rare species and habitat types are not included in current protected areas and are often on private lands.

Shafer, C. L. 1999. History of selection and system planning for US natural area national parks and monuments: beauty and biology. *Biodiversity and Conservation* 8: 189–204. Early efforts in U.S. park selection included attempts to protect species and special vegetation types.

Stattersfield, A. J., M. J. Crosby, A. J. Long, and D. C. Wege. 1998. *Endemic Bird Areas of the World: Priorities for Biodiversity Conservation.* BirdLife International, Cambridge. Highlights areas that need additional protection.

Stein, B. A., L. S. Kutner, and J. S. Adams. 2000. *Precious Heritage: The Status of Biodiversity in the United States.* Oxford University Press, New York. Beautiful book with information on the status of U.S. biodiversity.

Williams, P., D. Gibbons, C. Margules, A. Rebelo, et al. 1996. A comparison of richness hot spots, rarity hot spots, and complementary areas for conserving the diversity of British birds. *Conservation Biology* 10: 155–174. Elegant use of census data to pinpoint concentrations of rare species.

World Wildlife Fund. 2000. *The Global 200 Ecoregions: A User's Guide.* World Wildlife Fund. Gland, Switzerland. Detailed maps of biological communities with an evaluation of their distinctiveness and conservation status.

Wright, R., J. M. Scott, S. Mann, and M. Murray. 2001. Identifying unprotected and potentially at risk plant communities in the western USA. *Biological Conservation* 98: 97–106. This gap analysis study demonstrates that only one-third of vegetation types in the western United States are adequately protected; increased protection will have to be sought on other government lands and private lands.

Chapter *16*

Designing Networks of Protected Areas

I n this chapter we will examine some of the issues involved in designing effective protected areas. These issues
are currently being investigated by conservation biologists,
and they are providing insight into the best methods for establishing new protected areas. Although networks of parks
and conservation areas are often created in a haphazard fashion, dependent on the availability of money and land, a considerable body of ecological literature is now developing to
address the most efficient way to design networks of conservation areas that protect the full range of biological diversity
(Pressey et al. 1993; Shafer 1990, 1997; Poiani et al. 2000).
Such networks are needed because many protected areas are
required to protect examples of all species and biological
communities. (These concepts were described briefly in
Chapter 15.) The size and placement of protected areas
throughout the world are often determined by the distribution of people, potential land values, the political efforts of
conservation-minded citizens, and historical factors. In many
cases, lands are set aside for conservation protection because
they have no immediate commercial value—they are "the
lands that nobody wants" (Pressey 1994; Scott et al. 2001).

The largest parks usually occur in areas where few people live and where the land is considered unsuitable or too remote for agriculture, logging, urban development, or other human activities. Examples are the low heath forests on nutrient-poor soils at Bako National Park in Malaysia; the rugged, rocky mountain parks of Switzerland; the huge desert parks of the U.S. Southwest; and the one million km^2 of federal land in Alaska occupying tundra and mountains. Small conservation areas are common in large metropolitan areas and in densely settled and industrialized countries throughout Europe and in Japan. Many of the conservation areas and parks in metropolitan areas of Europe and North America were formerly estates of wealthy citizens and royalty. In the U.S. Midwest, a number of the prairie nature reserves are former railroad rights-of-way and other oddly shaped pieces with unusual histories.

In establishing new reserves, conservation biologists must consider the three "R's" of network design:

- *Representation:* All conservation units must be represented in the reserve.
- *Resiliency:* Reserves must be sufficiently large and well-protected to maintain all of the conservation units in a healthy condition for the foreseeable future.
- *Redundancy:* Reserves must protect enough examples of each conservation unit to ensure the long-term existence of the unit in the face of future uncertainties.

Issues of Reserve Design

Issues of reserve design have proved to be of great interest to governments, corporations, and private landowners, who are being urged—and mandated—to manage their properties for both the commercial production of natural resources and for the protection of biological diversity. However, consideration of such issues does not necessarily produce universal design guidelines: Conservation biologists have been cautioned against providing simplistic, overly general guidelines for designing nature reserves, because every conservation situation requires special consideration (Ehrenfeld 1989). In addition, all would benefit from more communication between the academic scientists who are developing theories of nature reserve design and the managers, planners, and policy makers who are actually creating new nature reserves (Prendergast et al. 1999). That said, questions about the following topics in reserve design can provide a useful starting point for discussions of the best way of protecting biodiversity and constructing networks of protected areas.

In this chapter we'll review the following issues of reserve design, which attempt to provide guidance to conservation managers:

1. How large must nature reserves be to protect species?
2. Is it better to have a single large reserve or many smaller reserves?

3. How many individuals of an endangered species must be protected in a reserve to prevent extinction?
4. What is the best shape for a nature reserve?
5. When several reserves are created, should they be close together or far apart, and should they be isolated from one another or connected by corridors?

Some of these issues are being explored using the island biogeography model of MacArthur and Wilson (1967), described in Chapter 8. Many of them also have originated from the insights of wildlife and park managers (Shafer 2001). The island biogeography approach makes the significant assumption, which is often invalid, that parks are habitat islands completely isolated by an unprotected matrix of inhospitable terrain. In fact, many species are capable of living and dispersing through this habitat matrix. Researchers working with island biogeography models and data from protected areas have proposed some answers to these questions, but they are still being debated (Figure 16.1).

Also, all of these issues have been viewed mainly with land vertebrates, higher plants, and large invertebrates in mind. The applicability of these ideas to aquatic nature reserves, where dispersal mechanisms are largely unknown, requires further investigation. Recent evidence suggests that many widespread marine species actually only disperse their offspring a short distance. If this proves true for many species, additional protected areas would have to be established to protect the genetic variation found in specific localities. Protecting marine nature reserves requires particular attention to pollution control because of its subtle and widespread destructive effects (Boersma and Parrish 1999). Various countries in the Caribbean and Pacific regions have made steps in the right direction: Many individual islands have half or even more of their coastlines designated as marine parks, and the entire island of Bonaire is a protected marine park, with ecotourism emerging as the leading industry.

Creating Adequately Sized Reserves

An early debate in conservation biology occurred over whether species richness is maximized in one large nature reserve or in several smaller ones of an equal total area (Simberloff and Abele 1982; Soulé and Simberloff 1986), known in the literature as the SLOSS debate (single large or several small). Is it better, for example, to set aside one reserve of 10,000 ha or four reserves of 2500 ha each? The proponents of large reserves argue that only large reserves have sufficient numbers of large, wide-ranging, low-density species (such as large carnivores) to maintain long-term populations (Figure 16.2). Large reserves also minimize the ratio of edge habitat to total habitat, encompass more species, and can have greater habitat diversity than small reserves.

Figure 16.1 Principles of reserve design that have been proposed based in part on theories of island biogeography. Imagine that the reserves are "islands" of the original ecosystem surrounded by land that has been made uninhabitable by human activities such as farming, ranching, or industrial development. The practical application of these principles is still being studied and debated, but in general the designs shown on the right are considered to be preferable to those on the left. (After Shafer 1997.)

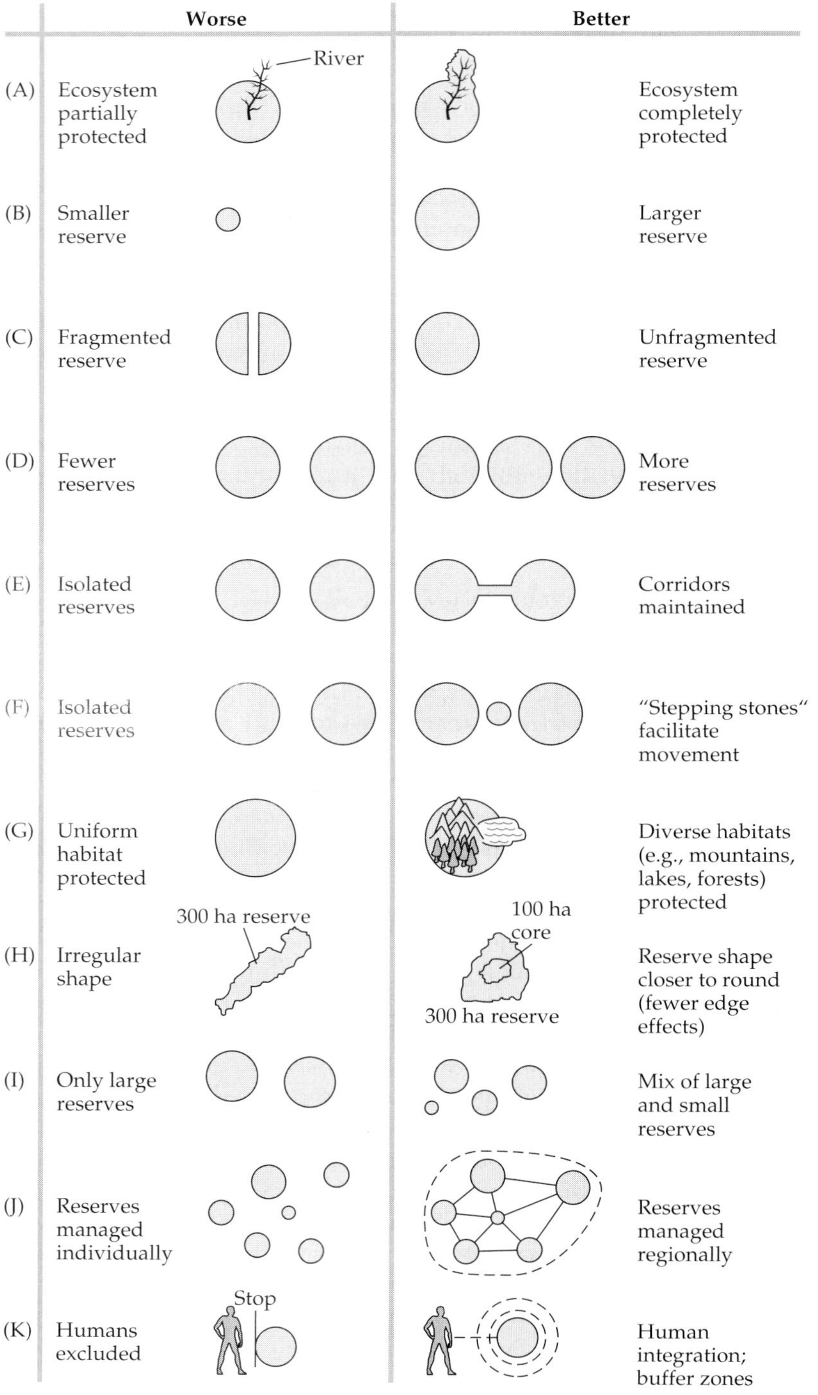

Worse
Better
River
(A) Ecosystem partially protected
Ecosystem completely protected
(B) Smaller reserve
Larger reserve
(C) Fragmented reserve
Unfragmented reserve
(D) Fewer reserves
More reserves
(E) Isolated reserves
Corridors maintained
(F) Isolated reserves
"Stepping stones" facilitate movement
(G) Uniform habitat protected
Diverse habitats (e.g., mountains, lakes, forests) protected
300 ha reserve
100 ha core
(H) Irregular shape
300 ha reserve
Reserve shape closer to round (fewer edge effects)
(I) Only large reserves
Mix of large and small reserves
(J) Reserves managed individually
Reserves managed regionally
Stop
(K) Humans excluded
Human integration; buffer zones

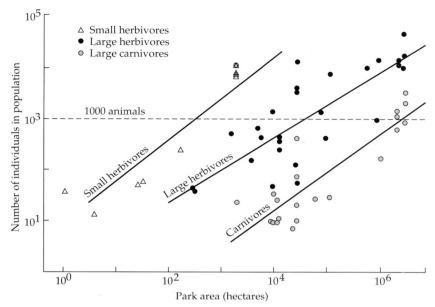

Figure 16.2 Population studies show that large parks and protected areas in Africa contain larger populations of each species than small parks; only the largest parks may contain long-term viable populations of many vertebrate species. Each symbol represents an animal population in a park. If the viable population size of a species is 1000 individuals (10^3; dashed line), parks of at least 100 ha (10^2) will be needed to protect small herbivores (e. g., rabbits, squirrels); parks of more than 10,000 ha will be needed to protect large herbivores (e. g., zebra, giraffes); and parks of at least 1 million ha will be needed to protect large carnivores (e. g., lions, hyenas). (From Schonewald-Cox 1983.)

The advantage of large parks is effectively demonstrated by an analysis of 299 mammal populations in 14 national parks in western North America (Figure 16.3) (Newmark 1995). Twenty-nine mammal species are now locally extinct and seven species have recolonized or newly colonized the parks. Extinction rates have been very low or zero in parks with area over 1000 km^2 and have been much higher in parks that are smaller than 1000 km^2. Extinction rates have been highest for species with low initial population numbers and small body size. Many of these extinctions are probably due to human activity, which is not included as an element of the biogeography model.

On the other hand, once a park reaches a certain size, the number of new species added with each increase in area starts to decline. At that point, creating a second large park, as well as a third or fourth park some distance away, may be an effective strategy for preserving additional species. The extreme proponents of large reserves argue that small re-

Figure 16.3 Each dot represents the extinction rate of animal populations for a particular U.S. national park. Mammals have higher extinction rates in smaller parks than in larger ones. (After Newmark 1995.)

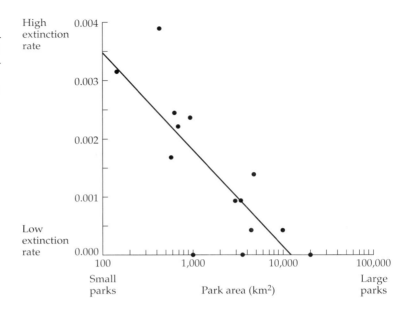

serves need not be maintained, because their inability to support long-term populations, ecosystem processes, and all successional stages, gives them little value for conservation purposes. Other conservation biologists argue that well-placed small reserves are able to include a greater variety of habitat types and more populations of rare species than one large block of the same area (Simberloff and Gotelli 1984; Shafer 1995). The value of several well-placed reserves in different habitats is demonstrated by a comparison of four national parks in the United States. The total number of large mammalian species in three national parks located in contrasting habitats (Big Bend in Texas, North Cascades in Washington, and Redwoods in California) is greater than the number of species in the largest U.S. park, Yellowstone, even though the area of Yellowstone is larger than the combined area of the other three parks. Creating more reserves, even if they are small ones, decreases the possibility of a single catastrophic force—such as an exotic animal, a disease, or fire—destroying an entire species.

The consensus now seems to be that strategies for reserve size depend on the group of species under consideration as well as the scientific circumstances. It generally is accepted that large reserves are better able to maintain many species because they have larger population sizes and greater variety of habitats. The research on extinction rates of populations in large parks has three practical implications:

1. When a new park is being established, it should be made as large as possible—to preserve as many species as possible, contain large pop-

ulations of each species, and provide a diversity of habitats and natural resources.

2. Whenever possible, land adjacent to protected areas should be acquired in order to reduce external threats to existing parks. Whenever possible, protected areas should be expanded to encompass an entire ecosystem (such as a watershed, a lake, or a mountain range), because the ecosystem is the most appropriate unit of management. Damage to an unprotected portion of the ecosystem could threaten the health of the whole. Legal control of a whole ecosystem allows park managers to defend it more effectively against destructive outside influences (Peres and Terborgh 1995).

3. Finally, if there is a choice between creating a new small park or a new large park in similar habitat types, the large park should be created. In conserving biodiversity, bigger is usually better. However, well-managed small nature reserves have value, particularly for the protection of many species of plants, invertebrates, and small vertebrates (Lesica and Allendorf 1992; Schwartz 1999). For example, woodland remnants in an Australian agricultural landscape retained some native insect species when they were as small as 50 m^2, an amazing demonstration of the conservation value of even extremely small habitat fragments (Abensperg-Traun and Smith 1999).

Often there is no choice but to accept the challenge of managing species and biological communities in small reserves (Schwartz 1997). Numerous countries have many more small protected areas (less than 100 ha) than medium and large ones, yet the combined area of these small reserves is only a tiny percentage of the total under protection (IUCN 1994). This is particularly true in places that have been intensively cultivated and settled for centuries, such as Europe, China, and Java. Bukit Timah Nature Reserve in Singapore is an excellent example of a small reserve that provides long-term protection for numerous species. This 50-ha forest reserve represents 0.2% of the original forested area on Singapore and has been isolated from other forests since 1860, yet it still protects 74% of the original flora, 72% of the original bird species, and 56% of the fish (Corlett and Turner 1996). In addition, small reserves located near populated areas make excellent conservation education and nature study centers that further the long-range goals of conservation biology by developing public awareness of important issues (Deardon 1995).

Reserve Design and Species Preservation

Because population size is the best predictor of extinction probability, reserves should be sufficient in area to preserve large populations of important species (rare and endangered species, keystone species, economically important species, etc.). The best evidence to date suggests that populations of at least several hundred reproductive individuals are needed to ensure the long-term viability of vertebrates, with several thousand individuals being a desirable goal (Lande 1995; see also Chapters 11 and 12). Having more than one population of a rare species within a protected area will increase the probability of survival for the species; if one population goes extinct, the species still remains in the reserve and can potentially recolonize its former range.

Several strategies exist to facilitate the survival of small populations of rare species in scattered, isolated nature reserves. They can be managed as one metapopulation, with efforts made to encourage natural migration between the nature reserves by maintaining connectivity among the reserves. Occasionally individuals can be collected from one nature reserve and added to the breeding population of another. Addressing the needs of wide-ranging species that cannot tolerate human disturbance is a more difficult aspect of ensuring viable populations in reserves. Ideally, a reserve should be large enough to include a viable population of the most wide-ranging species in it. Protection of the habitat of wide-ranging species, which are often large or conspicuous flagship species will often provide adequate protection for the other species in the community (see Chapter 15). Extensive areas of pine habitat surrounding the Savannah River nuclear processing plant in South Carolina are being protected to maintain the red-cockaded woodpecker (*Picoides borealis*), a species that needs large stands of mature longleaf pine trees (Figure 16.4). In the process, many endangered plant species are being protected as well.

The effective design of nature reserves requires a thorough knowledge of the natural history of important species and information on the distribution of biological communities. Knowledge about species' feeding requirements, nesting behavior, daily and seasonal movement patterns, potential predators and competitors, and susceptibility to disease and pests contributes to determining an effective conservation strategy. A balance has to be struck between focusing on the needs of the indicator or flagship species to the exclusion of all other species and managing only for maximum species diversity, which could result in the loss of the flagship species that interest the general public.

Minimizing Edge and Fragmentation Effects

It is generally agreed that parks should be designed to minimize harmful edge effects (see Chapter 9). Conservation areas that are rounded in shape minimize the edge-to-area ratio, and the center is farther from the edge than in other park shapes. Long, linear parks have the most edge, and all points in the park are close to the edge. Consequently, for parks with four straight sides, a square park is a better design than an elongated rectangle of the same area. Unfortunately, these ideas have rarely, if ever, been implemented. Most parks have irregular shapes because land acquisition is typically a matter of opportunity rather than a matter of design.

Figure 16.4 Longleaf pine habitat in the southeastern United States, including areas of South Carolina, North Carolina, and Georgia, are being managed to protect the endangered red-cockaded woodpecker. (A) In Francis Marion National Forest, South Carolina, heavily logged areas lack older trees with the nesting holes that the woodpecker requires, so artificial nesting holes are drilled in the trees. (B) Here a young woodpecker leaves the nest for its first flight. (Photographs© Derrick Hamrick.)

As discussed in Chapter 9, internal fragmentation of reserves by roads, fences, farming, logging, and other human activities should be avoided as much as possible, because fragmentation often divides a large population into two or more smaller populations, each of which is more vulnerable to extinction than is the large population (Schonewald-Cox and Buechner 1992). Fragmentation alters the climate inside forest reserves. Fragmentation also provides entry points for invasive species that may harm native species, creates more undesirable edge effects, and creates barriers to dispersal that reduce the probability of colonization of new sites.

The forces promoting fragmentation are powerful, because protected areas are often the only undeveloped land available for new projects such as agriculture, dams, and residential areas. This has been particularly true in densely settled areas such as Western Europe, where undeveloped land is scarce and there is intense pressure for development (Wallis deVries

1995). Undeveloped parkland near urban centers, for instance, may appear to be ideally positioned as a site for new industrial development, recreational facilities, schools, waste management sites, and government offices. In the eastern United States, many parks are crisscrossed by roads, railroad tracks, and power lines, which divide large areas of habitat like pieces of a roughly cut pie, in the process eliminating interior habitat needed by some species. Government planners often prefer to locate transportation networks and other infrastructure in protected areas because they assume there will be less political opposition to that than to locating the projects on privately owned, settled land. Indeed, park and forest supervisors are often rewarded for building infrastructure or increasing commodity production, regardless of whether it fragments their holdings and harms biodiversity. However, this situation is rapidly changing as conservation groups and some government officials become advocates for maintaining the integrity of protected areas.

Conservation Networks

Strategies do exist for aggregating small nature reserves into larger conservation networks. Nature reserves are often embedded in a larger matrix of habitat managed for resource extraction (such as timber forest, grazing land, and farmland). If conservation biologists can make management for the protection of biological diversity a secondary priority of these areas, then larger habitat areas can be included in conservation plans and the effects of fragmentation can be reduced (Soulé and Terborgh 1999). Habitat managed for resource extraction can sometimes also be managed as an important secondary site for wildlife and as dispersal corridors between isolated nature reserves. Whenever possible, populations of rare species should be managed as a large metapopulation to facilitate gene flow and migration among populations (Figure 16.5). Cooperation among public and private landowners is particularly important in developed metropolitan areas, where there are often many small, isolated parks under the control of a variety of different government agencies and private organizations (Kohm and Franklin 1997).

An excellent example of such cooperation is the Chicago Wilderness Project, which consists of 143 organizations collaborating to preserve more than 80,000 ha (200,000 acres) of tall-grass prairies, woodlands, rivers, streams, and other wetlands in metropolitan Chicago (Figure 16.6; Yaffee et al. 1996). These cooperating organizations include museums, zoos, forest preserve districts, national and local government agencies, and private conservation organizations. This network of natural areas is critical to the quality of life of residents, since it is the only undeveloped land available for recreation between the densely developed urban core of Chicago and the highly developed agricultural landscape outside of the metropolitan area. The Chicago Wilderness Biodiversity Council coordinates conservation efforts, facilitates communication among mem-

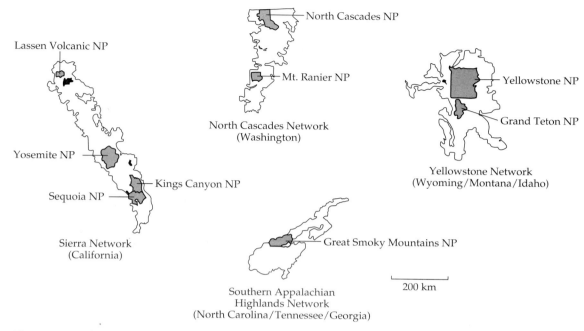

Figure 16.5 Often national parks (shaded areas) are adjacent to other areas of public lands (unshaded) that are managed by different agencies. The United States government is now managing large blocks of land that include national parks, national forests, and other federal lands as networks of natural areas in order to maintain populations of large and scarce wildlife. This illustration shows four such networks. Privately owned land is shown in black. (After Salwasser et al. 1987.)

bers, develops policy and strategy, directs scientific research, and encourages volunteer participation. Among its many educational initiatives, the council has produced *The Atlas of Biodiversity* to publicize the diversity of habitats and species in the Chicago Wilderness network and has established the Mighty Acorns program to teach nature stewardship to schoolchildren.

Linking Reserves with Habitat Corridors

One intriguing suggestion for designing a system of nature reserves has been to link isolated protected areas into one large system through the use of **habitat corridors:** strips of land running between the reserves (Simberloff et al. 1992; Rosenberg et al. 1997). Such habitat corridors, also known as conservation corridors or movement corridors, can allow plants and animals to disperse from one reserve to another, facilitating gene flow and colonization of suitable sites. Corridors can potentially transform a set of isolated protected areas by establishing a linked network, with populations interacting as metapopulations. Corridors also might help to preserve animals that must migrate seasonally among a series of

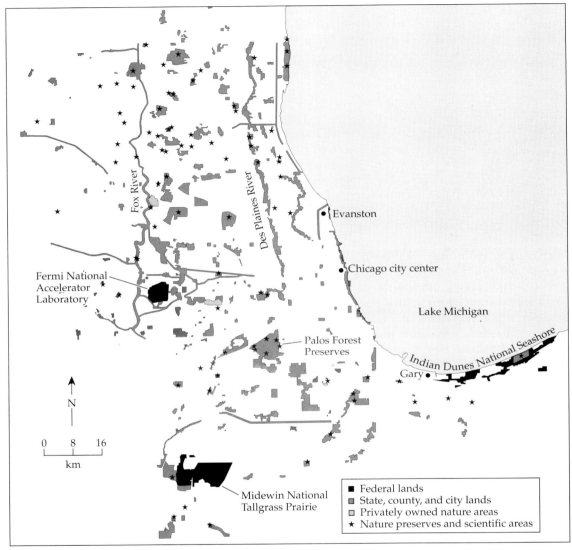

Figure 16.6 The Chicago Wilderness Project involves 143 organizations working together to preserve biodiversity and open space in the densely settled urban area, surrounded by agriculture. Many of the linear protected areas are trails and the banks of rivers. (After the Chicago Regional Biodiversity Council, 2001.)

different habitats to obtain food; if these animals were confined to a single reserve, they could starve. Observations on Brazilian arboreal mammals suggests that corridors of 30–40 m in width may be adequate for migration of most species and a corridor width of 200 m of primary forest will be adequate for all species (Laurance and Laurance 1999).

The idea of corridors has been embraced with enthusiasm by some park managers as a strategy for managing wide-ranging species. In Riverside, California, the preservation of dispersal corridors was a key component in a plan to establish a 17,400-ha reserve to protect the endangered Stephen's kangaroo rat, *Dipodomys stephensi* (Mann and Plummer 1995b). In Florida, millions of dollars have been spent to establish corridors between tracts of land occupied by the endangered Florida panther. In many areas, culverts, tunnels, and overpasses create passages under and over roads and railways that allow for dispersal between habitats for lizards, amphibians, and mammals (Yanes et al. 1995). An added benefit of these passageways is that collisions between animals and vehicles are reduced, which saves lives and money. In Canada's Banff National Park, road collisions involving deer, elk, and other large mammals declined by 96% after fences, overpasses, and underpasses were installed along a road (Figure 16.7).

The Wildlands Project has a detailed plan that would link all large protected areas in the United States by habitat corridors, creating a system that would allow large and currently declining mammals to coexist with

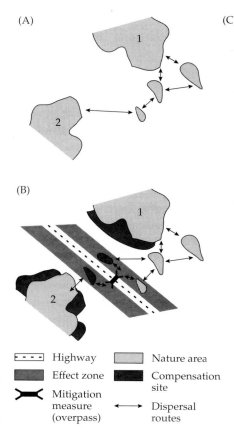

Figure 16.7 (A) Individuals of a species naturally disperse between two large protected areas (1 and 2) using smaller protected areas as "stepping-stones." (B) Habitat destruction and a large edge-effect zone caused by a new road block the migration route. To offset the effects of the road, compensation sites are added to the system of protected areas, and an overpass is built over the highway to allow dispersal. (A, B after Cuperus et al. 1999.) (C) An overpass is built over a divided, fenced-off highway to allow animals to migrate safely between two forested areas. (Photograph courtesy of Scott Jackson.)

human society (Soulé and Terborgh 1999). In eastern North America, there are over 2000 national, state, and provincial protected areas, but only 14 of them are over 2700 km^2, which is the approximate area needed to maintain populations of large mammals (Gurd et al. 2001). Linking the largest protected areas by corridors and managing them as single conservation systems would be an effective strategy to maintain rare species.

Corridors that facilitate natural patterns of migration will probably be the most successful at protecting species. For example, large grazing animals often migrate in regular patterns across a rangeland in search of water and the best vegetation. In seasonally dry savannah habitats, animals often migrate along the riparian forests that grow along streams and rivers (Spackman and Hughes 1995; Machtans et al. 1996). In mountainous areas, many bird and mammal species regularly migrate to higher elevations during the warmer months of the year. To protect migrating birds, a corridor was established in Costa Rica to link two wildlife reserves, the Braulio Carillo National Park and La Selva Biological Station. A 7700-ha corridor of forest several kilometers wide and 18 km long, known as La Zona Protectora, was set aside to provide an elevational link that allows at least 75 species of birds to migrate between the two large conservation areas (Bennett 1999).

As the global climate changes in the coming decade, many species will begin to migrate to higher elevations and to higher latitudes. Creating corridors to protect expected migration routes—such as north–south river valleys, ridges, and coastlines—would be a useful precaution. Extending existing protected areas in the direction of anticipated species movements would help to maintain long-term populations. Corridors that cross gradients of elevation, rainfall, and soils will also allow local migration of species to more favorable sites.

Although the idea of corridors is intuitively appealing, there are some possible drawbacks (Simberloff et al. 1992). Corridors may facilitate the movement of pest species and disease; thus a single infestation could quickly spread to all of the connected nature reserves and cause the extinction of all populations of a rare species. Also, animals dispersing along corridors may be exposed to greater risks of predation, because human hunters as well as animal predators tend to concentrate on routes used by wildlife.

Despite these concerns, the evidence to date tends to support the value of conservation corridors, though each case needs to be considered individually. In general, maintaining existing corridors is probably worthwhile, because many of them are along watercourses that may be biologically important habitats themselves. When new parks are being carved out of large blocks of undeveloped land, incorporating corridors by leaving small clumps of original habitat between large conservation areas may facilitate movement in a "stepping-stone" pattern. Similarly, forest species are more likely to disperse through a matrix of recovering secondary forest than through cleared farms and pastures. Corridors are most obviously needed along known migration routes. The abilities of different types of species to use corridors and intervening habitat areas to migrate between protected areas clearly needs to be more thoroughly assessed.

Habitat Corridor Case Studies

Several case studies serve to illustrate the concept and practical applications of habitat corridors, and some of the difficulties involved in establishing and maintaining such protected pathways.

CORRIDORS IN LOUISIANA WETLANDS   The Tensas River basin in northeastern Louisiana originally contained one million ha of flat, poorly drained forested land characteristic of the enormous Mississippi River floodplain (Gosselink et al. 1990). These floodplain forests are among the most productive in the United States for fish and wildlife and support large populations of migratory and resident birds. Large government flood control projects on the Mississippi River opened the land for development, and the Tensas River basin is now being fragmented by logging and conversion to agricultural fields for soybean, cotton, rice, and corn production. In 1957, 560,000 ha of forest remained, with the two largest blocks containing a total of 326,500 ha. By 1990, 157,000 ha remained, only 16% of the original forest, with four large patches (ranging in area from 10,000–30,000 ha) in protected areas and the remaining forest in smaller patches scattered throughout the basin. The Tensas River basin originally supported populations of the red wolf (*Canis rufus*), the Florida panther (*Felis concolor coryi*), and the ivory-billed woodpecker (*Campephilus principalis*), none of which are now found in the area; significant declines also have been observed in the total number of bird species and the abundance of one-third of forest-dependent bird species. Along with habitat destruction has come a decline in water quality, an increase in soil erosion, and flooding following heavy rainfall.

One strategy currently being pursued by The Nature Conservancy and federal, state, and local government departments involves protecting the biological diversity of the Tensas River basin through acquiring and protecting a system of corridors that will link the separate forest blocks into larger units (Llewellyn et al. 1996). Adding 400 ha of forest corridor would increase the size of the largest complex of connected forest from 50,000 ha to 100,000 ha. Adding 600 ha of corridors in the western edge of the basin would link together several large fragments, between 3000–10,000 ha in area, forming a 63,000-ha forest complex. These large forest blocks might be of sufficient size to protect some of the large wildlife species in the region, such as the black bear. In the process of repairing river banks and replanting bottomland habitat, there will be significant improvements in the ecosystem services provided by the river basin to nearby human settlements.

COMMUNITY BABOON SANCTUARY   Corridors may be valuable at a small scale, linking isolated forest patches. Such an approach has been undertaken at the 47 km² Community Baboon Sanctuary (CBS) in the village of

Bermudian Landing in Belize (Figure 16.8). Populations of black howler monkeys (*Alouatta pigra*) were declining because local landowners were clearing forest along the Belize River to create new agricultural land (Horwich and Lyon 1998), and the monkeys were unable to cross open fields between forest patches. As their food sources declined and their ability to move through the river forest became impaired, the monkey population underwent a serious decline. To reverse this trend, the 450 villagers living and owning land in the CBS agreed in 1985 to maintain corridors of forest approximately 20 m wide along the watercourses and property boundaries. Forest corridors also are being established across large fields and between forest patches. Other components of the plan include protecting trees that provide food for the monkeys and building aerial bridges over roads, so the monkeys can cross in safety. These measures appear to be successful, and the black howler population has been steadily increasing as their habitat is reconnected. Ecotourism associated with the project provides significant income to villagers, as described in Chapter 20.

(A)

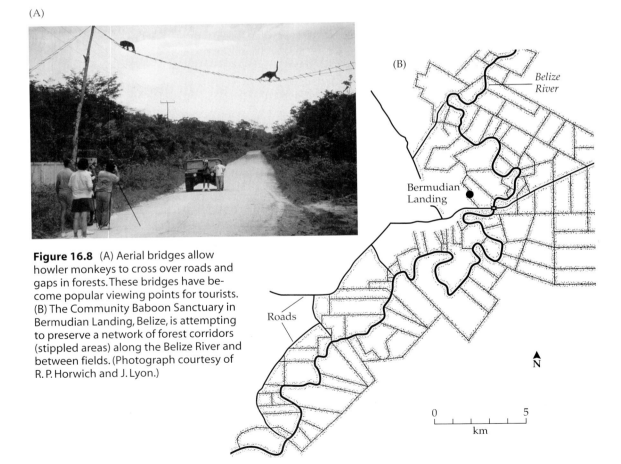

Figure 16.8 (A) Aerial bridges allow howler monkeys to cross over roads and gaps in forests. These bridges have become popular viewing points for tourists. (B) The Community Baboon Sanctuary in Bermudian Landing, Belize, is attempting to preserve a network of forest corridors (stippled areas) along the Belize River and between fields. (Photograph courtesy of R. P. Horwich and J. Lyon.)

Landscape Ecology and Park Design

The interaction of actual land-use patterns, conservation theory, and park design is evident in the discipline of **landscape ecology,** which investigates patterns of habitat types on a regional scale and their influence on species distribution and ecosystem processes (Hansson et al. 1995; Forman 1995; Turner et al. 2001). A landscape is defined by Forman and Godron (1981) as an "area where a cluster of interacting stands or ecosystems is repeated in similar form" (Figure 16.9).

Landscape ecology has been more intensively studied in the human-dominated environments of Europe, where long-term practices of traditional agricultural and forest management determine the landscape pattern, than in North America, where research has emphasized single habitat types that were minimally affected by people. In the European countryside, cultivated fields, pastures, woodlots, and hedges alternate to create a mosaic that affects the distribution of wild species. In the traditional Japanese landscape, known as *satoyama,* flooded rice fields, fields, villages, and forests provide a rich diversity of habitat for wetland species,

(A) Scattered patch landscapes

Open clearings
in a forest

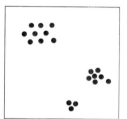

Groves of trees
in a field

(B) Network landscapes

Network of roads
in a large plantation

Riparian network of
rivers and tributaries
in a forest

(C) Interdigitated landscapes

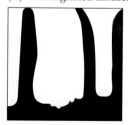

Tributary streams
running into a lake

Shifting
forest–grassland
borders

(D) Checkerboard landscapes

Farmland under
cultivation for
different crops

Lots in a residential
development

Figure 16.9 Renditions of four different landscape types where interacting ecosystems or other land uses form repetitive patterns. The discipline of landscape ecology focuses on such interactions rather than on a single habitat type. (After Zonneveld and Forman 1990.)

Figure 16.10 Traditional rural landscape near Tokyo, Japan, with an alternating pattern of villages (black); secondary forest (light gray shading); *padi*, or wet rice, fields (dark gray shading); and hay fields (white). Such landscapes were common in the past but are now becoming rare due to the increasing mechanization of Japanese agriculture, the movement of the population away from farms, and the urbanization of the Tokyo area. The area covered is approximately 4 km × 4 km. (After Yamaoko et al. 1977.)

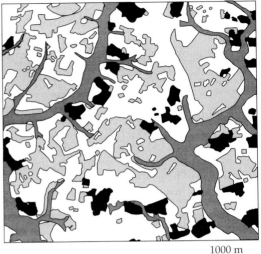

1000 m

such as dragonflies, amphibians, and waterfowl (Figure 16.10). In many areas of Europe and Asia, traditional patterns of farming, grazing, and forestry are being abandoned. In some places, rural people leave the land completely and migrate to urban areas, or their farming practices become more intensive, involving more machinery and inputs of fertilizer. In such cases, to protect biological communities, conservation biologists have to adopt strategies to maintain the traditional landscapes, in some cases by subsidizing traditional practices or having volunteers manage the land.

In such environments, many species are not confined to a single habitat, rather, they move between habitats or live on borders where two habitats meet. For these species, the patterns of habitat types on a regional scale are of critical importance. The presence and density of many species may be affected by the size of habitat patches and their degree of linkage. For example, the population size of a rare animal species will be different in two 100-ha parks, one with an alternating checkerboard of 100 patches of field and forest, each 1 ha in area, the other with a checkerboard of four patches, each 25 ha in area (Figure 16.11). These alternative landscape patterns may have very different effects on the microclimate (wind, temperature, humidity, and light), pest outbreaks, and animal movement patterns, as described in Chapter 9. Different land uses often result in dramatically contrasting landscape patterns. Forest areas cleared for shifting agriculture, permanent subsistence agriculture, plantation agriculture, or suburban development have differing distributions and sizes of remnant forest patches and different kinds of species.

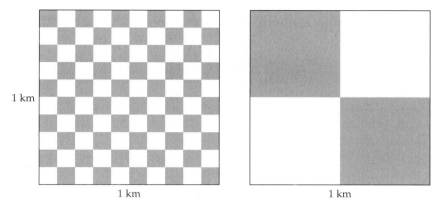

Figure 16.11 Two square nature reserves, each 100 ha in area (1 km on a side). They have equal areas of forest (shaded) and pasture (unshaded) but in very differently sized patches. Which landscape pattern benefits which species? This is a question managers must endeavor to answer.

To increase the number and diversity of animals, wildlife managers sometimes create the greatest amount of landscape variation possible within the confines of their game management unit (Yahner 1988). Fields and meadows are created and maintained, small thickets are encouraged, groups of fruit trees and crops are planted, patches of forests are periodically cut, little ponds and dams are developed, and numerous trails and dirt roads meander across and along all of the patches. Such landscaping is often appealing to the public, who are the main visitors and financial contributors to the park. The result is a park transformed into a mass of edges where transition zones abound. In one textbook on wildlife management, managers are advised to "develop as much edge as possible" because "wildlife is a product of the places where two habitats meet" (Yoakum and Dasmann 1971). This traditional approach is changing, as wildlife biologists include a broader set of goals in their management policies.

The goal of conservation biologists and wildlife biologists is not only to include as many species as possible within small nature reserves, but to protect those species most in danger of extinction as a result of human activity. Small reserves broken up into many subdivided habitat units within a compressed landscape (created in the past by wildlife managers) may have a large number of species, but these are likely to be principally common species that depend on human disturbance—in some cases, invasive species. A reserve that contains the maximum amount of edge may lack many rare interior species that survive only in large blocks of undisturbed habitat. The net result is that parks intensively managed for maximum wildlife and habitat diversity could be inhospitable to certain species of true conservation significance.

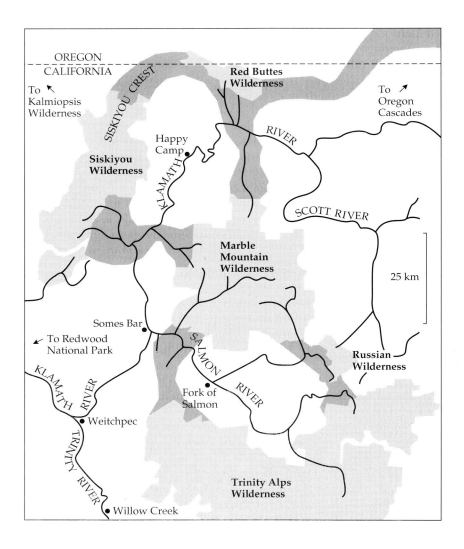

To remedy this localized approach, biological diversity needs to be managed on a regional landscape level, in which the size of the landscape units more closely approximates the natural size and migration patterns of the species (Cook and van Lier 1994; Grumbine 1994; Noss and Cooperrider 1994). An alternative to creating a miniature landscape of a variety of habitats on a small scale is to link all parks in an area in a regional plan, perhaps involving corridors, in which larger habitat units could be created (Figure 16.12). The Wildlands Project and the U.S. National Wildlife Refuge System are two such examples. Some of these larger habitat units would protect rare species, such as bears, wolves, and large cats, that are unable to tolerate human disturbance and need large areas to exist (Box 24).

◀ **Figure 16.12** In the Klamath National Forest of northern California and southern Oregon are five wilderness areas (light gray). Rather than managing these as independent protected areas, a proposal has been made to link them with corridors (darker gray). The region would then be managed as a single large conservation unit. A long-term goal would be to extend this regional management to nearby protected areas (arrows). (From Pace 1991.)

BOX 24 *National Wildlife Refuges*

When is protected land really protected? That question is being debated by managers of the National Wildlife Refuges (NWRs) scattered throughout the United States (Chadwick 1996). The first refuge was established in 1903, when President Theodore Roosevelt declared Pelican Island in Florida a protected area for birds. Since then 538 wildlife refuges covering a total of 1 million km² have been established—they are located in every state and in many territories. National Wildlife Refuges differ from national parks in that they are specifically set aside to benefit native flora and fauna rather than humans. Yet pressure from hunters, oil companies, and other special interest groups has influenced Congress to allow uses that may ultimately be incompatible with wildlife protection.

In many cases, NWRs provide the only protected habit for endangered species: panthers prowl the Florida Panther NWR; desert bighorn sheep and the Sonoran pronghorn roam in Cabeza Prieta NWR in Arizona; Lake Wales Ridge NWR protects a unique Florida scrub ecosystem; and sea turtles nest in the Culebra NWR, on the sandy beaches of Culebra, a tiny island off the coast of Puerto Rico. Wildlife refuges also provide essential habitat for species that are not endangered. Refuges dotting the north–south flyways used by migratory birds provide vital stopover habitats and nesting grounds and host countless other species. In total, the NWR system protects 168 threatened or endangered species.

Yet 60% of all NWRs allow activities harmful to wildlife. Over half of the nation's refuges allow hunting, which is justified on the grounds that permits and special stamps sold to hunters finance and maintain much of the NWR system; 207 NWRs also allow trapping. Ad-

Vast grasslands and herds of wildlife are a feature of the Arctic National Wildlife Refuge. Will the energy needs of the United States lead to oil explorations and extractions in this 60 million-ha wilderness? (Photograph © Tom Walker/Visuals Unlimited.)

BOX 24 *(continued)*

ditional moneys from the Land and Water Conservation Fund came with the primary mission to increase public space for recreation, rather than conservation. Some lands transferred from other federal organizations came with attendant drilling, mining, or grazing rights, which persisted under the National Wildlife Refuge title. The U.S. Fish and Wildlife Service, which is charged with managing the NWRs, must decide which activities are compatible with wildlife. Numerous Congressional committees have been unable to resolve this question. If trapping 1000 alligators every year in Sabine NWR is biologically sustainable, what about harvesting alligator eggs? If biologists ask ranchers to graze additional cattle to improve foraging conditions for geese in Merced NWR, why are grazing privileges being restricted in the Charles M. Russell NWR? Are the subsistence hunting and fishing privileges given to Yupik Eskimos substantially different from the hunting permits provided to duck hunters? Are power launches carrying bird-watchers different from boats towing water-skiers? Drawing the line is not easy, and shifting political winds make resolution more difficult.

The focus of emotional debate at present is the Arctic National Wildlife Refuge (ANWR), a pristine wilderness so remote that few humans have visited there, much less left any mark on the landscape. This area is sometimes referred to as "America's Serengeti," due to the abundant wildlife consisting of herds of caribou and musk oxen, nesting sites of tundra swans and seabirds, and bowhead whales just offshore. The ANWR sits on top of up to 7 billion barrels of oil, considered vital by many to the strategic energy needs of the United States. Environmentalists describe the potential for oil spills, the ugliness of drilling platforms, damage to the tundra, and the loss of a national treasure, while the business community, the Bush White House, and certain government officials emphasize the need to give the country additional options for energy independence. In the end, a compromise might allow oil extraction in limited areas of the refuge using methods that minimize the impact on the environment, such as slant drilling to reduce the number of drilling platforms and trucking in supplies only in winter when the tundra is frozen and roads can be made of ice. How this situation will be resolved is still being debated. However, whenever conservation ethics come up against business interests, any solution is bound to be imperfect.

Conclusion

Within the field of conservation biology, there is ongoing discussion of the optimal procedures for designing networks of protected areas. The publication of new research results and vigorous discussion are helping to provide greater insight into the various issues; some conservation biologists would argue that enough research has been done already. However, in describing the desire of conservation biologists to provide land managers with simplified general guidelines for designing networks of nature reserves, David Ehrenfeld (1989), a leading conservation scientist, states:

> I feel obliged to point out that there is a widespread obsession with a search for general rules of scientific conservation, the genetic code of conservation so to speak, and this finds expression in very general

statements about extinction rates, viable population sizes, ideal reserve designs, and so forth. . . . Yet this kind of generality is easily abused, especially when would-be conservationists become bewitched by models of their own making. When this happens, the sight of otherwise intelligent people trying to extract non-obvious general rules about extinction from their own polished and highly simplified versions of reality becomes a spectacle that would have interested Lewis Carroll. . . . We should not be surprised when different conservation problems call for qualitatively different solutions.

As of now, the managers of protected areas will still have to approach each land-acquisition decision on its individual merits. Managers need to be aware of the best examples and the appropriate models, but in the end the particular circumstances of a case, often involving such concerns as funding and politics, will determine the course of action. Probably the greatest challenge in designing systems of protected areas is to anticipate how the network will be managed to achieve its goals. In many cases, the management plan for the protected areas will be more important than the size and shape of the individual protected areas. In addition, people living nearby may help meet management objectives or come into conflict with park managers. This is the subject of the next chapter.

Summary

1. Conservation biologists are investigating the best way to design networks of protected areas. In some cases, investigations are based on the assumption that these areas have islandlike characteristics in a matrix of human-dominated landscape. The insight provided by these investigations can be combined with common sense and natural-history data to develop a useful approach.

2. Conservation biologists have debated whether it is better to create a single large park or several small parks comprising equivalent area; convincing arguments and evidence have been presented on both sides. In general, though, a large park will have more species than a small park of equivalent habitat.

3. Parks need to be designed to minimize harmful edge effects and, if possible, should contain an entire ecosystem. The tendency to fragment parks with roads, fences, and other human developments should be avoided, because they inhibit migration and facilitate the spread of exotic and other undesirable species and diseases. Whenever possible, government authorities and private landowners should coordinate their activities and manage adjoining small parcels of land as one large unit.

4. Habitat corridors have been proposed to link isolated conservation areas. These corridors may allow the movement of animals between protected areas, which would facilitate gene flow as well as dispersal and colonization of new sites. Habitat corridors will be most effective when they protect existing routes of migratory animals.

5. In the past, wildlife biologists advocated creating a mosaic of habitats with abundant edges. While this landscape design often increases the number of species and the overall abundance of animals, it may not favor some species of greatest conservation concern, which often occupy large blocks of undisturbed habitat.

For Discussion

1. The only known population of a rare beetle species has 50 individuals and exists in a 10 m × 10 m area in a 1-ha (100 m × 100 m) patch of metropolitan woodland. Should this woodland be established as a protected area or is it too small to protect the species? How would you make this determination? What suggestions could you make for designing and managing a park that would increase the chances of survival for this beetle species?

2. Obtain a map of a national park or protected area. How does the shape and location of the protected area differ from the ideal designs discussed in this chapter? What would it take to improve the design of the park and/or coordinate its management with surrounding landholders, so that it had a greater likelihood of preserving biodiversity?

3. Obtain a map of protected areas for a country or region. Consider how these protected areas could be linked by a system of habitat corridors. What would it accomplish? How much land would have to be acquired? How much would it cost? To complete this exercise, you might have to make many assumptions.

Suggested Readings

Bennett, A. F. 1999. *Linkages in the Landscape: The Role of Corridors and Connectivity in Wildlife Conservation.* IUCN, Gland, Switzerland. Book-length review of conservation corridors, with theory and examples.

Chadwick, D. H. 1996. Sanctuary: U.S. National Wildlife Refuges. *National Geographic* 190 (April): 2–35. A beautifully illustrated article, written in an accessible style.

Cook, E. A. and H. N. van Lier (eds.). 1994. *Landscape Planning and Ecological Networks.* Elsevier, Amsterdam. Conservation planning in a wide variety of ecosystems, with many European examples.

Deardon, P. 1995. Park literacy and conservation. *Conservation Biology* 9: 1654–1656. Excellent short essay on the role of protected areas as museums, zoos, playgrounds, cathedrals, reservoirs, laboratories, and schoolrooms.

Game, M. and G. F. Peterken. 1984. Nature reserve selection strategies in the woodlands of Central Lincolnshire, England. *Biological Conservation* 29: 157–181. Practical guide to land acquisition decisions.

Laurance, S. G. and W. F. Laurance. 1999. Tropical wildlife corridors: use of linear rainforest remnants by arboreal mammals. *Biological Conservation* 91: 231–239. This study from Australia shows that corridors 30–40m wide can be used by most arboreal mammals.

Poiani, K. A., B. D. Richter, M. G. Anderson, and H. E. Richter. 2000. Biodiversity conservation at multiple scales: Functional sites, landscapes and networks. *BioScience* 50: 133–146. Protecting biodiversity requires protecting the variation in natural processes, along with ecosystems and species.

Pressey, R. L., C. J. Humphries, C. R. Margules, R. I. Vane-Wright, and P. H. Williams. 1993. Beyond opportunism: Key principles for systematic reserve selection. *Trends in Ecology and Evolution* 8: 124–128. An alternative to the current haphazard approach to land acquisition.

Rosenberg, D. K., B. R. Noon, and E. C. Meslow. 1997. Biological corridors: Form, function, and efficiency. *BioScience* 47: 677–687. Many experiments are evaluating corridors and will hopefully determine their value to conservation efforts.

Schwartz, M. W. 1997. *Conservation in Highly Fragmented Landscapes.* Chapman & Hall, New York. Designing and managing nature reserves, with a particular emphasis on the U.S. Midwest. See the excellent chapter by Shafer.

Shafer, C. L. 1990. *Nature Reserves: Island Theory and Conservation Practice.* Smithsonian Institution Press, Washington, D.C. A comprehensive, well-illustrated review of the theories of reserve design, which presents evidence and counter-evidence for particular theories.

Shafer, C. L. 2001. Conservation biology trailblazers: George Wright, Ben Thompson and Joseph Dixon. *Conservation Biology* 15: 332–344. Many of the modern principles of conservation biology, park design, and wildlife management were practiced by past field biologists.

Soulé, M. E., and J. Terborgh. 1999. *Continental Conservation: Scientific Foundations of Regional Reserve Networks.* Island Press, Washington, D.C. Planning for conservation on a really big scale.

Turner, M. G., R. H. Garner, and R. V. O'Neill. 2001. *Landscape Ecology in Theory and Practice: Pattern and Process.* Springer-Verlag, New York.

Wallis deVries, M. F. 1995. Large herbivores and the design of large-scale nature reserves in Western Europe. *Conservation Biology* 9: 25–33. Excellent review of the difficulties of conserving large herbivores in a densely settled, highly developed region; strategies for designing better, larger protected areas.

17

Managing Protected Areas

P rotected areas have different objectives, depending on their legal status, establishment history, and individual characteristics. Some are designated to meet the needs of particular species. Others are designed to protect whole ecosystems, while other areas are protected for recreational and cultural values. Regardless of their objective, though, active management is often required for all kinds of protected areas, and it is important that the management be tailored to the goals of each individual protected area. This chapter examines some of the strategies employed in managing protected areas.

Although some people believe that "nature knows best" and that biodiversity is best served when humans do not intervene, the reality is often very different. In many cases, humans have already modified the environment so much that the remaining species and communities need human monitoring and intervention in order to survive. The world is littered with paper parks that have been created by government decree and then left to flounder without any management. These protected areas have gradually—and sometimes rapidly—lost species, and their habitat quality has been degraded. In some countries, people do not hesitate to farm, log, mine, hunt, and fish in protected areas because they feel that government land is owned by "everyone," "anybody" can take whatever they want, and "nobody" is willing to intervene. The crucial point is that often parks must be actively managed to prevent deterioration (Sutherland and Hill 1995; Halvorson and Davis 1996).

In addition, the most effective parks are usually those whose managers have the benefit of information provided by research and monitoring programs and have funds available to implement management plans. However, it is also true that sometimes management practices are ineffective or even detrimental. For example:

- Active management to promote the abundance of a game species such as deer has frequently involved eliminating top predators such as wolves and cougars; without predators to control them, game populations (and, incidentally, rodents) sometimes increase far beyond expectations. The result is overgrazing, habitat degradation, and a collapse of the animal and plant communities.
- Overenthusiastic park managers who remove hollow trees, dead standing trees, rotting logs, and underbrush to "improve" a park's appearance may unwittingly remove a critical resource needed by certain animal species for nesting and overwintering. Hollow trees, for instance, are the major nesting site for many bats and bears, and rotting logs are prime germination sites for the seeds of many orchids. In these instances, a "clean" park equals a biologically sterile park.
- In many parks, fire is part of the natural ecology of the area. Attempts to suppress fire completely are expensive and waste scarce management resources. They may eventually lead to loss of fire-dependent species and to massive, uncontrollable fires of unnatural intensity such as those that occurred in Yellowstone National Park in 1988.
- Attempts to reduce the illegal poaching of black and white rhinos by cutting off their valuable horns have apparently resulted in the inability of adult rhinos to chase away predators, greatly increasing mortality of rhino calves (Cunningham and Berger 1997).

In some countries, particularly Asian and European countries such as the United Kingdom and Japan, the habitats of interest, such as woodlands, meadows, and hedges, have been formed from hundreds and even thousands of years of human activity. These habitats support high species diversity as a result of traditional land-management practices, which must be maintained if the species are to persist. If these areas are not managed, they will undergo succession and lose many of their characteristic species. Many examples of successful park management come from the United Kingdom, where there is a history of scientists and volunteers successfully monitoring and managing small reserves such as the Monks Wood and Castle Hill Nature Reserves (Peterken 1996; Morris 2000). At these sites, the effects of different grazing methods (sheep vs. cattle, light vs. heavy grazing) on populations of wildflowers, butterflies, and birds are closely followed. For example, in montane grasslands at Ben Lawers National Nature Reserve in Scotland, the response of a rare alpine gentian has been studied in relation to the intensity of sheep grazing (Miller et al. 1999a). Gentian populations initially increase when sheep are excluded, but decline after three years due to an inability to compete with taller plants and a lack of open sites for seedling establishment. The presence of moderate sheep grazing is critical to the maintenance of this rare wildflower.

In a symposium volume entitled *The Scientific Management of Animal and Plant Communities for Conservation* (Duffey and Watts 1971), Michael Morris of Monks Wood concluded that

> There is no inherently right or wrong way to manage a nature reserve . . . the aptness of any method of management must be related to the objects of management for any particular site. . . . Only when objects of management have been formulated can results of scientific management be applied.

Small reserves, such as those found in long-settled areas and large cities, will generally require more active management than large reserves because they often are surrounded by an altered environment, have less interior habitat, and are more easily affected by exotic species and human activities. Even in large reserves, active management may be required to control hunting and to regulate the frequency of fire and the number of visitors. Simply maintaining the park boundaries may not be sufficient except in the largest and most remote areas.

Monitoring as a Management Tool

An important aspect of park management involves monitoring components that are crucial for biological diversity, such as the water level of ponds, the amount of soil being washed into streams, the number of individuals of rare and endangered species, the density of herbs, shrubs, and trees, the dates migratory animals arrive at and leave the park, and the amount of natural materials being removed by local people. Basic monitoring methods include recording standard observations, performing surveys of key elements, taking photographs from fixed points, and conducting interviews with park users (Danielson et al. 2000) (see Chapter 12). The exact types of information gathered depend on the goals of park management. Not only does monitoring allow managers to determine the health of the park, but it can suggest which management practices are working and which are not. With the right information, managers may be able to adjust park management practices to increase the chances of success.

One species that has been intensively monitored for decades is the giant cactus, or saguaro (*Carnegiea gigantea*), an icon of the desert land-

Figure 17.1 The same landscape, photographed in 1935, 1962, and 1986, showing ▶ the decline of a saguaro cactus population in the Rincon Mountain District, Saguaro National Park. The photographs depict the same population—there are no new saguaro plants visible in the photo, though there are many young plants. (Photographs by H. L. Shantz, J. R. Hastings, and R. M. Turner.)

scape (McAuliffe 1996). In 1933, the Saguaro National Monument was established east of Tucson, Arizona, to protect this flagship species. Detailed observations, combined with precise photographic records (Figure 17.1), show that stands of large saguaro are declining within the park. Investigations over an 80-year period suggest that adult cacti are damaged or killed by periods of subfreezing weather that occur about once a decade. Also, cattle grazing, which occurred from the 1880s until 1979, prevented regeneration by trampling seedlings and compacting the soil. Now that cattle grazing has stopped for over 20 years, permanent research plots within the park have recorded the establishment of large numbers of young saguaro plants. These will be closely watched to see if new cactus forests appear later this century.

Identifying and Managing Threats

Management of protected areas must take into account factors that threaten the biological diversity and ecological health of the park. These include many of the threats detailed in Chapters 9 and 10, including exotic species; low population size among rare species; habitat destruction, fragmentation, or degradation; and human use. In 1990, the World Conservation Monitoring Centre and UNESCO conducted a survey of 89 World Heritage sites to identify their management problems (WRI 1992). The responses showed a wide range of management problems as well as significant differences among continents. Threats to protected areas were generally greatest in South America and least in Europe. Illegal wildlife harvesting, fire, grazing, and cultivation were major threats in both South America and Africa. Inadequate park management was a particular problem in developing countries in Africa, Asia, and South America. The greatest threats faced by parks in industrialized countries were threats associated with major economic developments. Although these general patterns only provide an overview, they underscore how necessary it is to tailor management to individual parks, since any single park has its own unique problems—such as the illegal logging and hunting that plague many Central American parks, the vast number of tourists crowding into Yellowstone National Park during July and August, and the damage done to coral in tropical marine parks by pollution and unsupervised divers.

1935

1962

1986

Even in a well-regulated park, air pollution, acid rain, water pollution, global climate change, and the changing composition of atmospheric gases influence natural communities and cause some species to increase and others to decrease or be eliminated. Unfortunately, natural history studies show that invasive exotic species are likely to be the main beneficiaries of an altered environment since they tend to be adaptable, efficient dispersers and tolerant of disturbance. The ability of park managers to deal with these major, externally driven alterations in ecosystem processes is rather limited. Experiments are being conducted in which basic compounds such as lime are added to water bodies to prevent acidification; however, these measures will never take the place of needed environmental reforms to limit human production and consumption patterns.

Managing Invasive Species

Invasion by exotic species is now recognized as a threat to many protected areas, particularly wetlands, grasslands, and islands ecosystems. In many places, exotic species may already be present inside a park, and new exotic species may be invading along its boundaries. If these species are allowed to increase unchecked, native species and even entire communities might be eliminated from the park. Where an invasive species threatens native species, it should be removed or at least reduced in frequency (Myers et al. 2000). An exotic species that has just arrived and has known invasive tendencies should be aggressively removed while it is still at low densities. Removing invasive species each year is often highly cost-effective in comparison with the expensive massive eradication programs that are required when the population of an exotic species explodes (Chen 2001). European purple loosestrife (*Lythrum salicaria*), which invades North American wetlands, is an example of an invasive species that can outcompete many native plants, often forming pure stands along river and pond edges and in marshes. This species has a detrimental effect on wildlife, since it is not eaten by most waterfowl and crowds out beneficial species.

Once such an exotic species becomes established in an area, it may be difficult (if not impossible) to eliminate it. The recovery of previously declining populations of native plants and animals has often been linked to the elimination of exotic animal species such as goats, rats, rabbits, and sea gulls from islands and other management areas. Common methods involve poisoning, shooting, capturing, and preventing reproduction. In such cases, a major effort in public relations is needed to explain the goal of the intervention and to respond to the concerns of the public. As an example of pest management, colonies of three rare species of terns on an island off the Maine coast were displaced by expanding common sea gull populations (Anderson and Devlin 1999). When the sea gulls were removed by poisoning and shooting, the terns returned to the island and their numbers appear to be recovering. Constant vigilance is required, as the sea gulls would quickly return to the island if park managers did not shoot at them.

Managing Habitat

A park may have to be aggressively managed to ensure that the full range of original habitat types are maintained (Richards et al. 1999). Many species only occupy specific habitats and specific successional stages of habitat. When land is set aside as a protected area, often the pattern of disturbance and human usage changes so markedly that many species previously found on the site fail to persist. Natural disturbances, including fires, grazing, and tree falls, are key elements in the ecosystem required for the presence of certain rare species. In small parks, the full range of successional stages may not be present at a site, and many species may be missing for this reason. For example, in an isolated park dominated by old-growth trees, species characteristic of the early successional herb and shrub stage may be missing (Figure 17.2). If such a

Figure 17.2 A general model of the change in species diversity during forest succession following a major disturbance such as a fire, hurricane, or clear-cut logging. Early successional species are generally fast-growing and intolerant of shade; late successional species grow more slowly and are shade-tolerant. The full successional time span covers many years. (After Norse 1986.)

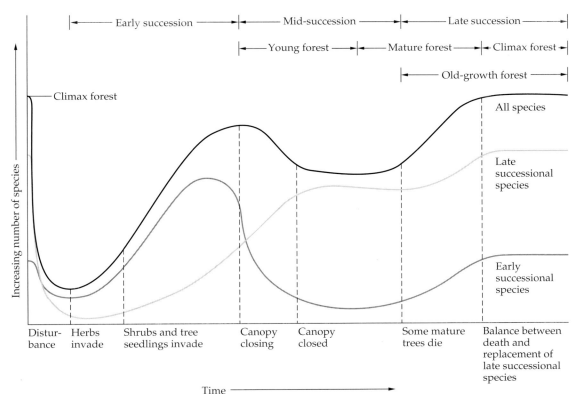

park is swept entirely by a fire or a windstorm, the species characteristic of old-growth forest may be eliminated. In many isolated protected areas in metropolitan areas, frequent human-caused fires and other human disturbances eliminate many of the late successional plant and animal species. However, early successional species may also be missing if they are not present in adjacent sites that serve as colonization sources.

Park managers sometimes must actively manage sites to ensure that all successional stages are present, so that species characteristic of each stage have a place to persist and thrive (Box 25). One common way to do this is to periodically set localized, controlled fires in grassland, shrublands, and forests to reinitiate the successional process (Fuhlendorf and Engle 2001). In some wildlife sanctuaries, grasslands and fields are maintained by livestock grazing, burning, mowing, or shallow plowing in order to retain open habitat in the landscape. For example, many of the unique wildflowers of Nantucket Island off the coast of Massachusetts are found in the scenic heathland areas. These heathlands were previously maintained by grazing sheep; now they must be burned every few years to prevent scrub oak forest from taking over and shading out the wildflowers (Figure 17.3A). The type and timing of management can also help in removing exotic species (Weiss 1999). In other situations, parts of protected areas must be carefully managed to minimize human disturbance and provide the conditions required by old-growth species (Figure 17.3B). For example, certain ground beetle species are found only in mature stands of boreal forest and disappear from lands managed under a system of clear-cut harvesting (Niemelå et al. 1993).

Fire appears to be important for maintaining species diversity in shrub ecosystems such as those found in the Mediterranean region, the chaparral of California, and the fynbos of South Africa. Speciation in response to the effects of fire appears to be primarily responsible for the development of the rich flora found in many shrubland communities. As humans have settled in shrubland areas, they have altered the natural fire regime (Pyne 1997). Frequent intentional fires to encourage the growth of young vegetation, combined with overgrazing, has led to severe soil erosion and desertification in many Mediterranean countries. However, complete suppression of fires also has negative effects, since a build-up of dead wood can result in infrequent accidental fires that are widespread, very hot, and destructive. A regular schedule of controlled burns appears to be the best strategy for maintaining species diversity and vegetation structure, and minimizing fire damage in shrubland vegetation (Brown et al. 1991).

Controlled disturbance is also necessary to maintain some species in English fens, a type of wet meadow or marshland. The fen violet, *Viola persicifolia*, has declined rapidly in Europe, as its habitat of open, alkaline, peaty areas (such as fens) has been drained and altered (Pullin and

BOX 25 *Habitat Management: The Key to Success in the Conservation of Endangered Butterflies*

In 1980 the heath fritillary butterfly (*Mellicta athalia*) had the dubious honor of being closer to extinction than any other butterfly species in England. The distribution of the species had declined steadily for 70 years as its preferred habitat became overgrown or was converted to farmland. The larvae of the heath fritillary feed on plants found in unimproved grasslands or where woodland has recently been cleared to create sunny glades. These habitats are ephemeral and patchy by nature; they require regular cutting of trees or grazing to maintain populations of the butterflies' food plants. The decline of traditional forestry practices and intensive farming have interrupted the natural processes that provide the necessary habitat (Warren 1991). The problem faced by the heath fritillary is similar to that of a number of butterfly species that must colonize specialized, ephemeral habitats —they survive as a network of temporary populations linked by dispersal, which is best described as a metapopulation. The silver-studded blue butterfly (*Plebejus argus*), found in the heathlands of East Anglia, and the bay checkerspot (*Euphydryas editha bayensis*), found in serpentine grasslands in the San Francisco Bay Area, are two species that share the heath fritillary's difficulties.

Long-term studies of the bay checkerspot have been particularly valuable in establishing key factors in the conservation and management of butterfly populations in habitat patches (Murphy et al. 1990). Many of these species have subtle, specialized habitat requirements that are best satisfied by extensive and diverse habitat in which natural processes can create favorable conditions. In the case of the silver-studded blue, the species is only found in young stands of bell heather, where adults feed on nectar and larvae feed on leaves (Ravenscroft 1990). The specialization goes even further because the larvae must be tended by a certain type of black ant (*Lasius* sp.) to survive, and the distribution of these ants is variable. When the butterflies' habitats are fragmented, these natural patterns may be interrupted. Species may be unable to locate new suitable habitat due to limited dispersal abilities. The silver-studded blue in particular seems to be unable to disperse more than 1 km from existing populations (Thomas 1995). Experimental attempts to establish new populations

Larvae of the heath fritillary butterfly *(Mellicta athalia)* feed on early succession plants and require the kind of patchy habitat that occurs when disturbances open up gaps in a forest. Intensive land use interrupts the natural processes that produce this habitat, endangering the survival of the species. (Photographs © Martin Warren.)

BOX 25 *(continued)*

by carrying adults to unoccupied sites have had some degree of success.

Detailed ecological studies have provided the basis for species-specific management strategies. Areas with heath fritillary populations are now managed to encourage the habitat types that the species prefers, such as newly felled woodland and unimproved grasslands. Assessment of the fritillary's progress after nearly a decade of intervention to maintain early-succession food plants demonstrates that human intervention has been a significant factor in the success of the colonies. Where habitat management did not occur, the majority of colonies became extinct (Warren 1991). Humans can simulate natural processes, as the case of the heath fritillary demonstrates, and intensive management has been generally successful in preventing the fritillary's extinction. However, the practice raises the disturbing issue of the extent to which endangered species depend on human action. The heath fritillary now appears to be utterly dependent on human intervention for survival; the fate of many other species probably rests entirely in our hands as well.

Many rare prairie butterfly species in North America are restricted to fragments that are maintained as nature reserves by government and conservation organizations (Swengel 1996). These prairies need to be burned, mown for hay, or grazed to maintain the prairie plants and vegetation, and each of these management regimens has significant effects on butterfly populations. In general, mowing is the most effective way to maintain populations of these rare species. In Iowa, roadsides dominated by exotic grasses are increasingly being replanted with native prairies species. While the original purpose of the program was to reduce maintenance costs, an indirect benefit has been a substantial increase in the abundance and diversity of rare butterfly species (Ries et al. 2001). The diversity of butterflies is most closely correlated with the diversity of prairie plants in flower.

Rare butterfly species such as the bay checkerspot and the silver-studded blue are often sensitive to changes in land-use practices. As people utilize more of the landscape for intensive agriculture, forest plantations, and human settlements, there will be less habitat suitable for butterflies. Butterflies are important to most human societies as symbols of beauty and freedom. If we want to have butterflies in our world, we need to include maintaining habitat for butterflies as an important management goal. In many cases this will mean continuing traditional land-use practices, particularly in European countries where the landscape has been strongly influenced by human activities, or even deliberately restoring habitat favored by butterflies.

Woodell 1987). At Woodwalton Fen National Nature Reserve, the species had apparently disappeared, but it was found again after considerable soil disturbance from the removal of scrub and commercial digging allowed seeds of the plant to germinate. A management policy involving removal of scrub and disturbance of soil appears to be necessary for the continued existence of the fen violet in England.

The type of controlled management that provides optimal results can be determined through field experiments. For example, chalk grasslands in Britain require specific management measures to maintain a biologically rich community. Experiments have shown that the number of species, the particular species present, and the species' relative abun-

(A)

(B)

Figure 17.3 Conservation management: intervention versus leave-it-alone. (A) Heathland in protected areas of Cape Cod, Massachusetts, is burned on a regular basis in order to maintain the open vegetation habitat and protect wildflowers and other rare species. (Photograph by Jackie Sones, Massachusetts Audubon Society.) (B) Sometimes management involves keeping human disturbance to an absolute minimum. This old-growth stand in the Olympic National Forest in Washington is the result of many years of solitude. (Photograph by Thomas Kitchin/Tom Stack & Associates.)

dance are determined by the management regime: whether the grassland is grazed, mowed, or burned; the time of year of the management; the amount of fertilizer applied; and whether the management is carried out continuously, annually, or rotationally (Morris 1971). Certain management regimes favor certain groups of species over others.

Managing Water

Rivers, lakes, swamps, estuaries, and all other types of wetlands must receive a sufficient supply of clean water to maintain their ecosystem processes. In particular, maintaining healthy wetlands is necessary for populations of waterbirds, fish, amphibians, aquatic plants, and a host of other species (Moyle and Leidy 1992; Pringle 2000). Yet parks may end up directly competing for water resources with irrigation projects, demands for residential and industrial water supplies, flood control schemes, and hydroelectric dams. Wetlands are often interconnected, so a decision affecting water levels and quality in one place has ramifications for other areas. One strategy for maintaining wetlands is to include an entire watershed within the protected area.

Biological reserves most likely to be affected by human alterations of hydrology are those located in the lower part of a watershed, whereas biological reserves located in the upper parts of a watershed are somewhat less likely to be affected. However, even remote sources of water are not exempt from human demands. In the mountains of Puerto Rico, water intakes in the Caribbean National Forest divert stream water for use as drinking water and for power generation (Figure 17.4; Pringle 2000). Six hundred thousand people are dependent on this diverted stream water. However, this means that more than 50% of the water is diverted on an average day, and many streams are dry for most of the year, resulting in a major impact on populations of fish and other aquatic animals, as well as ecological processes.

The water in nature reserves can be contaminated from nearby agricultural, residential, and industrial areas. Such a process can develop gradually over decades, as happened when the Everglades National Park in Florida was encircled by agricultural and urban development and its water source diverted and contaminated. An example of sudden contamination occurred in Spain in 1998 when a dam at a mine site collapsed, releasing approximately 150,000 m^3 of acid sludge with high concentrations of lead, zinc, and arsenic into the Doñana National Park wetlands. Huge numbers of fish and aquatic invertebrates died as a result. To deal with such situations, park managers may have to become politically sophisticated and effective at public relations to ensure that the wetlands under their supervision continue to receive the clean water they need to survive. A program of water-quality monitoring can help to document alterations in quality and quantity of water in ecosystems and to provide the information needed to convince government officials and the public of the seriousness of the problem.

Managing Keystone Resources

In the same way that natural patterns of disturbance may need to be artificially maintained, it may be necessary to preserve, maintain, and

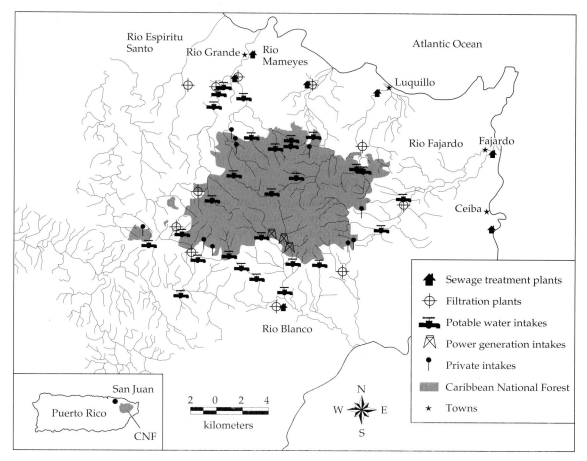

Figure 17.4 The Caribbean National Forest in the mountains of eastern Puerto Rico and its surroundings are the site of numerous intakes for drinking water, power generation, and private-use sewage treatment plants and water filtration plants. On an average day, these intakes divert more than half of the water in the streams, and as a result, some streams are typically dry. Note that water intakes are often in the mountains where the land is undeveloped and the water is clean, whereas the sewage treatment plants are near the coast, where the towns are located. (After Pringle 2000.)

supplement keystone resources on which many species depend. These include sources of food, water, minerals, natural shelter, and so forth. For example, fruits could be put on feeding platforms to replace a natural food source that was destroyed, or artificial pools could be built in streambeds to provide replacement water supplies. Keystone resources and keystone species can be enhanced in managed conservation areas to increase the populations of species whose members have declined. By planting native fruit trees and building an artificial pond, it might be possible to maintain vertebrate species in a smaller conservation area and at higher densities than would be predicted based on studies of species distribution in undisturbed habitat. Artificial ponds not only provide needed habitat for attractive insects such as dragonflies, but are important centers of public education in urban areas (Steytler and Samways 1995). Another example is providing nesting boxes or drilling nesting holes in trees for birds as a substitute resource when there are few dead trees with nesting cavities (see Figure 16.4). In this way a viable population of a rare species could be established, whereas without such interventions the population size of the rare species might be too small to persist. In each case a balance must be struck between establishing nature reserves free from human influence and creating seminatural gardens in which the plants and animals are dependent on people.

Managing Parks and People

Human use of the landscape is a reality that must be addressed in park design and management (Kramer et al. 1997; Redford and Sanderson 2000). People have been a part of virtually all the world's ecosystems for thousands of years, and excluding humans from nature reserves could have unforeseen consequences. For example, a savannah protected from cattle grazing and from fires set by people may change to forest, with a subsequent loss of the savannah species. When people who have traditionally used materials from inside a nature reserve are suddenly refused access to the area, they lose basic resources that they need to stay alive, and they will understandably be angry, frustrated, and unlikely to support the conservation effort. However, it is sometimes necessary to exclude local people from protected areas when resources are being overharvested to the point where the integrity of the biological communities is being threatened. This could result from overgrazing by cattle, excessive collection of fuelwood, or hunting with guns.

A possible solution to deal with a variety of conflicting demands on a protected area is **zoning**, which considers the overall management objectives for a park and sets aside designated areas that permit or give priority to certain activities. Some areas of a forest may be designated for timber production, hunting, wildlife protection, nature trails, or watershed maintenance. A marine reserve might allow fishing in certain areas and strictly prohibit it in others; certain areas might be designated for surfing, water-skiing, and recreational diving, but these sports may be prohibited elsewhere (Figure 17.5). Other commonly established zones are for the recovery of endangered species, restoration of degraded communities, and scientific research. For example, at the Cape Cod National Seashore in Massachusetts, protecting tern and piping plover nesting habitat on beaches has been given priority over the "rights" of people to drive off-road vehicles and to fish on the same beaches where birds

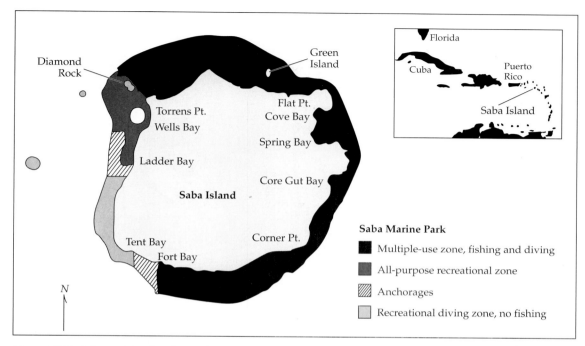

Figure 17.5 Saba, an island in the Caribbean under the jurisdiction of the Netherlands, has established a system of zoning to protect the marine environment and still allow fishing. The Saba Marine Park includes the entire coastal zone of the island. The designation of fishing exclusion zones is important to maintain the health of the coral reefs and fish populations that ecotourists come to see. (After Agardy 1997.)

are nesting (Figure 17.6). A hands-off policy by park managers that does not restrict beach access by fishermen and vehicles would result in the rapid destruction of the shorebird colonies. In this case, a compromise has been developed whereby prime nesting beaches are closed to human activities but other beaches open for recreational activities.

The challenge in zoning is to find a compromise that people are willing to accept that provides for the long-term, sustainable use of natural resources. Enforcement of zoning is often a major challenge for park personnel; for example, in marine reserves, fishermen will tend to move into the fishing-exclusion zones because this is where fishing is best. Only a combination of local involvement, publicity, education, clear posting of warning signs, and visible enforcement can guarantee the success of a zoning plan.

Ningaloo Marine Park, located off the west coast of Australia, provides an example of multiple-use zoning implemented to meet a variety of demands. This park protects the world's largest fringing coral bar-

Figure 17.6 Tern nesting habitat in the Cape Cod National Seashore and at nearby beaches is extremely vulnerable to the "wear and tear" that is inevitable in a heavily visited recreation area. Management is needed to reduce the impact on the birds from hikers, bicyclists, motorcyclists, dune-buggies, picnickers, and dog-walkers. (Photograph by David C. Twichell.)

rier reef, 250 km (156 miles) in length, including such notable species as dugongs (*Dugong dugong*), humpback whales (*Megaptera novaeangeliae*), and whale sharks (*Rhincodon typus*). More than 500 species of fish and 200 species of coral have been reported from the reef; this diversity is comparable to the well-known Great Barrier Reef off eastern Australia. The park has three primary zoning divisions: eight **sanctuary zones** in which human impact is minimized and only the viewing of marine life is permitted; seven **recreation zones** that can include swimming, boating, and recreational fishing; and one **general use zone** in which supervised commercial and recreational fishing is allowed.

Clear guidelines on the use of parks by local people and outside visitors must be a central part of any management plan, both in developed and developing countries (Kothari et al. 1996; Brandon et al. 1998). In Kenya, there has been an ongoing struggle between wildlife experts who advocate integrating local people into park management and others who favor excluding them from the parks. The result has been shifting policy which has left both wildlife officials and local people confused.

Many parks flourish or are destroyed depending on the degree of support, neglect, hostility, or exploitation they receive from the humans living nearby or within park boundaries. If the purpose of a protected area is explained to local residents, and most residents agree with the objectives and respect the rules of the park, then the area may have a better chance of maintaining its natural communities. In the most positive sce-

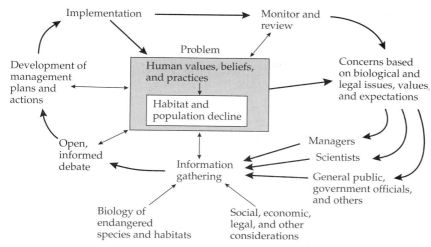

Figure 17.7 A model of an ideal management process for protected areas, emphasizing the stages of decision making. (After Cork et al. 2000.)

nario, local people become involved at the initial stages in park management and planning, are trained and employed by the park authority, and benefit from the protection and regulation of activity within the park (Figure 17.7). At the other extreme, if there is a history of bad relations and distrust between local people and the government, or if the purpose of the park is not explained adequately, the local people may reject the park and ignore park regulations. In this scenario, local people will clash with park personnel, to the detriment of the park. An extreme outcome of such a scenario might be the exclusion of local people from the park, with a conspicuously marked boundary patrolled by park guards. Such a situation has occurred at Nairobi National Park in Kenya and Keoladeo Ghana National Park in India.

There is now increasing recognition that involvement of local people is the crucial, missing element in many conservation management strategies. Top-down strategies, in which governments try to impose conservation plans, need to be integrated with bottom-up programs, in which villages and other local groups formulate and reach their own development goals (Clay 1991). As explained by Lewis (Lewis et al. 1990):

> If any lesson can be learned from past failures of conservation in Africa, it is that conservation implemented solely by government for the presumed benefit of its people will probably have limited success, especially in countries with weakened economies. Instead, conservation for the people and by the people with a largely service and supervisory role delegated to the government could foster a more cooperative relationship between government and the residents living with the re-

source. This might reduce the costs of law enforcement and increase revenues available to other aspects of wildlife management, which could help support the needs of conservation as well as those of the immediate community. Such an approach would have the added advantage of restoring to local residents a greater sense of traditional ownership and responsibility for this resource.

Reconciling the needs of local communities and conservation can be difficult, though. Sudden overconsumption of once-stable wildlife resources indicates that social change is underway. The traditional rules, practices, and agreements that kept local systems in a balance with nature are often swept away when roads, development projects, migrants, or a cash economy sweep into an area. A free-for-all may occur, with long-term residents trying to use what they view as "their" resources before outsiders come in and take them away. In such cases of rapid social change, public relations and enforcement become critical to protecting park resources before they disappear.

The United Nations Educational, Scientific, and Cultural Organization (UNESCO) has pioneered approaches to balance human needs and conservation with its Man and the Biosphere (MAB) Program (Figure 17.8). This program has designated hundreds of Biosphere Reserves worldwide in an attempt to integrate activities of local people, research, protection of the natural environment, and often tourism at a single location (Batisse 1997). The MAB concept depends on a system of zoning that defines a core area in which biological communities and ecosystems are strictly protected with a surrounding buffer zone in which nondestructive research is conducted and traditional human activities, such as the collection of thatch, medicinal plants, and small fuelwood, are carefully monitored for their impact on biodiversity. Surrounding the buffer zone is a transitional zone in which some forms of sustainable development (such as small-scale farming) are allowed, along with some extraction of natural resources (such as selective logging) and experimental research. In many areas, additional income is generated by providing food, lodging, and guiding services to tourists visiting the area. While these zones are easy to draw on paper, in practice it has been difficult to inform the local people who live in or near them where the zones are and what uses are allowed in them.

The general strategy of surrounding core conservation areas with buffer and transition zones is still being debated. The approach has benefits: local people may be more willing to support park activities, and certain desirable features of the landscape created by human use may be maintained (such as farms, gardens, and early stages of succession). Also, buffer zones may facilitate animal dispersal between highly protected core conservation areas and human-dominated transitional and protected areas (Figure 17.9). Yet zoning for multiple-use resource extraction including local people may only work if the core area is large

Opening conservation to man

Is the best way to protect a natural area to seal it off in a "closed jar" from the outside human world? Sooner or later such a policy can destroy the area it was intended to protect. Ecological and sociological pressures - both inside and outside - eventually may shatter the reserve.

Almost all natural areas have been modified by man: creating a reserve by excluding man can upset the ecological balance. Boundaries may not coincide with territorial areas and feeding grounds. Pressure builds up within the reserve. Jammed inside, some animals overbreed, others "eat themselves to starvation"

In some cases, nature reserves are created by excluding the local inhabitants from their traditional grazing and hunting areas. They have difficulty in accepting that these areas are only accessible to tourists. Gradually illicit hunting, grazing and cropping may encroach upon and eradicate the reserve.

MAB emphasizes man's partnership with nature. A reserve is open and interacts with its region. The local people can be its guardians.

It is not suggested that the traditional policy of conservation should be changed everywhere. Certainly some areas must remain untouched. But there are fewer and fewer natural areas left to conserve and certain reserves are being destroyed by these internal and external pressures. Opening conservation to man does not only apply to the Kenyan situation here but to many other countries. It may be a longer term solution.

The diagram (right) illustrates how a Kenyan specialist envisages integrating wildlife conservation, tourism and traditional land use through zonation into different use areas, research for rational management and participation of the local population. The term "biosphere reserve" was coined to identify reserves putting the "open" concept into practice.

MAN AND THE BIOSPHERE (MAB) PROGRAMME, UNESCO

Figure 17.8 Some parks try to protect natural areas by fencing them off from outside influences, analogous to sealing them off in a closed jar. Such policies may fail to recognize ecological and social forces that both maintain and threaten the ecosystem. UNESCO'S Man and the Biosphere (MAB) Program attempts to integrate the needs and cultures of local people in park planning and protection. (Poster from "Ecology in Action: An Exhibit," UNESCO, Paris, 1981.)

enough to protect viable populations of all key species, and if people are willing to respect the zones. Buffer zones may represent gray areas that quickly get treated as unowned and unmanaged lands. The success (or failure) of buffer zones seems to be closely tied to how well people are aware of and willing to obey their designated uses. This varies greatly in different parts of the world among different social situations. One of the ironies of integrating local people into park planning is that a well-run program that provides economic benefits will act as a magnet for poor people from neighboring areas, overwhelming the structure of the project and putting even more pressure on the protected areas.

Human populations will continue to increase dramatically in the coming decades, while resources such as fuelwood, medicinal plants, and wild meat will become harder to find. Managers of nature reserves in the developing world need to anticipate ever-greater demand for use of

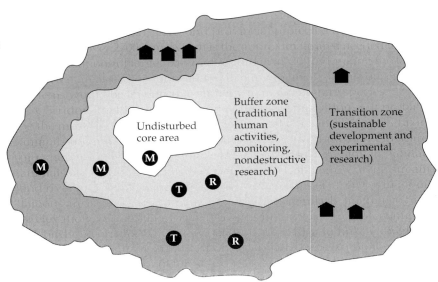

M Monitoring

T Tourism and recreation

⌂ Human settlements

R Research station, education, training

Figure 17.9 The general pattern of a MAB reserve: a core protected area is surrounded by a buffer zone, where human activities are monitored and managed and where research is carried out; this, in turn, is surrounded by a transition zone where sustainable development and experimental research take place.

the remaining patches of natural habitat. Conflict is inevitable as more people live and farm closer to high concentrations of wildlife that, during times of food scarcity, have nowhere to go but out of the park and into nearby agricultural fields and villages. Elephants, baboons, deer, peccaries, agoutis, and hornbills can all be significant crop raiders, while carnivores such as tigers pose a different set of challenges to nearby residents. Buffer zones linked to corridors can be important in mitigating human–wildlife conflicts, a fact appreciated by many traditional people who live near park boundaries.

Regulating Activities inside Protected Areas

Certain human activities are incompatible with maintaining biological diversity within a protected area. If these activities are allowed to continue, important elements of the biological communities eventually may be destroyed. The following activities within protected areas must be regulated, or abolished altogether:

- *Commercial harvesting of game and fish.* Some regulated hunting and fishing may be acceptable for personal consumption and sport, as long as it is sustainable, but harvesting for commercial sale frequently leads to the elimination of species. Commercial hunting and fishing within a reserve, if it is allowed at all, must be carefully monitored by park officials to ensure that animal populations are not depleted. Regulated hunting may also be necessary to control exotic animals and herbivore populations in areas with reduced populations of carnivore species. The problem with regulating hunting is that armed local hunters operating in remote areas of parks at night are extremely difficult to monitor, and they frequently intimidate park officials. Regulating hunting is most effective when there are clear checkpoints that hunters must pass through or when a village is so well organized and led that the community itself can regulate the hunting. The difficulties of regulating harvesting in parks is illustrated by the recent events in the Galapagos Islands of Ecuador, one of the world's premier national parks (Ferber 2000). Fishermen have refused to accept quotas on catches of lobster, sea cucumbers, sharks and other marine species, and have directed their anger at the park and scientists, threatening research workers, destroying park offices, research labs, equipment, and data books.

Establishment of marine reserves with regulated fishing or areas in which fishing is prohibited has proved an effective way to rebuild and maintain populations of fish (Figure 17.10) (Russ and Alcala 1996;

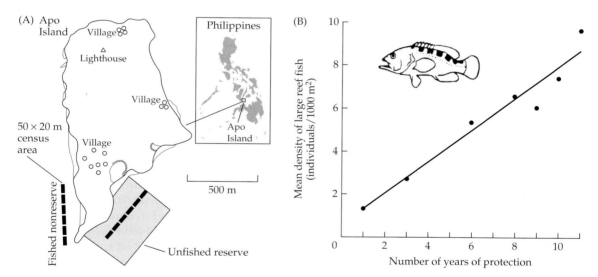

Figure 17.10 Large reef fish had been overharvested at Apo Island in the Philippines and were rarely seen. (A) In response to overharvesting, a reserve was set up (shaded area) on the eastern side of the island. Fishing continued at a nonreserve area on the western side of the island. A censusing study measured the number of large reef fish at each site (six underwater census areas are shown for each site). (B) Resulting data show that after the eastern part was protected as a marine reserve, the number of fish observed in the unfished reserve increased substantially; the number of fish in the nonreserve area did not increase because the fish were still being intensively harvested. (After Russ and Alcala 1996.)

Coblentz 1997). (These areas are also variously known as marine protected areas, marine parks, and no-fishing zones.) In comparison with nearby unprotected sites, marine parks in Kenya and Tanzania have greater weight of fish, greater density of commercially harvested fish, and greater coral reef cover (McClanahan et al. 1999; McClanahan and Arthur 2001). Unprotected and degraded reefs still retain most of their species and could be restored if they were also protected from overfishing and the use of dynamite in fishing. The hope is that juveniles and adults of species in protected areas will eventually disperse out and rebuild damaged and destroyed populations in nearby unprotected areas.

- *Intensive harvesting of natural plant products.* As with hunting and fishing, collection of natural plant products such as fruits, fibers, resins, and mushrooms for personal use may be acceptable, but commercial harvesting may be detrimental. Even personal collecting can be unacceptable in national parks with tens of thousands of visitors per year and where the local human population is large in relation to the area of the park. Monitoring of plant populations is needed to ensure that overharvesting does not occur. A surprisingly large number of people are sometimes found in remote areas of parks illegally collecting forest products such as medicinal plants, ornamental plants, and mushrooms. Dealing with such a situation represents a great challenge for park managers, particularly when the local people are armed and collecting at night.
- *Illegal logging and farming.* These activities degrade the habitat and eliminate species. Where these activities are large in scale, commercial in nature, and controlled by outside interests, they must be eliminated when possible. However, when the logging and farming are done by local people to supply basic human needs, banning these activities is very difficult and could be counterproductive. Some regulated harvesting and farming may even be useful to maintain successional stages and to preserve traditional agricultural systems.
- *Fire.* Occasional fires set accidentally or deliberately by local people to open up habitats, to provide forage for livestock and wildlife, and to reduce undesirable species may help to create a variety of successional stages. Fires that are more frequent than would occur naturally can dry out a habitat, cause soil erosion, and eliminate many native species. The combination of selective logging followed by fires to clear brush for farming can often result in widespread and highly destructive forest fires.
- *Recreational activities.* Popular recreational activities such as hiking off trails, camping outside designated areas, and riding motorcycles, off-road vehicles, and mountain bikes can eliminate sensitive plants and animals from protected lands and must be controlled and restricted to specified areas by park managers. Even such activities as birdwatching must sometimes be curtailed. In many heavily used parks,

frequent traffic by hikers wearing heavy boots has degraded vegetation along trails. Redwood trees in California, for instance, are harmed when park visitors compress the soil too tightly by walking around the redwood trunks. In many parks, people are not allowed to bring dogs for walks, because the dogs frighten and chase animals. In tropical marine parks, swimmers and divers are often restricted to specific areas or trails to prevent widespread damage to delicate branching corals (Tratalos and Austin 2001).

Park Management Resources

For park management to be effective, there must be adequate funding for a sufficient number of well-equipped, properly trained, and motivated park personnel who are willing to carry out park policy. Buildings, communications equipment, and other appropriate elements of infrastructure are necessary to manage a park. In many areas of the world, particularly in developing but also in developed countries, protected areas are understaffed, and they lack the equipment to patrol remote areas of the reserve. Without enough radios and vehicles, the park staff may be restricted to the vicinity of headquarters, unaware of what is happening in their own park. The importance of sufficient personnel and equipment should not be underestimated: In areas of Panama, for instance, the abundance of large mammals and the seed dispersal services they provide are directly related to the frequency of antipoaching patrols by park guards (Wright et al. 2000). In another study of 86 tropical parks, the parks that were most effective at maintaining the vegetation of the park in good conditions had: (1) the greatest number of guards per unit of area of the park, (2) clearly marked and maintained park borders, and (3) programs to compensate local people when park animals or other park activities damaged their crops (Bruner et al. 2001). (Interestingly, some parks were found to be effective at maintaining or even increasing the biological communities within their borders even with few park guards and poorly defined boundaries, because the legal designation of the national park prevented private land development.)

The majority of the evidence shows that park personnel and equipment are integral to a park's success, but funding for these resources is often a problem. For instance, compare the national parks and biological reserves of the United States and the Brazilian Amazon (Table 17.1) (Peres and Terborgh 1995). The United States employs 4002 park rangers, while Brazil, due to inadequate funding, employs only 23! That is a ratio of approximately one ranger per every 82 km^2 of park in the United States compared with one ranger for every 6053 km^2 of park in Brazil. Most of Brazil's parks lack even basic transportation, such as motorized boats, trucks, or jeeps; it is clearly impossible for Brazil's tiny park staff to adequately patrol large, rugged parks on foot or by canoe.

TABLE 17.1 Comparison of personnel and resources available for protecting national parks and biological reserves in the Brazilian Amazon and the United States

Feature	Brazilian Amazon	United States
Protected area (in km^2)	139,222	326,721
Number of park rangers	23	4002
Total number of park personnel[a]	65	19,000
Park ranger:km^2 ratio	1:6053	1:82
Park guard[b]	31	100
Administrative building[b]	45	100
Guard post[b]	52	100
Motor vehicle[b]	45	100

Source: After Peres and Terborgh 1995.
[a]Includes all office staff.
[b]Percentage of nature reserves with at least one.

It is an irony of our world that vast sums are spent on captive breeding and conservation programs by zoos and conservation organizations in the developed countries of the world, while the biologically rich parks of so many developing countries languish for lack of resources. For instance, the San Diego Zoological Society, largely occupied with keeping exotic animals on display for the public, has an annual budget of $70 million, which is about the same as the combined wildlife conservation budgets of all African countries south of the Sahara. In many cases, the annual management costs for endangered species and habitats are a bargain compared to the large costs of conservation efforts to save species on the verge of extinction or ecosystems on the verge of collapse (Wilcove and Chen 1998).

Throughout this chapter the principles and practices of management have been discussed. To implement management, people must be trained as conservation managers, learning both academic and practical skills. Positions for managers need to be created which provide a secure and adequate salary. These managers will then be in a position to carry out their responsibilities of protecting biological diversity.

Summary

1. Protected areas often must be managed to maintain biological diversity because the original conditions of the area have been and continue to be altered by human activities. Effective management begins with a clearly articulated statement of priorities. Monitoring can be used to determine whether management practices are working or need to be adjusted.

2. Parts of protected areas may have to be periodically burned, dug up, or otherwise disturbed by people to create the openings and successional stages that certain species need. Such management is crucial, for example, to some

endangered butterfly species that need early successional food plants to complete their life cycle.

3. Keystone resources such as nesting sites and water holes often need to be preserved, restored, or even added to protected areas in order to maintain populations of some species.

4. An effective management tool is zoning, allowing and prohibiting certain kinds of uses in different parts of a park. In Biosphere Reserves, a core area of strict protection is surrounded by buffer zones and transition zones in which various human activities are allowed.

5. For park management to be effective, protected areas must have an adequate staff and resources. In many cases, personnel and resources are insufficient to accomplish management objectives.

For Discussion

1. Think about a national park or nature reserve you have visited. In what ways was it well run or poorly run? What were the goals of the park or reserve, and how could they be achieved through better management?

2. Imagine a public nature preserve in a metropolitan area that protects a number of endangered species. Would the nature preserve be more effectively run by a government agency, a group of scientists, the local residents living near the reserve, a nongovernmental environmental organization (NGO), or by a council made up of all of them? What are the advantages and disadvantages of each of these possibilities?

3. Can you think of special challenges in the management of aquatic preserves, such as coastal estuaries, islands, or freshwater lakes, that would not be faced by managers of terrestrial protected areas?

4. Imagine you are a park ranger at Yellowstone National Park during the great fires of 1988. How would you explain the ecologically beneficial role of fire in mature lodgepole pine forests while reassuring park visitors that their park is not being destroyed?

Suggested Readings

Brandon, K., K. H. Redford, and S. E. Sanderson, (eds.). 1998. *Parks in Peril: People, Parks and Protected Areas.* Island Press, Washington, D.C. Managing national parks and providing for the needs of nearby people is a great challenge, and sometimes the problems are overwhelming.

Cooper, N. S. 2000. How natural is a nature reserve?: an ideological study of British nature conservation landscapes. *Biological Conservation* 9: 1131–1152. Protected areas in the United Kingdom have a diversity of objectives and management styles.

Costanza R., F. Andrade, P. Antunes, M. van den Belt, D. Boersma, et al. 1998. Principles for sustainable governance of the oceans. *Science* 281: 198–199. Oceans require special management methods.

Cunningham, C. and J. Berger. 1997. *Horn of Darkness: Rhinos on the Edge.* Oxford University Press, New York. The emotional story of evaluating Namibia's rhino protection program and the resulting tangle with government officials.

Duffy, E. and A. S. Watts (eds.). 1971. *The Scientific Management of Animal and Plant Communities for Conservation.* Blackwell Scientific Publications, Oxford. Examples of intensive management of small conservation areas.

Ferber, D. 2000. Galápagos station survives latest attack by fishers. *Science* 290: 2059–2060. The management plan for the Galápagos National Park has been resisted by the fishing community, who have taken out their frustration against scientists.

Halvorson, W. L. and G. E. Davis (eds.). 1996. *Science and Ecosystem Management in the National Parks.* University of Arizona Press, Tucson. Research, monitoring, and management are important in maintaining the health of protected areas.

McClanahan, T. R., N. A. Muthiga, A. T. Kamukuru, H. Machano, and R.W. Kiambo. 1999. The effects of marine parks and fishing on coral reefs of northern Tanzania. *Biological Conservation* 89: 161–182. Clear evidence is given that tropical marine parks protect fish and coral reefs.

Peterken, G. F. 1996. *Natural Woodland, Ecology and Conservation in Northern Temperate Regions.* Cambridge University Press, Cambridge. Authoritative description of natural processes and how they can be used in conservation management.

Pringle, C. M. 2001. Hydrological connectivity and the management of biological reserves: A global perspective. *Ecological Applications* 11: 981–998. The integrity of protected areas is constantly threatened by external sources of water pollution, dam construction, and the diversion of water.

Redford, K. H. and S. E. Sanderson. 2000. Extracting humans from nature. *Conservation Biology* 2000: 1362–1364. In a symposium, authors argue for the need to integrate local people in conservation strategies; other articles present case for excluding local people or for giving local people greater rights.

Ries, L., D. M. Debinski, and M. L. Wieland. 2001. Conservation value of roadside prairie restoration to butterfly communities. *Conservation Biology* 15: 401–411. Case study where restoring plant communities leads to an increase in native insects.

Spellerberg, I. F. 1994. *Evaluation and Assessment for Conservation: Ecological Guidelines for Determining Priorities for Nature Conservation.* Chapman and Hall, London. Methods for developing a management plan for conservation areas.

Sutherland, W. J. and D. A. Hill. 1995. *Managing Habitats for Conservation.* Cambridge University Press, Cambridge. An active approach is needed to maintain species and communities.

Chapter 18

Outside Protected Areas

A crucial component of conservation strategies must be the protection of biological diversity *outside* as well as inside protected areas. As David Western (1989), a leading conservation biologist based in Africa, says, "If we can't save nature outside protected areas, not much will survive inside." In the last chapter we discussed principles of managing protected areas. In this chapter, we explore strategies to include biodiversity protection as a management objective for both unprotected areas immediately outside protected areas and all other areas that are not protected. Protecting these areas is essential because more than 85% of the world's land will remain outside of protected areas, according to even the most optimistic predictions. Most of these unprotected lands are not used intensively by humans and still harbor some of their original biota. Strategies for reconciling human needs and conservation interests in unprotected areas are critical to the success of conservation plans (Western and Pearl 1989; Redford and Richter 1999; Berkes and Folke 2000). In almost every country, numerous rare species and biological communities will inevitably occur outside of protected areas. In the United States, 70% of the species listed under the U.S. Endangered Species Act occur on private land (Stein et al. 2000), and 10% occur exclusively on private lands. Even when endangered species occur on public land, it is often not land managed for biodiversity but rather managed primarily for timber harvesting, grazing, mining, or other economic uses. For many other countries as well, a gap exists in the protected-land system, with many rare and endangered ecosystems and species existing primarily or exclusively on private lands (Pressey et al. 2000).

It is shortsighted to rely solely on parks and reserves to protect biological diversity. Such reliance can create a paradoxical situation in which species and habitats inside the parks are protected while the same species and habitats outside are allowed to be damaged. Jeff McNeely (1989), an IUCN protected areas expert, suggests that the park boundary "is too often also a psychological boundary, suggesting that since nature is taken care of by the national park, we can abuse the surrounding lands, isolating the national park as an 'island' of habitat which is subject to the usual increased threats that go with insularity."

Some countries such as Brazil and Malaysia are establishing new, large national parks to deflect international criticism of their intensive development policies on areas outside of the parks. However, if the areas outside parks are degraded, then the biological diversity within the protected areas will decline as well (Table 18.1). This decline is due, in part, to the fact that many species must migrate across park boundaries to access resources that the park itself cannot provide. In general, the smaller a protected area is, the more it is dependent on neighboring unpro-

TABLE 18.1 Number of large herbivore species currently in some East African national parks and the number expected to remain if areas outside the parks become unavailable to wildlife

National park	Area (km²)	Number of herbivore species	
		Currently	If areas outside parks exclude wildlife[b]
Serengeti, Tanzania[a]	14,504	31	30
Mara, Kenya	1813	29	22
Meru, Kenya	1021	26	20
Amboseli, Kenya	388	24	18
Samburu, Kenya	298	25	17
Nairobi, Kenya	114	21	11

Source: Data from Western and Ssemakulu 1981.

[a]Serengeti National Park (the largest park) is able to maintain almost all of its large herbivore species, whereas Nairobi National Park (the smallest park) is able to maintain only half of its large herbivore species.

[b]Estimated number of species that will remain if areas outside the protected parks exclude wildlife due to agriculture, hunting, herding, or other human activities.

tected lands for the long-term maintenance of biological diversity. For example, in India, tigers sometimes leave the nature sanctuary in which they live to hunt in the surrounding human-dominated landscape (Seidensticker et al. 2000). Also, the number of individuals of any one species contained within park boundaries may be lower than the minimum viable population size. New national parks that are meant to compensate for a country's intensive development outside parks are attempts to mollify the international conservation community, but they are not solutions to the long-term problem.

The Value of Unprotected Habitat

Strategies that encourage private landowners and government land managers to protect rare species and biological communities are obviously essential to the long-term survival of many species. In many countries, government programs inform road builders and developers of the locations of rare species or threatened communities and help them modify their plans to avoid damage to the sites. Public education programs and even financial subsidies may be needed to encourage conservation efforts. The following examples illustrate the importance of land outside protected areas.

- *Mountain sheep.* Mountain sheep (*Ovis canadensis*) often occur in isolated populations on steep, open terrain surrounded by large areas of unsuitable habitat (Bleich et al. 1990). Since mountain sheep had been considered to be slow colonizers of new habitat, past conservation efforts focused on protecting known mountain sheep habitat and releasing sheep into areas that they had previously occupied. However, studies using radio telemetry have revealed that mountain sheep often move well outside their normal territories and even show considerable ability to move across inhospitable terrain between mountain ranges. The isolated mountain sheep populations are really parts of a large metapopulation that occupies a much greater area (see Figure 12.8). Thus, not only the land occupied by mountain sheep must be protected, but also the habitat between populations that acts as stepping-stones for dispersal, colonization, and gene flow.
- *The Florida panther.* The Florida panther (*Felis concolor coryi*) is an endangered subspecies of puma in South Florida with probably no more than 50 individuals (Maehr 1990; Maehr et al. 2001). This panther was designated the Florida state animal in 1982 and has since received a tremendous amount of government and research attention. Half of the present range of the panther is privately owned, and animals tracked with radio collars have all spent at least some of their time on private lands (Figure 18.1). The importance of private lands is illustrated by the fact that private lands typically are on better soils that support more prey species. Panthers that spend most of their time on private lands have a better diet and are in better condition than panthers on public land.

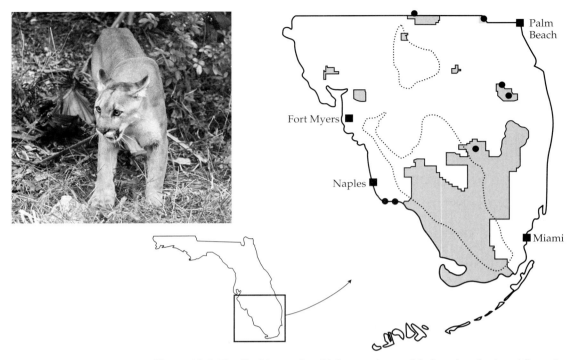

Figure 18.1 The Florida panther (*Felis concolor coryi*) is found on both public and private lands in South Florida. The dotted lines enclose areas known to be used by radio-collared panthers; the black dots represent sightings or other signs of uncollared panthers. Public lands are shaded. (After Maehr 1990. Photograph © Elizabeth DeLaney/Visuals Unlimited.)

Acquiring the 400,000 ha of private land occupied by the panther would cost around $2 billion, with management costs of around $30 million each year (Kautz and Cox 2001). Obviously, such a strategy would be financially and politically difficult. Even slowing down the pace of land development may be impractical. Two viable possibilities are educating private landowners on the value of conservation and paying willing landowners to practice management options that allow the continued existence of panthers—specifically, minimizing habitat fragmentation and maintaining preferred habitats of hardwood hammock forest, mixed hardwood swamp, and cypress swamp (Maehr and Cox 1995). In addition, building special road underpasses will help to reduce panther deaths from collisions with motor vehicles.

Native species often can continue to live in unprotected areas, especially when those areas are set aside or managed for some other purpose that is not harmful to the ecosystem. Forests that are either selectively logged on a long cutting cycle or are cut down for farming using traditional shifting cultivation methods may still contain a considerable percentage of their original biota and maintain most of their ecosystem services (Putz et al. 2000, 2001). In Malaysia, most forest bird species are still found in rain forests 25 years after selective logging has occurred, where undisturbed forest is available nearby to act as a source of colonists (Johns 1996). Primate species also appear to tolerate selective logging involving low levels of disturbance (Chapman et al. 2000).

Excellent examples of natural habitat occur on the large tracts of land surrounding nuclear processing facilities, such as the Savannah River site in South Carolina and on watersheds adjacent to metropolitan water supplies, such as the Quabbin Reservoir in Massachusetts. Although dams, reservoirs, canals, dredging operations, port facilities, and coastal development destroy and damage aquatic communities, some species are capable of adapting to altered conditions, particularly if the water is not polluted. In estuaries and seas managed for commercial fisheries, many native species remain because commercial and noncommercial species alike require that the chemical and physical environments remain undamaged.

In the United States, military reservations are particularly important habitats. Security zones surrounding government installations are some of the most outstanding natural areas in the world. The U.S. Department of Defense manages more than 10 million ha, much of it undeveloped, containing over 200 threatened and endangered species of plants and animals (Box 26). For example, the White Sands Missile Range in New Mexico is almost 1 million ha in area, about the same size as Yellowstone National Park. While certain sections of military reservations may be damaged by military activities, much of the habitat remains as an undeveloped buffer zone with restricted access.

Other areas that are not protected by law may retain species because the human population density and degree of utilization is typically very low. Border areas such as the demilitarized zone between North and South Korea often have an abundance of wildlife because they remain undeveloped and depopulated. Mountain areas, often too steep and inaccessible for development, are frequently managed by governments as valuable watersheds that produce a steady supply of water and prevent flooding; they also harbor important natural communities. Likewise, desert species may be at less risk than other unprotected communities because desert regions are considered marginal for human habitation and use.

In many parts of the world, wealthy individuals have acquired large tracts of land for their personal estates and for private hunting. These private estates are frequently used at very low intensity, often in a deliberate attempt by the landowner to maintain large wildlife populations. Some estates in Europe have preserved unique old-growth forests that have been owned and protected for hundreds of years by royal families.

Considerable biological diversity can also be maintained in traditional agricultural systems and forest plantations (see Chapter 20). Bird species are often more abundant in traditional agricultural landscapes, charac-

BOX 26 *In Defense of Wildlife . . . Send in the Marines!*

The thump of mortar fire and the thudding of tank treads hardly seem compatible with wildlife conservation, yet some of the largest expanses of undeveloped land in the United States are on military reservations located throughout the nation. The U.S. Department of Defense controls more than 10 million ha of land, nearly one-third the size of the 35 million ha of national park lands owned by the National Park Service. Whereas national parks host millions of visitors a year, access to military bases is limited to military personnel and authorized visitors; because of these restrictions, much of the land remains in its natural state. Moreover, the land used for military exercises often is not used intensively; for instance, the Air Force uses only 1250 ha of its 44,000-ha base in Avon Park, Florida, and similar small fractions are used at other sites (Boice 1996). As a result, many military bases have become de facto refuges for 130 species of endangered wildlife, many of which have their largest populations on military bases.

Rare and endangered desert tortoises, manatees, red-cockaded woodpeckers, bald eagles, Atlantic white cedars, and the least Bell's vireo all have found safe havens on military lands.

Obviously, military reservations differ from true wildlife refuges in one important aspect: They are sites for significant disturbances caused by military exercises. While much of the land may be left undisturbed as a security zone, large parts of the otherwise undeveloped land may be used periodically for acclimating troops to potential combat environments. Many bases contain toxic waste dumps and high levels of chemical pollutants, and human disturbance in the form of bomb explosions, artillery practice, or the use of heavy vehicles can have a significant effect on the resident wildlife.

The passage of the Legacy Resource Management Program in 1991 by Congress allowed the military to place greater emphasis on environmentally sound practices by giving them funding for research and conservation programs (Jacobson and Marynowski 1997). Recent programs have ranged from helping individual species to restoring entire habitats (Burger 2000; McKee and Berrens 2001). In

The endangered Hawaiian stilt (*Himantopus mexicanus knudseni*) lives on exposed mudflats in Nu'upia Wildlife Management Area of the Hawaii Marine Corps Base. The Marine Corps periodically uses amphibious assault vehicles to break up exotic woody plants that threaten to cover the mudflats and exclude the stilt. (Photographs courtesy of the Department of Defense.)

BOX 26 *(continued)*

some cases, conservation efforts simply mean protecting the stands of old-growth forest at the Jim Creek Radio Station in the Pacific Northwest, or the largest chunk of ungrazed tall-grass prairie in the West at Fort Sill, or the pine habitat that houses endangered red-cockaded woodpeckers at Fort Bragg. At the Naval Weapons Station at Charleston, South Carolina, Navy biologists have installed nest boxes and drilled holes in trees to provide future nest sites for the endangered red-cockaded woodpecker. Abandoned underground bunkers are being modified to provide habitat for bats. Construction of a pipeline in San Pedro, California, was halted when workers found a population of the Palos Verdes blue butterfly, formerly thought to be extinct. Navy biologists are now monitoring the population and restoring its coastal scrub habitat. Habitat is also being restored at numerous bases around the country as trees are replanted and bulldozers reshape land that has been pitted with bomb craters and gouged with vehicle tracks. Per-

sonnel at the Barksdale Air Force Base in Shreveport, Louisiana, have reflooded drained wetlands along the Red River, restoring 830 ha of wetlands for thousands of wading birds. Contaminated sites are being cleaned up. The Army's Rocky Mountain Arsenal in Colorado is even being transformed into the Rocky Mountain Wildlife Refuge, and an area of Fort Irwin in California, has been set aside to protect the endangered desert tortoise.

Habitat preservation on military lands isn't a perfect conservation solution: Conflict still arises when military commanders resist involvement in nonmilitary activities, when Congress questions funding such conservation activities, or when military activities appear to be incompatible with species protection. For the time being, though, military reservations are encouraging preservation. At Camp Pendleton in California, a clear message is being sent: A sign warns people away from a tern nesting site "by order of the base commander."

terized by a mixture of small fields, hedges and woodlands. In comparison with more intensive "modern" agricultural practices, these landscapes experience less exposure to herbicides, fertilizers, and pesticides (Freemark and Kirk 2001). In European countries, farmers are sometimes paid by the government to practice farming methods that allow birds to nest; new programs are being developed in which farmers are being paid for each clutch of birds produced (European Environment Agency 1998). Similar plans are being developed to maintain the traditional wildflowers of farmland, such as corn marigold (*Chrysanthemum sagetum*) and corn cockle (*Agrostemona githago*), which are eliminated by the applications of fertilizer and herbicides associated with intensive agriculture (Figure 18.2; Shardlow and Harper 2000).

Traditional tropical forest plantations often retain considerable species diversity. One notable example from tropical countries is traditional plantations of shade coffee, in which coffee is grown under a wide variety of shade trees, often as many as 40 tree species per farm (Figure 18.3A) (Perfecto et al. 1996). In northern Latin America alone, coffee plantations cover 2.7 million ha. These shade coffee plantations have structural complexity created by multiple vegetation layers and a diversity of birds and insects comparable to adjacent natural forest, and they represent a rich

Figure 18.2 The traditional wildflowers of European cultivated fields can be maintained when farmers are paid to reduce applications of herbicides and fertilizer. This wheat field in Dorset, England, has an abundance of uninvited corn marigold and poppy plants, but many of the other wildflowers of farmlands are now rare or extinct in England. (Photograph by Bob Gibbons/Natural Image.)

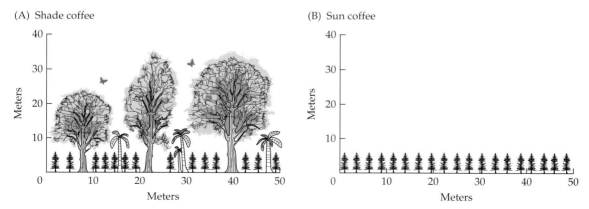

Figure 18.3 Two types of coffee management systems in the Central Valley of Costa Rica. (A) Shade coffee is grown under a diverse canopy of trees, providing a forest structure in which birds, insects, and other animals can live. (B) Sun coffee is grown as a monoculture, without shade trees. Animal life is greatly reduced. (After Fournier in Perfecto et al. 1996.)

repository of biodiversity (Roberts et al. 2000). However, they are rapidly being converted to high-yielding sun coffee plantations without shade trees, in which new coffee varieties are planted that require more pesticides and fertilizers (Figure 18.3B). These sun coffee plantations have only a tiny fraction of the species diversity found in shade coffee areas and are far more prone to water runoff and soil erosion. Therefore, maintaining species diversity in many tropical countries may mean subsidizing shade coffee farmers to maintain their traditional agriculture and possibly marketing their product at a premium price as "environmentally friendly" coffee.

Multiple-Use Habitat

In many countries, large parcels of government-owned land are designated for **multiple use:** They are managed to provide a variety of goods and services (Szaro and Johnston 1996; Johnson et al. 1999). The Bureau of Land Management in the United States oversees more than 110 million ha, including 83% of the state of Nevada and large amounts of Utah, Wyoming, Oregon, Idaho, and other western states (Figure 18.4). The U.S. National Forest covers over 83 million ha centered in the Rocky Mountains, the Cascade Range, the Sierra Nevada, the Appalachian Mountains, and the southern coast of Alaska. In the past, these lands have been managed for logging, mining, grazing, wildlife, and recreation. Increasingly, multiple-use lands also are being valued and managed for their ability to protect species, biological communities, and ecosystem services (Noss and Cooperrider 1994; Hunter 1999; Donahue 1999). The U.S. Endangered Species Act of 1973 and other similar laws require landowners, including government agencies, to avoid activities that threaten listed species.

Laws and court systems are now being used by conservation biologists to halt government-approved activities on public lands that threaten the survival of endangered species. In the late 1980s in Wisconsin, for instance, botanists questioned the way in which the U.S. Forest Service had been applying the multiple-use concept to the Nicolet and Chequamegon National Forests. These forests had been managed for a wide variety of natural resources by the U.S. Forest Service, but timber production and deer hunting were their two primary management priorities. Deer often increased in numbers following the fragmentation of forest blocks by logging because of vigorous plant growth along roads and in cut areas (Alverson et al. 1994). Deer populations were further encouraged when the Forest Service made "wildlife openings" in the forest, which were in effect deliberate fragmentations of the habitat. As a result, deer populations in those national forests had increased from their original density of 2–4 animals per km^2 to 5–12 animals per km^2. The enormous deer population was extensively overgrazing the forest understory, preventing the regeneration of many woody plant species. Overgrazing in the forests was threat-

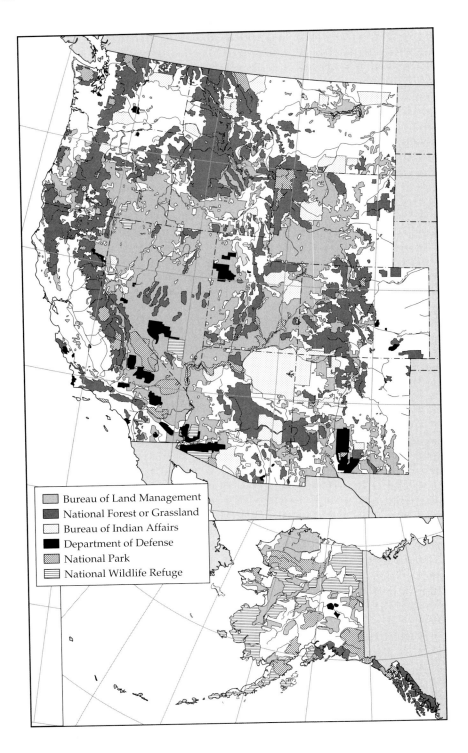

Bureau of Land Management
National Forest or Grassland
Bureau of Indian Affairs
Department of Defense
National Park
National Wildlife Refuge

◀ **Figure 18.4** In Alaska and the western states, agencies of the U.S. government own a large percentage of the land. (Data from National Geographic Society.)

ening the existence of 20 rare plant species protected under the 1976 National Forest Management Act, which provides for the protection of biodiversity as part of national policy (Mlot 1992).

The Wisconsin botanists had recommended to the U.S. Forest Service that to maintain biological diversity in these forests the best management strategy would be to forego all logging, road construction, and wildlife openings in blocks of land 200–400 km^2 in area that contained rare plant species to protect the interior of the blocks from overgrazing by deer. When the U.S. Forest Service rejected this suggestion and continued their management practices, the botanists felt they had no choice but to bring a lawsuit against them. Once the suit was filed in 1990, private conservation groups such as the Sierra Club and scientific organizations, including the American Institute of Biological Sciences and the Society for Conservation Biology, joined the botanists in the case. A coalition of interests representing logging, hunting, and snowmobiling groups organized to oppose the botanists. After many years, the U.S. Circuit Court finally ruled in 1995 that many of the concepts of conservation biology and biodiversity were too vague and imprecise to apply effectively, and that the U.S. Forest Service did not need to file an environmental impact statement for its management plan. Despite this apparent victory, because of all the publicity, lobbying, and discussion, the U.S. Forest Service actually changed its point of view and practices and began to protect the wildflower species in the manner recommended by the botanists.

Ecosystem Management

The unprotected lands adjacent to or near protected areas are often essential for the protected areas to achieve their objective of protecting biological diversity. Governments are encouraging the managers of protected areas to coordinate their conservation management activities with other government departments and private landowners. To achieve conservation objectives, many large blocks of land are now being managed in an integrated manner, termed **ecosystem management**. While there is no standard definition of this term, ecosystem management can be considered enhanced multiple-use management at the landscape scale that involves many stakeholders. The concept is defined by Grumbine (1994) as follows: "Ecosystem management integrates scientific knowledge of ecological relationships within a complex sociopolitical and values framework toward the general goal of protecting native ecosystem integrity over the long term." Public and private resource managers are increasingly being urged to expand their traditional emphasis on the maximum production of goods (such as volume of timber harvested) and services (such as number of park visitors) and instead take a broader perspective that includes the conservation of biological diversity and the protection of ecosystem services (Christensen et al. 1996; Yaffee 1999; Poiani et al. 2000).

Rather than each government agency, private conservation organization, business, or individual landowner acting in isolation, ecosystem management envisions them cooperating to achieve common conservation objectives (Holling and Meffe 1996; Machlis and Field 2000). For example, in a large forested watershed along the coast, ecosystem management would link all owners and users from the tops of the hills to the seashore—including foresters, farmers, conservation biologists, business groups, townspeople, and the fishing industry (Figure 18.5)—into an interconnected, cooperative force for conservation. Not all ecologists accept the ecosystem management paradigm, however; some consider it unlikely to change the human-oriented management practices that often lead to the overexploitation of natural resources (Stanley 1995). Despite the lack of universal agreement among ecologists, the concept of ecosystem management linked to the practice of conservation biology is being strongly embraced by certain government agencies, businesses, and conservation groups.

Important themes in ecosystem management include:

- Seeking and understanding connections between all levels and scales in the ecosystem hierarchy— from the individual organism to the species, the community, the ecosystem, and even to regional and global scales (Buck et al. 2001).
- Ensuring viable populations of all species, representative examples of all biological communities and successional stages, and healthy ecosystem functions.
- Monitoring significant components of the ecosystem (numbers of individuals of significant species, vegetation cover, water quality, etc.), gathering the needed data, and then using the results to adjust management in an adaptive manner (sometimes referred to as **adaptive management**) (Figure 18.6).
- Changing the rigid policies and practices of land-management agencies, which often result in a piecemeal approach and instead encouraging interagency cooperation and integration at the local, regional, national, and international levels, and cooperation and communication between public agencies and private organizations.
- Minimizing external threats to the ecosystem and maximizing sustainable benefits derived from it.
- Recognizing that humans are part of ecosystems and that human values influence management goals.

A detailed survey found at least 619 ecosystem management projects in the United States with ecosystem preservation and restoration as their

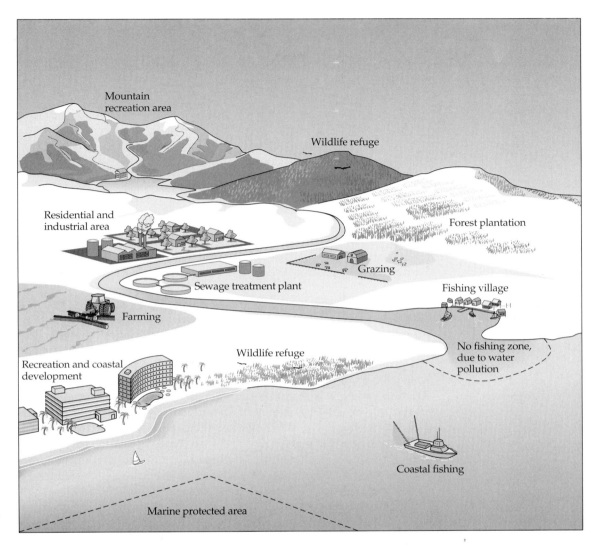

Figure 18.5 Ecosystem management involves linking all of the stakeholders that affect a large ecosystem and receive benefits from it. In this case, a watershed needs to be managed for a wide variety of purposes, many of which influence each other. (After Miller 1996.)

major goals (Yaffee 1996). Most of them have only been around since 1991. Land ownership is predominantly private for 41% of the projects, predominantly public for 31%, and mixed for 27%. Projects on private land predominated in the Northeast, Midwest, and Southeast, while projects on public land were more common in the Northwest and Southwest. Ecosystem management has also been embraced by the Ontario

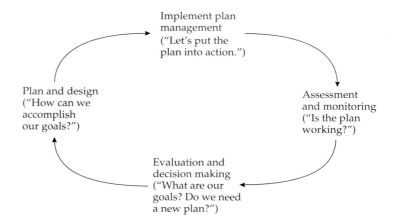

Figure 18.6 Adaptive management involves a cycle of planning and design, implementation, assessment and monitoring, and evaluation and decision-making. (After Comiskey et al. 2001.)

Park System in Canada as a method for large-scale management (Zorn et al. 2001).

One example of ecosystem management is the Malpai Borderlands Group, a cooperative enterprise of ranchers and local landowners who promote collaboration between private landowners, government agencies, and conservation organizations such as The Nature Conservancy. The group is working to develop a network of cooperation across nearly 400,000 ha of unique, rugged mountain and desert habitat along the Arizona and New Mexican border (Glenn 1997). This country of isolated mountains, or "sky islands," includes the Animas and Peloncillo Mountains. This is one of the richest biological areas in the United States, supporting Mexican jaguars, 265 species of birds, and 90 species of mammals (Figure 18.7). It includes 19 listed threatened and endangered species, and dozens of other rare and endemic species, such as the New Mexico ridge-nosed rattlesnake, the lesser long-nosed bat, and the Yaqui chub fish. The Malpai Borderlands Group is using controlled burning as a range management tool, reintroducing native grasses, applying innovative approaches to cattle grazing, incorporating scientific research into management plans, and taking action to avoid habitat fragmentation by using conservation easements (agreements not to develop land) to prevent residential development. Their goal is to create "a healthy, unfragmented landscape to support a diverse, flourishing community of human, plant and animal life in the Borderlands Region" (Yaffee 1996).

As might be expected from such a relatively new and ambitious approach, many ecosystem management projects have experienced difficulties. Many attempts at ecosystem management have not succeeded due to distrust among the participating groups (Rigg 2001). Certain groups, such as real-estate developers and conservation activists, often have fundamentally different objectives. Forcing conservation-minded

Figure 18.7 The Malpai Borderlands Group encourages ecosystem management for 400,000 ha of desert and mountains in southern Arizona and New Mexico. Numerous rare and endangered species, including the Mexican jaguar (*Panthera onca*), are protected in the process. (Photograph by Warner Glenn, from *Eyes of Fire: Encounter with a Borderland Jaguar*.)

groups into alliances might weaken their ability to lobby the government for conservation measures and prevent them from taking cases to court.

A logical extension of ecosystem management is **bioregional management**, which often focuses on a single large ecosystem such as the Caribbean Sea, the Great Barrier Reef of Australia, or a series of linked ecosystems such as the protected areas of Central America (Miller 1996). A bioregional approach is particularly appropriate where there is a single, continuous, large ecosystem that crosses international boundaries or when activity in one country or region will directly affect an ecosystem in another country. For the 16 countries that participate in the Mediterranean Action Plan, for example, bioregional cooperation is absolutely necessary because the enclosed Mediterranean Sea has weak tides that cannot quickly remove pollution resulting from deforestation and soil erosion, high human populations along the coasts, and heavy oil tanker traffic (Figure 18.8). This combination of problems threat-

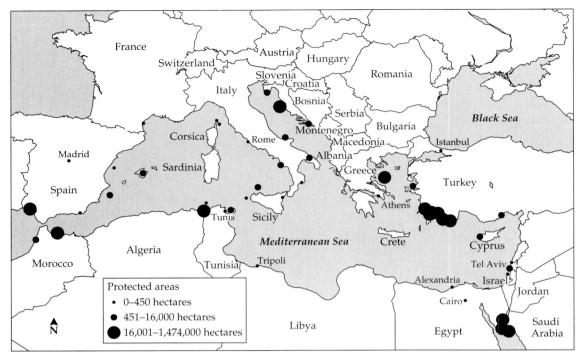

Figure 18.8 The countries participating in the Mediterranean Action Plan cooperate in monitoring and controlling pollution and coordinating their protected areas. Major protected areas along the coast are shown as dots. Note that there are no major protected areas on the coasts of France, Libya, and Egypt. (After Miller 1995.)

ens the health of the entire Mediterranean ecosystem, including the sea, its surrounding lands, and its associated tourist and fishing industries. Cross-boundary management is also necessary because pollution from one country can significantly damage the natural resources of neighboring countries. Participants in the plan agree to cooperate in monitoring and controlling pollution, carrying out research, and developing new pollution control methods.

Case Studies

Throughout the world, the protection of biological diversity is being incorporated as an important objective of land management. We conclude the chapter by examining three case studies that demonstrate the problems of managing biological diversity outside protected areas—old-growth forests in the Pacific Northwest of the United States, Kenya's large wildlife populations outside its parks, and a successful community-based program in Zambia.

Managed Coniferous Forests

The coniferous forests of the Pacific Northwest of the United States are managed for a variety of natural resources, but timber production traditionally has been considered the most important (Hansen et al. 1991, 1995; Halpern and Spies 1995). In this ecosystem, the issue of timber production versus the conservation of unique species—the northern spotted owl (*Strix occidentalis caurina*), the marbled murrelet (*Brachyramphus marmoratus*), as well as the salmon—has been a highly emotional and political debate billed as "owls versus jobs." Some environmentalists want to stop all cutting in old-growth forests, while many local citizens want the logging industry to continue current practices without outside interference. A regional compromise is now emerging in which logging will largely cease in national forests, which will act as a core reserve for biodiversity. Logging will continue to a limited extent on state and private lands, but in a way that minimally affects rare and endangered species.

Research on forest management techniques has contributed to this compromise solution: Many of the species characteristic of old-growth forests over 200 years old, including cavity-nesting birds such as the northern spotted owl, are also found at lower densities in young forests following natural disturbances (because even very young forests have at least a few old, large trees, some dead, standing trees, and fallen trees that remain after fires and storms). These resources are sufficient to support a complex community of plants and animals. However, clear-cutting techniques that remove living and dead trees of all ages in order to maximize wood production eliminate the places and resources that certain animals and plants need to live. Further, clear-cutting damages the adjacent streams and rivers, leading to the loss of salmon and other aquatic animals. In managed forests of the Pacific Northwest, the past practice of clear-cut, staggered patches of timber produced a landscape pattern that was a mosaic of forest fragments, with different tree ages across fragments and uniform ages within them (Figure 18.9).

Research has been used to develop an approach in which conifer forests could be managed to both produce timber and maintain the most important elements of biodiversity. These lessons have been incorporated into the "new forestry" or "ecological forestry" now being practiced in the Pacific Northwest (Kohm and Franklin 1997; Carey 2000). This method essentially involves removing most trees in the areas that are designated for logging, but leaving a low density of large live trees, standing dead trees, and some fallen trees to provide structural complexity and to serve as habitat for animal species in the next forest cycle (Figure 18.10). Typically around 18% of the trees remain after this type of logging, but up to 40% of the trees can remain, if necessary. By avoiding logging near streams, water quality and other ecosystem services can also be protected.

Figure 18.9 Staggered harvesting of trees in managed forests of the Pacific Northwest produces a striking mosaic landscape of forest fragments. Within each patch, all vegetation is at the same successional stage. (Photograph by A. Levno.)

This change in logging has had major economic consequences. Large areas of national forest are now off-limits to logging, and ecological forestry is now practiced in the remaining areas of state and private forest. Ecological forestry requires a reduced harvest of timber at the time of cutting and a somewhat longer cutting cycle, resulting in a lower profit for the timber industry. Although strict environmentalists are still not satisfied because some old-growth "big trees" continue to be cut down, United States citizens and their government have reached a hard-won compromise on the use of these forests and the development of the entire region.

African Wildlife outside Parks

East African countries such as Kenya are famous for the spectacular wildlife populations found in their national parks, which are the basis of a valuable ecotourist industry. Despite the fame of the parks, about three-fourths of Kenya's 2,000,000 large animals live in rangelands outside the parks' boundaries (Western 1989). The rangelands of Kenya occupy 700,000 km^2, or about 40% of the country. Among the well-known species found predominantly outside the parks are the giraffe (89%), the

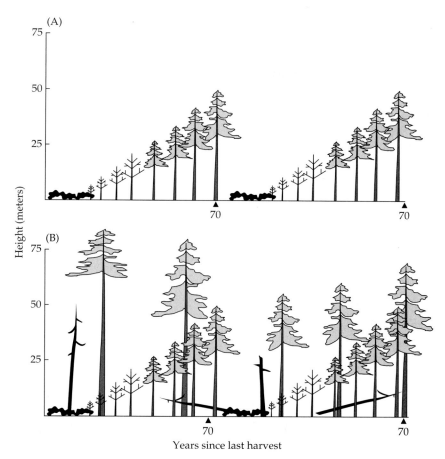

Figure 18.10 (A) Conventional clear-cutting (pictured in Figure 18.9) involves removing all trees from an area on a 70-year cycle, thus reducing the structural diversity of the forest. (B) New practices better maintain structural diversity by leaving behind some old trees, standing dead trees, and fallen trees. (After Hansen et al. 1991.)

impala (72%), Grevy's zebra (99%), the oryx (73%), and the ostrich (92%). Only the rhinoceros, elephant, and wildebeest are found predominantly inside the parks; rhinos and elephants are concentrated in parks because poachers seeking ivory, horn, and hides have virtually eliminated external populations of these animals. The large herbivores found in the parks often graze seasonally outside them. However, the rangelands outside the parks are increasingly unavailable to wildlife due to fences, poaching, and agricultural development.

In Kenya and in other African countries, areas surrounding national parks are often used as rangeland for domestic cattle. It may seem intuitive to conclude that the cattle compete with wildlife species for range, water, and vegetation; however, studies have shown that the main factor determining the productivity and number of Kenyan wildlife species is not competition from livestock but the amount of rainfall. The productivity of the rangelands, as measured by the weight of animals produced per km^2, per year, increases in a linear fashion with rainfall; the number of species on the land is highest with intermediate amounts of rainfall. The presence of livestock outside the parks does not affect the number of wildlife species present and has only a slight effect on productivity. It would appear that limited grazing of livestock may be compatible with wildlife conservation in some circumstances and that commercial range may extend the effective area of a wildlife preserve. Even in areas where there is commercial ranching, there appears to be little change in the types of wildlife species present. To support this point, Western (1989) has noted that human communities that raise livestock, such as the Masai in Tanzania, have lived in East Africa for over 3000 years without even one large herbivore going extinct. The Masai even have social prohibitions against hunting and eating wildlife, relying solely on their cattle for food instead.

The continued existence of wild species on some unprotected African lands appears to be attributable to a stable social structure and secure land tenure in the local human population. These tend to be characteristic of both traditional and highly developed societies. In these situations, control of resources is highly regulated by a recognized authority and current needs can be deferred to enhance future production of resources. Countries in which there is migration, poverty, unclear ownership of resources, and a breakdown of authority are likely to experience the greatest environmental deterioration and destruction of biological communities, because in these circumstances people focus on their immediate needs with little concern for the future value of resources. In some unstable countries, there is an unregulated proliferation of guns in rural areas and an inability to control poaching. In a study of factors affecting the status of the African elephant, the most important were the scope of civilian disruption, and to a lesser extent, the socioeconomic status of the people (Burrill et al. 1986). This study concluded that elephant populations in stable countries are increasing by 2.5% per year, while in unstable countries they are declining by 16% per year.

In areas of East Africa with substantial rural settlement, a number of factors contribute to the persistence of wildlife in unprotected areas (Western 1989). Many wildlife species are valued for their meat, so their presence on rangeland is encouraged. Private ranching, in which wildlife and livestock are managed together, is often more profitable than managing livestock alone. Some wildlife species are present in very low numbers; some are elusive and ignored by ranchers. Some areas containing wildlife are not used by people because they are inaccessible, have an inadequate water supply, or exist in the presence of warfare or disease.

In these locations wildlife exists without interference. Some species such as elephants are tolerated since they open up woody vegetation for grassland and enhance the habitat for livestock. Some species are protected outside parks by laws against hunting and trading, which are enforced by wildlife officials. Finally, others persist simply because people enjoy them, find them beautiful or amusing, and so encourage (or at least tolerate) their presence.

In Kenya and neighboring countries, a change in government policy is allowing rural communities and landowners to profit directly from the presence of large game animals (Western 1997). With assistance from international donor agencies, local ecotourist businesses—geared toward hiking, photography, canoeing, and horseback safaris, for example—are being established. When the land is adequately stocked with animals, trophy hunting is also allowed for high fees; sale of the meat and hide from hunting expeditions provides additional revenue. The most well-known programs, which combine community development with tourism and wildlife conservation, are CAMPFIRE in Zimbabwe and ADMADE in Zambia (Getz et al. 1999). The programs apparently are successful at combining conservation and community development, but they have been criticized by animal rights groups because they allow trophy hunting. Further, the programs depend on continuing subsidies from outside donor agencies; only a small percentage of funding actually reaches the village level. When outside subsidies cease, the programs often end, indicating the weakness of the local economy, the instability of the local ecotourism industry, and ineffective government policies.

Community-Based Wildlife Management in Zambia

In many areas of Africa, wildlife has declined dramatically during the last several decades due to hunting and agricultural development, despite attempts by national governments to impose top-down conservation policies and to establish effective national parks. Local residents and conservation officers are now working together to increase the level of community involvement in national park wildlife management. One example of how community involvement might work in Africa comes from the ADMADE (Administrative Management Design for game management areas) program, which was initiated to resolve conflicts in the Luangwa River Valley in eastern Zambia (Lewis 1995). The Luangwa River Valley supports a world-famous concentration of wildlife and contains four national parks in which people are not allowed to live or hunt (Lewis et al. 1990). Surrounding the parks and occupying a much greater total area are game management areas in which tribal people live and in which hunting is currently allowed only with permits.

In the 1970s and 1980s, the situation was out of balance, with wildlife providing no benefit to the local people. Hunting licenses were so expensive that they were bought only by safari hunters. Local residents, who could not afford them, were angry that they were prevented from obtaining the meat they needed to feed their families while sport hunters were allowed to shoot animals for trophies. (From a national economic perspective, the single greatest revenue earner in these game management areas was at that time, and still is, the license fees paid by foreign safari hunters—but at that time less than 1% of this revenue was returned to the economy of the local villages.) Not surprisingly, local residents in the Luangwa River Valley came to resent the parks, the tourists, and the safaris. Chief Matama (quoted in Lewis et al. 1990) summarized the feelings of his people in a speech:

> Tourists come here to enjoy the lodges and to view the wildlife. Safari companies come here to kill animals and make money. We are forgotten. . . . Employment here is too low. Luangwa Lodge employs only about 4 people, and safari hunting employs no one. How can you ask us to cooperate with conservation when this is so?

As a result of these attitudes, illegal poaching of elephants, rhinos, and other animals increased dramatically during the 1970s and 1980s, and wildlife populations plummeted. Personnel from the National Parks and Wildlife Service (NPWS) were ineffective at stopping the poaching; since they were not from the local area, they were unwelcome in the villages, and they did not actively patrol the game management areas. Local people perceived NPWS personnel as acting only in the interests of the safari companies and having little regard for local concerns. Poaching provided necessary meat and the chance to make some money.

To remedy this deteriorating situation, the experimental ADMADE program was initiated in 1987 in the Lupande Game Management Area, which occupies 4849 km^2 in the Luangwa Valley and has 20,000 people. The program has the following key elements:

1. Local residents are hired and trained as scouts. These scouts are to remain in their own village areas to act as wildlife custodians.
2. The NPWS personnel live with the community, supervising the scouts, explaining the goals of the program to the villagers, and promoting community participation.
3. All workers hired in the program for construction of buildings, wildlife maintenance, and seasonal work come from the local villages.
4. Revenues are provided to the program by allowing safari companies to bid for hunting rights. Sixty-eight percent of this revenue is returned to local villages for community projects, and the remainder is used for carrying out wildlife management. Additional revenue is provided by sustained-yield harvesting of hippos and commercial sale of meat, hides, and teeth.
5. Decisions on wildlife management and employment practices are made following discussions with tribal chiefs and village leaders. Village leaders and community members themselves decide how best to spend the community development funds.

Fifteen years later, this community-based program appears to be successful at addressing many of the earlier problems of wildlife management. In 1988 the ADMADE program was extended throughout the entire country and includes 70,000 km^2 under active management as of 1998. The National Parks and Wildlife Service also set up the Institute for Community-Based Resource Management, where more than 500 village scouts have been trained and research is carried out. These village scouts patrol actively, catching poachers and seizing firearms; as a result, illegal killing of elephants and black rhinos has declined in some areas by 90%. Poachers from outside the area are reported to the village scouts since they are now seen as a threat to a community resource. Local people have begun to benefit from the employment opportunities and revenue provided by the program. Community funds have been used to build and renovate schools, medical clinics, and wells, and to purchase village-owned vehicles. The income generated through regulated, sustainable safari hunting and tourism (currently around $1.5 million per year), supplemented by aid from foreign governments, provides for most of the expenses of the program. One of the most innovative features of this program involves collaboration with local leaders to develop Geographical Information System maps of their lands using data provided by village scouts, wildlife officers, and outside researchers (Figure 18.11). These maps can be used to show changes in wildlife density, animal migration routes, land-use patterns, and patrol routes (Lewis

Figure 18.11 Community leaders in the ADMADE program use maps in their discussions on wildlife management. These maps are prepared using a Geographic Information Systems (GIS) analysis incorporating data collected by village scouts, licensed hunters, and researchers. (Photograph courtesy of ADMADE, Zambia.)

1995). Local leaders have used them to develop long-range management plans that represent the best compromise between national wildlife policy and the economic needs of the local people. These plans include monitoring wildlife to ensure that hunting is done sustainably, which is known as the "Green Bullet" program.

Since 1993, the revenues from wildlife-based industries in ADMADE areas have been growing at about 20% per year, and wildlife stocks and habitat are protected where the program is effectively administered. As a result of strong public support for ADMADE, the Zambian government has revised its Wildlife Act to give legal status to local communities as the rightful management authority for wildlife in game management areas. The ADMADE Program demonstrates how involving local people in wildlife management and revenue sharing offers a potentially effective way of reconciling conflicts outside of protected areas. However, it is uncertain if this project could be replicated elsewhere without external sources of funding from international donors and without the high fees paid by safari hunters.

Summary

1. Considerable biological diversity exists outside of protected areas, particularly in habitat managed for multiple-use resource extraction. Such unprotected habitats are vital for conservation because in all countries, protected areas account for only a small percentage of total area. Animal species living in protected areas often forage on or migrate to unprotected land where they are vulnerable to hunting, habitat loss, and other threats from humans. Governments are increasingly including the protection of biological diversity as a priority on multiple-use land.

2. Government agencies, private conservation organizations, businesses, and private landowners are cooperating on a large scale to achieve conservation objectives and to use natural resources sustainably. Over 600 such ecosystem management projects are currently underway in the United States.

3. In temperate forest ecosystems, biological diversity can be enhanced if logging operations minimize fragmentation, and if some late-successional components are left, including living trees, standing dead trees, and fallen trees.

4. In Africa, many of the characteristic large animals are found predominantly in rangeland outside the parks. Local people and landowners often maintain wildlife on their land for a variety of purposes; further incentives are being developed to encourage this practice.

For Discussion

1. Consider a national forest that has been used for decades for logging, hunting, and mining. If endangered plant species are discovered in this forest, should these activities be stopped? Can logging, hunting, and mining coexist with endangered species and, if so, how? If logging has to be stopped or scaled back, do logging companies or their employees deserve any compensation?

2. Imagine that you are informed by the government that the endangered Florida panther lives on a piece of land that you own and were planning to develop as a golf course. Are you happy, angry, confused, or proud? What are

your options? What would be a fair compromise that would protect your rights, the rights of the public, and the rights of the panther?

3. Choose a large aquatic ecosystem that includes more than one country, such as the Black Sea, the Rhine River, the Caribbean, the St. Lawrence River, or the South China Sea. What agencies or organizations have responsibility for ensuring the long-term health of the ecosystem? In what ways do they, or could they, cooperate in managing the area?

Suggested Readings

Berkes, F. and C. Folke (eds.). 2000. *Linking Social and Ecological Systems: Management Practices and Social Mechanisms for Building Resilience.* Cambridge University Press, New York. Case studies of social responses to ecosystem changes.

Boice, L. P. 1996. Endangered species management on U.S. Air Force lands. *Endangered Species Update* 13(9): 6–8. The U.S. military is getting involved in conservation; see also other issues of the excellent magazine.

Buck, L. E., C. C. Geisler, J. Schelhas, and E. Wollenberg. 2001. *Biological Diversity: Balancing Interests through Adaptive Collaborative Management.* CRC Press, Tampa, Florida. Managers and scientists are developing flexible management approaches that reconcile local, regional, national, and global needs.

Christensen, N. L., L. A. M. Bartuska, J. H. Brown, S. Carpenter, et al. 1996. The report of the Ecological Society of America committee on the scientific basis for ecosystem management. *Ecological Applications* 6: 665–691. A special issue of the journal devoted to this topic, with many excellent articles.

European Environment Agency. 1998. *Europe's Environment. The Second Assessment.* Elsevier Science, Oxford. Land use policies, particularly those relating to agriculture, greatly influence biological diversity in Europe.

Freemark, K. E. and D. A. Kirk. 2001. Birds on organic and conventional farms in Ontario: partitioning effects of habitat and practices on species composition and abundance. *Biological Conservation* 101: 337–350. Governments and conservation organizations are developing programs to directly pay farmers for maintaining bird species on their land.

Holling, C. S. and G. K. Meffe. 1996. Command and control and the pathology of natural resource management. *Conservation Biology* 10: 328–337. The need for government agencies to be more flexible.

Hunter, M. L., Jr. (ed.). 1999. *Maintaining Biodiversity in Forest Ecosystems.* Cambridge University Press, New York. Obtaining benefits from forests while maintaining biodiversity.

Johnson, N. C., A. J. Malk, and R. C. Szaro. 1999. *Ecological Stewardship. A Common Reference for Ecosystem Management.* Elsevier Science, New York. An integration of ecological, economic, and social factors in management.

Machlis, G. E. and D. R. Field. 2000. *National Parks and Rural Development: Practice and Policy in the United States.* Island Press, Washington, D.C. National parks and rural communities are intertwined in terms of their goals and economy, so cooperation is important.

Putz, F. E., G. M. Blate, K. H. Redford, R. Fimel, and J. Robinson. 2001. Tropical forest management and conservation of biodiversity: An overview. *Conservation Biology* 15: 7–20. Leaders in the field argue that carefully managed selectively logged forests can help preserve biodiversity.

Seidensticker, J., S. Christie, and P. Jackson (eds.). 1999. *Riding the Tiger: Tiger Conservation in Human Dominated Landscapes.* Cambridge University Press, London. Tigers are often in conflict for survival with the people in densely settled landscapes; this book discusses strategies for coexistence.

Western, D. and M. Pearl (eds.) 1989. *Conservation for the Twenty-First Century.* Oxford University Press, New York. Leading authorities contribute essays, many of which are related to conservation outside protected areas.

Wondolleck, J. M. and S. L. Yaffee. 2000. *Making Collaboration Work: Lessons from Innovation in Natural Resource Management.* Island Press, Washington, D.C. Advice on how to develop a collaborative approach.

Yaffee, S. L. 1996. *Ecosystem Management in the United States: An Assessment of Current Experience.* Island Press, Washington, D.C. Summary descriptions of 105 selected projects, along with listings and contact information for 619 projects. A great source of information.

Zorn, P., W. Stephensen, and P. Grigoriev. 2001. An ecosystem management program and assessment process for Ontario National Parks. *Conservation Biology* 15: 353–362. Park lands and neighboring lands are being managed as large ecosystems.

Chapter 19

Restoration Ecology

D amaged and degraded ecosystems provide an important opportunity for conservation biologists to put research findings into practice by restoring original species and communities (Daily 1995; Whisenant 1999; Allen et al. 2001). Rebuilding damaged ecosystems has great potential for enlarging, enhancing, and connecting the current system of protected areas. **Ecological restoration** is the practice of restoration and is defined as "the process of intentionally altering a site to establish a defined, indigenous, historic ecosystem. The goal of this process is to emulate the structure, function, diversity, and dynamics of the specified ecosystem" (Society of Ecological Restoration 1991). **Restoration ecology** is the science of restoration and refers to research and scientific study of restored populations, communities and ecosystems (Cairns and Heckman 1996). These are overlapping disciplines, as ecological restoration provides useful scientific data in the process of its work, and restoration ecology interprets and evaluates restoration projects in a way that can lead to improved methods. In this chapter we examine these interconnected disciplines and the effects their practices are having on protecting biological diversity.

There are many different situations in which restoration ecology plays an important role. For instance, in many cases, businesses are required by law to restore habitats they have degraded through activities such as strip mining or water pollution. Governments must restore ecosystems damaged by their own activities, including the dumping of sewage into rivers and estuaries by municipalities or chemical pollution on military bases. Restoration efforts are sometimes part of the mitigation process, in which a new site, often incorporating wetland communities, is created or rehabilitated as a substitute for a site that has been destroyed by development (Zedler 1996). At other times, ecological processes such as annual floods and fires that have been disrupted by dams, levees, and fire-suppression efforts need to be restored.

Ecological restoration has its origins in older applied technologies that attempted to restore ecosystem functions or species of known economic value, such as: wetland replication (to prevent flooding), mine site reclamation (to prevent soil erosion), range management of overgrazed lands (to increase production of grasses), and tree planting on cleared land (for timber, recreational, and ecosystem values) (Urbanska et al. 1997; Gilbert and Anderson 1998). However, these technologies often produce only simplified biological communities or communities that cannot maintain themselves. As concern for biological diversity has grown, restoration plans have included as a major goal the reestablishment of original species assemblages and communities. The input of conservation biologists is needed to make these efforts succeed.

Damage and Restoration

Ecosystems can be damaged by natural phenomena such as volcanic eruptions, hurricanes, and fires triggered by lightning, but they typically recover to their original biomass, community structure, and even a similar species composition through the process of succession. However, some ecosystems have been so degraded by human activity that their ability to recover on their own is severely limited. For example, the original plant species will not be able to grow at a site if the soil has been washed away by erosion. Recovery is particularly unlikely when the damaging agent is still present in the ecosystem. For example, restoration of degraded savannah woodlands in western Costa Rica and the western United States is not possible as long as the land continues to be overgrazed by introduced cattle; reduction of the grazing pressure is obviously the key starting point in these restoration efforts (Fleischner 1994).

Once the damaging agent is removed or controlled, the original communities may reestablish themselves by natural successional processes from remnant populations. However, recovery is unlikely when many of the original species have been eliminated over a large area so that there is no source of colonists. Prairie species, for instance, were eliminated from huge areas of the United States when the land was converted to agriculture. Even when an isolated patch of land is no longer cultivated, the original community is unlikely to reestablish itself because there is no source of seeds and no potential colonizing animals of the original species. The site also may be dominated by invasive species, which often become established in disturbed areas; invasive species must be removed before native species can recover. Recovery also is unlikely when the physical environment has been so altered that the original species can no longer survive there; an example is mine sites, where the restoration of natural communities may be delayed by decades or even centuries due to soil erosion and the heavy-metal toxicity and low nutrient status of the remaining soil (Figure 19.1). Restoration in these habitats requires modification of the physical environment by adding soil, nutrients, and water, by removing invasive species, and by reintroducing original species to the point where the natural process of succession and recovery can begin. These restored sites then need to be monitored for years, even decades, to determine how well management goals are being achieved and if further intervention is required.

In certain cases entirely new environments are created by human activity, such as reservoirs, canals, landfills, and industrial sites. If these sites are neglected, they often become dominated by invasive species, resulting in biological communities that are not useful to people, not typical of the surrounding areas, valueless or even damaging from a conservation perspective, and aesthetically unappealing. If these sites are

Figure 19.1 To speed the recovery of this devastated coal mine site in Wyoming, crews planted 120,000 shrubs. Mining sites often need a great deal of human help in order to recover even a semblance of biodiversity. (Photograph from Jordan et al. 1990.)

properly prepared and native species are reintroduced, native communities possibly can be restored. New habitat is often deliberately created as part of a **mitigation process** to compensate for habitats damaged or destroyed elsewhere. The goal of these and other restoration efforts often is to create new habitats that are comparable in ecosystem functions or species composition to existing **reference sites** (Stephenson 1999; Swetnam et al. 1999; Kloor 2000; Egan and Howell 2001). Reference sites provide explicit goals for restoration and supply quantitative measures of the success of a project. Indeed, reference sites act as control sites and are central to the very concept of restoration. To determine whether the goals of restoration projects are being achieved, both the restoration and the reference sites need to be monitored over time.

Ecological Restoration Techniques

Restoration ecology provides theory and techniques to restore various types of degraded ecosystems. Four main approaches are available in restoring biological communities and ecosystems (Figure 19.2) (Bradshaw 1990; Cairns and Heckman 1996; Whisenant 1999):

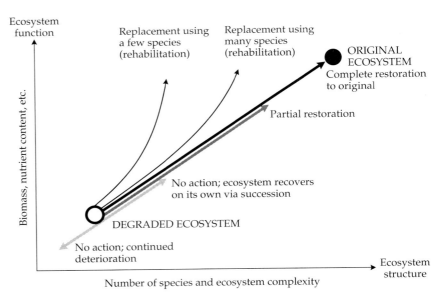

Figure 19.2 Degraded ecosystems have lost both their structure (in terms of species and their interactions with the physical and biological environments) and their function (the accumulation of biomass and soil, water, and nutrient processes). In evaluating sites for restoration, scientists must decide whether the best course of action is to restore the site completely, partially restore the site, rehabilitate the site with different species, or take no action. (After Bradshaw 1990.)

1. *No action:* Restoration is deemed too expensive, previous attempts have failed, or experience has shown that the ecosystem will recover on its own. Letting the ecosystem recover on its own, also known as passive restoration, is typical of old agricultural fields in eastern North America, which return to forest within a few decades after being abandoned for agriculture.

2. *Rehabilitation:* Replacing a degraded ecosystem with another productive type, using just a few or many species. An example of this is replacing a degraded forest area with a productive pasture. Replacement at least establishes a biological community on a site and restores ecological functions such as flood control and soil retention. In the future the new community might eventually come to incorporate a larger number of native species than its original had.

3. *Partial restoration:* Restoring at least some of the ecosystem functions and some of the original, dominant species. An example is replacing a degraded forest with a tree plantation or replanting a degraded grassland with a few species that can survive. Partial restoration typically focuses on dominant species or particularly resilient species that are critical to ecosystem function, delaying action on the rare and less common species that are part of a complete restoration program.

4. *Complete restoration:* Restoring the area to its original species composition and structure by an active program of site modification and reintroduction of the original species. Restoration must first determine and reduce the source of ecological degradation. For example, a source of pollution must be controlled before a lake ecosystem can be restored. Natural ecological processes must be reestablished and allowed to heal the system.

Practical Considerations

Restoration ecology projects often involve professionals from other fields who lend their expertise. These practitioners often have different goals than conservation biologists. For instance, civil engineers involved in major projects seek to find economical ways to permanently stabilize land surfaces, prevent soil erosion, make the site look better to neighbors and the general public, and if possible, restore the productive value of the land (Daily 1995). Sewage treatment plants must be built as part of the restoration of lakes, rivers, and estuaries. To restore wetland communities needed for flood control and wildlife habitat, dams and channels may have to be altered to establish the original water flow patterns. Ecologists contribute to these restoration efforts by developing ways to restore the original communities in terms of species diversity, species composition, vegetation structure, and ecosystem function. To be practical, ecological restoration must also consider the speed of restoration, the cost, the reliability of results, and the ability of the final community to persist with little or no further maintenance. Practitioners of ecological restoration must have a clear grasp of how natural systems work and what methods of restoration are feasible (Clewell and Rieger 1997; Allen et al. 2001; Zedler et al. 2001). Considerations of the cost and availability of seeds, when to water plants, how much fertilizer to add, how to remove invasive species, and how to prepare the surface soil may become paramount in determining a project's success. Dealing with such practical details generally has not been the focus of academic biologists in the past, but these details must be considered in ecological restoration.

Restoration ecology, the science of restoration, is valuable to the science of ecology because it provides a test of how well we understand a biological community and the extent to which we can successfully reassemble a functioning community from its component parts demonstrates the depth of our knowledge and points out deficiencies. As Bradshaw (1990) has said, "Ecologists working in the field of ecosystem restoration are in the construction business, and like their engineering colleagues, can soon discover if their theory is correct by whether the airplane falls out of the sky, the bridge collapses, or the ecosystem fails to flourish." In this sense, restoration ecology can be viewed as an experimental methodology that complements existing basic research on intact systems. In addition to its role as a conservation strategy, restoration projects provide opportunities to completely reassemble communities in different ways, to see how well they function, and to test ideas on a larger scale than would be possible otherwise (Baldwin et al. 1994; Dobson 1997; Young et al. 2001).

Efforts to restore degraded terrestrial communities generally have emphasized the establishment of the original plant community. This emphasis is appropriate because the plant community typically contains the majority of the biomass and provides structure for the rest of the community. However, in the future, restoration ecology needs to devote more attention to the other major components of the community. Fungi (see Box 8 in Chapter 5) and bacteria play a vital role in soil decomposition and nutrient cycling; soil invertebrates are important in creating soil structure; herbivorous animals are important in reducing plant competition and maintaining species diversity; birds and insects are often essential pollinators; and many birds and mammals have vital functions as insect predators, soil diggers, and seed dispersers. Many of these nonplant species can be transferred to a restored site in sod samples. If an area is going to be destroyed and then restored later, as might occur during strip mining, the top layer of soil, which contains the majority of buried seeds, soil invertebrates, and other soil organisms can be carefully removed and stored for later use in restoration efforts (Urbanska et al. 1997; Allen et al. 1999, 2001). While these methods are a step in the right direction, many species will still be lost during this process and the community structure will be completely altered. Large animals and aboveground invertebrates may have to be deliberately caught in sufficient numbers and then released onto restored sites to establish new populations, if they are not able to disperse to the site on their own.

Restoration ecology will play an increasingly important role in the conservation of biological communities if degraded lands and aquatic communities can be restored to their original species composition and added to the limited existing area under protection. Because degraded areas are unproductive and of little economic value, governments may be willing to restore them and increase their productive and conservation value.

Case Studies

The following case studies illustrate some of the problems and successes of ecological restoration.

Wetlands Restoration in Japan

An informative example of wetlands restoration comes from Japan, where parents, teachers, and children have built over 500 small dragonfly ponds next to schools and in public parks to provide habitat for dragonflies and other native aquatic species (Primack et al. 2000). Dragonflies are an important symbol in Japanese culture, and are useful as a starting point for teaching zoology, ecology, chemistry, and principles of conservation. These ponds provide a focus for an entire science and math curriculum. The ponds are planted with aquatic plants; many dragonflies colonize them on their own, and some species are carried in as nymphs from other ponds. The schoolchildren are responsible for the regular weeding and maintenance of these "living laboratories," which helps them to feel an ownership of the project and to develop environmental awareness (Figure 19.3).

The Grand Canyon–Colorado River Ecosystem

One high-profile case of restoration in the United States involves the Grand Canyon. In 1996, scientists were challenged to come up with exactly the right methodology to restore the Colorado River ecosystem where it flows through the Grand Canyon. The river had been drastically altered in 1963 by the construction of the Glen Canyon Dam and the filling-in of Lake Powell. While those projects did provide water and electricity throughout the region, less water flowed into the river. Most significantly, the loss of water greatly reduced the spring floods that once surged through the canyon creating new beaches and habitat for the unique Grand Canyon fish species. Without the flooding to carry new sediment and scour the banks, beaches and banks were either worn away or became overgrown with woody vegetation, and introduced game fish began to replace native fish. To restore this crucial flooding event, the Bureau of Reclamation, after extended discussion with scientists and engineers, released an experimental flood of 900 million m^3 over the course of one week in March 1996 (Schmidt et al. 1998). The flood was effective

(A)

(B)

(C)

Figure 19.3 (A) Children in Yokohama, Japan, are building a dragonfly pond next to their school. Activities involved in its construction include excavating the site, packing the bottom with clay, and reinforcing the banks with wooden posts; later, when the pond is completed, the children will fill it with aquatic plants and release dragonfly larvae. (B) A group of children and adults uses butterfly nets to check for the diversity and abundance of dragonflies at a Yokohama city pond during a city-sponsored maintenance day. They will also remove excess aquatic plants and exotic fish species from the pond. (C) This publicity poster (which exclaims "Let's build a dragonfly pond!"), along with an extensive offering of brochures and practical manuals, is part of government efforts to interest schoolchildren and the general public to participate in programs to restore and enhance the environment. (Photographs courtesy of Seiwa Mori and Yokohama City Environmental Protection Bureau.)

in creating new beaches and habitat for native fish species, but by 2002 the river had mostly returned to its pre-flood condition. More experimental floods are being discussed.

Restoration in Urban Areas

Highly visible restoration efforts are also taking place in many urban areas, to reduce the intense human impact on ecosystems and enhance the quality of life for city dwellers. Local citizen groups often welcome the opportunity to work with government agencies and conservation groups to restore degraded urban areas. Unattractive drainage canals in concrete culverts can be replaced with winding streams bordered with large rocks and planted with native wetland species. Vacant lots and neglected lands can be replanted with native shrubs, trees, and wildflowers. Gravel pits can be packed with soil and restored as ponds. These efforts have the additional benefits of fostering neighborhood pride, creating a sense of community, and enhancing property value.

Restoring native communities on huge urban landfills presents one of the most unusual opportunities. In the United States, 150 million tons of trash are being buried in over 5000 active landfills each year. These eyesores can be the focus of conservation efforts. When they have reached their maximum capacity, these landfills are usually capped by sheets of plastic and layers of clay to prevent toxic chemicals and pollutants from seeping out. If these sites are left alone, they are often colonized by weedy, exotic species. However, planting native shrubs and trees attracts birds and mammals that will bring in and disperse the seeds of a wide range of native species.

Consider the ongoing restoration of the Fresh Kills landfill on Staten Island in New York City (Young 1995). The site occupies over 1000 ha, has a volume 25 times that of the Great Pyramid of Giza, and has garbage mounds as tall as the Statue of Liberty. Certain sections of the landfill have reached their maximum capacity and are now undergoing restoration to create native biological communities. The project began by using bulldozers to contour the site, creating an appearance and drainage similar to natural coastal dunes. Next, 52,000 individuals of 18 species of trees and shrubs were planted to create distinctive native plant communities: an oak scrub forest, a pine-oak forest, and a low shrubland. Herbs were planted within these communities. Right away, the trees provided perching places for fruit-eating birds that brought seeds of many new species to the site. After just one year, seedlings of 32 additional woody plant species had appeared on the site. The site appears to be on its way to establishing a native ecosystem. Native birds of conservation interest such as ospreys, hawks, and egrets nest and feed there. The eventual goal is to create a new park with abundant wildlife, open to the citizens of this huge city.

Restoration of Some Major Communities

Many efforts to restore ecological communities have focused on wetlands, lakes, prairies, and forests. These environments have suffered severe alteration from human activities and are good candidates for restoration work, as described below.

Wetlands

Some of the most extensive restoration work has been done on wetlands, including swamps and marshes (Zedler 1996; Karr and Chu 1998). Wetlands are often damaged or even filled in because their importance in flood control, maintenance of water quality, and preservation of biological communities is either not known or not appreciated. More than half of the original wetlands in the United States have already been lost, and in heavily populated states such as California, over 90% have been lost (Cairns and Heckman 1996). Because of wetland protection under the Clean Water Act and the U.S. government policy of "no net loss of wetlands," large development projects that damage wetlands must repair them or create new wetlands to compensate for those damaged beyond repair (Box 27). The focus of these efforts has been on recreating the original hydrology of the area and then planting native species. Experience has shown that such efforts to restore wetlands often do not closely match the species composition or hydrologic characteristics of reference sites. The subtleties of species composition, water movement, and soils, as well as the site history, are too difficult to match. Often the restored wetlands are dominated by exotic, invasive species. However, the restored wetlands often do have some of the wetland plant species, or at least similar ones, and can be considered to have some degree of functional equivalency to the reference sites. The restored wetlands also have some of the beneficial ecosystem characteristics such as flood control and pollution reduction, and they are often valuable for wildlife habitat. Further study and research of restoration methods may result in further improvement.

Lakes

Limnologists (scientists who study the chemistry, biology, and physics of freshwater bodies) involved in multibillion-dollar efforts to restore lakes are already gaining valuable insights into community ecology and trophic structure that otherwise would not be possible (Welch and Cooke 1990; MacKenzie 1996). One of the most common types of damage to lakes and ponds is **cultural eutrophication,** which is eutrophication caused by the excess mineral nutrients that are the products of human activity. Signs of eutrophication include increases in the algae population (particularly surface scums of blue-green algae), lowered water clarity, lowered oxygen content of the water, fish kills, and an eventual increase in the growth of floating plants and other water weeds.

Attempts to restore eutrophic lakes have not only provided practical management information, but have also provided insight into the basic science of limnology. In many lakes, the eutrophication process can be reversed by reducing amounts of mineral nutrients entering the water through better sewage treatment or by diverting polluted water; this approach is known as bottom-up control. In other lakes, improvement does not occur, suggesting that the lake has internal mechanisms that are recycling excess nutrients from the sediment to the water column and keeping the nutrient levels artificially high.

One possible mechanism for the continual presence of excess nutrients in the water column involves fish species such as the carp (*Cypri-*

BOX 27 *Easier Said Than Done: Restoring the Kissimmee River*

The Kissimmee River was formerly a long, meandering river that flowed from Lake Kissimmee to Lake Okeechobee in central Florida. Its loops and bends created a mosaic of wetlands and floodplains that supported a highly diverse community of waterfowl, wading birds, fish, and other wildlife. The hydrology of the Kissimmee River was unique. The large number of headwater lakes and streams that drain into the Kissimmee River, combined with flat floodplains, low riverbanks, and poor drainage lead to frequent, prolonged flooding, dense vegetation and outstanding wildlife habitat.

But the annual floods that created such a unique ecosystem were not considered compatible with the rapid expansion of urban and agricultural development in the 1950s and

The Kissimmee River Restoration project involves removing two water control structures (S-65B and S-65C) and backfilling the 37 km of canal between them. In the process, 72 km of continuous river channel will be restored, and floodwaters will cover the floodplain once again. In Phase I, completed in 2001, control structure S-65B was removed, 24 km of the river channel was restored, and 15 km of channel was filled in. The map is not to scale. The distance from Lake Kisimmee to Lake Okeechobee is around 90 km. (Data from the South Florida Water Management District, 2001.)

BOX 27 *(continued)*

1960s. In response to the growing demand for flood protection, the Kissimmee River was channelized. The U.S. Army Corps of Engineers dug a 90-km long drainage canal, built levees, and regulated water flow from the feeder lakes. Two-thirds of the wetlands were drained, one-third of the river's natural channel was destroyed, and much of the drained land was converted to rangeland for cattle. As the water flow was diverted through the canal, oxygen concentrations in the water declined. An ecosystem that had been characterized by highly variable water levels and patchy, diverse habitats became a stable, homogeneous environment. The impacts were immediate: Overwintering bird populations declined to 10% of their original size, habitat for game fish was degraded, and a diverse natural community of wading birds and fish was replaced by a few dominant species such as cattle egrets, gar, and bowfin (Toth 1996). Intensive agriculture on former wetlands transported high levels of nutrients into the channelized river and eventually into Lake Okeechobee, accelerating the eutrophication process.

As the impact of the channelization became apparent, public pressure from conservation groups mounted to restore the Kissimmee River to its original state. Initial plans focused on restoring certain target species or functions of the river. Fishermen lobbied for restoration of the largemouth bass fishery. Residents clamored for improving water quality by restoring the filtering function of the wetlands. Hunters and bird-watchers focused on improving conditions for waterfowl. Ultimately it became clear that efforts needed to focus on restoring the ecological integrity of the whole ecosystem, rather than on individual characteristics such as species abundance (Toth and Aumen 1994).

A demonstration project in 1984 used a dam across the canal to direct river water into the former wetland, recreating marshland and reestablishing old river channels. Within one year, wetland plant communities were reestablished and fish and bird populations increased dramatically in the reflooded areas. This demonstration project and other restoration studies and modeling efforts provided evidence that the restoration of the Kissimmee River was technically feasible.

In 1992, the U.S. Congress authorized the restoration of the Kissimmee River, through backfilling 37 km of the flood-control canal, removing two water control structures, and re-carving 15 km of old river channel. In the process, 11,000 ha of wetlands and 72 continuous km of the twisting river channel will be restored. To accomplish this, approximately 40,000 ha of land are being acquired by the government. Important habitat will be provided for over 300 fish and wildlife species, including the endangered bald eagle, snail kite, and wood stork. The first phase of the reconstruction was completed between 1999 and 2001. It restored 24 km of river channel and 4400 ha of floodplain. Future phases of the restoration project are scheduled to be completed by 2010. A major component of the project involves continuous ecological evaluation to determine the degree of success at each phase, and the opportunity for fine-tuning the plan along the way. The final project cost is estimated to be $500 million, shared equally between the federal government and the state of Florida. While this cost may seem enormous, the totality of ecosystem services provided by a healthy, restored Kissimmee River will be immensely valuable and will reestablish a significant part of Florida's natural heritage. The project might also serve as a tutorial for the far larger Comprehensive Everglades Restoration Plan—begun in 2001 and slated to cost $8 billion—which is designed to rebuild this degraded, world-famous wetland of south Florida (Schrope 2001).

---

nus carpio) and the brown bullhead (*Ictalurus nebulosus*). These species eat nutrient-rich organic matter on the lake bottom and then excrete these nutrients into the water column. This hypothesis is supported by the declines in phosphorus concentration that occurs after carp populations are reduced in eutrophic lakes. The composition of the fish community also can affect the eutrophication process through predator–prey relationships. In some eutrophic lakes, planktonic invertebrates (such as the crustacean *Daphnia*) that eat algae are rapidly consumed by the fish, allowing the algae to grow unchecked. If predatory fish (which feed on other fish) are added to the lake, the populations of zooplankton-eating fish often drop, crustacean populations increase, the abundance of algae decreases, and water quality improves. Improvements in water quality achieved through manipulations of fish populations are referred to as top-down control, illustrating how restorationists can take advantage of natural processes of recovery and reestablishment of ecosystem dynamics.

One of the most dramatic and expensive examples of lake restoration has been the effort to restore Lake Erie (Makarewicz and Bertram 1991). Lake Erie was the most polluted of the Great Lakes in the 1950s and 1960s, characterized by deteriorating water quality, extensive algal blooms, declining indigenous fish populations, the collapse of commercial fisheries, and oxygen depletion in deeper waters. To address this problem, the United States and Canadian governments have invested more than $7.5 billion since 1972 in wastewater treatment facilities, reducing the annual discharge of phosphorus into the lake from 15,260 tons in 1972 to 2449 tons in 1985. Once water quality began to improve in the mid-1970s and the 1980s, stocks of the native commercial walleye pike (*Stizostedion vitreum vitreum*), a predatory fish, began to increase on their own. Other predatory and game fish were added to the lake by state agencies. As a result, both bottom-up and top-down control agents worked to improve lake quality. The 1980s saw continued improvement in Lake Erie water quality, as shown by lower concentrations of phosphorus, lower phytoplankton (algal) abundance, and a shift in the trophic community toward higher relative numbers of algal-feeding zooplankton and predatory fish, and lower numbers of zooplankton-feeding fish (Figure 19.4). There is even some evidence of improvement in oxygen levels at the lower depths of the lake. Even though the lake may never return to its original condition because of altered water chemistry and the large number of exotic species present, the combination of bottom-up and top-down controls—and the investment of billions of dollars—has resulted in a significant degree of restoration in this large, highly managed ecosystem.

Prairies

Many small parcels of former agricultural land in North America have been restored as prairies. Because they are species-rich, have many beautiful wildflowers, and can be established within a few years, prairies represent ideal subjects for restoration work (Samson and Knopf 1996; Packard and Mutel 1997). Also, the techniques used for prairie restoration are similar to common gardening and agriculture and are well suited to volun-

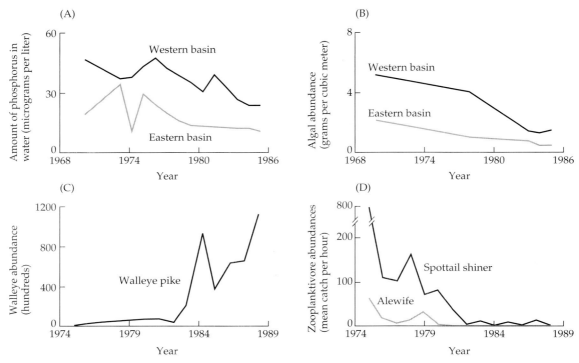

Figure 19.4 Signs of recovery in Lake Erie. (A) Levels of phosphorus at the eastern and western ends of the lake. Phosphorus levels were lowered during the 1970s and early 1980s by treating the sewage and other human effluents that entered the lake. (B) Algal abundance. Algal blooms, which lower the water quality and eliminate other species, have declined over time as the levels of phosphorus decline. (C) Walleye pike abundance, as measured by the sport fishermen catch, has increased once algal levels declined and water quality improved. Walleye are predatory fish that feed on zooplanktivorous fish such as alewife and spottail shiners; adding walleye to the lake is one way to increase the population of crustaceans and other zooplankton, which in turn feed on the algae. (D) The abundance of alewife and shiners, measured by the catch per hour in Lake Erie fishing trawlers. When populations of these fish reach overly high levels, they decimate the zooplankton population; with fewer zooplankton to feed on them, algal blooms flourish even more. Alewife and shiner populations declined after walleye and other introduced predatory fish began to increase. (After Makarewicz and Bertram 1991.)

teer labor. Of course, reestablishing the full range of plant species, soil structure, and invertebrates could take centuries or may never occur.

Some of the most extensive research on the restoration of prairies has been carried out in Wisconsin, starting in the 1930s. A wide variety of techniques has been used in these prairie restoration attempts, but the basic method involves a site preparation of shallow plowing, burning, and raking, if prairie species are present, or eliminating all vegetation by plowing or applying herbicides, if only exotics are present. Native plant species are then established by transplanting them in prairie sods obtained elsewhere, planting individuals grown from seed, or scattering prairie seed collected from the wild or from cultivated plants (Figure 19.5). The simplest method is gathering hay from a native prairie and sowing it on the prepared site.

(A)

(B)

Figure 19.5 (A) In the late 1930s, members of the Civilian Conservation Corps (one of the organizations created by President Franklin Roosevelt in order to boost employment during the Great Depression) participated in a University of Wisconsin project to restore the wild species of a Midwestern prairie. (B) The prairie as it looked 50 years later. (Photographs from the University of Wisconsin Arboretum and Archives.)

One of the most ambitious proposed restorations involves re-creating a short-grass prairie ecosystem, or "buffalo commons," on about 380,000 km^2 of the Plains states, from the Dakotas to Texas and from Wyoming to Nebraska (Popper and Popper 1991; Mathews 1992). This land is currently used for environmentally damaging and often unprofitable agriculture and grazing that is supported by government subsidies. The human population of this region is declining as farmers and townspeople go out of business and young people move away. From the ecological, sociological, and even economic perspectives, the best long-term use of much of the region might be as a restored prairie ecosystem. The human population of the region could stabilize around nondamaging core industries such as tourism, wildlife management, and low-level grazing by cattle and bison, leaving only the best lands in agriculture. The proposed project is controversial because the farmers and ranchers still living in the region do not want to be told to move. On a somewhat smaller scale, a project in Siberia is being planned to restore the original steppe grasslands ecosystem, including bison, wild horses, and other large grazers, on 160 km^2 of land.

Prairie restoration projects are also useful for their educational value and for their ability to excite urban dwellers eager to be involved in conservation efforts. The Chicago metropolitan area is particularly well known for such projects; some involve creating prairie grasslands with native prairie species, rather than lawns, in suburban neighborhoods. In concluding his essay on five decades of Wisconsin experiments, Cottam (1990) says, "Prairie restoration is an exciting and rewarding enterprise. It is full of surprises, fantastic successes, and abysmal failures. You learn a lot—usually more about what not to do than what to do. Success is seldom high, but prairie plants are resilient, and even a poor beginning will in time result in a beautiful prairie."

Tropical Dry Forest in Costa Rica

An exciting experiment in restoration ecology is currently taking place in northwestern Costa Rica. The tropical dry forests of Central America have long suffered from large-scale conversion to cattle ranches and farms. Only a few fragments remain. Even in these fragments, logging and hunting threaten remaining species. This destruction has gone largely unnoticed as international scientific and public attention has focused on the more glamorous rain forests elsewhere. The American ecologist Daniel Janzen has been working with Costa Rica's National Park Service and resident staff to restore 110,000 ha of land in the Area de Conservación Guanacaste (ACG) (Figure 19.6) (Allen 1988; Janzen 1988b, 2000).

Restoration of this area of marginal ranches, low-quality pastures, and forest fragments includes planting both native and exotic trees to shade out introduced invasive grasses, eliminating human-caused fires, and banning logging and hunting. Livestock grazing is initially used to lower

(A)

(B)

(C)

Figure 19.6 (A) The Area de Conservación Guanacaste is an experiment in restoration ecology—an attempt to restore the devastated and fragmented tropical dry forest of Costa Rica. (B) Eight years of fire suppression allowed native trees and other species to become established once again, turning a barren grassland (left) into a young forest (right). (Photographs by C. R. Carroll.) (C) Daniel Janzen, an ecologist from the United States, is a driving force behind the restoration project in Guanacaste. Here he inspects moth specimens from the study area. (Photograph by William H. Allen.)

the abundance of grasses. Grazing is then phased out as the forest invades through natural animal- and wind-borne seed dispersal. In just 15 years, this process has converted 60,000 ha of pastures to a species-rich, dense young forest. While this process reestablishes the dry forest ecosystem and benefits the adjacent rain forest to which animals of the dry forest seasonally migrate, it will require an estimated 200–500 years to regain the original forest structure.

An innovative aspect of this restoration is that all 130 members of the staff and administration of the ACG are Costa Ricans and reside in the area. The ACG offers training and advancement for its staff, educational opportunities for their children, and the best economic use of these marginal lands, which were formerly ranch and farm lands. ACG employees are selected from the local community, rather than spending scarce resources on imported consultants. A key element in the restoration plan is what has been termed **biocultural restoration**, meaning that the ACG teaches basic biology in the field to all students in grades four through six in the neighboring schools and gives presentations to citizen groups. Janzen (quoted in Allen 1988) believes that, in rural areas such as Guanacaste, providing an opportunity for learning about nature can be one of the most valuable functions of national parks and restored areas:

> The public is starving for and responds immediately to presentations of complexity of all kinds—biology, music, literature, politics, education, et cetera. . . . The goal of biocultural restoration is to give back to people the understanding of the natural history around them that their grandparents had. These people are now just as culturally deprived as if they could no longer read, hear music, or see color.

This educational effort has created a community literate in conservation issues as well as a local viewpoint that the ACG offers something of value to all. Residents have begun to view the ACG as if it were a large ranch producing "wildland resources" for the community rather than an exclusionary "national park." The ACG is welcomed and acknowledged as being as important as the traditional agricultural countryside it replaced (Janzen 1999, 2000). Both the staff and neighboring residents have become strong supporters of the ACG.

Funding for land purchases and park management for the ACG restoration project, totaling $45 million as of 2001, comes from the Costa Rican government and donations from over 4000 individuals, institutions, and private international foundations. In the future, operating income to pay for the $1.2 million annual budget will increasingly come from fees paid by foreign and Costa Rican scientists working at the biological field stations. Also, the proximity of the park to the Pan American Highway makes it an ideal location for ecotourism. Employment in these expanding research, tourist, and educational facilities will provide a significant source of income for the local community, particularly for those who are interested in nature and education. For continued success, the ACG must ensure that the plan for park development and management provides the proper integration of community needs and restoration needs in a way that satisfactorily fulfills both. Also, by having scientists involved in the design and implementation of the project, basic and applied information will be obtained that can be used to advance the science of restoration ecology.

In the final analysis, this restoration effort has been so successful and has attracted so much media attention in large part because a highly articulate, well-known individual—Daniel Janzen—committed all his time and resources to a cause in which he passionately believed. His enthusiasm and vision have inspired many other people to join his cause, and he is a classic example of how potent a force for conservation one individual can be.

The Future of Restoration Ecology

Restoration ecology is becoming one of the major growth areas in conservation biology, and has its own scientific society, the Society for Ecological Restoration, and journals, *Restoration Ecology* and *Ecological Restoration*. Scientists are increasingly able to synthesize the growing range of published studies and suggest improvements in how to carry out restoration projects. However, conservation biologists in this field must take care to ensure that restoration efforts are legitimate, rather than just a public-relations cover by environmentally damaging industrial corporations only interested in continuing business as usual (Falk and Olwell 1992; Zedler 1996). A 5-ha "demonstration" project in a highly visible location does not compensate for thousands or tens of thousands of hectares damaged elsewhere and should not be accepted as such by conservation biologists. The best long-term strategy still is to protect and manage biological communities where they are found naturally; only in these places can we be sure that the requirements for the long-term survival of all species are available.

Summary

1. Ecological restoration is the practice of reestablishing populations and whole communities in degraded, damaged, or even destroyed habitat. Restoration ecology is the scientific study of such restorations. Partial restoration of certain species or ecosystem functions may be an appropriate goal if complete restoration is impossible or too expensive. Establishment of new communities such as wetlands, forests, and prairies on degraded or abandoned sites provides an opportunity to enhance biological diversity in habitats that have little other value and can improve the quality of life of people living in the area. Restoration ecology can also provide insight into community ecology by reassembling a biological community from its original species.

2. Restoration projects begin by eliminating or neutralizing factors that prevent the system from recovering. Then some combination of site preparation, habitat management, and reintroduction of original species gradually allows the community to regain the species and ecosystem characteristics of designated reference sites. Restoration efforts are usually concerned with the soil, plants, and hydrology of the site, but animals, symbiotic fungi, and bacteria also are increasingly included in restoration plans.

3. Most attempts to restore severely degraded habitat have had only limited success in restoring the original species composition and ecosystem function. Creating new habitat in one place to compensate for the destruction of a similar habitat elsewhere, known as mitigation, is often not an effective conservation strategy; the best strategy is to protect populations and communities where they currently occur.

For Discussion

1. Restoration ecologists are becoming more successful at restoring biological communities. Does this mean that biological communities can be moved around the landscape and positioned in convenient places that do not inhibit further expansion of human activities?

2. How would you evaluate the success of a project that is currently restoring a biological community? What criteria and techniques would you use? How much time would you need to monitor the restored community?

3. What do you think are some of the easiest natural communities to restore? The most difficult? Why?

4. Conservation efforts are particularly difficult in areas of Africa where there is an increasing human population coupled with poverty, warfare, and environmental damage. Consider the plight of the mountain gorilla living in the Virunga Mountains of Africa. If it is not possible to protect this species in its native locality, why not use a range of African plants to restore a degraded site in a more stable place, such as the mountains of Costa Rica, Mexico, or Puerto Rico, and then release a population of gorillas onto the site? Is this feasible? What about extending the concept to create an entire African savannah ecosystem, complete with herds of grazing animals and predators, on degraded rangelands in Mexico? What are the advantages and disadvantages of such a restoration approach?

Suggested Readings

Allen, E., M. Allen, and J. S. Brown. 2001. Restoration of animal, plant, and microbial diversity. In *Encyclopedia of Biodiversity*, S. A. Levin (ed.), Vol. 5, pp. 185–202. Academic Press, San Diego, CA. Restoration projects can include animals and microbes.

Cairns, J. and J. R. Heckman. 1996. Restoration ecology: The state of an emerging field. *Annual Review of Energy and the Environment* 21: 167–189. Excellent summary of the field.

Dobson, A. P., A. D. Bradshaw, and A. J. M. Baker. 1997. Hopes for the future: restoration ecology and conservation biology. *Science* 277: 515–522. Overview of the field in a special edition of *Science* devoted to human impact on the planet.

Galatowitsch, S. M. and A. G. Van der Valk. 1996. *Restoring Prairie Wetlands: An Ecological Approach*. Iowa State University Press, Ames, IA. Practical guide on how to restore prairies and how to see whether it worked.

Gilbert, O. L. and P. Anderson. 1998. *Habitat Creation and Repair*. Oxford University Press, Oxford. Practical guide to restoration, with many examples from the United Kingdom.

Janzen, D. H. 1988. Tropical ecological and biocultural restoration. *Science* 239: 243–244. Unique integration of ecology and public education.

Karr, J. R. and E. W. Chu. 1998. *Restoring Life in Running Waters*. Island Press, Washington, D.C. Presents a system for monitoring and improving rivers.

Mathews, A. 1992. *Where the Buffalo Roam*. Grove Weidenfeld, New York. Superb popular account of the controversial "buffalo commons" proposal.

Restoration Ecology and *Ecological Restoration*. Check out these journals to see what is really happening in the field. Available from most college and university libraries and from the Society for Ecological Restoration, 1955 W. Grant Road #150, Tucson AZ 85745 U.S.A.; or contact the society at www.ser.org.

Schrope, M. 2001. Save our swamp. *Nature* 409: 128–130. An $8 billion wetlands restoration plan for the Florida Everglades may not succeed due to a lack of clean water.

Swetnam, T. W., C. D. Allen, and J. L. Betancourt. 1999. Applied historical ecology: using the past to manage the future. *Ecological Applications* 9(4): 1189–1206.

Toth, L. A., J. W. Koebel, Jr., A. G. Warne, and J. Chamberlain. 2002. Implications of reestablishing prolonged flood pulse characteristics of the Kissimmee River and floodplain ecosystem. In *Flood Pulsing in Wetlands: Restoring the Natural Hydrological Balance*, Beth Middleton (ed.), pp. 191–221. John Wiley & Sons, Inc., New York.

Whisenant, S. G. 1999. *Repairing Damaged Wildlands*. Cambridge University Press, Cambridge. Restoration emphasizing natural recovery processes.

White, P. S. and J. L. Walker. 1997. Approximating nature's variation: selecting and using reference information in restoration ecology. *Restoration Ecology* 5: 338–349. Selecting reference sites is difficult because no two sites are exactly the same; see other excellent articles in this special edition of the journal.

Young, T. P., J. M. Chase, and R. T. Huddleston. 2001. Community succession and assembly. *Ecological Restoration* 19(1): 5–18.

Zedler, J. B. 1996. Ecological issues in wetland mitigation: An introduction to the forum. *Ecological Applications* 6: 33–37. A special issue of *Ecological Applications* provides excellent information on the creation of new wetlands.

PART VI

Conservation and Human Societies

Chapter 20

Conservation and Sustainable Development at the Local and National Levels

As we have seen, many problems in conservation biology require a multidisciplinary approach that addresses the need to protect biological diversity while simultaneously providing for the economic welfare of people. The sea turtle conservation program described in Box 1 in Chapter 1 illustrates such an approach: Conservation biologists in Brazil are employing fisher groups at the *local level* as conservation workers, developing tourist facilities and educational materials, providing medical care and aquaculture training for the local people, and supplying the information the national government needs to establish new protected areas and conservation laws. Conservation biologists throughout the world are actively working at the local and national levels to develop such innovative approaches. This chapter examines some of the strategies employed at the local and national levels to promote conservation, strategies that often involve action by government and by private conservation organizations. The chapter also explores the efforts by traditional people to protect their lands, which is an important component of protecting biodiversity, since many traditional peoples live in the most biologically diverse areas of the world. Finally, the chapter concludes with a brief evaluation of some of these efforts and suggests possible improvements.

As has been discussed, efforts to preserve biological diversity sometimes conflict with both real and perceived human needs (Figure 20.1). Increasingly, many conservation biologists, policy makers, and land managers are recognizing the need for **sustainable development**—economic development that satisfies both present and future needs for resources and employment while minimizing its impact on biological diversity (Lubchenco et al. 1991; Lee 2001). As defined by some environmental economists, **economic development** implies improvements in efficiency and organization but not necessarily increases in resource consumption. Economic development is clearly distinguished from **economic growth,** which is defined as material increases in the amount of resources used. Sustainable development is a useful and important concept in conservation biology because it emphasizes *improving current development and limiting growth.* By this definition, investing in national park infrastructure to improve protection of biological diversity and provide revenue opportunities for local communities would be an example of move-

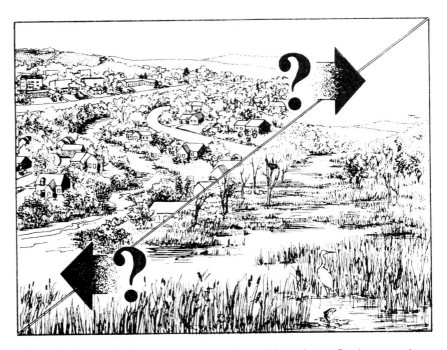

Figure 20.1 Sustainable development seeks to address the conflict between development to meet human needs and the preservation of the natural world. (From Gersh and Pickert 1991; drawing by Tamara Sayre.)

ment toward sustainable development, as would implementation of less destructive logging and fishing practices.

Unfortunately, the concept of sustainable development is often misappropriated. Many large corporations and the policy organizations that they fund have misused the concept of sustainable development to "greenwash" their industrial activities without any change in practice (Willers 1994). For instance, a plan to establish a huge mining complex in the middle of a forest wilderness cannot justifiably be called "sustainable development" simply because a small percentage of the land area is set aside as a park. Alternatively, some conservation biologists champion the opposite extreme, claiming that sustainable development means that vast areas of the world must be kept off limits to all development and should be allowed to remain or return to wilderness. As with all such disputes, informed scientists and citizens must study the issues carefully, identify which groups are advocating which positions and why and then make careful decisions that best meet the seemingly contradictory needs of human society and the protection of biological diversity. Such apparent contradiction necessitates compromise, and in most cases, compromises form the basis of government policy and laws, with conflicts resolved by government agencies and courts.

Conservation at the Local Level

One of the most powerful strategies in protecting biological diversity at the local level is the designation of intact biological communities as nature reserves or conservation land. Governments often set aside public lands for various conservation purposes and to preserve future options. Government bodies buy land as local parks for recreation, conservation areas to maintain biological diversity, forests for timber production and other uses, and watersheds to protect water supplies. In some cases, land is purchased outright, but often it is donated to conservation organizations by public-spirited citizens. Many of these citizens receive significant tax benefits from the government to encourage these donations.

Land Trusts

In many countries, private conservation organizations are among the leaders in acquiring land for conservation (Dwyer and Hodge 1996). In the Netherlands about half of the protected areas are privately owned. In the United States alone, over 6 million ha of land are protected at a local level by land trusts, which are private, nonprofit corporations established to protect land and natural resources. There are around 3000 private conservation organizations in the United States, many of which have land protection, public education, and political lobbying as major objectives. At a national level, major organizations such as The Nature

Conservancy and the Audubon Society have protected an additional 3 million ha in the United States.

Land trusts are particularly common in Europe. In Britain, the National Trust has more than 2.7 million members and owns around 248,000 ha of land, much of it farmland, including 26 National Nature Reserves, 466 Sites of Special Scientific Interest, 355 properties of Outstanding National Beauty, and 40,000 archaeological sites (Figure 20.2). Among the many private land trusts in Britain, one of the most notable is the Royal Society for the Protection of Birds (RSPB), which has almost 900,000 members and manages 130 reserves with an area of 92,000 ha. A major emphasis of many of these reserves is nature conservation, often linked to school programs. The RSPB has an annual income of about $45 million and is active in bird conservation issues around the world. These private reserve networks are collectively referred to as CARTs—Conservation, Amenity, and Recreation Trusts, a name that reflects their varied objectives. Jean Hocker (in Elfring 1989), executive director of the Land Trust Exchange, an association of land trust organizations, explains:

> Different land trusts may save different types of land for different reasons. Some preserve farmland to maintain economic opportunities for local farmers. Some preserve wildlife habitat to ensure the existence of an endangered species. Some protect land in watersheds to improve or maintain water quality. Whether biologic, economic, productive, aesthetic, spiritual, educational, or ethical, the reasons for protecting land are as diverse as the landscape itself.

In addition to outright purchase of land, both governments and conservation organizations protect land through **conservation easements**, in which landowners give up the right to develop, build on, or subdivide their property in exchange for a sum of money, lower real-estate taxes, or

Figure 20.2 Membership in the British National Trust has been undergoing a dramatic increase, with a corresponding increase in landownership. (After Dwyer and Hodge 1996.)

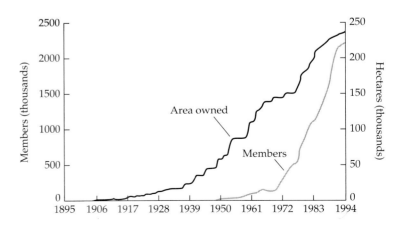

some other tax benefit. Sometimes the government or conservation organization purchases the development rights to the land, compensating the landowner for not selling it to developers. For many landowners, accepting a conservation easement is an attractive option: They receive a financial advantage while still owning their land and are able to feel that they are assisting conservation objectives. Of course, the offer of lower taxes or money is not always necessary; many landowners will voluntarily accept conservation restrictions without compensation.

Another strategy that land trusts and governments use is **limited development**: A landowner, property developer, and a conservation organization reach a compromise that allows part of the land to be commercially developed while the remainder is protected by a conservation easement. Limited development projects are often successful because the value of the developed lands is usually enhanced by being adjacent to conservation land. Limited development also allows the construction of necessary buildings and other infrastructure for an expanding human society.

Governments and conservation organizations can further encourage conservation on private lands through other mechanisms, including compensating private landowners for desisting from some damaging activity and implementing some positive activity (Bowers 1999; Environmental Defense 2000). **Conservation leasing** involves providing payments to private landowners who actively manage their land for biodiversity protection. Tax deductions and payments could also apply to any costs of restoration or management, including weeding, controlled burning, establishing nest holes, and planting native species. In some cases, private landowners may still be allowed to develop their land later, even if endangered species come to live on the land. A related idea is **conservation banking**, in which a landowner deliberately preserves an endangered species or a protected habitat type such as wetlands, or even restores degraded habitat and creates new habitat. A developer can then pay the landowner or a conservation organization to protect this new habitat in compensation for a similar habitat that is being destroyed elsewhere by a construction project (Bean and Dwyer 2000). The funds paid by the developer for such habitat mitigation can be used to pay for the management of the newly created, restored, or preserved habitat and endangered species living there.

Local efforts by land trusts to protect land are sometimes criticized as being elitist because they provide tax breaks only to those wealthy enough to take advantage of them, in addition to lowering the revenue collected from land and property taxes. Others argue that land used in other ways, such as for agriculture or to build shopping malls, is more productive. While land in trust may initially yield lower tax revenues, loss of tax revenue from land acquired by a land trust is often offset by the increased value and consequent increased property taxes of houses and land adjacent to the conservation area. In addition, the employment, recreational activities, tourist spending and student projects associated with nature reserves, national parks, wildlife refuges, and other protected areas generate revenue throughout the local economy, which benefits the community. Finally, by preserving important features of the landscape and natural communities, local nature reserves also preserve and enhance the cultural heritage of the local society, a consideration that must be valued for sustainable development to be achieved.

Local Legislation

Most efforts to find the right balance between the preservation of species and habitats and the needs of society rely on initiatives from concerned citizens, conservation organizations, and government officials. The result of these initiatives often end up codified into environmental regulations or laws. These efforts may take many forms, but they begin with individual and group decisions to prevent the destruction of habitats and species in order to preserve something of perceived economic, cultural, biological, scientific, or recreational value.

In modern societies, local (city and town) and regional (county, state, and provincial) governments pass laws to provide effective protection for species and habitats and at the same time provide development for the continued needs of society (Buck 1996; Press et al. 1996; Saterson 2001). Often, but not always, these local and regional laws are comparable to or stricter than national laws. Such laws are passed because citizens and political leaders feel that they represent the will of the majority and provide long-term benefits to society. Conservation laws regulate activities that directly affect species and ecosystems. The most prominent of these laws governs when and where hunting and fishing can occur; the size, number, and species of animals that can be taken; and the types of weapons, traps, and other equipment that can be used. Restrictions are enforced through licensing requirements and patrols by game wardens and police. In some settled and protected areas, hunting and fishing are banned entirely. Similar laws affect the harvesting of plants, seaweed, and shellfish. Related legislation includes prohibitions on trade in wild-collected animals and plants. Certification of origin of biological products may be required to ensure that wild populations are not depleted by illegal collection or harvest. These restrictions have long applied to certain animals such as trout and deer and plants of horticultural interest such as rhododendrons, azaleas, and cacti. New initiatives are being developed to certify the origin of additional products such as ornamental fish and wood.

Laws that control the ways in which land is used are another means of protecting biological diversity. These laws include restrictions on the extent of land use or access, type of land use, and generation of pollution. For example, vehicles and even people on foot may be restricted from habitats and resources that are sensitive to damage, such as bird-nesting areas, bogs, sand dunes, wildflower patches, and sources of drinking water. Uncontrolled fires may severely damage habitats, so practices such as campfires that contribute to accidental fires are often rigidly controlled. Zoning laws sometimes prevent construction in sensitive areas such as barrier beaches and floodplains. Wetlands are often strongly protected because of their recognized value for flood protection, preserving water quality and maintaining wildlife. Even where development is permitted, building permits are reviewed with increasing scrutiny to ensure that damage is not done to endangered species or ecosystems, particularly wetlands. For major regional and national projects, such as dams, canals, mining and smelting operations, oil extraction, and highway construction, environmental impact statements must be prepared describing the damage that such projects could cause. To prevent inadvertent damage to natural resources and human health, it is essential to consider the full potential environmental impacts before projects are initiated. The passage and enforcement of conservation-related laws on a local level can become an emotional experience that divides a community and even leads to violence. To avoid such counterproductive outcomes, conservationists must be able to convince the public that using resources in a thoughtful and sustainable manner creates the greatest long-term benefit for the community. The general public must be made to look beyond the immediate benefits that come with rapid and destructive exploitation of resources. For example, towns often need to restrict development in watershed areas to protect water supplies; this may mean that houses and businesses are not built in these sensitive areas and landowners may have to be compensated for these lost opportunities. It is essential that conservation biologists clearly communicate the reasons for these restrictions. Those affected by the restrictions can become allies in the protection of resources if they understand the importance and long-term benefits of reduced access. These people must be kept informed and consulted throughout the decision-making process. The ability to negotiate, compromise, and explain positions, regulations, and restrictions—often using the best scientific evidence available—are important skills for conservationists to develop. A fervent belief in one's cause is not enough.

Conservation at the National Level

Throughout much of the modern world, national governments play a leading role in conservation activities (Saterson 2001). Governments can use their revenues to buy new lands for conservation. Areas particularly targeted for conservation are the watersheds that protect drinking water, open lands near densely settled urban areas, areas occupied by endangered species, and lands adjacent to existing protected areas. In the United States, special funding mechanisms, such as the Land Legacy Initiative and the Land and Water Conservation Fund, have been established to purchase land for conservation purposes. National governments can also strongly influence conservation practices on private land through the payment of cash subsidies and the granting of tax deductions to landowners who manage their lands for biological diversity.

The establishment of national parks is a particularly important conservation strategy. National parks are the single largest source of protected lands in many countries. For example, Costa Rica's national parks protect more than half a million hectares, or about 8% of the nation's land area, and 14% of the land receives some type of protection (WRI 2000). Outside the protected areas, deforestation is proceeding rapidly, and soon national parks may represent the only undisturbed habitat and source of natural products, such as timber, in the whole country. As of 1998, the U.S. National Park system, with more than 380 sites, protected around 34 million ha.

National Legislation

National legislatures and governing agencies are the principal bodies for developing standards that limit environmental pollution. Laws regulating aerial emissions, sewage treatment, waste dumping, and development of wetlands are often enacted to protect human health and property and resources such as drinking water, forests, and commercial and sport fisheries. The level of enforcement of these laws demonstrates a nation's determination to protect the health of its citizens and the integrity of its natural resources. At the same time, these laws protect biological communities that would otherwise be destroyed by pollution. The air pollution that exacerbates human respiratory disease, for instance, also damages commercial forests and biological communities; pollution that ruins drinking water also kills terrestrial and aquatic species such as turtles and fish.

National governments can also have a substantial effect on the protection of biological diversity through the control of their borders, ports, and commerce. To protect forests and regulate their use, governments can ban logging, as was done in Thailand following disastrous flooding; they can restrict the export of logs, as was done in Indonesia; and they can penalize timber companies that damage the environment. Certain kinds of environmental destructive mining can be banned. Methods of shipping oil and toxic chemicals can be regulated.

To prevent the exploitation of rare species, governments can restrict the possession of certain species and control all imports and exports of the species through laws and agreements such as the Convention on International Trade in Endangered Species (CITES). For example, the U.S. government restricts trade in endangered tropical parrots through the enforcement of CITES and the Wild Bird Conservation Act. Persons caught violating these laws can be fined or imprisoned. National governments can also regulate the importation of all exotic species into their countries as a way of preventing the accidental or intentional introduction of invasive species.

Finally, national governments can identify endangered species within their borders and take steps to conserve them, such as protecting and acquiring habitat for the species, controlling use of the species, developing research programs, and implementing in situ and ex situ recovery plans (Figure 20.3). In European countries, for example, endangered species conservation is accomplished through domestic enforcement of international agreements such as CITES and the Ramsar Wetlands Convention. International Red Lists of endangered species prepared by the International Union for the Conservation of Nature and national Red Data books also highlight priorities for conservation. In Europe, countries protect species and habitats through directives adopted by the European Union; these directives implement the earlier Bern Convention (Bouchet et al. 1999). Some countries may have additional laws, such as the National Parks and Access to the Countryside Act of 1981 in the United Kingdom, which protects habitat occupied by endangered species.

It is interesting to note that national legal efforts to protect species are subject to cultural factors: Some species with cultural appeal receive extensive protection, while other species equally in danger may not get the protection they need. In the United Kingdom, for example, the beloved and relatively common hedgehog (*Erinaceous europaeus*) and the badger (*Meles meles*) receive far greater protection than many truly rare species of insects (Harrop 1999). Also, dilemmas may arise when con-

Figure 20.3 Whooping cranes are protected by the U. S. Endangered Species Act and are intensively managed. Here captive-born juvenile whooping cranes are taught foraging and flying skills by a crane expert in a whooping crane costume. The birds will eventually join a flock in the wild without ever having seen an "unmasked" human. (Photograph courtesy of the International Crane Foundation.)

servation efforts for one endangered species would be detrimental to a second endangered species living in the same site. For example, one species may require protection from fires to survive, while another species may require frequent fire to maintain their populations.

The U.S. Endangered Species Act

In the United States, the principal conservation law protecting species is the Endangered Species Act (ESA), passed in 1973 and subsequently amended in 1978 and 1982. This legislation has been a model for other countries, though its implementation has often been controversial (Chadwick 1995; Bean 1999; Czech and Krausman 2001). The ESA was created by the U.S. Congress to "provide a means whereby the ecosystems upon which endangered species and threatened species depend may be conserved [and] to provide a program for the conservation of such species." Species are protected under the ESA if they are on the official list of endangered and threatened species. In addition, a recovery plan is generally required for each listed species (Boersma et al. 2001).

As defined by law, "endangered species" are those likely to become extinct as a result of human activities and/or natural causes in all or a major portion of their range; "threatened species" are those likely to become endangered in the near future. The Secretary of the Interior, acting through the U.S. Fish and Wildlife Service (FWS), and the Secretary of Commerce, acting through the National Marine Fisheries Service (NMFS), can add and remove species from the list based on information available to them. Since 1973, more than 1200 U.S. species have been added to the list, in addition to about 550 endangered species from elsewhere in the world that may be imported into the United States.

The ESA requires all U.S. government agencies to consult with the FWS and the NMFS to determine whether their activities will affect listed species, and it prohibits activities that will harm these species and their habitat—a critical feature, since many of the threats to species comes from activities on federal lands, such as logging, cattle grazing, and mining. The ESA also prevents private individuals, businesses, and local governments from harming or "taking" listed species and damaging their habitat and prohibits all trade in listed species (Boersma et al. 2001). These restrictions on private land are important to species recovery because around 10% of endangered species are found exclusively on private land (Stein et al. 2000). By protecting habitats, the ESA in effect uses listed species as indicator species to protect entire biological communities and the thousands of species that they contain.

An analysis of the listing process for the U.S. Endangered Species Act shows a number of revealing trends. The great majority of U.S. species listed under the ESA are plants (712 species) and vertebrates (336 species), despite the fact that most of the world's species are insects and other invertebrates. More than 40% of the 300 mussel species found in the United States are extinct or in danger of extinction, yet only 70 species are listed under the ESA. Clearly, greater efforts must be made to study the lesser known and underappreciated invertebrate groups and extend listing to those endangered species whenever necessary. Another study of species covered by the ESA has shown that on average only about 1000 individuals remain at the time a given animal is listed, while plants have fewer than 120 individuals remaining when they are added to the list (Wilcove et al. 1993). Thirty-nine species were listed when they had 10 or fewer individuals remaining and one freshwater mussel species was listed when it had only a single remaining population that was not reproducing. Species with dramatically reduced populations such as these may encounter genetic and demographic problems that can impede or prevent recovery. For the ESA to be most effective, endangered species must be given protection under the ESA before they decline to the point where recovery becomes virtually impossible. An early listing of a declining species might allow it to recover and thus become a candidate for removal from the list more quickly than if authorities were to wait for its status to worsen before adding it to the list.

Despite some challenges in the two decades since its enactment, the ESA has become an increasingly important conservation tool. It has provided the legal basis for protecting some of the most well-known animal species in the United States, such as the grizzly bear, the bald eagle, the whooping crane, and the gray wolf. Because the law protects the ecosystems in which endangered species live, entire biological communities and thousands of species have been protected at the same time (Carroll et al. 1996).

The ESA has become a source of contention between conservation and some business interests in the United States. The conservation opinion is expressed by Bill Reffalt of the Wilderness Society (in Horton 1992): "The Endangered Species Act is a safety net for species we've put in jeopardy while we get our act together to take care of the planet. Ultimately we've got to convince people that human progress running counter to the existence of species simply is not sustainable." The best long-term success for the legal protection of species is preventing the habitat loss that causes species to be endangered in the first place. This point is emphasized by Randall Snodgrass of the National Audubon Society: "If the Act is truly to prevent further species loss it's got to evolve into a next generation wildlife law instead of [an emergency] law that just recovers species from the brink."

The prevailing business view is that natural resources should be used to provide the greatest benefit to people without worrying about obscure plants and animals. Further, the government should not be telling landowners what they can and cannot do on private property. The protection afforded to species listed under the ESA is so strong that business interests and landowners often lobby strenuously against the listing of species in their area. At the extreme are landowners who destroy endangered species on their property to evade the provisions of the ESA, a practice informally known as "shoot, shovel, and shut up." Such was the fate of half of the only known population of the St. Thomas Island prickly ash, which was deliberately destroyed in 1985 before it was added to the list of protected species (Mann and Plummer 1995a).

The economic implications of protecting listed species can be staggering. These economics have propelled pro-business groups to form, which employ environmentally friendly–sounding rhetoric to argue against the ESA, promoting instead "wise use" of natural resources—in most cases, uses that prioritize human needs for jobs, raw materials, and economic development over the requirements of species or ecosystems. This issue is best illustrated by the 2.8 million ha of old-growth forest in the Pacific Northwest, potentially worth billions of dollars, which have been designated as critical protected habitat for the endangered northern spotted owl. Limitations on logging in this region, strongly advocated by environmental organizations, were fiercely resisted by business and citizen groups in the region, as well as by many politicians. After years of negotiations, logging has finally ceased on most federal land, and restrictions have been placed on logging activities on state and private lands. The federal government lands are providing a core area for biodiversity protection. In addition, the public is recognizing that intact watersheds are needed to provide abundant clean water for residential and business use, to reduce the risk of flooding, and to maintain salmon populations and the valuable commercial and sport fisheries they support.

THE ESA AND RECOVERY   At present almost 250 species are candidates under consideration for listing; while awaiting official decision, some of these species have probably gone extinct. The reluctance of government agencies to put species on the list is caused primarily by the restrictions it places on economic activity, even though economic costs are not supposed to be a factor in listing. Another important obstacle to listing is the difficulty of species recovery—rehabilitating species or reducing the threats to species to the point where they can be removed from listing under the ESA, or "de-listed" (Doremus and Pagel 2001). So far, only 23 of more than 1200 listed U.S. species have been de-listed. The most notable successes include the brown pelican, the American peregrine falcon, and the American alligator (Figure 20.4). In 1994, with great fanfare, the bald eagle was moved from the highly regulated "endangered" category to the less critical "threatened" category because its numbers in the lower 48 states had increased from 400 breeding pairs in the 1960s to the current 5800 pairs. Seven species have been de-listed because they went extinct, and eleven species were de-listed either because new populations were found or because biologists decided that they were not truly distinct species. Overall, approximately one-third of the listed species are still declining in numbers, one-third are stable or increasing and, most surprisingly, one-third are of unknown status (Wilcove et al. 1996).

Figure 20.4 The American alligator is a conservation success story. It is one of the few species in the United States that has been de-listed under the Endangered Species Act, having been judged no longer threatened or in need of strict protection. (Photograph by Brian Parker/ Tom Stack & Associates.)

The difficulty of implementing recovery plans for so many species is often not primarily biological but, rather, political, administrative, and ultimately financial. For example, an endangered river clam species might need to be protected from pollution and the effects of an existing dam. Installing sewage treatment facilities and removing a dam are theoretically straightforward actions, but expensive and difficult to carry out in practice. The U.S. Fish and Wildlife Service annually spends only around $350 million per year on activities related to the ESA; most of these funds are used for land acquisition and legal expenses. One estimate suggests that increasing funding to $650 million per year would be needed to create a truly effective program, one that would implement effective recovery programs for all listed species (Miller et al. 2002). The cost eventually might be higher if the U.S. government grants private landowners financial compensation for ESA-imposed restrictions on the use of their property, an option that is periodically discussed in the U.S. Congress.

While funding for the ESA has been growing steadily over the past 20 years, the number of species protected under the ESA has been growing even faster. As a result, there is less money available per species in need of recovery now than ever before (Figure 20.5). The importance of adequate funding for species recovery is shown by a study demonstrating that species that receive a higher proportion of requested funding for their recovery plans have a higher probability of reaching a stable or improved status than species that receive a lower proportion of funding (Miller et al. 2002). But as the species best suited to current management techniques respond to conservation efforts, the remaining species will represent the most difficult and most expensive cases to deal with (Abbitt and Scott 2001).

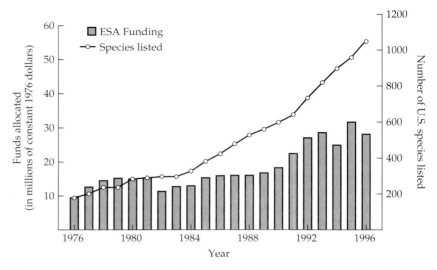

Figure 20.5 The number of species protected by the U.S. Endangered Species Act has been increasing at a faster rate than the funding available to protect these species (expressed in 1976 dollars). As a result, the money available per species is declining. (From Wilcove et al. 1996.)

Even though funding is supposed to be allocated on a priority system according to the degree of threat a species faces, its potential for recovery, and its taxonomic distinctiveness, certain species often receive disproportionately large funding because they are widely recognizable bird and mammal species with strong public support (such as the bald eagle, the American peregrine flacon, the Florida panther, the grey wolf, and the West Indian manatee) or because they are umbrella species whose protection is linked to the protection of economically valuable ecosystems (such as the red-cockaded woodpecker in Southeastern pine forests, the northern spotted owl in old-growth forests of the Pacific Northwest, and the California gnatcatcher in California coastal sagebrush habitat). Other species are substantially underfunded because they are relatively unknown to the public, they have restricted distributions, they are not birds and mammals, and they are from geographical areas with weak or no political representation; examples include the Virgin Islands tree boa, the Red Hills salamander, the Puerto Rican nightjar, and the Florida salt marsh vole (Restani and Marzluff 2002).

CONFLICT AND THE ESA: COMPROMISE SOLUTIONS   An attempt was made to find compromises between the economic interests of the country and conservation priorities during a controversy over whether the protection of the snail darter, a small endangered fish species, should block a major dam project. As a result, the ESA was amended in 1978 to allow a cabinet-level committee, the so-called "God Squad" to exclude certain populations of endangered species from protection.

Despite the God-Squad amendment to the ESA, concerns about the implications of ESA protection have often forced business organizations, conservation groups, and governments to develop compromises that reconcile both conservation and business interests (Hoffman et al. 1997; James 1999). To provide a legal mechanism to achieve this goal, Congress amended the ESA in 1982 to allow the design of Habitat Conservation Plans (HCPs). HCPs are regional plans that allow development in designated areas but also protect remnants of biological communities or ecosystems that contain groups of actual or potentially endangered species (Noss et al. 1997). These plans are drawn up by the concerned parties—developers, conservation groups, and local governments—and given final approval by the U.S. Fish and Wildlife Service. An important feature of these plans is a "no surprises" clause, whereby developers have only limited financial responsibility if the conservation plan does not succeed in protecting the designated endangered species. Also, if any changes to the plan are subsequently needed, the government agrees to pay for them. Over 380 HCPs covering 12 million ha and 200 species have been approved as of 2001. In one case, an innovative program in Riverside County, California, allows developers to build within the historic range of the endangered Stephen's kangaroo rat (*Dipodomys stephensi*) if they contribute to a fund that will be used to buy wildlife sanctuaries. Already, more than $42 million has been used to secure 41,000 ha, with a long-term goal of raising $100 million. In this case and others, the result is a compromise in which developers may proceed after paying additional fees into the fund to support conservation activities. Such plans need to be carefully monitored to determine if they are meeting their stated objectives.

In 1991 the state of California passed the Natural Community Conservation Planning Act, emphasizing habitat conservation and the protection of species on a regional scale in a manner similar to that of HCPs. Natural Community Conservation Planning has been applied to the contentious issue of development in the coastal sage scrub habitat of southern California. This area includes almost 100 rare, sensitive, threatened, or endangered plants and animals, most notably the coastal California gnatcatcher (*Polioptila californica californica*), protected under the U.S. Endangered Species Act, and the coastal cactus wren (*Campylorhynchus brunnecapillus sandiegensis*). As a result of agricultural development and more recent urban development, less than 20% of the original coastal sage scrub habitat still exists, divided into small habitat fragments. The remaining habitat includes some of the country's most valuable land for real-estate development. Without some regional plan, continuing development of the remaining scrub would almost certainly result in the extinction of the endangered coastal California gnatcatcher (Figure 20.6).

(A)

(B)

Figure 20.6   (A) In southern California, a Natural Community Conservation Plan has been established to protect the California gnatcatcher, shown here at a nest with its chicks. (Photograph by Robb Hirsch.) (B) Protecting large blocks of coastal sage scrub community from uncontrolled development and fragmentation is key to the plan. (Photograph by Reed Noss.)

Rather than face the severe restrictions of the ESA, a Natural Community Conservation Plan has been developed for a southern California region that includes 160,000 ha of habitat. Negotiating the plan has proved to be a challenge, since three-fourths of the habitat is privately owned and the planning area includes 50 cities and five counties. The largest public landowner in the area—the U.S. Department of Defense—uses its portion of the land for military exercises. The Natural Community Conservation Plan that has been developed for the area involves surveying and monitoring coastal sage scrub communities—in particular, their endangered bird species—with the goal of protecting permanent reserves in high-quality habitat. Some limited development will continue during this planning process, allowing regions within the plan to lose up to 5% of their lower-quality habitat. This development is being directed away from the areas likely to be designated as permanent reserves.

While habitat conservation plans are not perfect, they are at least attempts to create the next generation of conservation planning: approaches that seek to protect many species, entire ecosystems, or whole communities, and that extend over a wide geographic region that includes many projects, landowners, and jurisdictions. The difficulty with such an approach is that attempting to create a consensus among groups with clearly different goals prevents conservation biologists from pursuing their goals with single-minded intensity. Indeed, in some cases, conservation biologists have been incorporated into ineffective bureaucratic structures without having had a significant impact on protecting endangered species (Brower et al. 2001).

Traditional Societies, Conservation, and Sustainable Use

In this section of the chapter we'll examine the attitudes held by traditional societies toward conservation, discuss how some traditional societies police their own resource use, and review some conservation projects that involve traditional societies. Human activities are not automatically incompatible with biological diversity. There are a number of highly diverse biological communities that exist in places where people have practiced a traditional way of life for many generations, using the resources of their environment in a sustainable manner. Local people practicing a traditional way of life in rural areas, with relatively little outside influence in terms of modern technology, are variously referred to as tribal people, indigenous people, native people, or traditional people (Dasmann 1991).These people regard themselves as the original inhabitants of the region and are often organized at the community or village level. It is necessary to distinguish these established indigenous people from more recent settlers, who may not be as concerned with the health of surrounding biological communities or as knowledgeable about the species present. In many countries, such as India and Mexico, there is a striking correspondence between areas occupied by local people and the areas of high conservation value and intact forest (Toledo 2001). Local people often have established local systems of rights to natural resources, which sometimes are recognized by their governments; potentially they are important partners in conservation efforts. Worldwide, there are approximately 300 million indigenous people living in more than 70 countries, occupying 12–19% of the Earth's land surface (Redford and Mansour 1996). However, indigenous people who practice their traditional culture are on the decline. In most areas of the world, local people are increasingly coming into contact with the modern world, resulting in changing belief systems (particularly among the younger members of society) and greater use of outside manufactured goods. Sometimes this shift can lead to a weakening of ties to the land and conservation ethics.

People have lived as hunters, fishers, farmers, and gatherers in nearly every terrestrial ecosystem of the world for thousands of years. Even remote tropical rain forests that are designated as "wilderness" by governments and conservation groups often have a small, sparse human population. In fact, tropical areas of the world have coexisted with human societies for thousands of years because the Tropics have been free of glaciation and are particularly amenable to human settlement, and until now, in most places humans did not substantially or irreversibly damage the biological diversity of their surroundings. Traditional societies utilizing innovative irrigation methods and a mixture of crops were often able to support relatively high human population densities without destroying the environment or the surrounding biological communities. For example, areas of the Maya lowlands in Mexico, Belize, Guatemala, and Honduras are lightly settled at present, with only about 5 people per km^2; the area is covered by forests and has many unique species and biological communities. However, at the height of Maya civilization, approximately 1200 years ago, the region had densities of up to 500 people per km^2 and the range of species apparently was maintained (Figure 20.7) (Gomez-Pompa and Kaus 1992). The low population densities among traditional societies of many Neotropical rain forest areas today

Figure 20.7 A thousand years ago, Maya farms and cities occupied a wide area of the Central American lowlands, with no apparent loss of species. Today the ruined cities are overgrown by tropical forests. (Photograph by R. Primack.)

are an artifact of the repeated episodes of disease, exploitation, and fighting during the 500 years since the arrival of Europeans. Populations of these traditional people have been reduced to less than 10% of their levels prior to contact with Europeans.

Rather than being a threat to the "pristine" environment in which they live, traditional peoples have been an integral part of these environments for thousands of years. The present mixture and relative densities of plants and animals in many biological communities may reflect the historic activities—such as fishing, selective hunting of game animals, and planting of useful plant species—of people in the area. In tropical forests, the commonly practiced agricultural system, known variously as swidden agriculture, shifting cultivation, or slash-and-burn agriculture, also affects forest structure and species composition by creating a mosaic of forest patches of different ages. In this system, the trees in an area are cut down, the fallen plant material is burned, and crops are planted in the nutrient-rich ash. After one or several harvests, the nutrients are washed out of the soil by the rain; the farmer then abandons the field and cuts down a new patch of forest for planting. This system works well and does not degrade the environment as long as human population density is low and there is abundant forest land.

As populations of local people increase and as they join the modern economy, their impact on biodiversity will similarly increase. The necessity to reconcile the needs of local people and conservation is illustrated by the example of the endangered red panda (*Ailurus fulgens*) in Langtang National Park, Nepal (see Figure 12.1). Villagers live inside the park boundary and keep herds of livestock, including yak (a type of Asian ox) and cows. Most of the areas where red pandas live are grazed by livestock. Villagers are now increasing their herds to supply milk to the towns and the tourist industry (Figure 20.8). While people, livestock, and pandas currently coexist in the park, the increasing grazing pressure will eventually overtake the remaining habitat and eliminate red pandas from the area unless a compromise is found.

Conservation Ethics

The conservation ethics of traditional societies have been viewed in a variety of perspectives by Western civilization. At one extreme, local people are viewed as destroyers of biological diversity who cut down forests and overharvest game. This destruction is accelerated when these people acquire guns, chainsaws, and outboard motors. At the other extreme, traditional peoples are viewed as "noble savages" living in harmony with nature and minimally disturbing the natural environment. An emerging middle view is that traditional societies are highly varied, and there is no one simple description of their relationship to their environment that fits all groups (Redford and Sanderson 2000). In addition to the variation among traditional societies, these societies also vary from within; they are changing rapidly as they encounter outside

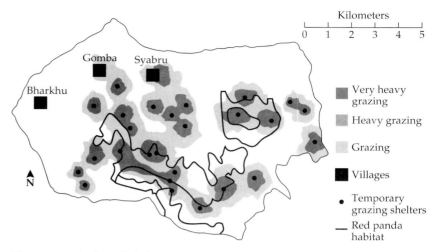

Figure 20.8 Red panda habitat in Langtang National Park, Nepal, overlaps areas grazed by cattle and frequented by herders and their dogs. A compromise needs to be developed so that people and wildlife can coexist, otherwise human needs will drive the red panda to extinction. (After Fox et al. 1996.)

influences, and there are often sharp differences between older and younger generations.

Many traditional societies do have strong conservation ethics. These ethics are subtler and less clearly stated than Western conservation beliefs, but they tend to affect people's actions in their day-to-day lives, perhaps more than Western beliefs (Posey 1992; Western 1997; Berkes et al. 2000; Folke and Colding 2001). In such societies, people use their traditional ecological knowledge to create management practices that are linked to belief systems and enforced by village consent and the authority of leaders. These practices might include restricting certain locations from harvesting or restricting the ages, size, and sex of animals harvested, and restricting harvesting seasons and methods of farming. One well-documented example of such a conservation perspective is that of the Tukano Indians of northwest Brazil (Chernela 1987), who live on a diet of root crops and river fish (Figure 20.9). They have strong religious and cultural prohibitions against cutting the forest along the Upper Río Negro, which they recognize as important to the maintenance of fish populations. The Tukano believe that these forests belong to the fish and cannot be cut by people. They have also designated extensive refuges for fish and permit fishing along less than 40% of the river margin. Anthropologist Janet M. Chernela observes, "As fishermen dependent upon river systems, the Tukano are aware of the relationship between their environment and the life cycles of the fish, particularly the role played by the adjacent forest in providing nutrient sources that maintain vital fisheries."

Figure 20.9 River fish are the main source of protein for the Tukano people of the Amazon basin, who have a strong conservation ethic grounded in their cultural and religious beliefs. They do not cut the forest along the riverbanks because they believe that this forest belongs to the fish. (Photograph by Paul Patmore.)

In addition to coexisting with their environments without destroying them, local people can also manage the environment to maintain biological diversity, as shown by the traditional agroecosystems and forests of the Huastec Indians of northeastern Mexico (Alcorn 1984). In addition to their permanent agricultural fields and swidden agriculture, the Huastec maintain managed forests known as *te'lom,* on slopes, along watercourses, and in other areas that are either fragile or unsuitable for intensive agriculture (Figure 20.10). These forests contain more than 300 species of plants from which the people obtain food, wood, and other products. Species composition in the forest is altered in favor of useful species by planting and periodic selective weeding. Forest resources provide Huastec families with the means to survive the failure of their cultivated crops should they encounter a season of bad weather or an insect outbreak. Comparable examples of intensively managed village forests exist in traditional societies throughout the world (Oldfield and Alcorn 1991; Stone and D'Andrea 2002).

Local people who support conservation are often inspired to take the lead in protecting biological diversity. For instance, the destruction of communally owned forests by government-sanctioned logging operations has been a frequent target of protests by traditional people through-

Figure 20.10 A Huastec Indian woman at a *te'lom,* an indigenous managed forest in northeastern Mexico. Here she collects sapote fruit (*Manilkara achras*) and cuttings of a frangipani tree (*Plumeria rubra*) for planting. (From Alcorn 1984; photograph by Janis Alcorn.)

out the world. In India, followers of the Chipko movement hug trees to prevent logging (Gadgil and Guha 1992). In Borneo, the Penans, a small tribe of hunter-gatherers, have attracted worldwide attention by blockading logging roads that enter their traditional forests. In Thailand, Buddhist priests are working with villagers to protect communal forests and sacred groves from commercial logging operations (Figure 20.11). As stated by a Tambon leader in Thailand,

> This is our community forest that was just put inside the new national park. No one consulted us. We protected this forest before the roads were put in. We set up a roadblock on the new road to stop the illegal logging. We caught the district police chief and arrested him for logging. We warned him not to come again. (Alcorn 1991)

Empowering such local people and helping them to obtain **legal title**— right to ownership of the land that is recognized by the government— to their traditionally owned lands is often an important component of efforts to establish locally managed protected areas in developing countries.

Figure 20.11 Buddhist priests in Thailand offer prayers and blessings to protect communal forests and sacred groves from commercial logging operations. (Photograph by Project for Ecological Recovery, Bangkok.)

Conservation Efforts That Involve Traditional Societies

In the developing world and even in many developed countries such as Australia and Canada, it is often not possible to create a rigid separation between lands used by local people to obtain natural resources and those designated by governments as protected areas. Local people often live in and/or traditionally use the resources found in protected areas. Also, considerable biological diversity often occurs on traditionally managed land owned by local people. For example, indigenous communities own 97% of the land in Papua New Guinea, and Ameridian reserves in the Amazon basin occupy over 100 million ha of incredibly diverse habitats. The Inuit people (formerly known as the Eskimos) govern one-fifth of Canada. In Australia, tribal people control 90 million ha, including many of the most important areas for conservation. The challenge, then, is to develop strategies for incorporating these local people in conservation programs and policy development. Such new approaches have been developed in an effort to avoid **ecocolonialism,** the common practice by some governments and conservation organizations of disregarding the traditional rights and practices of local people in order to establish new conservation areas, so called because of its similarity to the historical abuses of native rights by colonial powers of past eras (Cox and Elmqvist 1993, 1997).

There are many examples of reserves in which people are allowed to enter protected areas periodically to obtain natural products or are compensated for preserving and managing biological diversity. In Biosphere Reserves, an international land-use designation, local people are allowed to use resources from designated buffer zones. For instance, in Chitwan National Park in Nepal, local people are allowed to collect canes and thatch in buffer zones (see Figure 17.6). In addition, large game animals are periodically harvested for meat in many African game reserves. Agreements have been negotiated between local people and governments allowing cattle to graze inside certain African parks in exchange for agreement from the local people not to harm wild animals outside the parks.

Through such compromises, the economic needs of local people are included in conservation management plans, to the benefit of both the people and the reserves. Such compromises, known as **Integrated Conservation–Development Projects** (**ICDPs**), are now regarded as worthy of serious consideration, though in practice they are often problematic to implement, as described later in the chapter (Alpert 1995; Primack et al. 1998; Redford and Sanderson 2000; Salafsky et al. 2001a). There are many possible strategies for combining the protection of biological diversity, the customs of traditional societies, the genetic variation of traditional crops, and economic development that could be classified as ICDPs (Caldecott 1996; Maser 1997). A large number of such programs have been initiated over the last decade, which have provided opportunities for evaluation and improvement (Salafsky and Margoluis 1999). A critical component of these projects must be the ongoing monitoring of biological, social, and economic factors to determine how effective they are in meeting their goals. Involving local people in these monitoring efforts may be an important source of information and will also help to indicate how the people themselves perceive the benefits and problems of the project. Following are some examples of the types of ICDPs currently in practice:

BIOSPHERE RESERVES   UNESCO's Man and the Biosphere Program (MAB), described in Chapter 17, includes among its goals the maintenance of "samples of varied and harmonious landscapes resulting from long-established land use patterns" (Batisse 1997). This program is an extremely successful example of an ICDP; there are 368 Biosphere Reserves in 87 countries, covering over 260 million ha (Figure 20.12). The MAB Program recognizes the role of people in shaping the natural landscape, as well as the need to find ways in which people can sustainably use natural resources without degrading the environment. The research framework, applied in its worldwide network of designated Biosphere Reserves, integrates natural science and social science research. It in-

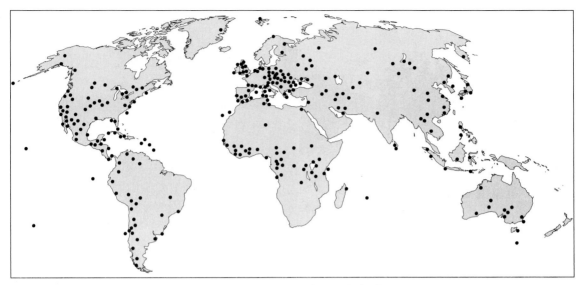

Figure 20.12 Locations of recognized Biosphere Reserves (dots). A lack of reserves is apparent in biologically important regions such as New Guinea, the Indian subcontinent, South Africa, and Amazonia. (Data from UNESCO 1996.)

cludes investigations of how biological communities respond to different human activities, how humans respond to changes in their natural environment, and how degraded ecosystems can be restored to their former condition. A desirable feature of Biosphere Reserves is a system of zonation in which there are varying levels of use, from complete protection to areas where farming and logging are permitted.

One instructive example of a Biosphere Reserve is the Kuna Yala Indigenous Reserve on the northeast coast of Panama. In this protected area comprising 60,000 ha of tropical forest and coral islands, 50,000 Kuna people in 60 villages practice traditional medicine, agriculture, and forestry, with documentation and research undertaken by scientists from outside institutions (Figure 20.13). The Kuna carefully regulate the levels of scientific research in the reserve, insist on local training and local guides to accompany the visiting scientists, and require the payment of research fees and the presentation of reports before scientists leave the area. The boundaries of the reserve are recognized by the Panamanian government. The Kuna even control the type and rate of economic development in the reserve and have their own paid, outside advisors. The level of empowerment of the Kuna is unusual, and it illustrates the potential for traditional people to take control of their destiny, their way of life, and their environment. However, it is not clear how long the Kuna will retain their high level of control over the re-

Figure 20.13 Kuna park guards patrolling the boundary of the Kuna Yala Indigenous Reserve, a Biosphere Reserve. (Photograph courtesy of Mac Chapin.)

serve. A change appears to be occurring in the Kuna: Traditional conservation beliefs are eroding in the face of outside influences, and younger Kuna are beginning to question the need to rigidly protect the reserve (Redford and Mansour 1996). Also, the Kuna people have had difficulties establishing a stable organization that can administer the program and work with external conservation and donor groups. Unfortunately, empowering traditional people is no guarantee that biodiversity will be preserved. This is particularly true when traditions change or disappear, economic pressures for exploitation increase, and programs are mismanaged (Oates 1999).

IN SITU AGRICULTURAL CONSERVATION   The long-term health of modern agriculture depends on the preservation of the genetic variability maintained in local varieties of crops maintained by traditional farmers (see Chapter 14). One innovative suggestion has been for an international agricultural body, such as the Consultative Group on International Agricultural Research, to subsidize villages as in situ (in place) landrace custodians (Nabhan 1985; Altieri and Anderson 1992). The cost of subsidizing villages to maintain the genetic variation of major crops such as wheat, maize, and potatoes would be a relatively modest investment in the long-term health of world agriculture.

Programs incorporating in situ practices have already been initiated in some places (Figure 20.14). In Mexico, a number of development programs are attempting to integrate traditional agriculture, conservation, and research (Benz et al. 1990; Toledo 1991). One example is the 140,000-ha Sierra de Manantlán Biosphere Reserve in western Mexico, which was established to preserve the only known populations of *Zea diploperennis*, a perennial relative of maize (corn) with resistance to many pests of cultivated maize (Figure 20.15). This perennial, occurring only in abandoned *milpas* (fields planted using traditional shifting agricultural methods), is of great potential value in efforts to introduce new genetic variation into the annual domesticated corn crop, which is valued at $55 billion per year. Imagine a disease-resistant perennial corn crop that did not have to be replanted each year, which would cut down on

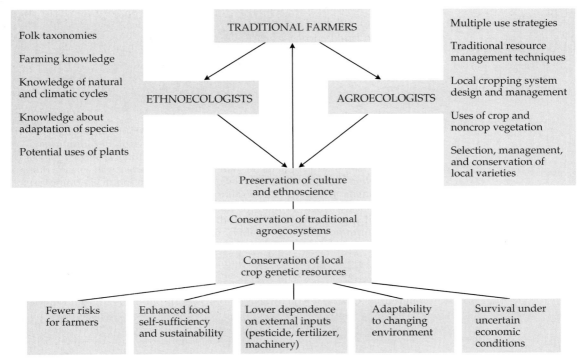

Figure 20.14 It is useful to view traditional agricultural practices both from a human cultural and an agricultural perspective. A synthesis of these viewpoints can lead to theoretical and methodological approaches that seek to conserve the environment, the culture, and the genetic variation found in these traditional agroecosystems. (After Altieri and Anderson 1992.)

Figure 20.15 *Zea diploperennis* is a perennial relative of maize, shown here growing on the edge of a traditional maize field in the Sierra de Manantlán Biosphere Reserve in Mexico. American scientist Mike Nee holds a bundle of harvested *Zea diploperennis*. (Photograph by Hugh Iltis.)

the costs of plowing and herbicide use and reduce soil erosion. In this instance, the long-term protection of *Z. diploperennis* depends on encouraging local farmers to remain on the land and continue their traditional cultivation practices.

A different approach used in arid regions of the American Southwest involves linking traditional agriculture and genetic conservation, with a focus on dryland crops with drought tolerance (Nabhan 1989). A private organization, Native Seeds/SEARCH, collects the seeds of traditional crop cultivars for long-term preservation. The organization also encourages a network of 4600 farmers and other members to grow traditional crops, provides them with the seeds of traditional cultivars, and buys their unsold production.

Countries have also established special reserves to conserve areas containing wild relatives and ancient landraces of commercial crops. Species reserves protect the wild relatives of wheat, oats, and barley in Israel and citrus in India, and 127 such reserves have been created in the former Soviet Union to protect cold-adapted landraces.

EXTRACTIVE RESERVES   In many areas of the world, indigenous people have extracted products from natural communities for decades and even centuries. The sale and barter of these natural products are a major part of people's livelihoods. Understandably, local people are very concerned about retaining their rights to continue collecting natural products from the surrounding countryside (Box 28) (Western et al. 1994). In areas where such collection represents an integral part of indigenous society, the establishment of a national park that excludes the traditional collection of products will meet with as much resistance from the local community as will a land-grab that involves exploitation of the natural resources and their conversion to other uses. A type of protected area known as an **extractive reserve** may present a sustainable solution to this problem. However, these programs need to be evaluated to determine if they are able to maintain a sustainable level of harvesting and not damage the underlying resource base.

The Brazilian government is trying to address the legitimate demands of local citizens through extractive reserves, from which settled people collect natural materials such as wood products, edible seeds, rubber, resins, and Brazil nuts in ways that minimize damage to the forest ecosystem (Wunder 1999). Such extractive areas in Brazil, which comprise about 3 million ha, guarantee the ability of local people to continue their way of life and guard against the possible conversion of the land to cattle ranching and farming. At the same time, the government protection afforded to the local population also serves to protect the biological diversity of the area because the ecosystem remains basically intact (Nepstad and Schwartzman 1992).

Extractive reserves appear to be appropriate to the Amazon rain forests, where about 68,000 rubber tapper families live. The rubber tappers live at a density of only about one family per 300–500 ha, of which they clear only a few hectares for growing food. Commercial rubber tapping has been going on in the Amazon for over 100 years, and rubber-tapping areas presently occupy 4–7% of the Amazon area. The efforts of Chico Mendes and his subsequent assassination in 1988 drew worldwide attention to the plight of the rubber tappers (see Box 31 in Chapter 22). In response to both local and international concern, the Brazilian government established extractive reserves in rubber-tapping areas. To many people, establishing the reserves made sense because the rubber collection system was already in place. The hope was that the rubber tappers themselves would have a strong vested interest against habitat destruction because it also would destroy their livelihood.

The Brazilian experiment has indicated that extractive reserves are a possible mechanism to preserve biological diversity, but it has also illustrated a number of major limitations (Wunder 1999). First, these reserves occupy only a small percentage of the Amazon; conservation efforts aimed at protecting the Amazon really need to concentrate on

BOX 28 *People-Friendly Conservation in the Hills of Southwest India*

There is no question that human activities play an overwhelming role in the decline of many species and habitats. All too often, however, conservation activists forget that human beings are among the potential victims of the worldwide biological diversity crisis. Some rural societies have already been affected by the decline of leaves, fruits, roots, and other nontimber forest products (NTFPs) traditionally harvested for household use and for sale in local markets. For some of these people, natural products represent a crucial subset of their income, and some may be essential for food preparation, medicines, or rituals. In many cases, external political or economic pressures have damaged or destroyed the social mechanisms that traditionally prevented overuse of a particular resource so that many NTFPs that were once harvested in a sustainable manner are now becoming depleted. As forests shrink in size and become degraded through increased pressure on both timber and nontimber resources, it is uncertain whether NTFP collection is sustainable in particular areas—if not, alternative sources of income and supplies must be found to support rural families. Although it is a vital first step in determining sustainable harvesting levels, few efforts have been made to document and mon-

itor the methods and amounts of different NTFPs taken (Peters 1994). An important case study is underway in the Biligiri Rangaswamy Temple (BRT) Sanctuary in southwestern India. This study began by determining the amount of NTFPs taken from the BRT, but then took a huge step beyond by training the local people to monitor the health of the forest and to process and sell the forest products themselves.

This hilly, forested area contains species from both the Western and Eastern Ghats mountain chains and is known for the density and diversity of its wildlife (Bawa et al. 1998). The inhabitants of the BRT forests, the Soliga people, are the remaining members of a tribe that has survived in this remote area since ancient times. The Soligas lived in the region for centuries as shifting cultivators but became sedentary agriculturists during the past century, a result of efforts by first the British colonial government and later the Indian government to curtail shifting cultivation and preserve the forest. Since the 540-km^2 BRT Sanctuary was established in 1974, shifting cultivation has been completely banned. Instead, many of the Soligas farm small pieces of land (1–2 ha) and collect NTFPs for their own use and for sale through government-

Soliga villagers collect nontimber forest products from the nature sanctuary. (Photograph courtesy of Kamal Bawa.)

BOX 28 *(continued)*

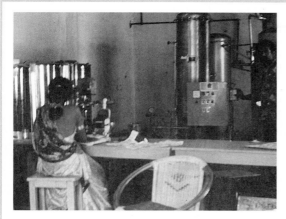

A local worker processes honey in a factory established in the village. (Photograph courtesy of Kamal Bawa.)

sponsored cooperatives. At present, some 4500 Soligas occupy 25 settlements within and around the sanctuary.

A study of NTFP harvesting by the Soligas has been underway since 1993, involving researchers from both India and the United States. The format and goals of this study are a significant departure from the commonplace conservation methodology, which tends to focus first upon a species, habitat, or ecosystem. Although the primary goal of the study is the conservation of biological resources in the BRT forest, the study is uncommon in that it approaches the problem from a sociological and economic perspective rather than a strictly biological perspective. Most conservationists would agree that conservation efforts cannot succeed if they do not make some provision for the people who depend on a threatened resource, but it is unusual for the people to be the principal focus of a biological conservation project.

The project began by using extensive surveys to determine whether NTFPs truly play a vital role in the Soliga household economy (Hegde et al. 1996). Nontimber forest products constitute as much as 50% of an average Soliga household's annual income, but the study found that commonplace NTFP extraction practices are neither sustainable nor efficient, nor do they produce maximum benefits for the Soligas, even though many local products have great potential market value. The BRT forests contain a number of edible and medicinal plant species, many of which the Soligas regularly collect for home use and for sale. Other natural products such as honey provide supplemental income, although they can be difficult to collect—honey collectors in particular risk not only bee stings but also more serious injuries related to falls from the large trees where the bees nest.

Moreover, because there is open access to these unregulated resources, collection of NTFPs often occurs at the wrong time of year to promote regeneration, or is done using methods that damage the resource. In the case of honey collection, for instance, collection from a nest ideally should take place after bee larvae have matured to the point when they will not suffer from the loss of the honey. If the honey is collected too soon in the bees' growth

A display of Soliga products in a village store. (Photograph courtesy of Kamal Bawa.)

BOX 28   *(continued)*

cycle, the larvae may die, and fewer bees in the hive mean that less honey is produced—and the resource begins a slow downward spiral of depletion. Such problems have also been seen in certain plant resources. Medicinal plants have been overharvested near the villages so that people must go ever farther to find plants to collect. Tree species with edible or medicinal fruits have few saplings or young trees to constitute the next generation when the older trees die. Inadequate regeneration is not entirely due to overharvesting; fire, invasive species, and other disturbances also play an important role.

Another problem is that local people sell raw materials through the government-controlled cooperatives, although the greatest amount of profit comes only after the product is processed and marketed. Thus, the Soligas do not receive the greatest possible return from the forest products they harvest and can only increase their income by collecting greater amounts of raw materials.

In response to these concerns, researchers have begun to create enterprises that improve the Soligas' ability to make a living from forest products without overharvesting them. The idea behind this project is simple: If the Soligas process the raw materials themselves, they can eliminate the middlemen between them and the consumers. The Soligas can increase their income by marketing and selling the products directly in nearby towns and cities. By doing this, they can earn a much higher rate per unit of raw materials they harvest and therefore will need to harvest less to make ends meet.

Several enterprises are already underway. The first involves collecting and processing honey from both wild and domestic apiaries. This honey is sold directly to consumers using the Soligas' own brand name (*Prakruti,* which means "nature"). The second project produces jams and pickles for sale, using the fruits of forest species. A third produces and markets herbal medicines using both wild herbs collected from the forest and herbs cultivated in gardens. The researchers and the Soligas have also started to restore some degraded lands in the sanctuary with native species, primarily those that produce commercial products other than timber.

Finally, the Soligas and the researchers have joined forces to develop a management team that monitors the forests and the financial well-being of the enterprises. In other words, the Soligas are assuming responsibility for the long-term maintenance of the resource base as well as the functioning of the factories. When monitoring reveals that a particular NTFP is being depleted, harvesting levels can be reduced until the resource base recovers. As the economic ventures started by this program gain momentum, hopefully more and more of the local residents will find that conserving forest resources is in their best interest. Those concerned with the conservation of species and habitat could ask for nothing more.

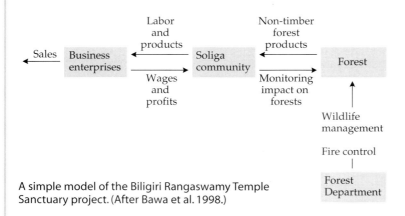

A simple model of the Biligiri Rangaswamy Temple Sanctuary project. (After Bawa et al. 1998.)

reducing the rates of deforestation caused by ranching and farming activities, which already occupy more than one-quarter of the northern Amazon region. Second, extractive reserves provide occupations for only a tiny percentage of the millions of Brazilians who need a livelihood. Third, populations of large animals in extractive reserves are often substantially reduced due to subsistence hunting. The real challenge for rubber tappers and their Brazilian and international allies is to develop products that can be collected and sold at a good market price, perhaps even at a premium as "rain forest products." If the local people cannot survive by collecting and selling natural products, they might be forced, out of economic desperation, to cut down their forests for timber and use the land for agriculture. Because many extractive reserves are only able to operate with the support of outside subsidies, the economic viability of these reserves is still unknown. However, the decade-long decline in prices paid for wild-collected rubber and Brazil nuts suggest that these reserves may not be economically viable.

These sorts of efforts are not limited to Latin America. Many countries in east and southern Africa are aggressively applying community development and sustainable harvesting strategies in their efforts to preserve wildlife populations. The government of Zimbabwe in particular has developed a series of innovative programs for generating income from wildlife that is used to run wildlife programs and provide clear benefits to local people (Taylor and Dunstone 1996; Getz et al. 1999). Much of the funding to support, develop, and administer these programs comes from foreign government agencies, such as the U.S. Agency for International Development. One of the most prominent programs is CAMPFIRE (Communal Area Management Programme for Indigenous Resources), in which local communities working with the government sell sport-hunting rights to safari companies. Revenue is also generated through the sale of live animals and ecotourism.

In this program, uncontrolled subsistence harvesting and poaching have declined as people realized the benefits of joining the program. The result is far greater densities of animals, including elephants, crocodiles, ostriches, and buffaloes, and greater benefits to local people. Approximately 82,000 households with 600,000 people participate in CAMPFIRE to manage 1 million ha. The program generates Z$10 million per year in revenue, more than 50% of which is returned to the people for both personal income and to build needed community infrastructure such as school rooms and grinding mills. Within villages, people are involved in protecting the wildlife and the habitat it occupies because they know it is the key to maintaining the long-term income of the village. At a village meeting, during which wildlife revenues were being distributed, one leader stated, "This money comes to you from your wildlife. It is your money. The decision is yours. You cannot wait for the government. You can develop your community according to how you decide." Despite the apparent success of this program, questions have been raised by animal rights organizations as to why foreign governments are subsidizing a program that depends on the desire of wealthy safari hunters to kill animals. They wonder if such a program is really a good example of conservation. Also, it is unknown how long the program would persist if the substantial subsidies provided by foreign governments were reduced or withdrawn. And finally, it is unclear if wildlife populations could be maintained in the face of constant levels of harvesting. Future generations of conservation biologists will need to evaluate these programs to determine if they are meeting their stated short- and long-term goals.

COMMUNITY-BASED INITIATIVES   In many cases, local people already protect biological communities such as forests, wildlife, rivers, and coastal waters in the vicinity of their homes. Such protection is often enforced by village elders on the basis of religious and traditional beliefs. Governments and conservation organizations can assist local conservation initiatives by providing legal title to traditional lands, access to scientific expertise, and financial assistance to develop needed infrastructure. One example is the Baboon Sanctuary in eastern Belize, created by a collective agreement among a group of villages to maintain the forest habitat required by the local population of black howler monkeys (see Figure 16.9) (Horwich and Lyon 1998). Ecotourists visiting the sanctuary pay a fee to the village organization and additional payments are made if they stay overnight and eat meals with a local family. Conservation biologists working at the site have provided training for local nature guides, a body of scientific information on the local wildlife, funds for a local natural history museum, and business training for the village leaders.

In the Pacific islands of Samoa, much of the rain forest land is under "customary ownership"—it is owned by communities of indigenous people (Cox 1997). Villagers are under increasing pressure to sell logs from their forests to pay for schools and other necessities. Despite this situation, the local people have a strong desire to preserve the land because of the forest's religious and cultural significance, as well as its value for medicinal plants and other products. A variety of solutions are being developed to meet these conflicting needs: In American, or Eastern, Samoa, the U.S. government in 1988 leased forest and coastal land from the villages to establish a new national park. In this case, the villages retained ownership of the land and traditional hunting and collecting rights (Figure 20.16). Village elders were also assigned places on the park advisory board so they would have a voice in issues of governance and management. In Western Samoa, international conservation organizations and various donors agreed to build schools, medical clinics, and other public works projects that the villages needed in exchange for stopping all commercial logging. Thus, each dollar donated did double service, both protecting the forest and providing humanitarian aid to the villages.

Figure 20.16 In Samoa, the U.S. Park Service leases communally owned land and marine habitat for a national park, while local families maintain their rights to collect traditional products. (Photograph © Kip F. Evans.)

Evaluating Conservation Initiatives That Involve Traditional Societies

A key element in the success of many of the projects discussed in the preceding section is the opportunity for conservation biologists to build on and work with stable, flexible, local communities with effective leaders and competent government agencies (Barrett et al. 2001; Salafsky et al. 2001b). However, in many cases a local community may have internal conflicts and poor leadership, making it incapable of administering a successful conservation program. Also, many government agencies are ineffective or even corrupt. These factors will tend to prevent conservation programs from succeeding. An additional negative factor is the increasing population pressure that is generated not only by high birth rates but by the tendency of successful programs to attract immigrants to the area. This increasing population leads to further environmental degradation and a breakdown of social structures (Attwell and Cotterill 2000; Homer-Dixon 2001). Conservation initiatives involving recent immigrants or impoverished, disorganized local people are generally even more difficult. Consequently, while working with local people may be a desirable goal, in some cases this simply is not possible. Sometimes the only way to preserve biological diversity is to exclude people from protected areas and rigorously patrol their boundaries (Terborgh 2000).

In many cases, projects that have initially appeared very promising were terminated when external funding and management ended. Even for projects that appear successful, there is often no monitoring of ecological and social parameters to determine if project goals are being achieved (Newmark and Hough 2000). It is essential for any conservation program design to include mechanisms for evaluating the progress and success of measures taken. Projects can also be undermined by external forces, such as political instability and economic downturns. A creative strategy being developed involves direct payments to individual landowners and local communities that protect critical ecosystems, in effect paying the community to be good land stewards (Ferraro 2001). Such an approach has the advantage of greater simplicity than programs that attempt to link conservation with economic development.

The catchphrase "think globally, act locally," is a true measure of how conservation must work. In the preceding examples, one factor is consistently true: Whether they are supporting conservation activities or opposing them, ordinary people with no strong feelings about conservation are more likely to respond to issues that affect their day-to-day lives. If people learn that a species or habitat to which they are accustomed to having access might be taken away from them because of pressures to develop the land (or to conserve a species), they may feel compelled to take direct action. This reaction can be a double-edged sword; when harm to the environment is viewed by local inhabitants as a threat to their well-being, it can be used to the advantage of conservation, but it is often the case that conservation activities are initially perceived as threatening the local way of life or obstructing the community from beneficial economic development. The challenge for conservation biologists is to energize local people in support of conservation while recognizing and addressing the objections of those who oppose it. In many cases, improving the economic conditions of people's lives and helping them obtain secure rights to their land is essential to preserving biological diversity in developing countries.

Summary

1. Legal efforts to protect biodiversity occur at local, regional, and national levels, and regulate activities affecting both privately and publicly owned lands. Governments and private land trusts may buy land for conservation purposes or acquire conservation easements and development rights for future protection. Associated laws limit pollution, curtail or ban certain types of development, and set rules for hunting and other recreational activities—all with the aim of preserving biodiversity and protecting human health.

2. National governments protect biodiversity by establishing national parks, controlling imports and exports at their borders, and creating regulations for air and water pollution. The most effective law in the United States for protecting species is the Endangered Species Act. The protection afforded under the Act is so strong that pro-business and development groups are often forced to work with biologists to develop compromises that protect species and allow some development.

3. Conservation biologists are collaborating with local people to achieve the combined objectives of protecting biological diversity, preserving cultural diversity, and providing new economic opportunities. Initiatives that allow people to use park resources in a sustainable manner without harming biological diversity are sometimes called Integrated Conservation–Development Projects.

For Discussion

1. Apply the concepts of development and growth to aspects of the economy that you know about. Are there industries practicing or at least approaching sustainable development? Are there industries or aspects of the economy that are clearly not sustainable? Are development and growth always linked, or can there be growth without development, or development without growth? Consider industries such as logging, mining, education, road construction, home construction, and nature tourism.

2. What are the roles of government agencies, private conservation organizations, businesses, community groups, and individuals in the conservation of biological diversity? Can they work together, or are their interests necessarily opposed to each other?

3. Imagine that a new tribe of hunting-and-gathering people is discovered in a remote area of the Amazon that has previously been designated for logging and mining. The area is also found to contain numerous species new to science. Should the project go forward as planned and the people be given whatever employment they are suited for? Should the area be closed to all outsiders and the people and new species allowed to live undisturbed? Should the tribe be contacted by social workers, educated in special schools, and eventually incorporated into modern society? Can you think of a possible compromise that would integrate conservation and development? In such a case, who should decide what actions should be taken?

4. CAMPFIRE involves a rural area in Africa generating income through safari hunting, nature photography, and wildlife viewing. Elephants are hunted in this program despite the fact that they are a protected species under the Convention on International Trade in Endangered Species. What ethical, economic, political, ecological, and social issues are raised by this high-profile program?

Suggested Readings

Berkes, F., J. Colding, and C. Folke. 2000. Rediscovery of traditional ecological knowledge as adaptive management. *Ecological Applications* 10 (5): 1251–1262. An article from a symposium on traditional ecological knowledge; describes how local people use their own observations to manage wildlife and other natural resources.

Caldecott, J. 1996. *Designing Conservation Projects*. Cambridge University Press, Cambridge. Practical advice on setting up conservation projects, from initial concept to implementation. Includes development options and case studies.

Cox, P. A. 1997. *Nafanua: Saving the Samoan Rain Forest*. W. H. Freeman and Company, New York. Exciting and beautiful account of a scientist's efforts to save a forest and help a village.

Czech, B. and P. R. Krausman. 2001. *Endangered Species Act: History, Conservation Biology, and Public Policy*. Johns Hopkins University Press, Baltimore, MD. An analysis of the ESA, combining policy, law, and ecology.

Doremus, H. and J. E. Pagel. 2001. Why listing may be forever: Perspectives on delisting under the U.S. Endangered Species Act. *Conservation Biology* 15: 1258–1268. In a special symposium issue on the Endangered Species Act, this article argues that species require continued protection because the original threats often remain.

Dwyer, J. C. and I. D. Hodge. 1996. *Countryside in Trust: Land Management by Conservation, Recreation and Amenity Organisations.* John Wiley and Sons, Chichester. Description of the enormous growth of land trusts in Britain.

Ferraro, P. J. 2001. Global habitat protection: Limitations of development interventions and a role for conservation performance payments. *Conservation Biology* 15(4): 990–1000. Rather than linking conservation and economic development, perhaps payments should be made directly to the local people for good conservation practices.

Hoffman, A. J., M. H. Bazerman, and S. L. Yaffee. 1997. Balancing business interests and endangered species protection. *Sloan Management Review* 39 (1): 59–73. Business and conservation groups can sometimes work together for mutual benefit.

Homer-Dixon, T. F. 2001. *Environment, Scarcity, and Violence.* Princeton University Press, Princeton, New Jersey. In many countries of the developing world, environmental degradation and habitat loss are linked to poverty and violence.

McNeely, J. A. and W. S. Keeton. 1995. The interaction between biological and cultural diversity. In *Cultural Landscapes of Universal Value*, B. von Droste, H. Plachter, G. Fisher, and M. Rossler (eds.). Gustav Fischer Verlag, New York, pp. 25–37. Excellent essay with many examples.

Miller, J. K., J. M. Scott, C. R. Miller, and L. P Waits. 2002. The endangered species act: Dollars and sense? *BioScience* 52: 163–168. Species are allocated funds based on surprising criteria.

Oates, J. F. 1999. *Myth and Reality in the Rainforest: How Conservation Strategies Are Failing in West Africa.* University of California Press, Berkeley. A skeptic argues that many sustainable development projects do not live up to expectations.

Press, D., D. F. Doak, and P. Steinberg. 1996. The role of local government in the conservation of rare species. *Conservation Biology* 10: 1538–1548. Action at the local level is often the appropriate scale for protecting small populations of rare species and particular sites of special interest.

Primack, R., D. Bray, H. Galletti, and I. Ponciano (eds.). 1998. *Timber, Tourists and Temples: Conservation and Development in the Maya Forest of Belize, Guatemala, and Mexico.* Island Press, Washington, D.C. Intricate social, political, and economic factors affect conservation issues in this important region.

Redford, K. H. and S. E. Sanderson. 2000. Extracting humans from nature. *Conservation Biology* 14: 1362–1364. An article in a special issue debating the role of indigenous people in protected areas.

Stone, R. D. and C. D'Andrea. 2002. *Tropical Forests and the Human Spirit.* University of California Press, Berkeley, CA. Strongly argues for the role of empowering local people to protect tropical forests.

Western, D. 1997. *In the Dust of Kilimanjaro.* Island Press, Washington, D.C. The former Director of the Kenya Wildlife Service provides a personal view of the need for integration of people and wildlife on the African landscape.

Chapter

21

An International Approach to Conservation and Sustainable Development

Much biological diversity is concentrated in the countries of the developing world, many of which are relatively poor, suffering from political instability, and experiencing rapid rates of population growth, development, and habitat destruction. Despite these problems, developing countries are not averse to preserving biological diversity—many have established protected areas and have ratified the Convention on Biological Diversity (discussed in detail later in this chapter). Ultimately it is the responsibility of each country to protect its own natural environment, which is the source of products, ecosystem services, recreation, and culture—since many species are a source of national pride and figure prominently in stories, songs, and art. However, until their economies are stronger, developing countries may require outside assistance to help pay for the habitat preservation, research, and management required for the task. It is appropriate for the developed countries of the world (including the United States, Canada, Japan, Australia, and many of the European nations) to provide such assistance, since they rely on the biological diversity of the Tropics to supply genetic material and natural products for agriculture, medicine, and industry. The question we examine in this chapter is, how can countries work together to preserve biological diversity?

It is essential that this question be considered at the level of nations. The protection of biological diversity is a topic that must be addressed at multiple levels of government. While the major control mechanisms that presently exist in the world are based within individual countries, international agreements are increasingly being used to protect species and habitats. International cooperation is an absolute requirement for several reasons:

1. *Species migrate across international borders.* Conservation efforts must protect species at all points in their ranges; efforts in one country will be ineffective if critical habitats are destroyed in a second country to which an animal migrates. For example, efforts to protect migratory bird species in northern Europe will not work if the birds' overwintering habitat in Africa is destroyed. Efforts to protect whales in U.S. coastal waters will not be effective if these species are killed or harmed in international waters. Species are particularly vulnerable when they are migrating, as they may be more conspicuous, more tired, or more desperately in need of food and water.

2. *International trade in biological products is commonplace.* A strong demand for a product in another country can result in the overexploitation of the species by a poor country to supply this demand. When people are willing to pay high prices for exotic pets and esoteric wildlife products such as tiger bones, rhino horn, and bear gallbladders, poachers or poor, desperate people will take or kill even the very last animal to obtain this income. To prevent overexploitation, education is needed, along with economic alternatives for the people involved and control and management of the trade at both the points of export and import.

3. *The benefits of biological diversity are of international importance.* The community of nations is helped by the species and varieties that can be used in agriculture, medicine, and industry; the ecosystems that help regulate climate; and the national parks and biosphere reserves of international scientific and tourist value. Biological diversity is also widely recognized to have intrinsic value, existence value, and option value. The countries of the world that use and rely on the value from biological diversity need to be willing to help the less wealthy countries of the world preserve it.

4. *Many problems of environmental pollution that threaten ecosystems are international in scope and require international cooperation.* Such threats include atmospheric pollution and acid rain; the pollution of lakes, rivers, and oceans; greenhouse gas production exchange and global climate change; and ozone depletion. Consider the River Danube, which flows through Germany, Austria, the Slovak Republic, Hungary, Croatia, Yugoslavia, Bulgaria, Moldova, and Romania, and car-

ries the pollution of a vast agricultural and industrial region before emptying into the Black Sea—another international body of water, this one bordered by four additional countries. Only countries working together can solve problems such as these.

International Agreements to Protect Species

We begin by discussing the key international agreements that exist to protect species. One of the most important treaties protecting species at an international level is the **Convention on International Trade in Endangered Species (CITES)**, established in 1973 in association with the United Nations Environmental Program (UNEP) (Hemley 1994; Saterson 2001). The treaty has currently been ratified by more than 150 countries. CITES, headquartered in Switzerland, establishes lists (known as Appendices) of species for which international trade is to be controlled or monitored. Member countries agree to restrict trade in and destructive exploitation of these species. Appendix I includes approximately 675 animals and plants for which commercial trade is prohibited. Appendix II includes about 3700 animals and 21,000 plants whose international trade is regulated and monitored. For plants, Appendices I and II cover important horticultural species such as orchids, cycads, cacti, carnivorous plants, and tree ferns; timber species and wild-collected seeds are increasingly being considered for regulation as well. For animals, closely regulated groups include parrots, large cat species, whales, sea turtles, birds of prey, rhinos, bears, and primates. Species collected for the pet, zoo, and aquarium trades and species harvested for their fur, skin, or other commercial products also are closely monitored.

International treaties such as CITES are implemented when a country signing the treaty passes laws to enforce it. Countries may also establish Red Data Books of endangered species, which are national versions of the international Red Lists prepared by the IUCN. Laws may protect both species listed by CITES and the national Red Data books. Once species protection laws are passed within a country, police, customs inspectors, wildlife officers, and other government agents can arrest and prosecute individuals possessing or trading in protected species and seize the products or organisms involved (Figure 21.1). In one case in Florida, an individual was sentenced to 13 months in jail for attempting to smuggle an orangutan into the United States. The CITES Secretariat periodically sends out bulletins aimed at publicizing specific illegal activities. Recently the CITES Secretariat has recommended temporarily halting wildlife trade with Vietnam and Fiji because of their unwillingness to restrict the illegal export of wildlife from their territories.

Member countries are required to establish their own management and scientific authorities to implement their CITES obligations. Technical advice is provided by nongovernment organizations such as the **Interna-**

Figure 21.1 In August of 1995 Belgian customs inspectors seized an enormous shipment of contraband wildlife items. The haul contained many items banned by the CITES treaty, including monkey skulls, stuffed specimens of rare bird species, and tiger pelts. Parts from over 2000 individual animals were identified in the shipment. (AP Photo/Pierre Thielemans.)

tional Union for the Conservation of Nature (IUCN) **Wildlife Trade Specialist Group**, the **World Wildlife Fund (WWF) TRAFFIC network**, and the **World Conservation Monitoring Centre (WCMC) Wildlife Trade Monitoring Unit**, which is part of the United Nations. CITES is particularly active in encouraging cooperation among countries in addition to fostering conservation efforts by development agencies. The treaty has been instrumental in restricting the trade in certain endangered wildlife species. Its most notable success has been a global ban on the ivory trade when poaching was causing severe declines in African elephant populations (Box 29). Now countries in southern Africa with increasing elephant populations are requesting a resumption of limited ivory sales. A difficulty with enforcing CITES is that shipments of both living plants and animals and preserved parts of plants and animals are often mislabeled, due to either an ignorance of species names or a deliberate attempt to avoid the restrictions of the treaty. Also, sometimes countries fail to enforce the restrictions of the treaty due to a lack of trained staff, or corruption.

Another key treaty is the Convention on Conservation of Migratory Species of Wild Animals, often referred to as the Bonn Convention, signed in 1979, with a primary focus on bird species. This convention serves as an important complement to CITES by encouraging international efforts to conserve bird species that migrate across international borders and by emphasizing regional approaches to research, management, and hunting regulations. The Convention now includes protection of bats and their habitats and cetaceans in the Baltic and North Seas. However, only 36 countries have signed this Convention and its budget is very limited.

BOX 29   *The War for the Elephant: Is the Armistice Over?*

onservationists must occasionally take radical steps to save an overexploited species from extinction. For those concerned with the fate of the African elephant (*Loxodonta africana*) in the 1970s and 1980s, the measures employed to preserve the species sometimes amounted to actual warfare. Park rangers who wanted to prevent the elephant's extinction had to protect the animals with drawn weapons. At the center of the conflict was the demand for elephant ivory, which grew rapidly during the 1970s and early 1980s because of the rising buying power of East Asian consumers. Over 800 tons of ivory were required annually to meet market demands (Jones 1990). Most elephant poaching was not done by impoverished small-time hunters, but by organized bands of poachers carrying automatic weapons. In a few cases, the poachers were even the same people whose job it was to protect the animals: the game wardens themselves.

Under these circumstances it is hardly surprising that the total elephant population on the African continent dropped from 1.3 million in the late 1970s to under 600,000 by the late 1980s. Poaching accounted for 80% of elephant mortality in Kenya's Tsavo ecosystem in the 1980s as the price of ivory rose in world markets. East Africa's elephant populations were decimated: Kenya lost an estimated 85% of its elephant herd, Uganda nearly 90%—some 150,000 animals in less than a decade. In contrast, the large, well-protected herds of Zimbabwe, Botswana, South Africa, Malawi, and Namibia maintained their numbers. To deal with the threat, the wildlife service of Kenya and neighboring countries instituted a harsh policy toward poachers: Patrols of armed game wardens would aggressively search for and arrest poachers, shooting back if the poachers resisted arrest. This new policy, combined with other incentives, including higher pay, increased the commitment of game wardens to their job.

At the same time, the East African countries joined together to ask the member nations of CITES to halt ivory imports. Under the existing system, the ivory trade was officially regulated by the CITES treaty, and each country was allocated a specified maximum export quota. The reality was that countries that had reached their quota freely passed additional ivory to neighboring countries, where it was reexported with official permits. It has been estimated that more than 80% of the

Elephant tusks confiscated from poachers are kept under heavily armed guard in South Africa. Many East African countries and international organizations fear that legalizing the sale of ivory would lead to increased poaching and illegal smuggling across borders. (Photograph © R. de la Harpe/Biological Photo Service.)

BOX 29 *(continued)*

ivory being exported from Africa in the late 1980s came from elephants killed by poachers (Dobson and Poole 1992). When the ban was finally instituted in 1989, the price of ivory dropped dramatically, and so did the rate of poaching.

The damage done to the East African elephant herds by three decades of unrestricted hunting is more than a matter of mere numbers. First, elephants are social animals with complex behaviors that are taught to younger elephants by their elders (Poole 1996). Because the poachers selectively killed the elephants with the largest tusks—in other words, the older elephants, generally between 25 and 60 years of age—the transmission of knowledge from mature animals to the next generation relating to sources of food and water has been disrupted.

Second, elephants have a profound impact on the development of microhabitats on which many other animals depend. Elephants strip leaves, knock down trees, and trample brush as they feed, opening up habitat for other kinds of vegetation. The elephants' foraging patterns initiate succession phases, opening up forest areas of East African bush for grazing animals such as gazelle, zebra, and wildebeest, and, in West and Central Africa, encourage the growth of vegetation favored by gorillas and other forest animals. With fewer elephants available to perform this service, less open habitat is created, and the other species suffer as a consequence.

The efforts to save the elephant have had a significant, positive impact. The ivory ban and antipoaching patrols appear to have worked—the price of ivory has dropped precipitously, and elephant herds in East Africa are increasing. Yet, the elephant is not entirely safe; countries in southern Africa with stable and even increasing elephant herds have requested a partial lifting of the trade ban, claiming that the sale of elephant products would provide financial support for their successful elephant management programs. But in other parts of Africa, wildlife officers and conservation biologists are concerned about the impact of a partially lifted ban. Will the measures designed to prevent poaching work? Or will the slaughter that has so badly damaged many elephant populations in East Africa be renewed—this time killing the remaining elephant families? Only time can tell for certain, but the eyes of many people concerned with the fate of these majestic animals will be watching closely.

Other important international agreements that protect species include:

- Convention on Conservation of Antarctic Marine Living Resources
- International Convention for the Regulation of Whaling, which established the International Whaling Commission
- International Convention for the Protection of Birds and the Benelux Convention on the Hunting and Protection of Birds
- Convention on Fishing and Conservation of Living Resources in the Baltic Sea and the Belts
- Convention on the Conservation and Management of Highly Migrating Fish Stocks in the Western and Central Pacific Oceans
- Miscellaneous agreements protecting specific groups of animals, such as prawns, lobsters, crabs, fur seals, Antarctic seals, salmon, and vicuña

A weakness of all these international treaties is that they operate through consensus, so strong, necessary measures are often not adopted if one or more countries are opposed to the measures. Also, any nation's participation is voluntary and countries can ignore these conventions to pursue their own interests when they find the conditions of compliance too difficult. This flaw was highlighted when several countries decided not to comply with the International Whaling Commission's 1986 ban on whale hunting. Persuasion and public pressure are the principal means used to induce countries to enforce treaty provisions and prosecute violators, though funding through treaty organizations can also help.

International Agreements to Protect Habitat

Habitat conventions at the international level complement species conventions by emphasizing unique biological communities and ecosystem features that need to be protected (and within these habitats, a multitude of individual species can be protected). Three of the most important are the **Convention on Wetlands of International Importance Especially as Waterfowl Habitat** (or the **Ramsar Convention on Wetlands**), the **Convention Concerning the Protection of the World Cultural and Natural Heritage** (or the **World Heritage Convention**), and the **UNESCO Man and the Biosphere Program** (or the **Biosphere Reserves Program**). Countries designating protected areas under these Conventions voluntarily agree to administer them under the terms of the conventions; countries do not give up sovereignty over these areas to an international body but retain full control over them.

The Ramsar Convention on Wetlands was established in 1971 to halt the continued destruction of wetlands, particularly those that support migratory waterfowl, and to recognize the ecological, scientific, economic, cultural, and recreational values of wetlands (Hails 1996). The Ramsar Convention covers freshwater, estuarine, and coastal marine habitats, and includes 1150 sites with a total area of more than 96.3 million ha (Figure 21.2). The 131 countries that have signed the Ramsar Convention agree to conserve and protect their wetland resources and designate for conservation purposes at least one wetland site of international significance. Twenty-eight Ramsar countries in the Mediterranean have joined together to form a Wetlands Forum for regional cooperation. A comparable program, the Western Hemisphere Shorebird Reserve Network, focuses on protecting the declining wetland habitat of the Americas.

The World Heritage Convention is associated with UNESCO, IUCN, and the International Council on Monuments and Sites (von Droste et al. 1995; Sayer et al. 2000). This Convention has received unusually wide support, with 170 countries participating. The goal of the Convention is to protect cultural areas and natural areas of international significance through its World Heritage Site Program. The Convention is unusual because it emphasizes the cultural as well as biological significance of nat-

Figure 21.2 Izunuma is a Ramsar-listed wetland in Japan. Rice paddies, roads, and buildings come right up to the edge of the lake. More than 25,000 geese overwinter on the lake and feed in the rice paddies. (Photograph by M. Kunimoto.)

ural areas and recognizes that the world community has an obligation to support the sites financially. Limited funding for World Heritage Sites comes from a special United Nations foundation, which also supplies technical assistance. As with the Ramsar Convention, this Convention seeks to give international recognition and support to protected areas that are established initially by national legislation. The 144 World Heritage Sites protecting natural areas cover around 142 million ha and include some of the world's premier conservation areas (Figure 21.3): Serengeti National Park in Tanzania, Sinharaja Forest Reserve in Sri Lanka, Iguaçu Falls in Brazil, Manu National Park in Peru, the Queensland Rain Forest of Australia, Komodo National Park in Indonesia, Ha Long Bay in Vietnam, and Great Smoky Mountains National Park in the United States, to name a few.

UNESCO's Man and the Biosphere Program (MAB) began in 1971. Biosphere reserves are designed to be models that demonstrate the compatibility of conservation efforts and sustainable development for the benefit of local people, as described in Chapter 20. As of 2002, a total of 408 biosphere reserves had been created in 94 countries, covering more than 263 million ha, and including 44 reserves in the United States, 20 in Russia, 17 in Bulgaria, 16 in China, 14 in Germany, and 11 in Mexico (see Figure 20.11). The largest designated biosphere is 70 million ha in area, located in Greenland.

(A)

(B)

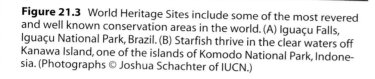

Figure 21.3 World Heritage Sites include some of the most revered and well known conservation areas in the world. (A) Iguaçu Falls, Iguaçu National Park, Brazil. (B) Starfish thrive in the clear waters off Kanawa Island, one of the islands of Komodo National Park, Indonesia. (Photographs © Joshua Schachter of IUCN.)

These three Conventions and provisions of the Convention on Biological Diversity establish an overarching consensus regarding appropriate conservation of protected areas and certain habitat types. More limited international agreements protect unique ecosystems and habitats in particular regions, including the Western Hemisphere, the Antarctic biota, the South Pacific, Africa, the Caribbean, and the European Union (WRI 1994). Other international agreements have been ratified to prevent or limit pollution that poses regional and international threats to the environment. The Convention on Long-Range Trans-Boundary Air Pollution in the European Region recognizes the role that long-range transport of air pollution plays in acid rain, lake acidification, and forest dieback. The Convention on the Protection of the Ozone Layer was signed in 1985 to regulate and phase out the use of chlorofluorocarbons.

Conservation measures can also potentially provide for promoting cooperation between governments. Such is often the case when countries need to manage areas collectively. In many areas of the world, rugged, undeveloped border areas mark the boundaries between countries. Often, the region is managed by artificial units marked by political boundaries rather than as a single natural ecosystem. An alternative to this situation is to establish transfrontier parks that include larger areas (Zbicz and Green 1997; Mackinnon 2000). Park personnel from the countries involved can manage the park resources collectively and promote conservation on a larger scale (Godwin 2001). An early example of this collaboration was the decision to manage Glacier National Park in the United States and Waterton Lakes National Park in Canada as the Glacier International Peace Park. Today, intensive efforts are being made to link national parks and protected areas in Zimbabwe, Mozambique, and South Africa into larger management units (Figure 21.4). This joint management would have the added advantage of protecting the seasonal migratory routes of large animals.

Marine pollution is another area of vital concern because of the extensive areas of international waters not under national control and the ease with which pollutants released in one area can spread to another area. Agreements covering marine pollution include the Convention on

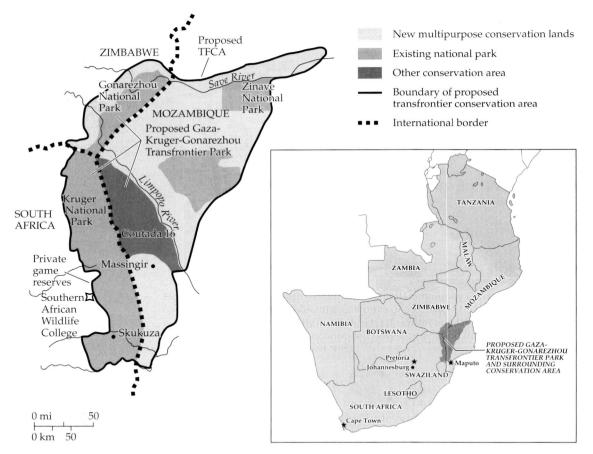

Figure 21.4 Proposed Gaza-Kruger-Gonarezhov Transfrontier Park will unite wildlife management activities in national parks and conservation areas of South Africa, Mozambique, and Zimbabwe. A larger conservation area will include national parks, private game reserves, and private farms and ranches. (After Godwin 2001.)

the Prevention of Marine Pollution by Dumping of Wastes and Other Matters, the Convention on the Law of the Sea, and the Regional Seas Program of the United Nations Environmental Program (UNEP). Regional agreements cover the northeastern Atlantic, the Baltic, and other specific locations, particularly in the North Atlantic region.

The Earth Summit, 1992

Protecting the environment is ultimately a global task. Despite continued destruction of key resources and ecosystems, significant strides have been made in adopting a global approach to sound environmental management. One of the most significant hallmarks of this progress was the international conferences held for 12 days in June, 1992 in Rio de Janeiro, Brazil. Known officially as the United Nations Conference on Environment and Development (UNCED), and unofficially as the Earth Summit, or the Rio Summit, the conference brought together representatives from 178 countries, including heads of state, leaders of the United Nations, and major nongovernment and conservation organizations. Their purpose was to discuss ways of combining increased protection of the environment with more effective economic development in less wealthy countries (United Nations 1993a,b). The conference successfully heightened awareness of the seriousness of the environmental crisis by placing the issue at the center of world attention. Also, the conference established a clear linkage between the protection of the environment and the need to alleviate poverty in the developing world through increased levels of financial assistance from developed countries (Figure 21.5). While the developed countries of the world potentially have the resources to provide for their citizens and protect the environment, for many of the poor countries, the immediate use of natural resources is often a prerequisite to raising the standard of living of an impoverished population. At the Earth Summit, the developed countries collectively agreed that they would assist the developing countries of the world in protecting the global environment and biodiversity. The central achievement of the Earth Summit was the willingness of the participants to work together on long-term goals, as stated by UNCED Secretary-General Maurice F. Strong (quoted in Haas et al. 1992): "The Earth Summit is not an end in itself, but a new beginning. The measures you agree on here will be but the first steps on a new pathway to our common future. Thus, the results of this conference will ultimately depend on the credibility and effectiveness of its follow-up."

In addition to initiating many new projects, conference participants discussed, and most eventually signed, six major documents:

1. *The Rio Declaration.* This nonbinding Declaration provides general principles to guide the actions of both wealthy and poor nations on issues of the environment and development. The right of nations to

Social Impacts   Linkages   Environmental Impacts

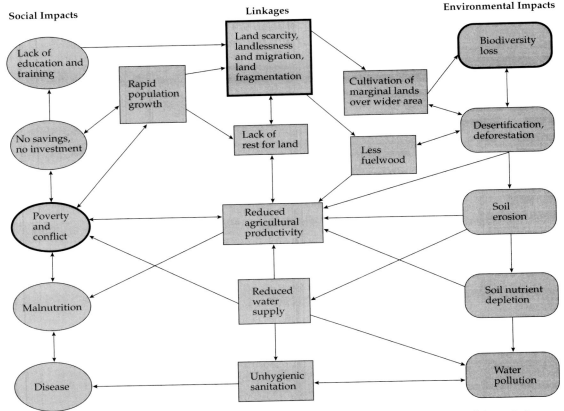

Figure 21.5 Some linkages between poverty and environmental degradation. Breaking the linkages is a focus of national and international funding efforts by the World Bank and other donor organizations. (After Goodland 1994.)

utilize their own resources for economic and social development is recognized, as long as the environments of other nations are not harmed in the process. The Declaration affirms the "polluter pays" principle, in which companies and governments take financial responsibility for the environmental damage that they cause. As stated in the Declaration, "States shall cooperate in a spirit of global partnership to conserve, protect, and restore the health and integrity of the earth's ecosystem. In view of the different contributions to global environmental degradation, states have common, but differentiated responsibilities."

2. *Convention on Climate Change.* This agreement requires industrialized countries to reduce their emissions of carbon dioxide and other greenhouse gases and to make regular reports on their progress. While specific emission limits were not decided upon, the Convention states

that greenhouse gases should be stabilized at levels that will not interfere with the Earth's climate. The United States, the world's major user of fossil fuels, has continued to resist the provisions of this convention, along with Australia, Canada, China, and the oil-producing states of the Middle East.

3. *Convention on Biological Diversity.* The Convention on Biological Diversity has three objectives: protecting the various components of biological diversity, using them sustainably, and sharing the benefits of new products made with genetic resources of wild and domestic species (Glowka et al. 1994; Raustiala and Victor 1996). The first two objectives recognize that countries have an obligation to protect their biological diversity and to use it in a responsible manner. While individual countries have the primary responsibility of protecting their own biological diversity, substantial international funding has been provided to assist developing countries in these efforts. The Convention also recognizes that indigenous people should share in the benefits derived from biological diversity, particularly when they have contributed their own local knowledge about the species. Developing international intellectual property rights laws that fairly share the financial benefits of biological diversity among countries, biotechnology companies, and local people is proving to be a major challenge to the Convention, with some progress and some roadblocks still to overcome (Posey 1996). In many cases, developing countries have severely restricted or even halted the removal of any biological materials from their countries. This has had the unexpected effect of hindering international scientific research unrelated to biological prospecting. In fact, the United States Congress has delayed ratifying the treaty, in part because of potential restrictions on its enormous biotechnology industry.

4. *Statement on Forest Principles.* An agreement on the management of forests proved difficult to negotiate, with strong differences of opinion between tropical and temperate countries. The resulting non-binding agreement calls for the sustainable management of forests, but does not impose conditions to ensure that this occurs. Protection of forests will most likely come from individual governments, local communities, private companies, and conservation organizations rather than from a single, all-encompassing agreement.

5. *Agenda 21.* This 800-page document is an innovative attempt to describe in a comprehensive manner the policies needed for environmentally sound development. Agenda 21 links the environment with other development issues that are often considered separately, such as child welfare, poverty, gender issues, technology transfer, and the unequal division of wealth. Plans of action are described to address problems of the atmosphere, land degradation and desertification, mountain development, agriculture and rural development, defor-

estation, aquatic environments, and pollution. Financial, institutional, technological, and legal mechanisms for implementing these action plans are also described.

6. *Convention to Combat Desertification.* This convention has the goals of protecting dryland environments and improving the living standards of people. Specific activities involve land reform, improving agriculture and livestock management, better forestry practices, soil and water conservation, and wildlife protection. Over 130 countries have ratified the Convention and many countries have submitted action plans describing how they would combat desertification. However, funding to implement these plans has not been forthcoming.

The most contentious issue resulting from the Summit has been deciding how to fund the Earth Summit programs, particularly the Convention on Biological Diversity and Agenda 21. At the time, the cost of these programs was estimated to be about $600 billion per year, of which $125 billion was to come from the developed countries as overseas development assistance (ODA). Because the level of ODA from all countries in the early 1990s totaled approximately $60 billion per year, implementing these Conventions would have required a severalfold increase of the aid commitment at that time. The developed countries did not agree to this increase in funding, and as an alternative proposal, the Group of 77 (a group of developing countries) had suggested that industrialized countries increase their level of foreign assistance to 0.7% of their Gross National Product (GNP) by the year 2000, which would have roughly doubled their level of assistance. While the major developed countries agreed in principle to this figure, no schedule was set to meet the target date. Of 21 donor countries, only a few wealthy northern European countries have met these target percentages of GNP given as foreign assistance as of the year 2000, most notably Norway (1.4%), Denmark (0.96%), Sweden (0.92%), the Netherlands (0.88%), and Finland (0.76%). Many of the larger developed countries, including the United States, at 0.17% of GNP, have actually lowered the percentage of GNP that they give as foreign assistance over the past 10 years.

The inability of the major industrial countries to allocate funds to implement the six conference agreements has been disappointing. However, the fact remains that two important agreements—the Convention on Biological Diversity and the Convention on Climate—were ratified by many countries and have formed the basis for many specific actions on the part of governments and conservation organizations. Follow-up meetings through 1997 indicated a willingness on the part of governments to continue the discussion (Figure 21.6). The most notable success is the international agreement, reached at Kyoto in December of 1997, to reduce global greenhouse gas emissions to below 1990 levels. However, many countries, most notably China, Russia, Japan, Australia, Canada, and Saudi

Figure 21.6 World leaders met in 1997 for "Rio +5," a follow-up of the Earth Summit. At the meeting, Mikhail Gorbachev, the former president of the Soviet Union, addressed a forum that included prominent political and environmental leaders. (Photograph by Hiromi Kobori.)

Arabia, have not ratified the Kyoto treaty, and the United States, which has not ratified the treaty, has recently decided to withdraw from it.

International Funding

Following the Earth Summit, international funding for conservation has increased dramatically. What is the process that identifies projects for funding? Often it begins when a conservation biologist, conservation organization, or government identifies a conservation need, such as protecting a species, establishing a nature reserve, or training park personnel. This often initiates a lengthy process of analysis, discussion, planning, project design, proposal writing, fundraising, and implementation that involves different types of conservation organizations. Private foundations (e.g., the MacArthur Foundation), international organizations (e.g., the World Bank), and government agencies (e.g., U.S. Agency for International Development) often provide money for conservation programs through direct grants to the institutions that implement the projects (e.g., Colorado State University, Missouri Botanical Garden, the governments of developing countries). In some cases, foundations and government agencies give money to major conservation **nongovernment organizations** (**NGOs**) (e.g., the World Wildlife Fund, Conservation International), which in turn provide grants and technical assistance to local conservation organizations. The major international conservation organizations are often active in establishing, strengthening, and funding local NGOs as well as government programs in the developing world that run conservation programs. From the perspective of an international conservation organization such as the World Wildlife Fund, working with local organizations in developing countries is an effective strategy because it trains and supports groups of citizens within the country, who can then be advocates for conservation for years to come.

A common funding pattern is for an active local conservation program in a developing country to receive money from one or more conservation foundations and foreign governments, maintain scientific links to international conservation NGOs, and have affiliations with local and overseas research institutions. In such a manner, the world conservation community is knit together through networks of money, expertise, and mutual interests. The Program for Belize (PFB) is a good example of this. At first glance the PFB is a Belizean organization, staffed by Belizean personnel, with the main purpose of managing a Belizean conservation facility, the Rio Bravo Conservation and Management Area. However, the PFB has an extensive network of research, institutional, and financial connections to government agencies (e.g., the U.S. Agency for International Development) and private organizations (e.g., the Manomet Center for Conservation Sciences and the Audubon Society in Massachusetts) in other countries.

The World Bank and the Global Environment Facility

Increasingly, groups in the developed countries recognize that if they want to preserve biological diversity in species-rich but cash-poor countries, they cannot simply provide advice: a financial commitment is also required. Approximately $5 billion is currently spent per year worldwide on biodiversity protection by governments and conservation organizations (Myers 2001). One of the single largest sources for the protection of biological diversity is the Global Environment Facility (GEF), created in 1991 and currently managed by the World Bank in Washington, D.C., in cooperation with the United Nations Development Program (UNDP) and the United Nations Environmental Program (UNEP). In addition, the World Bank itself and related international banks began to increase their own funding of conservation projects at around the same time. By the year 2000, the World Bank was managing 226 conservation programs worth $2.6 billion in countries throughout the world (Figure 21.7). Funding is expected to increase to over $3.5 billion by 2002, and perhaps to as much as $5 billion. Other programs within the GEF are targeted toward addressing global climate change, protecting the

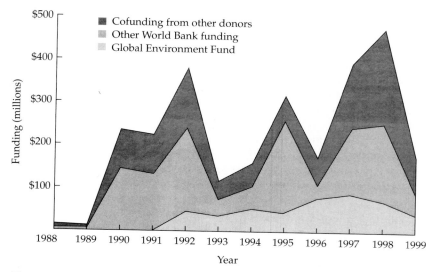

Figure 21.7 World Bank funding for biodiversity projects on an annual basis for the period 1988 to 1999. The total portfolio of 226 projects is valued at $2.6 billion, with $450 million coming from the Global Environment Facility (medium gray) and $1.2 billion in co-funding (light gray) from other donors, including governments, foundations, and conservation organizations. (After World Bank 2000.)

ozone layer, the sustainable use of forests, and managing freshwater and marine resources. On average, new biodiversity grants worth $250 million are funded each year by the GEF and the World Bank. Examples of projects sponsored by the GEF are the following:

- *Zimbabwe.* The Wildlife Management and Environmental Conservation Project supports local communities in obtaining greater economic value from wildlife.
- *Ghana.* Conservation of coastal wetlands critical to birds migrating along the East Atlantic Flyway through better design of sewage treatment facilities and support of sustainable community projects.
- *Turkey.* Creating crop management zones and forest gene resource zones to conserve traditional varieties and wild ancestors of grain, legume, and fruit tree species that are vital to the maintenance of modern agriculture.
- *Vietnam.* Provide training for managers of protected areas, park guards, and forest rangers.
- *Brazil.* Changes in land reform policy and tax subsidies are being developed to protect the remaining fragments of Brazil's Atlantic Forest.

Case Study: Funding in Latin America
A recent report published by the World Wildlife Fund provides a detailed picture of biodiversity funding for the Latin American and

Caribbean region (Castro et al. 2000). Between 1990 and 1997, 65 major donor organizations, including national governments, international development banks, conservation organizations, foundations, and research institutions funded 3489 conservation projects in Latin America and the Caribbean region, at a total cost of $3.26 billion. The six largest donors were the World Bank ($544 million), the Inter-American Development Bank ($361 million), German Technical Cooperation ($287 million), the U.S. Agency for International Development ($196 million), the Global Environment Facility ($187 million), and the Canadian International Development Agency ($157 million). Brazil received the largest share of funding ($898 million, or 31% of the total), followed by Mexico ($421 million), Venezuela ($225 million), Honduras ($145 million), and Guatemala ($127 million).

National governments and international banks provided 90% of the aid funding to Latin America, demonstrating the great importance of those institutions to funding international conservation. Although foundations and conservation organizations provided only 9.6% of the funding for Latin America, they are often able to fund innovative small projects and provide more intensive management. The growing importance of private funding throughout the world is illustrated by the recent $260 million donation given by the Moore Foundation to the conservation organization Conservation International. Conservation International is in turn cooperating with the World Bank, the Global Environment Facility, the MacArthur Foundation, and the Japanese government to establish the $150 million Critical Ecosystem Partnership Fund to protect threatened global hot spots and biological diversity.

Is the Funding Adequate and Effective?

While funding levels for conservation in developing countries are generally increasing each year, the amount of money being spent is still not sufficient to protect the great storehouse of biological riches needed for the long-term prosperity of human societies. Compared with the $13 billion spent each year on the U.S. space program and the $315 million spent each year on the Human Genome Project, the approximately $100 million per year being spent by U.S. institutions on biological diversity in developing countries is meager indeed.

Evaluations of the GEF have judged the projects funded so far to be a mixed success. On the positive side, the GEF provided increased funding for conservation and biodiversity projects, reviewing biodiversity-related legislation, transferring conservation information, planning national biodiversity strategies, identifying and protecting important ecosystems and habitats, and enhancing the capacity to carry out biodiversity projects (Keohane and Levy 1996). However, the lack of participation by community groups, local scientists and government leaders, and an overreliance on foreign consultants were identified as major problems (Bowles and Prickett 1994; Global Environment Facility 1999a). An additional problem was the mismatch of large-scale funding over short periods with the long-term needs of poor countries.

It has to be recognized that many environmental projects supported by international aid do not provide lasting solutions to the problems because of failure to deal with the "4 Cs"—concern, contracts, capacity, and causes (see Rabinowitz [1995] for an instructive case study). Environmental aid will be effective only when applied to situations in which both donors and recipients have a genuine *concern* to solve the problems (Do key people really want the project to be successful, or do they just want the money?); when mutually satisfactory and enforceable *contracts* for the project can be agreed on (Will the work actually be done once the money is given out?); where there is the *capacity* to undertake the project in terms of institutions, personnel, and infrastructure (Do people have the skills to do the work, and do they have the necessary resources, such as vehicles, research equipment, buildings, and libraries, to carry out the work?); and when the *causes* of the problem are addressed (Will the project treat the underlying causes of the problem or just provide temporary relief of the symptoms?). Despite these problems, international funding of conservation projects continues. Hopefully, past experiences will allow new projects to be more effective.

National Environmental Funds

In addition to direct grants for projects, an increasingly important mechanism used to provide secure, long-term support for conservation activities in developing countries is the **national environmental fund** (**NEF**). NEFs are typically set up as conservation trust funds or foundations in which a board of trustees—composed of representatives of the host government, conservation organizations, and donor agencies—allocates the annual income from an endowment to support inadequately funded government departments and nongovernment conservation organizations and activities. NEFs have been established in over 50 developing countries with funds contributed by developed countries and by major organizations such as the World Bank, the Global Environment Facility, and the World Wildlife Fund (Mikitin and Osgood 1994; Global Environment Facility 1999b).

One important early example of an NEF, the Bhutan Trust Fund for Environmental Conservation (BTF), was established in 1991 by the government of Bhutan in cooperation with the World Bank and the World Wildlife Fund. The BTF has already received about $26 million, (exceeding its goal of $20 million) with the Global Environment Facility its largest donor. The fund provides $1 million per year for surveying the rich biological resources of this eastern Himalayan country, training foresters, ecologists, and other environmental professionals; promoting environmental education; establishing and managing protected areas; and designing and implementing integrated conservation development projects.

Debt-for-Nature Swaps

Many countries in the developing world have accumulated huge international debts. Collectively, these countries owe about $1.3 trillion to international financial institutions, an amount that represents 44% of their combined GNPs (Dogsé and von Droste 1990; Thapa 1998). In many sub-Saharan countries, annual payments on their foreign debt can amount to over half of their GNP. Various factors have combined to make repayment of these loans difficult or impossible for many countries. Some developing countries have rescheduled their loan payments, unilaterally reduced them, or have stopped making them altogether. Because of the low expectation of repayment, the commercial banks that hold these debts are selling the debts at a steep discount on the international secondary debt market. For example, Brazilian debt has traded for about 22% of its face value, Costa Rican debt for 14–18%, and Peruvian for as little as 5%. In the case of Peru, this would mean that a $1 million loan owed to a bank could be purchased for $50,000 on the international secondary debt market.

In a creative approach, debt from the developing world is being used as a vehicle for financing projects to protect biological diversity, so-called **debt-for-nature swaps.** These swaps appear to offer great opportunities for all participants, they have great public relations appeal, and they are relatively simple in theory.

In one common type of debt-for-nature swap, an NGO in the developed world (such as Conservation International) cooperates with the government of a debtor country (such as Bolivia) in developing a proposal involving an environmental activity. This activity could involve land acquisition for conservation purposes, park management, development of park facilities, conservation education, or sustainable development projects. The international NGO negotiates with a local NGO or a local government agency that is willing to actually implement the environmental program. The international NGO then finds a bank that has a loan from the debtor country that it is willing to donate or sell the loan to the NGO at a large discount. This debt must be for an amount and of a form that is acceptable to the debtor country. After the international NGO has acquired the loan, the loan is returned to the debtor country so that no more payments have to be made on the debt. In exchange, the debtor country agrees to supply a certain amount of local currency for the agreed-on conservation activities, often by issuing bonds that pay a fixed annual amount for the project.

In other swaps, governments of developed countries owed money directly by developing countries may decide to cancel a certain percentage of the debt if the developing country will agree to contribute to a national environmental fund or to some other conservation activity. Such programs have converted debt valued at $1.5 billion for conservation and sustainable development activities in Colombia, Poland, the Philippines, and Madagascar, and a dozen other countries. In one program, Spain agreed to allow Latin American countries to convert $70 million in debt to conservation programs of equivalent value. Debt swaps are being incorporated into major foreign assistance programs such as the Enterprise for the Americas. Despite this, the total amount of debt involved in debt-for-nature swaps is only about 0.1% of the total debt owed by developing countries, so their overall effect in reducing indebtedness so far has been minimal.

Costa Rica has taken the lead in debt swaps. Outside conservation organizations have spent $12 million to purchase more than $79 million of Costa Rican debt, which has then been exchanged for $42 million in bonds for use in conservation activities at La Amistad Biosphere Reserve, Braulio Carillo National Park, Corcovado National Park, Guanacaste National Park, Tortuguero National Park, and Monteverde Cloud Forest, a private reserve. The interest on the bonds is used to establish a fund administered by the Costa Rican government and several local NGOs, including the Costa Rican Parks Foundation. This money has been used to acquire land for parks, to develop and institute a plan for managing these reserves, and to establish projects in sustainable development.

While debt-for-nature swaps have great potential advantages, they present a number of potential limitations to both the donor and the recipient (Patterson 1990; Roodman 2001). Debt swaps will not change the underlying problems that led to environmental degradation in the first place. Farmers still need land to farm, timber industries continue to log, and cash-hungry developing countries still have a motivation to exploit the environment for profit. Where land degradation is being driven by poor, landless farmers, debt-for-nature swaps need to support programs for poverty alleviation and land reform. Also, spending money on conservation programs might divert money from other necessary domestic programs such as medical care, schools, and agricultural development.

Marine Environments

Innovative funding programs such as NEFs and debt-for-nature swaps are particularly needed for marine protected areas, which have lagged behind terrestrial protected areas in conservation efforts (Hooten and Hatziolos 1995). The ease with which the marine environment can be polluted, the high value of seashore real estate, and the open access to marine resources mean that such protected areas will require special attention. Establishing low-impact ecotourism facilities and restricted fishing zones are among the possibilities that need to be examined and given increased funding in the immediate future.

International Development Banks and Ecosystem Damage

The rates of tropical deforestation, habitat destruction, and the loss of aquatic ecosystems have often been greatly accelerated by poorly conceived large-scale projects that are internationally financed, which sometimes involve dams, roads, mines, and resettlements. These projects may be financed by the international development agencies of major industrial nations, as well as the four major **multilateral development banks** (**MDBs**) controlled by those nations. These MDBs include the World Bank, which lends to developing countries in all regions of the globe, and the regional MDBs, including the Inter-American Development Bank (IDB), the Asian Development Bank (ADB), and the African Development Bank (AFDB).

Multilateral development banks annually loan more than $25 billion to 151 countries to finance development projects (Rich 1990; Roessler 2000). The impact of the MDBs is actually even greater since their funding is often linked to financing from donor countries, private banks, and other government agencies; the $25 billion funding of the MDBs attracts about another $50 billion in loans, which makes the MDBs major players in the developing world. Related to the MDBs are international financial institutions, such as the International Monetary Fund (IMF) and the International Finance Corporation, and government-supported export credit agencies, such as the U.S. Export-Import Bank, Japan's Export-Import Bank, Germany's Hermes Guarantee, Britain's Export Credits and Guarantee Department, France's COFACE, and Italy's SACE. These international institutions collectively support $400 billion of foreign investments and exports each year, or almost 8% of total world trade (Kapur et al. 1997; Rich 2000). These export credit agencies exist primarily to support the corporations of developed countries in selling manufactured goods and services to developing countries.

While the official goal of the MDBs is sustainable economic development and poverty alleviation, many of the projects they fund actually exploit natural resources to create exports for international markets. In many cases, these MDB-funded projects have resulted in the destruction of ecosystems over a wide area, involving soil erosion, flooding, water pollution, health problems, loss of income for local people, and loss of biological diversity. A World Bank study of its own projects found that 37% of the projects it funded could not be considered satisfactory if environmental criteria were included in the project evaluation (WRI 1994; UNDP 1994). Outside reviewers have been even more skeptical of World Bank projects (Rich 1990, 1994; Kapur et al. 1997).

Development Lending Case Studies

Among the most highly publicized examples of environmental destruction resulting from MDB and World Bank lending are the transmigration program in Indonesia; road construction, agricultural development, and industrialization projects in Brazilian Amazonia; and large dam construction in places such as Indonesia, India, China, Nepal, and Pakistan.

INDONESIAN RESETTLEMENT   From the 1970s to the late 1980s, the World Bank loaned $560 million to the Indonesian government to resettle millions of people from the densely populated inner islands of Java, Bali, and Lombok to the sparsely inhabited, heavily forested outer islands of Borneo (Kalimantan), New Guinea (Irian Jaya), and Sulawesi. The relocated farm families were supposed to raise crops to feed themselves as well as cash crops, such as rubber, oil-palm, and cacao, that could be exported, allowing Indonesia to pay off the loans. Known as the transmigration program, this activity has been an environmental and economic failure: The poor tropical forest soils on these outer islands are often unsuitable for the intensive agriculture practiced by these farmers (Whitten 1987). In addition, the infrastructure the farmers needed for their plantations did not develop, in part due to corruption and mismanagement. As a result, many of the farmers have become impoverished and have been forced to practice shifting agriculture. The production of export crops to pay off the World Bank loans has not occurred. In addition, at least 2 million ha and possibly up to 6 million ha of tropical rain forests have been destroyed by the transmigrating settlers (Rich 1990). The rate of this deforestation accelerated in 1997 and 1998 because the combination of unusually dry weather, legal and illegal logging, and clearing forest and scrub lands for agriculture by burning has resulted in forest fires over an enormous area. In addition, the presence of large numbers of new settlers in remote rural locations has contributed to political instability and ethnic violence.

BRAZILIAN HIGHWAYS   Many of the large Brazilian projects financed by the World Bank and other banks have failed to take into account the loss of biological diversity that results from their activities. Agricultural, industrial, and transportation projects have consistently been launched without comprehensive environmental impact studies or land-use studies to determine their feasibility.

The highway project in the Brazilian state of Rondonia is a classic example of a development program gone awry—on a colossal scale. The World Bank and the Inter-American Development Bank have loaned hundreds of millions of dollars to Brazil since 1981 to build roads and settlement areas as part of the Northwest Development Program. The eventual cost of the program will be more than $1.6 billion (Fearnside 1990; Kapur et al. 1997). Most of these funds were spent on the construction of a 1500-km section of road connecting Cuiabá, capital of Mato Grasso, to Porto Velho, capital of Rondonia. The remaining funds were used for building secondary and feeder roads and settlement areas, with only 3% of the budget allocated for biological and Amerindian reserves and 0.5% for research. Once this highway was opened, farmers from southern and northeastern Brazil, who had been displaced from the land by increasing mechanization and land ownership laws that favored the wealthy, were encouraged by the government to move to Rondonia and receive free land. The farmers and ranchers who migrated to the region cut down huge areas of forest near the roads to establish new farms and ranches. As a result, during the 1980s, Rondonia had one of the most rapid rates of deforestation in the world. At the peak of deforestation in 1987, 20 million ha—2.5% of Brazil's total land area—were burned in one of the world's most massive episodes of environmental devastation.

Much of the land in this region of Brazil was unsuitable for agriculture, but was often cleared to establish land claims; this practice was often facilitated by tax subsidies supporting cattle ranching. In its haste to develop the region, the Brazilian government also built roads across Amerindian reserves and biological reserves that were supposed to be completely protected, effectively opening up even these areas to deforestation. The Ianomãmi Indians, for instance, were given legal rights to only 30% of the land that they occupied and this holding was eventually fragmented into 19 separate pieces by roads and other developments. In general, the cattle ranches and tree plantations that were supposed to pay for the loans failed after the modern-day colonists abandoned their plots, resulting in the increased indebtedness of the Brazilian government. The overall result has been environmental devastation with minor, fleeting economic benefits. Despite the lack of environmental safeguards, the World Bank continues to fund road construction in Rondonia (Kapur et al. 1997). Massive forest destruction in Rondonia and elsewhere in Brazil continued through the 1990s, with particularly high rates of clearing and forest fires in 1997 and 1998 (Nepstad et al. 1999, 2001). A massive new round of construction of 6245 km of roads funded by international development banks is just beginning, doubling the amount of forest area accessible by road and the potential to substantially increase forest fragmentation and clearing (Figure 21.8). An alternative to spending billions of dollars on roads into the rain forest would be to intensify agriculture in existing cultivated regions, improve the quality of life for poor people, and take measures to reduce forest fires.

DAM PROJECTS   A major class of projects financed by MDBs is the construction of dam and irrigation systems that provide water for agricultural activities and generate hydroelectric power (Goodland 1990). While dams provide important benefits, these projects destroy free, wild rivers and often damage large aquatic ecosystems by changing water depth and current watershed patterns, increasing sedimentation and creating barriers to dispersal. As a result of these changes, many species are no longer able to survive in the altered environment (Box 30). In addition, all of the

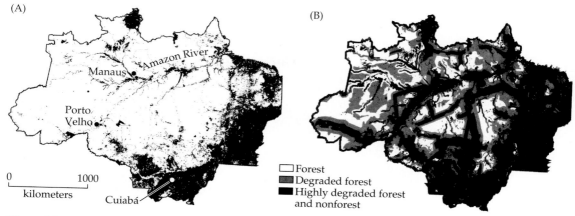

Figure 21.8 (A) A current map of the Brazilian Amazon showing forest (white) and deforested, degraded, and savannah areas (black). Note that deforestation occurs along rivers and roads and in eastern and southern populated areas. (B) When Brazil completes its proposed system of new roads by the year 2020, the amount of pristine forest cover (white) far from roads is predicted to be dramatically reduced, with much of the land lightly and moderately degraded (gray) and deforested, highly degraded, or converted to savannahs (black). If strong conservation measures are implemented by the government, the levels of degradation and deforestation could be somewhat reduced. (After Laurance et al. 2001.)

people living in the area to be flooded are displaced, which often causes them to become impoverished and forces them to move to cities.

Ironically, research indicates that the long-term success of some of the large international dam projects that threaten aquatic ecosystems may depend on preserving the forest ecosystem surrounding the project site. The loss of plant cover on the slopes above water projects often results in soil erosion and siltation, with resulting loss of efficiency, higher maintenance costs, and damage to irrigation systems and dams. Protecting the forests and other natural vegetation in the watersheds is now widely recognized as an important and relatively inexpensive way to ensure the efficiency and longevity of these water projects, while at the same time preserving large areas of natural habitat (Figure 21.9). In one study of irrigation projects in Indonesia, it was found that the cost of protecting watersheds ranged only from 1–10% of the total cost of the project, in contrast to an estimated 30–40% drop in efficiency due to siltation if the forests were not protected (MacKinnon 1983).

One of the most successful examples of an effective environmental investment is the $1.2 million loan by the World Bank to assist in the development and protection of Dumoga–Bone National Park in northern Sulawesi, Indonesia (McNeely et al. 1990). A 278,700-ha primary rain forest, which included the catchment area on the slopes above a $60 million

Figure 21.9 Hydroelectric dam on the Volta River in Ghana. The watersheds around such dams must be protected if the dams are to operate efficiently, but displaced peoples may try to farm there. (Photograph courtesy of FAO.)

irrigation project that was financed by the World Bank, was converted into a national park (Figure 21.10). In this particular case, the World Bank was able to protect its original investment through less than 2% of the project's cost and create a significant new national park in the process.

Reforming Development Lending

If many of the large international development projects are so economically unsuccessful and so environmentally harmful, why do host countries want them and why do the MDBs agree to finance them? Why are big projects approved? Projects are often funded because economists, engineers, and government officials make overly optimistic predictions on construction schedules and costs and prices of commodities and minimize potential problems; surveys and pilot studies are not undertaken or their results are disregarded; comparable projects elsewhere are not evaluated; finally, the environmental and social costs of projects are often ignored or minimized, since these variables are considered external to economic analysis (see Chapter 4).

Host governments often want large projects to proceed since the projects provide temporary jobs, temporary economic prosperity, and some

BOX 30 *How Much Will the Three Gorges Dam Really Cost?*

On the surface, it sounds like a great idea: build a dam to control flooding, improve navigation, and provide clean hydroelectric power to millions of people. The Yangtze River is one of the largest rivers in the world, running from the Tibetan plateau through China and emptying into the East China Sea. Flooding is a serious problem for the people living near the Yangtze: A series of floods in 1954 killed more than 30,000 people, and flooding in 1991 claimed at least another 3000 victims (Edmonds 1991). The area is economically depressed and per capita income is low. In 1992, the Chinese government gave final approval to build a dam downriver of the Three Gorges area of the Yangtze River in central China, with the aims of improving navigation, protecting approximately 10 million people from floods, and generating electricity for industrial development. Construction of the main dams has already begun, with completion expected in 2009. It is estimated that the electricity generated by the dam will reduce coal consumption (the primary source of electricity) by 30–50 million tons each year, which will significantly reduce air pollution (Jingling 1993). Slower currents and a more stable water flow would also improve navigability for shipping.

But the costs of building the dam are high—construction will cost over US\$60 billion, and perhaps as much as \$70 billion. In addition to funding by Chinese banks, substantial funding is coming from government-sponsored finance agencies such as Germany's Hermes Guarantee and Japan's Export-Import Bank, with private banks such as Citigroup, Chase Manhattan Bank, Credit Suisse, First Boston, Merrill Lynch, Deutsche Bank and Barclays Capital assisting with placing Chinese government bonds for the project. And as the reservoir behind the dam fills, it is flooding low-lying areas, necessitating the resettlement of entire villages, towns, and cities—eventually over a million people in all (Chau 1995). The long,

A photograph of the dam under construction gives a sense of the magnitude of the undertaking. (Photograph © 1998 Bob Sacha.)

BOX 30 *(continued)*

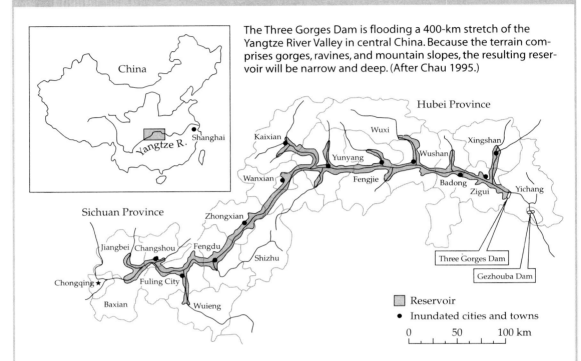

The Three Gorges Dam is flooding a 400-km stretch of the Yangtze River Valley in central China. Because the terrain comprises gorges, ravines, and mountain slopes, the resulting reservoir will be narrow and deep. (After Chau 1995.)

China

Yangtze R. Shanghai

Sichuan Province

Jiangbei Changshou Fengdu

Chongqing ★ Fuling City

Baxian Wuieng

Zhongxian

Shizhu

Kaixian Wuxi Hubei Province

Wanxian Yunyang Xingshan

Fengjie Wushan

Badong Yichang

Zigui

Three Gorges Dam

Gezhouba Dam

■ Reservoir

• Inundated cities and towns

0   50   100 km

narrow reservoir will stretch across more than 400 km of the Yangtze valley, from Yichang westward to Chongqing, one of China's largest cities. Temples, pagodas, and other important cultural sites are being submerged by up to 175 m of water. The Yangtze River basin also contains a freshwater fishery that provides two-thirds of the country's catch, and agricultural lands that yield 40% of the country's crops—much of which will be affected by the dam. The dam's effect on natural communities is also likely to be profound and detrimental.

Previous water projects involving human resettlement have been less than successful. Often people are resettled in areas so far from their original homes that they have had trouble adjusting. To avoid this problem, the plan is to move one million people uphill from their current location. However, those uphill sites that are not already in use are typically steep, covered with thin, infertile soil, and lack sufficient water for agriculture. It is estimated that five

times the present farmlands will be needed to yield the same amount of food. As steep hillsides are deforested, erosion will accelerate, increasing the build-up of silt behind the dam.

Dams have a fairly predictable impact on the environment. They block the movement of nutrients downriver, slow water flow, and decrease variations in the water level. Slower currents decrease oxygen levels and decrease the ability of the river to flush out pollutants. As the hydrology changes, so does the composition of the plant and animal communities. With the construction of the Three Gorges Dam, the rare Chinese sturgeon (*Acipenser sinensis*) probably will be unable to swim up the Yangtze River to spawn. The endangered Chinese river dolphin (*Lipotes vexillifer*), a species with only about 300 individuals left, moves up and down the river with rising and falling water levels and may have difficulty moving in conditions of stable water levels. Countless other species will be affected as well.

BOX 30 *(continued)*

Some of these concerns have been addressed by the dam's planners. Millions of dollars have been spent to terrace steep slopes for agriculture, and large tracts of uncultivated land on the margins of the areas to be flooded have been set aside for relocation efforts. Electricity provided by the dam should reduce deforestation caused by collection of fuelwood. Reforestation efforts have been planned to reduce erosion and deposition of silt in the river. Little is known, however, about how suitable marginal lands are for farming, how fast silt will build-up behind the dam, or how endangered species in the drainage basin will adapt to the altered hydrology. Perhaps the best emblem of the Three Gorges Dam is the endangered Siberian crane (*Grus leucogeranus*), symbolic of well-being among the Chinese, that feeds in shallow waters along the Yangtze River basin. Changing water levels may affect its survival—and the prosperity of the Chinese people as well.

release from social tensions for the duration of the project. Local business leaders, especially those with close links to the government, endorse the projects because they can make large profits on project contracts. Industrialized countries that support the banks often encourage these loans to stabilize governments in host countries—governments that are friend-

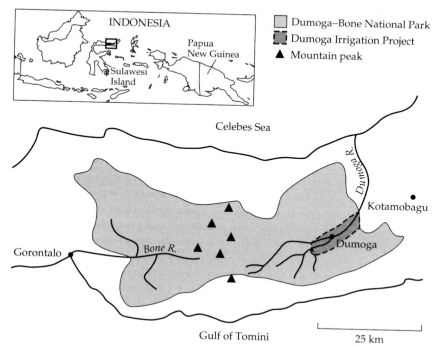

Figure 21.10 The Dumoga–Bone National Park on the northern arm of Sulawesi Island, Indonesia, protects the watershed above the Bone River and the Dumoga River, including the Dumoga Irrigation Project. (After Wells and Brandon 1992.)

ly to their interests, but which may lack popular support. And lastly, bank officials themselves want to make big loans because that is their business, and they continue to make loans for projects that experience should tell them are not environmentally sound or suitable for the long-term economic goals of the country.

There are several steps that MDBs should take to operate more responsibly. First, they should not fund environmentally destructive projects. This step would require the MDBs to develop cost–benefit models for development projects that take into account the environmental and ecological effects of those projects. Also, banks need to encourage open public discussions from all interested parties before projects are implemented (Goodland 1992; Roessler 2000). The MDBs are moving in this direction by allowing public examination, independent evaluations, and discussion of environmental impact reports by local organizations affected by projects being considered for funding.

Because the MDBs are primarily financed by the governments of the major developed countries, their policies can be scrutinized by the elected representatives of the MDB member countries, the national media, and conservation organizations. As past projects have been publicly criticized, the World Bank has reacted by required new projects to be more environmentally responsible; they have hired ecological and environmental staff to review new and ongoing projects, conducted more thorough environmental analyses, and adopted a management policy called "new environmentalism" that recognizes the linkages between economic development and environmental sustainability (Steer 1996).

This new environmentalism recognizes that there is a high environmental cost for inappropriate economic policies, reducing poverty is often crucial to protecting the environment, and economic growth must incorporate environmental values. To implement this policy, the World Bank has dramatically increased its lending in the area of biodiversity protection. As of 1999, the Bank has investments of $2.6 billion for 226 biodiversity projects in over 60 countries (World Bank 2000). This increased biodiversity investment has attracted another $1.2 billion from other sources, bringing the total investment to $3.8 billion. Around 8% of its recent investments are for environmental projects, with a major focus on pollution abatement and control, but they also include funding for biodiversity conservation, forest management, and the conservation of natural resources. A recent trend is toward funding a larger number of smaller projects, which often have more specific goals and are managed on a local level.

For the remaining 92% of its recent investments, the World Bank now requires environmental impact assessments as well as careful review by its environmental staff. In many cases, projects must include actions to mitigate their negative environmental impacts. Many conservation organizations remain skeptical that the World Bank will apply this new environmentalism policy to the bulk of its investments as time goes on. Careful scrutiny of its actions in the future is required, particularly the lending done by the affiliated International Finance Corporation and import-export banks, which lend to the private sector. It will be crucial to monitor the funding decisions of the MDBs and the projects they undertake rather than heed their speeches and reports, since they have proven to be extremely effective at public relations even as they continue their damaging activities (Roessler 2000).

One such project to watch is the mammoth Hidrovia Project in South America, in which the Paraguay-Parana River would be dredged and channeled so that large ships could carry cargo from Buenos Aires on the Argentina coast 3000 km north into Bolivia, Paraguay, and Brazil and then return carrying soybeans and other agricultural products from southern Brazil to world markets (Eckstrom 1996). This river system drains the Pantanal in South America, the world's largest wetland, covering nearly 200,000 km^2 in southwestern Brazil, eastern Bolivia, and northeastern Paraguay—an area larger than England, Wales, and the Netherlands combined. The wetland consists of a vast, unspoiled everglades, fabulously rich in endangered wildlife such as jaguars, tapirs, maned wolves, and giant otters. Environmentalists believe the Hidrovia Project will completely alter the hydrology of the area, submerging some areas, drying out others, and leading to an enormous loss of biological diversity. In Argentina, unprecedented flooding downriver could result, though maintenance of wetlands could minimize some of the adverse impacts. The final cost of the project is estimated to be $1 billion, with $3 billion in added maintenance costs over the next 25 years. The preliminary engineering and environmental impact study has already cost around $10 million, sponsored by the Inter-American Bank and the UNDP. The area is also being surveyed for a natural gas pipeline from Bolivia to the coast of Brazil. Funding, publicity, and opposition to the project go through cycles, in which the project moves forward, is cancelled, then starts again in a somewhat different form.

It remains to be seen whether the MDBs will change their basic practices or merely their rhetoric, choosing to publicize their "showcase" projects (Roessler 2000). It should also be noted that the MDBs have no enforcement authority: Once they hand the money over, countries can choose to ignore the environmental provisions in an agreement despite local and international protests. In such instances, one of the MDBs' few effective options is to cancel further stages of funding for these projects and delay new projects. As Rich (1990) pointed out more than ten years ago:

> Real reform in the MDBs will not occur without steady and increased political pressure. What has been won so far is an unprecedented and undeniable place for citizen activism, the only force that can bring accountability to the agencies controlling the international development agenda. But the fact that the World Bank and the IDB have un-

dertaken some bureaucratic reforms does not mean that environmentalists can assume that their case is won, or even that their ideas will get a sympathetic hearing. New posts have been created in the past without disrupting 'business as usual.' Environmentalists should remember that for any bank or bureaucracy, let alone the MDBs, nothing is cheaper than words.

The MDBs have shown some commitment to reducing environmental degradation in two instances. In Papua New Guinea, the World Bank refused to provide development loans until the government carried out a number of measures that would ensure more prudent forest management practices, which led to a full review of forestry practices and a subsequent moratorium on opening additional areas for logging. In Cambodia, a related international bank, the International Monetary Fund, withheld a loan until the government showed similar willingness to address serious problems related to its timber industry. These cases show the ability of the MDBs to foster responsible use of the globe's resources. Unfortunately, another trend is for the World Bank and the MDBs to finance "clean" projects that can be publicly justified on environmental and social grounds, while the far larger import-export banks quietly support the huge projects that damage the environment and benefit large corporations. Conservation biologists will have to wait and see which direction the MDBs will pursue in the future.

Increased Funding Is Necessary for the Future

The need for increased funding for biodiversity remains great at the local, national, and international levels. At present, about $4 billion is spent each year on budgets for protected areas, yet $17 billion would be required for managing the world's biological diversity adequately (WCMC 1992; Heywood 1995). While $17 billion is an enormous amount of money, it is small relative to the whopping $245 billion spent each year on agricultural subsidies and the $1 trillion spent on military defense. Certainly the world's priorities could be modestly adjusted to give more resources to the protection of biological diversity. Instead of countries rushing forward in a race to supply themselves the next generation of fighter aircraft, missiles, and other weapons systems, what about spending what it takes to protect biological diversity? Instead of the world's affluent consumers buying the latest round of consumer luxuries and electronic gadgets to replace things that still work, what about contributing more money to conservation organizations and causes?

There is also a role to be played by conservation organizations and businesses working together to market "green products." Already the Forest Stewardship Council and similar organizations are certifying wood products as having come from sustainably managed forests, and coffee companies are marketing shade-grown coffee. If consumers are educated to buy these products at a somewhat higher price, this could be a strong force in international conservation efforts.

Summary

1. International agreements and conventions that protect biological diversity are needed for the following reasons: species migrate across borders, there is an international trade in biological products, the benefits of biological diversity are of international importance, and the threats to diversity are often international in scope and require international cooperation. The Convention on International Trade in Endangered Species (CITES) was enacted to prevent destructive trade in endangered species. CITES prohibits trade in some species and regulates and monitors trade in others. Other international agreements protect habitat, such as the Ramsar Convention on Wetlands, the World Heritage Convention, and the UNESCO Biosphere Reserves Program.

2. Six major environmental documents were signed at the 1992 Earth Summit, the most important of which are the Convention on Biological Diversity and the Convention on Global Climate Change. The World Bank is managing biodiversity projects worth $2.6 billion, funded to implement the provisions of these treaties.

3. Conservation groups and governments in developed countries are providing substantial funding to protect biological diversity in developing countries. While the increased levels of international funding are welcome, the amount of money is still not sufficient to deal with the loss of biological diversity that is taking place. In the end, countries must take the primary responsibility for protecting biological diversity within their borders.

4. Innovative approaches are being developed to finance the preservation of biodiversity. One approach involves setting up national environmental funds (NEFs) in which the annual income from an endowment is used to finance conservation activities. A second approach involves debt-for-nature swaps, in which the foreign debt obligations of a government are canceled in exchange for the government providing increased conservation funding.

5. International development banks, including the World Bank, have often funded massive projects in developing countries that cause widespread environmental damage. The World Bank is now attempting to be more environmentally responsible in its lending policies; environmental groups will be watching to see if the change really occurs.

For Discussion

1. Imagine that Brazil, Indonesia, China, or Canada builds an expensive dam to provide electricity and water for irrigation. The project will take decades to pay back the costs of construction and lost ecosystem services—or it may never pay back the costs. Who are the winners with such a project and who are the losers? Consider the local people who had to move, newly arrived settlers, construction companies, timber companies, local banks, international banks, the urban poor, government leaders, environmental organizations, and anyone else that you think will be affected. Consider also the animals and plants that lived in the watershed before the dam was built. Can they survive in the same region? Can they migrate to another place?

2. Are poverty and the conservation of biological diversity linked, and if so, how? Should these problems be attacked together or separately?

3. How do national governments decide on an acceptable amount of money to spend on protecting biological diversity? How much money should a particular country spend on protecting biological diversity? Can you calculate an amount? What are the most cost-effective measures governments can take to protect biological diversity?

4. Suppose a species was discovered in Peru that could potentially cure a major disease affecting millions of people if it were grown on a large scale in cultivation and then widely marketed. If the government of Peru did not show interest in protecting this wonderful species, what could the international community do to protect the species and to fairly compensate the country for doing so? Come up with a variety of offers, suggestions, or alternatives that could be used to convince the government and people of Peru to protect the species and to become involved in its commercial development.

5. Do you think that the purchase of "green," environmentally responsible products is an effective way to promote the conservation of biodiversity? Would people by willing to spend more money for wood, coffee, and other products that have been produced in a sustainable manner, and if so, how much more? How could you determine if the purchase of such products was really making a difference?

Suggested Readings

Castro, G., I. Locker, V. Russell, L. Cornwell, and E. Fajer. 2000. *Mapping Conservation Investments: An Assessment of Biodiversity Funding in Latin America and the Caribbean.* World Wildlife Fund, Inc., Washington, D.C. Summary and analysis of international conservation investments in Latin America.

Christen, C. A. and J. Allen. 2001. *A Vested Interest: BSP Experiences with Developing and Managing Grant Portfolios.* World Wildlife Fund, Inc., Washington, D.C. The U.S. Biodiversity Support Program summarizes a decade of funding conservation projects worldwide.

Eckstrom, C. K. 1996. A wilderness of water: Pantanal. *Audubon* 98(2): 54–65. An enormous South American wetland is on the verge of development. What can be protected?

Environment Department of the World Bank. 2000. *The World Bank and The Global Environment: A Progress Report.* World Bank, Washington, D.C. An official statement of the World Bank's effort on behalf of the environment.

Godwin, P. 2001. Wildlife without borders. National Geographic 200(3): 2–31. Potential benefits and problems of establishing transfrontier protected areas.

Hails, A. J. (ed.). 1996. *Wetlands, Biodiversity, and the Ramsar Convention: The Role of the Convention on Wetlands in the Conservation and Wise Use of Biodiversity.* Ramsar Convention Bureau, Gland, Switzerland. Overview of the convention with many featured examples.

Kapur, D., J. P. Lewis, and R. Webb (eds.). 1997. *The World Bank: Its First Half-Century.* The Brookings Institute, Washington, D.C. Thorough, critical examination of the World Bank's lending policies.

Laurance, W. F., M. A. Cochrane, S. Bergen, P. M. Fearnside, et al. 2001. The future of the Brazilian Amazon. *Science* 291: 438-439. Road construction in the Amazon will lead to the rapid loss of forest cover.

Poole, A. 1996. *Coming of Age with Elephants: A Memoir.* Hyperion, New York. Personal account of how studies of elephants in Kenya led to involvement in their protection.

Posey, D. A. 1996. Protecting indigenous peoples' rights to biodiversity. *Environment* 38 (8): 6–9, 37–45. Innovative new methods are being developed to compensate local people for their knowledge of and protection of biological diversity.

Rabinowitz, A. 1995. Helping a species go extinct: The Sumatran rhino in Borneo. *Conservation Biology* 9: 482–488. Spending money on high-profile projects sometimes hides an unwillingness to tackle tough problems on the ground.

Roessler, T. 2000. The World Bank's lending policy and environmental standards. *North Carolina Journal of International Law and Commercial Regulation* 26: 105–137. An objective view of World Bank policy.

Roodman, D. M. 2001. *Still Waiting For the Jubilee: Pragmatic Solutions for the Third World Debt Crisis*. Worldwatch Institute, Washington, D.C. Debt-for-nature swaps have not delivered all that they promised.

Sayer, J., N. Ishwaran, J. Thorsell, and T. Sigaty. 2000. Tropical forest biodiversity and the World Heritage Convention. *Ambio* 29: 302–309. The Convention provides a powerful international approach for protecting biodiversity.

Thapa, B. 1998. Debt-for-nature swaps: an overview. *International Journal of. Sustainable Development and World Ecology* 5: 249–262. Debt-for-nature swaps are an important mechanism, providing $1.5 billion for conservation projects, but the amount is still tiny in comparison to the foreign debt of developing countries.

Zbicz, D. C. and M. J. B. Green. 1997. Status of the world's transfrontier protected areas. *Parks* 7(3): 5–10. In a few areas of the world countries are experimenting with cooperative park management.

An Agenda for the Future

s we have seen throughout this book, there is no mystery as to why biological diversity is showing a rapid, worldwide decline. Biological communities are destroyed and species are driven to extinction because of human resource use, which is propelled by the need of poor people to survive, the excessive consumption of resources by affluent people and countries, and the desire to make money. The destruction may be caused by local people in the region, recent arrivals from outside the region, local business interests, large businesses in urban centers, multinational corporations in other countries, or governments. People may also be unaware of the impact of human activities on the natural world, or they may be apathetic. In order for conservation policies to work, people at all levels of society must see that it is in their own interest to work for conservation (Myers 1996). If conservationists can demonstrate that the protection of biological diversity has more value than its destruction, people and their governments will be more willing to preserve biological diversity. This assessment should include not only monetary value, but also existence value, option value, and intrinsic value.

Ongoing Problems and Possible Solutions

There is a consensus among conservation biologists that there are a number of major problems involved in preserving biological diversity and that certain changes in policies and practices are needed. We list these problems, and suggested solutions, below.

Problem: Protecting biological diversity is difficult when most of the world's species remain undescribed by scientists and are not known by the general public. Further, most biological communities are not being monitored to determine how they are changing over time.

Solution: More scientists and enthusiastic nonscientists need to be trained to identify, classify, and monitor species and biological communities, and funding should be increased in this area (Raven and Wilson 1992; Wilson 1992, 1994). There is a particular need for training more scientists and establishing research institutes in developing countries. Enthusiastic nonscientists can often play an important role in protecting biodiversity once they are given some training and guidance by scientists. People interested in conservation biology should be taught basic skills, such as species identification and environmental monitoring techniques, and should join and support local, national, and international conservation organizations. Information on biological diversity must be made more accessible; this may be accomplished in part through the new Global Biodiversity Information Facility, which will serve as a central clearinghouse for data from 29 industrialized countries and be accessible via the Internet (Redfearn 1999).

Problem: Many conservation issues are global in scope, involving many countries.

Solution: Countries are increasingly willing to discuss international conservation issues, as shown by the 1992 Earth Summit and the 1997 Climate Change Conference in Kyoto. Nations are also more willing to sign and implement treaties such as the Convention on Biological Diversity, the Convention on Global Climate Change, and the Convention on International Trade in Endangered Species. International conservation efforts are expanding, and further participation in these activities by conservation biologists and the general public should be encouraged. One positive development is the trend toward establishing transfrontier parks that straddle borders; these parks are good for wildlife and encourage cooperation between countries. Citizens and governments of developed countries must also become aware that they bear a direct responsibility for the destruction of biological diversity through their overconsumption of the world's resources (Figure 22.1). Conservation professionals need to demonstrate how changes in the actions and lifestyles of individuals on the local level can have a positive influence far beyond their immediate community.

Figure 22.1 In one year, an average U.S. family of four with a typical American lifestyle consumes approximately 3785 liters (1000 gallons) of oil, shown here in barrels, for fueling its two cars and heating its home. The same family burns about 2270 kg (5000 pounds) of coal, shown here in a pile in the right foreground, to generate the electricity to power lights, refrigerators, air conditioners, and other home appliances. The air and water pollution that results from this consumption of resources directly harms biological diversity, and creates an "ecological footprint" that extends far beyond their home. Regulating such consumption must be addressed in a comprehensive conservation strategy at individual, local, regional, national, and global scales. (Photograph by Robert Schoen/ Northeast Sustainable Energy Association.)

Problem: Developing countries often want to protect their biological diversity but are under pressure to develop their natural resources.

Solution: Conservation organizations, zoos, aquariums, and botanical gardens in developed countries should continue to provide financial support to developing countries for conservation activities, in particular establishing and maintaining national parks and other protected areas. This support should continue until countries are able to protect biodiversity with their own resources. This is fair and reasonable since developed countries have the funds to support these parks and make use of the protected biological resources in their agriculture, industry, research programs, zoos, aquaria, botanical gardens, and educational systems. Economic and social problems in developing countries must be addressed at the same time, particularly those relating to poverty and war. Reducing or forgiving foreign debt payments, debt-for-nature swaps, and environmental trust funds may be additional mechanisms to achieve these goals. Individual citizens can donate money and participate in organizations that further advance these conservation goals.

Problem: Economic analyses often paint a falsely encouraging picture of development projects that are environmentally damaging.

Solution: Comprehensive cost–benefit analyses must be used that compare potential project benefits with environmental and human costs such as soil erosion, water pollution, loss of natural products, loss of traditional knowledge with potential economic value, loss of tourist potential, loss of species of possible future value, and loss of places for people to live. In particular, the effects of large projects on local people typically have been ignored in economic analyses and should be given more attention. Environmental impact analyses also need to include comparative studies of similar projects completed elsewhere and the probabilities and costs of possible worst-case scenarios. Local communities and the general public should be presented with this information and asked to provide input into the decision process.

Problem: Ecosystem services are often not assigned value in economic decision-making.

Solution: Economic activities that affect the environment should be linked to the maintenance of ecosystem services through fees, penalties, and the establishment of nearby protected areas. Industry and human communities must become morally and financially responsible for the resources that they use and the pollution that they cause. The "polluter pays" principle must be adopted, in which industries, governments, and individual citizens pay for cleaning up the environmental damage their activities have caused (Bernow et al. 1998; Wolbarts 2001). A step in this direction are the increased rates utilities are now charging customers for water and sewer use, rates that better reflect the actual costs of providing these services. Financial subsidies to industries that damage the environment—such as the pesticide, petrochemical, logging, fishing, and tobacco industries—should end, particularly to the industries that damage human health as well, and those funds should be redirected to activities that enhance the environment and human well-being.

Problem: Much of the destruction of the world's biological diversity is caused by people who are poor who are simply trying to survive.

Solution: Conservation biologists and charitable and humanitarian organizations need to assist local people in organizing and developing sustainable economic activities that do not damage biological diversity.

Integrated conservation–development projects (ICDPs) represent one approach. Foreign assistance programs need to be carefully planned to help the rural poor rather than primarily benefiting urban elites, as they often do. Because the funds of conservationists are limited and problems are urgent, conservation efforts should concentrate on people who are affecting areas of major biological importance. Conservation biologists and organizations are increasing their participation in programs for poor rural areas that promote smaller families, reduced population growth, and more training. These programs should be closely linked to efforts aimed at improving economic opportunities and halting environmental degradation (Dasgupta 1995). Supporting more intensive forms of permanent agriculture and local industries may also provide an alternative to additional land clearing (Goklany 1998). Providing financial support for education for all school-aged children in these communities can also ease dire economic situations by providing local people with additional skills and alternatives for future employment that are not be dependent on local biological resources.

Problem: Decisions about land conservation and the establishment of protected areas are often made by central governments with little input from people and local organizations in the region being affected. Consequently, local people sometimes feel alienated from conservation projects and do not support them.

Solution: In order for a conservation project to be successful, it is imperative that local people believe that they will benefit from it and that their involvement is important. To achieve this goal, environmental impact statements and other project information should be publicly available to encourage open discussion at all steps of a project. Local people should be provided with whatever assistance they may need in order to understand and evaluate the implications of the project being presented to them. Mechanisms should be established to ensure that the rights, responsibilities, and if possible, the decisions for management are shared between government agencies, conservation organizations, and local communities and businesses (Salafsky et al. 2001b). Conservation biologists working in national parks should periodically explain the purpose and results of their work to nearby communities and school groups and listen to what the local people have to say. In some cases, a regional strategy such as a habitat conservation plan or a natural community conservation plan may have to be developed to reconcile the need for some development (and resulting loss of habitat) with the need to protect species and biological communities.

Problem: Revenues, business activities, and scientific research associated with national parks and other protected areas do not directly benefit surrounding communities.

Solution: Whenever possible, local people should be trained and employed in parks as a way of utilizing local knowledge and providing income to local people. A portion of park revenues should be used to fund local community projects such as schools, clinics, roads, cultural activities, sports programs and facilities, and community businesses—infrastructure that benefits a whole village, town, or region.

Problem: National parks and conservation areas often have inadequate budgets to pay for conservation activities.

Solution: It is often possible to increase funds for park management by raising rates for admission, lodging, or meals—so that rates reflect the actual cost of maintaining the area. Concessions selling goods and services may be required to contribute a percentage of their income to the park's operation. Also, zoos and conservation organizations in the developed world should continue to make direct financial contributions to conservation efforts in developing countries. For example, members of the American Zoo and Aquarium Association and their partners supported over 1300 *in situ* conservation projects in 80 countries worldwide from 1999 to 2000.

Problem: Many endangered species and biological communities are on private land and on government land that is managed for timber production, grazing, mining, and other activities. Timber companies that lease forests and ranchers that rent rangeland from the government often damage biological diversity and reduce the productive capacity of the land in pursuit of short-term profits. Private landowners often regard endangered species on their land as restrictions on the use of it.

Solution: Change the laws so that people can obtain leases to harvest trees and use rangelands only as long as the health of the biological community is maintained (Davis and Wali 1994). Eliminate tax subsidies that encourage the overexploitation of natural resources, and establish payments for land management that enhances conservation efforts (Losos et al. 1995; Environmental Defense 2000). Alternatively, educate landowners to protect endangered species and praise them publicly for their efforts.

Problem: In many countries, governments are inefficient and are bound by excessive regulation. Consequently, governments are often slow and ineffective at protecting biological communities.

Solution: Local NGOs and citizen groups are often the most effective agents for promoting conservation. Accordingly, these groups should be encouraged and supported politically, scientifically, and financially. Conservation biologists need to educate individual citizens about local environmental issues and encourage them to take action when necessary. New foundations should be started by individuals, organizations, and businesses to financially support conservation efforts.

Figure 22.2 Demonstrations such as this protest led by Julia "Butterfly" Hill against the extensive logging of old-growth forests in northern California can focus media attention on environmental problems that society must not ignore. This demonstration is peaceful, but other environmental demonstrations have been confrontational and even violent. (Photograph by Shaun Walker.)

Problem: Many businesses, banks, and governments are uninterested in and unresponsive to conservation issues.

Solution: Lobbying efforts may be effective at changing the policies of unresponsive institutions because most will want to avoid bad publicity. Petitions, rallies, letter-writing campaigns, and economic boycotts all have their place when requests for change are ignored (Figure 22.2; Box 31). Conservationists need to be realistic and keep a long-term perspective. However, unrealistic demands for immediate change sometimes also have value in eliciting realistic counterproposals from previously unresponsive institutions. In many situations, radical environmental groups such as Greenpeace and EarthFirst! dominate media attention with dramatic, publicity-grabbing actions, while mainstream conservation organizations such as The Nature Conservancy, Conservation International, Environmental Defense, and the World Wildlife Fund follow behind to negotiate a compromise.

Conservation Biologists' Role in Protecting Biodiversity

The problems and solutions we just discussed underscore the importance of conservation biologists—they will be the primary participants in solving those problems. Conservation biology differs from many other

BOX 31   *Environmental Activism Confronts the Opposition*

he past two decades have witnessed a tremendous increase in popular awareness of environmental issues (Gore 1992). Many conservation organizations such as the Sierra Club, the World Wildlife Fund, and The Nature Conservancy, to name only a few, have gained hundreds of thousands of new members. Greenpeace International, one of the most active organizations in protesting environmental destruction, has approximately 2.6 million members and an annual budget of around $100 million. The surge in environmental awareness, however, has triggered a disturbing backlash from those industries, business interests, labor organizations, and even some governments that resent and fear any restrictions on the exploitation of natural resources (Motavelli 1995; Ehrlich and Ehrlich 1996; Kurlansky 1996). Conservation of natural resources may be linked, in some peoples' minds, to a loss in profits and job opportunities. When people fear losing their jobs or businesses because of conservation measures, they feel anger toward environmental activists. This perception tends to be more prevalent in a slow economy. Incidents of intimidation, threats, and physical harassment,

sometimes frighteningly violent, have been reported worldwide by environmental activists.

Perhaps the best-known violent incident occurred in 1988, when Chico Mendes, a Brazilian activist organizing rubber tappers to resist the encroachment of cattle ranching and logging in the Amazon rain forest, was assassinated by ranchers. Mendes's martyrdom created a worldwide uproar and focused global attention on the destruction of the rain forest. The conviction of the rancher who allegedly ordered the murder was an initial victory for Mendes's supporters; before this incident, large landowners, loggers, and miners could—and did—act with impunity against activists, labor leaders, native people, and anyone else who stood in the way of the exploitation of Brazil's forests (Toufexis 1992). The victory, however, was short-lived; the conviction was overturned on appeal. Moreover, many other activists in Brazil have been beaten or killed, both before and since Mendes's death. Activists claim that hit lists circulate openly among developers, loggers, and ranchers, groups whom the government often seems unable to control.

Environmentalists in many countries often face arrest and abuse at the hands of their own governments. People who protest destructive activities have been branded as subversives, traitors, or foreign agents for fighting government policies that

Greenpeace ships have attracted global media attention during high-profile confrontations with ships involved in illegal fishing and whaling operations, or activities considered by them to be immoral. (Photograph courtesy of Greenpeace.)

BOX 31 *(continued)*

promote unrestricted development at the expense of the environment. Based on these and other charges, some activists have been interrogated, jailed, beaten, and tortured. In 1995, nine environmental activists were hanged in Nigeria after a secret trial; they were members of the Ogoni tribe, whose land is being destroyed by a massive oil production operation sanctioned by the Nigerian government. Such incidents occur even in countries considered progressive with regard to conservation.

The persecution and injustices faced by environmental activists are by no means limited to developing nations. Individual activists fighting industrial pollution and the destruction of important biological communities in North America and Europe have also been victims of persecution, ranging from arson to assault to attempted murder. On occasion, authorities responsible for investigating the crimes have responded with either indifference or overt antagonism toward the victims. In a famous incident, French government agents were convicted in the 1985 bombing in New Zealand of the Greenpeace flagship *Rainbow Warrior,* in which a crew member died. The ship was being readied to leave for the South Pacific to protest the French nuclear weapons testing program.

In Northern California, members of Earth First! have staged many nonviolent protests against logging in a 24,000-ha region known as the Headwaters Forest. This area is one of the last remaining unprotected old-growth redwood forests and is a home for the federally endangered marbled murrelet. Activists and local residents have become alarmed by the Pacific Logging Company's dramatic increases in the rate of clear-cutting. Clear-cutting of trees on steep slopes has led to massive landslides, destroying homes and silting up streams. Protesters from Earth First! and other groups have been arrested for trespassing, have had their eyes dabbed with painful pepper spray by police, and have been threatened with violence by area residents. In 1997, national media attention was drawn to a young, articulate woman, Julia "Butterfly" Hill, who decided to protest the logging by sitting and living in a tall redwood tree until the logging company agreed to end cutting in the Headwaters region. After two years of sitting in the 1000-year-old tree she named "Luna" and ever-increasing levels of publicity and tension, Julia Butterfly finally descended from her tree perch when the Pacific Logging Company agreed to stop logging in some of the old-growth forests. Earth First! regards this as only a partial victory on the way to complete conservation protection for the Headwaters Forest, and protests and tree-sits continue (see Figure 22.2).

Environmental activists work to persuade or, if that fails, to force society to accept the limitations that must be imposed on human consumption if the biosphere is to survive. Activists interested in protecting the environment and biological diversity are joining the entire spectrum of organizations, from mainstream political parties, including newly formed Green Parties, to hard-line confrontational groups. In some cases, this has meant undertaking acts of civil disobedience, such as blocking trucks and occupying trees to stop the chain saw. In a few extreme cases, protestors have engaged in ecosabotage, destroying vehicles and buildings (Taylor 1995; Maher 1999). Business organizations and conservative elements in the labor movement are increasingly lobbying and forming action groups to counter conservation groups. In an interesting twist, these prodevelopment groups often use environmental rhetoric to argue for the "wise use" of natural resources. "Wise use" in this case often refers to unlimited grazing, logging, and mining, and other unrestricted resource utilization.

Unfortunately, open discussion can give way to anger, confrontation, and intimidation, in some cases resulting in violence. Conservation biologists must help to develop innovative approaches that inform, educate, and organize diverse groups of people to find solutions to environmental problems and to de-fuse the tensions and violence that often surrounds these issues.

scientific disciplines in that it plays an active role in the preservation of biological diversity in all its forms: species, genetic variability, biological communities, and ecosystem functions. Members of the diverse disciplines that contribute to conservation biology share the common goal of protecting biological diversity in practice, rather than simply investigating it and talking about it (Norton 1991; Barry and Oelschlaeger 1996; Robertson and Hull 2001).

Challenges for Conservation Biologists

The ideas and theories of conservation biology are increasingly being incorporated into decisions about park management and species protection. At the same time, botanical gardens, museums, nature centers, zoos, national parks, and aquariums are reorienting their programs to meet the challenges of protecting biological diversity. The need for large parks and the need to protect large populations of endangered species are two particular topics that have received widespread attention in both academic and popular literature. The vulnerability of small populations to local extinction, even when they are carefully protected and managed, and the alarming rates of species extinction and destruction of unique biological communities worldwide have also been highly publicized. As a result of this publicity, the need to protect biological diversity is entering political debate and has been targeted as a priority for government conservation programs.

One of the most serious challenges facing conservation biology is reconciling the needs of local people and the need to preserve biological diversity. How can poor people—particularly in the developing world but also in rural areas of developed countries—be convinced to forgo the exploitation of nature reserves and biological diversity when they are desperate to obtain the food, wood, and other natural products that they need for their daily survival? Park managers in particular need to find compromises, such as those exemplified by biosphere reserves and integrated conservation–development projects, that allow people to obtain the natural resources that they need to support their families yet not damage the park's natural communities. In each place, a balance has to be achieved between excluding people to protect vulnerable species and encouraging people to freely use park resources. At national and international levels, the world's resources must be distributed more fairly to end the inequalities that exist today. Effective programs must be established to stabilize the world's human population. At the same time, the destruction of natural resources by industries must be halted, so that the short-term quest for profits does not lead to a long-term ecological catastrophe (Goodland 1992). Management strategies to preserve biological diversity also need to be developed for the 90% of the terrestrial environment that will remain outside of protected areas, as well as for the vast, largely unexplored marine environment.

Achieving the Agenda

If these challenges are to be met successfully, conservation biologists must take on several active roles. They must become more effective *educators* in the public forum as well as in the classroom. Conservation biologists need to educate as broad a range of people as possible about the problems that stem from loss of biological diversity (Collett and Karakashain 1996). They need to convey a positive message about what has been accomplished and what can be accomplished to protect biological diversity, by delivering a sense of realistic optimism to counter the pessimism and passivity so frequently encountered in modern society.

Conservation biologists often teach college students and write technical papers addressing these issues, but they reach only a limited audience in this way: Remember that only a few hundred or a few thousand people read most scientific papers. In contrast, millions of adults watch nature programs on television, especially ones produced by the National Geographic Society, the Public Broadcasting Service, and the British Broadcasting Corporation, and tens of millions of children watch the television channel Animal Planet, programs such as *Zoboomafoo* and movies such as *Fern Gully*, which often have powerful conservation themes. Conservation biologists need to reach a wider range of people through speaking in villages, towns, cities, elementary and secondary schools, parks, and neighborhood gatherings. Also, the themes of conservation need to be even more widely incorporated into public discussions. Conservation biologists must spend more of their time writing articles and editorials for newspapers and magazines, as well as speaking on radio, television, and other mass media. Conservation biologists need to make a special effort to talk to children's groups and to write versions of their work that children can read. Hundreds of millions of people visit zoos, aquariums and botanical gardens, making these another prime venue for communicating conservation messages to the public. Conservation biologists must continue to seek out creative ways to reach wider audiences and avoid repeatedly "preaching to the converted."

The efforts of Merlin Tuttle and Bat Conservation International (BCI) illustrate how public attitudes toward even unpopular species can be changed. BCI has campaigned throughout the United States and the world to educate people on the importance of bats in ecosystem health, emphasizing their roles as insect eaters, pollinators, and seed dispersers. A valuable part of this effort has involved producing bat photographs and films of exceptional beauty. In Austin, Texas, Tuttle intervened when citizens petitioned the city government to exterminate the hundreds of thousands of Mexican freetail bats (*Tadarida brasiliensis*) that lived under a downtown bridge. He and his colleagues were able to convince people that the bats were both fun to watch and critical in controlling noxious insect populations over a wide area. The situation has changed so drastically that now the government protects the bats as a matter of civic

Figure 22.3 Citizens and tourists gather in the evening to watch bats emerge from their roosts on the underside of a bridge in Austin, Texas. Merlin Tuttle and his organization Bat Conservation International have successfully changed many people's opinions about bats, animals that are generally unpopular with the public. (Photograph by Merlin Tuttle, Bat Conservation International.)

pride and practical pest control, and citizens and tourists gather every night to watch the bats emerge from under the bridge on their nightly expeditions (Figure 22.3).

Conservation biologists must also become *politically active* and influence public policy. Involvement in the political process allows conservation biologists to influence the passage of new laws to support the preservation of biological diversity or to argue against legislation that would prove harmful to species or ecosystems (Brown 2000; Clark 2001). An important first step in this process is joining conservation organizations or mainstream political parties to gain strength by working in a group and to learn more about the issues. It is important to note that there is also room for people who prefer to work by themselves. Recent difficulties in getting the U.S. Congress to reauthorize the Endangered Species Act and to ratify the Convention on Biological Diversity and the Convention on Global Climate Change dramatically illustrate the need for greater political activism on the part of scientists who understand the implications of not taking action now. Though much of the political process is time-consuming and tedious, it is often the only way to accomplish major conservation goals such as acquiring new land for reserves or preventing overexploitation of old-growth forests. Conservation biologists need to master the language and methods of the legal process and form effective alliances with environmental lawyers, citizen groups, and politicians.

Conservation biologists need to become *organizers* within the scientific community. Many professional biologists in universities, colleges, museums, high schools, and government agencies concentrate their energies on the specialized needs of their professional niche. They may feel that their institutions want them to concentrate on "pure science" and "not get involved in politics." These biologists may not realize that the world's biological diversity is under imminent threat of destruction, and their contributions are urgently needed to save it (Huenneke 1995). Or they may imagine that they are too busy with career goals or too unimportant to get involved in the struggle. By stimulating interest in this problem among their colleagues, conservation biologists can increase the ranks of trained professional advocates fighting the destruction of natural resources; these professional biologists may also find their involvement to be personally and professionally beneficial, as their new interests may result in heightened scientific creativity and more inspired teaching.

Conservation biologists need to become *motivators,* convincing a range of people to support conservation efforts. At a local level, conservation programs have to be created and presented in ways that provide incentives for local people to support them. Local people need to be shown that protecting the environment not only saves species and biological communities but also improves the long-term health of their families, their own economic well-being, and their quality of life (WRI 1998; McMichael et al. 1999). Public discussions, education, and publicity need to be a major part of any such program. Careful attention must be devoted in particular to convincing business leaders and politicians to support conservation efforts. Many of these people will support conservation efforts when they are presented in the right way. Sometimes conservation is perceived to have good publicity value, or supporting it is perceived to be better than a confrontation that may otherwise result. National leaders may be among the most difficult people to convince, since they must respond to a diversity of interests. However, whether it is due to reason, sentiment, or professional self-interest, once converted to the conservation cause, these leaders may be in a position to make major contributions.

Finally, and most important, conservation biologists need to become effective *managers* and *practitioners* of conservation projects (Bohlen 1993; Sutherland 1998; Rabinowitz 2001). They must be willing to walk on the land and go out on the water to find out what is really happening, to get dirty, to talk with local people, to knock on doors, and to take risks. Conservation biologists must learn everything they can about the species and communities that they are trying to protect and then make that knowledge available to others (Clark 1999; Latta 2000). If conservation biologists are willing to put their ideas into practice, and to work with park managers, land-use planners, politicians, and local people, then progress will follow. Getting the right mix of models, new theories, innovative approaches, and practical examples is necessary for the success of the discipline. Once this balance is found, conservation biologists working with an energized citizenry will be in a position to protect the world's biological diversity during this unprecedented era of change.

Summary

1. There are major problems involved in protecting biological diversity; to address these problems, many changes must be made in policies and practices. These changes must occur at local, national, and international levels and require action on the part of individuals, conservation organizations, and governments.

2. Conservation biologists must demonstrate the validity of the theories and approaches of their new discipline and actively work with all components of society to protect biological diversity and restore the degraded elements of the environment.

For Discussion

1. Is conservation biology fundamentally different from other branches of biology such as physiology, genetics, or cell biology? Does conservation biology have underlying assumptions that are distinct from other fields of biology?

2. As a result of studying conservation biology, have you decided to change your lifestyle or your level of political activity? Do you think you can make a difference in the world, and if so, in what way?

3. Go to the library or search online to find articles that interest you in journals such as *Conservation Biology, Biological Diversity, BioScience, Biodiversity and Conservation, Ecological Applications,* and *National Geographic.* What is appealing about the articles you selected?

Suggested Readings

Barry, D. and M. Oelschlaeger. 1996. A science for survival: Values for conservation biology. *Conservation Biology* 10: 905–911. This excellent article and others, in a special section of this issue, assert that advocacy for the protection of biological diversity is an important part of the discipline.

Bohlen, J. T. 1993. *For the Wild Places: Profiles in Conservation.* Island Press, Washington, D.C. Patricia Chapple Wright, David Western, George Archibold, Louis Diego Gomez, and Rick Steiner have made major accomplishments in conservation.

Brown, K. 2000. Transforming a discipline: A new breed of scientist-advocate emerges. *Science* 287:1192–1193. Several articles in this issue describe how conservation biologists and ecologists are working with the government to affect policy.

Collett, J. and S. Karakashain (eds.). 1996. Greening the College Curriculum: A Guide to Environmental Teaching in the Liberal Arts. Island Press. Washington, D.C. Environmental and conservation issues can be a theme unifying many university courses and programs of study.

Ehrlich, A. H. and P. R. Ehrlich. 1996. *Betrayal of Science and Reason: How Anti-Environmental Rhetoric Threatens Our Future.* Island Press, Washington, D.C. Environmental arguments are being criticized and countered by strong arguments from groups favoring development.

Giono, J. 1989. *The Man Who Planted Trees.* Collins Dove, Melbourne, Australia. Simple, beautiful story about how one person can make a change in society.

Huenneke, L. F. 1995. Involving academic scientists in conservation research: Perspectives of a plant ecologist. *Ecological Applications* 5: 205–214. Academic scientists need to involve themselves in practical problems and the political process.

Meine, C. and R. L. Knight (eds.). 1999. *The Essential Aldo Leopold: Quotations and Commentaries.* University of Wisconsin Press, Madison, WI. Superb collection of Leopold quotations allows readers to follow the evolution of his conservation philosophy in a wide variety of areas.

Meffe, G. K. and C. R. Carroll. 1997. *Principles of Conservation Biology,* 2nd ed. Sinauer Associates, Sunderland, MA. Excellent advanced textbook.

Middleton, S. and D. Littschwager. 1994. *Witness: Endangered Species of North America.* Chronicle Books, San Francisco. Superb photographs; also watch this team on discussion-provoking video: *America's Endangered Species: Don't Say Good-Bye.* National Geographic Video. 1997. Directed by Robert Kenner.

Rabinowitz, A. 2001. *Beyond the Last Village. A Journey of Asia's Forbidden Wilderness.* Island Press, Washington, D.C. A personal account of wildlife research and conservation in a remote area of Burma.

Soulé, M. E. and G. H. Orians. (eds.). 2001. *Conservation Biology: Research Priorities for the Next Decade.* Island Press, Washington, D.C. Leaders in the field describe future directions for research and action.

Stearns, B. P. and S. C. Stearns. 1999. *Watching, from the Edge of Extinction.* Yale University Press, New Haven, CT. Captures the drama, excitement, and frustrations of conservation biologists involved in last-ditch efforts to save species.

Sutherland, W. J. (ed.). 1998. *Conservation Science and Action.* Blackwell Science, Oxford. Practical ways of conducting conservation projects.

Wilson, E. O. 1992. *The Diversity of Life.* Belknap Press, Cambridge, MA. The best popular book on the biodiversity crisis, eminently suitable to recommend or give to interested people.

Wolbarts, A. B. (ed.). 2001. *Solutions for an Environment in Peril.* The Johns Hopkins University Press, Baltimore, Maryland. How to deal with the environmental crisis.

APPENDIX
Selected Environmental Organizations and Sources of Information

The best single reference on conservation activities is the *Conservation Directory*, (www.nwf.org/conservationdirectory). This directory lists thousands of local, national, and international conservation organizations; conservation publications; and leaders in the field of conservation. Other publications of interest include *The Complete Guide to Environmental Careers in the 21st Century* (1998), published by Island Press, 1718 Connecticut Avenue N.W., Suite 300, Washington, D.C. 20009-1148; *Environmental Profiles: A Global Guide to Projects and People* (1993), published by Garland Publishing, 29 W. 35th Street, New York, NY 10001; and *World's Who's Who and Does What in Environment and Conservation* (1997), by N. Polunin and L. M. Curme, published by St. Martin's Press, New York. Additionally, the *Web of Science* (www.webofscience.com), available through libraries and online by subscription, provides a powerful way to search for published research by subject, author, and title.

The following is a list of some major organizations and resources:

American Zoo and Aquarium Association
8403 Colesville Road, Suite 710
Silver Spring, MD 20910-3314 U.S.A.
www.aza.org
  Preservation and propagation of captive wildlife.

Bern Convention Secretariat
Council of Europe
67075 Strasbourg-Cedex, France
www.nature.coe.int/english/cadres/bern.htm
  Conservation of the flora, fauna, and habitats of European nations.

BirdLife International
Wellbrook Court
Girton Road
Cambridge, CB3 0NA, U. K.
www.birdlife.org.uk
  Determines conservation status and priorities for birds throughout the world.

Center for Marine Conservation
1725 DeSales St., Suite 600
Washington, D.C. 20036 U.S.A.
www.oceanconservancy.org
  Focuses on marine wildlife and ocean and coastal habitats.

Convention on Biological Diversity Secretariat
Secretariat of the Convention on Biological Diversity
World Trade Centre
393 Saint Jacques Street, Office 300
Montreal, Quebec, Canada
H2Y 1N9
www.biodiv.org
  Promotes the goals of the CBD: sustainable development, biodiversity conservation, and equitable sharing of genetic resources.

CITES Secretariat of Wild Fauna and Flora
International Environment House
15 Chemin des Anémones
CH-1219 Châtelaine-Geneva, Switzerland
www.cites.org
Regulates trade in endangered species.

Conservation International
1919 M Street NW Suite 600
Washington, D.C. 20036
www.conservation.org
Active in conservation efforts and in working for sustainable development.

Earthwatch Institute
3 Clock Tower Place, Suite 100
P.O. Box 75
Maynard, MA 01754
www.earthwatch.org
Clearinghouse for international conservation projects in which volunteers can work with scientists.

European Center for Nature Conservation
P.O. Box 1352
5004 BJ Tilburg
The Netherlands
www.ecnc.nl
Provides the scientific expertise that is required for making conservation policy.

Environmental Data Research Institute
1655 Elmwood Ave., Suite 225
Rochester, NY 14620-3426 U.S.A.
Publishes *Environmental Granting Foundations,* a comprehensive guide to funding sources.

Environmental Defense
257 Park Avenue South
New York, NY 10010 U.S.A.
www.environmentaldefense.org
Involved in scientific, legal, and economic issues.

Fauna & Flora International
Great Eastern House
Tenison Road
Cambridge CB1 2TT U.K.
www.fauna-flora.org
Long-established international conservation body acting to protect species and ecosystems.

Food and Agriculture Organization of the United Nations
Viale delle Terme di Caracalla
00100 Rome, Italy
www.fao.org
A UN agency supporting sustainable agriculture, rural development, and resource management.

Friends of the Earth
1025 Vermont Avenue N.W.
Washington, D.C. 20005-6303 U.S.A.
www.foe.org
International organization working to improve and expand environmental public policy.

Global Environmental Facility Secretariat
1818 H Street, NW
Washington, D.C. 20433 U.S.A.
www.gefweb.org
Funds international biodiversity and environmental projects.

Greenpeace U.S.A.
702 H Street N.W. Suite 300
Washington, D.C. 20001 U.S.A.
www.greenpeace.org
Activist organization, known for grassroots efforts and dramatic protests against environmental damage.

International Union for the Conservation of Nature and Natural Resources (IUCN)
Rue Mauverney 28
CH-1196, Gland, Switzerland
www.iucn.org
> This is the premier coordinating body for international conservation efforts. Produces directories of specialists and the Red Lists of endangered species.

Missouri Botanical Garden/Center for Plant Conservation
P.O. Box 299
St. Louis, MO 63166-0299 U.S.A.
www.mobot.org
> Major centers for worldwide plant conservation activities.

National Audubon Society
700 Broadway
New York, N.Y. 10003 U.S.A.
www.audubon.org
> Extensive program, including wildlife conservation, public education, research, and political lobbying.

National Council for Science and the Environment (NCSE)
1725 K Street, N.W., Suite 212
Washington, DC 20006-1401 U.S.A.
www.cnie.org
> Formerly the Committee for the National Institute for the Environment. Works to improve the scientific basis for environmental decision making; their website provides extensive environmental information.

National Wildlife Federation
11100 Wildlife Center Drive
Reston, VA 20190-5362 U.S.A.
www.nwf.org
> Advocates for wildlife conservation. Publishes the *Conservation Directory*, as well as the outstanding children's publications *Ranger Rick* and *Your Big Backyard*.

Natural Resources Defense Council
40 West 20th Street
New York, NY 10011 U.S.A.
www.nrdc.org
> Uses legal and scientific methods to monitor and influence government actions and legislation.

The Nature Conservancy (TNC)
International Headquarters
4245 North Fairfax Drive, Suite 100
Arlington, VA 22203-1606 U.S.A.
www.nature.org
> Emphasizes land preservation. Maintains extensive records on rare species distribution in the Americas, particularly North America.

The New York Botanical Garden/Institute for Economic Botany
200th Street and Kazimiroff Boulevard
Bronx, NY 10458 U.S.A.
www.nybg.org
> Conducts research and conservation programs involving plants that are useful to people.

Rainforest Action Network
221 Pine Street, Suite 500
San Francisco, CA 94104 U.S.A.
www.ran.org
> Works actively for rain forest conservation and human rights.

The Ramsar Convention Bureau
Rue Mauverney 28
CH-1196 Gland, Switzerland
www.ramsar.org
> Promotes international conservation of wetlands.

Royal Botanic Gardens, Kew
Richmond Surrey TW9 3AB, United Kingdom
www.rbgkew.org.uk
> The famous "Kew Gardens" are home to a leading botanical research institute and an enormous plant collection.

Sierra Club
85 Second Street, Second Floor
San Francisco, CA 94105-3441 U.S.A.
www.sierraclub.org
> Leading advocate for the preservation of wilderness and open space.

Smithsonian Institution/National Zoological Park
3001 Connecticut Ave., N.W.
Washington, D.C. 20008 U.S.A.
www.natzoo.si.edu
> The National Zoo and the nearby U.S. National Museum of Natural History represent a vast resource of literature, biological materials, and skilled professionals.

Society for Conservation Biology
4245 N Fairfax Drive
Arlington, VA 22203 U.S.A.
www.conbio.net/scb
> Leading scientific society for the field. Develops and publicizes new ideas and scientific results through the journal *Conservation Biology*.

Student Conservation Association (SCA)
689 River Road P.O. Box 550
Charlestown, NH 03603
www.sca-inc.org
> Places volunteers and interns with conservation organizations and public agencies.

United Nations Development Programme (UNDP)
One United Nations Plaza
New York, NY 10017 U.S.A.
www.undp.org
> Funds and coordinates international economic development activities, particularly those that use natural resources in a responsible way.

United Nations Environment Programme (UNEP)
United Nations Avenue, Gigiri
P.O. Box 30552, Nairobi, Kenya
www.unep.org
> International program of research and management relating to major environmental problems.

United States Fish and Wildlife Service
Department of the Interior
1849 C Street N.W.
Washington, D.C. 20240 U.S.A.
www.fws.gov
> The leading U.S. government agency in the conservation of endangered species, with a vast research and management network. Major activities also take place within other federal government units, such as the National Marine Fisheries Service and the U.S. Forest Service. The Agency for International Development is active in many developing nations. Individual state governments have comparable units, with National Heritage programs being especially relevant. The *Conservation Directory*, mentioned above, shows how these units are organized.

Wetlands International
P.O. Box 471
6700 AL Wageningen
The Netherlands
www.wetlands.org
> Focus on the conservation and sustainable management of wetlands.

The Wilderness Society
1615 M Street N.W.
Washington D.C. 20036 U.S.A.
www.tws.org
  Organization devoted to preserving wilderness and wildlife.

Wildlife Conservation Society/New York Zoological Society
2300 Southern Boulevard
Bronx, NY 10460-1099 U.S.A.
www.wcs.org
  Leaders in wildlife conservation and research.

World Bank
1818 H Street N.W.
Washington, D.C. 20433 U.S.A.
www.worldbank.org
  A multinational bank involved in economic development; increasingly concerned with environmental issues.

World Conservation Monitoring Centre (WCMC)
Information Office
219 Huntingdon Road
Cambridge CB3 0DL, United Kingdom
www.unep-wcmc.org
  Monitors global wildlife trade, the status of endangered species, natural resource use, and protected areas.

World Resources Institute (WRI)
10 G Street N.E., Suite 800
Washington, D.C. 20002 U.S.A.
www.wri.org
  Research center producing excellent papers on environmental, conservation, and development topics.

World Wildlife Fund (WWF)
1250 Twenty-Fourth Street N.W.
P.O. Box 97180
Washington, D.C. 20077-7180 U.S.A.
www.worldwildlife.org or www.wwf.org
  Major conservation organization, with branches throughout the world. Active both in research and in the management of national parks.

Xerces Society
4828 Southeast Hawthorne Boulevard
Portland, OR 97215-3252 U.S.A.
www.xerces.org
  Focuses on the conservation of insects and other invertebrates.

Zoological Society of London
Regent's Park
London NW1 4RY, U. K.
www.zsl.org
  Center for worldwide activities to preserve nature.

Bibliography

Abbitt, R. J. F. and J. M. Scott. 2001. Examining differences between recovered and declining endangered species. *Conservation Biology* 15: 1274–1284.

Abbitt, R. J. F., J. M. Scott, and D. S. Wilcove. 2000. The geography of vulnerability: incorporating species geography and human development patterns into conservation planning. *Biological Conservation* 96: 169–175.

Abensperg-Traun, M. and G. T. Smith. 1999. How small is too small for small animals? Four terrestrial arthropod species in different-sized remnant woodlands in agricultural Western Australia. *Biodiversity and Conservation* 8: 709–726.

Adams, D. and M. Carwardine. 1990. *Last Chance to See.* Harmony Books, New York.

Agardy, T. 1999. Creating havens for marine life. *Issues in Science and Technology* 16: 37–44.

Agardy, T. S. 1997. *Marine Protected Areas and Ocean Conservation.* R. G. Landes Company, Austin, TX.

Aguirre, A. A. and E. E. Starkey. 1994. Wildlife disease in U.S. National Parks: Historical and coevolutionary perspectives. *Conservation Biology* 8: 654–661.

Akçakaya, H. R. 1990. Bald ibis *Geronticus eremita* population in Turkey: An evaluation of the captive breeding project for reintroduction. *Biological Conservation* 51: 225–237.

Akçakaya, H. R., M. A. Burgman, and L. R. Ginzburg. 1997. *Applied Population Ecology: Using RAMAS® EcoLab.* Applied Biomathematics, Setauket, NY.

Akçakaya, H. R., M. A. Burgman, and L. R. Ginzburg. 1999. *Applied Population Ecology: Principles and Computer Exercises Using RAMAS® EcoLab.* Sinauer Associates, Sunderland, MA.

Alcock, J. 2002. *Animal Behavior: An Evolutionary Approach*, 6th ed. Sinauer Associates, Sunderland, MA.

Alcorn, J. B. 1984. Development policy, forests and peasant farms: Reflections on Huastec-managed forests' contributions to commercial production and resource conservation. *Economic Botany* 38: 389–406.

Alcorn, J. B. 1991. Ethics, economies and conservation. *In* M. L. Oldfield and J. B. Alcorn (eds.), *Biodiversity: Culture, Conservation and Ecodevelopment*, pp. 317–349. Westview Press, Boulder, CO.

Alcorn, J. B. 1993. Indigenous peoples and conservation. *Conservation Biology* 7: 424–426.

Alford, R. A. and S. J. Richards. 1999. Global amphibian declines: A problem in applied ecology. *Annual Review of Ecology and Systematics* 30: 133–165.

Alford, R. A., P. M. Dixon, and J. H. K. Pechmann. 2001. Global amphibian population declines. *Nature* 412: 499–500.

Allan, T. and A. Warren (eds.). 1993. *Deserts, the Encroaching Wilderness: A World Conservation Atlas.* Oxford University Press, London.

Allen, C., R. S. Lutz, and S. Demarais. 1995. Red imported fire ant impacts on Northern bobwhite populations. *Ecological Applications* 5: 632–638.

Allen, E. B., J. S. Brown, and M. F. Allen. 2001. Restoration of animal, plant, and microbial diversity. *In* S. A. Levin (ed.), *Encyclopedia of Biodiversity,* 5: 185–202. Academic Press, San Diego, CA.

Allen, M. F., E. B. Allen, T. A. Zink, S. Harney, et al. 1999. Soil microorganisms. *In* L. R. Walker (ed.), *Ecosystems of Disturbed Ground, Ecosystems of the World 16*, pp. 521–544. Elsevier Press, Amsterdam.

Allen, W. H. 1988. Biocultural restoration of a tropical forest: Architects of Costa Rica's emerging Guanacaste National Park plan to make it an integral part of local culture. *BioScience* 38: 156–161.

Allendorf, F. W. and R. F. Leary. 1986. Heterozygosity and fitness in natural populations of animals. *In* M. E. Soulé (ed.), *Conservation Biology: The Science of Scarcity and Diversity*, pp. 57–76. Sinauer Associates, Sunderland, MA.

Alpert, P. 1995. Applying ecological research at integrated conservation and development projects. *Ecological Applications* 5: 857–861.

Altieri, M. A. and M. K. Anderson. 1992. Peasant farming systems, agricultural modernization and the conservation of crop genetic resources in Latin America. *In* P. L. Fiedler and S. K. Jain (eds.), *Conservation Biology: The Theory and Practice of Nature Conservation, Preservation and Management*, pp. 49–64. Chapman and Hall, New York.

Alverson, W. S., W. Kuhlmann, and D. M. Waller. 1994. *Wild Forests: Conservation Biology and Public Policy.* Island Press, Washington, D.C.

Ames, M. H. 1991. Saving some cetaceans may require breeding in captivity. *BioScience* 41: 746–749.

Anderson, J. G. T. and C. M. Devlin. 1999. Restoration of a multi-species seabird colony. *Biological Conservation* 90: 175–181.

Antonovics, J. 1976. The nature of limits to natural selection. *Annals of the Missouri Botanical Garden* 63: 224–247.

Araujo, R. and M. A. Ramos. 2000. Status and conservation of the giant European freshwater pearl mussel (*Margaritifera auricularia*) (Spengler, 1793) (Bivalvia: Unionoidea). *Biological Conservation* 96: 233–239.

Arita, H. T., J. G. Robinson, and K. H. Redford. 1990. Rarity in Neotropical forest mammals and its ecological correlates. *Conservation Biology* 4: 181–192.

Armbruster, P. and R. Lande. 1993. A population viability analysis for African elephant (*Loxodonta africana*): How big should reserves be? *Conservation Biology* 7: 602–610.

Armstrong, S. and R. Botzler (eds.). 1998. *Environmental Ethics: Divergence and Convergence*. McGraw-Hill, New York.

Arnold, A. E., Z. Maynard, G. Gilbert, P. D. Coley, and T. A. Kursar. 2000. Are tropical fungal endophytes hyperdiverse? *Ecology Letters* 3: 267–274.

Arnolds, E. 1991. Decline of ectomycorrhizal fungi in Europe. *Agriculture Ecosystems and Environment* 35: 209–244.

Aron, J. L. and J. A. Patz (eds.). 2001. *Ecosystem Change and Public Health: A Global Perspective*. The John Hopkins University Press, Baltimore, Maryland.

Arrow, K., B. Bolin, R. Costanza, P. Dasgupta, C. Folke, et al. 1995. Economic growth, carrying capacity and the environment. *Science* 268: 520–522.

Ashley, M. V., D. J. Melnick, and D. Western. 1990. Conservation genetics of the black rhinoceros (*Diceros bicornis*). 1. Evidence from the mitochondrial DNA of three populations. *Conservation Biology* 4: 71–77.

Askins, R. A. 2000. *Restoring North America's Birds: Lessons from Landscape Ecology*. Yale University Press, New Haven, CT.

Attwell, C. A. M. and F. P. D. Cotterill. 2000. Postmodernism and African conservation science. *Biodiversity and Conservation* 9: 559–577.

Avise, J. C. and J. L. Hamrick (eds.). 1996. *Conservation Genetics: Case Histories from Nature*. Chapman and Hall, New York.

Ayres, E. 1999. *God's Last Offer: Negotiating for a Sustainable Future*. Four Walls Eight Windows, New York.

Baker, C. S. and S. R. Palumbi. 1994. Which whales are hunted? A molecular genetic approach to monitoring whaling. *Science* 265: 1538–1539.

Baldwin, A. D., J. de Luca, and C. Pletsch (eds.). 1994. *Beyond Preservation: Restoring and Inventing Landscapes*. University of Minnesota Press, Minneapolis, MN.

Balick, M. J. and P. A. Cox. 1996. *Plants, People and Culture: The Science of Ethnobotany*. Scientific American Library, New York.

Balick, M. J., E. Elisabetsky, and S. A. Laird (eds.). 1996. *Medicinal Resources of the Tropical Forest: Biodiversity and Its Importance to Human Health*. Columbia University Press, New York.

Balmford, A. 1996. Extinction filters and current resilience: The significance of past selection pressures for conservation biology. *Trends in Ecology and Evolution* 11: 193–196.

Balmford, A. and A. Long. 1994. Avian endemism and forest loss. *Nature* 372: 623–624.

Balmford, A. and K. J. Gaston. 1999. Why biodiversity surveys are good value. *Nature* 398: 204–205.

Balmford, A., G. M. Mace, and N. Leader-Williams. 1996. Designing the ark: Setting priorities for captive breeding. *Conservation Biology* 10: 719–728.

Baltz, D. M. 1991. Introduced fishes in marine systems and inland seas. *Biological Conservation* 56: 151–177.

Barbier, E. B. 1993. Valuation of environmental resources and impacts in developing countries. *In* R. K. Turner (ed.), *Sustainable Environmental Economics and Management*, pp. 319–337. Belhaven Press, New York.

Barbier, E. B., J. C. Burgess, and C. Folke. 1994. *Paradise Lost? The Ecological Economics of Biodiversity*. Earthscan Publications, London.

Barinaga, M. 1995. New study provides some good news for fisheries. *Science* 269: 1043.

Barrett, C. B., K. Brandon, C. Gibson, and H. Gjertsen. 2001. Conserving tropical biodiversity amid weak institutions. *BioScience* 51: 497–502.

Barrett, S. C. H. and J. R. Kohn. 1991. Genetic and evolutionary consequences of small population size in plants: Implications for conservation. *In* D. A. Falk and K. E. Holsinger (eds.), *Genetics and Conservation of Rare Plants*, pp. 3–30. Oxford University Press, New York.

Barry, D. and M. Oelschlaeger. 1996. A science for survival: Values for conservation biology. *Conservation Biology* 10: 905–911.

Baskin, Y. 1994. There's a new wildlife policy in Kenya: Use it or lose it. *Science* 265: 733–734.

Baskin, Y. 1997. *The Work of Nature: How the Diversity of Life Sustains Us*. Island Press, Washington, D.C.

Bassett, L. (ed.). 2000. *Faith and Earth: A Book of Reflection for Action*. United Nations Environment Programme, New York.

Batisse, M. 1997. A challenge for biodiversity conservation and regional development. *Environment* 39: 7–33.

Bawa, K. S. 1990. Plant-pollinator interactions in tropical rainforests. *Annual Review of Ecology and Systematics* 21: 399–422.

Bawa, K. S. and A. Markham. 1995. Climate change and tropical forests. *Trends in Ecology and Evolution* 10: 348–349.

Bawa, K. S. and S. Dayanandan. 1997. Socioeconomic factors and tropical deforestation. *Nature* 386: 562–563.

Bawa, K. S. and S. Menon. 1997. Biodiversity monitoring: The missing ingredients. *Trends in Ecology and Evolution* 12: 42.

Bawa, K. S., S. Lele, K. S. Murali, and B. Ganesan. 1998. Extraction of non-timber forest products in Biligiri Rangan Hills, India: Monitoring of a community-based project. *In* K. Saterson, R. Margolis, and N. Salafsky (eds.), *Measuring Conservation Impact: Proceedings from a Symposium at the 1996 Joint Meeting of the Society for Conservation Biology and the Ecological Society of America, Providence, RI*. Biodiversity Support Program, Washington, D.C.

Bax, N., J. T. Carlton, A. Mathews-Amos, R. L. Haedrich, F. G. Howarth, et al. 2001. The control of biological invasions in the world's oceans. *Conservation Biology* 15: 1234–1246.

Bazzaz, F. A. and E. D. Fajer. 1992. Plant life in a CO_2–rich world. *Scientific American* 266(1): 68–74.

Bean, M. J. 1999. Endangered species, endangered act? *Environment* 41: 13–38.

Bean, M. J. and L. E. Dwyer. 2000. Mitigation banking as an endangered species conservation tool. *ELR News and Analysis* 30: 10537–10556.

Beccaloni, G. W. and K. J. Gaston. 1995. Predicting the species richness of neotropical forest butterflies: Ithomiinae (*Lepidoptera nymphalidae*) as indicators. *Biological Conservation* 71: 77–86.

Beck, B. B., L. G. Rapport, M. R. Stanley Price, and A. C. Wilson. 1994. Reintroduction of captive-born animals. *In* P. J. Olney, G. M. Mace, and A. T. C. Feistner (eds.), *Creative Conservation: Interactive Management of Wild and Captive Animals*, pp. 265–286. Chapman and Hall, London.

Beddington, J. 2001. Resource exploitation, fisheries. *In* S. A. Levin (ed.), *Encyclopedia of Biodiversity*, 5: 161–172. Academic Press, San Diego, CA.

Beebee, T. J. C. 1996. *Ecology and Conservation of Amphibians*. Chapman and Hall, London.

Béland, P. 1996. The beluga whales of the St. Lawrence River. *Scientific American* 274(5): 74–81.

Benitez-Malvido, J. 1998. Impact of forest fragmentation on seedling abundance in a tropical rain forest. *Conservation Biology* 12: 380–389.

Bennett, A. F. 1999. *Linkages in the Landscape: The Role of Corridors and Connectivity in Wildlife Conservation*. IUCN, Gland, Switzerland.

Bennett, E. L. and J. G. Robinson. 2000. *Hunting of Wildlife in Tropical Forests: Implications for Biodiversity and Forest Peoples*. The World Bank, Washington, D.C.

Benstead, J. P., J. G. March, and C. M. Pringle. 2000. Estuarine larval development and upstream post-larval migration of freshwater shrimps in two tropical rivers of Puerto Rico. *Biotropica* 32: 545–548.

Benz, B. F., L. R. Sánchez-Velásquez, and F. J. Santana Michel. 1990. Ecology and ethnobotany of *Zea diploperennis*: Preliminary investigations. *Maydica* 35: 85–98.

Berger, J. 1990. Persistence of different-sized populations: An empirical assessment of rapid extinctions in bighorn sheep. *Conservation Biology* 4: 91–98.

Berger, J. 1999. Intervention and persistence in small populations of bighorn sheep. *Conservation Biology* 13: 432–435.

Berger, J., P. B. Stacey, L. Bellis, and M. P. Johnson. 2001. A mammalian predator-prey imbalance: Grizzly bear and wolf extinction affect neotropical migrants. *Ecological Applications* 11: 947–960.

Berkes, F. 1999. *Sacred Ecology. Traditional Ecological Knowledge and Resource Management*. Taylor and Francis, Philadelphia and London.

Berkes, F. 2001. Religious traditions and biodiversity. *In* S. A. Levin (ed.), *Encyclopedia of Biodiversity*, 5: 109–120. Academic Press, San Diego, CA.

Berkes, F. and C. Folke (eds.). 2000. *Linking Social and Ecological Systems: Management Practices and Social Mechanisms for Building Resilience*. Cambridge University Press, New York.

Berkes, F., J. Colding, and C. Folke. 2000. Rediscovery of traditional ecological knowledge as adaptive management. *Ecological Applications* 10: 1251–1262.

Bernow, S., R. Costanza, H. Daly, R. DeGennaro, et al. 1998. Ecological tax reform. *BioScience* 48: 193–196.

Bibby, C. J. 1992. *Putting Biodiversity on the Map: Priority Areas for Global Conservation*. International Council for Bird Preservation, Cambridge.

Bierregaard, R. O., T. E. Lovejoy, V. Kapos, A. A. Dos Santos, and R. W. Hutchings. 1992. The biological dynamics of tropical rainforest fragments. *BioScience* 42: 859–866.

Biggins, D. E., A. Vargas, J. L. Godbey, and S. H. Anderson. 1999. Influence of prerelease experience on reintroduced black-footed ferrets (*Mustela nigripes*). *Biological Conservation* 89: 121–129.

Billington, H. L. 1991. Effect of population size on genetic variation in a dioecious conifer. *Conservation Biology* 5: 115–119.

Birkeland, C. (ed.). 1997. *The Life and Death of Coral Reefs*. Chapman and Hall, New York.

Bisby, F. A. 2000. The quiet revolution: Biodiversity informatics and the internet. *Science* 289: 2309–2314.

Blaustein, A. R. and D. B. Wake. 1995. The puzzle of declining amphibian populations. *Scientific American* 272(4): 52–57.

Bleich, V. C., J. D. Wehausen, and S. A. Holl. 1990. Desert-dwelling mountain sheep: Conservation implications of a naturally fragmented distribution. *Conservation Biology* 4: 383–389.

Bodmer, R. E., J. F. Eisenberg, and K. H. Redford. 1997. Hunting and the likelihood of extinction of Amazonian mammals. *Conservation Biology* 11: 460–466.

Boersma, P. D. and J. K. Parrish. 1999. Limiting abuse: Marine protected areas, a limited solution. *Ecological Economics* 31: 287–304.

Boersma, P. D., P. Kareiva, W. F. Fagan, J. A. Clark, and J. M. Hoekstra. 2001. How good are endangered species recovery plans? *BioScience* 51: 643–649.

Bohlen, J. T. 1993. *For the Wild Places: Profiles in Conservation*. Island Press, Washington, D.C.

Boice, L. P. 1996. Endangered species management on U.S. Air Force lands. *Endangered Species Update* 13: 6–7.

Boucher, G. and P. J. D. Lambshead. 1995. Ecological biodiversity of marine nematodes in samples from temperate, tropical and deep-sea regions. *Conservation Biology* 9: 1594–1605.

Bouchet, P., G. Falkner, and M. B. Seddon. 1999. Lists of protected land and freshwater molluscs in the Bern Convention and European Habitats Directive: Are they relevant to conservation? *Biological Conservation* 90: 21–31.

Bowers, J. 1999. Policy instruments for the conservation of remnant vegetation on private land. *Biological Conservation* 87: 327–339.

Bowles, I. A. and G. T. Prickett. 1994. *Reframing the Green Window: An Analysis of the GEF Pilot Phase Approach to Biodiversity and Global Warming and Recommendations for the Operational Phase.* Conservation International/National Resources Defense Council, Washington, D.C.

Bowles, M. L. and C. J. Whelan. 1994. *Restoration of Endangered Species: Conceptual Issues, Planning and Implementation.* Cambridge University Press, Cambridge.

Bradbury, R. B., R. J. H. Payne, J. D. Wilson, and J. R. Krebs. 2001. Predicting population responses to resource management. *Trends in Ecology and Evolution* 16: 440–445.

Bradshaw, A. D. 1990. The reclamation of derelict land and the ecology of ecosystems. *In* W. R. Jordan III, M. E. Gilpin, and J. D. Aber (eds.), *Restoration Ecology: A Synthetic Approach to Ecological Research*, pp. 53–74. Cambridge University Press, Cambridge.

Braithwaite, R. W. 2001. Tourism, role of. *In* S. A. Levin (ed.), *Encyclopedia of Biodiversity*. 5: 667–679. Academic Press, San Diego, CA.

Brandon, K., K. H. Redford, and S. E. Sanderson, (eds.). 1998. *Parks in Peril: People, Politics and Protected Areas.* Island Press, Washington, D.C.

Briggs, J. C. 1995. *Global Biogeography.* Elsevier, Amsterdam.

Briscoe, D. A., J. M. Malpica, A. Robertson, G. J. Smith, et al. 1992. Rapid loss of genetic variation in large captive populations of *Drosophila* flies: Implications for the genetic management of captive populations. *Conservation Biology* 6: 416–425.

Brooks, T. M., S. L. Pimm, and J. O. Oyugi. 1999. Time lag between deforestation and bird extinction in tropical forest fragments. *Conservation Biology* 13: 1140–1150.

Brooks, T. M., A. Balmford, N. Burgess, J. Fjeldså, et al. 2001. Toward a blueprint for conservation in Africa. *Bioscience* 51: 613–624.

Brower, A., C. Reedy, and J. Yelin-Kefers. 2001. Consensus versus conservation in the Upper Colorado River Basin recovery implementation program. *Conservation Biology* 15: 1001–1007.

Brown, G. M. 1993. The economic value of elephants. *In* E. B. Barbier (ed.), *Economics and Ecology: New Frontiers in Sustainable Development*, pp. 146–155. Chapman and Hall, London.

Brown, K. S. 2000. Transforming a discipline: A new breed of scientist-advocate emerges. *Science* 287: 1192–1193.

Brownlow, C. A. 1996. Molecular taxonomy and the conservation of the red wolf and other endangered carnivores. *Conservation Biology* 10: 390–396.

Bruner, A. G., R. E. Gullison, R. E. Rice, and G. A. B. da Fonseca. 2001. Effectiveness of parks in protecting tropical biodiversity. *Science* 291: 125–128.

Brush, S. B. and D. Stabinsky (eds.). 1996. *Valuing Local Knowledge: Indigenous People and Intellectual Property Rights.* Island Press, Washington, D.C.

Bryant, D., D. Nelson, and L. Tangley. 1997. *The Last Frontier Forests: Ecosystems and Economies on the Edge.* World Resources Institute, Washington, D.C.

Buchmann, S. L. and G. P. Nabhan. 1997. *The Forgotten Pollinators.* Island Press, Washington, D.C.

Buck, L. E., C. C. Geisler, J. Schelhas, and E. Wollenberg. 2001. *Biological Diversity: Balancing Interests through Adaptive Collaborative Management.* CRC Press LLL, Tampa, Florida.

Buck, S. J. 1996. *Understanding Environmental Administration and Law.* Island Press, Washington, D.C.

Bulte, E. H. and G. C. van Kooten. 2000. Economic science, endangered species, and biodiversity loss. *Conservation Biology* 14: 113–119.

Bulte, E. H. and G. C. van Kooten. 2001. State intervention to protect endangered species: Why history and bad luck matter. *Conservation Biology* 15: 1799–1803.

Burbidge, A. A. and N. L. McKenzie. 1989. Patterns in the modern decline of Western Australia's vertebrate fauna: Causes and conservation implications. *Biological Conservation* 50: 143–198.

Burger, J. 2000. Integrating environmental restoration: Long-term stewardship at the Department of Energy. *Environmental Management* 26: 469–478.

Burks, D. C. (ed.). 1994. *Place of the Wild: A Wildlands Anthology.* Island Press/Shearwater, Washington, D.C.

Burrill, A., I. Douglas-Hamilton, and J. MacKinnon. 1986. Protected areas as refuges for elephants. *In* J. MacKinnon and K. MacKinnon (eds.), *Protected Areas Systems Review of the Afrotropical Realm*, IUCN, Gland, Switzerland.

Bush, G. L. 2001. Speciation, process of. *In* S. A. Levin (ed.), *Encyclopedia of Biodiversity*, 5: 371–382. Academic Press, San Diego, CA.

Buzas, M. A. and S. J. Culver. 1991. Species diversity and dispersal of benthic Foraminifera. *BioScience* 41: 483–489.

Cabeza, M. and A. Moilanen. 2001. Design of reserve networks and the persistence of biodiversity. *Trends in Ecology and Evolution* 16: 242–248.

Cade, T. J., J. H. Endersone, C. G. Thelander, and C. M. White (eds.). 1998. *Peregrine Falcon Populations: Their Management and Recovery.* The Peregrine Fund, Boise, ID.

Cairns, J. and J. R. Heckman. 1996. Restoration ecology: The state of an emerging field. *Annual Review of Energy and the Environment* 21: 167–189.

Caldecott, J. 1988. *Hunting and Wildlife Management in Sarawak.* IUCN, Gland, Switzerland.

Caldecott, J. 1996. *Designing Conservation Projects.* Cambridge University Press, Cambridge.

Callicott, J. B. 1990. Whither conservation ethics? *Conservation Biology* 4: 15–20.

Callicott, J. B. 1994. *Earth's Insights: A Multicultural Survey of Ecological Ethics from the Mediterranean Basin to the Australian Outback.* University of California Press, Berkeley, CA.

Canby, T. Y. 1993. Bacteria: Teaching old bugs new tricks. *National Geographic* 184(August): 36–60.

Carey, A. B. 2000. Effects of new forest management strategies on squirrel populations. *Ecological Applications* 10: 248–257.

Carlton, J. T. 2001. Endangered marine invertebrates. *In* S. A. Levin (ed.), *Encyclopedia of Biodiversity*, 2: 455–464. Academic Press, San Diego, CA.

Carlton, J. T. and J. B. Geller. 1993. Ecological roulette: The global transport of nonindigenous marine organisms. *Science* 261: 78–82.

Carlton, J. T., J. B. Geller, M. L. Reaka-Kudla, and E. A. Norse. 1999. Historical extinction in the sea. *Annual Review of Ecology and Systematics* 30: 515–538.

Carroll, C. R. 1992. Ecological management of sensitive natural areas. *In* P. L. Fiedler and S. K. Jain (eds.), *Conservation Biology: The Theory and Practice of Nature Conservation, Preservation and Management*, pp. 347–372. Chapman and Hall, New York.

Carroll, C. R., C. Augspurger, A. Dobson, J. Franklin, et al. 1996. Strengthening the use of science in achieving the goals of the Endangered Species Act: An assessment by the Ecological Society of America. *Ecological Applications* 6: 1–12.

Carson, R. 1962. *Silent Spring*. Reprinted 1982 by Penguin, Harmondsworth, UK.

Carte, B. K. 1996. Biomedical potential of marine natural products: Marine organisms are yielding novel molecules for use in basic research and medical applications. *BioScience* 46: 271–286.

Castelletta, M., N. S. Sodhi, and R. Subaraj. 2000. Heavy extinctions of forest avifauna in Singapore: Lessons for biodiversity conservation in Southeast Asia. *Conservation Biology* 14: 1870–1880.

Castro, G., I. Locker, V. Russell, L. Cornwell, and E. Fajer. 2000. *Mapping Conservation Investments: An Assessment of Biodiversity Funding in Latin America and the Caribbean*. World Wildlife Fund, Inc., Washington, D.C.

Caswell, H. 2001. *Matrix Population Models*, 2nd ed. Sinauer Associates. Sunderland, MA.

Caughley, G. and A. Gunn. 1996. *Conservation Biology in Theory and Practice*. Blackwell Science, Malden, MA.

Caulfield, C. 1985. *In the Rainforest*. Alfred A. Knopf, New York.

Ceballos-Lascuráin, H. (ed.). 1993. *Tourism and Protected Areas*. IUCN, Gland, Switzerland.

Center for Plant Conservation. 1991. Genetic sampling guidelines for conservation collections of endangered plants. *In* D. A. Falk and K. E. Holsinger (eds.), *Genetics and Conservation of Rare Plants*, pp. 224–238. Oxford University Press, New York.

Chadwick, D. H. 1993. American prairie: Roots of the sky. *National Geographic* 184(October): 90–119.

Chadwick, D. H. 1995. Dead or alive: The Endangered Species Act. *National Geographic* 187(March): 2–41.

Chadwick, D. H. 1996. Sanctuary: U.S. National Wildlife Refuges. *National Geographic* 190(October): 2–35.

Chapin III, F. S., O. E. Sala, I. C. Burke, J. P. Grime, et al. 1998. Ecosystem consequences of changing biodiversity. *BioScience* 48: 45–52.

Chapin, F. S., E. S. Zavaleta, V. T. Eviner, R. L. Naylor, et al. 2000. Consequences of changing biodiversity. *Nature* 405: 234–242.

Chapman, C. A. and C. A. Peres. 2001. Primate conservation in the new millennium: The role of scientists. *Evolutionary Anthropology* 10: 16–33.

Chapman, C. A., S. R. Balcomb, T. R. Gillespie, J. P. Skorupa, and T. T. Struhsaker. 2000. Long-term effects of logging on African primate communities: A 28-year comparison from Kibale National Park, Uganda. *Conservation Biology* 14: 207–217.

Chau, K. 1995. The Three Gorges Project of China: Resettlement prospects and problems. *Ambio* 24: 98–102.

Chen, L. Y. 2001. Cost savings from properly managing endangered species habitats. *Natural Areas Journal* 21: 197–203.

Cherfas, J. 1991. Disappearing mushrooms: Another mass extinction? *Science* 254: 1458.

Cherfas, J. 1993. Backgarden biodiversity. *Conservation Biology* 7: 6–7.

Cherfas, J. 1996. Forbidden fruit and vegetables. *Plant Talk* 5: 17–19.

Chernela, J. 1987. Endangered ideologies: Tukano fishing taboos. *Cultural Survival Quarterly* 11: 50–52.

Chester, C. C. 1996. Controversy over the Yellowstone's biological resources. *Environment* 38: 10–15, 34–36.

Chicago Regional Biodiversity Council. 2001. *Chicago Wilderness, An Atlas of Biodiversity*. Chicago Regional Biodiversity Council, Chicago, IL.

Chichilnisky, G. 1996. The economic value of Earth's resources. *Trends in Ecology and Evolution* 11: 135–140.

Chown, S. L. and K. J. Gaston. 2000. Areas, cradles and museums: the latitudinal gradient in species richness. *Trends in Ecology and Evolution* 15: 311–315.

Christen, C. A. and J. Allen. 2001. *A Vested Interest: BSP Experiences with Developing and Managing Grant Portfolios*. World Wildlife Fund, Inc., Washington, D.C.

Christensen, N. L., A. M. Bartuska, J. H. Brown, S. Carpenter, et al. 1996. The report of the Ecological Society of America Committee on the scientific basis for ecosystem management. *Ecological Applications* 6: 665–691.

Chu, E. W. and J. R. Karr. 2001. Environmental impact, concept and measurement of. *In* S. A. Levin (ed.), *Encyclopedia of Biodiversity*, 2: 557–577. Academic Press, San Diego, CA.

Cincotta, R. P. and R. Engelman. 2000. *Nature's Place: Human Population and the Future of Biological Diversity*. Population Action International, Washington, D.C.

Cincotta, R. P., J. Wisnewski, and R. Engelman. 2000. Human population in biodiversity hotspots. *Nature* 404: 990–992.

Clark, C. 1992. Empirical evidence for the effect of tropical deforestation on climatic change. *Environmental Conservation* 19: 39–47.

Clark, J. R. 1999. The ecosystem approach from a practical point of view. *Conservation Biology* 13: 679–681.

Clark, T. W. 2001. Developing policy-oriented curricula for conservation biology: Professional and leadership education in the public interest. *Conservation Biology* 15: 31–39.

Clark, W. C. 1989. Managing planet Earth. *Scientific American* 261(3): 47–54.

Clay, J. 1991. Cultural survival and conservation: Lessons from the past twenty years. *In* M. L. Oldfield and J. B. Alcorn (eds.), *Biodiversity: Culture, Conservation and Ecodevelopment*, pp. 248–273. Westview Press, Boulder, CO.

Clemmons, J. R. and R. Buchholz (eds.). 1997. *Behavioral Approaches to Conservation in the Wild*. Cambridge University Press, New York.

Clewell, A. and J. Rieger. 1997. What practitioners need from restoration ecologists. *Restoration Ecology* 5: 350–354.

Coblentz, B. E. 1990. Exotic organisms: A dilemma for conservation biology. *Conservation Biology* 4: 261–265.

Coblentz, B. E. 1997. Subsistence consumption of coral reef fish suggests non-sustainable extraction. *Conservation Biology* 11: 559–561.

Cochrane, M. A., A. Alencar, M. D. Schulze, C. M. Souza, et al. 1999. Postive feedbacks in the fire dynamics of closed canopy tropical forests. *Science* 284: 1832–1835.

Cohn, J. P. 1991. New focus on wildlife health. *BioScience* 41: 448–450.

Colding, J. and C. Folke. 2001. Social taboos: "Invisible" systems of local resource management and biological conservation. *Ecological Applications* 11: 584–600.

Coleman, D. C. 2001. Soil biota, soil systems, and processes. *In* S. A. Levin (ed.), *Encyclopedia of Biodiversity*, 5: 305–314. Academic Press, San Diego, CA.

Collett, J. and S. Karakashain (eds.). 1996. *Greening the College Curriculum: A Guide to Environmental Teaching in the Liberal Arts*. Island Press, Washington, D.C.

Colwell, R. K. 1986. Community biology and sexual selection: Lessons from hummingbird flower mites. *In* T. J. Case and J. Diamond (eds.), *Ecological Communities*, pp. 406–424. Harper and Row Publishers, New York.

Colyvan, M., M. A. Burgman, C. R. Todd, H. R. Akçakaya, and C. Boek. 1999. The treatment of uncertainty and the structure of the IUCN threatened species categories. *Biological Conservation* 89: 245–249.

Comiskey, J. A., F. Dallmeier, and A. Alonso. 2001. Framework for assessment and monitoring of biodiversity. *In* S. A. Levin (ed.), *Encyclopedia of Biodiversity*, 3: 63–74. Academic Press, San Diego, CA.

Commoner, B. 1971. *The Closing Circle*. Alfred A. Knopf, New York.

Condit, R., S. P. Hubbel, and R. B. Foster. 1992. Short-term dynamics of a Neotropical forest. *BioScience* 42: 822–828.

Connor, E. F. and E. D. McCoy. 1979. The statistics and biology of the species-area relationship. *American Naturalist* 13: 791–833.

Connor, E. F. and E. D. McCoy. 2001. Species-area relationships. *In* S. A. Levin (ed.), *Encyclopedia of Biodiversity*, 5: 397–412. Academic Press, San Diego, CA.

Conservation International. 1990. *The Rain Forest Imperative*. Conservation International, Washington, D.C.

Conway, W. G., M. Hutchins, M. Souza, Y. Kapentanakos, and E. Paul. 2001. *The AZA Field Conservation Resource Guide*. Zoo Atlanta, Atlanta, Georgia.

Cook, E. A. and N. H. van Lier (eds.). 1994. *Landscape Planning and Ecological Networks*. Elsevier, Amsterdam.

Cooper, D. S. and C. M. Francis. 1998. Nest predation in a Malaysian lowland rain forest. *Biological Conservation* 85: 199–202.

Cooper, N. S. 2000. How natural is a nature reserve?: An ideological study of British nature conservation landscapes. *Biological Conservation* 9: 1131–1152.

Cork, S. J., T. W. Clark, and N. Mazur. 2000. Introduction: An interdisciplinary effort for koala conservation. *Conservation Biology* 14: 606–609.

Corlett, R. T. and I. M. Turner. 1996. The conservation value of small, isolated fragments of lowland tropical rain forest. *Trends in Ecology and Evolution* 11: 330–333.

Costanza, R., O. Segurea, and J. Martinez-Alier. 1996. *Getting Down to Earth: Practical Applications of Ecological Economics*. Island Press, Washington, D.C.

Costanza, R., R. d'Arge, R. de Groot, S. Farber, et al. 1997. The value of the world's ecosystem services and natural capital. *Nature* 387: 253–260.

Costanza R., F. Andrade, P. Antunes, M. van den Belt, et al. 1998. Principles for sustainable governance of the oceans. *Science* 281: 198–199.

Cottam, G. 1990. Community dynamics on an artificial prairie. *In* W. R. Jordan III, M. E. Gilpin, and J. D. Aber (eds.), *Restoration Ecology: A Synthetic Approach to Ecological Research*, pp. 257–270. Cambridge University Press, Cambridge.

Couzin, J. 1999. Landscape changes make regional climate run hot and cold. *Science* 283: 317–318.

Cowling, R. M., P. W. Rundel, B. B. Lamont, M. K. Arroyo, and M. Arianoutsou. 1996. Plant diversity in mediterranean-climate regions. *Trends in Ecology and Evolution* 11: 362–366.

Cox, G. W. 1993. *Conservation Ecology*. W. C. Brown, Dubuque, IA.

Cox, P. A. 1997. *Nafanua: Saving the Samoan Rain Forest*. W. H. Freeman, New York.

Cox, P. A. 2001. Pharmacology, biodiversity and. *In* S. A. Levin (ed.), *Encyclopedia of Biodiversity*, 4: 523–536. Academic Press, San Diego, CA.

Cox, P. A. and T. Elmqvist. 1993. Ecocolonialism and indigenous knowledge systems: Village controlled rainforest preserves in Samoa. *Pacific Conservation Biology* 1: 6–13.

Cox, P. A. and M. J. Balick. 1994. The ethnobotanical approach to drug discovery. *Scientific American* 270(6): 82–87.

Cox, P. A. and T. Elmqvist. 1997. Ecocolonialism and indigenous-controlled rainforest preserves in Samoa. *Ambio* 26: 84–89.

Crooks K. R., A. V. Suarez, D. T. Bolger, and M. E. Soulé. 2001. Extinction and colonization of birds on habitat islands. *Conservation Biology* 15: 159–172.

Crosby, A. W. 1986. *Ecological Imperialism: The Biological Expansion of Europe 900–1900*. Cambridge University Press, Cambridge.

Cuarón, A. D. 2000. A global perspective on habitat disturbance and tropical rainforest mammals. *Conservation Biology* 14: 1574–1579.

Cully, A. 1996. Knowlton's cactus (*Pediocactus knowltonii*) reintroduction. *In* D. A. Falk, C. Miller, and M. Olwell (eds.), *Restoring Diversity: Strategies for Reintroduction of Endangered Plants*, pp. 403–410. Island Press, Washington, D.C.

Cunningham, C. and J. Berger. 1997. *Horn of Darkness: Rhinos on the Edge.* Oxford University Press, New York.

Cuperus, R., K. J. Canters, H. A. U. de Hars, and D. S. Friedman. 1999. Guidelines for ecological compensation associated with highways. *Biological Conservation* 90: 41–51.

Czech, B. and P. R. Krausman. 2001. *Endangered Species Act. History, Conservation Biology, and Public Policy.* Johns Hopkins University Press, Baltimore, MD.

Daily, G. C. 1995. Restoring value to the world's degraded lands. *Science* 269: 350–354.

Daily, G. C. (ed.). 1997. *Nature's Services: Societal Dependence on Ecosystem Services.* Island Press, Washington, D.C.

Daily, G. C. and S. Dasgupta. 2001. Ecosystem services, concept of. *In* S. A. Levin (ed.), *Encyclopedia of Biodiversity*, 2: 353–362. Academic Press, San Diego, CA.

Daily, G. C. and K. E. Ellison. 2002. *New Economy of Nature: The Quest to Make Conservation Profitable.* Island Press, Washington, D.C.

Dallmeier, F. (ed.). 1992. *Long-Term Monitoring of Biological Diversity in Tropical Forest Areas.* MAB Digest No. 11. UNESCO, Paris.

Daly, H. E. and J. B. Cobb, Jr. 1989. *For the Common Good: Redirecting the Economy Toward Community, the Environment and a Sustainable Future.* Beacon Press, Boston MA.

Danielsen, F., D. S. Balete, M. K. Poulsen, M. Enghoff, et al. 2000. A simple system for monitoring biodiversity in protected areas of a developing country. *Biodiversity and Conservation* 9: 1671–1705.

Darling, J. D. 1988. Working with whales. *National Geographic* 174(December): 886–908.

Darwin, C. R. 1859. *On the Origin of Species.* John Murray, London.

Dasgupta, P. 2001. Economic value of biodiversity, overview. *In* S. A. Levin (ed.), *Encyclopedia of Biodiversity*, 2: 291–304. Academic Press, San Diego, CA.

Dasgupta, P. S. 1995. Population, poverty and the local environment. *Scientific American* 272(2): 40–45.

Dasmann, R. F. 1987. World parks, people and land use. *In* R. Hermann and T. B. Craig (eds.), *Conference on Science in National Parks: The Fourth Triennial Conference on Research in National Parks and Equivalent Reserves*, pp. 122–127. The George Wright Society and the U.S. National Parks Service.

Dasmann, R. F. 1991. The importance of cultural and biological diversity. *In* M. L. Oldfield and J. B. Alcorn (eds.), *Biodiversity: Culture, Conservation and Ecodevelopment*, pp. 7–15. Westview Press, Boulder, CO.

Daszak, P. and A. A. Cunningham. 1999. Extinction by infection. *Trends in Ecology and Evolution* 14: 279.

Daszak, P., A. A. Cunningham, and A. D. Hyatt. 2000. Emerging infectious diseases of wildlife—threats to biodiversity and human health. *Science* 287: 443–449.

Daugherty, C. H., A. Cree, J. M. Hay, and M. B. Thompson. 1990. Neglected taxonomy and continuing extinctions of tuatara (*Sphenodon*). *Science* 347: 177–179.

Davey, A. G. 1998. *National System Planning for Protected Areas.* IUCN, World Conservation Union, Gland, Switzerland.

Davidson, C., H. B. Shaffer, and M. R. Jennings. 2001. Declines of the California red-legged frog: Climate, UV-B, habitat, and pesticides hypotheses. *Ecological Applications* 11: 464–479.

Davidson, E. A. 2000. *You can't Eat GNP. Economics as if it Mattered.* Perseus Publishing, Cambridge, MA.

Davis, M. B. and C. Zabinski. 1992. Changes in geographical range resulting from greenhouse warming: Effects on biodiversity in forests. *In* R. Peters and T. E. Lovejoy (eds.), *Global Warming and Biological Diversity*, pp. 297–308. Yale University Press, New Haven, CT.

Davis, S. H. and A. Wali. 1994. Indigenous land tenure and tropical forest management in Latin America. *Ambio* 23: 485–490.

Davradou, M. and G. Namkoong. 2001. Science, ethical arguments, and management in the preservation of land for grizzly bear conservation. *Conservation Biology* 15: 570–577.

Deardon, P. 1995. Park literacy and conservation. *Conservation Biology* 9: 1654–1656.

Debinski, D. M. and R. D. Holt. 2000. A survey and overview of habitat fragmentation experiments. *Conservation Biology* 14: 342–355.

Decker, D. J., M. E. Krasny, G. R. Goff, C. R. Smith, and D. W. Gross (eds.). 1991. *Challenges in the Conservation of Biological Resources: A Practitioner's Guide.* Westview Press, Boulder, CO.

Deem, S. L., W. B. Karesh, and W. Weisman. 2001. Putting theory into practice: Wildlife health in conservation. *Conservation Biology* 15: 1224–1233.

Del Tredici, P. 1991. Ginkgos and people: A thousand years of interaction. *Arnoldia* 51: 2–15.

De Mauro, M. M. 1993. Relationship of breeding system to rarity in the lakeside daisy (*Hymenoxys acaulis* var. *glabra*). *Conservation Biology* 7: 542–550.

Diamond, A. W. 1985. The selection of critical areas and current conservation efforts in tropical forest birds. *In* A. W. Diamond and T. E. Lovejoy (eds.), *Conservation of Tropical Forest Birds*, pp. 33–48. Technical Publication No. 4, International Council for Bird Preservation, Cambridge, UK.

Diamond, J. 1999. *Guns, Germs and Steel: The Fates of Human Societies.* W. W. Norton & Company, New York.

Diamond, J. M. 1984. "Normal" extinctions of isolated populations. *In* M. H. Nitecki (ed.), *Extinctions*, pp. 191–245. University of Chicago Press, Chicago IL.

Diamond, J. M. 1986. The design of a nature reserve system for Indonesian New Guinea. *In* M. E. Soulé (ed.), *Conservation Biology: The Science of Scarcity and Diversity*, pp. 485–503. Sinauer Associates, Sunderland, MA.

Diamond, J. M., K. D. Bishop, and S. van Balen. 1987. Bird survival in an isolated Java woodland: Island or mirror? *Conservation Biology* 4: 417–422.

Diaz, S. 2001. Ecosystem function measurement, terrestrial communities. *In* S. A. Levin (ed.), *Encyclopedia of Biodiversity*, 2: 321–344. Academic Press, San Diego, CA.

Dinerstein, E. and G. F. McCracken. 1990. Endangered greater one-horned rhinoceros carry high levels of genetic variation. *Conservation Biology* 4: 417–422.

Dinerstein, E. and E. D. Wikramanayake. 1993. Beyond hotspots: How to prioritize investments to conserve biodiversity in the Indo-Pacific region. *Conservation Biology* 7: 53–65.

Dingwall, P., J. Harrison, and J. A. McNeely (eds.). 1994. *Protecting Nature: Regional Reviews of Protected Areas*. IUCN Publications, Gland, Switzerland.

Dobson, A. 1995. Biodiversity and human health. *Trends in Ecology and Evolution* 10: 390–392.

Dobson, A. 1998. *Conservation and Biodiversity*. Scientific American Library, No. 59. W. H. Freeman and Co., New York.

Dobson, A. P. and J. H. Poole. 1992. Ivory: Why the ban must stay! *Conservation Biology* 6: 149–151.

Dobson, A. P., A. D. Bradshaw, and A. J. M. Baker. 1997. Hopes for the future: Restoration ecology and conservation biology. *Science* 277: 515–522.

Dobson, A. P., J. P. Rodriguez, W. M. Roberts, and D. S. Wilcove. 1997. Geographic distribution of endangered species in the United States. *Science* 275: 550–554.

Docherty, D. E. and R. I. Romaine. 1983. Inclusion body disease of cranes: A serological follow-up to the 1978 die-off. *Avian Diseases* 27: 830–835.

Dogsé, P. and B. von Droste. 1990. *Debt-For-Nature Exchanges and Biosphere Reserves*. UNESCO, Paris.

Donahue, D. L. 1999. *Western Range Revisited: Removing Livestock from Public Lands to Conserve Native Biodiversity*. University of Oklahoma Press, Norman, OK.

Donoghue, M. J. and W. S. Alverson. 2000. A new age of discovery. *Annals of the Missouri Botanical Garden* 87: 110–126.

Donovan, T. M. and C. W. Welden. 2002. *Spreadsheet Exercises in Conservation Biology and Landscape Ecology*. Sinauer Associates, Sunderland, MA.

Doremus, H. and J. E. Pagel. 2001. Why listing may be forever: Perspectives on delisting under the U.S. Endangered Species Act. *Conservation Biology* 15: 1258–1268.

Dover, G. 2001. Dear Mr. Darwin: Help! *Trends in Ecology and Evolution* 16: 126.

Dowling, T. E. and M. R. Childs. 1992. Impact of hybridization on a threatened trout of the south-western United States. *Conservation Biology* 6: 355–364.

Drayton, B. and R. Primack. 1996. Plant species lost in an isolated conservation area in metropolitan Boston from 1894 to 1993. *Conservation Biology* 10: 30–40.

Drayton, B. and R. B. Primack. 1999. Experimental extinction of garlic mustard (*Alliaria petiolata*) populations: Implications for weed science and conservation biology. *Biological Invasions* 1: 159–167.

Driscoll, D. A. 1999. Genetic neighbourhood and effective population size for two endangered frogs. *Biological Conservation* 88: 221–229.

Drost, C. A. and G. M. Fellers. 1996. Collapse of a regional frog fauna in the Yosemite Area of the California Sierra Nevada, USA. *Conservation Biology* 10: 414–426.

Duffus, D. A. and P. Dearden. 1990. Non-consumptive wildlife-oriented recreation: A conceptual framework. *Biological Conservation* 53: 213–231.

Duffy, E. and A. S. Watts (eds.). 1971. *The Scientific Management of Animal and Plant Communities for Conservation*. Blackwell Scientific Publications, Oxford.

Dugan, P. (ed.). 1993. *Wetlands in Danger: A World Conservation Atlas*. Oxford University Press, New York.

Duncan, J. R. and J. L. Lockwood. 2001. Extinction in a field of bullets: A search for causes in the decline of the world's freshwater fishes. *Biological Conservation* 102: 97–105.

Dunham, J. B. and W. L. Minckley. 1998. Allozymic variation in desert pupfish from natural and artificial habitats: Genetic conservation in fluctuating populations. *Biological Conservation* 84: 7–15.

Dunlap, P. V. 2001. Microbial diversity. *In* S. A. Levin (ed.), *Encyclopedia of Biodiversity*, 4: 191–206. Academic Press, San Diego, CA.

Dwyer, J. C. and I. D. Hodge. 1996. *Countryside in Trust: Land Management by Conservation, Recreation and Amenity Organizations*. John Wiley and Sons, Chichester, UK.

Earle, S. 1996. *Sea Change: A Message of the Oceans*. Ballantine Books, New York.

Echelle, A. A. and A. F. Echelle. 1997. Genetic introgression of endemic taxa by non-natives: a case study with Leon Springs pupfish and sheepshead minnow. *Conservation Biology* 11: 153–161.

Eckstrom, C. K. 1996. A wilderness of water: Pantanal. *Audubon* 98: 54–65.

Edmonds, R. L. 1991. The Sanxia (Three Gorges) project: The environmental argument surrounding China's super dam. *Global Ecology and Biogeography Letters* 1: 105–125.

Edwards, J. L., M. A. Lane, and E. S. Nielsen. 2000. Interoperability of biodiversity databases: Biodiversity information on every desktop. *Science* 289: 2312–2314.

Edwards, M. 1994. Pollution in the former USSR: Lethal legacy. *National Geographic* 186(August): 70–99.

Egan, D. and E. Howell (eds.). 2001. *The Historical Ecology Handbook: A Restorationist's Guide to Reference Ecosystems*. Island Press, Washington, D.C.

Ehrenfeld, D. W. 1970. *Biological Conservation*. Holt, Rinehart and Winston, New York.

Ehrenfeld, D. W. 1978. *The Arrogance of Humanism*. Oxford University Press, New York.

Ehrenfeld, D. W. 1989. Hard times for diversity. *In* D. Western and M. Pearl (eds.), *Conservation for the Twenty-first Century*, pp. 247–250. Oxford University Press, New York.

Ehrlich, A. H. and P. R. Ehrlich. 1996. *Betrayal of Science and Reason: How Anti-Environmental Rhetoric Threatens Our Future*. Island Press, Washington, D.C.

Ehrlich, P. R. and A. H. Ehrlich. 1968. *The Population Bomb.* Amereon, Mattituck, NY.

Ehrlich, P. R. and A. H. Ehrlich. 1981. *Extinction: The Causes and Consequences of the Disappearance of Species.* Random House, New York.

Eisner, T. 1991. Chemical prospecting: A proposal for action. *In* F. H. Bormann and S. R. Kellert (eds.), *Ecology, Economics, Ethics: The Broken Circle,* pp. 196–202. Yale University Press, New Haven, CT.

Elfring, C. 1989. Preserving land through local land trusts. *BioScience* 39: 71–74.

Elliot, R. 1992. Intrinsic value, environmental obligation and naturalness. *The Monist* 75: 138–160.

Ellstrand, N. C. 1992. Gene flow by pollen: Implications for plant conservation genetics. *Oikos* 63: 77–86.

Elzinga, C. L., D. W. Salzer, J. W. Willoughby, and J. P. Gibbs. 2001. *Monitoring Plant and Animal Populations.* Blackwell Scientific, Oxford.

Emerson, R. W. 1836. *Nature.* James Monroe and Co., Boston, MA.

Enderson, J. H., W. Heinrich, L. Kiff, and C. M. White. 1995. Population changes in North American peregrines. *Transactions of the 60th North American Wildlife and Natural Resource Conference,* pp. 142–161. Wildlife Management Institute, Washington, D.C.

Engelhardt, K. A. M and M. E. Ritchie. 2001. Effects of macrophyte species richness on wetland ecosystem functioning and services. *Nature* 411: 687–689.

Entwistle, A. and N. Dunstone (eds.). 2000. *Priorities for the Conservation of Mammalian Diversity: Has the Panda had its Day?* Cambridge University Press, Cambridge, UK.

Environmental Defense. 2000. *Progress on the Back Forty: An Analysis of the Incentive-Based Approaches to Endangered Species Conservation on Private Land.* Washington, D.C.

Epstein, P. R. 1998. *Marine Ecosystems: Emerging Diseases as Indicators of change: Health of the Ocean from Labrador to Venezuela.* Harvard Medical School, Boston.

Epstein, P. R. (ed.). 1999. *Extreme Weather Events: The Health and Economic Consequences of the 1997/98 El Niño and La Niña.* Harvard Medical School, Boston.

Erdelen, W. 1988. Forest ecosystems and nature conservation in Sri Lanka. *Biological Conservation* 43: 115–135.

Erwin, T. L. 1982. Tropical forests: Their richness in Coleoptera and other arthropod species. *Coleopterists Bulletin.* 36: 74–75.

Esler, D. 2000. Applying metapopulation theory to conservation of migratory birds. *Conservation Biology* 14: 366–372.

Essington, T. E. 2001. The precautionary approach in fisheries management: The devil is in the details. *Trends in Ecology and Evolution* 16: 121–122.

Estes, J. A. 1996. The influence of large, mobile predators in aquatic food webs: Examples from sea otters and kelp forests. *In* S. P. R. Greenstreet and M. L. Tasker (eds.), *Aquatic Predators and Their Prey,* pp. 65–72. Fishing News Books, Blackwell Scientific Publications, Malden, MA.

Estes, J. A., K. Crooks, and R. Holt. 2001. Predators, ecological role of. *In* S. A. Levin (ed.), *Encyclopedia of Biodiversity,* 4: 857–878. Academic Press, San Diego, CA.

European Environment Agency. 1998. *Europe's Environment. The Second Assessment.* European Environment Agency, Office for the Official Publications of the European Community. Elsevier Science, Oxford.

Evans, M. E. K., R. W. Dolan, E. S. Menges, and D. R. Gordon. 2000. Genetic diversity and reproductive biology in *Warea carteri* (Brassicaceae), a narrowly endemic Florida scrub annual. *American Journal of Botany* 87: 372–381.

Faith, D. P. 1994. Phylogenetic diversity: A general framework for the prediction of future diversity. *In* P. L. Forey, C. J. Humphries, and R. I. Vane-Wright (eds.), *Systematics and Conservation Evaluation,* pp. 251–268. Oxford University Press, New York.

Falk, D. A. 1991. Joining biological and economic models for conserving plant genetic diversity. *In* D. A. Falk and K. E. Holsinger (eds.), *Genetics and Conservation of Rare Plants,* pp. 209–224. Oxford University Press, New York.

Falk, D. A. and K. E. Holsinger (eds.). 1991. *Genetics and Conservation of Rare Plants.* Oxford University Press, New York.

Falk, D. A. and P. Olwell. 1992. Scientific and policy considerations in restoration and reintroduction of endangered species. *Rhodora* 94: 287–315.

Falk, D. A., C. I. Millar, and M. Olwell (eds.). 1996. *Restoring Diversity: Strategies for Reintroduction of Endangered Plants.* Island Press, Washington, D.C.

Farnsworth, E. J. and J. Rosovsky. 1993. The ethics of ecological field experimentation. *Conservation Biology* 7: 463–472.

Fearnside, P. M. 1990. Predominant land uses in Brazilian Amazonia. *In* A. Anderson (ed.), *Alternatives to Deforestation: Steps Toward Sustainable Use of the Amazon Rain Forest,* pp. 233–251. Columbia University Press, Irvington, NY.

Fearnside, P. M. and J. Ferraz. 1995. A conservation gap analysis of Brazil's Amazonian vegetation. *Conservation Biology* 9: 1134–1148.

Fearnside, P. M., J. A. Sayer, D. Cleary, R. O. Bierregaard, Jr., and G. Prance. 1996. Brazil. *In* C. S. Harcourt and J. A. Sayer (eds.), *The Conservation Atlas of Tropical Forests: The Americas,* pp. 229–248. Simon and Schuster, New York.

Feinsinger, P. 2001. *Designing Field Studies for Biodiversity Conservation.* Island Press, Washington, D.C.

Ferber, D. 2000. Galápagos station survives latest attack by fishers. *Science* 290: 2059–2060.

Ferraro, P. J. 2001. Global habitat protection: Limitations of development interventions and a role for conservation performance payments. *Conservation Biology* 15: 990–1000.

Ferry, L. 1995. *The New Ecological Order.* University of Chicago Press, Chicago.

Ferson, S. and M. Burgman (eds.). 2000. *Quantitative Methods for Conservation Biology.* Springer-Verlag, New York.

Fischer, A. G. 1960. Latitudinal variations in organic diversity. *Evolution* 14: 64–81.

Fischer, H. 1995. *Wolf Wars: The Remarkable Inside Story of the Restoration of Wolves to Yellowstone.* Falcon Press, Helena, MT.

Fischer, J. and D. B. Lindenmayer. 2000. An assessment of published results of animal relocations. *Biological Conservation* 96: 1–11.

Fisk, M. R., S. J. Giovannoni, and I. H. Thorseth. 1998. Alteration of oceanic volcanic glass: Textural evidence of microbial activity. *Science* 281: 978–980.

Fitzgerald, S. 1989. *International Wildlife Trade: Whose Business Is It?* World Wildlife Fund, Washington, D.C.

Fitzgibbon, C. D., H. Mogaka, and J. H. Fanshawe. 1995. Subsistence hunting in Arabuko-Sokoke Forest, Kenya and its effects on mammal populations. *Conservation Biology* 9: 1116–1127.

Fiumera, A. C., P. G. Parker, and P. A. Fuerst. 2000. Effective population size and maintenance of genetic diversity in captive-bred populations of a Lake Victoria cichlid. *Conservation Biology* 14: 886–892.

Flather, C. H., M. S. Knowles, and I. A. Kendall. 1998. Threatened and endangered species geography. *BioScience* 48: 365–376.

Fleischner, T. L. 1994. Ecological costs of livestock grazing in western North America. *Conservation Biology* 8: 629–644.

Folke, C. and J. Colding. 2001. Traditional conservation practices. *In* S. A. Levin (ed.), *Encyclopedia of Biodiversity,* 5: 681–694. Academic Press, San Diego, CA.

Foose, T. J. 1983. The relevance of captive populations to the conservation of biotic diversity. *In* C. M. Schonewald-Cox, S. M. Chambers, B. MacBryde, and L. Thomas (eds.). *Genetics and Conservation,* pp. 374–401. Benjamin/Cummings, Menlo Park, CA.

Forman, R. T. 1995. *Land Mosaics: The Ecology of Landscapes and Regions.* Cambridge University Press, New York.

Forman, R. T. and M. Godron. 1981. Patches and structural components for a landscape ecology. *BioScience* 31: 733–740.

Fossey, D. 1990. *Gorillas in the Mist.* Houghton Mifflin, Boston.

Fowler, S. L. 2000. Basking shark (*Cetorhinus maximus*). *In* R. P. Reading and B. Miller (eds.), *Endangered Animals,* pp. 49–53. Greenwood Press, Westport, CT.

Fox, J., P. Yonzon, and N. Podger. 1996. Mapping conflicts between biodiversity and human needs in Langtang National Park. *Conservation Biology* 10: 562–569.

Frankel, O., A. Brown, and J. Burdon. 1995. *The Conservation of Plants.* Cambridge University Press, Cambridge.

Frankham, R. 1996. Relationships of genetic variation to population size in wildlife. *Conservation Biology* 10: 1500–1508.

Franklin, I. R. 1980. Evolutionary change in small populations. *In* M. E. Soulé and B. A. Wilcox (eds.), *Conservation Biology: An Evolutionary-Ecological Perspective,* pp. 135–149. Sinauer, Sunderland, MA.

Frazier, J. 2000. Kemp's Ridley sea turtle (*Lepidochelys kempii*). *In* R. P. Reading and B. Miller (eds.), *Endangered Animals,* pp. 164–170. Greenwood Press, Westport, CT.

Fredrickson, J. K. and T. C. Onstott. 1996. Microbes deep inside Earth. *Scientific American* 275(4): 68–73.

Freemark, K. E. and D. A. Kirk. 2001. Birds on organic and conventional farms in Ontario: partitioning effects of habitat and practices on species composition and abundance. *Biological Conservation* 101: 337–350.

Freese, C. H. (ed.). 1997. *Harvesting Wild Species: Implications for Biodiversity Conservation.* Johns Hopkins University Press, Baltimore, MD.

Fricke, H. and K. Hissmann. 1990. Natural habitat of the coelocanths. *Nature* 346: 323–324.

Frohlich, J. and K. D. Hyde. 1999. Biodiversity of palm fungi in the tropics: are global fungal diversity estimates realistic? *Biodiversity and Conservation* 8: 977–1004.

Fuccilo, D., L. Sears, and P. Stapleton. 1998. *Biodiversity in Trust: Conservation and Use of Plant Genetic Resources in CGIAR Centres.* Cambridge University Press, New York.

Fuhlendorf, S. D. and D. M. Engle. 2001. Restoring heterogeneity on rangelands: Ecosystem management based on evolutionary grazing patterns. *BioScience* 51: 625–632.

Fujita, M. S. and M. D. Tuttle. 1991. Flying foxes (Chiroptera: Pteropodidae): Threatened animals of key ecological and economic importance. *Conservation Biology* 5: 455–463.

Fuller, R. B. 1970. *Operating Manual for Spaceship Earth.* Touchstone, New York.

Fullerton, D. and R. Stavins. 1998. How economists see the environment. *Nature* 395: 433–434.

Funch, P. and R. Kristensen. 1995. Cycliophora is a new phylum with affinities to Entoprocta and Ectoprocta (*Symbion pandora*). *Nature* 378: 711–714.

Futuyma, D. J. 1995. *Science on Trial: The Case for Evolution,* revised edition. Sinauer Associates, Sunderland, MA.

Futuyma, D. J. 1998. *Evolutionary Biology,* 3rd ed. Sinauer Associates, Sunderland, MA.

Gadgil, M. and R. Guha. 1992. *This Fissured Land: An Ecological History of India.* Oxford University Press, Oxford.

Gage, J. D. and P. A. Tyler. 1991. *Deep-Sea Biology: A Natural History of Organisms at the Deep Seafloor.* Cambridge University Press, Cambridge.

Galatowitsch, S. M. and A. G. Van der Valk. 1996. *Restoring Prairie Wetlands: An Ecological Approach.* Iowa State University Press, Ames, IA.

Galbraith, C. A., P. V. Grice, G. P. Mudge, S. Parr, and M. W. Pienkowski. 1998. The role of statutory bodies in ornithological conservation. *Ibis* 137: S224-S231.

Galdikas, B. 1995. *Reflections of Eden: My Years with the Orangutans of Borneo.* Little Brown, Boston.

Game, M. and G. F. Peterken. 1984. Nature reserve selection strategies in the woodlands of Central Lincolnshire, England. *Biological Conservation* 29: 157–181.

Gärdenfors, U. 2001. Classifying threatened species at national versus global levels. *Trends in Ecology and Evolution* 16: 511–516.

Gascon, C., T. E. Lovejoy, R. O. Bierregaard, J. R. Malcolm, et al. 1999. Matrix habitat and species richness in tropical forest remnants. *Biological Conservation* 91: 223–229.

Gaston, K. J. 1991. The magnitude of global insect species richness. *Conservation Biology* 5: 283–296.

Gaston, K. J. 1994. Spatial patterns of species description: How is our knowledge of the global insect fauna growing? *Biological Conservation* 67: 37–40.

Gaston, K. J. 2000. Global patterns in biodiversity. *Nature* 405: 220–227.

Gates, D. M. 1993. *Climate Change and Its Biological Consequences*. Sinauer Associates, Sunderland, MA.

Gentry, A. H. 1986. Endemism in tropical versus temperate plant communities. *In* M. E. Soulé (ed.), *Conservation Biology: The Science of Scarcity and Diversity*, pp. 153–181. Sinauer Associates, Sunderland, MA.

Gerrodette, T. and W. G. Gilmartin. 1990. Demographic consequences of changing pupping and hauling sites of the Hawaiian monk seal. *Conservation Biology* 4: 423–430.

Gersh, J. and R. Pickert. 1991. Land-use modeling: Accommodating growth while conserving biological resources in Dutchess County, New York. *In* D. J. Decker, M. E. Krasnyk, G. R. Goff, C. R. Smith, and D. W. Gross (eds.), *Challenges in the Conservation of Biological Resources: A Practitioner's Guide*, pp. 233–242. Westview Press, Boulder, CO.

Gerwick, W. H., B. Marquez, K. Milligan, L. Tong Tan, and T. Williamson. 2001. Plant sources of drugs and chemicals. *In* S. A. Levin (ed.), *Encyclopedia of Biodiversity*, 4: 711–722. Academic Press, San Diego, CA.

Getz, W. M., L. Fortmann, D. Cumming, J. du Toit, et al. 1999. Sustaining natural and human capital: Villagers and scientists. *Science* 283: 1855–1856.

Gibbons, A. 1992. Conservation biology in the fast lane. *Science* 255: 20–22.

Gibbs, W. W. 2001. The Arctic oil and wildlife refuge. *Scientific American* 284(5): 63–69.

Giese, M. 1996. Effects of human activity on adelie penguin *Pygoscelis adeliae* breeding success. *Biological Conservation* 75: 157–164.

Gigon, A., R. Langenauer, C. Meier, and B. Nievergelt. 2000. Blue Lists of threatened species with stabilized or increasing abundance: A new instrument for conservation. *Conservation Biology* 14: 402–413.

Gilbert, G. S. and S. P. Hubbell. 1996. Plant diseases and the conservation of tropical forests. *BioScience* 46: 98–106.

Gilbert, O. L. and P. Anderson. 1998. *Habitat Creation and Repair*. Oxford University Press, Oxford.

Gilpin, M. E. and M. E. Soulé. 1986. Minimum viable populations: Processes of species extinction. *In* M. E. Soulé (ed.), *Conservation Biology: The Science of Scarcity and Diversity*, pp. 19–34. Sinauer Associates, Sunderland, MA.

Giono, J. 1989. *The Man Who Planted Trees*. Collins Dove, Melbourne, Australia.

Giovannoni, S. J., T. B. Britschgi, C. L. Moyer, and K. G. Field. 1990. Genetic diversity in Sargasso Sea bacterioplankton. *Nature* 345: 60–63.

Gittleman, J. L. 1994. Are the pandas successful specialists of evolutionary failures? *Bioscience* 44: 456–464.

Gittleman, J. L., S. M. Funk, D. McDonald, and R. K. Wayne (eds.). 2000. *Carnivore Conservation*. Cambridge University Press, Cambridge.

Given, D. R. 1995. *Principles and Practice of Plant Conservation*. Timber Press, Portland, OR.

Glazer, A. N. 2001. Natural reserves and preserves. *In* S. A. Levin (ed.), *Encyclopedia of Biodiversity*, 4: 317–328. Academic Press, San Diego, CA.

Glenn, W. 1997. A model for cooperative land management: The Malpai Borderlands Group. *Society for Conservation Biology Newsletter* 4: 1–2.

Global Environment Facility. 1999a. *Experience with Conservation Trusts*. World Bank, New York.

Global Environment Facility. 1999b. *Interim Assessment of Biodiversity Enabling Activities*. World Bank, New York.

Glowka, L., F. Burhenne-Guilman, and H. Synge. 1994. *A Guide to the Convention on Biological Diversity*. IUCN, Gland, Switzerland.

Godoy, R. A. 2001. *Indians, Markets and Rainforests: Theoretical, Comparative, and Quantitative Explorations in the Neotropics*. Columbia University Press, New York.

Godoy, R. A., R. Lubowski, and A. Markandya. 1993. A method for the economic valuation of non-timber tropical forest products. *Economic Botany* 47: 220–233.

Godwin, P. 2001. Wildlife without borders. *National Geographic* 200(September): 2–31.

Goerck, J. M. 1997. Patterns of rarity in the birds of the Atlantic forest of Brazil. *Conservation Biology* 11: 112–118.

Goklany, I. M. 1998. Saving habitat and conserving biodiversity on a crowded planet. *BioScience* 48: 941–953.

Goldammer, J. G. 1999. Forests on fire. *Science* 284: 1782–1783.

Goldman, B. and F. H. Talbot. 1976. Aspects of the ecology of coral reef fishes. *In* O. A. Jones and R. Endean (eds.), *Biology and Geology of Coral Reefs*, 3: 125–154. Academic Press, New York.

Goldschmidt, T. 1996. *Darwin's Dreampond: Drama in Lake Victoria*. MIT Press, Cambridge, MA.

Goldsmith, B. (ed.). 1991. *Monitoring for Conservation and Ecology*. Chapman and Hall, New York.

Gomez-Pompa, A. and A. Kaus. 1992. Taming the wilderness myth. *BioScience* 42: 271–279.

Goodland, R. J. A. 1990. The World Bank's new environmental policy for dams and reservoirs. *Water Resources Development* 6: 226–239.

Goodland, R. J. A. 1992. Environmental priorities for financing institutions. *Environmental Conservation* 19: 9–22.

Gore, A. 1992. *Earth in the Balance: Ecology and the Human Spirit*. Houghton Mifflin, New York.

Gosselink, J. G., G. P. Shaffer, L. C. Lee, D. M. Burdick, et al. 1990. Landscape conservation in a forested wetland watershed. *BioScience* 40: 588–600.

Gössling, S. 1999. Ecotourism: a means to safeguard biodiversity and ecosystem functions? *Ecological Economics* 29: 303–320.

Gotelli, N. J. 2001. *A Primer of Ecology,* 3rd ed. Sinauer Associates, Sunderland, MA.

Gram, W. K., V. L. Sork, R. J. Marquis, R. B. Renken, et al. 2001. Evaluating the effects of ecosystem management: a case study in a Missouri Ozark forest. *Ecological Applications* 11: 1667–1679.

Grant, P. R. and B. R. Grant. 1992. Darwin's finches: Genetically effective population sizes. *Ecology* 73: 766–784.

Grant, P. R. and B. R. Grant. 1997. The rarest of Darwin's finches. *Conservation Biology* 11: 119–126.

Grassle, J. F. 1991. Deep-sea benthic biodiversity. *BioScience* 41: 464–469.

Grassle, J. F. 2001. Marine ecosystems. *In* S. A. Levin (ed.), *Encyclopedia of Biodiversity,* 4: 13–26. Academic Press, San Diego, CA.

Greenberg, R. and S. Droege. 1999. On the decline of the rusty blackbird and the use of ornithological literature to document long-term population trends. *Conservation Biology* 13: 553–559.

Gregg, W. P., Jr. 1991. MAB Biosphere reserves and conservation of traditional land use systems. *In* M. L. Oldfield and J. B. Alcorn (eds.), *Biodiversity: Culture, Conservation and Ecodevelopment*, pp. 274–294. Westview Press, Boulder, CO.

Greuter, W. 1995. Extinction in Mediterranean areas. *In* J. H. Lawton and R. M. May. *Extinction Rates*, pp. 88–97. Oxford University Press, Oxford.

Griffith, B., J. M. Scott, J. W. Carpenter, and C. Reed. 1989. Translocation as a species conservation tool: Status and strategy. *Science* 245: 477–480.

Grifo, F. and J. Rosenthal (eds.). 1997. *Biodiversity and Human Health.* Island Press, Washington, D.C.

Grigg, R. W. and D. Epp. 1989. Critical depth for the survival of coral islands: Effects on the Hawaiian archipelago. *Science* 243: 638–641.

Groombridge, J. J., C. G. Jones, M. W. Bruford, and R. A. Nichols. 2000. Conservation biology- "Ghost" alleles of the Mauritius kestrel. *Nature* 403: 616.

Grove, N. 1988. Quietly conserving nature. *National Geographic* 174(December): 818–844.

Grove, R. H. 1992. Origins of Western environmentalism. *Scientific American* 267(1): 42–47.

Grumbine, E. R. 1994. What is ecosystem management? *Conservation Biology* 8: 27–38.

Guerrant, E. O. 1992. Genetic and demographic considerations in the sampling and reintroduction of rare plants. *In* P. L. Fiedler and S. K. Jain (eds.), *Conservation Biology: The Theory and Practice of Nature Conservation, Preservation and Management*, pp. 321–344. Chapman and Hall, New York.

Guerrant, E. O. and B. M. Pavlik. 1998. Reintroduction of rare plants: Genetics, demography and the role of *ex-situ* conservation methods. *In* P. L. Fiedler and P. M. Kareiva (eds.), *Conservation Biology: For the Coming Decade*, pp. 80–108. Chapman and Hall, New York.

Gurd, D. B., T. D. Nudds, and D. H. Rivard. 2001. Conservation of mammals in Eastern North American wildlife reserves: How small is too small? *Conservation Biology* 15: 1355–1363.

Haas, P. M., M. A. Levy, and E. A. Parson. 1992. Appraising the Earth Summit: How should we judge UNCED's success? *Environment* 34: 7–35.

Hails, A. J. (ed.). 1996. *Wetlands, Biodiversity and the Ramsar Convention: The Role of the Convention on Wetlands in the Conservation and Wise Use of Biodiversity.* Ramsar Convention Bureau, Gland, Switzerland.

Hair, J. D. 1988. The economics of conserving wetlands: A widening circle. Paper presented at Workshop in Economics, IUCN General Assembly, 4–5 February 1988, Costa Rica.

Hall, S. J. G. and J. Ruane. 1993. Livestock breeds and their conservation: A global overview. *Conservation Biology* 7: 815–826.

Halliday, T. 1998. A declining amphibian conundrum. *Nature* 394: 418–419.

Halpern, C. B. and T. A. Spies. 1995. Plant diversity in natural and managed forests of the Pacific Northwest. *Ecological Applications* 5: 913–935.

Halvorson, W. L. and G. E. Davis (eds.). 1996. *Science and Ecosystem Management in the National Parks.* University of Arizona, Tucson.

Hamilton, M. B. 1994. Ex situ conservation of wild plant species: Time to reassess the genetic assumptions and implications of seed banks. *Conservation Biology* 8: 39–49.

Hammond, P. M. 1992. Species Inventory. *In* WCMC, *Global Diversity: Status of the Earth's Living Resources*, pp. 17–39. Chapman and Hall, London.

Hamrick, J. L. and M. J. W. Godt. 1989. Allozyme diversity in plant species. *In* A. H. D. Brown, M. T. Clegg, A. L. Kahler, and B. S. Weirs (eds.), *Plant Population Genetics, Breeding, and Genetic Resources*, pp. 43–63. Sinauer Associates, Sunderland, MA.

Hamrick, J. L., M. J. W. Godt, D. A. Murawski, and M. D. Loveless. 1991. Correlations between species traits and allozyme diversity: Implications for conservation biology. *In* D. A. Falk and K. E. Holsinger (eds.), *Genetics and Conservation of Rare Plants*, pp. 75–86. Oxford University Press, New York.

Hancocks, D. 2001. *A Different Nature: The Paradoxical World of Zoos and Their Uncertain Future.* University of California Press. Berkeley, CA.

Hanley, N. and C. Splash. 1994. *Cost-Benefit Analysis and the Environment.* Edward Elgar Publishing, Cheltenham, UK.

Hannah, L., J. L. Carr, and A. Landerani. 1995. Human disturbance and natural habitat: A biome level analysis of a global set. *Biodiversity and Conservation* 4: 128–155.

Hansen, A. J., T. A. Spies, F. J. Swanson, and J. L. Ohmann. 1991. Conserving biodiversity in managed forests. *BioScience* 41: 382–392.

Hansen, A. J., S. L. Garman, J. F. Weigand, D. L. Urban, W. C. McComb, and M. G. Raphael. 1995. Alternative silvicultural regimes in the Pacific Northwest: Simulations of ecological and economic effects. *Ecological Applications* 5: 535–555.

Hansen, A. J., R. P. Neilson, V. H. Dale, C. H. Flather, et al. 2001. Global change in forests: Responses of species, communities, and biomes. *BioScience* 51: 765–779.

Hanski, I. and D. Simberloff. 1997. The metapopulation approach, its history, conceptual domain and application to conservation. *In* I. Hanski and D. Simberloff (eds.), *Metapopulation Biology*, pp. 5–26. Academic Press, Inc., San Diego, CA.

Hanski, I., A. Moilanen, and M. Gyllenberg. 1996. Minimum viable metapopulation size. *American Naturalist* 147: 527–541.

Hansson, L., L. Fahrig, and G. Merriam (eds.). 1995. *Mosaic Landscapes and Ecological Processes*. Chapman and Hall, London.

Harcourt, A. H. 1995. Population viability estimates: Theory and practice for a wild gorilla population. *Conservation Biology* 9: 134–142.

Hardin, G. 1968. The tragedy of the commons. *Science* 162: 1243–1248.

Hardin, G. 1985. *Filters Against Folly: How to Survive Despite Economists, Ecologists and the Merely Eloquent*. Viking Press, New York.

Hardin, G. 1993. *Living Within Limits: Ecology, Economics and Population Taboos*. Oxford University Press, New York.

Harms, K. E., S. J. Wright, A. Calderón, A. Hernández, and E. A. Herre. 2000. Pervasive density-dependent recruitment enhances seedling diversity in a tropical forest. *Nature* 404: 493–495.

Harper, J. L. 1977. *Population Biology of Plants*. Academic Press, New York.

Harrison, I. J. and M. L. J. Stiassny. 1999. The quiet crisis: A preliminary listing of the freshwater fishes of the world that are extinct or "missing in action." *In* R. D. E MacPhee (ed.), *Extinctions in Near Time*, pp. 271–329. Kluwer Academic/Plenum Publishers, New York.

Harrison, J. L. 1968. The effect of forest clearance on small mammals. *In Conservation in Tropical Southeast Asia*. IUCN, Morges, Switzerland.

Harrop, S. R. 1999. Conservation regulation: A backward step for biodiversity? *Biodiversity and Conservation* 8: 679–707.

Harte, J. and R. Shaw. 1995. Shifting dominance within a montane vegetation community: Results of a climate-warming experiment. *Science* 267: 876–879.

Harwood, J. 2000. Risk assessment and decision analysis in conservation. *Biological Conservation* 95: 219–226.

Hassan, H. and H. E. Dregne. 1997. *Natural Habitats and Ecosystems Management in Drylands: An Overview*. Environment Department Paper No. 51: The World Bank, Washington, D.C.

Hausfater, G. and K. Kennedy. 1986. Dian Fossey (1932–1985). *American Anthropologist* 88: 956–965.

Hawksworth, D. L. 1990. The long-term effects of air pollutants on lichen communities in Europe and North America. *In* G. M. Woodwell (ed.), *The Earth in Transition: Patterns and Processes of Biotic Impoverishment*, pp. 45–64. Cambridge University Press, Cambridge.

Hawksworth, D. L. 1991. *The Biodiversity of Microorganisms and Invertebrates: Its Role in Sustainable Agriculture*. CAB International, Wallingford, UK.

Hawksworth, D. L. 2001. Nomenclature, systems of. *In* S. A. Levin (ed.), *Encyclopedia of Biodiversity*, 4: 389–402. Academic Press, San Diego, CA.

Hawksworth, D. L., P. M. Kirk, and S. D. Clark (eds.). 1997. *Biodiversity Information*. Oxford University Press, New York.

Heal, G. 2000. *Nature and the Marketplace: Capturing the Value of Ecosystem Services*. Island Press, Washington, D.C.

Hedrick, P. W. 2000. *Genetics of Populations*, 2nd ed. Jones and Bartlett Publishers, Sudbury, MA.

Hegde, R., S. Suryaprakash, L. Achoth, and K. S. Bawa. 1996. Extraction of non-timber forest products in the forests of Biligiri Rangan Hills, India. *Economic Botany* 50: 243–251.

Hellmann, J. J. 2001. Species interactions. *In* S. A. Levin (ed.), *Encyclopedia of Biodiversity*, 5: 453-466. Academic Press, San Diego, CA.

Hellmann J. J. and G. W. Fowler. 1999. Bias, precision, and accuracy of four measures of species richness. *Ecological Applications* 9: 824–834.

Hemley, G. (ed.). 1994. *International Wildlife Trade: A CITES Sourcebook*. Island Press, Washington, D.C.

Hendrey G. 2001. Acid rain and deposition. *In* S. A. Levin (ed.), *Encyclopedia of Biodiversity*, 1: 1–16. Academic Press, San Diego, CA.

Hendrickson D. A. and J. E. Brooks. 1991. Transplanting short-lived fishes in North American deserts: Review, assessment and recommendations. *In* W. L. Minckley and J. E. Deacon (eds.), *Battle Against Extinction: Native Fish Management in the American West*, pp. 283–302. University of Arizona Press, Tucson.

Heschel, M. S. and K. N. Paige. 1995. Inbreeding depression, environmental stress and population size variation in Scarlet Gilia (*Ipomopsis aggregata*). *Conservation Biology* 9: 126–133.

Heyer, W. R., M. A. Donnelly, R. W. McDiarmid, L. -A. C. Hayek, and M. S. Foster (eds.). 1994. *Measuring and Monitoring Biological Diversity: Standard Methods for Amphibians*. Smithsonian Institution Press, Washington, D.C.

Heywood, I., S. Cornelius, and S. Carver. 1998. *An Introduction to Geographical Information Systems*. Prentice Hall, New Jersey.

Heywood, V. H. (ed.). 1995. *Global Diversity and Assessment*. Cambridge University Press, New York.

Hilton-Taylor, C. 2000. *2000 IUCN Red List of Threatened Species*. IUCN/SSC, Gland, Switzerland and Cambridge, UK.

Hodgson, G. and J. A. Dixon. 1988. Logging versus fisheries and tourism in Palawan. *East-West Environmental Policy Institute Occasional Paper No. 7*. East-West Center, Honolulu.

Hoffman, A. J., M. H. Bazerman, and S. L. Yaffee. 1997. Balancing business interests and endangered species protection. *Sloan Management Review* 39: 59–73.

Hofman, R. J. 1995. The changing focus of marine mammal conservation. *Trends in Ecology and Evolution* 10: 462–465.

Hokit, D. G., B. M. Stith, and L. C. Branch. 2001. Comparison of two types of metapopulation models in real and artificial landscapes. *Conservation Biology* 15: 1102–1113.

Holl, K. D., G. C. Daily, and P. R. Ehrlich. 1995. Knowledge and perceptions in Costa Rica regarding environment, population and biodiversity issues. *Conservation Biology* 9: 1548–1558.

Holling, C. S. and G. K. Meffe. 1996. Command and control and the pathology of natural resource management. *Conservation Biology* 10: 328–338.

Holloway, M. 1994. Nurturing nature. *Scientific American* 270(4): 98–108.

Homer-Dixon, T. F. 2001. *Environment, Scarcity, and Violence.* Princeton University Press, Princeton, NJ.

Hooten, A. J. and M. E. Hatziolos (eds.). 1995. *Sustainable Financing Mechanisms for Coral Reef Conservation. Environmentally Sustainable Development Proceedings Series* No. 9. The World Bank, Washington, D.C.

Hornocker, M. G. 1992. Learning to live with mountain lions. *National Geographic* 182(July): 52–65.

Horton, T. 1992. The Endangered Species Act: Too tough, too weak, or too late? *Audubon* 94: 68–74.

Horwich, R. H. and J. Lyon. 1998. Community-based development as a conservation tool: The Community Baboon Sanctuary and the Gales Point Manatee Reserve. *In* R. B. Primack, D. Bray, H. A. Galletti, and I. Ponciano (eds.), *Timber, Tourists, and Temples: Conservation and Development in the Maya Forest of Belize, Guatemala, and Mexico*, pp. 343–364. Island Press, Washington, D.C.

Houghton, J. T., L. G. Meira Filho, B. A. Callander, N. Harris, A. Katttenberg, and K. Maskell. 1996. *Climate Change 1995. The Science of Climate Change.* Cambridge University Press, Cambridge, U.K.

Hourigan, T. F. and E. S. Reese. 1987. Mid-ocean isolation and the evolution of Hawaiian Reef fishes. *Trends in Ecology and Evolution* 2: 187–191.

Howarth, F. G. 1990. Hawaiian terrestrial arthropods: An overview. *Bishop Museum Occasional Papers* 30: 4–26.

Howarth, W. 2001. Literary perspectives on biodiversity. *In* S. A. Levin (ed.), *Encyclopedia of Biodiversity*, 3: 739–746. Academic Press, San Diego, CA.

Hoyt, E. 1988. *Conserving the Wild Relatives of Crops.* IBPGR, IUCN, WWF, Rome.

Hubbell, S. P. 2001. *The Unified Neutral Theory of Biodiversity and Biogeography.* Princeton University Press, Princeton, NJ.

Huenneke, L. F. 1995. Involving academic scientists in conservation research: Perspectives of a plant ecologist. *Ecological Applications* 5: 209–214.

Hughes, J. B. and J. Roughgarden. 2000. Species diversity and biomass stability. *The American Naturalist* 155: 618–627.

Hughes, T. P. 1994. Catastrophes, phase shifts and large-scale degradation of a Caribbean coral reef. *Science* 265: 1547–1551.

Hulse, D. and R. Ribe. 2000. Land conversion and the production of wealth. *Ecological Applications* 10: 679–682.

Hunter, M. L., Jr. (ed.). 1999. *Maintaining Biodiversity in Forested Ecosystems.* Cambridge University Press, NY.

Huston, M. A. 1994. *Biological Diversity: The Coexistence of Species on Changing Landscapes.* Cambridge University Press, Cambridge.

Hutchings, M. J. 1987. The population biology of the early spider orchid, *Ophrys sphegodes* Mill. 1. A demographic study from 1975–1984. *Journal of Ecology* 75: 711–727.

Huxel, G. R. 1999. Rapid displacement of native species by invasive species: effects of hybridization. *Biological Conservation* 89: 143–152.

Huxel, G. R. and G. Polis. 2001. Food webs. *In* S.A. Levin (ed.), *Encyclopedia of Biodiversity*, 3: 1–18. Academic Press, San Diego, CA.

Iltis, H. H. 1988. Serendipity in the exploration of biodiversity: What good are weedy tomatoes? *In* E. O. Wilson and F. M. Peter (eds.), *Biodiversity*, pp. 98–105. National Academy Press, Washington, D.C.

Ingvarsson, P. K. 2001. Restoration of genetic variation lost- The genetic rescue hypothesis. *Trends in Ecology and Evolution* 16: 62–63.

Intergovernmental Panel on Climate Change (IPCC). 1996. *Climate Change 1995: The Science of Climate Change.* World Meteorological Organization and United Nations Environmental Program.

Intergovernmental Panel on Climate Change (IPCC). 2001. *Climate Change 2001: Synthesis Report.* Cambridge University Press, Cambridge.

Irwin, A. 2001. Wild at heart. *New Scientist* 169: 28–31.

IUCN. 1994. *Guidelines for Protected Area Management Categories.* IUCN, Gland, Switzerland.

IUCN. 1996. *1996 IUCN Red List of Threatened Animals.* IUCN, Gland, Switzerland.

IUCN. 2000. *Species: Newsletter of the Species Survival Commission.* Gland, Switzerland.

IUCN/UNEP. 1986. *Review of the Protected Areas System in the Afrotropical Realm.* IUCN, Gland, Switzerland.

IUCN/UNEP. 1988. *Coral Reefs of the World.* 3 Volumes. IUCN, Gland, Switzerland.

IUCN/WWF. 1989. *The Botanic Gardens Conservation Strategy.* IUCN, Gland, Switzerland.

Jacobson, S. K. and S. Marynowski. 1997. Public attitudes and knowledge about ecosystem management of Department of Defense lands in Florida. *Conservation Biology* 11: 770–778.

Jacobson, S. K., E. Vaughan, and S. W. Miller. 1995. New directions in conservation biology: Graduate programs. *Conservation Biology* 9: 5–17.

Jaffe, M. 1994. *And No Birds Sing.* Simon and Schuster, New York, NY.

James, F. C. 1999. Lessons learned from a study of habitat conservation planning. *BioScience* 49: 871–874.

James, F. C., C. E. McCulloch, and D. A. Wiedenfeld. 1996. New approaches to the analysis of population trends in land birds. *Ecology* 77: 13–27.

Janzen, D. H. 1983. No park is an island: Increase in interference from outside park as size decreases. *Oikos* 41: 402–410.

Janzen, D. H. 1986. The eternal external threat. *In* M. Soulé (ed.), *Conservation Biology: The Science of Scarcity and Diversity*, pp. 286–303. Sinauer Associates, Sunderland, MA.

Janzen, D. H. 1988a. Tropical dry forests: The most endangered major tropical ecosystem. *In* E. O. Wilson and F. M. Peter (eds.), *Biodiversity*, pp. 130–137. National Academy Press, Washington, D.C.

Janzen, D. H. 1988b. Tropical ecological and biocultural restoration. *Science* 239: 243–244.

Janzen, D. H. 1999. Gardenification of tropical conserved wildlands: Multitasking, multicropping, and multiusers. *Proceedings of the National Academy of Sciences of the United States* 96: 5987–5994.

Janzen, D. H. 2000. How to grow a wildland. The gardenification of nature. *In* P. H. Raven and T. Williams (eds.), *Nature and Human Society*, pp. 521–529. National Academy Presses, Washington, D.C.

Janzen, D. H. 2001. Latent extinctions- the living dead. *In* S.A. Levin (ed.), *Encyclopedia of Biodiversity*, 3: 689–700. Academic Press, San Diego, CA.

Jenkins, R. E. 1996. Natural Heritage Data Center Network: Managing information for managing biodiversity. *In* R. C. Szaro and D. W. Johnston (eds.), *Biodiversity in Managed Landscapes: Theory and Practice*, pp. 176–192. Oxford University Press, New York.

Jingling, T. 1993. The features of the Three Gorges Reservoir. *In* S. Luk and J. Whitney (eds.), *Megaproject: A Case Study of China's Three Gorges Project*, pp. 63–70. Armonk, New York.

Johannes, R. E. 1978. Traditional marine conservation methods in Oceania and their demise. *Annual Review of Ecology and Systematics* 9: 49–64.

Johns, A. D. 1996. Bird population persistence in Sabahan logging concessions. *Biological Conservation* 75: 3–10.

Johnson, N. 1995. *Biodiversity in the Balance: Approaches to Setting Geographic Conservation Priorities*. Biodiversity Support Program, World Wildlife Fund, Washington, D.C.

Johnson, N. C., A. J. Malk, and R. C. Szaro. 1999. *Ecological Stewardship. A Common Reference for Ecosystem Management*. Elsevier Science, New York.

Jones, A. T. and M. J. Hayes. 1999. Increasing floristic diversity in grassland: The effects of management regime and provenance on species introduction. *Biological Conservation* 87: 381–390.

Jones, H. L. and J. M. Diamond. 1976. Short-time-base studies of turnover in breeding birds of the California Channel Islands. *Condor* 76: 526–549.

Jones, R. F. 1990. Farewell to Africa. *Audubon* 92: 1547–1551.

Jordan, W. R., III, M. E. Gilpin, and J. D. Aber (eds.). 1990. *Restoration Ecology: A Synthetic Approach to Ecological Research*. Cambridge University Press, Cambridge.

Kappelle, M., M. M. I. van Vuuren, and P. Baas. 1999. Effects of climate change on biodiversity: a review and identification of key research issues. *Biodiversity and Conservation* 8: 1383–1397.

Kapur, D., J. P. Lewis, and R. Webb (eds.). 1997. *The World Bank: Its First Half-Century*. The Brookings Institute, Washington, D.C.

Karl, T., N. Nicholls, and J. Gregory. 1997. The coming climate. *Scientific American* 276(5): 78–83.

Karr, J. R. and E. W. Chu. 1998. *Restoring Life in Running Waters*. Island Press, Washington, D.C.

Kaufman, L. 1992. Catastrophic change in a species-rich freshwater ecosystem: Lessons from Lake Victoria. *BioScience* 42: 846–858.

Kaufman, L. and A. S. Cohen. 1993. The great lakes of Africa. *Conservation Biology* 7: 632–633.

Kauffman, J. B. and D. A. Pyke. 2001. Range ecology, global livestock influences. *In* S. A. Levin (ed.), *Encyclopedia of Biodiversity*, 5: 33–52. Academic Press, San Diego, CA.

Kautz, R. S. and J. A. Cox. 2001. Strategic habitats for biodiversity conservation in Florida. *Conservation Biology* 15: 55–77.

Kavanaugh M., A. A. Rahim, and C. J. Hails. 1989. *Rainforest Conservation in Sarawak: An International Policy for WWF*. WWF Malaysia, Kuala Lumpur.

Keitt, T. H., M. A. Lewis, and R. D. Holt. 2001. Allee effects, invasion pinning, and species' borders. *American Naturalist* 157: 203–216.

Keller, L. F., P. Arcese, J. N. M. Smith, W. M. Hochachka, and S. C. Stearns. 1994. Selection against inbred song sparrows during a natural population bottleneck. *Nature* 372: 356–357.

Kellert, S. R. 1996. *The Value of Life: Biological Diversity and Human Society*. Island Press/Shearwater Books, Washington, D.C.

Kellert, S. R. and E. O. Wilson (eds.). 1993. *The Biophilia Hypothesis*. Island Press, Washington, D.C.

Kelly, B. T. and M. K. Phillips. 2000. Red wolf (*Canis rufus*). In R. P. Reading and B. Miller (eds.), *Endangered Animals*, pp. 247–252. Greenwood Press, Westport, CT.

Kelly, P. K. 1994. *Thinking Green: Essays on Environmentalism, Feminism and Nonviolence*. Parallax Press, Berkeley, CA.

Kenchington, R. A. and M. T. Agardy. 1990. Achieving marine conservation through biosphere reserve planning and management. *Environmental Conservation* 17: 39–44.

Kendrick, R. 1995. Diminishing returns. *National Geographic* 188(November): 2–37.

Keohane, R. O. and M. A. Levy (eds.). 1996. *Institutions for Environmental Aid: Pitfalls and Promises*. MIT Press, Cambridge, MA.

Kerr, R. A. 1998. Acid rain control: Success on the cheap. *Science* 282: 1024–1027.

Kienast, F., O. Wilki, and B. Brzeziecki. 1998. Potential impacts of climate change on species richness in mountain forests- an ecological risk assessment. *Biological Conservation* 83: 291–305.

Kiew, R. 1991. *The State of Nature Conservation in Malaysia.* Malayan Nature Society, Kuala Lumpur.

Kimura, M. and J. F. Crow. 1963. The measurement of effective population numbers. *Evolution* 17: 279–288.

Kirkpatrick, M. and P. Jarne. 2000. The effects of a bottleneck on inbreeding depression and the genetic load. *American Naturalist* 155: 154–167.

Klass, K. D., O. Zompro, N. P. Kristensen, and J. Adis. 2002. Mantophasmatodea: A new insect order with extant members in the Afrotropics. *Science* 296: 1456–1459.

Kleiman, D. G. 1989. Reintroduction of captive mammals for conservation. *BioScience* 39: 152–161.

Kleiman, D. G., M. E. Allen, K. V. Thompson, and S. Lumpkin. 1996. *Wild Mammals in Captivity: Principles and Techniques.* University of Chicago Press, Chicago.

Klein, B. C. 1989. Effects of forest fragmentation on dung and carrion beetle communities in central Amazonia. *Ecology* 70: 1715–1725.

Klein, M. L., S. R. Humphrey, and H. F. Percival. 1995. Effects of ecotourism on distribution of waterbirds in wildlife refuge. *Conservation Biology* 9: 1454–1465.

Kloor, K. 2000. Ecology - Everglades restoration plan hits rough waters. *Science* 288: 1166–1167.

Kohm, K. and J. F. Franklin (eds.). 1997. *Creating a Forestry for the 21st Century: The Science of Ecosystem Management.* Island Press, Washington, D.C.

Komers, P. E. and G. P. Curman. 2000. The effect of demographic characteristics on the success of ungulate re-introductions. *Biological Conservation* 93: 187–193.

Koopowitz, H., A. D. Thornhill, and M. Andersen. 1994. A general stochastic model for the prediction of biodiversity losses based on habitat conversion. *Conservation Biology* 8: 425–438.

Kothari, A., N. Singh, and S. Suri (eds.). 1996. *People and Protected Areas: Toward Participatory Conservation in India.* Sage Publications, New Delhi.

Kramer, R., C. van Shaik, and J. Johnson (eds.). 1997. *Last Stand: Protected Areas and Defense of Tropical Biodiversity.* Oxford University Press, New York.

Kratochwil, A. (ed.). 2000. *Biodiversity in Ecosystems.* Kluwer Academic Publishers, Dordrecht, Netherlands.

Krebs, J. R., J. D. Wilson, R. B. Bradbury, and B. M. Siriwardena. 1999. The second silent spring? *Nature* 400: 611–612.

Kremen, C., A. M. Merenlender, and D. D. Murphy. 1994. Ecological monitoring: A vital need for integrated conservation and development programs in the tropics. *Conservation Biology* 8: 388–397.

Kremen, C., V. Razafimahatratra, R. P. Guillery, J. Rakotomalala, et al. 1999. Designing the Masoala National Park in Madagascar based on biological and socioeconomic data. *Conservation Biology* 13: 1055–1068.

Kristensen, R. M. 1983. Loricifera, a new phylum with Aschelminthes characters from the meiobenthos. *Zeitschrift fur Zoologische Systematik* 21: 163–180.

Kurlansky, M. 1996. Oil, toil and tyranny. *Audubon* 98: 128.

Kushmaro, A., M. Fine, and E. Rosenberg. 1996. Bacterial infection and coral bleaching. *Nature* 380: 396.

Kuylenstierna, J. C. I., H. Rodhe, S. Cinderby, and K. Hicks. 2001. Acidification in developing countries: Ecosystem sensitivity and the critical load approach on a global scale. *Ambio* 30: 20–28.

Lacy, R. C. 1987. Loss of genetic diversity from managed populations: Interacting effects of drift, mutation, immigration, selection and population subdivision. *Conservation Biology* 1: 143–158.

Lacy, R. C. and D. B. Lindenmayer. 1995. A simulation study of the impacts of population subdivision on the mountain brushtail possum *Trichosurus caninus* Ogilby (Phalangeridae: Marsupialia), in south-eastern Australia: Loss of genetic variation within and between subpopulations. *Biological Conservation* 73: 131–142.

Lambshead, J. and P. Schalk. 2001. Invertebrates, marine, overview. *In* S. A. Levin (ed.), *Encyclopedia of Biodiversity,* 3: 543–560. Academic Press, San Diego, CA.

Lande, R. 1988. Genetics and demography in biological conservation. *Science* 241: 1455–1460.

Lande, R. 1995. Mutation and conservation. *Conservation Biology* 9: 782–792.

Lande, R. and G. F. Barrowclough. 1987. Effective population size, genetic variation and their use in population management. *In* M. E. Soulé (ed.), *Viable Populations for Management,* pp. 87–124. Cambridge University Press, Cambridge.

Lanza, R. P., B. L. Dresser, and P. Damiani. 2000. Cloning Noah's Ark. *Scientific American* 283(5): 84–89.

Latta, S. C. 2000. Making the leap from researcher to planner: Lessons from avian conservation planning in the Dominican Republic. *Conservation Biology* 14: 132–139.

Laurance, S. G. and W. F. Laurance. 1999. Tropical wildlife corridors: Use of linear rainforest remnants by arboreal mammals. *Biological Conservation* 91: 231–239.

Laurance, W. F. 1991. Ecological correlates of extinction proneness in Australian tropical rain forest mammals. *Conservation Biology* 5: 79–89.

Laurance, W. F. 1999. Reflections on the tropical deforestation crisis. *Biological Conservation* 91: 109–117.

Laurance, W. F. and R. O. Bierregaard, Jr. (eds.). 1997. *Tropical Forest Remnants: Ecology, Management and Conservation of Fragmented Communities.* The University of Chicago Press, Chicago, IL.

Laurance, W. F. and M. A. Cochrane. 2001. Synergistic effects in fragmented landscapes (introduction to a special section). *Conservation Biology* 15: 1488–1489.

Laurance, W. F. and G. B. Williamson. 2001. Positive feedback among forest fragmentation, drought and climate change in the Amazon. *Conservation Biology* 15: 1529–1535.

Laurance, W. F., K. R. McDonald, and R. Speare. 1996. Epidemic disease and the catastrophic decline of Australian rain forest frogs. *Conservation Biology* 10: 406–414.

Laurance, W. F., L. V. Ferreira, J. M. Rankin-de Merona, and S. G. Laurance. 1998. Rain forest fragmentation and the dynamics of Amazonian tree communities. *Ecology* 79: 2032–2040.

Laurance, W. F., M. A. Cochrane, S. Bergen, P. M. Fearnside, et al. 2001. The future of the Brazilian Amazon. *Science* 291: 438–439.

Lawton, J. H. and R. M. May (eds.). 1995. *Extinction Rates.* Oxford University Press, Oxford.

Lawton, J. H. and K. Gaston. 2001. Indicator species. *In* S. A. Levin (ed.), *Encyclopedia of Biodiversity*, 3: 437–450. Academic Press, San Diego, CA.

Leader-Williams, N. 1990. Black rhinos and African elephants: Lessons for conservation funding. *Oryx* 24: 23–29.

Leakey, R. and R. Lewin. 1996. *The Sixth Extinction: Patterns of Life and the Future of Humankind.* Doubleday, Anchor, New York.

Ledig, F. T. 1988. The conservation of diversity in forest trees. *BioScience* 38: 471–479.

Lee, K. 1996. The source and locus of intrinsic value. *Environmental Ethics* 18: 297–308.

Lee, K. N. 2001. Sustainability, concept and practice of. *In* S. A. Levin (ed.), *Encyclopedia of Biodiversity*, 5: 553–568. Academic Press, San Diego, CA.

Leitner, W. and W. R. Turner. 2001. Measurement and analysis of biodiversity. *In* S. A. Levin (ed.), *Encyclopedia of Biodiversity*, 4: 123–144. Academic Press, San Diego, CA.

Lemonick, M. D. 1997. Under attack: It's humans, not sharks, who are nature's most fearsome predators. *Time* 150: 59–64.

Leopold, A. 1939a. A biotic view of land. *Journal of Forestry* 37: 113–116.

Leopold, A. 1939b. The farmer as a conservationist. *American Forests* 45: 294–299, 316, 323.

Leopold, A. 1949. *A Sand County Almanac and Sketches Here and There.* Oxford University Press, New York.

Lesica, P. and F. W. Allendorf. 1992. Are small populations of plants worth preserving? *Conservation Biology* 6: 135–139.

Lesica, P., R. F. Leary, F. W. Allendorf, and D. E. Bilderback. 1988. Lack of genetic diversity within and among populations of an endangered plant, *Howellia aquatilis. Conservation Biology* 2: 275–282.

Levin, S. A. 1996. Economic growth and environmental quality. *Ecological Applications* 6: 12.

Levin, S. A. (ed.). 2001. *Encyclopedia of Biodiversity.* Academic Press, San Diego, CA.

Levitus, S., J. I. Antonov, T. P. Boyer, and C. Stephens. 2000. Warming of the world ocean. *Science* 287: 2225–2229.

Lewis, D. M. 1995. Importance of GIS to community-based management of wildlife: Lessons from Zambia. *Ecological Applications* 5: 861–872.

Lewis, D. M., G. B. Kaweche, and A. Mwenya. 1990. Wildlife conservation outside protected areas—lessons from an experiment in Zambia. *Conservation Biology* 4: 171–180.

Li, L., C. Kato, and K. Horikoshi. 1999. Bacterial diversity in deep-sea sediments from different depths. *Biodiversity and Conservation* 8: 659–677.

Likens, G. E. 1991. Toxic winds: Whose responsibility? *In* F. H. Bormann and S. R. Kellert (eds.), *Ecology, Economics, Ethics: The Broken Circle*, pp. 136–152. Yale University Press, New Haven, CT.

Lilleskov, E. A., T. J. Fahey, and G. M. Lovett. 2001. Ectomycorrhizal fungal aboveground community change over an atmospheric nitrogen deposition gradient. *Ecological Applications* 11: 397–410.

Lin, S. C. and L. P. Yuan. 1980. *Hybrid rice breeding in China.* International Rice Research Institute, Innovative Approaches to Rice Breeding. Manila, Philippines.

Lindberg, K. 1991. *Policies for Maximizing Nature Tourism's Ecological and Economic Benefits.* World Resources Institute, Washington, D.C.

Linden, E. 1994. Ancient creature in a lost world. *Time*(June): 52–54.

Lindenmayer, D. B. 2000. Factors at multiple scales affecting distribution patterns and their implications for animal conservation- Leadbeater's Possum as a case study. *Biodiversity and Conservation* 9: 15–35.

Lindenmayer, D. B. and R. C. Lacy. 1995. Metapopulation viability of arboreal marsupials in fragmented old-growth forests: Comparison among species. *Ecological Applications* 5: 183–199.

Lindenmayer, D. B., M. A. Burgman, H. R. Akçakaya, R. C. Lacy, et al. 1995. A review of the generic computer-programs ALEX, RAMAS/SPACE and VORTEX for modeling the viability of wildlife metapopulations. *Ecological Modeling* 82: 161–174.

Lindholm, J. and B. Barr. 2001. Comparison of marine and terrestrial protected areas under federal jurisdiction in the United States. *Conservation Biology* 15: 1441–1444.

Line, L. 1993. Silence of the songbirds. *National Geographic* 183(June): 68–91.

Linington, S. and H. Pritchard. 2001. Gene banks. *In* S.A. Levin (ed.), *Encyclopedia of Biodiversity*, 3: 165–182. Academic Press, San Diego, CA.

Linnell, J. D. C., J. E. Swenson, and R. Anderson. 2000. Conservation of biodiversity in Scandanavian boreal forests: large carnivores as flagships, umbrellas, indicators, or keystones? *Biodiversity and Conservation* 9: 857–868.

List, P. C. 1993. *Radical Environmentalism: Philosophy and Tactics.* Wadsworth Publishing Co., Belmont, CA.

List, P. C. (ed.). 2000. *Environmental Ethics and Forestry: A Reader.* Temple University Press, Philadelphia.

Llewellyn, D. W., G. P. Shaffer, N. J. Craig, L. Creasman, et al. 1996. A decision-support system for prioritizing restoration sites on the Mississippi River alluvial plain. *Conservation Biology* 7: 1446–1456.

Lloyd, B. D and R. G. Powlesland. 1994. The decline of kakapo *Strigops habroptilus* and attempts at conservation by translocation. *Biological Conservation* 69: 75–85.

Loehle, G. and B. Li. 1996. Habitat destruction and the extinction debt revisited. *Ecological Applications* 6: 665–692.

Loeschcke, V., J. Tomiuk, and S. K. Jain (eds.). 1994. *Conservation Genetics.* Birkhauser Verlag, Basel, Switzerland.

Loope, L. L. 1995. Strategies for long-term protection of biological diversity in rainforests of Haleakala National Park and East Maui, Hawaii. *Endangered Species Update* 12: 1–5.

Loope, L. L., O. Hamann, and C. P. Stone. 1988. Comparative conservation biology of oceanic archipelagoes: Hawaii and the Galápagos. *BioScience* 38: 272–282.

Loreau, M. and A. Hector. 2001. Partitioning selection and complementarity in biodiversity experiments. *Nature* 412: 72–76.

Losos, E., J. Haynes, A. Phillips, and C. Alkiere. 1995. Taxpayer-subsidized resource extraction harms species. *BioScience* 45: 446–455.

Lövei, G. 2001. Extinctions, modern examples of. 2001. *In* S. A. Levin (ed.), *Encyclopedia of Biodiversity*, 2: 731–744. Academic Press, San Diego, CA.

Lovelock, J. 1988. *The Ages of Gaia.* W. W. Norton & Company, New York.

Lowman, M. D. 1999. *Life in the Treetops: Adventures of a Woman in Field Biology.* Yale University Press, New London, CT.

Loye, J. and S. Carroll. 1995. Birds, bugs and blood-Avian parasitism and conservation. *Trends in Ecology and Evolution* 10: 232–235.

Lubchenco, J. 1991. The Sustainable Biosphere Initiative: An ecological research agenda. *Ecology* 72: 371–412.

Ludwig, D., R. Hilborn, and C. Walters. 1993. Uncertainty, resource exploitation and conservation: Lessons from history. *Science* 260: 17, 36.

Luper-Foy, S. 1992. Justice and natural resources. *Environmental Values* 1: 47–64.

Lyles, A. M. 2001. Zoos and zoological parks. *In* S.A. Levin (ed.), *Encyclopedia of Biodiversity*, 5: 901–912. Academic Press, San Diego, CA.

Lynch, J. A., V. C. Bowersox, and J. W. Grimm. 2000. Acid rain reduced in eastern United States. *Environmental Science and Technology* 6: 940–949.

MacArthur, R. H. and E. O. Wilson. 1967. *The Theory of Island Biogeography.* Princeton University Press, Princeton, NJ.

Mace, G. M. 1994. Classifying threatened species: Means and ends. *Philosophical Transactions of the Royal Society of London: Series B* 344: 91–97.

Mace, G. M. 1995. Classification of threatened species and its role in conservation planning. *In* J. H. Lawton and R. M. May (eds.), *Extinction Rates*, pp. 131–146. Oxford University Press, Oxford.

Mace, G. M and E. J. Hudson. 1999. Attitudes toward sustainability and extinction. *Conservation Biology* 13: 242–246.

Machlis, G. E. and D. R. Field. 2000. *National Parks and Rural Development: Practice and Policy in the United States.* Island Press, Washington, D.C.

Machtans, G. S., M. Villard, and S. J. Hannon. 1996. Use of riparian buffer strips as movement corridors by forest birds. *Conservation Biology* 7: 1366–1380.

Mack, R. N., D. Simberloff, W. M. Lonsdale, H. Evans, et al. 2000. Biotic invasions: causes, epidemiology, global consequences, and control. *Ecological Applications* 10: 689–710.

MacKenzie, D. 2000. Sick to death. *New Scientist* 167: 32–35.

MacKenzie, S. H. 1996. *Integrated Resource Planning and Management: The Resource Approach in the Great Lakes Basin.* Island Press, Washington, D.C.

MacKinnon, J. 1983. *Irrigation & Watershed Protection in Indonesia.* Report to IBRD Regional Office, Jakarta.

MacKinnon, K. 2000. *Transboundary Reserves. World Bank Implementation of the Ecosystem Approach.* World Bank, New York.

Mader, H. J. 1984. Animal habitat isolation by roads and agricultural fields. *Biological Conservation* 29: 81–96.

Maehr, D. S. 1990. The Florida panther and private lands. *Conservation Biology* 4: 167–170.

Maehr, D. S. and J. A. Cox. 1995. Landscape features and panthers in Florida. *Conservation Biology* 9: 1008–1020.

Maehr, D. S., R. F. Noss, and J. L. Larkin (eds.). 2001. *Large Mammal Restoration. Ecological and Sociological Challenges in the 21st Century.* Island Press, Washington, D.C.

Magnuson, J. J. 1990. Long-term ecological research and the invisible present. *BioScience* 40: 495–501.

Maher, H. 1999. Driven to Violence: ABCNEWS.com's Heather Maher on Ecoterrorism. www.abcnews.com.

Makarewicz, J. C. and P. Bertram. 1991. Evidence for the restoration of the Lake Erie ecosystem. *BioScience* 41: 216–223.

Malakoff, D. 1998. Death by suffocation in the Gulf of Mexico. *Conservation Biology* 281: 190–192.

Mangel, M. and C. Tier. 1994. Four facts every conservation biologist should know about persistence. *Ecology* 75: 607–614.

Mann, C. C. and M. L. Plummer. 1995a. Is Endangered Species Act in danger? *Science* 267: 1256–1258.

Mann, C. C. and M. L. Plummer. 1995b. Are wildlife corridors on the right path? *Science* 270: 1428–1430.

Mann, C. C. and M. L. Plummer. 1999. A species' fate, by the numbers. *Science* 284: 36–37.

Marcovaldi, M. A. and G. G. dei Marcovaldi. 1999. Marine turtles of Brazil: The history and structure of Projeto TAMAR-IBAMA. *Biological Conservation* 91: 35–41.

Mares, M. A. 1992. Neotropical mammals and the myth of Amazonian biodiversity. *Science* 255: 976–979.

Margules, C. R. and R. L. Pressey. 2000. Systematic conservation planning. *Nature* 405: 243–253.

Marsh, G. P. 1864. *Man and Nature; or, Physical Geography as Modified by Human Action.* Reprinted in 1965, D. Lowenthal (ed.), Harvard University Press, Cambridge, MA.

Marsh, D. M. 2001. Fluctuations in amphibian populations: A meta-analysis. *Biological Conservation* 101: 327–335.

Martin, P. S. 2001. Mammals (late Quaternary), extinctions of. *In* S. A. Levin (ed.), *Encyclopedia of Biodiversity,* 3: 825–840. Academic Press, San Diego, CA.

Maser, C. 1997. *Sustainable Community Development: Principles and Practices.* St. Lucie Press, Delray Beach, FL.

Masood, E. and L. Garwin. 1998. Costing the earth: When ecology meets economics. *Nature* 395: 426–430.

Mateo, N., W. Nader, and G. Tamayo. 2001. Bioprospecting. *In* S. A. Levin (ed.), *Encyclopedia of Biodiversity,* 1: 471–488. Academic Press, San Diego, CA.

Mathews, A. 1992. *Where the Buffalo Roam.* Grove Weidenfeld, New York.

Mathiessen, P. 2000. *Tigers in the Snow.* North Point Press, New York.

Mauchamp, A. 1997. Threats from alien plant species in the Galapagos Islands. *Conservation Biology* 11: 260–263.

Maunder, M. 2001. Plant conservation, overview. *In* S. A. Levin (ed.), *Encyclopedia of Biodiversity,* 4: 645–658. Academic Press, San Diego, CA.

Maxted, N. 2001. *Ex Situ, In Situ* Conservation. *In* S. A. Levin (ed.), *Encyclopedia of Biodiversity,* 2: 683–696. Academic Press, San Diego, CA.

May, R. M. 1992. How many species inhabit the Earth? *Scientific American* 267(4): 42–48.

Mayr, E. 1991. *One Long Argument: Charles Darwin and the Genesis of Modern Evolutionary Thought.* Harvard University Press, Cambridge.

McAuliffe, J. R. 1996. Saguaro cactus dynamics. *In* W. Halvorson and G. Davis (eds.), *Science and Ecosystem Management in the National Parks,* pp. 96–131. University of Arizona Press, Tucson.

McCallum, H. and A. Dobson. 1995. Detecting disease and parasite threats to endangered species and ecosystems. *Trends in Ecology and Evolution* 10: 190–194.

McCann, K. S. 2000. The diversity-stability debate. *Nature* 405: 228–233.

McCarty, J. P. 2001. Ecological consequences of recent climate change. *Conservation Biology* 15: 320–331.

McClanahan, T. R. and R. Arthur. 2001. The effect of marine reserves and habitat on populations of East African coral reef fishes. *Ecological Applications* 11: 559–569.

McClanahan, T. R., N. A. Muthiga, A. T. Kamukuru, H. Machano, and R. W. Kiambo. 1999. The effects of marine parks and fishing on coral reefs of northern Tanzania. *Biological Conservation* 89: 161–182.

McCullough, D. R. (ed.). 1996. *Metapopulations and Wildlife Conservation.* Island Press, Washington, D.C.

McKee, M. and R. P. Berrens. 2001. Balancing army and endangered species concerns: Green vs. Green. *Environmental Management* 27: 123–133.

McKibben, B. 1996. What good is a forest? *Audubon* 98: 54–65.

McLachlan, J. A. and S. F. Arnold. 1996. Environmental estrogens. *American Scientist* 84: 452–461.

McLaren, B. E. and R. O. Peterson. 1994. Wolves, moose and tree rings on Isle Royale. *Science* 266: 1555–1558.

McLaughlin, A. 1993. *Regarding Nature: Industrialism and Deep Ecology.* State University of New York Press, Albany.

McLean, H. E. 1995. Smart maps: Forestry's newest frontier. *American Forests* (March/April): 13–21.

McMichael, A. J., B. Bolin, R. Costanza, G. C. Daily, et al. 1999. Globalization and the sustainability of human health. *BioScience* 49: 205–210.

McNeely, J. 2001. Social and cultural factors. *In* S. A. Levin (ed.), *Encyclopedia of Biodiversity,* 5: 285–294. Academic Press, San Diego, CA.

McNeely, J. A. 1989. Protected areas and human ecology: How national parks can contribute to sustaining societies of the twenty-first century. *In* D. Western and M. Pearl (eds.), *Conservation for the Twenty-first Century,* pp. 150–165. Oxford University Press, New York.

McNeely, J. A. and W. S. Keeton. 1995. The interaction between biological and cultural diversity. *In* B. von Droste, H. Plachter, G. Fisher, and M. Rossler (eds.), *Cultural Landscapes of Universal Value,* pp. 25–37. Gustav Fischer Verlag, New York.

McNeely, J. A., J. Harrison, and P. Dingwall (eds.). 1994. *Protecting Nature: Regional Reviews of Protected Areas.* IUCN, Cambridge.

McNeely, J. A., K. R. Miller, W. Reid, R. Mittermeier, et al. 1990. *Conserving the World's Biological Diversity.* IUCN, World Resources Institute, CI, WWF-US, the World Bank, Gland, Switzerland and Washington, D.C.

McPhee, J. 1971. *Encounters with the Archdruid.* Farrar, Straus and Giroux, New York.

Medina, E. and O. Huber. 1992. The role of biodiversity in the function of savannah ecosystems. *In* O. T. Solbrig, H. M. van Emden, and P. G. W. J. van Oordt (eds.), *Biodiversity and Global Change,* pp. 139–158. International Union of Biological Sciences, Paris.

Meffe, G. C. and C. R. Carroll. 1997. *Principles of Conservation Biology,* 2nd ed. Sinauer Associates, Sunderland, MA.

Meine, C. 2001. Conservation movement, historical. *In* S. A. Levin (ed.), *Encyclopedia of Biodiversity,* 1: 883–896. Academic Press, San Diego, CA.

Meine, C. and R. L. Knight (eds.). 1999. *The Essential Aldo Leopold: Quotations and Commentaries.* University of Wisconsin Press, Madison.

Menge, B. and T. Freidenburg. 2001. Keystone species. *In* S. A. Levin (ed.), *Encyclopedia of Biodiversity,* 3: 613–632. Academic Press, San Diego, CA.

Menges, E. S. 1990. Population viability analysis for an endangered plant. *Conservation Biology* 4: 52–62.

Menges, E. S. 1992. Stochastic modeling of extinction in plant populations. *In* P. L. Fiedler and S. K. Jain (eds.), *Conservation Biology: The Theory and Practice of Nature Conservation, Preservation and Management,* pp. 253–275. Chapman and Hall, New York.

Menges, E. S. 2000. Population variability analyses in plants: Challenges and opportunities. *Trends in Ecology and Evolution* 15: 51–56.

Meyers, N. 1997. Consumption in relation to population, environment and development. *The Environmentalist* 17: 33–44.

Middleton, S. and D. Littschwager. 1994. *Witness: Endangered Species in North America*. Chronicle Books, San Francisco.

Middleton, S. and D. Littschwager. 1997. *America's Endangered Species: Don't Say Good-Bye*. National Geographic Video.

Miller, B., R. P. Reading, and S. Forrest. 1996. *Prairie Night: Black-Footed Ferret and the Recovery of Endangered Species*. Smithsonian Institution Press, Washington, D.C.

Miller, B., R. P. Reading, and T. W. Clark. 2000. Black-footed ferret (*Mustela nigripes*). In R. P. Reading and B. Miller (eds.), *Endangered Animals*, pp. 54–59. Greenwood Press, Westport, CT.

Miller, G. H., J. W. Magee, B. J. Johnson, M. L. Fogel, et al. 1999b. Pleistocene extinction of *Genyornis newtoni*: Human impact on Australian megafauna. *Science* 283: 205–208.

Miller, G. R., C. Geddes, and D. K. Mardon. 1999a. Response of the alpine gentian *Gentiana nivalis* L. to protection from grazing by sheep. *Biological Conservation* 87: 311–318.

Miller, J. K., J. M. Scott, C. R. Miller, and L. P Waits. 2002. The endangered species act: Dollars and sense? *BioScience* 52: 163–168.

Miller, K. R. 1996. *Balancing the Scales: Guidelines for Increasing Biodiversity's Chances Through Bioregional Management*. World Resources Institute, Washington, D.C.

Miller, P. 1995. Crusading for chimps and humans: Jane Goodall. *National Geographic* 188(December): 102.

Mills, E. L., H. H. Leach, J. T. Carlton, and C. L. Secor. 1994. Exotic species and the integrity of the Great Lakes. *BioScience* 44: 666–676.

Mills, L. S. and F. W. Allendorf. 1996. The one-migrant-per-generation rule in conservation and management. *Conservation Biology* 10: 1509–1518.

Milton, S. J., W. R. J. Dean, M. A. du Plessis, and W. R. Siegfried. 1994. A conceptual model of arid rangeland degradation. *BioScience* 44: 70–76.

Milton, S. J., W. J. Bond, M. A. DuPleiss, D. Gibbs, et al. 1999. A protocol for plant conservation by translocation in threatened lowlands Fynbos. *Conservation Biology* 13: 735–743.

Minckley, W. L. 1995. Translocation as a tool for conserving imperiled fishes: Experiences in western United States. *Biological Conservation* 72: 297–309.

Mitchell, J. G. 1992. Our disappearing wetlands. *National Geographic* 182(October): 3–45.

Mitchell, J. G. 1994. Our national parks. *National Geographic* 186(April): 2–55.

Mitikin, K. and D. Osgood. 1994. *Issues and Options in the Design of Global Environment Facility-Supported Trust Funds for Biodiversity Conservation*. World Bank, Washington, D.C.

Mittermeier, R. A., P. R. Gil, and C. G. Mittermeier. 1997. *Megadiversity: Earth's Biologically Wealthiest Nations*. Conservation International, Washington, D.C.

Mittermeier, R. A., N. Myers, P. R. Gil, and C. G. Mittermeier. 1999. *Hotspots: Earth's Richest and Most Endangered Terrestrial Ecoregions*. Agrupacion Sierra Madre, S. C., Mexico City, Mexico.

Mlot, C. 1992. Botanists sue Forest Service to preserve biodiversity. *Science* 257: 1618–1619.

Moffat, M. W. 1994. *The High Frontier: Exploring the Tropical Rainforest Canopy*. Harvard University Press, Cambridge, MA.

Moiseenko, T. 1994. Acidification and critical loads for surface waters: Kola, northern Russia. *Ambio* 23: 418–424.

Montalvo, A. M. and N. C. Ellstrand. 2001. Nonlocal transplantation and outbreeding depression in the subshrub *Lotus scoparius* (Fabaceae). *American Journal of Botany* 88: 28–269.

Mooney, H. A. and R. J. Hobbs (eds.). 2000. *Invasive Species in a Changing World*. Island Press, Washington, D.C.

Moore, D., M. M. Nauta, S. E. Evans, and M. Rotheroe (eds.). 2001. *Fungal Conservation: Issues and Solutions*. Cambridge University Press, United Kingdom.

Morales, J. C., P. M. Andau, J. Supriatna, Z. Z. Zainuddin, and D. J. Melnick. 1997. Mitochondrial DNA variability and conservation genetics of the Sumatran rhinoceros. *Conservation Biology* 11: 539–543.

Morell, V. 1986. Dian Fossey: Field science and death in Africa. *Science* 86: 17–21.

Morell, V. 1993. Primatology: Called 'trimates,' three bold women shaped their field (Dian Fossey, Jane Goodall and Birute Galdikas). *Science* 260: 420–425.

Morell, V. 1994. Serengeti's big cats going to the dogs. *Science* 264: 23.

Morell, V. 1996. New mammals discovered by biology's new explorers. *Science* 273: 1491.

Morell, V. 1999. Variety of life. *National Geographic* 195(February): 6–32.

Morris, M. G. 2000. The effects of structure and its dynamics on the ecology and conservation of arthropods in British grasslands. *Biological Conservation* 95: 129–142.

Morris, W. F. and D. F. Doak. 2002. *Quantitative Conservation Biology: Theory and Practice of Population Viability Analysis*. Sinauer Associates, Sunderland, MA.

Mosquin, T., P. G. Whiting, and D. E. McAllister. 1995. *Canada's Biodiversity: The Value of Life, Its Status, Economic Benefits, Conservation Costs and Unmet Needs*. Canadian Museum of Nature, Ottawa.

Motavelli, J. 1995. In harms' way. *E: The Environmental Magazine* 6: 28–37.

Mousson, L., G. Nève, and M. Baguette. 1999. Metapopulation structure and conservation of the cranberry fritillary *Boloria aquilonaris* (Lepidoptera, Nymphalidae) in Belgium. *Biological Conservation* 87: 285–293.

Mowat, F. 1984. *Sea of Slaughter*. McClelland and Stewart, Toronto.

Moyle, P. B. 1995. Conservation of native freshwater fishes in the Mediterranean-type climate of California, USA: A review. *Biological Conservation* 72: 271–279.

Moyle, P. B. and R. A. Leidy. 1992. Loss of biodiversity in aquatic ecosystems: Evidence from fish faunas. *In* P. L. Fiedler and S. K. Jain (eds.), *Conservation Biology: The Theory and Practice of Nature Conservation, Preservation and Management,* pp. 127–169. Chapman and Hall, New York.

Muir, J. 1901. *Our National Parks.* Houghton Mifflin, Boston, MA.

Muir, J. 1916. *A Thousand Mile Walk to the Gulf.* Houghton Mifflin, Boston, MA.

Murphy, D. D., D. E. Freas, and S. B. Weiss. 1990. An environment-metapopulation approach to population viability analysis for a threatened invertebrate. *Conservation Biology* 4: 41–51.

Mustart, P, J. Juritz, C. Makua, S. W. Van der Merwe, and N. Wessels. 1995. Restoration of the clanwilliam cedar *Widdringtonia cedarbergensis*: The importance of monitoring seedlings planted in the Cederberg, South Africa. *Biological Conservation* 72: 73–76.

Muths, E. and M. P. Scott. 2000. American Burying Beetle (*Nicrophorus americanus*). In R. P. Reading and B. Miller (eds.), *Endangered Animals,* pp. 10–15. Greenwood Press, Westport, CT.

Myers, J. H., D. Simberloff, A. M. Kuris, and J. R. Carey. 2000. Eradication revisited: dealing with exotic species. *Trends in Ecology and Evolution* 15: 316–320.

Myers, N. 1980. *Conversion of Tropical Moist Forests.* National Academy of Sciences, Washington, D.C.

Myers, N. 1983. *A Wealth of Wild Species.* Westview Press, Boulder, CO.

Myers, N. 1986. Tropical deforestation and a mega-extinction spasm. *In* M. E. Soulé, (ed.), *Conservation Biology: The Science of Scarcity and Diversity,* pp. 394–409. Sinauer Associates, Sunderland, MA.

Myers, N. 1987. The extinction spasm impending: Synergisms at work. *Conservation Biology* 1: 14–21.

Myers, N. 1988. Tropical forests: Much more than stocks of wood. *Journal of Tropical Ecology* 4: 209–221.

Myers, N. 1991. Tropical deforestation: The latest situation. *BioScience* 41: 282.

Myers, N. 1993. Sharing the earth with whales. *In* L. Kaufman and K. Mallory (eds.), *The Last Extinction,* pp. 179–194. MIT Press, Cambridge, MA.

Myers, N. 1996. *Ultimate Security: The Environmental Basis of Political Stability.* Island Press, Washington, D.C.

Myers, N. 1997. Consumption in relation to population, environment and development. *The Environmentalist* 17: 34–44.

Myers, N. 1998. Lifting the veil on perverse subsidies. *Nature* 392: 327–328.

Myers, N. (In Press). The biodiversity outlook: Endangered species and endangered ideas. *In* J. F. Shogren and J. Tschirari (eds.), *Social Order and Endangered Species Preservation.* Cambridge University Press, New York.

Myers, N. and J. Kent. 2001. *Perverse Subsidies: How Tax Dollars Can Undercut the Environment and the Economy.* Island Press, Washington, D.C.

Myers, N. and A. Knoll. 2001. The biotic crisis and the future of evolution. *Proceedings of the National Academy of Sciences of the United States* 98: 5389–5392.

Myneni, R. B., C. D. Keeling, C. J. Tucker, G. Asrar, and R. R. Nemani. 1997. Increased plant growth in the northern high latitudes from 1981 to 1991. *Nature* 386: 698–702.

Nabhan, G. P. 1985. Native crop diversity in Aridoamerica: Conservation of regional gene pools. *Economic Botany* 39: 387–399.

Nabhan, G. P. 1989. *Enduring Seeds: Native American Agriculture and Wild Plant Conservation.* North Point Press, San Francisco.

Naess, A. 1986. Intrinsic value: Will the defenders of nature please rise? *In* M. E. Soulé (ed.), *Conservation Biology: The Science of Scarcity and Diversity,* pp. 153–181. Sinauer Associates, Sunderland, MA.

Naess, A. 1989. *Ecology, Community and Lifestyle.* Cambridge University Press, Cambridge.

Naiman, R. J., J. J. Magnuson, D. M. McKnight, J. A. Stanford, and J. R. Karr. 1995. Fresh-water ecosystems and their management- A national initiative. *Science* 270: 584–585.

Nash, J. A. 1991a. *Loving Nature: Ecological Integrity and Christian Responsibility.* Abington, Nashville.

Nash, R. 1982. *Wilderness and the American Mind.* Yale University Press, New Haven, CT.

Nash, R. 1990. *American Environmentalism: Readings in Conservation Biology,* 3rd ed. McGraw-Hill, New York.

Nash, S. 1991b. What price nature? *BioScience* 41: 677–680.

National Research Council (NRC). 1996. *Ecologically Based Pest Management: New Solutions for a New Century.* National Academy Press, Washington, D.C.

Nature Conservancy, The. 1996. *Designing a Geography of Hope: Guidelines for an Ecoregion-Based Conservation in The Nature Conservancy.* The Nature Conservancy, Arlington, VA.

Naylor, R. L., R. J. Goldburg, H. Mooney, M. Beveridge, et al. 1998. Nature's subsidies to shrimp and salmon farming. *Science* 282: 883–884.

Nei, M., T. Maruyama, and R. Chakraborty. 1975. The bottleneck effect and genetic variability in populations. *Evolution* 29: 1–10.

Nellemann, C., I. Vistnes, P. Jordhoy, and O. Strand. 2001. Winter distribution of wild reindeer in relation to power lines, roads, and resorts. *Biological Conservation* 101: 351–360.

Nepstad, D. C. and S. Schwartzmann (eds.). 1992. *Non-Timber Products from Tropical Forests: Evaluation of a Conservation and Development Strategy.* The New York Botanical Garden, Bronx, NY.

Nepstad, D. C., A. Verissimo, A. Alencar, C. Nobre, et al. 1999. Large-scale impoverishment of Amazonian forests by logging and fire. *Nature* 398: 505–508.

Nepstad, D., G. Carvalho, A. C. Barros, A. Alencar, et al. 2001. Road paving, fire regime feedbacks, and the future of Amazon forests. *Forest Ecology and Management* 5524: 1–13.

Neto, R. B. and D. Dickson. 1999. $3 m deal launches major hunt for drug deals in Brazil. *Nature* 400: 302.

Neuenschwander, P. 2001. Biological control of the cassava mealybug in Africa: A review. *Biological Control* 21: 214–229.

Newmark, W. D. 1995. Extinction of mammal populations in western North American national parks. *Conservation Biology* 9: 512–527.

Newmark, W. D. and J. L. Hough. 2000. Conserving wildlife in Africa: Integrated conservation and development projects and beyond. *BioScience* 50: 585–592.

Newton, I. 1994. The role of nest sites in limiting the numbers of hole-nesting birds: A review. *Biological Conservation* 70: 265–276.

Nias, R. C. 2001 Endangered ecosystems. *In* S. A. Levin (ed.), *Encyclopedia of Biodiversity*, 2: 407–424. Academic Press, San Diego, CA.

Niemelä, J., D. Langor, and J. R. Spence. 1993. Effects of clear cut harvesting on boreal ground-beetle assemblages (Coleoptera: Carabidae) in Western Canada. *Conservation Biology* 7: 551–561.

Nieminen, M., M. C. Singer, W. Fortelius, K. Schops, and I. Hanski. 2001. Experimental confirmation that inbreeding depression increases extinction risk in butterfly populations. *American Naturalist* 157: 237–244.

Nilsson, S. G., U. Arup, R. Baranowski, and S. Ekman. 1995. Tree-dependent lichens and beetles as indicators in conservation forests. *Conservation Biology* 9: 1208–1216.

Noble, I. and S. Roxburgh. 2001. Terrestrial ecosystems. *In* S. A. Levin (ed.), *Encyclopedia of Biodiversity*, 5: 637–646. Academic Press, San Diego, CA.

Norris, S. 2000. A Year for Biodiversity. *BioScience* 50: 103–107.

Norse, E. A. 1986. *Conserving Biological Diversity in Our National Forests*. The Wilderness Society, Washington, D.C.

Norse, E. A. (ed.). 1993. *Global Marine Biological Diversity: A Strategy for Building Conservation into Decision Making*. Island Press, Washington, D.C.

Norton, B. G. 1991. *Toward Unity Among Environmentalists*. Oxford University Press, New York.

Norton, B. G. 2000. Biodiversity and environmental values: in search of a universal earth ethic. *Biodiversity and Conservation* 9: 1029–1044.

Norton, B. G., M. Hutchins, E. F. Stevens, and T. L. Maple. 1995. *Ethics on the Ark: Zoos, Animal Welfare and Wildlife Conservation*. Smithsonian Institution Press, Washington, D.C.

Noss, R. F. 1992. Essay: Issues of scale in conservation biology. *In* P. L. Fiedler and S. K. Jain (eds.), *Conservation Biology: The Theory and Practice of Nature Conservation, Preservation and Management*, pp. 239–250. Chapman and Hall, New York.

Noss, R. F. and A. Y. Cooperrider. 1994. *Saving Nature's Legacy: Protecting and Restoring Biodiversity*. Island Press, Washington, D.C.

Noss, R. F., E. T. La Roe III, and J. M. Scott. 1995. *Endangered Ecosystems of the United States: A Preliminary Assessment of Loss and Degradation*. Biological Report 28. Washington: U.S. Department of Interior, National Biological Service.

Noss, R. F., M. A. O'Connell, and D. D. Murphy. 1997. *The Science of Conservation Planning: Habitat Conservation Under the Endangered Species Act*. Island Press, Washington, D.C.

NOVA. 1997. *Kingdom of the Seahorse*, WGBH Science Unit, Boston, MA.

Nunney, L. and D. R. Elam. 1994. Estimating the effective population size of conserved populations. *Conservation Biology* 8: 175–184.

Oates, J. F. 1999. *Myth and Reality in the Rainforest: How Conservation Strategies Are Failing in West Africa*. University of California Press, Berkeley.

Oates, J. F., M. Abedi-Lartey, W. S. McGraw, T. T. Struhsaker, and G. H. Whitesides. 2000. Extinction of a West African Red Colubus monkey. *Conservation Biology* 14: 1526–1532.

Odum, E. P. 1997. *Ecology: A Bridge Between Science and Society*. Sinauer Associates, Sunderland, MA.

Oelschlaeger, M. 1994. *Caring for Creation: An Ecumenical Approach to the Environmental Crisis*. Yale University Press, New Haven, CT.

Office of Technology Assessment of the U.S. Congress (OTA). 1987. *Technologies to Maintain Biological Diversity*. OTA-F-330. U.S. Government Printing Office, Washington, D.C.

Oldfield, M. L. and J. B. Alcorn (eds.). 1991. *Biodiversity: Culture, Conservation and Ecodevelopment*. Westview Press, Boulder, CO.

Oliver, I. and A. J. Beattie. 1993. A possible method for the rapid assessment of biodiversity. *Conservation Biology* 7: 562–568.

Oliver, I. and A. J. Beattie. 1996. Invertebrate morphospecies as surrogates for species: A case study. *Conservation Biology* 10: 99–110.

Olney, P. J. S. and P. Ellis (eds.). 1995. *1994 International Zoo Yearbook*, 35. Zoological Society of London, London.

Olson, D. M. and E. Dinerstein. 1998. The Global 200: A representation approach to conserving the Earth's most biologically valuable ecoregions. *Conservation Biology* 12: 502–515.

Olson, S. L. 1989. Extinction on islands: Man as a catastrophe. *In* M. Pearl and D. Western (eds.), *Conservation Biology for the Twenty-first Century*, pp. 50–53. Oxford University Press, Oxford.

Orr, D. W. 1994. *Ecological Literacy: Education and the Transition to a Postmodern World*. State University of New York Press, Albany.

Osborn, F. 1948. *Our Plundered Planet*. Little, Brown Company, Boston.

Pace, F. 1991. The Klamath corridors: Preserving biodiversity in the Klamath National Forest. *In* W. E. Hudson (ed.), *Landscape Linkages and Biodiversity*, pp. 105–116. Island Press, Washington, D.C.

Packard, S. and C. Mutel (eds.). 1997. *Tallgrass Prairie Restoration Handbook*. Island Press, Washington, D.C.

Packer, C. 1992. Captives in the wild. *National Geographic* 181(April): 122–136.

Packer, C. 1997. Viruses of the Serengeti: Patterns of infection and mortality in African lions. *Journal of Animal Ecology* 68: 1161–1178.

Packer, C., A. E. Pusey, H. Rowley, D. A. Gilbert, et al. 1991. Case study of a population bottleneck: Lions of the Ngorongoro Crater. *Conservation Biology* 5: 219–230.

Paddack, M. J. and J. A. Estes. 2000. Kelp forest fish populations in marine reserves and adjacent exploited areas of central California. *Ecological Applications* 10: 855–870.

Paine, R. T. 1966. Food web complexity and species diversity. *American Naturalist* 100: 65–75.

Panayotou, T. and P. S. Ashton. 1992. *Not by Timber Alone: Economics and Ecology for Sustaining Tropical Forests.* Island Press, Washington, D.C.

Parfit, M. 1995. Diminishing returns: Exploiting the ocean's bounty. *National Geographic* 188(May): 2–56.

Parkes, R. J., B. A. Cragg, S. J. Bale, S. M. Getliff, et al. 1994. Deep bacterial biosphere in Pacific Ocean sediments. *Nature* 371: 410–413.

Parmesan, C., N. Ryrholm, C. Stefanescu, J. K. Hill, et al. 1999. Poleward shifts in geographical ranges of butterfly species associated with regional warming. *Nature* 399: 579–583.

Paton, P. W. C. 1994. The effect of edge on avian nest success: How strong is the evidence? *Conservation Biology* 8: 17–26.

Patterson, A. 1990. Debt for nature swaps and the need for alternatives. *Environment* 32: 5–32.

Pearson, D. L. and F. Cassola. 1992. World-wide species richness patterns of tiger beetles (Coleoptera: Cicindelidae): Indicator taxon for biodiversity and conservation studies. *Conservation Biology* 6: 376–391.

Pechmann, J. H. K., D. E. Scott, R. D. Semlitsch, J. P. Caldwell, et al. 1991. Declining amphibian populations: The problems of separating human impacts from natural fluctuations. *Science* 253: 892–895.

Pechmann, J. H. K. and H. M. Wilbur. 1994. Putting declining amphibian populations in perspective- natural fluctuation and human impacts. *Herpetologica* 50: 65–84.

Peluso, N. L. 1992. The Ironwood problem: The (mis)management and development of an extractive rain forest product. *Conservation Biology* 6: 210–219.

Peres, C. A. and J. W. Terborgh. 1995. Amazonian nature reserves: An analysis of the defensibility status of existing conservation units and design criteria for the future. *Conservation Biology* 9: 34–46.

Perfecto, I., R. A. Rice, R. Greenberg, and M. E. Van der Voort. 1996. Shade coffee: A disappearing refuge for biodiversity. *BioScience* 46: 598–608.

Perrings, C. 1995. Economic values of biodiversity. *In* V. H. Heywood (ed.), *Global Biodiversity Assessment*, pp. 823–914. Cambridge University Press, Cambridge.

Persson, N. J., J. Axelman, and D. Broman. 2000. Validating possible effects of eutrophication using PCB concentrations in bivalves and sediment of the US musselwatch and benthic surveillance programs. *Ambio* 29: 246–251.

Peterken, G. F. 1996. *Natural Woodland, Ecology and Conservation in Northern Temperate Regions.* Cambridge University Press, Cambridge.

Peters, C. M. 1994. *Sustainable Harvest of Non-timber Plant Resources in Tropical Moist Forest: An Ecological Primer.* Biodiversity Support Program, Washington, D.C.

Peters, C. M., A. H. Gentry, and R. Mendelsohn. 1989. Valuation of a tropical forest in Peruvian Amazonia. *Nature* 339: 655–656.

Peters, R. L. and T. E. Lovejoy (eds.). 1992. *Global Warming and Biological Diversity.* Yale University Press, Boulder, CO.

Pfab, M. F. and E. T. F. Witkowski. 2000. A simple population viability analysis of the Critically Endangered *Euphorbia clivicola* R. A. Dyer under four management scenarios. *Biological Conservation* 96: 263–270.

Philippart, J. C. 1995. Is captive breeding an effective solution for the preservation of endemic species? *Biological Conservation* 72: 281–295.

Phillips, K. 1990. Where have all the frogs and toads gone? *BioScience* 40: 422–424.

Pimentel, D., L. Westra, and R. F. Noss (eds.). 2000a. *Ecological Integrity: Integrating Environment, Conservation, and Health.* Island Press, Washington, D.C.

Pimentel, D., L. Lach, R. Zuniga, and D. Morrison. 2000b. Environmental and economic costs of nonindigenous species in the United States. *BioScience* 50: 53–65.

Pimentel, D., C. Harvey, P. Resosudarmo, K. Sinclair, et al. 1995. Environmental and economic costs of soil erosion and conservation benefits. *Science* 267: 1117–1121.

Pimentel, D., C. Wilson, C. McCullum, R. Huang, et al. 1997. Economic and environmental benefits of diversity. *BioScience* 47: 747–757.

Pimm, S. L. 1991. *The Balance of Nature?* University of Chicago Press, Chicago.

Pimm, S. L. and R. A. Askins. 1995. Forest losses predict bird extinctions in eastern North America. *Proceedings of the National Academy of Sciences* 92: 9343–9347.

Pimm, S. L. and P. Raven. 2000. Biodiversity- Extinction by numbers. *Nature* 403: 843–845.

Pimm, S. L., H. L. Jones, and J. Diamond. 1988. On the risk of extinction. *American Naturalist* 132: 757–785.

Pimm, S. L., M. P. Moulton, and L. J. Justice. 1995. Bird extinction in the Central Pacific. *In* J. H. Lawton and R. M. May (eds.), *Extinction Rates*, pp. 75–87. Oxford University Press, Oxford.

Pinchot, G. 1947. *Breaking New Ground.* Harcourt, Brace, New York.

Piñero, D., M. Martinez-Ramos, and J. Sarukhan. 1984. A population model of *Astrocaryum mexicanum* and a sensitivity analysis of its finite rate of increase. *Journal of Ecology* 72: 977–991.

Platenberg, R. J. and R. A. Griffiths. 1999. Translocation of slow-worms (*Anguis fragilis*) as a mitigation strategy: A case-study from south-east England. *Biological Conservation* 90: 125–132.

Plissner, J. H. and S. M. Haig. 2000. Viability of piping plover *Charadrius melodus* metapopulations. *Biological Conservation* 92: 163–173

Plotkin, M. J. 1993. *Tales of a Shaman's Apprentice.* Viking/Penguin, New York.

Plucknett, D. L., N. J. H. Smith, J. T. Williams, and N. M. Anishetty. 1987. *Gene Banks and the World's Food.* Princeton University Press, Princeton, NJ.

Poffenberger, M. (ed.). 1990. *Keepers of the Forest.* Kumarian, West Hartford, CT.

Poiani, K. A., B. D. Richter, M. G. Anderson, and H. E. Richter. 2000. Biodiversity conservation at multiple scales: Functional sites, landscapes and networks. *BioScience* 50: 133–146.

Poole, A. 1996. *Coming of Age with Elephants: A Memoir.* Hyperion, New York.

Popper, F. J. and D. E. Popper. 1991. The reinvention of the American frontier. *Amicus Journal* (Summer): 4–7.

Porazinska, D. L. and D. Wall. 2001. Soil Conservation. *In* S. A. Levin (ed.), *Encyclopedia of Biodiversity,* 5: 315–326. Academic Press, San Diego, CA.

Porteous, P. L. 1992. Eagles on the rise. *National Geographic* 182(November): 42–55.

Porter, J. and J. Tougas. 2001. Reef ecosystems: Threats to their biodiversity. *In* S. A. Levin (ed.), *Encyclopedia of Biodiversity,* 5: 73–96. Academic Press, San Diego, CA.

Porter, S. D. and D. A. Savignano. 1990. Invasion of polygyne fire ants decimates native ants and disrupts arthropod communities. *Ecology* 71: 2095–2106.

Posey, D. A. 1992. Traditional knowledge, conservation and "the rain forest harvest". *In* M. Plotkin and L. Famolare (eds.), *Sustainable Harvest and Marketing of Rain Forest Products,* pp. 46–50. Island Press, Washington, D.C.

Posey, D. A. 1996. Protecting indigenous peoples' rights to biodiversity. *Environment* 38: 6–9, 37–45.

Possingham, H., D. B. Lindenmayer, and M. A. McCarthy. 2001. Population viability analysis. *In* S. A. Levin (ed.), *Encyclopedia of Biodiversity,* 4: 831–844. Academic Press, San Diego, CA.

Poten, C. J. 1991. A shameful harvest: America's illegal wildlife trade. *National Geographic* 180(September): 106–132.

Powell, A. N. and F. J. Cuthbert. 1993. Augmenting small populations of plovers: An assessment of cross-fostering and captive-rearing. *Conservation Biology* 7: 160–168.

Powell, J. R. and J. P. Gibbs. 1995. A report from Galapagos. *Trends in Ecology and Evolution* 10: 351–354.

Power, M. E., D. Tilman, J. A. Estes, B. A. Menge, et al. 1996. Challenges in the quest for keystones. *BioScience* 46: 609–620.

Power, T. M. 1991. Ecosystem preservation and the economy in the Greater Yellowstone area. *Conservation Biology* 5: 395–404.

Power, T. M. and R. N. Barret. 2001. *Post-Cowboy Economics: Pay and Prosperity in the New American West.* Island Press, Washington, D.C.

Prance, G. T., W. Balée, B. M. Boom and R. L. Carneiro. 1987. Quantitative ethnobotany and the case for conservation in Amazonia. *Conservation Biology* 1: 296–310.

Prendergast, J. R., R. M. Quinn, and J. H. Lawton. 1999. The gap between theory and practice in selecting nature reserves. *Conservation Biology* 13: 484–492.

Prescott-Allen, C. and R. Prescott-Allen. 1986. *The First Resource: Wild Species in the North American Economy.* Yale University Press, New Haven, CT.

Press, D., D. F. Doak, and P. Steinberg. 1996. The role of local government in the conservation of rare species. *Conservation Biology* 10: 1538–1548.

Pressey, R. L. 1994. Ad hoc reservations: Forward or backward steps in developing representative reserve systems. *Conservation Biology* 8: 662–668.

Pressey, R. L., C. J. Humphries, C. R. Margules, R. I. Vane-Wright, and P. H. Williams. 1993. Beyond opportunism: Key principles for systematic reserve selection. *Trends in Ecology and Evolution* 8: 124–128.

Pressey, R. L., T. C. Hager, K. M. Ryan, J. Schwarz, et al. 2000. Using abiotic data for conservation assessments over extensive regions: quantitative methods applied across New South Wales, Australia. *Biological Conservation* 96: 55–82.

Primack, R. B. 1988. Forestry in Fujian province (People's Republic of China) during the Cultural Revolution. *Arnoldia* 48: 26–29.

Primack, R. B. 1992. Tropical community dynamics and conservation biology. *BioScience* 42: 818–820.

Primack, R. B. 1996. Lessons from ecological theory: Dispersal, establishment and population structure. *In* D. A. Falk, C. I. Millar, and M. Olwell (eds.), *Restoring Diversity: Strategies for Reintroduction of Endangered Plants.* Island Press, Washington, D.C.

Primack, R. B. 1998. Monitoring rare plants. *Plant Talk.* 15: 29–35.

Primack, R. B. and P. Cafaro. 2001. Environmental ethics. *In* S. A. Levin (ed.), *Encyclopedia of Biodiversity,* 2: 545–556. Academic Press, San Diego, CA.

Primack, R. B. and B. Drayton. 1997. The experimental ecology of reintroduction. *Plant Talk* 11: 25–28.

Primack, R. B. and P. Hall. 1992. Biodiversity and forest change in Malaysian Borneo. *BioScience* 42: 829–837.

Primack, R. B. and S. L. Miao. 1992. Dispersal can limit local plant distribution. *Conservation Biology* 6: 513–519.

Primack, R. B. and T. Lovejoy (eds.). 1995. *Ecology, Conservation and Management of Southeast Asian Rainforests.* Yale University Press, New Haven, CT.

Primack, R. B., E. Hendry, and P. Del Tredici. 1986. Current status of *Magnolia virginiana* in Massachusetts. *Rhodora* 88: 357–365.

Primack, R. B., H. Kobori, and S. Mori. 2000. Dragonfly pond restoration promotes conservation awareness in Japan. *Conservation Biology* 14: 1553–1554.

Primack, R. B., D. Bray, H. Galetti, and J. Ponciano (eds.). 1998. *Timber, Tourists and Temples: Conservation and Development in the Maya Forest of Belize, Guatemala and Mexico.* Island Press, Washington, D.C.

Pringle, C. M. 2000. Threats to U.S. public lands from cumulative hydrologic alterations outside of their boundaries. *Ecological Applications* 10: 971–989.

Pullin, A. S. and S. R. J. Woodell. 1987. Response of the fen violet, *Viola persicifolia* Schreber, to different management regimes at Woodwalton Fen National Nature Reserve, Cambridgeshire, England. *Biological Conservation* 41: 203–217.

Purvis, A. and A. Hector. 2000. Getting the measure of biodiversity. *Nature* 405: 212–219.

Putz, F. E., D. P. Dykstra, and R. Heinrich. 2000. Why poor logging practices persist in the tropics. *Conservation Biology* 14: 951–956.

Putz, F. E., G. M. Blate, K. H. Redford, R. Fimbel, and J. Robinson. 2001. Tropical forest management and conservation of biodiversity: An overview. *Conservation Biology* 15: 7–20.

Pyne, S. J. 1997. *Fire in America: A Cultural History of Wildland and Rural Fire.* The University of Washington Press, Seattle.

Quammen, D. 1996. *The Song of the Dodo: Island Biogeography in an Age of Extinctions.* Scribner, New York.

Quinn, R. M., J. H. Lawton, B. C. Eversham, and S. N. Wood. 1994. The biogeography of scarce vascular plants in Britain with respect to habitat preference, dispersal ability and reproductive biology. *Biological Conservation* 70: 149–157.

Rabinowitz, A. 1993. *Wildlife Field Research and Conservation Training Manual.* International Wildlife Conservation Park, New York.

Rabinowitz, A. 1995. Helping a species go extinct: The Sumatran rhino in Borneo. *Conservation Biology* 9: 482–488.

Rabinowitz, A. 2000. *Jaguar. One Man's Struggle to Establish the World's First Jaguar Preserve.* Island Press, Covelo, CA.

Rabinowitz, A. 2001. *Beyond the Last Village. A Journey of Asia's Forbidden Wilderness.* Island Press, Washington, D.C.

Rabinowitz, D., S. Cairns, and T. Dillon. 1986. Seven forms of rarity and their frequency in the flora of the British Isles. *In* M. E. Soulé (ed.), *Conservation Biology: The Science of Scarcity and Diversity*, pp. 182–204. Sinauer Associates, Sunderland, MA.

Radmer, R. J. 1996. Algal diversity and commercial algal products: New and valuable products from diverse algae may soon increase the already large market for algal products. *BioScience* 46: 263–270.

Ralls, K. and R. L. Brownell. 1989. Protected species: Research permits and the value of basic research. *BioScience* 39: 394–396.

Ralls, K., P. H. Harvey, and A. M. Lyles. 1986. Inbreeding in natural populations of birds and mammals. *In* M. Soulé (ed.), *Conservation Biology: The Science of Scarcity and Diversity*, pp. 35–56. Sinauer Associates, Sunderland, MA.

Ralls, K., J. D. Ballou, and A. Templeton. 1988. Estimates of lethal equivalents and the cost of inbreeding in mammals. *Conservation Biology* 2: 185–193.

Ralls, K. S., R. Frankham, and J. Ballou. 2001. Inbreeding and outbreeding. *In* S. A. Levin (ed.), *Encyclopedia of Biodiversity*, 3: 427–436. Academic Press, San Diego, CA.

Raup, D. M. 1979. Size of the Permo-Triassic bottleneck and its evolutionary implications. *Science* 206: 217–218.

Raup, D. M. 1992. *Extinction: Bad Genes or Bad Luck?* W. W. Norton & Company, New York.

Raustiala, K. and D. G. Victor. 1996. Biodiversity since Rio: The future of the Convention on Biological Diversity. *Environment* 38: 16–26, 37–45.

Raven, P. H. 1981. Research in botanical gardens. *Botanisches. Jahrbücher für Systematik.* 102: 53–72.

Raven, P. H. and E. O. Wilson. 1992. A fifty-year plan for biodiversity surveys. *Science* 258: 1099–1100.

Ravenscroft, N. O. M. 1990. The ecology and conservation of the silver-studded blue butterfly *Plejebus argus* L. on the sandlings of East Anglia, England. *Biological Conservation* 53: 21–36.

Ray, G. C. and W. P. Gregg, Jr. 1991. Establishing biosphere reserves for coastal barrier ecosystems. *BioScience* 41: 301–309.

Reading, R. P. and S. R. Kellert. 1993. Attitudes toward a proposed reintroduction of black-footed ferrets (*Mustela nigripes*). *Conservation Biology* 7: 569–580.

Reaka-Kudla, M. L., D. W. Wilson, and E. O. Wilson (eds.). 1996. *Biodiversity II: Understanding and Protecting our Natural Resources.* National Academy Press, Washington, D.C.

Real, L. A. 1996. Sustainability and the ecology of infectious disease: Diseases and their pathogenic agents must be viewed as important parts of any ecosystem management strategy. *BioScience* 46: 88–96.

Redefining Progress. 2001. http://www.rprogress.org/

Redfearn, J. 1999. OECD to set up global facility on biodiversity. *Science* 285: 22–23.

Redford, K. H. 1992. The empty forest. *BioScience* 42: 412–422.

Redford, K. H. and J. A. Mansour (eds.). 1996. *Traditional Peoples and Biodiversity Conservation in Large Tropical Landscapes.* The Nature Conservancy, Arlington, VA.

Redford, K. H. and B. D. Richter. 1999. Conservation of biodiversity in a world of use. *Conservation Biology* 13: 1246–1256.

Redford, K. H. and S. E. Sanderson. 2000. Extracting humans from nature. *Conservation Biology* 14: 1362–1364.

Reed, J. M. 1999. The role of behavior in recent avian extinctions and endangerments. *Conservation Biology* 13: 232–241.

Reed, J. M., C. S. Elphick, and L. W. Oring. 1998. Life-history and viability analysis of the endangered Hawaiian stilt. *Biological Conservation* 84: 35–45.

Reed, R. A., J. Johnson-Barnard, and W. L. Baker. 1996. Contribution of roads to forest fragmentation in the Rocky Mountains. *Conservation Biology* 10: 1098–1107.

Rees, W. 2001. Ecological footprint, concept of. *In* S. A. Levin (ed.), *Encyclopedia of Biodiversity*, 2: 229–244. Academic Press, San Diego, CA.

Regan, H. M., M. Colyvan, and M. A. Burgman. 2000. A proposal for fuzzy International Union for the Conservation of Nature (IUCN) categories and criteria. *Biological Conservation* 92: 101–108.

Regan, H. M., R. Lupia, A. N. Drinan, and M. A. Burgman. 2001. The currency and tempo of extinction. *American Naturalist* 157: 1–10.

Regan, T. 1992. Does environmental ethics rest on a mistake? *The Monist* 75: 161–182.

Reid, W. V. and K. R. Miller. 1989. *Keeping Options Alive: The Scientific Basis for Conserving Biodiversity*. World Resources Institute, Washington, D.C.

Reid, W. V., S. A. Laird, R. Gamez, A. Sittenfeld, et al. (eds.). 1993. *Biodiversity Prospecting*. World Resources Institute, Washington, D.C.

Reinartz, J. A. 1995. Planting state-listed endangered and threatened plants. *Conservation Biology* 9: 771–781.

Reinthal, P. N. and M. L. J. Stiassny. 1991. The freshwater fishes of Madagascar: A study of endangered fauna with recommendations for a conservation strategy. *Conservation Biology* 5: 231–243.

Repetto, R. 1990. *Promoting Environmentally Sound Economic Progress: What the North Can Do*. World Resources Institute, Washington, D.C.

Repetto, R. 1992. Accounting for environmental assets. *Scientific American* 266(6): 94–100.

Restani, M. and M. Marzluff. 2002. Funding extinction? Biological needs and political realities in the allocation of resources to endangered species recovery. *Bioscience* 52: 169–177.

Rex, M. A. 1997. An oblique slant on deep-sea biodiversity. *Nature* 385: 577–590.

Reynolds, J. F. 2001. Desertification, *In* S. A. Levin (ed.), *Encyclopedia of Biodiversity*, 2: 61–78. Academic Press, San Diego, CA.

Rhoades, R. E. 1991. World's food supply at risk. *National Geographic* 179(April): 74–105.

Rich, B. 1990. Multilateral development banks and tropical deforestation. *In* S. Head and R. Heinzman (eds.), *Lessons of the Rainforest*, pp. 118–130. Sierra Club Books, San Francisco.

Rich, B. 1994. *Mortgaging the Earth*. Beacon Press, Boston.

Rich, B. 2000. Trading in dubious practices: OECD countries must stop export credit agencies funding environmentally damaging and immoral projects. *Financial Times* February: 13.

Rich, T. C. G. and E. R. Woodruff. 1996. Changes in the vascular plant floras of England and Scotland between 1930–1960 and 1987–1988: The BSBI monitoring scheme. *Biological Conservation* 75: 217–229.

Richards, S. A., H. P. Possingham, and J. Tizard. 1999. Optimal fire management for maintaining community diversity. *Ecological Applications* 9: 880–892.

Richardson, J. E., F. M. Weitz, M. F. Fay, Q. C. B. Cronk, et al. 2001. Rapid and recent origin of species richness in the Cape flora of South Africa. *Nature* 412: 181–183.

Richman, L. K., K. J. Montali, R. L. Garber, M. A. Kennedy, et al. 1999. Novel endotheliotropic herpes viruses fatal for Asian and African elephants. *Science* 283: 1171–1176.

Ricketts, T. H., E. Dinerstein, D. M. Olson, C. J. Loucks, et al. 1999. *Terrestrial Ecoregions of North America. A Conservation Assessment*. Island Press, Washington, D.C.

Ricklefs, R. E. 2001. *The Economy of Nature*, 5th ed. W. H. Freeman and Co., New York.

Ries, L., D. M. Debinski, and M. L. Wieland. 2001. Conservation value of roadside prairie restoration to butterfly communities. *Conservation Biology* 15: 401–411.

Rigg, C. M. 2001. Orchestrating ecosystem management: Challenges and lessons from Sequoia National Forest. *Conservation Biology* 15: 78–90.

Roberts, D. L, R. J. Cooper, and L. J. Petit. 2000. Use of premontane moist forest and shade coffee agrosystems by army ants in Western Panama. *Conservation Biology* 15: 192–199.

Robertson, D. P. and R. B. Hull. 2001. Beyond biology: toward a more public ecology for conservation. *Conservation Biology* 15: 970–979.

Robinson, J. G., K. H. Redford, and E. L. Bennett. 1999. Wildlife harvest in logged tropical forests. *Science* 284: 595–596.

Robinson, M. H. 1992. Global change, the future of biodiversity and the future of zoos. *Biotropica* (Special Issue) 24: 345–352.

Rochelle, J. A., L. A. Lehman, and J. Wisniewski (eds.). 1999. *Forest Fragmentation: Wildlife and Management Implications*. Koninkliijke Brill NV, Leiden, Netherlands.

Roessler, T. 2000. The World Bank's lending policy and environmental standards. *North Carolina Journal of International Law and Commercial Regulation* 26: 105–137.

Rogers, D. L. and F. T. Ledig. 1996. *The Status of Temperate North American Forest Genetic Resources*. U.S. Department of Agriculture Forest Service and Genetic Resources Conservation Program, University of California, Davis.

Roldán, G. 1988. *Guía para el Estudio de los Macroinvertebrados Acuáticos del Departamento de Antioquia*. Fondo-FEN Colombia, Editorial Presencia, Santa fe de Bogotá.

Rolston, H. III. 1988. *Environmental Ethics: Values In and Duties To the Natural World*. Temple University Press, Philadelphia.

Rolston, H. III. 1989. *Philosophy Gone Wild: Essays on Environmental Ethics*. Prometheus Books, Buffalo, NY.

Rolston, H. III. 1994. *Conserving Natural Value*. Columbia University Press, New York.

Rolston, H. III. 1995. Duties to endangered species. *In* W. A. Nierenberg (ed.), *Encyclopedia of Environmental Biology*, 1: 517–528. Harcourt/Academic Press, San Diego.

Rolston, H. III. 2000. The land ethic at the turn of the millennium. *Biodiversity and Conservation* 9: 1045–1058.

Roodman, D. M. 2001. *Still Waiting for the Jubilee: Pragmatic Solutions for the Third World Debt Crisis*. Worldwatch Institute, Washington, D.C., Worldwatch Paper 155.

Rosenberg, D. K., B. R. Noon, and E. C. Meslow. 1997. Biological corridors: Form, function, and efficacy. *BioScience* 47: 677–687.

Ruckelshaus, W. D. 1989. Toward a sustainable world. *Scientific American* 261(3): 166–175.

Ruiz, G. M., J. T. Carlton, E. D. Grosholz, and A. H. Hines. 1997. Global invasions of marine and estuarine habitats by non-indigenous species: mechanisms, extent, and consequences. *American Zoologist* 37: 621–632.

Ruiz, G. M., T. K. Rawlings, F. C. Dobbs, L. A. Drake, et al. 2000. Global spread of microorganisms by ships. *Nature* 408: 49.

Rundel, P. W. 2001. Mediterranean-climate ecosystems. *In* S. A. Levin (ed.), *Encyclopedia of Biodiversity*, 4: 145–160. Academic Press, San Diego.

Russ, G. R. and A. C. Alcala. 1996. Marine reserves: Rates and patterns of recovery and decline of large predatory fish. *Ecological Applications* 6: 947–962.

Ryder, O. A., A. McLaren, S. Brenner, Y. P. Zhang, and K. Benirschke. 2000. Ecology- DNA banks for endangered animal species. *Science* 288: 275.

Sæther, B. 1999. Top dogs maintain diversity. *Nature* 400: 510–511.

Safina, C. 1993. Bluefin tuna in the West Atlantic: Negligent management and the making of an endangered species. *Conservation Biology* 7: 229–234.

Safina, C. 2001. Fish conservation. *In* S. A. Levin (ed.), *Encyclopedia of Biodiversity*, 2: 783–800. Academic Press, San Diego, CA.

Sala, O. E., F. S. Chapin III, J. J. Armesto, E. Berlow, et al. 2000. Global biodiversity scenarios for the year 2100. *Science* 287: 1770–1774.

Salafsky, N. and R. Margoluis. 1999. Threat reduction assessment: A practical and cost-effective approach to evaluating conservation and development projects. *Conservation Biology* 13: 830–841.

Salafsky, N., R. Margoluis, and K. Redford. 2001b. *Adaptive Management: A Tool for Conservation Practitioners*. Biodiversity Support Program, Washington, D.C.

Salafsky, N., H. Cauley, G. Balachander, B. Cordes, et al. 2001a. A systematic test of an enterprise strategy for community-based biodiversity conservation. *Conservation Biology* 15: 1585–1595.

Saltz, D. 2001. Wildlife management. *In* S. A. Levin (ed.), *Encyclopedia of Biodiversity*, 5: 823–830. Academic Press, San Diego, CA.

Salwasser, H., C. M. Schonewald-Cox, and R. Baker. 1987. The role of interagency cooperation in managing for viable populations. *In* M. E. Soulé (ed.), *Viable Populations for Conservation*, pp. 159–173. Cambridge University Press, Cambridge.

Sample, V. A. 1994. *Remote Sensing and GIS in Ecosystem Management*. Island Press, Washington, D.C.

Samson, F. B. and F. L. Knopf (eds.). 1996. *Prairie Conservation: Preserving America's Most Endangered Ecosystem*. Island Press, Washington, D.C.

Santos, T and J. L. Telleria. 1994. Influence of forest fragmentation on seed consumption and dispersal of Spanish juniper *Juniperus thurifera*. *Biological Conservation* 70: 129–134.

Sapp, J. 1999. *What is Natural? Coral Reef Crisis*. Oxford University Press, New York.

Saterson, K. 2001. Government legislation and regulation. *In* S. A. Levin (ed.), *Encyclopedia of Biodiversity*, 3: 233–246. Academic Press, San Diego, CA.

Savidge, J. A., 1987. Extinction of an island forest avifauna by an introduced snake. *Ecology* 68: 660–668.

Sawhill, J. C. 1996. Conservation science comes of age. *Nature Conservancy* (January/February): 5–9.

Sayer, J., N. Ishwaran, J. Thorsell, and T. Sigaty. 2000. Tropical forest biodiversity and the World Heritage Convention. *Ambio* 29: 302–309.

Sayer, J. A. and T. C. Whitmore. 1991. Tropical moist forests: Destruction and species extinction. *Biological Conservation* 55: 199–213.

Schaller, G. B. 1993. *The Last Panda*. University of Chicago Press, Chicago.

Schaller, G. B. and L. Wulin. 1996. Distribution, status and conservation of wild yak *Bos grunniens*. *Biological Conservation* 76: 1–8.

Scheiner, S. M. and J. M. Rey-Benayas. 1994. Global patterns of plant diversity. *Evolutionary Ecology* 8: 331–347.

Schelhas, J. and R. Greenberg (eds.). 1996. *Forest Patches in Tropical Landscapes*. Island Press, Washington, D.C.

Schemske, D. W., B. C. Husband, M. H. Ruckelshaus, C. Goodwillie, et al. 1994. Evaluating approaches to the conservation of rare and endangered plants. *Ecology* 75: 584–606.

Schmidt, J. C., R. H. Webb, R. A. Valdez, G. R. Marzolf, and L. E. Stevens. 1998. Science and values in river restoration in the Grand Canyon. *BioScience* 48: 735–747.

Schmidt, K. 1997. Life on the brink. *Earth* 26–33.

Schmidtz, D. and E. Willott (eds.). 2001. *Environmental Ethics: What Really Matters, What Really Works*. Oxford University Press, New York.

Schneider, D. 1995. Down and out in the Gulf of Mexico. *Scientific American* 272(4): 29.

Schneider, S. 1998. *Laboratory Earth: The Planetary Gamble We Can't Afford to Lose*. Basic Books, New York, NY.

Schneider, S. H. 1989. The changing climate. *Scientific American* 261(3): 70–79.

Schneider, S. H. and T. L. Root. 2001. *Wildlife Response to Climate Change: North American Case Studies*. Island Press, Washington, D.C.

Schonewald-Cox, C. M. 1983. Conclusions: Guidelines to management: A beginning attempt. *In* C. M. Schonewald-Cox, S. M. Chambers, B. MacBryde, and L. Thomas (eds.), *Genetics and Conservation: A Reference for Managing Wild Animal and Plant Populations*, pp. 414–445. Benjamin/Cummings, Menlo Park, CA.

Schonewald-Cox, C. M. and M. Buechner. 1992. Park protection and public roads. *In* P. L. Fiedler and S. K. Jain (eds.), *Conservation Biology: The Theory and Practice of Nature Conservation, Preservation and Management*, pp. 373–396. Chapman and Hall, New York.

Schrope, M. 2001. Save our swamp. *Nature* 409: 128–130.

Schultes, R. E. and R. F. Raffauf. 1990. *The Healing Forest: Medicinal and Toxic Plants of the Northwest Amazonia*. Dioscorides Press, Portland.

Schulz, H. N., T. Brinkhoff, T. G. Ferdelman, M. H. Marine, et al. 1999. Dense populations of a giant sulfur bacterium in Namibian shelf sediments. *Science* 284: 493–495.

Schwartz, M. W. 1997. *Conservation in Highly Fragmented Landscapes*. Chapman & Hall, New York.

Schwartz, M. W. 1999. Choosing the appropriate scale of reserves for conservation. *Annual Review of Ecology and Systematics* 30: 83–108.

Schwartz, M. W., S. M. Hermann, and P. J. van Mantgem. 2000. Estimating the magnitude of decline of the Florida torreya (*Torreya taxifolia* Arn.). *Biological Conservation* 95: 77–84.

Scott, J. M., B. Csuti, and F. Davis. 1991. Gap analysis: An application of Geographic Information Systems for wildlife species. *In* D. J. Decker, M. E. Krasny, G. R. Goff, C. R. Smith, and D. W. Gross (eds.), *Challenges in the Conservation of Biological Resources: A Practitioner's Guide*, pp. 167–179. Westview Press, Boulder, CO.

Scott, J. M., C. B. Kepler, C. van Riper III, and S. I. Fefer. 1988. Conservation of Hawaii's vanishing avifauna. *BioScience* 38: 232–253.

Scott, J. M., F. W. Davis, R. G. McGhie, R. G. Wright, et al. 2001. Nature reserves: Do they capture the full range of America's biological diversity? *Ambio* 11: 999–1007.

Scott, M. E. 1988. The impact of infection and disease on animal populations: Implications for conservation biology. *Conservation Biology* 2: 40–56.

Sea World. 2000. *Appendix: Population estimates*. Data from http://www.seaworld.org/infobooks/Baleen/estimatesbw.html.

Seidensticker, J., S. Christie, and P. Jackson (eds.). 1999. *Riding the Tiger: Tiger Conservation in Human Dominated Landscapes*. Cambridge University Press, London.

Seip, H. M., P. Aagaard, V. Angell, O. Eilersten, et al. 1999. Acidification in China: Assessment based on studies at forested sites from Chongqing to Guanzhou. *Ambio* 28: 522–528.

Sessions, G. (ed.). 1995. *Deep Ecology for the 21st Century: Readings on the Philosophy and Practice of the New Environmentalism*. Shambala Books, Boston.

Shafer, C. L. 1990. *Nature Reserves: Island Theory and Conservation Practice*. Smithsonian Institution Press, Washington, D.C.

Shafer, C. L. 1995. Values and shortcomings of small reserves. *BioScience* 45: 80–88.

Shafer, C. L. 1997. Terrestrial nature reserve design at the urban/rural interface. *In* M. W. Schwartz (ed.), *Conservation in Highly Fragmented Landscapes*, pp. 345–378. Chapman and Hall, New York.

Shafer, C. L. 1999. History of selection and system planning for US natural area national parks and monuments: Beauty and biology. *Biodiversity and Conservation* 8: 189–204.

Shafer, C. L. 2001. Conservation biology trailblazers: George Wright, Ben Thompson, and Joseph Dixon. *Conservation Biology* 15: 332–344.

Shaffer, M. L. 1981. Minimum population sizes for species conservation. *BioScience* 31: 131–134.

Shardlow M. and M. Harper. 2000. Compassion for competitors: saving wild arable plants. *Plant Talk*. 22/23: 39–42.

Shi, D. E. 1985. *The Simple Life: Plain Living and High Thinking*. Oxford University Press, New York.

Shulman, S. 1986. Seeds of controversy. *BioScience* 36: 647–651.

Shultz, S., A. E. Dunham, K. V. Root, S. L. Soucy, et al. 1999. *Conservation Biology with RAMAS® EcoLab Software*. Sinauer Associates, Sunderland, MA.

Simberloff, D. 2001. Introduced species, effect and distribution. *In* S. A. Levin (ed.), *Encyclopedia of Biodiversity*, 3: 517–530. Academic Press, San Diego, CA.

Simberloff, D. S. 1986. Are we on the verge of a mass extinction in tropical rainforests? In D. K. Elliott (ed.), *Dynamics of Extinction*, pp. 165–180. John Wiley & Sons, New York.

Simberloff, D. S. 1992. Do species-area curves predict extinction in fragmented forest? *In* T. C. Whitmore and J. A. Sayer (eds.), *Tropical Deforestation and Species Extinction*, pp. 75–89. Chapman and Hall, London.

Simberloff, D. S. and L. G. Abele. 1982. Refuge design and island biogeographic theory: Effects of fragmentation. *American Naturalist* 120: 41–50.

Simberloff, D. S. and N. Gotelli. 1984. Effects of insularization on plant species richness in the prairie-forest ecotone. *Biological Conservation* 29: 27–46.

Simberloff, D. S., J. A. Farr, J. Cox, and D. W. Mehlman. 1992. Movement corridors: Conservation bargains or poor investments? *Conservation Biology* 6: 493–505.

Simberloff, D. S., D. C. Schmitz, and T. C. Brown. (eds.). 1997. *Strangers in Paradise: Impact and Management of Nonindigenous Species in Florida*. Island Press, Washington, D.C.

Simmons, R. E. 1996. Population declines, variable breeding areas and management options for flamingos in Southern Africa. *Conservation Biology* 10: 504–515.

Simonetti, J. A. and E. Rivera-Milla. In press. Conocimiento de la fauna de chilena. *In* G. Halffter and J. A. Simonetti (eds.), *La Diversidad Biológica de Iberoamérica*. Instituto de Ecología, Xalapa Mexico.

Simpson, S. 2001. Fishy business. *Scientific American* 285(1): 82–89.

Singer, F. J., L. C. Zeigenfuss, and L. Spicer. 2001. Role of patch size, disease, and movement in rapid extinction of bighorn sheep. *Conservation Biology* 15: 1347–1354.

Singer, P. 1979. Not for humans only. *In* K. E. Goodpaster and K. M. Sayre (eds.), *Ethics and Problems of the Twenty-first Century*, pp. 191–206. University of Notre Dame, Notre Dame, IN.

Smith, A. 1909. *An Inquiry into the Nature and Causes of the Wealth of Nations*. Bullock, J. L. (ed.), P. F. Collier & Sons, New York.

Smith, D. W., K. M. Murphy, and D. S. Guernsey. 2001. *Yellowstone Wolf Project: Annual Report, 2000*. National Park Service, Yellowstone Center for Resources, Yellowstone National Park, Wyoming.

Smith, F. D. M., R. M. May, R. Pellew, T. H. Johnson, and K. R. Walter. 1993. How much do we know about the current extinction rate? *Trends in Ecology and Evolution* 8: 375–378.

Smith, T. B., S. Kark, C. J. Schneider, R. K. Wayne, and C. Moritz. 2001. Biodiversity hotspots and beyond: The need for preserving environmental transitions. *Trends in Ecology and Evolution* 16: 431.

Smith, W. H. 2001. Pollution, overview. *In* S. A. Levin (ed.), *Encyclopedia of Biodiversity*, 4: 731–744. Academic Press, San Diego, CA.

Snyder, N. and H. Snyder. 2000. *The California Condor: A Saga of Natural History and Conservation*. Academic Press, San Diego, CA.

Snyder, N. F., S. R. Derrickson, S. R. Beissinger, J. W. Wiley, et al. 1996. Limitations of captive breeding in endangered species recovery. *Conservation Biology* 10: 338–349.

Society of Ecological Restoration. 1991. *Program and abstracts, 3rd Annual Conference*. Orlando, FL. 18–23 May.

Sokolow, R. 1992. America's first food writer. *Natural History* 101: 68–71.

Soulé, M. 1985. What is conservation biology? *BioScience* 35: 727–734.

Soulé, M. (ed.). 1987. *Viable Populations for Conservation*. Cambridge University Press, Cambridge, UK.

Soulé, M. 1990. The onslaught of alien species and other challenges in the coming decades. *Conservation Biology* 4: 233–239.

Soulé, M. and D. Simberloff. 1986. What do genetics and ecology tell us about the design of nature reserves? *Biological Conservation* 35: 19–40.

Soulé, M. E. 1980. Thresholds for survival: Maintaining fitness and evolutionary potential. *In* M. E. Soulé and B. A. Wilcox (eds.), *Conservation Biology: An Evolutionary-Ecological Perspective*, pp. 151–170. Sinauer Associates, Sunderland, MA.

Soulé, M. E., and J. Terborgh. 1999. *Continental Conservation. Scientific Foundations of Regional Reserve Networks*. Island Press, Washington, D.C.

Soulé, M. E. and G. H. Orians. (eds.). 2001. *Conservation Biology: Research Priorities for the Next Decade*. Island Press, Washington, D.C.

Southgate, D. and H. L. Clark. 1993. Can conservation projects save biodiversity in South America? *Ambio* 22: 163–166.

Spackman, S. C. and J. W. Hughes. 1995. Assessment of minimum stream corridor width for biological conservation: Species richness and distribution along mid-order streams in Vermont, USA. *Biological Conservation* 71: 325–332.

Spalding, M. D., C. Ravilious, and E. P. Green. 2001. *World Atlas of Coral Reefs*. The University of California Press, Berkely, CA.

Spellerberg, I. F. 1994. *Evaluation and Assessment for Conservation: Ecological Guidelines for Determining Priorities for Nature Conservation*. Chapman and Hall, London.

Spencer, C. N., B. R. McClelland, and J. A. Stanford. 1991. Shrimp stocking, salmon collapse and eagle displacement. *BioScience* 41: 14–21.

Stanley, T. 1995. Ecosystem management and the arrogance of humanism. *Conservation Biology* 9: 254–262.

Stanley-Price, M. R. 1989. *Animal Re-introductions: The Arabian Oryx in Oman*. Cambridge University Press, Cambridge.

Stattersfield, A. J., M. J. Crosby, A. J. Long, and D. C. Wege. 1998. *Endemic Bird Areas of the World: Priorities for Biodiversity Conservation*. Birdlife International, Cambridge.

Stearns, B. P. and S. C. Stearns. 1999. *Watching, From the Edge of Extinction*. Yale University Press, New Haven, CT.

Steer, A. 1996. Ten principles of the New Environmentalism. *Finance and Development* 33: 4–7.

Stein, B. A. and S. R. Flack. 1997. *Species Report Card: The State of U.S. Plants and Animals*. The Nature Conservancy, Arlington, VA.

Stein, B. A., L. S. Kutner, and J. S. Adams (eds.). 2000. *Precious Heritage: The Status of Biodiversity in the United States*. Oxford University Press, New York.

Stephenson, N. L. 1999. Reference conditions for giant sequoia forest restoration: Structure, process, and precision. *Ecological Applications* 9: 1253–1265.

Stevens, S. M. and T. P. Husband. 1998. The influence of edge on small mammals: Evidence from Brazilian Atlantic forest fragments. *Biological Conservation* 85: 1–8.

Steytler, N. S. and M. J. Samways. 1995. Biotope selection by adult male dragonflies (Odonata) at an artificial lake created for insect conservation in South Africa. *Biological Conservation* 72: 381–386.

Stiassny, M. L. J. 1996. An overview of freshwater biodiversity: With some lessons from African fishes. *Fisheries* 21: 7–13.

Stohlgren, T. J. 2001. Endangered plants. *In* S. A. Levin (ed.), *Encyclopedia of Biodiversity*, 2: 465–478. Academic Press, San Diego, CA.

Stolzenburg, W. 1992. The mussels' message. *Nature Conservancy* 42: 16–23.

Stolzenburg, W. 1996. Aquatic animals in danger. *Nature Conservancy* 46: 7.

Stone, C. P. and L. L. Loope. 1996. Alien species in Hawaiian national parks. *In* W. L. Halvorson and G. E. Davis (eds.), *Science and Ecosystem Management in the National Parks*, pp. 132–183. The University of Arizona Press, Tucson.

Stone, R. D. and C. D'Andrea. 2002. *Tropical Forests and the Human Spirit*. University of California Press, Berkeley, CA.

Strayer, D. L. 2001. Endangered freshwater invertebrates. *In* S. A. Levin (ed.), *Encyclopedia of Biodiversity*, 2: 425–440. Academic Press, San Diego, CA.

Strayer, D. L., N. F. Caraco, J. J. Cole, S. Findlay, and M. L. Pace. 1999. Transformation of freshwater ecosystems by bivalves. *BioScience* 49: 19–27.

Sutherland, W. J. (ed.). 1998. *Conservation Science and Action*. Blackwell Science, Oxford.

Sutherland, W. J. and D. A. Hill. 1995. *Managing Habitats for Conservation*. Cambridge University Press, Cambridge.

Svarstad, H., H. C. Bugge, and S. S. Dhillion. 2000. From Norway to Novartis: Cyclosporin from *Tolypocladium inflatum* in an open access bioprospecting regime. *Biodiversity and Conservation* 9: 1521–1541.

Swengel, A. B. 1996. Effects of fire and hay management on abundance of prairie butterflies. *Biological Conservation* 76: 73–85.

Swetnam, T. W., C. D. Allen, and J. L. Betancourt. 1999. Applied historical ecology: using the past to manage the future. *Ecological Applications* 9: 1189–1206.

Szafer, W. 1968. The ure-ox, extinct in Europe since the seventeenth century: An attempt at conservation that failed. *Biological Conservation* 1: 45–47.

Szaro, R. C. and D. W. Johnston (eds.). 1996. *Biodiversity in Managed Landscapes: Theory and Practice*. Oxford University Press, New York.

Takacs, D. 1996. *The Idea of Biodiversity*. The Johns Hopkins University Press, Baltimore.

Tamarin, R. H. 2001. *Principles of Genetics*, 7th ed. Wm. C. Brown, Dubuque, IA.

Tarpy, C. 1993. Zoos: Taking down the bars. *National Geographic* 184(July): 2–37.

Taylor, B. R. (ed.). 1995. *Ecological Resistance Movements*. State University of New York Press, Albany.

Taylor, V. J. and N. Dunstone (eds.). 1996. *The Exploitation of Mammal Populations*. Chapman and Hall, London.

Tear, T. H., J. M. Scott, P. H. Hayward, and B. Griffith. 1993. Status and prospects for success of the Endangered Species Act: A look at recovery plans. *Science* 262: 976–977.

Temple, S. A. 1991. Conservation biology: New goals and new partners for managers of biological resources. *In* D. J. Decker et al. (eds.), *Challenges in the Conservation of Biological Resources: A Practitioner's Guide*, pp. 45–54. Westview Press, Boulder, CO.

Terborgh, J. 1974. Preservation of natural diversity: The problem of extinction prone species. *BioScience* 24: 715–722.

Terborgh, J. 1986. Keystone plant resources in the tropical forest. *In* M. E. Soulé (ed.), *Conservation Biology: The Science of Scarcity and Diversity*, pp. 330–344. Sinauer Associates, Sunderland, MA.

Terborgh, J. 1999. *Requiem for Nature*. Island Press, Washington, D.C.

Terborgh, J. 2000. The fate of tropical forests: A matter of stewardship. *Conservation Biology* 14: 1358–1361.

Terborgh, J. and B. Winter. 1983. A method for siting parks and reserves with special reference to Colombia and Ecuador. *Biological Conservation* 27: 45–58.

Thapa, B. 1998. Debt-for-nature swaps: An overview. *International Journal of Sustainable Development and World Ecology* 5: 249–262.

Thiollay, J. M. 1989. Area requirements for the conservation of rainforest raptors and game birds in French Guiana. *Conservation Biology* 3: 128–137.

Thomas, A. 1995. Genotypic inference with the Gibbs sampler. *In* J. Ballou, M. Gilpin, and T. J. Foose (eds.), *Population Management for Survival and Recovery*, pp. 261–272. Columbia University Press, New York.

Thomas, C. D. 1990. What do real population dynamics tell us about minimum viable population sizes? *Conservation Biology* 4: 324–327.

Thomas, C. D. and J. C. G. Abery. 1995. Estimating rates of butterfly decline from distribution maps: The effect of scale. *Biological Conservation* 73: 59–65.

Thomas, K. S. 1991. *Living Fossil: The Story of the Coelocanth*. Norton, New York.

Thomashow, M. 1996. *Ecological Identity: Becoming a Reflective Environmentalist*. MIT Press, Cambridge.

Thoreau, H. D. 1863. *Excursions*. Ticknor and Fields, Boston, MA.

Thoreau, H. D. 1971. *Walden*. Princeton University Press, Princeton.

Thorne, E. T. and E. S. Williams. 1988. Disease and endangered species: The black-footed ferret as a recent example. *Conservation Biology* 2: 66–74.

Thornhill, N. W. (ed.). 1993. *The Natural History of Inbreeding and Outbreeding*. University of Chicago Press, Chicago, IL.

Tilman, D. 1999. The ecological consequences of change in biodiversity: A search for general principles. *Ecology* 80: 1455–1474.

Tilman, D., D. Wedin, and J. Knops. 1996. Productivity and sustainability influenced by biodiversity in grassland ecosystems. *Nature* 379: 718–720.

Tilman, D., R. M. May, C. L. Lehman, and M. A. Nowak. 1994. Habitat destruction and the extinction debt. *Nature* 371: 65.

Toft, R. J., R. J. Harris, and P. A. Williams. 2001. Impacts of the weed *Tradescantia fluminensis* on insect communities in fragmented forests in New Zealand. *Biological Conservation* 102: 31–46.

Toledo, V. M. 2001. Indigenous peoples, biodiversity and. *In* S. A. Levin (ed.), *Encyclopedia of Biodiversity* 3: 451–464. Academic Press, San Diego, CA.

Toth, L. A. 1996. Restoring the hydrogeomorphology of the channelized Kissimmee River. *In* A. Brookes and F. D. Shields, Jr. (eds.), *River Channel Restoration: Guiding Principles for Sustainable Projects*, pp. 369–383. John Wiley and Sons, Chichester, England.

Toth, L. A. and N. G. Aumen. 1994. Integration of multiple issues in environmental restoration and resource enhancement in south central Florida. *In* J. Cairns, Jr., T. V. Crawford, and H. Salwasser (eds.), *Implementing Integrated Environmental Management*, pp. 61–78. Virginia Polytechnic Institute and State University, Blacksburg, VA.

Toth, L. A., J. W. Koebel Jr., A. G. Warne, and J. Chamberlain. 2002. Implications of reestablishing prolonged flood pulse characteristics of the Kissimmee River and floodplain ecosystem, pp. 191–221. *In* B. Middleton (ed.), *Flood Pulsing in Wetlands: Restoring the Natural Hydrological Balance*, pp. 191–122. John Wiley & Sons, Inc., New York, NY.

Toufexis, A. 1992. A new endangered species: Human protectors of the planet put their lives on the line. *Time* 139: 48–50.

Tratalos, J. A. and T. J. Austin. 2001. Impacts of recreational SCUBA diving on coral communities of the Caribbean island of Grand Cayman. *Biological Conservation* 102: 67–75.

Travis, J. 1993. Invader threatens Black, Azov Seas. *Science* 262: 1336–1337.

Trombulak, S. C. and C. A. Frissell. 2000. Review of ecological effects of roads on terrestrial and aquatic communities. *Conservation Biology* 14: 18–30.

Tucker, R. P. 2000. *Insatiable Appetite: the United States and the Ecological Degradation of the Tropical World.* The University of California Press, Berkeley.

Tudge, C. 1992. Last stand for Society snails. *New Scientist* 135: 25–29.

Turner, M. G., R. H. Garner, and R. V. O'Neill. 2001. *Landscape Ecology in Theory and Practice: Pattern and Process.* Springer-Verlag, New York.

Tuxill, J. 1999. *Nature's Cornucopia: Our Stake in Plant Diversity.* World Watch Institute, Washington, D.C.

Twiss, J. R. and R. R. Reeves (eds.). 1999. *Conservation and Management of Marine Mammals.* Smithsonian Institution Press, Washington, D.C.

UNDP/UNEP/World Bank. 1994. *Global Environment Facility: Independent Evaluation of the Pilot Phase.* The World Bank, Washington, D.C.

UNESCO. 1996. *The World Network of Biosphere Reserves.* UNESCO, Paris, France.

Union of Concerned Scientists. 1999. *Global Warming: Early Warning Signs.* Union of Concerned Scientists. Cambridge, MA.

United Nations. 1993a. *Agenda 21: Rio Declaration and Forest Principles.* Post-Rio Edition. United Nations Publications, New York.

United Nations. 1993b. *The Global Partnership for Environment and Development.* United Nations Publications, New York.

Urbanska, K. M., N. R. Webb, and P. J. Edwards (eds.). 1997. *Restoration Ecology and Sustainable Development.* Cambridge University Press, Cambridge.

Valutis, L. L. and J. M. Marzluff. 1999. The appropriateness of puppet-rearing birds for reintroduction. *Conservation Biology* 13: 584–591.

Van de Veer, D. and C. Pierce. 1994. *The Environmental Ethics and Policy Book: Philosophy, Ecology, Economics.* Wadsworth Publishing Company, Belmont, CA.

Van Driesche, R. G. and T. J. Bellows. 1996. *Biological Control.* Chapman and Hall, New York.

Van Driesche, J. and R. Van Driesche. 2000. *Nature Out of Place: Biological Invasions in the Global Age.* Island Press, Washington, D.C.

Van Swaay, C. A. M. 1990. An assessment of the changes in butterfly abundance in the Netherlands during the twentieth century. *Biological Conservation* 52: 287–302.

Van Wensveen, L. 2000. *Dirty Virtues: The Emergence of Ecological Virtue Ethics.* Prometheus, New York.

Vane-Wright, R. I., C. R. Smith, and I. J. Kitching. 1994. A scientific basis for establishing networks of protected areas. *In* P. L. Forey, C. J. Humphries, and R. I. Vane-Wright (eds.), *Systematics and Conservation Evaluation,* pp. 327–350. Oxford University Press, New York.

Veith, M., J. Kosuch, R. Feldmann, H. Martens, and A. Seitz. 2000. A test for correct species declaration of frog legs imports from Indonesia into the European Union. *Biodiversity and Conservation* 9: 333–341.

Vincent, A. C. J. 1994. The improbable seahorse. *National Geographic* 186(April): 37–52.

Vincent, A. C. J. and H. J. Hall. 1996. The threatened status of marine fishes. *Trends in Ecology and Evolution* 11: 360–361.

Visscher, P. M., D. Smith, S. J. G. Hall, and J. A. Williams. 2001. A viable herd of genetically uniform cattle-Deleterious alleles seem to have been purged in a feral strain of inbred cows. *Nature* 409: 303.

Vitousek, P. M. 1994. Beyond global warming: ecology and global change. *Ecology* 75: 1861–1876.

Vitousek, P. M. 1997. Human domination of Earth's ecosystems. *Science* 278: 21.

Vitousek, P. M., C. M. D'Antonio, L. L. Loope, and R. Westerbrooks. 1996. Biological invasions as global environmental change. *American Scientist* 84: 468–478.

Vitousek, P. M., J. D. Aber, R. W. Howarth, G.E. Likens, et al. 1997. Human alteration of the global nitrogen cycle: Sources and consequences. *Ecological Applications* 7: 737–750.

Volk, T. 1997. *Gaia's Body: A Physiology of the Earth.* Copernicus Press, New York.

von Droste, B., H. Plachter, and M. Rossler (eds.). 1995. *Cultural Landscapes of Universal Value.* Gustav Fischer Verlag, New York.

Wallenda, T. and I. Kottke. 1998. Nitrogen deposition and ectomycorrhizas. *New Phytologist* 139: 169–187.

Waller, G. (ed.). 1996. *Sealife: A Guide to the Marine Environment.* Smithsonian Institution Press, Washington, D.C.

Wallis deVries, M. F. 1995. Large herbivores and the design of large-scale nature reserves in Western Europe. *Conservation Biology* 9: 25–33.

Walpole, M. J., H. J. Goodwin, and K. G. R. Ward. 2001. Pricing policy for tourism in protected areas: Lessons from Komodo National Park, Indonesia. *Conservation Biology* 15: 218–227.

Walther, G. R., E. Post, P. Convey, A. Menzel, et al. 2002. Ecological responses to recent climate change. *Nature* 416: 389–395.

Waples, R. S. and D. J. Teel. 1990. Conservation genetics of Pacific salmon: Temporal changes in allele frequency. *Conservation Biology* 4: 144–156.

Ward, D. M., R. Weller, and M. M. Bateson. 1990. 16 rRNA sequences reveal numerous uncultured microorganisms in a natural community. *Nature* 345: 63–65.

Ward, G. C. 1992. India's wildlife dilemma. *National Geographic* 181(May): 2–29.

Warren, M. S. 1991. The successful conservation of an endangered species, the heath fritillary butterfly *Mellicta athalia,* in Britain. *Biological Conservation* 55: 37–56.

Watling, L. and E. A. Norse. 1998. Disturbance of the seabed by mobile fishing gear: A comparison to forest clearcutting. *Conservation Biology* 12: 1180–1197.

Weber, P. D. 1993. Reviving coral reefs. *In* L. R. Brown (ed.), *State of the World 1993,* pp. 42–60. Norton, New York.

Weber, W., L. J. T. White, A. Vedder, and L. Naughton-Treves (eds.). 2001. *African Rain Forest Ecology and Conservation: An Interdisciplinary Perspective.* Yale University Press, New Haven, CT.

Webster, D. 1997. The looting and smuggling and fencing and hoarding of impossibly precious feathered and scaly wild things. *The New York Times Magazine*, February 16, 1997, pp. 26–33, 48–49, 53, 61.

Weiss, S. B. 1999. Cars, cows, and checkerspot butterflies: Nitrogen deposition and the management of nutrient-poor grasslands for a threatened species. *Conservation Biology* 13: 1476–1486.

Welch, E. B. and G. D. Cooke. 1990. Lakes. In W. R. Jordan III, M. E. Gilpin, and J. D. Aber (eds.), *Restoration Ecology: A Synthetic Approach to Ecological Research*, pp. 109–129. Cambridge University Press, Cambridge.

Wells, M. and K. Brandon. 1992. *People and Parks: Linking Protected Area Management with Local Communities*. The World Bank/WWF/USAID, Washington, D.C.

Wells, S. and N. Hanna. 1992. *The Greenpeace Book on Coral Reefs*. Greenpeace, Washington, D.C.

Westemeier, R. L., J. D. Brown, S. A. Simpson, T. L. Esker, et al. 1998. Tracking the long-term decline and recovery of an isolated population. *Science* 282: 1695–1698.

Western, D. 1989. Conservation without parks: Wildlife in the rural landscape. In D. Western and M. Pearl (eds.), *Conservation for the Twenty-first Century*, pp. 158–165. Oxford University Press, New York.

Western, D. 1997. *In the Dust of Kilimanjaro*. Island Press, Washington, D.C.

Western, D. and W. Henry. 1979. Economics and conservation in Third World national parks. *BioScience* 29: 414–418.

Western, D. and J. Ssemakula. 1981. The future of the savannah ecosystem: Ecological islands or faunal enclaves? *African Journal of Ecology* 19: 7–19.

Western, D. and M. Pearl (eds.). 1989. *Conservation for the Twenty-First Century*. Oxford University Press, New York.

Western, D., R. M. Wright, and S. C. Strum (eds.). 1994. *Natural Connections: Perspectives in Community-Based Conservation*. Island Press, Washington, D.C.

Westra, L. and P. Wenz. 1995. *The Faces of Environmental Racism: the Global Equity Issues*. Rowman Littlefield, Lanham, MD.

Whisenant, S. G. 1999. *Repairing Damaged Wetlands*. Cambridge University Press.

White, P. S. 1996. Spatial and biological scales in reintroduction. In D. A. Falk, C. I. Millar, and M. Olwell (eds.), *Restoring Diversity: Strategies for Reintroduction of Endangered Plants*, pp. 49–86. Island Press, Washington, D.C.

White, P. S. and J. L. Walker. 1997. Approximating nature's variation: Selecting and using reference information in restoration ecology. *Restoration Ecology* 5: 338–349.

Whiten, A. and C. Boesch. 2001. The cultures of chimpanzees. *Scientific American* 284(1): 61–67.

Whitmore, T. C. 1990. *An Introduction to Tropical Rain Forests*. Clarendon Press, Oxford.

Whitten, A. J. 1987. Indonesia's transmigration program and its role in the loss of tropical rain forests. *Conservation Biology* 1: 239–246.

Whitten, A. J., K. D. Bishop, S. V. Nash, and L. Clayton. 1987. One or more extinctions from Sulawesi, Indonesia? *Conservation Biology* 1: 42–48.

Wiese, R. J. and M. Hutchins. 1994. *Species Survival Plans: Strategies for Wildlife Conservation*. American Zoo and Aquarium Association, Bethesda, MD.

Wilcove, D., M. J. Bean, R. Bonnie, and M. McMillan. 1996. *Rebuilding the Ark: Toward a More Effective Endangered Species Act for Private Land*. Environmental Defense Fund, Washington, D.C.

Wilcove, D. S. 1999. *The Condor's Shadow: The Loss and Recovery of Wildlife in America*. W. H. Freeman, New York.

Wilcove, D. S. and L. Y. Chen. 1998. Management costs for endangered species. *Conservation Biology* 12: 1405–1407.

Wilcove, D. S., M. McMillan, and K. C. Winston. 1993. What exactly is an endangered species? An analysis of the U.S. Endangered Species List: 1985–1991. *Conservation Biology* 7: 87–93.

Wilcove, D. S., D. Rothstein, J. Dubow, A. Phillips, and E. Losos. 1998. Quantifying threats to imperiled species in the United States. *BioScience* 48: 607–615.

Wilkie, D. S. and J. F. Carpenter. 1999. Bushmeat hunting in the Congo Basin: An assessment of impacts and options for mitigation. *Biodiversity and Conservation* 8: 927–955.

Wilkinson, C., O. Linden, H. Cesar, G. Hodgson, et al. 1999. Ecological and socioeconomic impacts of 1998 coral mortality in the Indian Ocean: An ENSO impact and a warning of future change? *Ambio* 28: 188–196.

Willers, B. 1994. Sustainable development: A New World deception. *Conservation Biology* 8: 1146–1148.

Williams, J. D. and R. M. Nowak. 1993. Vanishing species in our own backyard: Extinct fish and wildlife of the United States and Canada. In L. Kaufman and K. Mallory (eds.), *The Last Extinction*, pp. 107–140. MIT Press, Cambridge, MA.

Williams, P., D. Gibbons, C. Margules, A. Rebelo, et al. 1996. A comparison of richness hotspots, rarity hotspots and complementary areas for conserving the diversity of British birds. *Conservation Biology* 10: 155–174.

Willig, M. 2001. Latitude, common trends within. In S. A. Levin (ed.), *Encyclopedia of Biodiversity*, 3: 701–714. Academic Press, San Diego, CA.

Wilson, D. E. and R. F. Cole. 1998. *Measuring and Monitoring Biological Diversity: Standard Methods for Mammals*. Smithsonian Institution Press, Washington, D.C.

Wilson, E. O. 1984. *Biophilia*. Harvard University Press, Cambridge, MA.

Wilson, E. O. 1987. The little things that run the world: The importance and conservation of invertebrates. *Conservation Biology* 1: 344–346.

Wilson, E. O. 1989. Threats to biodiversity. *Scientific American* 261(3): 108–116.

Wilson, E. O. 1991. Rain forest canopy: The high frontier. *National Geographic* 180(December): 78–107.

Wilson, E. O. 1992. *The Diversity of Life*. The Belknap Press of Harvard University Press, Cambridge, MA.

Wilson, E. O. 1994. *Naturalist*. Island Press, Washington, D.C.

Wilson, E. O. and D. L. Perlmann. 1999. *Conserving Earth's Biodiversity*. Island Press, Washington, D.C.

Wilson, M. A. and S. R. Carpenter. 1999. Economic valuation of freshwater ecosystem services in the United States: 1971–1997. *Ecological Applications* 9: 772–783.

Wolbarts, A. B. (ed.). 2001. *Solutions for an Environment in Peril*. The Johns Hopkins University Press, Baltimore, Maryland.

Wolf, C. M., T. Garland, and B. Griffith. 1998. Predictors of avian and mammalian translocation success: Re-analysis with phylogenetically independent contrasts. *Biological Conservation* 86: 243–255.

Wolf, C. M., B. Griffith, C. Reed, and S. A. Temple. 1996. Avian and mammalian translocations: Update and re-analysis of 1987 survey data. *Conservation Biology* 10: 1142–1155.

Wolkomir, R. 1995. California sea otters. *National Geographic* 187(June): 42–61.

Wondolleck, J. M. and S. L. Yaffee. 2000. *Making Collaborations Work: Lessons from Innovation in Natural Resource Management*. Island Press, Washington, D.C.

Woodard, C. 2000. *Ocean's End: Travels though Endangered Seas*. Basic Books (Perseus Books Group), New York.

Woodford, J. 2000. *The Wollemi Pine*. Text Publishing House.

Woodruff, D. S. 2001. Populations, species, and conservation genetics. *In* S. A. Levin (ed.), *Encyclopedia of Biodiversity*, 4: 811–818. Academic Press, San Diego, CA.

World Bank. 2000b. *Supporting the Web of Life. The World Bank and Biodiversity- A Portfolio Update (1988–1999)*. The World Bank, Washington, D.C.

World Bank. 2000b. *The World Bank and The Global Environment: A Progress Report*. World Bank, Washington, D.C.

World Commission on Environment and Development (WCED). 1987. *Our Common Future*. Oxford University Press, Oxford.

World Conservation Monitoring Centre (WCMC). 1992. *Global Biodiversity: Status of the Earth's Living Resources*. Compiled by the World Conservation Monitoring Centre, Chapman and Hall, London.

World Resources Institute (WRI). 1992. *World Resources 1992–93*. Oxford University Press, New York.

World Resources Institute (WRI). 1994. *World Resources 1994–1995: A Guide to the Global Environment*. Oxford University Press, New York.

World Resources Institute (WRI) 1998. *World Resources 1998–99*. Oxford University Press, New York.

World Resources Institute/IUCN/UNEP. 1992. *Global Biodiversity Strategy: Guidelines for Action to Save, Study and Use Earth's Biotic Wealth Sustainably and Equitably*. WRI, Washington, D.C.

World Resources Institute. (WRI) 2000. *World Resources 2000–2001*. World Resources Institute, Washington, D.C.

World Wildlife Fund (WWF). 1999. *Religion and Conservation*. Full Circle Press, New Delhi.

World Wildlife Fund (WWF). 2000. *The Global 200 Ecoregions: A User's Guide*. WWF, Gland, Switzerland.

World Wildlife Fund for Nature. 1989. *The Importance of Biological Diversity*. WWF, Gland, Switzerland.

World Wildlife/IUCN. 1997. Centres of Plant Diversity: A guide and strategy for their conservation, 3: North America, Middle America, South America, Caribbean Islands. WWF, Information Press, Oxford, UK.

Wright, R., J. M. Scott, S. Mann, and M. Murray. 2001. Identifying unprotected and potentially at risk plant communities in the western USA. *Biological Conservation* 98: 97–106.

Wright, S. 1931. Evolution in Mendelian populations. *Genetics* 16: 97–159.

Wright, S. J., H. Zeballos, I. Domínguez, M. M. Gallardo, et al. 2000. Poachers alter mammal abundance, seed dispersal, and seed predation in a neotropical forest. *Conservation Biology* 14: 227–239.

Wunder, S. 1999. *Value Determinants of Plant Extractivism in Brazil*. Instituto de Pesquisa Econômica Aplicada, Rio de Janeiro, Brazil.

Yaffee, S. L. 1996. *Ecosystem Management in the United States: An Assessment of Current Experience*. Island Press, Washington, D.C.

Yaffee, S. L. 1999. Three faces of ecosystem management. *Conservation Biology* 13: 713–725.

Yahner, R. H. 1988. Changes in wildlife communities near edges. *Conservation Biology* 2: 333–339.

Yamaoko, K., H. Moriyama, and T. Shigematsu. 1977. Ecological role of secondary forests in the traditional farming area in Japan. *Bulletin of Tokyo University* 20: 373–384.

Yanes, M, J. M. Velasco, and F. Suarez. 1995. Permeability of roads and railways to vertebrates- The importance of culverts. *Biological Conservation* 7: 217–222.

Yoakum, J. and W. P. Dasmann. 1971. Habitat manipulation practices. *In* R. H. Giles (ed.), *Wildlife Management Techniques*, pp. 173–231. The Wildlife Society, Washington, D.C.

Yodzis, P. 2001. Trophic levels. *In* S. A. Levin (ed.), *Encyclopedia of Biodiversity*, 5: 695–700. Academic Press, San Diego, CA.

Yonzon, P. B. and M. L. Hunter, Jr. 1991. Cheese, tourists and red pandas in the Nepal Himalayas. *Conservation Biology* 5: 196–202.

Young, A. G. and G. M. Clarke (eds.). 2001. *Genetics, Demography, and Viability of Fragmented Populations*. Cambridge University Press, New York.

Young, R. A., D. J. P. Swift, T. L. Clarke, G. R. Harvey, and P. R. Betzer. 1985. Dispersal pathways for particle-associated pollutants. *Science* 229: 431–435.

Young, T. P. 1994. Natural die-offs of large mammals: Implications for conservation. *Conservation Biology* 8: 410–418.

Young, T. P., J. M. Chase, R. T. Huddleston. 2001. Community succession and assembly. *Ecological Restoration* 19: 5–18.

Young, W. 1995. A dump no more. *American Forests* 101: 58–59.

Zbicz, D. C. and M. J. B. Green. 1997. Status of the world's transfrontier protected areas. *Parks* 7: 5–10.

Zeddies, J., R. P. Schaab, P. Neuenschwander, and H. R. Herren. 2001. Economics of biological control of the cassava mealybug in Africa. *Agricultural Economics* 24: 209–219.

Zedler, J. B. 1996. Ecological issues in wetland mitigation: An introduction to the forum. *Ecological Applications* 6: 33–37.

Zedler, J. B., R. Lindig-Cisneros, C. Bonilla-Warford, and I. Woo. 2001. Restoration of biodiversity, overview. *In* S. A. Levin (ed.), *Encyclopedia of Biodiversity*, 5: 203–212. Academic Press, San Diego, CA.

Zhi, L., P. Wenshi, Zhu Xiaojian, W. Dajun, and W. Hao. 2000. What has the panda taught us? *In* A. Entwistle and N. Dunstone (eds.), *Priorities for the Conservation of Mammalian Diversity: Has the Panda had its Day?*, pp. 325–334. Cambridge University Press, Cambridge.

Zonneveld, I. S. and R. T. Forman (eds.). 1990. *Changing Landscapes: An Ecological Perspective.* Springer-Verlag, New York.

Zorn, P., W. Stephenson, and P. Grigoriev. 2001. An ecosystem management program and assessment process for Ontario National Parks. *Conservation Biology* 15: 353–362.

Index

About the Author

Richard B. Primack is a Professor in the Biology Department at Boston University and the former Associate Director of the Environmental Studies Program. He received his B.A. at Harvard University in 1972 and his Ph.D. at Duke University in 1976. He then completed a postdoctoral fellowship at the University of Canterbury in New Zealand and sabbatical fellowships at Harvard University. Previous books published include: *A Field Guide to Poisonous Plants and Mushrooms of North America* (with Charles K. Levy); *A Forester's Guide to the Moraceae of Sarawak*; *A Primer of Conservation Biology*, Second Edition; *Ecology, Conservation and Management of Southeast Asian Rainforests* (edited with Thomas Lovejoy); and *Timber, Tourists, and Temples: Conservation and Development in the Maya Forest of Belize, Guatemala and Mexico* (edited with David Bray, Hugo Galletti, and Ismael Ponciano).

Dr. Primack's research interests include rare plant conservation and restoration; the ecology, conservation, and management of tropical forests in Southeast Asia; conservation biology education; and the natural history of orchids. He is the President-Elect of The Association for Tropical Biology.

About the Book

Editor: Andrew D. Sinauer
Project Editor: Kerry L. Falvey
Editorial Assistant: Sydney Carroll
Production Manager: Christopher Small
Book Design: Jefferson Johnson
Book Layout and Composition: Michele Ruschhaupt/The Format Group
Cover Design: Jefferson Johnson
Book and Cover Manufacture: Courier Companies, Inc.